RIDING THE DRAGON

A journey through every Chinese province

Chris Taylor

For Martha and Molly - Wo de xiao pengyou

...and for Justine for all her support

A NOTE ON THE TEXT

My trips to China were haphazard and contained a certain random quality that seemed to me to be an important part of my reasons for being there - to see what turned up and to avoid a predetermined and preconceived idea of what the country would be.

And so I hopscotched from province to province, from Mongolian border to the Himalayan foothills and onto cities and suburbs, villages and temples, rivers and ocean. My journey jumped from season to season too; sometimes it was hot and humid and sometimes it rained like it might never stop. Other times the weather was bone crackingly cold and I felt that I would never be warm again. Each chapter describes a different province, each of which can be located on the map at the front of the book for those who yearn for a sense of place.

Your journey through this book can be as random as mine and there is no need to read these chapters in sequence for there is none. I have tried to create some sense of order by separating the provinces into three distinct sections and have used the Yangtze River as my demarcation line between North and South, just as the Chinese do. The third section refers to those western provinces that retain a sense of wild remoteness due in the main to the extremes of desert, jungle and mountains. But the chapters are all stand alone and as distinct from each other as the provinces they describe, so if you wish to jump from Shanghai to Sichuan or from Tianjin to Tibet then feel free to do so, since the author did much the same.

TABLE OF CONTENTS

PREFACE

My fascination with China began after my arrival in Hong Kong in 2003 from England and I suppose these chapters are a tribute to my attachment.

I came as a British teacher of European History and was told that I would be teaching History to international students. This was no problem, but there was a catch. The history I would be delivering would be about China, about revolution and famine and about men called Mao and Deng of whom I knew nothing. But I came to love my new teaching topic and I hope instilled a love of China in my students too, though often their interest was tainted with horror and disbelief and confusion since 20th Century Chinese History has this effect on people.

I visited Beijing in the depths of winter in my first year to see the Great Wall and Mao's embalmed body and have returned to China dozens of times since; to the jungles of Yunnan, the mountains of Tibet, the deserts of Gansu and the casinos of Macau, for China is nothing if not varied.

We cannot afford to get China wrong and my book contributes to the current debate about the growing power of a country that many in Hong Kong and the West have grave misgivings about and equate with threat. I'm no apologist for China's unpleasant aspects but we need to understand that a nation is more than the sum total of crisis and disaster that we are fed and more also than the autocratic and corrupt government system that the people of China – the real heartbeat of the nation - continue to endure.

China fascinates me but I hope that this is a book without bouquets and is no weak-at-the-knees exaltation to the object of my affection. Sometimes I get thoroughly sick of her. She can be capricious, unpredictable and exasperating. She smokes and spits and farts. She can be unhelpful, bossy and inclined to authoritarianism and sometimes I think of leaving her for someone else....I've heard India is nice. But then a shaft of sunlight hits a deserted temple courtyard, the wind blows a flurry of sand from a Gobi desert dune, the sun slowly rises over the Himalayan foothills or the ice sparkles on a frozen river in the North and my affection is renewed.

China has her problems to be sure; corruption, separatism, and destruction of the environment are chief amongst these but in the last three decades, she has made rapid strides and recovered her robust good health after the terminal decline and tragedy of 100 years of invasion, war and famine.

More than anything, it is the people who bring me back; the unfailingly generous and resilient billion Chinese, some of whom I have met in every one of her 33 provinces. And it's also the solitude, the wide open unspoiled spaces of a nation with an astonishing variety of natural beauty, for though China is the most populous nation on earth, she is far from the most densely populated.

So I'll keep going back because China is a nation on the up. There's an optimism and opportunism and a can do mentality there that is as energizing and exhausting and thrilling as the first throes of love. Arise, arise, millions of hearts with one mind. March on! March on! So says the Chinese national anthem and it feels that our romance is still alive....

PART 1

NORTH OF THE YANGTZE

JILIN

吉林

186 528sq km
Population 27.2 million

" 'Man' was the very first word I learned to read... but I had never understood its meaning before. Only today, with the communist party and the policy of remoulding criminals, have I learned the significance of this magnificent word and become a real man."

Aisin-Gioro Pu Yi, the Last Emperor of China (1965)

Football was born in the old cotton making, ship building industrial heartland of Britain where stadiums sat incongruous beside terraced houses. Black-and-white photo matchstalk Lowry men trudged to the match under slate grey skies and endured Depression and Blitz, swaying and jostling in great heaving terraced masses and throwing their flat caps in the air to celebrate that great cannonball heavy leather football in the back of the net.

The North East is China's industrial heartland. The Japanese army came here for iron and coal and conquest, and Soviet industrial advisers helped build literal and figurative bridges after the Japanese had left. Industry has declined and the north-east is now China's rust belt, but in football, northern China is still king. Dalian Shide from Liaoning province is China's most successful team, but Changchun Yatai have also won the Chinese Super League, and it was in Changchun that I met my first real Chinese football fans.

They were sheltering from the bitter cold like me in one of the local jiaozi dumpling shops, where little pastry ingots of pork and beef are served by the dozen on hotplates - part of the unfussy and uncomplicated cuisine that reflects the character of the North Eastern people. They spoke English and invited me to join them, and this was welcome since their table was furthest from the door through which an icy blast and needles of frost blew whenever a customer entered the shop. Like all proper football fans these men had a single conversation topic and when they heard I was English wanted to know which team I followed. They were Changchun Yatai supporters naturally but despite the success of their team, these were not happy fans.

Chinese soccer is a mess and the national team a source of embarrassment and disgrace. 'We play soccer like the Brazilians play ping-pong' laughed one of my new friends through a mouthful of jiaozi and another told me there are only two things wrong with the Chinese national players: their left feet and their right feet. I'd heard this joke before and I remembered also reading a Changchun newspaper headline that reported China's loss to Iraq in 2008 that eliminated the team from World Cup qualification. 'The national team lost again', the headline despaired. 'We have nothing to say'. There was no other text or mention of the game throughout the rest of the paper, since if you ignore something long enough it might go away.

It is remarkable that a nation of 1.3 billion should be so bad at a sport in which they desperately want to excel, since a winning soccer team gains more global respect than even a parade of missiles. China's failures are especially painful since she claims to have invented the sport. Notwithstanding the nation's rather exhausting claim to have invented nearly everything[1], there is a grain (rice grain cultivation was also invented by China) of truth in this since Chinese soldiers enjoyed playing a football style game called Cuju using a leather ball stuffed with human hair, as early as the third century BC, though they eventually lost on a disputed offside decision to Genghis Khan's Mongolia.

China might have had a fighting chance if there had been a World Cup held 300 years before the birth of Christ, but it's been a sorry tale of ineptitude and failure and non-qualification since then. In fact China has traditionally opted out of team sports altogether. Expertise in wushu martial arts and ping-pong is hardly transferable to the soccer field and some Chinese have attempted to intellectualize and justify their failure. Perhaps as they say, the Chinese are dextrous and coordinated rather than strong. Perhaps the decline of Confucianism has created too great an emphasis on the individual at the expense of the team. Perhaps the net theory is right; that the Chinese do best in sports where they are separated from the enemy by a lattice, like table tennis and badminton.

The real problem is that Chinese soccer is better at passing brown envelopes than the ball. Illegal gambling, match fixing and bribery among coaches, players and 'black whistle' corrupt referees is endemic in the game and stifles all attempts at systematic development of the sport. In addition, Chinese fans are notoriously obnoxious and I wondered how many of my new dumpling companions had participated in the shouted obscenities involving animal genitalia at matches that had so exercised the national press. China has increasingly adopted Western notions of nationalism and competitiveness in sport without the sportsmanship. Fans in Beijing rioted after China lost a World Cup qualifier in 1985 to Hong Kong; this defeat was a victory for imperialism and capitalism instead of merely 22 men running for 90 minutes on a

---

1   see gunpowder, paper, kites, bridges, compasses, printing, bells, coffins, forks, lacquerware, oars, noodles, silk, banknotes, acupuncture, toothbrushes, golf, matches, porcelain, stirrups, toilet paper, wheelbarrows.

muddy field. But it is defeat to Japan that rankles the most. Every game against Japan is an opportunity to boo her anthem, throw garbage at the Japanese players, smash the windows of Japanese cars, chase the Japanese team bus shouting 'Kill, Kill, Kill' or unfurl a huge banner saying 'May a big sword chop off Japanese heads' (all of these things happened at the Asian cup tournament in 2004.) It doesn't help that Japan usually wins.

The success of the women's Chinese soccer team only makes things worse. The 'Iron Roses' made it to the final of the women's World Cup in 1999 where they lost to the USA but most Chinese soccer fans prefer the men's game and female success draws male failure into sharp relief. I asked my friends about this as we ate the final dumplings and drank the last of the beer. 'It's because we're going through a period of yin female power' pontificated the man who had drunk the most beer. 'What is wrong with our yang?'

I had misplaced my manly yang too on the journey to Changchun. I bought the cheapest ticket possible from Shenyang since the journey was only three hours, so that I could sit on a hard seat and enjoy the earthy unfussy, uncomplicated jiaozi mentality of the North East. It was December and the temperature had dropped to extravagantly low levels as I traveled further north and I was *cold*, though the children and old ladies on my carriage were cheerful, full of yang and coping just fine.

An hour into the trip, frost was covering the inside of the window and great fangs of ice hung from the outside of the train. I replaced the hat and gloves that I had removed earlier in accordance with my mother's childhood mantra that 'I wouldn't feel the benefit' when I went outside if I wore them inside too. I wandered to the buffet car to break the monotony of gazing at fields made brittle with ice and rutted, deathtrap frozen country roads, but mostly in search of tea or something, *anything* that was warm. 'Mei you cha' said the waitress and I wondered what train this was that had no tea, that most indispensable of commodities, more widely available in China than anything else apart from cheap cigarettes and dishonest taxi drivers.

The police came to my rescue. Officers ride every train in China; they wander the carriages self-importantly ready to reject the ticketless and the undesirable and on overnight journeys they lick their fingers to examine my passport and leave a greasy smear, a certificate of travel, on every page. But checking foreign passports doesn't take long this far north, since it would be a fool indeed who would come to China's rust belt in the middle of winter, and for most of this trip the police could be found lounging feet up or head asleep on a pillow of arms in the buffet car. This burly policeman raised himself from his slumbers, saw a fellow passenger in tea-less distress and poured me a glass from his own flask. We had a stilted, limited Chinese conversation throughout which he turned a couple of walnuts continuously in his hand. I took this as a form of stress relief but it served equally well as an allegory for most of my dealings with China's police force where I stand sheepish and vulnerable and wait for a visa stamp or permission to enter or to stay or to leave from a grumpy official who could pronounce my request impossible at any moment and who has me by the balls.

This man was different. He asked if I liked 'our China' and if I wanted more tea. He grinned a row of yellow teeth, announced that he could speak English and bellowed 'Rades an Zhenmen' at the top of his voice several times, which I finally came to understand as 'Ladies and Gentlemen', a singularly useless phrase on a frozen northern train and more suited to a circus big top than a buffet car clunking through a frozen landscape. But I smiled and gave a big thumbs up anyway, mindful of the walnuts rotating, twisting, crunching in his massive hand.

By the time I returned to my seat, satiated with Chinese police tea, the passengers in the seat opposite me had resolved to become talkative. I spoke loudly over the rattling wheels about the weather since I had learned the Chinese words for cold, freezing, ice and snow though I regretted not knowing brass and monkeys. My companions were students and spoke a little English. I asked how, and they replied that they had learned it at school together and I wondered if they had been in the same class. They replied yes, there had been 70 students in their class room and I took this to mean they had got their English vocabulary wrong. 'You mean 70 in your school' I said and they replied no, they meant what they said. 70 students in one class was a preposterously high number, ill designed to teach anything meaningful at all. I tried to imagine the poor teacher marching between serried ranks of desks reciting irregular verbs to 70 puzzled faces and answering the questions of 70 raised hands. Yet these students had learned enough at least for a stilted conversation about the weather with a foreigner on a train.

In the end, this low price, hard seat journey was just the same as any train I've been on in China except everyone wore a hat and I could see my breath. All passengers were engaged in the serious business of eating as they always are on trains, and as on all trains the passengers to Changchun favoured snacks that pass the time. Chief amongst these are sunflower seeds and the carriage was filled with the sound of kernels cracking in teeth, a growing mound of splintered shells littering every patch of plastic table and carpeting the floor between the passengers booted feet. Just as on all trains, constant and repeated announcements of weather conditions, arrival times and delays drowned the noise of hungry locals chewing upon shells, though unlike on a sleeper carriage, on this train I had no way of turning the sound off. Passengers played offensively loud appalling Chinese pop music on their garishly lit mobile phones and on this train as on all others, men stood between the carriages and sucked hungrily on cigarettes though today their refuge was covered in frosted ice and they took care to avoid touching the metal with nicotine fingers lest they stuck to the train and couldn't get off till spring.

An hour from Changchun the heaters came to life, the ice melted from the windows and a trail of water on the floor made rafts of the discarded shells. We were a convivial bunch in our refuge of heat and light that trundled through the brutal cold of a Jilin countryside made more forbidding by darkness. I began to wish this was an overnight journey since there is no better feeling than swaying through the night, safe and warm on what Paul Theroux calls 'the cast-iron cradle' and waking to breakfast and the excitement of a new town.

But by 7pm the blackness outside had given way to the lights of Changchun; hats were thrust onto infant heads and for the first time in my experience on a Chinese train there was no pushing and shoving, bag-as-a-weapon stampede to get off, for the train was warm and outside was cold. The station clock read -22°C and I almost became a casualty of winter, my body frozen into grotesque shapes like Sitting Bull in the snow at the Battle of Wounded Knee since my companions

8

were eager to use a little more of their 70 in a room English and help me catch a cab, a task I was perfectly capable of achieving alone. They reasoned rightly that the taxis at the station exit would be overpriced so we walked a numbing five minutes to the main road and waited on a street corner for a further excruciating 10 minutes while I lost all sensation in my ears and face. My hat was at the bottom of my bag because I had imagined my passage from train to taxi to hotel would be ruthlessly efficient and there was no way I was going to remove a glove to find it.

Finally a cab was procured and my helpers loaded my bag and cheerfully waved me away, announcing in my frozen ear with great solemnity and nod and a wink confidentiality that their local knowledge, their hardheaded bargaining, their thrifty freeze the balls off a brass monkey negotiations had saved me the sum of three yuan. A bargain indeed, though as they told me in a final flourish of English, it was 'not necessary to thank'.

Changchun was the seat of Japanese power in Manchuria (Japan renamed the region Manchukuo) for 14 years between 1931 and 1945 which is why the Japanese get booed at football matches by the fans of Changchun Yatai. The city was called Hsinking then (the new name means 'Eternal Spring' which seemed laughingly inappropriate on this freezing day) and the occupiers, conscious of hatred and resentment from the occupied, attempted to lend their conquest an air of legitimacy by installing the deposed Chinese Qing emperor Pu-Yi as titular head of state. Pu-Yi's acceptance of the post was disastrous to any lingering hopes he had ever to return to his throne in the Forbidden City and he was soon derided as a puppet of the Japanese, a traitor to his country.

Pu-Yi's estate from where he nominally ran the affairs of Manchukuo is in Changchun. The last Emperor moved here in 1932 and it's a grand enough place with its racecourse white with snow today and an open-air pool drained of water the use of which seemed unimaginable, for how could summer ever come to this place? It's a monument to self-delusion and known as 'The Puppet Emperor's Palace' and the first interrogatory information board in the first room left me in no doubt how this place was to be viewed. 'Why can some people make much

9

resistance at all costs and finally become national heroes when the state faces invasion and crisis?' I was asked. 'On the contrast, other people betray themselves to their enemies. Being servile they become guilty men…. we display some officials of the Puppet Manchurian regime and their ugly looks'.

The tokenism of his ugly Emperor status must have been clear to Pu-Yi though he was excessively short sighted. The Emperor had no real power and seems to have led a rather indolent and boring life in Changchun while the Japanese murdered and burned and looted their way through China. The museum tried to be informative and non-partisan but the authors of the information boards were filled with righteous fury and rarely resisted a dig at the disgraced Emperor. 'Here Pu-Yi played badminton, though his courtiers let him win'. 'Here Pu-Yi sunbathed while others swam'. 'Here Pu-Yi played drums, here he played piano, to take his mind off the depression of being a puppet'.

Photos of Pu-Yi litter the Puppet Palace though he is rarely dressed in Qing Dynasty finery. Usually he is in suit and tie with Brylcreemed hair like some 1930s fop or Clark Gable marionette, heavy circular tortoise shell glasses framing his boyish goofy face. In Russia the murdered Czar has been rehabilitated and raised to sainthood, but Pu-Yi's cause is forlorn because he looks so *unheroic* and such a geek; hardly strong enough to crack a sunflower seed.

Yet this scrawny, sand in the face four eyed weakling always had a beautiful woman on his arm. Pu-Yi in tennis slacks carrying a wooden racket, Pu-Yi leaning on a sit up and beg bicycle, Pu-Yi lounging on a rug in his Japanese garden (though never Pu-Yi attending to affairs of state or Pu-Yi offering comfort to the victims of bombing raids); always a woman with thoroughly modern cropped hair by his side. The story of Pu-Yi's post-war arrest, happy conversion to communism (did he have a choice?) and final years as a gardener in Beijing are well documented, but this Puppet Palace is a record of the life of the women in the Emperor's life as much as the Emperor himself.

Pu-Yi's fourth wife lived here; her quarters are labeled 'The Imperial Concubine rooms' though Li Yuqin slept in the large bed beneath sumptuous tapestries for only a very short time since she arrived as a 15-year-old in 1943 just two years before the Japanese defeat. This left her with hardly enough time for a swim or a game of badminton or to hear her husband's puppet escapist tinkling on the piano. Li Yuqin finished her life in gainful employ just like her gardening ex-husband, as a librarian in Changchun. Pu-Yi didn't want a divorce but Li Yuqin was determined. Her son from a second marriage commented after her death 'my mother had the right to pursue her own happiness'.

The Emperor's first wife Wan Rong ('Beautiful Countenance') enjoyed no such happiness. Her marriage to the Emperor produced no heirs; it is rumoured that Pu-Yi was infertile, though this may have been a delicate way of avoiding discussion of his sexuality; so more Noel Coward than Clark Gable then. The Imperial Consort moved to the Forbidden City when she was 17 and was an opium addict by the time she and her husband arrived in Changchun. She had separate rooms in the Puppet Palace and rarely came out to speak to or eat with a husband she despised. By 1940 Wan Rong was consuming 2 ounces of opium a day. In the same year her baby girl born to one of the house servants was killed by lethal injection, the trauma of which drove her further into addiction. She died in prison in 1946 from malnutrition and opium withdrawal, aged 39. Pu-Yi received the news three years later.

I walked from this dysfunctional house back towards Changchun and past the road to the First Automobile Works, for this is a city at the heart of Chinese car production. China's first Liberation trucks were made here but production is given over now to Audis with black windows owned by party leaders and businessmen and Volkswagens driven at breakneck pace by taxi drivers all over the country. Red Flag (Hongqi) limousines are made here too, that big black brand beloved of communist leaders from Mao onwards. It was a specially commissioned Red Flag limo that was Richard Nixon's transport on his visit to China in 1972 and another, registration 2009, that carried Hu Jintao during the 60th anniversary parade day in Beijing and from which he addressed troops. 'Comrades you have worked hard!' he bellowed while helicopters and fighter jets buzzed overhead and missiles and tanks trundled behind in a display of Chinese muscle so conspicuously lacking in Pu-Yi. Such bravado allowed all of China to forget how bad they are at football if just for one day .

I walked through Nanhu Park and over the South Lake frozen to tarmac where skaters pirouetted and children screamed and rode bicycles whose front wheel had been yanked off and replaced by a short ski. A fog of vapour like Wan Rong opium smoke billowed from my mouth and froze into ice on my scarf but the walk made me warm and I was unperturbed by the bank of clouds that blew over the First Automobile Works and delivered tiny flakes of snow that floated in the air and refused to land since they were too light and it was too cold to snow properly.

It was no less cold the following day in Jilin City to where I caught another slow train from Changchun's massive station of steel and glass. The train was late which was no surprise in this weather- it seemed a wonder that the trains were running at all - and everyone began to overheat in the waiting hall in fur hat and thick boots. We were all reluctant to remove a single item of clothing lest the train arrive, the gates spring open leaving us to join the mad rush for a seat on to the platform and into the freezing air with a bare head.

The train traveled through a landscape made almost featureless by a covering of snow. There were few towns and no sign even of farms and crops, though for a while we traveled beside the huge concrete pillars of an unfinished flyover at odds with the rural surrounds that went nowhere and that had been abandoned so long that tufts of grass grew defiantly on top of each one. A watery sun was out and offered a little warmth through the window where I rested my head, listlessly watched the scenery slide past and listened to the crack, crack, crack of sunflower seeds.

Jilin City is small and industrial and rather ugly, except for the Songhua River that flows slow and broad in a great arc through the centre of town. The river would be pleasant enough in summertime with its sturdy bridge and tree-lined promenade along each bank, but in the frozen bitter winter the Songhua becomes the city's most compelling feature by far.

The reason for the Songhua's fame is steam. There is a hydroelectric dam built by the Japanese upstream from which sufficient hot water debouches into the river to keep it ice free throughout the winter. The consequence of all this warm water is a mass of steam drifting off the river like banks of autumnal fog or the smoke of deep buried seismic activity as if the whole town is about to explode. When the wind is light the steam hits the trees that line the riverbank and settles as rime on every branch and twig, turning them into astonishing brittle things of beauty; jewelled trees, trees made of coral.

This unique spectacle raises the city from the mundane. The Chinese call it 'shugua' and travel to Jilin from all over the country to take photos and my riverside hotel had tapped into this national enthusiasm with an ingenious electronic 'rimeometer' in the lobby. The board gave an opinion on wind speed, temperature, amount of steam and quality of rime with a series of stars. Today was a five-star wind and temperature day though perplexingly the two star quality of steam had led to a disappointing one star verdict on rime. And the rimeometer was right. A quick glance from the window suggested the river had steam enough, but the trees were brown and bare of ice and looked like the barebones gnarly trees I had seen from the train window on my journey through the Jilin countryside.

I asked the receptionist if the trees would be shinier and rimier the next day but I could get little sense from her. Her eyes were rimmed red and she could barely talk through great gasping sobs of despair; perhaps she was disappointed about today's paucity of rime? The doorman, liveried in a threadbare uniform told me the trees are better in the early morning. He added with venom that there was no point at all in talking to *her* and suddenly I felt like Alice down the rabbit hole where everyone is either glum or angry and Alice has no idea at all how to deal with the angry Duchess or the desperate tears of Mock Turtle sadness.

But the doorman knew his rime. The crushing cold of dawn arrived, the rimeometer signaled five glowing stars and outside the trees were suspended in fragile glass. I was Alice no more but through the wardrobe in a Narnia enchanted by a witch's wintry spell.

My photos would have been better if it hadn't been so cold. I flapped at the shutter button with my mittened flippers and paid scant attention to flash, focus and shutter speed as the shattering cold seeped through my clothes and made shugua of my bones. But there, as I prepared to flee back to the hotel, was an apparition, a mirage, an ice maiden floating between the trees, her black tresses spilling down her back, her slippered feet tripping lightly over the sugary snow.

I had seen wedding photos in unlikely places in China, but this was beyond belief. Photographers in down jackets and ski boots were shouting instructions to a bride who, safe in the warm glow of romance, needed nothing but a sleeveless and backless wedding dress to keep her warm. The groom looked unhappy in patent shoes and white suit but he at least had a jacket on and if he just pulled that cummerbund down a few inches more it might afford some protection for those parts of his body so essential to a happy marriage. I would have spoken to the bride but this might have necessitated the removal of one of the scarves I had tied across my face and I didn't want to ruin the transitory beauty of the moment and make flesh this apparition, this floating paradigm of loveliness with base conversation. Also I did not know the Chinese words for hypothermia, frostbite or corpse.

The road out of town was corrugated with ice but my taxi driver put his foot to the floor regardless and we bumped and slithered our way to Zhuque Shan, threatening at any moment to career into the steamy Songhua. This country park is called Rose Finch Mountain after the songbirds that chatter in the trees when the ice has melted and the shugua trees have budded into leaf. Locals go to Rose Finch to ski and I knew that I would find inadequately dressed amateurs sprawled across the snow here, for if there is one sport that the Chinese are worse at than football, it's skiing.

There was a mechanical contraption pulling tyre inner tubes to the top of the hill from where staff muffled in hoods and salopettes pushed them down, extra hard and with a sneaky spin to add a little glamour to the cold monotony of the job. Even these squealing beginners couldn't fail to stay on board though and as they arrived panting at the bottom, ran across to the hoist shouting 'again, again!'. I gave the tyres a go but the rush of air covered my ears in rime so I was content to sit with a cup of brown liquid that might have been coffee on a heated kang and watch a tour group from sunny Indonesia stamp their feet and wail as they tried to make sense of this icy planet so far from equatorial home.

There were sleds pulled by dogs here too, homemade contraptions of metal pipes and tarpaulin with a national flag fluttering on top. Each was harnessed to a hairy mastiff dog whose shaggy muzzle was coated in frost and who lay panting on the snow without a care for a belly on frigid ice. Some of these junkyard toboggans were attached to two dogs and in one case a dog and a sheep were tethered together, the dog looking sheepish and the sheep looking dogged. I wondered if the sheep/dog combination would be faster than two dogs. I wondered if the fleecy sheep was warmer than the hairy dog. I wondered why the dog didn't just eat the sheep. I think the cold was getting to me.

Jilin means 'auspicious forest' and though this sounds somewhat bohemian, new age and free spirited, it's not inappropriate for a city of meteorites and cosmic space dust. An unearthly shower fell on Jilin in March 1976, including a whopping two tonne meteorite that is now on display in the town's meteorite shower museum. This may have been the dullest museum I ever visited in China (there is some serious competition for this accolade) - it's a fine line between a meteorite and a lump of rock after all - though it was warm inside and I learnt that these extra special extra terrestrial stones consist chiefly of olivine and orthopyroxene with minor kamacite toenite and troilite, that the ratio of olivine to orthopyroxene is 1:1:7. The texture of the rock can be described as spherultic, glassy, devitrified-spherultic and monospherultic. This was all ineffably dull but the long words took on a fascinating importance whenever I considered the prospect of a return outdoors.

There was more age of aquarius hippiedom in evidence at the Sky Temple on the edge of town where foreigners who make it to this off the tourist trail place can attend Kung Fu classes and where I had my fortune told from the ripples of water in a bronze bowl. This ancient practice works on the principle of throwing a pebble into still water and counting the ripples; an even number means yes, and an odd number no. Or was it even is no and odd is yes? Couldn't be clearer, but I remember my fortune teller was very exacting about the type of bowl.

There are other methods of water divination, all of which possess a gratifying degree of random unquantifiable chance designed to reinforce the cynicism of an empirical Westerner like me. Ripples were the cheapest fortune on offer, but I could have tried a number of others all of which can be safely tackled at home.

1, Water gazing. Sit with your back to the light in a darkened room. Gaze into but not *at* the water and interpret the symbols that appear therein.

2, Divination by floating. Ask a yes/no question as you throw an object into the water. If it sinks the answer is yes, if it floats the answer is no. This system is clearly open to abuse. Choose a rock for 'will I be wealthy?' and a feather for 'will I become ill and die?'

3, Divination by steam. Hang a mirror on a wall. Boil a pot of water. Place it in front of the mirror. Steam will cloud the mirror much like the desires of your heart. Gaze into the steam. The drips will form letters that should be clues. Give up spotting letters and gaze at your reflection; is that spinach in my teeth? Am I getting grey whiskers in my beard? Should I trim the hair sprouting from my nose?

4, Interpret the river. Study the whirls in a river til truths be known unto you. This should be done alone and at night but only by women.

So there was little point in my returning to the Songhua River in the chill of night to watch the eddys between the clouds of hydroelectric steam what with me being a boy and all, and I went for dumplings instead. The xinxingyuan jiaoziguan restaurant was packed with the heat of locals and the steam of the kitchen and I ate my fill. Here the questions were more to my liking; would you like more food? Will you drink some beer? Yes and yes.

Jilin's renowned dumpling shop is close to the most famous building in town, the old 1917 Catholic Church. The church has a chequered past and was ransacked and nearly destroyed in the Cultural Revolution, before restoration began in the 1980s which is ongoing still. It's a microcosm of the relationship between Chinese Communism and Christianity which was derided as a foreign imperialist conceit, then brutalized by those who saw no room for other beliefs in their blinkered Marxist dogma. But Christianity is now tolerated and freedom of worship, like the church itself, is repaired and restored, though this too is an ongoing project.

The Red Guard firebrands had their gospel too, but they were wrong when they thought they could destroy the church. Marx called religion the people's opium - a phrase that must have had particular resonance with the Chinese who had been subjected to the British immorality of The Opium Wars - and Mao said; 'Communism is not love. Communism is a hammer which we use to crush our enemy' which could hardly be further from Christ's turn the other cheek philosophy. The Chairman believed in miracles but these would be achieved by class struggle not by the word of God.

But here on the wintry streets of Jilin was a Catholic Church, its bricks a tribute to endurance and its bells caroling defiance across the steaming river. The church's very existence, its tower piercing the frigid air, is a benediction and its flourishes and cupolas break the monotony and the drab functionality of the rest of town. Yet perhaps the survival of Christianity in China should come as no surprise. The Bible says 'He hath put down the mighty from their seats and exalted them of low degree' (Luke 1:52) Doesn't this make Jesus a Communist too?

ANHUI

安徽

142 450 sq km
Population 65.2 million

'Great things are done when men and mountains meet; this is not done when jostling in the street'

William Blake

One moment the little girl on the bus sitting on her grandma's knees was giggling and hiding her eyes as I smiled at her and pulled faces and the next she was vomiting on the floor. This was okay; there was hardly a straight line on these roads between vegetable plots through white washed Southern Anhui villages and the driver *was* driving a little fast as bus drivers are inclined to do all over China. She was only a little girl, and it was only a little vomit, and the sight of my face can be a little sickening I suppose. So Grandma dabbed the girl's chin with a tissue, fingers of watery vomit trickled and expanded across the floor and our journey continued.

Then she *really* vomited. There was an audible gasp from the passengers as a great looping arc of milky foam was projected from her mouth with astonishing force fully 2 metres across the bus. Seats were strafed, bags were blitzed, clothes were carpet bombed. This was bad enough but that same refluxive cascade also headed unerringly towards our driver, hitting his back, his neck, the little box of coins he kept by the gearstick and pebble dashing the bus dials and instruments so that although we still knew he was driving too fast, we didn't know by how much.This was impressive from so small a child and I was tempted to applaud but as the driver felt the warm wetness of the toddlers stomach contents seep through his shirt and swung his vehicle to a halt I waited for him to erupt with similar violence to the girl. Grandmother and child were invited to leave the bus and we left them dripping and forlorn beneath a cluster of top-heavy bamboo and drove on. I could hardly blame the driver for expelling the pair - the vomit was beginning to really stink - but what I failed to realise was that this was not abandonment but an example of all that is best about China. The driver parked the bus by a stream and rose soggily from his seat. By the time he had returned to the bus with a bucket full of river water a passenger had extracted an old work shirt from her bag to give him to wear. Newly attired he set to work with a mop cheerfully chatting with the passengers who opened windows for fresh air, pulled out tissues to help with the mopping and remarked on how unfortunate this was for the poor child. Everyone was cheerful and helpful and I tried to imagine the reaction of a grumpy bus driver back home if one of his passengers had chundered on him or his bus.

By the time we drove back to pick up the granny and sick child, no one would have known that the bus had been slick with sick just moments before. This community of care was delightful. The Chinese can be infuriatingly over interested and voyeuristic, but here that was preferable to non-involvement or indifference or furious disapproval.

No one cared about the smell or the diversion or the delay, the little girl was all that mattered. Everyone asked if she was okay as she re-boarded and Grandma said she was thank you even as she wiped flecks of vomit from her cardigan. We were soon once more on our way in the bright sunshine, bumping and swerving on pretty rural lanes. The girl was happy again though she didn't giggle as hard but buried her face in her grandma's breast when I looked at her. All was right with the world. Children laughed and birds sang. And then the girl vomited again.

The villages in southern Anhui are some of the most delightful in all China. This rural idyll is largely untouched by modernisation; the village houses that we swerved through and vomited by are largely of Qing and Ming construction, some are 13th century Song dynasty, and the fields of rape seed and vegetables are still tended by straw hat bare-foot peasants and buffalo. This region is called Huizhou and was home to successful merchants who were sent to do business elsewhere, re-turning home just once a year. These merchants funnelled their profits home into lavish, solid residences and ancestral halls rather than uproot their families and disrespect their ancestral clans. The result is village after village of solidly uniform houses all painted white and blotched by grey mildew; a world away from the drab concrete utilitarianism of most Chinese villages.

The grey tiles of most houses end in the flourish of a horse head gable silhouetted in a curl against the bright sky. These were originally designed to prevent fire (and burglars) jumping from one house to an-other but are now a means of decoration. Much of what was functional in these villages is now decorative. Heavy wooden doors gleam with the patina of centuries of polishing, bubbling streams run alongside and between the houses and the streets are cobbled with hard wearing, ir-regular round stones that are too bumpy for motorbikes and too narrow for cars which adds to the villages' tranquility and timelessness. There are decorative arches called 'paifeng'[2] in these villages too. Sometimes over 10 metres high, these arches were built to celebrate virtuous behav-iour or family success or an important event. They gave social standing

---

2 A female arch is called a 'pailou'. Roads often go through a paifeng but always around a pailou so that a man can never be below a woman.

to merchants whose grubby commercialism placed them on the bottom rung of the Confucian social ladder where scholarship and learning were paramount and teachers had more value than shopkeepers.

I left my band of brothers and the vomiting girl who had perked up again now at the 11th century village of Xidi where a huge paifeng towers above the buildings on the main square beside the river. The square and the labyrinthine alleys beneath the horse head gables were dotted with young Chinese artists who sat with easel and paints in a frenzy of sketching, sucking the end of their brush and cocking their heads to one side. They were trying to capture the antiquity of the stones, the geometry of the squat square windows and the vigour of the women who sat on haunches outside their houses scrubbing vegetables and socks in the stream or plucking chickens whose angular feet stuck like tridents from cooking pots.

Most left off painting to say hello to the foreigner and a group of strikingly pretty female art students asked to have a picture with me because I was 'so handsome' which was a reminder of how good China can be for the ego. I ate in a 400-year-old building called the 'Pig's Heaven Inn' and though the food was rather functional and dull, I enjoyed sitting on the third floor terrace bathed in sunlight where I gazed down on the grey roofs of the village. I could see no artists or shops or even alleyways from my rooftop perch, just a sea of ancient grey tiles framed by soaring green hills. The only noise from up here was the sound of chattering birds and the rush of the river (and possibly, very faint in the distance, the retching of a small girl on a public bus) and I felt that if I'd had an easel I might have painted a picture too.

It was probably inevitable that I would fall asleep and I have a horrible feeling still that a thread of saliva might have been hanging from my mouth when I was awoken with a tug on my sleeve by a woman who wondered if I might like to pay my bill. I mumbled apologies and that I loved the view and shuffled down the narrow stone steps worn smooth by dynasties of feet and on, on over the cobbles and out of Xidi.

I took a two yuan bus ride to the neighbouring village of Hongcun, 10 km upstream. Local public buses are one of the few true bargains left in China at a time of modernisation and inflation. Two or three yuan will get you almost anywhere - on-board entertainment, singing, bodily fluids, smoking, livestock, arguments, delays, bags of offal, white knuckle terror, steaming radiators and punctures are all included at no extra charge. It's good that the ride was so cheap since Hongcun and Xidi each cost an extortionate 80 yuan to enter. Yet the second village was if anything even prettier than the first. The same solid merchant homes, the same gabled roofs and polished cobbled lanes, but Hongcun has water too - two famous lakes that give the village balance and proportion and that were causing greater numbers of artists still to reach for their watercolours to capture the scene. The lakes form part of Hongcun's plan that is supposed to resemble the body of a buffalo. Moon and Sun Ponds are the buffalo stomachs and two ancient ginkgo and red poplar trees at the village entrance are the buffalo horns, the streams and canals its intestines. I'm unsure what the thrustingly erect stone marker in the centre of the village is designed to represent.

Such is the picture book prettiness of Hongcun that it was chosen by Ang Lee as the setting for his movie 'Crouching Tiger, Hidden Dragon'. Moon Lake, where I watched a woman in ankle length wellies washing a basket of green leaves, is the very same body of water that Michelle Yeoh leapt so extravagantly in the movie, above the carp who circled in the green water below. These fish swam lethargically in the clear water and have become astonishingly plump like many of the villagers who have grown fat and comfortable on Crouching Tiger 80 yuan entrance ticket fame.

The villagers of Hongcun certainly knew how to turn a dollar. There was a tourist market on the edge of Sun Lake and many house front doors were thrown open to accommodate a table laden with fans and coins, teapots and paintbrushes for sale. I wasn't buying but I enjoyed the glimpses into people's homes, their battered chairs and bicycles and posters of ancestors and Mao Zedong hanging from crumbly whitewashed walls. Some had photos too of President Jiang Zemin because he visited the village once and declared it beautiful. Jiang is the only man to my knowledge who wears his trousers so high that his belt might be mistaken for a cravat, though Mao himself wore his waistband disturbingly high too.

There were old women in Hongcun selling chestnuts on street corners. I bought some from a jawdroppingly ancient crone whose brown gnarly face was more walnut than chestnut and we made a deal, that I would buy if she allowed me to photograph that astonishingly wrinkled face. She agreed, took my money, but then covered her face with wrinkled arthritic hands so that I could not photograph her and the self-esteem I gained from the pretty art students in Xidi drained away as I realised I'd been outwitted by a 100-year-old.

Hongcun may be full of tourist shops, cheating grannies and corpulent carp, but it wasn't always like this in Anhui. The Chinese refer to the province as 'nongye dasheng' - the big agricultural province - which is a euphemism for somewhere very poor. It's still the poorest province in eastern China, a victim of geography because the north of this landlocked place is arid and eroded and the south is very mountainous. The central belt of Anhui around the Yangtze River is regularly flooded; the river has been hindrance and hardship for Anhui rather than a helpful source of industry and trade, indeed the river has traditionally divided Anhui so profoundly that north and south have barely seemed like a coherent entity at all.[3] Only Sichuan suffered more terribly in the great famine of 1959-61 when the death rate in Anhui rose by 250% and the birthrate fell by 80%. The old gnarly woman with the chestnuts would have remembered all that so I could hardly begrudge her my cash gained by small deception.

Anhui is more comfortable now. The Yangtze was finally bridged in the province in 1995; buses are full, the fish are fat, young people have time to paint. Much of the investment in the province has come in recent years on the urging of Premier Hu Jintao. He is a native of southern Anhui and I wonder if this is the response of a Huizhou merchant made good - sent away to Beijing but still determined to send some profit home and respect his ancestors.

If Huizhou villages are renowned for their beauty though, this is as nothing compared to the ecstasies of Huangshan. There are holy and ancient mountains round every corner in China; though the mountains of Huangshan have no Buddhist or Taoist traditions like those at Emei or Tai Shan (See Sichuan and Shandong chapters), Huangshan outstrips them all in popularity.

---

3   Anhui was only created as a province in the 17th century.

It is said that every person in China should visit Huangshan at least once and on the sunny autumn Sunday when I went, it seemed that the whole population had come at once. I had been warned about the crowds and did everything I could to avoid them. I awoke at 5am in my hostel 30 km from the foot of the hill and crept around to avoid waking the other residents, though this was near impossible on the creaky stairs. Remarkably the breakfast I had been promised was ready for me and steaming on the table, that strange collection of soggy white toast, an alarmingly pink sausage and a slice of orange that Chinese hostels call an 'American breakfast' though I have yet to meet an American who would claim to eat such a meal in Texas, Ohio or Maine.

My plan for a dawn raid was going well but the scheme was in tatters by the time I arrived at Huangshan. I should have known better. The bus was late and no self-respecting driver in China would travel 30 km with a single fare. So we waited for more business and drove slowly around town like some red light kerb crawler and then waited some more and by the time we arrived at the mountain, the sun was high in the sky and the queues for the cable cars were of biblical proportions, though the driver had at least secured one more 10 yuan paying fare for his bus.

It hadn't been sunny on the way to the mountain. The mist had been swirling low amongst the Huizhou merchant houses and rice fields and I considered turning back for though Huangshan is famous for its ethereal mists clinging to pine trees and swirling amongst dramatic granite, this was a pea-souper and not ethereal at all. But it burnt off and with it went my last chance of avoiding the crowds. My day on Huangshan became an exercise in people watching, a fascinating insight into the burgeoning Chinese domestic tourist industry, a test of my ability to cope in a crowd. But as a day on the mountain, in the clear cold air, as communion with nature and discovering inner peace, frankly it was rubbish.

I queued for an hour to pay 310 yuan to enter the scenic area and board a cable car to the top. The information boards that I had plenty of time to read told me that these are the hills that inspired the movie Avatar and I wondered if this meant they were simply overblown and overrated - it would certainly explain the crowds of people queueing up because they had been told they should, though there were perfectly fine and less popular (and less *expensive*) mountains elsewhere.

The cable car went some way to restoring my faith in the worth of Huangshan. As we gained height the vertical granite and otherworldliness of these hills became clearer and at least in my little steel cocoon hanging from a wire there was for a while only five other people so I could forget about the crowds who would be waiting above. It was impossible to make sense of the wooden signs at the top that had no scale or point of reference and taught me only that I should go to Lotus Flower Rock, Refreshing Terrace, White Goose Ridge and Beginning to Believe Peak, so for a while I wandered aimlessly and got hopelessly lost. But this was no bad thing, and for a while I avoided the crowds and wandered precipitous paths on the edge of yawning drops by pine trees that grew improbably from the vertical rock.

The path through Huangshan's 'Grand Canyon' was particularly fine and the number of people lessened as the steps became steeper and more exposed. For a moment I thought I'd lost my way since no tourist path should be this vertiginous and I began to feel a strange desire to fling myself off and save myself the queue for the cable car down. I was reassured by the arrival of a group of middle-aged heavily made up Korean women who were running up and down the vertical steps, laughing hysterically and pretending to throw each other off, oblivious to the risk of death or snagging a brightly coloured stocking.

I thought someone *had* fallen when I heard lusty screams and cries rebounding from the rocks but this was merely a group of Chinese tourists leaning over the guard rail and shouting into the gaping jaws of the valley below in order to listen to their voices rebounding from the granite. 'Hello-Hello-Hello'. 'I'm disturbing everyones peace and quiet-quiet-quiet and being very annoying-ing-ing-ing'.

Little did I realise that this was as much peace and quiet-quiet-quiet I would get on Huangshan today. I climbed out of the Grand Canyon through a bomb blasted dark tunnel that went through a protuberance of rock so steep that even middle-aged Koreans couldn't climb round it and began to climb towards Bright Summit Peak. The summit is the highest point of Huangshan – what O-Level geography teachers would call a 'honeypot' -and it was *crawling* with people gathered like ants attracted by sweet views and the scent of somewhere famous. My descent to the western route past 'Flower Blooming on a Brush Tip', 'Purple Cloud Peak' and 'Mobile Phone Rock'[4] was slow beyond belief as 10,000 tourists shuffled and pushed their way along a mountain path in search of mountain solitude. The crawling was exacerbated because we all had to squeeze through a narrow rock fissure called 'The Gleam of Sky' (another poetic name) and such was the press of bodies that my mind turned to football crowds, Indian temple worshippers, Meccan pilgrims and the frantic stampede of disaster.

This was more like Disneyland than a mountain adventure. There were further delays as 10,000 people stopped to photograph the Welcoming Guest Pine - one of the thousands of wind contorted trees on Huangshan. This tree looked much the same as many others and I was unable to see why it had been so singled out for fame and reproduction on countless scroll paintings, cigarette packets and beer bottles, but I stopped and looked at the forlorn tree perched on the rocks above too because in this crowd I had no choice.

By the time I boarded a cable car down (another 80 yuan on this financially ruinous mountain) it had taken me three hours to shuffle 2 km from Bright Summit Peak and I was exhausted by frustration rather than physical effort with a sense of wasted time on these otherworldly rocks like I had just sat through a screening of Avatar. My snail speed companions had been as frustrated as me; 'tai dou ren' they had said – 'too many people' and I have never seen so many arguments and posturing in China as I saw on Huangshan that day as people accused other people of pushing in, getting in the way, going too slow, spoiling their trip to China's famous mountain.

It is this fame that is at the heart of Huangshan's problems. The Chinese believe that such is the beauty of Huangshan, that once climbed, a man will never want to climb another mountain and even in this throng of people I was still asked what I thought of Huangshan and told what a fine mountain it was. I agreed, too weary to argue

---

4   the names of peaks and rocks on Huangshan are a kind of poetry, 'Mobile Phone Rock' excepted.

and conscious that I should avoid offending people with whom I was likely to be walking shoulder to shoulder and experiencing unwelcome physical intimacy for at least the next hour. I said I also felt that after Huangshan I might never want to climb another mountain, though I didn't mean this as a compliment to Anhui's famous hills.

Huangshan's reputation stems from its significance in Chinese art and literature. The weird granite shapes have inspired artists and songwriters through the centuries (a whole school of ink painting is named after the mountain) and 20,000 poems have been written about Huangshan[5] which is about one for every person on the path on a typical sunny Sunday. It is the exponential rise of China's domestic tourism coupled with Huangshan's fame that combined to create my get-me-out-of-here-I-can't-stand-it-any-longer feeling that I have rarely experienced before outside of a Chinese train station or public toilet. Traveling China has become much easier in recent years with the lifting of restrictions, massive investment in roads, railways and airlines and the rapid rise of incomes. The number of domestic tourist trips increased from 695 million in 1998 to around 1 billion in 2010 creating a revenue of 1¼ trillion yuan. As a consequence all the honeypots are crowded, the Great Wall deluged, Forbidden City swamped, terracotta warriors thronged, Hong Kong crammed, Huangshan sardined. It would be impossible for such numbers to be low impact but discreet and subtle these tourists are not.

Megaphones, litter, flags and massive tour groups lead the way in economy of scale Chinese tourism. Other countries are starting to feel the economic benefit of Chinese tourism too; foreign trips for Chinese tourists rose from 3,000,000 to 12,000,000 in 2002-2010[6] and by 2020 China is projected to produce 100 million outbound trips, making it the largest exporter of tourists in the world by far. From the Amazon to the Outback, the Pyramids to the Taj Mahal, let the megaphones ring out and the tour flags fly!

---

5   The eighth century poet Li Bai is said to have given the mountain its name.

6   Though most outbound tourists only go to Hong Kong and Macau. Only 5% of Chinese tourists go to Europe and fewer still to the USA which did not receive 'approved tourist status' until June 2008.

As I inched closer to the cable car building along the crowded mountain path, I stared with everyone else at eyeball to eyeball shouting matches that erupted all around, since there was little else to do apart from exclaim 'tai dou ren' and muse whether it might be physically possible to shove a megaphone down the throat of a tour guide. A woman stepped on my foot and another tried to push past so in the interest of cultural assimilation I began to argue too. The woman complained loudly that I wouldn't let her past and I shouted back and soon others were joining in on my side so that the argument was raging long after I had left it and I finally boarded a car with the self same woman who had tried to push past me. All was forgiven on the gentle swaying ride through the rocks when the crowds had gone and the view was filled with a jumble of peaks and boulders, too wild and steep and inhospitable for crowds and megaphones.

It was possible to see why Huangshan causes such a stir as the shadows lengthened and the rock turned gold in the late afternoon sun. If it had been permissible to simply ride up and down Huangshan in a cable car all day and not get out to fight the crowds I might have liked the place much more, and as I boarded a bus back to the villages and fields I decided that, like a Huizhou merchant, it was time to find my fortune elsewhere.

TIANJIN

天津

11 399 sq km
Population 10.23 million

"It is too early to say"

Zhou En-Lai, when asked about the effects of the 1789 French Revolution.

On 27th July1976, thousands of chickens in Baiguantuan, 100km North-East of Tianjin refused to eat and ran around in wild concentric circles scratching uselessly at the ground and clucking noisily in bug-eyed terror. This seems like normal chicken behaviour to me, but hens were not the only creatures exhibiting foul conduct that night.

31

Mr. Yao Guangqing, a city official from nearby Tangshan in Hebei province said "The weather was very hot and close, and dogs and chickens refused to go inside buildings. As I walked home, I passed a pond and noticed that fish were jumping out of the water." Residents in the same town talked of alarmed owners grasping their wildly flapping and clearly suicidal goldfish which leapt repeatedly from their bowls. Chickens dashing hither and thither are one thing, but fish leaping from water is another matter entirely. Clearly something was wrong in North East China on that July night.

The behaviour of local residents seems to have been little better than the chickens. It took a total of 4 hours to show a movie at Tangshan open air cinema that night as numerous fights broke out in the audience. The short temperedness of movie goers may have been caused by the strange lights and loud sounds reported by people all over town. Witnesses tell of fireballs racing across the sky followed by loud roaring noises louder than a plane. No wonder customers were so distracted since it seems likely that these celestial lights and sounds would have been much more interesting than the film.

The leaping fish and chaotic chickens, the preternatural lights in the night sky were auguries of the most devastating natural disaster of the 20th century. Rumblings began at 3.42am on the morning of 28th July 1976 and within 15 seconds a powerful earthquake, measuring 7.8 on the Richter scale, had destroyed 90% of Tangshan's buildings. Initial estimates suggest that over 600 000 people were killed in the calamity, though this was subsequently revised to 250 000. Either figure confirms that the earthquake at Tangshan was deadly in a way that none had been since the Shaanxi Chinese quake killed a reported 830 000 in January 1556.

The tragedy centered on the coal mining town of Tangshan, 60 miles North of Tianjin. Here, buildings were flattened over a five square mile area and the devastation was such that pictures from the town at the time are like those black and white photographs of Dresden or Berlin at the end of World War II. The death count was so high because the city is built on unstable alluvial soil and because the tremor struck in the early hours of the morning when most people were fast asleep. A total of 1,951 miners died though The New York Times reported that it was a miner called Li Yulin who first brought word of the devastation to Beijing. Dirty and exhausted, Li drove in an ambulance for 6 hours, right up to the party leaders' compound at Zhongnanhai adjacent to the Forbidden City, where he reported that Tangshan had been destroyed.

The government responded by spraying the ruins with disinfectant and dropping biscuits to the hungry survivors. PLA troops arrived at the double and scratched uselessly at the ruins with bare hands. Casualties were greater still due to a number of aftershocks and because corpses were buried quickly close to the residences in which they perished. This caused health problems after summer rainfall when the bodies were exposed. Troops left their digging and had to find these impromptu graves, exhume the bodies and organise reburial outside of the city. Long term rebuilding was started almost straight away, foreign aid refused and street committees began organising widows and widowers into marriages of convenience in order to maintain social harmony. "It worked out very well for me", said one determinedly optimistic, and opportunistic old lady interviewed years later by local TV who had been married to a worker from a nearby street. "I got on much better with my new husband than the one who died in the earthquake".

Tangshan was the epicenter of the seismic shift but I first became aware of the magnitude of the quake sitting by the earthquake memorial in the center of Tianjin, China's 4th largest city. By the standards of Chinese municipal art, the memorial is an unusually tasteful tribute to the 23 938 who died here on 28th July 1976. There are the usual statues of defiant we-won't-let-this-beat-us lantern-jawed military, but here also is a statue of a mother, head bowed in grief for her children, set amidst beds of azaleas beneath the steel and glass of Tianjin's burgeoning skyline. When the summer humidity rises in North-Eastern China, men beat the heat by turning up their vests and trouser legs to expose as much flesh as possible to the occasional breath of wind and in the memorial park there was no shortage of old men ventilating themselves as they crouched over their Chinese Chess boards. I asked if they remembered this 'thing', since I didn't know the Chinese word for earthquake, and pointed to the pale stones of the monument. One of the bare-bellied, rolled-up trousers, socks-and-shoes old men lifted his head from his game and answered in English. "No one cried" he said "the deaths were too many".

The political aftershocks of the event were equally huge and in a century of political turbulence, the year 1976 stands as a watershed in modern Chinese history. This was the summer of the USA bicentennial, of Nadia Comoneci's perfect scores at the Montreal Olympics and the Great British heat wave. Such events seem frivolous compared to China where the summer of that year marked the tenth anniversary of the chaos, infighting, Red Guard wanton destruction and virtual civil war of the Cultural Revolution which claimed a total of 1 million lives. Mao's life was nearing its end - the earthquake came to be seen as a portent of his death just 6 weeks later - and China was entering a period of political struggle the outcome of which would determine the direction the country would take for the next 10 years.

On one side were the moderates led by Deng Xiaoping who desired the introduction of openness and reform. Deng had been denounced from his death bed by Mao and sent into internal exile by the radical 'Gang of Four', led by Mao's wife Jiang Qing, who was in no mood to let the trifle of an earthquake derail her plans for China and denunciation of Deng. "There were merely several hundred thousand deaths. So what? Denouncing Deng Xiaoping concerns 800 million people" opined Mao's missus. The new Premier and Mao look-a-like Hua Guofeng was less brutally insensitive and, consummate politician that he was, Hua visited the sites affected by the quake where he shook hands and patted babies' heads. Despite Mad Madam Mao's warnings to 'Be alert to Deng Xiaoping's criminal attempt to exploit earthquake phobia to suppress revolution", the battle for hearts and minds was won. Hua arrested the Gang of Four in October 1976, Deng was rehabilitated and China embarked on a series of reforms and modernizations which, though imperfect, were infinitely preferable to the mayhem of a second Cultural Revolution. In this way, the cataclysmic events of Tangshan and Tianjin of 28 July became both a taker and a saver of lives.

The death of Mao, fall of the Gang of Four and July earthquake; profound moments all, but ask a native of Tianjin what he remembers most about 1976 and he'll tell you 'The death of Zhou En-Lai'. At least

I *think* that's what he'll tell you, since the Tianjin dialect is so distinct. I had been warned about the eloquent, humorous Tianjin native with his thick accent and rapid speech. Other Chinese talk of 'weizuizu', which roughly translates as 'the Tianjin mouth' and I was helpfully advised by other Chinese to approximate the local speech by speaking standard Mandarin or Putonghua with orange pips in my mouth, though I suppose any seeds might serve the purpose. One nation it might be, but Chinese across the country derive considerable amusement from the idiosyncrasies of each others' speech and in a place this size, this can mean a whole different language. Thus I have had Hebei taxi drivers in tucks of laughter and radioing their friends in delight by speaking a few words in Cantonese and a Sichuanese farmer who hooted and slapped the fat backside of his buffalo when I asked the way with the slurred tone of a Beijinger.

Zhou En-Lai died on 8 January 1976. The Gang of Four had ordered that displays of public grief were inappropriate for such a 'capitalist roader', but despite this, hundreds of thousands of defiant mourners crowded Tiananmen Square in Beijing to express their sorrow at the passing of this much loved man who had been Premier since the creation of the People's Republic in 1949. Zhou and his wife Deng Yingchao were not born in Tianjin but spent much of their youth here as students and post World War I protesters against Japanese interference in China and such was their affection for the town that a portion of their mortal remains were scattered in Tianjin's river, the Haihe. Tianjin has returned the compliment by the building of the Zhou and Deng Memorial Hall on the city outskirts.

This place, opened in 1998, has received 4 million visitors to date and is "a place to behold a great man with awe, where the elegant demeanor of these two great persons can be highlighted" according to Tianjin tourist information literature. There's a certain amount of awe in the entrance lobby where I had to surrender my bottle of mineral water "in case you make a bomb" according to the security guard. Here, past the Ilyushin passenger jet presented to Zhou by the Soviet Union in 1957 (no leader should be without one) is a huge white marble statue of Zhou and Deng called 'deep love full of the rivers and mountains', framed by the 'broad sea and smooth cloud' wall hanging.

Yet the majority of the nine sections of the exhibition – charisma, pursuit of truth, saving China, State affairs, women's movements, turning the tide, great causes, living forever and last wishes – are rather more concerned with the friendship and love of this man and woman united by revolution, than with great deeds of state. So here are photos of the 2 in warm embrace on the porch of a house in Tianjin, or in wicker chairs outside Zhou's cave dwelling in the loess hills of Shaanxi province at the end of the Long March in 1935. A smiling, smoking Mao is often in the photos and sometimes armed guards and lines of red flags fluttering in the breeze, but Zhou and Deng have eyes only for each other.

The couple married in 1925 and remained childless though, like a Far Eastern Brad Pitt and Angelina Jolie, they adopted several orphaned children of 'revolutionary martyrs', including future Premier Li Peng. Deng outlived her husband by 20 years and kept herself busy with any number of good Socialist causes, but despite all her revolutionary committees and women's movements, the old revolutionary must have missed her comrade terribly.

Zhou was certainly no under achiever. By the age of 4 he could read and write several hundred Chinese characters, which may explain his tenacity in defending this complicated script in the 1950s when other leaders, including Mao, were convinced it should be abandoned as an impediment to peasant literacy. I can hear the old curmudgeon in Politburo meetings now… "If I learnt it by the age of 4, then 800 million peasants can jolly well learn it now". By his mid twenties, Zhou had been Head of Tianjin Students Union, a trainee teacher and organiser of the Chinese Communist movement across Western Europe after he fled to Paris like most good 20th century Asian revolutionaries. Many a night Zhou must have shared croissants and some ripe Brie with Ho Chi Minh and Pol Pot who were also there at the time as Edith Piaf lilted from a gramophone through a latticed window on a warm spring evening in Montmartre. Well, possibly. I hardly dare make a comparison with my achievements by the same age, but it seems Zhou could organize a revolution in the same time it takes me to get the shopping in, dead head the roses or hang that picture that has leaned against the wall behind the sofa for the past three weeks.

Zhou's political career after 1949 is a stellar succession of political campaigns, economic reforms and, in particular, diplomatic missions abroad. These culminated in the 1972 visit to China by Richard Nixon when the President famously remarked that Beijing really had a 'great wall' and Zhou took centre stage in the absence of an ailing Mao. He was ailing himself the following year and eventually succumbed to bladder cancer but is remembered for his dedication as a skilled negotiator with an unusual attention to detail. A man at the head of a revolution certainly, but Zhou was more like a Mandarin bureaucrat in the Confucian tradition. Caught in a paradox, China's Premier was at once conservative and radical, pragmatic and ideological, with a belief in harmony and order while simultaneously extolling rebellion. His role in the Great Proletarian Cultural Revolution is shrouded in controversy and highlights how Zhou was pulled in two directions. He personally intervened to curb the excesses of the Red Guards and used his influence to protect some of China's oldest treasures including the Potala Palace in Lhasa. Yet he survived the purges and in photos of Red Guard rallies of the time, he's usually there standing behind Mao and waving his Little Red Book; sensibly pragmatic perhaps, but Zhou fully appreciated the benefits of self preservation. Still, handsome and charismatic, the Memorial Hall exonerates him as a man who 'tried his best' during China's difficult years and perhaps that is enough.

Tianjin's taxi drivers don't have a bad word for Deng or Zhou but were delighted by my summary of Mao as 'sometimes good and sometimes bad'. All were united in their condemnation of China's then current boss Hu Jintao who is 'suspicious and untrustworthy' and who should clearly take some man-of-the-people lessons from the life of old Zhou. Taxis are a good shorthand method of understanding the status of a city in China. In the undeveloped far West, you're as likely to ride in a donkey cart as a car and in modern Hong Kong the cabs are ubiquitous, efficient and clean and the drivers don't try to extract a few extra yuan by claiming the meter is broken. Tianjin is a city in the middle of feverish reconstruction and redevelopment and a short distance from the center of power in Beijing. It sits at the northern end of the Sui dynasty Grand Canal which still provides links with the Yangtze and towns further south and such is its size and prominence that this former capital of Hebei province is one of only four cities given the status of separate municipality. But despite all this, here the taxis are cramped and the seat belts don't work and the meter starts at a bargain five yuan. In Shanghai; big, brash, infamous, decadent Shanghai, they start at 10 yuan (13 at night), which makes the Paris of the East exactly twice as exclusive, desirable and stylish as this city that no one has really heard of and which is completely overshadowed by its big brother Beijing 120 km away.

But it wasn't always so. Tianjin means 'Heavenly Ford' after the fording of the Haihe here by Emperor Yongle in 1404, though it was the 19th and 20th centuries that for a while placed the city at the centre of Chinese affairs. This may be a cause of some regret to locals who regard the invasion by foreign devils at this time as a cause of shameful regret, but the evidence of European occupation of the city is everywhere.

19th century Britain seems to have had a superabundance of stiff upper lipped naval officers who were convinced of the need to educate the savages; a term that can be defined as anyone who could not play billiards or who lived more than a couple of hundred miles from the Home Counties in any direction. As a consequence armed vessels were dispatched to make mischief across the globe in a policy called 'gunboat diplomacy'. It was Tianjin's turn in 1858 when Admiral Sir Michael Seymour took his starched uniform and extravagant moustaches and captured Tientsin (as it was then called) in the opening skirmishes of the Second Opium War. Seymour's gunboat was sufficiently persuasive to encourage the Emperor of China to ratify the Treaties of Tientsin in 1860 which opened the city to foreign trade and the establishment of concessions.

Many Chinese cities were subject to such humiliation at this time which partly explains the revolution and rapid industrialization of China in the 20th century, since Mao's peculiar brand of Communism was as much nationalist as socialist. When he announced that China had 'stood up' from Tiananmen gate in 1949, he meant that she had managed to stand up to the bullying and land grabbing of the rest of the world in China that had happened over the preceding 100 years. Tientsin was unique because the whole of the industrialized world took a nibble from the city and established an enclave where Chinese law and culture did not apply and which provided a home from home for privileged and rather superior expat communities. Britain had a concession here of course, but so did France, Germany, Italy, Japan and Russia. Even Austria-Hungary and Belgium got in on the act.

Considering the inequities of the system, the concession era was remarkably peaceful in Tientsin and the majority population turned a blind eye as the invaders established their own prisons, barracks, schools, hospitals and pink gin drinks cabinets. The settlers began a sort of unofficial competition in building the most grandiose and ostentatious images of permanence that they could in their enclave and it is these hubristic symbols that constitute Tianjin's most notable feature today. British concession buildings are all ionic columns and marble porticos in that curious high Victorian mix of classicism with a gothic flourish. Two blocks away, the visitor enters the wrought iron balconied world of Paris, while 10 minutes walk further, the Italianate flourishes of rococo and grandeur of Rome prevails. The old German quarter is all red tiled Bavaria and here also is Kiesselings century old bakery where the pinafored staff continues to serve gingerbread, black forest gateaux and high tea.

I couldn't help but admire the grandiose ambition of these men and the stability and statement of their architectural legacy that had survived Japanese invasion and Communist revolution. The interior of the buildings is often more impressive still, especially along the Jiefang Bielu where the grand old buildings give an illusion of walking through Victorian Manchester, or Delhi or Shanghai for that matter. These buildings had mostly been banks and Tianjin's municipal council had chosen to celebrate them with a series of plaques and notice boards detailing their history and an invitation to go inside where acres of stained glass, fat stone cherubs and vaulted ceilings dwarfed the routine of China Post Office workers or insurance clerks shuffling papers below. I felt an irrational pride in these places, like I had in some way been involved in their construction, but above all I just *liked* them with that same comfort of familiarity a long way from home that German colonialists must have felt when they bought an apple strudel from Kiesselings.

If Tianjin has come to terms with its colonial legacy, this wasn't always the case and life in the concessions occasionally got a bit scary. In June 1870, Wanghailou Church, built by French Catholic missionaries one year before, was attacked and burned to the ground along with the nearby French Consulate by an angry Chinese mob. Confusion seems to have arisen regarding a literal interpretation of Catholic theology when the nuns were suspected of consuming real blood and flesh at Holy Communion. The confusion was compounded by the sighting of several jars of pickled onions and the inevitable conclusion that the ghoulish nuns were making preserves of childrens' eyes. After the 'incident of the pickled eyeballs' as the event isn't, but really should be known, the Qing government agreed to pay compensation to France as if a church in rural Brittany had been razed rather than one in the heart of China.

More trouble was to come. In 1900, a mystical anti foreigner group who believed themselves immune to bullets called the Society of Right and Harmonious Fists, or 'Boxers' occupied Tientsin and laid siege to those foreign blights on the Chinese escutcheon. A joint European and Japanese force intervened and executed many of the Boxers before handing control of the city back to the Qing government 2 years later, no doubt with a great deal of patronizing advice exhorting Empress Cixi to look after the place better in future.

In July 1937, the city fell to Japan and this gave rise to the Tientsin incident of June 1939 when the Imperial Japanese Army surrounded and blockaded the British concession after Britain's refusal to hand over six Chinese men who had assassinated a prominent local collaborator and taken refuge there. The incident looked likely to cause an Anglo-Japanese war until the British Prime Minister decided that he had enough on his hands with Hitler and gave up the unfortunate refugees who were promptly executed by the Japanese. Tientsin's troubles continued after the Japanese surrender when the city became a base for American forces. In 1946, a series of rapes of Chinese girls caused huge demonstrations and eventually the withdrawal of US troops in 1947; after 87 years of colonial interference, China finally had her city back.

Despite such unwelcome intrusion for so long, the people of Tianjin are remarkably hospitable to and interested in `waiguoren' or 'outside people'. I was causing quite a stir as I sat in the Gaubouli Dumpling

Shop and the giggling waitress brought me a free glass of green tea with my meal. I naturally interpreted this as an apology for that nasty business at Wanchouli Church in 1870 and I in turn left a tip as a mark of regret for my country's arrogantly imperialist policies and imposition of the scourge of opium on the Chinese population in the mid nineteenth century. Gaubouli is a venerable Tianjin institution in a city that is serious about its dumplings. These delicate savoury parcels of meat and vegetables can be enjoyed in almost any restaurant, hotel or from a myriad of street vendors across the city, though Goubouli are considered to be the finest purveyors of xiaolongbao. The name means 'dogs won't touch it', but my waitress, though generous with her green tea, was unable to tell me why. The manager was summoned to answer the waiguoren's question and he told me that it was a reference to the ugliness of the original proprietor rather than the quality of the dumplings which are excellent and would I like some more tea?

Even The Astor on Jiefung Bielu had dumplings on its menu. This venerable hotel used to be the swankiest in Tianjin; the first in China to have telephones, electric lights and elevators, though now its colonial ambience, pictures of old Tientsin and dark wood interior have been superseded by the chrome and natural light of top end international hotels. In 1924, the last Emperor of the Qing dynasty, Pu-Yi, was forced to leave the Forbidden City and licked his wounds in the Astor until the Japanese moved him on to Dalian in Liaoning province in 1931. Poor Pu-Yi; as if losing the eternal dragon throne held by his ancestors for hundreds of years and being ordered around by the Japanese wasn't enough, he also suffered the ignominy of rejection in Tianjin, when the Imperial concubine Wenxiu divorced him. This was the first time such a thing had happened to an Emperor, though you can understand Wenxiu's point of view. She had after all signed up to a life of unparalleled luxury in the company of subservient eunuchs in the opulent surroundings of the Forbidden City; the mini bar in the Astor Hotel just doesn't seem to cut it by comparison. Rarely can a man have suffered such a fall from grace. (For more details on the life of Pu-Yi see Liaoning chapter).

My foreign face was equally well received at the main Tianjin market of Guwan Shichang, though this had much to do with the likelihood that my pockets would be deeper and my negotiating skills less refined than the average local with his Tianjin mouth on the hunt for a bargain. Guwan Shichang is exactly what you would expect of a Chinese antique market and you're more likely to pick up something cheap here in provincial Tianjin than in the tourist markets of Beijing and Shanghai. Here on a few chaotic streets in the centre of the old town, hundreds of tradesman lay out their wares on old blankets and bargain hard. There is an extraordinary collection of bird cages, pottery, Mao statues, watches, cigarette cards, fans, tiny lotus shoes for bound feet, lacquer ware and pipes here, interspersed with hand drawn barrels selling sweet potatoes, corn and dumplings. I was drawn to the colour stills from Cultural Revolutionary ballets; pirouetting Red Guard dancers clutching hand grenades and Long Marchers pas de deuxing on the bodies of defeated Landlords but eventually settled on a Hitler doll at a knock down price.

This action figure rippling with muscles and dressed in black leather trench coat was a sort of homoerotic Fascist fantasy doll and the stall holder wasn't going to let me get away easily after registering my interest. 'Xitele, Xitele!' he cried, removed Adolf's leather boots and demonstrated the moving joints of this far right Barbie doll. There was no matching Goebbels Playmobil set or Tiger Tank Barbie accessories unfortunately, but the game commenced. "Special price 200 yuan, where you come from?' asked the owner of this National Socialist Toys R Us stall. 'Hong Kong - Oh, they speak funny there, OK for you today 100 yuan, I like you very much 80 yuan, no problem 50 yuan final price" and Xitele was mine.

Chinese attitudes to Hitler are difficult to fathom in the West and as I guiltily threw Adolf into my rucksack, I was reminded of the bar in Hong Kong I had stumbled into while escaping a sudden downpour. In there the walls were decorated with swastikas and a huge picture of the Wehrmacht cavalry riding through the Arc de Triomphe after the fall of Paris where the dartboard or picture of dogs playing snooker should have been. The owner explained that he was an admirer of Hitler and interested in German history and would I like to see his SS dagger before I ordered my beer?

I had met a German tourist in rural Shanxi province the year before and told her that the Chinese name for Germany is 'Deguo' which means 'virtuous country'. She said this was all well and good but that she told most Chinese she met that she was from Belgium or Holland or France, since if she mentioned Germany she invariably received the same reply. "Oh Germany", they would say "Xitele, Xitele, very good!" and give a resounding thumbs up.

I think this is because the Chinese see Hitler as a strong leader and a man of action. He is also someone who looked funny with that little moustache, like Charlie Chaplin and who waved his arms around a lot. Admiration of Hitler doesn't imply any degree of anti-Semitism. Rather, he was a man who made many mistakes but did great things too and in a country still under the sway of Maoism, this is something that many Chinese can simply relate to.

Tianjin has been rebuilt and remodeled since the tragedy of 1976. But it's not all shopping malls and spruced up colonial follies; the city has its fair share of temples too, though most sit incongruously in the shadow of immense high rises. On the river bank and surrounded by the faux Ming dynasty hutongs of Ancient Culture Street is Tianshan Temple, a tribute to Mazu, the goddess of the sea where once the grandest Mazu Temple Fair in all of China was held. Dabeichan Yuan or The Monastery of Deep Compassion is Tianjin's most important Buddhist temple and is reached through an extraordinary market of prayer beads, candles, statues, talismans and gifts for the huge Sakyamuni and Guanyin statues inside. Damaged in the Cultural Revolution, the temple was unscathed by the earthquake of 1976. Inside, hundreds of Tianjin mouths were joined in a recitation of the ancient Diamond Sutra in celebration of a centuries old faith as they murmured responses to the incantations of a monk. In that instant, colonial invasion, war, Communist revolution and natural disaster seemed transitory and illusive and to have hardly changed the city at all. The monks shuffled across the worn stone of the temple courtyard, candles were lit and Tianjin was for a moment old Tientsin again.

BEIJING

北京

17 000 sq km
Population 15.5 million

*'Only one more indispensable massacre of Capitalists or
Communists or Fascists or Christians or Heretics, and there we are
- there we are in the Golden Future'*

Aldous Huxley

I'm rarely happier in China than when I'm sitting firmly in a saddle and
turning the pedals of a bicycle. Better still if the bike is a proper old-
fashioned Chinese model and I'm out early enough to avoid the traffic.
So it was that I came to be cycling past Tiananmen Square at 6.30 in

the morning on 30 kg of solid 'Forever' brand bike, whose frame announced it was' made in Shanghai'. This is the sort of bike that adopts a momentum of its own and on which the rider sits up and begs and feels toweringly tall. So I free wheeled through the crisp morning Beijing air and seemed to be almost at Mao's eye line as he stared impassively from his portrait on Tiananmen Gate.

The country lane, provincial city pedaling of my youth was more mundane than this and it felt thrilling to be in the iconic centre of this iconic city. Beijing is sophisticated and world-weary; so much so that even the sight of a hairy foreigner sitting bolt upright and wobbling along on a Shanghai bike created hardly a murmur of surprise. Only one man waved enthusiastically and gave a cheery 'Ni Hao', but I might have wobbled and lost control of my Forever iron horse if I had let go and waved back.

Mao's enormous portrait on Tiananmen Gate is the most famous image in Beijing and possibly in all of China. I dismounted here and took photos of the gate, of people taking photos of people in front of the gate and of my shiny black bicycle in front of the gate; one solid, overweight and unpredictable Chinese icon in front of another.

Gate and portrait are scrupulously clean and freshly painted. Verges are neatly trimmed and abundantly floral and highly polished rhetoric on either side of the portrait trumpets 'Long live the People's Republic of China' and ' Long live the unity of the peoples of the world'. The gate is so immaculately presented since it has huge political significance at the entrance to the Forbidden City though it wasn't always Mao who hung here; the gate has been the repository for a number of objects of veneration. Sun Yat Sen once adorned the masonry and also Lenin, Stalin, Marx and his buddy Engels. I'm pleased that Engels once had a space on the gate too since he is the forgotten man who co-wrote the *Communist Manifesto* in 1848 - a sort of George Harrison overshadowed by John Lenin. He deserves his place in history since his beard was extraordinarily fine and more luxuriant even than that of the hirsute Marx. When his portrait gazed down upon Beijing, I wonder if the Chinese thought that all foreigners must be this hairy.

The granite sets on Tiananmen Square are strong enough to withstand the weight of tanks, though my chunky bike seemed to give the security guards palpitations and I was told in no uncertain terms that my Forever was not welcome here. So, I swung across Chang'an Lu, planted the bike onto its stand and took to the square on foot.

I was early enough to see the daily flag raising ceremony where clockwork soldiers march past at 108 paces per minute, each pace exactly 75 cm long. The saluting soldiers, the red flag with its yellow stars fluttering in the early Beijing breeze and partly obscuring the now-you-see-him-now-you-don't portrait and framed by all of that Tiananmen granite seemed about as far away from the deserts of Gansu and mountains in Yunnan as China could get. But like the wild parts of the West, Tiananmen also glories in wide-open spaces. There's 100 acres of square here, which makes Tiananmen the largest urban space in the world and big enough for all those millions of Red Guards who came to worship at the altar of Mao with their Little Red Bibles in the 1960s. It's a desert of granite with neither benches nor trees and I could see all the way south to that other massive edifice called Qianmen – literally 'front gate'.

The uniformity of Tiananmen Square is broken by the 38 metre high Monument to the People's Heroes, but I barely broke stride here to look at Mao's calligraphy ('eternal glory to the People's heroes') or the bas reliefs of famous patriotic events such as Lin Zexu's destruction of opium (see Fujian chapter). No, I was off to see a Chinese hero in the flesh.

Considerable controversy followed the government decision to embalm the body of Mao after his death in 1976 and stick it in a squat mausoleum where it could be respectfully viewed by an adoring public. The building was very expensive and is rather ugly and the Chinese were not entirely sure how to do the preserving. The mausoleum is certainly impressive and was finished in double quick time by enthusiastic voluntary labour. It's heavy on symbolism and contains granite from Sichuan, porcelain from Guangdong, wood from Shanxi, Earth from the quake stricken Tangshan (see Tianjin chapter) and rock from Mount Everest. Mao rests on black stone from the holy Taoist mountain of Tai Shan in Shandong in reference to the ancient philosopher Sima Qian's remark that 'One's life can be weightier than Mount Tai or lighter than a goose feather'. There's even sand here from the Taiwan Straits in a crushingly unsubtle reference to China's claim to her lost province.

China's post Mao transient Chairman Hua Guofeng was able to announce that "Chairman Mao will always be with us" at the opening ceremony just one year after China had lost her Great Helmsman. But the extravagant cost of the place was a stick with which to beat Hua and he was soon replaced by more economy minded leaders and anyway, it's doubtful that Mao wanted to be always with the Chinese people at all. Mao acknowledged in 1956 that "we all have to die, whether crushed by a house or blown to smithereens by an atom bomb" - though I'm hoping for a more peaceful death than either of these options. He pronounced "after people die, they shouldn't be allowed to occupy any more space. We should all be burnt ... used for fertilizer".

This eminently practical approach to death is rooted in good peasant common sense and contrasts sharply with China's first emperor Shi Huang Di who moved heaven and earth and swallowed mercury to achieve immortality, but they went ahead and pickled him anyway. Mao's physician Liu Zhisui was horrified since the China of the 1970s didn't have the necessary embalming technologies and had to borrow expertise from Vietnam who had preserved Ho Chi Minh six years before.

Liu claims they made a mess of things in his book 'The private lives of Chairman Mao'. Such accounts don't inspire confidence and I queued outside the over budgeted mausoleum in a state of excitement, since it's not everyday that I get to see a long dead, badly preserved corpse in a crystal coffin. Security is tight in the queue; no bags, no cameras and plenty of heavy-handed frisking by teenage guards in poorly fitted uniforms. I was momentarily shaken when one of the smooth faced guardians asked to see 'my backside', though fortunately he simply meant that I should turn around rather than bare my hairy buttocks in some arcane tribute to Mao. There have been attempts to vandalize the place such as when a hapless protester tried to smuggle grenades inside but was betrayed by the wooden handles protruding from his pockets. Guards were commended for 'discovering' this terrorist attempt at corpse destruction, though it seems to me that spotting several wooden sticks in a man's pockets would take little discovery at all.

So, camera, bag and grenade free, I wandered through the enormous doors, past a statue of Mao all white, seated and Lincoln like and into the hushed inner sanctum itself. The first thing the visitor notices here is the speed with which everyone is hurried along. Eyes fixed on the corpse, I was soon traveling at a pace that equated to a jog and the whole thing lasted less than three minutes. This gives credence to those naysayers who argue that I wasn't looking at Mao's body at all but a waxwork replica since the original was so badly preserved; perhaps the authorities rush everyone through in the hope that no one will notice the waxy skin or the glassy eyes.

Mao certainly did look weird and waxy draped in a red flag with hammer and sickle, but, that a 30-year-old preserved body should look a bit strange or lifeless seems a statement of the obvious. Let's face it, the whole *idea* is weird. Some Chinese have recognised this too and in recent years university professors have written to the government asking to have the body removed and cremated in accordance with Mao's wishes and because such idol worship is not conducive to generating respect of Chinese culture in the world community. They were ignored but many of China's growing middle classes would agree and in addition there is a feeling that the enormous mausoleum ruins the feng shui of Tiananmen Square. Yet the variety of accents of the pilgrims in the queue that snakes around the building and across the square everyday are testament to the enduring appeal of Mao who continues to unify the nation like no one else. Or maybe they come for the tacky gift shop at the back of the mausoleum, for where else is one to get hold of a lucky Mao Charm or a cigarette lighter that plays 'The East is Red'?

Writing about Tiananmen Square and ignoring the repression of democratic protest here in 1989 would be to ignore a very large elephant in the room. Estimating the death toll of the massacre is futile indeed since figures range from 200 to 3000; images of those events of 4 June have a powerful resonance since it was all so unexpected after the peaceful protests and gentle decline of communism in most of Eastern Europe that culminated in the fall of the Berlin Wall six months later. The events provided a defining image; of a single man with his plastic carrier bags in front of the tank - a neat and newsworthy encapsulation of heroic and futile resistance against overbearing might.

The protests were sparked by the death of former secretary-general Hu Yaobang whom protesters wanted to mourn. Hu had been reform minded and openly critical of excess. The struggle was given added impetus by the arrival in the Beijing summer of 1989 of that other reform minded politician Mikhail Gorbachev. A third reformer, general secretary Zhao Ziyang visited the square on 19 May to urge the students to end their hunger strike, for which he was placed under house arrest until his death in 2005. Zhao famously said to the protesters "We are already old, it doesn't matter to us anymore". He is a reminder that the Chinese government is not uniformly repressive. Men like Hu and Zhao have achieved high office in the past, it's just that hardliners continue to dominate the present.

No one was more hardline in 1989 than Premier Li Peng and the tanks, the smashing of the protesters' 'Goddess of democracy' and the bloodshed were probably instigated by the man some call 'The Butcher of Beijing'. There is irony in this since Li is the adopted son of former premier Zhou Enlai, the best loved and most famous moderate during China's Cultural Revolution, that time when the hardliners dominated as never before. There was another massacre in the square in 1976 when protesters were denied the opportunity to place wreaths and chrysanthemums on the Monument to the People's Heroes, to mourn Zhou's death and I wonder if Li thought of his adopted father as the tanks rolled in 1989. (For more information on Zhou, see Tianjin chapter).

I walked underneath the strings of flying kites and back to my bike by the gate; how different the rosy painted face of Mao looked to the embalmed features in his coffin. Authorities have several of these enormous likenesses ready to be pressed into service should the need arise and the need had been urgent in 1989 when three protesters threw paint filled eggs at the portrait, splattering Mao's face and shirt. Protesters helped the police arrest the perpetrators which is a fascinating insight into the mentality of the Chinese who seem to have respected Mao even as they demanded a change of government. The egg throwers are called Lu Ducheng, Yu Dongyue and Yu Zhijian and were sentenced to labour camp for life, 20 years and 16 years. Lu and Yu Zhijian were freed after 11 years but Yu Dongyue was not released until 2006 on medical grounds. He had been treated brutally and kept in solitary confinement for years and was described as 'uncooperative' by prison officials since he had continued to make 'reactionary statements'. On his release, Yu appeared deranged and no longer recognized members of his family and this story seemed sadder than ever to me as I stood close to where Yu had thrown his paint and made his gesture.

Chang'an Lu is a huge street designed for military parades and the traffic was hotting up, so I steered my bike into the road that separates the Forbidden City from Zhongnanhai. I love the contrast here between the old imperial seat of power and the high vermilion walls of Beijing's Kremlin across the road at Zhongnanhai where the current leadership lives. There is strictly no entry to Zhongnanhai and the irony of this so close to the aloof and forbidden Kingdom of the emperors seems entirely lost on this modern and theoretically egalitarian communist state.

Inside the high walls and past the stern guards it's all rather lovely inside Zhongnanhai; a verdant and bucolic oasis of lakes, parklands and pavilions that was originally an Imperial leisure Garden. The gates to the kingdom were briefly thrown open after the death of Mao but since the spot of bother on the nearby square, the leadership has retreated into it's shell. Indeed it was here in the 'Palace steeped in Compassion' that the party planned the crushing of the democratic movement in 1989; never has a building being less deserving of its name. It's forbidden even to stop outside the gates now and I was waved on and shouted at when I slowed down my bike - clearly the guard had forgotten how difficult it is to maintain a constant speed on a Forever bicycle.

The walled compound ends at the hill of Jingshan which was created with the soil excavated from the lakes inside. There is a tree here from which the last Ming emperor Chongzhen hanged himself in 1644 after writing his final testimony and killing his 15-year-old daughter and concubines as peasant rebels swarmed into the city. An old tree is commemorated inside the park but it's probably not the same one that Chongzhen chose and the real reason for visiting Jingshan lies at the top of the stairs that climb through many more trees behind. For the view up here has the Forbidden City spread out below - a reminder that the Ming Dynasty might have been Beijing's greatest era despite its inglorious end hanging from the branches of a tree, for this most famous, gigantic and beautiful palace is the creation of the Ming.

It was Emperor Yongle who constructed modern Beijing in the 15th century after the town had been flattened by Genghis Khan 200 years before. Yongle's city was the largest in the world until 1650 and the Forbidden City was its crowning glory. It still felt that way as I parked my bike, paid my fee and walked through the massive gates. Mao's mausoleum is stuffed with symbolism but it's got nothing on this place. The gates I passed through had 81 studs each since odd numbers represent masculine qualities and the highest digit is nine and 9x9 is 81, so these gates were about as loaded with testosterone as a gate could be. The city has a total of 9999 rooms and there are nine Dragons on the huge and famous screen inside.

Just about the only thing that wasn't oozing imperial yang masculinity in the city were its 3000 eunuchs who attended the needs of the emperor and delivered concubines to him wrapped up like some fragrant wet dream parcel in yellow silk. The eunuchs carried their yang around their necks, since by keeping their balls in a decorative pouch, they could still be buried whole and secure entry to heaven.

No man can hear this detail without wincing and checking his own testicles are intact, and I did this instinctively as I learned the fundamentals of Ming Dynasty gonads and every conceivable detail about the Forbidden City from my audio guide, which also swung in a pouch from my neck. I was quite taken with this device that delivered an endless litany of facts appropriate to my location in the palace and knew exactly where I was no matter how often I backtracked and changed location and tried to outwit it.

The first time I visited Gugang there was no such audio sophistication, it was the middle of winter and the water in the huge metal vats traditionally used to combat fire was iced over. I remembered how welcome the Starbucks coffee shop in the palace was that day, but even as I warmed myself I was aware of the incongruity of hot milk latte with a splash of vanilla in this most famous and Chinese of buildings. Like putting an advert for Nike on Stonehenge, this American coffee shop destroyed the aesthetics of the place, and much as I wanted a hot drink after my early start on the iron horse I was relieved to see it gone. The steam machine, Mochaccinos, chocolate sprinklers and ambient jazz CDs were packed away because of a Chinese online campaign that collected 500,000 signatures and accused the cafe of ruining the solemnity of the palace. Starbucks left gracefully enough and the store is now full of Chinese books and cards, miniature Qin Dynasty Emperor dolls and 'I love Beijing' T-shirts. No more solemn perhaps, but certainly more Chinese.

So I had to go elsewhere for coffee and ended in McDonald's where the smiling have-a-nice-day waitresses were dressed in baseball caps quite unlike the red guard uniforms of their parents 40 years before; it seemed that the retreat of Starbucks is only a temporary defeat for the American dream. Happy from my meal, I climbed back aboard Shanghai's finest and cycled the route from Forbidden City to the other great Ming creation in Beiing, the Temple of Heaven.

I tried to stick as closely to the route that 24 emperors took twice a year from Palace to Temple to make a sacrifice inside the Hall of Prayer for good harvests. Commoners had to stay inside when the Emperor passed and no one was allowed to remain upstairs since this would put his head higher than that of the Lord of a thousand years. Aisin Gioro Pu-Yi was the last Emperor to take this walk before the overthrow of the Qing dynasty in 1911, though it must have felt like quite a trek to the boy emperor who was still only six years old at the time of his abdication. Poor Pu-Yi was overthrown and made a puppet of the Japanese. His thoughts were reformed in prison for 10 years and he ended his life as a common gardener in Beijing's Botanical Gardens, dying of cancer unmourned in a Beijing hospital in 1967. This story has a happy ending of sorts when he was reprieved and had his ashes transferred to the Western Qing tombs in 1995 following the success of Bertolucci's 'The last Emperor' movie and a sort of sanitised revival of Manchu culture in Beijing when Qing Dynasty style banquets became briefly all the rage.

Diminutive, bespectacled Pu-Yi could no doubt find his way from Forbidden City to Temple of Heaven but he didn't have to deal with the destruction of the old route and the creation of monumental buildings and roads by the Communist party anxious to give form to their socialist city. I arrived panting and hot and with taxi drivers' curses ringing in my ears following my negotiation of the Beijing traffic. The city had lost its early-morning serenity by this time and the Temple's Echo wall where a whispered poem or Confucian verse can be heard clearly from one end to the other was crowded with coughing and spitting Chinese tourists who bellowed their Ni Haos to their friends. "Ni keyi ting wo ma?", "can you hear me?" screamed one man to another. Of course he can I thought; the lifeless corpse of Chairman Mao can probably hear you.

Yet there is no denying the serenity of the main hall which is fantastically decorated and elaborately constructed with neither nails nor cement. The original Hall of Prayer for Good Harvests was destroyed by lightning in 1889 (the official reason for this divine intervention was as punishment for a sacrilegious caterpillar which climbed almost to the top of the roof) but the new one looks beautiful too. The Chinese call their country Zhongguo - the Middle Kingdom - since their nation was the centre of the world and what could lie beyond but barbarians and backwardness? Beijing was the middle of the Middle Kingdom, the Temple of Heaven in the middle of Beijing and the round altar where the emperor made his sacrifice the centre of the Temple; truly the absolute centre of the whole universe.

I trundled back towards my guesthouse, resolved to park the Forever forever since the sheer weight of the thing was taking its toll and the saddle, despite its oversize springs that would have looked more at home on a sofa, was playing havoc with the backside that I'd thought the mausoleum guard had wanted to see. All of this history, this middle of the Kingdom culture had once been protected by stout city walls though you'd be hard pressed to see them now because they were dismantled brick by brick in the 1950s to make room for a ring road and the Metro in one of the most shortsighted decisions any government anywhere has ever made. And they really were dismantled and reused in a most Chinese thrifty, make do and mend way; the bricks were used in factories and housing, and ditches vacated by the huge ramparts became tunnels for the Metro. When the dismantling process was complete and the remaining walls were declared a cultural heritage, only a few watchtowers and short sections of the inner wall remained.

The wall must once have been magnificent and stretched 40 km linking watchtowers, sentry posts, arches and gates before the Communist Party deemed it a hindrance to traffic. Old Peking photos show a wall that really looked as if it could defend a city and it's a great shame that it's gone. What's more, the traffic in Beijing is horrendous anyway rendering the stated purpose of the destruction of the walls futile.

The party didn't just tear things down in the 1950s and 1960s. They also embarked on an ambitious project of tunnel building underneath the city to keep Beijing's citizens safe from attack. Relations with the Soviet Union had become so bitter by the 1960s that war seemed inevitable so a vast city of underground shelters and tunnels were built. The Metro system was part of this and the technique of digging, then building the roof afterwards is the reason why the walls had to go. The underground city or 'Dixia Cheng' was designed to withstand a nuclear attack and allow China's leaders to flee safely to military bases in the hills. The 6 million citizens meanwhile would stay underground and make use of the restaurants, schools, theatres, factories, warehouses and farms there... Mao also thoughtfully included a roller skating rink. The tunnels were mostly dug by hand by 300,000 local volunteers including schoolchildren and provide a link to every part of the city. According to some reports they stretch all the way to Tianjin, a mere 130 km away.

It's difficult to verify any of this since most of the network cannot be explored and the small part that can was closed for maintenance when I last went. The tiny locked wooden entrance on a Beijing side street was most unprepossessing and gave little hint of the vast complex that must lie beyond. I would especially liked to have tried some subterranean speleological skating.

My route to the hotel lay through that region north of the Forbidden City that is crowded with traditional Beijing dwellings called hutong. The name originally meant 'water wells' but has come to mean the straight alleyways that connect Beijing's old city. The hutong are lined with siheyuan houses and lie East-West so that doorways are North-South in order to provide good feng shui. Siheyuan literally means a courtyard surrounded by four buildings and conforms to a classic Chinese design; main house on the north of the courtyard and facing south and connected to the other buildings by decorated pathways that provide a cool place and shelter from the summer sun and winter rains. The entrance gate is usually painted the same vermilion as the Forbidden City and large lion headed copper door knockers add to the notion of grandeur in miniature. The whole is a microcosm of feng shui and Confucian ethics where family members were assigned different buildings in the complex according to their rank.

So it transpires that the hutong are as architecturally impressive and culturally important as the old city walls, and yet just like the walls the siheyuan are being knocked down at a rapid rate to make way for that which is newer and better. One likes to assume that the destruction of cultural relics is aberration of the past and of less enlightened times, but in Beijing it goes on.

The hutong are perfect for riding a bike through. No traffic and a constant succession of photogenic entrance ways, doorstep scrubbing locals and tiny songbirds in cages. My bike was right at home here and my photos of the old-fashioned black machine leaning against a stone doorway or beneath a red lantern could have come from any time in the last 50 years. It's easy to get lost in this narrow maze of streets and soon I was bouncing over cobbles down an alley that was narrower than the rest and ended in a cul-de-sac. The communal function of the hutong is evident down these small alleys where a single siheyuan is divided into four houses and residents sit together in the courtyard and play mahjong. No running water perhaps, but probably preferable to the anonymous high-rises in the Beijing suburbs that hutong dwellers are being moved to while the siheyuan are knocked down around them.

I wasn't part of the community and as I veered into an old man's backyard a furious pug dog charged towards me on his stumpy legs and barked his disapproval. I apologised to the old man and backed up (not an easy thing on a Shanghai bike) and tried not to notice that the old fella' was dressed only in voluminous pyjama bottoms pulled up too high in that way old men do the world over.

Public pyjama wearing is big news in Beijing and Shanghai; not just any old jim-jams but neat and respectable enough to pop to the corner shop or chat on a public bench. It's probably a way for locals to show they live in the area and are not migrants and serves a valuable role in the creation of local identity and ownership. Or maybe it's an affirmation of prosperity showing that they don't have to sleep in their clothes? On the other hand, it might be a bit of 'my pyjamas are nicer than yours' urban one-upmanship in a classless society, or perhaps it's just a way of keeping cool on hot summer Beijing nights while retaining a degree of modesty?

Whatever the reasons, pyjama wearing has become a tradition in summery Beijing, though like the Hutong and the walls it's part of the city's culture that is under attack. Authorities have had enough and the PJ police are now out in force. It's already impossible to go into the main shopping district in pyjamas but the Hutongs remain a last preserve of public nightwear fashion. I'm unclear why the authorities disapprove so, though I suppose such behaviour is neither modern nor sophisticated. I liked it though, and was always careful to give a cheerful 'hello' to pyjama wearers and decided that if I ever move to Beijing, I would buy a pair of pyjamas too.

I was not unhappy to park my bike back at the hotel and set off on foot through the Hutong for lunch. The siheyuan in some quarters are unlikely to be knocked down where the whole block has been turned into a trendy area of restaurants, bars and guesthouses. Indeed, I had slept that night in a stone courtyard house and dreamed of marching with the guards in Tiananmen Square in my pyjamas. There's plenty of street food available around; here can be found the ubiquitous and mundane youtiao, a deep-fried stick of dough that Beijingers munch on their way to work, but the stalls and steaming woks can also provide jianbang pancakes, zhou porridge, cooked bread filled with pork called roubing, malatang spicy soup, hongshou baked sweet potatoes and dozens of other fresh cooked delicacies from spicy braised pigs intestines (tastier than it sounds), to fish balls, though these put me in mind of those poor Forbidden City eunuchs rather too much.

My exertions on the bike had earned me a sit down lunch so I ducked into a siheyuan that had been converted into a Tibetan café. There's irony in the current fashion amongst young urban Chinese for all things Tibetan; while the region enjoys little political freedom, interest in the exoticism, natural environment and romance of the land of snows appear stronger than ever. This Tibet chic is best seen in the boom in visitor numbers to Tibet - 4 million went in 2008, a 60% increase from two years before, and most of these are people from the big eastern cities on a spiritual quest who return with Tibetan music, jewellery, literature, prayer flags, Buddha statues, rugs and beads and wear T-shirts decorated with Tibetan script. Perhaps young Beijingers need some spiritualism in their lives and want to believe in something, though this kleptomania might be nothing more than mindless tourism and it's questionable whether the Tibetan people derive much benefit from the re-packaging of their entire culture.

The cafe I chose was different since it was owned by a Tibetan and not a Beijinger who had simply tapped into the trend. I ordered Tibetan damje rice with yak meat, raisins and yoghurt and Momo dumplings though really this was an urban approximation of a Tibetan meal; when I traveled in remote Tibet the food I ate was far more basic than this and raisins had been as much of a rumour as the yeti. I asked the proprietor how she felt about living in a Han city. She answered that she would tell me, though she wouldn't give her name and suddenly I felt subversive, political and grown up, like a real journalist instead of a bloke charging around Beijing on his bike and shouting hello to people in their pyjamas.

"I miss my homeland" she said, "but I came to Beijing to work because there is none in Tibet". But did she like it here I wondered? "Not at all - there are too many people, but my cafe is peaceful and reminds me of home". The cafe was a shrine to Tibet, the prayer flags and mantras playing were a world away from the Hutong outside. The nameless owner told me that she loved to walk in the western hills of Beijing since they reminded her of her hometown in Tibet, "though you will say it is in Gansu since this is the Chinese name for it". Of all the injustice meted out to Tibet, the re drawing of her borders seems to rankle with Tibetans the most. In the 1950s the new province of Qinghai was created and parts of Tibet were assimilated into Gansu and Sichuan in order to reduce the size and cultural influence of that troublesome region.

There was nothing too controversial here, and I wondered why she wouldn't give her name, though there was understandable resentment from a woman who had reluctantly left a home whose name had been changed. Yet she had been able to come to the heart of Han China and open a cafe that was a profitable and going concern. I hope that the assimilation and popularity of Tibetan culture in China might lead to an appreciation of its value rather than its destruction and dilution and anyway it's much more difficult to destroy a culture than to tear down some city walls.

This area of hutong by Qianhai Lake and surrounding Nanluogu Xiang is very trendy indeed. Next to the Tibet cafe was a bookshop; further along clothing, gift shops and bars lined the main street. The bookshop was filled with postcards of old Beijing (city walls intact) and a coffee bar, and there was a whole section devoted to the works of Mao and biographies of party elders. The shop owner said these were his bestsellers and reckoned his small shop was an attempt to stem the tide of liberalism in Beijing. "I miss the equality of Mao's time" he said, in much the same way that Italians mourn the era of Mussolini when the trains ran on time. The gift shop suggested a surge in Mao's popularity too, though I'm not sure if the cultural revolutionary mugs, 'we are all soldiers' beer glasses, Mao puppets and 'celebrate with great joy and enthusiasm the publication of the Constitution of the People's Republic of China' T-shirts on sale in shops full of industrial chic and ambient jazz would have been quite what the chairman would have wanted.

My cycling was over for the day and I hailed a taxi at the main road. Catching a cab is never an easy prospect in Beijing because the drivers are remorseless and resourceful in maximising their profits. They sit inside specially constructed metal cages and I'm never clear whether these are to protect drivers from passengers or the other way round. Beijing taxi meters must be the most unreliable machines in China since every time I enter a cab in the city the meter doesn't work. "It's 85 yuan on the meter but I'll do a special price of 81 because you are a visitor". How kind, but I insisted I would rather pay the meter price anyway. The game was in full flow now; "but my meter is broken" he replies, but by this time we are out in the flow of traffic and there was no going back so I settled down for the ride. On arrival I slid 30 yuan through the bars of his cage and I said I knew this ride should cost no more, he grinned sheepishly and the smile meant I should hardly blame him for chancing his luck as he sped off.

I rather enjoy these exchanges in China and usually win by speaking a little Chinese and surprising the driver. Even when you lose, a few yuan makes very little difference, though I imagine that if I lived in Beijing and had to deal with this game every single time that I caught a cab, I would be driven to distraction more often than to my destination. I had a similar experience on the return when there was a paucity of cabs and a feverish crowd was pushing it's way onto a bus. This driver wanted 100 yuan and I laughed with mock indignation, but he refused to move or switch on the meter until I promised that is what he would get. I told him he was only charging me this because I was a waiguoren - literally an outside country person, a foreigner - to which he said 'Yes'.

So I got out and approached a policeman who I told that this driver was refusing to accept my fare and trying to overcharge me simply because I was not Chinese. The policeman simply shrugged his shoulders and in that shrug was absolute withering 'I couldn't care less about your problem, just go and pay the fare, wealthy waiguoren and stop bothering me' contempt. I pondered my options, joined the fight to board the bus to who knows where, paid my one yuan and got off two stops later at a taxi rank where the driver cheerfully clicked the meter which had not crept to even 20 yuan by the end of my journey. A triumph indeed, but these are the reasons why independent travel in China can be so exhausting; the constant round of negotiations, the language difficulties and the pressing crowds. It's the fear of this that drives most visitors to join tour groups and stray no further than Beijing, Shanghai or Xi'an. But the hassle is really a state of mind and a part of the adventure. After all, what would be the point of coming if it wasn't all so very different?

All those taxi hassles would bring me to the Luguo Bridge. This is a 12th century bridge that Marco Polo described as "a very fine stone bridge, so fine indeed that it has very few equals in the world", though if it wasn't for an incident here in 1937, the bridge might be forgotten, for all Marco Polo's rapture. It was in this exact place that the war with Japan began on 7 July 1937 when the Chinese garrison was alarmed by Japanese army manoeuvres on the other side. Thinking a Japanese invasion was underway, the soldiers fired a few ineffectual rifle shots. After a series of skirmishes and ceasefires, a full-scale attack began on 14 July and the bridge and the whole of Beijing were in Japanese hands a few days later. This was the culmination of six years of Japanese occupation of Chinese territory north of Beijing which the nationalist Chinese government had been powerless to prevent. All of this was a source of great shame to the Chinese and when the attack began and full-scale war ensued, it might have felt almost like a relief that at least they could fight and resist, though it would take eight more years to finally drive the invading Kwantung army from Chinese soil.

The walls of the bridge and of Wanping fortress beyond are still pockmarked with shell holes, and what self-respecting traveler could resist running his fingers over these and imagining what had happened here? Beijing authorities have built the memorial hall of the war of resistance against Japan here, full of grisly reminders of the conflict, but it is the bridge that is the main attraction. Its 266 metres long and has a look of great antiquity; hundreds of stone Ming, Qing, Yuan and Jin lions line both sides and no one seems to agree how many lions there are. Estimates range from 482 to 496, though records state that there were originally 627; confusion reigns because there are small lions hiding on the head and back of the bigger lions and smaller lions hiding under the paws of these and teeny tiny lions under the belly of these.

There were student guides at the entrance to the bridge who were keen to practice their English and I willingly took up the offer of a guided tour. I asked if they got many Japanese visitors here and my guide said that they did and proceeded to give the most balanced and fair minded analysis of the conflict that I had ever heard. "Japan sees it all from their view" said this 15-year-old "and they believed they were helping China, and in some ways they were since we modernised and became independent because of the trouble then and who's to say who is right and who is wrong?" How different to the common (and probably understandable) attitude to the war and the fury that Japan is perceived to be lacking in contrition.

As the rain began to fall on the Marco Polo Bridge, my guide scurried away and brought me back an umbrella; political balance *and* shelter for a refugee? Surely this girl should be working for the United Nations? I thanked her, strolled the 266 metres to the end of the bridge trying to count the lions and promptly slipped on the 12th century granite polished smooth by the footsteps of Beijingers and Japanese soldiers. I lay flat on my back on the soaking stone, another casualty of war on the Luguo Bridge, the water seeping through and muddying my clothes. Perhaps this is why the taxi driver wanted 100 yuan to let me into his cab?

It's nearly impossible to visit Beijing without a visit to the Great Wall and in the end, the incessant offers of bargain tours, the look of wild surprise that I wasn't going wore me down and I went. You see, I decided that I'd already seen the wall in a much more authentic state,crumbling into the desert in Gansu and Shanxi or abutting the ocean in Hebei.

But I was wrong; the wall might be touristy and over restored so close to the capital, but its magnificent here too: after all how could any section of this towering and iconic 6500 km structure be anything other than magnificent? It's not *quite* as magnificent as the shopkeeper selling mini replicas of the wall here was inclined to think however. He told me that the wall would stretch from Los Angeles to New York City and also the singularly useless statistic that if all the bricks were made into a single barrier 5 m high, they would encircle the Earth. Who works these things out? But his final statistic, the drum roll and finale to beat all the rest was the tired old claim that the wall can be seen from the moon. This can't be true, since its only 9 m wide and the same colour of the soil surrounding it. The moon is 384,393 km from Earth; viewing a dun coloured wall on a dun coloured landscape from up there would be like viewing a human hair from 2 miles away. You'd need vision thousands of times more powerful than normal to see the wall from the moon and no astronaut yet has claimed to have spotted it because it *can't be seen.*

The shopkeeper shook his head and smiled, for the wall cannot be reduced to a scientific equation to the Chinese. I pondered this as I sat atop the ancient stones and stared north across dry hills and a scattering of hamlets. The wall is not so much masonry as a symbol, an idea and a philosophy of greatness of a kingdom at the middle of the Earth. No matter that it cannot be seen from space after all and that it wasn't even fit for purpose since it was breached by Mongols and Manchus any number of times. Perhaps this flawed defence was not the fault of the wall at all however, since if the enemy attacked at night the defenders from Beijing would surely have been unprepared and dressed in nothing but their pyjamas.

SHANDONG

山东

156 000 sq km
Population 94 million

'Hold faithfulness and sincerity as first principles'

Confucius

My boarding card to Shandong told me to 'feel easy and considerate at all times'. But it was hard to feel either with a three hour airport delay watching red jacket waitresses line up for inspection at the start of their shift as if they were on some military campaign. Their supervisor shuffled round his team, keys jangling from his belt, barking orders and inspecting fingernails. The girls chanted that they would work hard and serve the customer, but after the Major-General had gone, they slumped back into their chairs, gossiping and chatting on mobile phones and filing their clean, approved fingernails since they had absolutely no customers.

The delay was due to the southern China rain; great sheets of warm wetness making lakes of the aeroplane tarmac, raining like it would never end. But Confucius said 'It does not matter how slowly you go as long as you do not stop' and soon enough we were bursting through the fat grey clouds that looked impervious to planes and into the forgotten blue sky Kingdom above. Shandong was a haven of warm sun and cool north of the Yangtze air after the cheerless swelter of the South and my taxi driver was as sunny and accommodating as the weather.

This taxi switched on his meter unhesitatingly, avoiding the usual wearying haggle over the fare. The driver spoke some English and had seized upon the word 'etcetera' as the most fundamentally useful term in the English language. "I'm here to see Shandong and practice my Chinese" I said. "Ah, congratulations etcetera" he replied.

What was this place with expansive blue skies and friendly drivers' etcetera? The secret to his good behaviour lay in the airport system that forbade me to enter a taxi until a uniformed man had spoken to the driver and given me a card. The man's badge told me he was from the 'Municipal transportation and Communications commission'; a dispassionate sovereign body that was here to regulate taxis and ensure fair play. The card he handed me provided a telephone number in big black digits, below which I was told 'if phenomenons happen on you such as luggage or goods loss, unfriendly service attitude of driver, overcharge, unnormal use on mileage fare meter and resist for hire, you have a right to dial this number to complain'.

This just about covered every aspect of a taxi drivers fun dammit. But the driver was reassuringly and familiarly clueless about how to find my destination and as I was set down at the train station and the mileage fare meter that had been used so normally was switched off, he was no longer subject to the cloying attention of the municipal bureaucratic Commissioner. The driver asked if I had enjoyed the ride and then his best behaviour broke at last;

"I am a poor man, you give me a little more money etcetera". But Confucius says 'He who will not economise will have to agonise' so I gave the driver only what the meter said, though his complaints were ringing in my ears, and bought a cheap hard seat ticket for the train to Qufu etcetera.

Confucius was born and lived in Qufu for most of his life. Over 2000 years later the town is still a place of pilgrimage and veneration of the great sage. I hired a guide called Carrie to show me the Confucius Temple and Kong mansion since I knew both would be piled high with symbolism and allegory which I would otherwise have little prospect of understanding. Confucius lived from 551 to 479 BC though he achieved high office only briefly in late middle age before wandering rootless around Shandong pontificating and musing and preaching his message of social harmony.

The temple built in his honour is a grand place and in China is second only to the Forbidden City in scale. Confucius knows his place; his temple is deliberately and respectfully one brick lower than the Hall of Supreme Harmony in Beijing and the studs on the doors number in rows of seven since nine is the perfect number and reserved for the Emperor. Yet the Qufu Temple is in many ways more impressive than the sterile and over renovated one in Beijing. This temple had atmosphere, 1800-year-old cypress trees and ancient carved stone stelae on the backs of patient bixi turtle guardians. Carrie also delightedly showed me the temple's cheeky claim to superiority; there are pillars (though Carrie called them pillows) carved intricately in the shape of dragons supporting the main temple in Qufu which had to be covered in folds of silk whenever an Emperor visited[7] in order to avoid a royal tantrum since only the Emperor was allowed dragons.

It puzzled me why the Emperor didn't ask 'what's under the silk boys?' But Carrie didn't know; it seems to me that Chinese dynastic emperors may have had a mandate from heaven but were a singularly un-inquisitive bunch and very easily fooled. Carrie did know a lot of other stuff though. Here was the Gate of Double Glory used for emperor visits and here the 198 stone stelae inscribed with names of the

---

7   Which was quite often; the Qing Emperor Qianlou alone visited eight times.

50,000 successful candidates in imperial examinations. Next was the Apricot Pavilion from where Confucius instructed his students and the Lu wall inside where Confucius books had been hidden when Emperor Qin had wanted to burn them.[8]

The recovered books, called the Analects (Lunyu in Chinese), are the very basis of Confucian thought. They are a collection of 497 aphorisms, little nuggets of wisdom, upon which Chinese political life was organised for over 2000 years. For two millennia, knowledge of the Analects was the basic requirement for all civil service exams and entry to the vast and powerful Chinese political bureaucracy. Ancient China must have been filled with unhappy young men reluctantly poring over a copy of the Analects on sunny days and moaning that they could be outside flying a kite or playing with newly invented gunpowder.

The Emperor too was required to practice Confucian values. Confucius said 'the wisest sage should rule' and this wisdom was based upon the five Confucian virtues of benevolence, righteousness, propriety, wisdom and trustworthiness; consistent application of these would make force unnecessary. Of course, not all Chinese rulers have applied the five virtues consistently, but the idea is a good one. Confucius compared emperors to the wind under the force of which the grass of the common people must bend, but even a rudimentary knowledge of Chinese history reveals that the benevolent wind of the imperial mandate has sometimes been more akin to a hurricane, ripping the grass up by its roots and scattering it in wild turbulent gusts.

Confucius believed that man is capable of perfection and has no need of gods. The most fundamental golden rule of Confucianism is 'you be nice to me and I'll be nice to you' but underpinning this is a belief that excess in anything - religion, money, fun - is bad. It's all rather puritanical and joyless and grounded in strict obedience; ruler to ruled, son to father, younger brother to older, wife to husband. Friendships are important too - Confucius said 'have no friends not equal to yourself' - but there is little room for frivolity in the Analects; the sage is mostly preoccupied with hard work, respect for the past and above all, education - the first word on the first page of the analects is 'xue' - study.

---

8   They were discovered and extracted years later by workmen in the Han dynasty.

All this emphasis on the past and demands of feudal obedience were anathema to the Communists. Mao declared Confucius 'China's number one hooligan' and rejected the old social age, class and gender boundaries, blowing harder and more destructively on the grass of the common people than any other Emperor had before. Carrie showed me the damage wrought on the temple by Mao's Red Guards - stelae cracked and the main sculptural image of Confucius entirely destroyed. As ever, the selectivity of Red Guard destruction was puzzling. Some stelae had been left alone for very specific reasons, this one because it praised Emperor Zhu Yuan Zhang who had started life as a simple farmer and was therefore deemed politically acceptable, another said 'Apricot Pavilion' and was unmolested because it was carved by a man called Dang, a word that was also shorthand for the Communist Party.

The Cultural Revolution has long passed and been discredited and China has changed. Confucius said 'ignorance is the night of the mind, but a night without moon and star'; the Sage is a celestial body in China once more, praised by the government and held as a paradigm of virtue. The rehabilitation was clear at the opening ceremony of the Olympics in 2008 in Beijing when 3000 men dressed as Confucian disciples banged drums and chanted 'Friends have come from afar, how happy we are', another of the great man's cute sayings. The current leadership's emphasis on 'harmonious society' is a very Confucian concept, though I suspect this new Confucianism has less to do with ancient concepts of virtue than as a means of cementing the status quo of the voiceless masses ruled by a new imperial elite. What better way to ensure conformity in a time of rapid economic and technological change than with an emphasis on obedience and a healthy dollop of national pride and military power? 'The superior man, when resting in safety, does not forget that danger may come. Thus his person is not endangered and his states and all their clans are preserved'. Confucius said that too and might have approved of Beijing's modern parades of thundering tanks and gleaming missiles.

Carrie showed me the new statue that has replaced the one smashed in the 1960s by those whose respect for virtue and the past had been smashed by blind obedience and political dogma. The new image is based on Tang Dynasty paintings of the man and for all that Confucius was learned and wise with a good turn of phrase and a catchy line in axioms, he was a remarkably ugly man with hunched shoulders, goofy teeth and a dyspeptic expression that suggests virtue and kindness are concepts that concern people other than him.

Carrie insisted that Confucius was 'eunuch' which puzzled me until I realised she meant unique, though the former might have accounted for his pained expression. She agreed that he was indeed very ugly which was magnanimous of her since Confucius was a distant relative. Carrie's surname was Kong; she said she was born in Qufu and 'I will die here', a sudden melodramatic outburst that was entirely out of keeping with her demure appreciation of stelae and learned discourse on silk wrapped pillows. But she let slip that she had gone to find work in Guangzhou last year and come home not because she missed her hometown but because the big southern city was 'too big, too busy, too hot, too scary' - a sentiment I entirely agree with. (See Guangdong chapter)

I discovered later that everyone in Qufu has the name Kong and claims descent from Confucius – the K section in the local phone book must be huge. A Chinese university offered DNA testing in 2008 to establish who really *was* a descendant, but the townspeople understandably refused since it would be a shame to discover you are merely a Smith, Jones or Chan. I could hardly blame Carrie for her familial aspirations since the Kong clan were long regarded as 'the first family under heaven' and occupied an extravagant mansion that abuts the main Confucius Temple. The direct male descendant was given the title Yansheng Duke, was exempt from tax and the only man apart from the Emperor permitted to ride a horse in the Forbidden City, though his visits there would be rare for why would you travel to Beijing when you could enjoy 196 course banquets and dragon pillows back home?

The mansion is as full of symbolism as the temple and based on severe Confucian ethics; any young family member who offended an older was beaten 20 times with a bamboo club and there was such strict delineation in the mansion that an 1887 fire raged for three days because only 12 of the Kong's 500 servants were permitted to enter that part of the mansion to fight the flames where the fire had broken out.

The last of the Kong line fled to Taiwan in 1947 so he missed out on commemoration in the Kong Forest in Qufu. I took a taxi the short distance to the forest the next day since the sky was still blue, the sun had turned the day to 37°C of heat and it was too hot to walk. Confucius said 'everything has its beauty but not everyone sees it' but there was no pleasure beneath the wilting sun and I was glad to be in the cool of the trees. Carrie told me that the forest is unique for its lack of snakes and a particular type of heron that nests there. I can confirm that I saw not a single snake, though they would have been unwise to come out in this heat, and the herons were nesting in the trees in a corner of the forest depositing guano over the branches and forest floor and leaving an overwhelming stench that even Confucius would have struggled to see beauty in.

The herons were outnumbered only by the proliferation of overweight and pasty bare-chested middle-aged Chinese tourists sucking on ice creams, though away from the main path the forest was remarkably peaceful with ancient graves covered in tiny characters standing aslant between the trees. Beams of sunlight laden with dust pierced the canopy and butterflies flapped from leaf to leaf, lazy in the heat. I like a good graveyard and was the only student who enjoyed the brass rubbings on school trips to English Mediaeval churches as the other boys shared a packet of cigarettes behind a flying buttress or snogged Tracy Beck behind the rood screen. I'd taken the dutiful student pilgrimage to Pere Lachaise, looked at the tomb of Oscar Wilde and Marcel Proust and listened to Doors tapes by the grave of Jim Morrison. Highgate Cemetery had been closed when I went so I scaled the wall to look at the grave of Karl Marx. A security guard found me there and shone a torch in my face, telling me this was private property. 'Ah, but all property is theft' I smugly replied, though as the police were called to deal with this smart arse student I concluded that Marx may have been wrong.

Confucius' tomb was less grand than the huge stone edifice of Marx's giant head, shoulders and bushy beard in Highgate and less covered in the stubs of candles and beer can offerings on the grave of Jim Morrison. It's a simple, ancient and rather affecting piece of stone. Nearby is a hut where his disciples would spend three years each tending and contemplating his grave. There is a second grave here, that of Confucius' son who died before his great father and seems to have achieved little in his short life. Confucius acknowledged that 'by nature men are nearly alike; by practice they get to be wide apart', but the epitaph on his son's grave – 'he died before his father without making any noteworthy achievements' - seemed unduly harsh.

Qufu had been a sombre and reverential place, a town of philosophical thought and rumination. The seaside town of Qingdao was its breezy antithesis with its bracing sea air, plastic buckets and spades and crowds of locals enjoying the beach. In Qingdao I hired that rarest thing in China, a bicycle that actually fitted me, and spent a glorious day cycling the coast breathing deeply the wind from the Yellow Sea with its tang of salt and seaweed.

I rode along the 40 km 'Qingdao scenic route' - a trail signed and designed to enjoy the great outdoors is another rare thing in China-towards the mountains of Lao Shan from where clear mineral water is extracted and used to give the local beer its unique flavor. Past the old warship and submarine I breezed where signs prohibiting photos of these antique pieces seemed excessively sensitive. Past too the World of Jellyfish and wedding couples outside ugly three star hotels where lion dancers skipped around not quite clean stretch limos while drum troupes consisting entirely of old ladies tapped out a staccato tattoo of wedded bliss. I stayed to watch; until lions, drums and pensioners were packed up with indecent haste for the next job the moment the bride had been spun round beneath an inflatable arch and carried into the hotel's underwhelming lobby.

The town centre beaches by the Chunqiao Pier were hopelessly crowded with people fossicking in rock pools since there was little enough sand to sit on; bodies were so tightly packed that it seemed unlikely there would be room to get a tan. But further from town the coast became wilder and emptier and I could hear the crash of the waves and the crunch of my tyres on gravel. Wires on the flagpoles of every nation at the Olympic sailing centre were pinging in the onshore breeze but there were few other signs of life in this abandoned place where the Sailors Bar, the Helmsman's Club and the Captain's Cabin restaurants were padlocked and aimless since the Olympic regatta had absconded. A great deal of money had been lavished on the neat boardwalks and harbour here, but it was impossible to keep it relevant and soon the weather that had filled the spinnakers of Olympian boats will wear the place down and it will look destitute and awful.

Further still from the crowds of town centre beach sun worshippers I encountered several old men dressed head to toe in rubber. I initially assumed this was a meeting of the Shandong fetishist club but in fact these prophylactic pensioners were diving for seaweed. They clambered over rocks, took a deep draught of Shandong oxygen and submerged with wire baskets, emerging a few seconds later (no heroic deep diving astonishing feats of breath holding here) with handfuls of bladder wrack and kelp. Occasionally an old fella would bob into view waving a hand in triumph, a sea urchin or anemone in his hand.

It would have been difficult for these old men to look good in their rubber livery, but the sight was made less enchanting still because everything was so baggy. The reason for this became clear when each man finished accumulating his inedible looking crop, snapped off his mask and peeled off his suit, the commodious size of which had enabled each old-timer to keep on his nylon slacks, shirt and tank top so that he could slip on his shoes, mount his bike and cycle his harvest away.

I rode back to town through Badaguan district. The air was cool and balmy here, seasoned by the myrtles, cedars and peach trees that lined the road in front of early 20th-century European villas where German colonists once lived. Kiautschau had been a German colony from 1897 to 1914 because Kaiser Wilhelm was determined to keep up with the British Empire building Joneses next door. The Germans achieved a remarkable amount in 17 years. The centre of Qingdao is full of sturdy brick German architecture, cobbled streets and churches and gives a unique character sadly lacking in most knock-it-down, build-it-up homogenous Chinese cities. Germany put a sewage system beneath the streets[9], installed electricity and connected Qingdao to the rest of Shandong by rail. There were more students in Qingdao than any other place in China during German rule and the churches they built are particularly lovely. I chained my bike to stout German railings and went inside the simple Protestant church with its stuccoed yellow

---

9   an event precipitated not by a desire to save the locals but by the death of the second German governor of Kiautschau of typhus.

walls, climbed the tower behind the art nouveau clock face and gazed back along the coast to the villas, the abandoned Olympic Village and the rubbery old men harvesting their catch.

St Michael's Church is a bigger, grander statement of devotion, as Catholic churches often are. In the Protestant church I could hear only wood pigeons in the trees outside, but St Michael's was full of Sunday worshippers and young girls with plastic flowers holding their first confirmation while the congregation opened their throats and sang Jesu, Joy of Man's Desire in fractured English; an appropriately German hymn for an old German church. I lingered for the rest of the service to rest my saddle sore behind on a sturdy wooden pew but also because I enjoyed the staged call and response companionship of the service. When I see Buddhist or Taoist temples in China, I feel like a voyeur, a tourist; they interest me but they don't *move* me. But this Christian church did, because of its comforting familiarity, because I was alone in a foreign land and because it reminded me of when I was a child. There were huge religious murals on the walls of the church of a resolutely blue eyed and Caucasian Jesus and I wondered if Catholicism felt like a very *foreign* religion to the worshippers, though the Aryan superman Christ in his blindingly white robes and sad eyes seemed ready to accept all creeds with his outstretched arms. I don't like save-the-natives proselytising which is often merely an excuse to steal the peoples' land while their eyes are closed in prayer. But the worshippers were singing hard, and the confirmation girls were flushed with pride. Confucius said 'wherever you go, go with all your heart'; this was a very fine church and I was glad to be here.

The service ended with a great pealing of bells. The sign outside said that 'the voices of the bells are melodious and concrete'; certainly the noise thundered around the old town in a solid and tangible way, though the sign also reported that even this venerable old church had been seriously damaged in the Cultural Revolution, without comment or emotion, just a statement of fact. The Germans came to Qingdao because the Kaiser wanted his place in the sun, but also because of the killing of two German Christian missionaries in 1897. The German Emperor's response was a hysterical speech which coined the phrase 'Yellow Peril' (Gelbe Gefahr) for the first time. Wilhelm commissioned a picture to accompany his speech, called Yellow Peril in which the Archangel Michael, looking even more Aryan than Jesus on the walls of Qingdao Cathedral, stands ready to protect Europe's womanhood and confront the looming menace of a great golden Buddha across the sea.

This fear of the East was very real for Europeans in the early 20th century; the Fraus and Frauleins in the villas of Badaguan must have been a little frightened living amongst so many godless Chinese (though the churches were built to fix that) while their menfolk played God behind handlebar moustaches, enterprising and improving, complacently unaware of the 20th century catastrophes that would befall their nation. When he wasn't writing about the call of the wild, Jack London was considering the threat of the growing Chinese population too and how the West might launch biological warfare, kill them all and occupy China in his 1910 story 'The Unparalleled Invasion'. Sax Rohmer's sinister Fu Manchu character is also typical of the time, the archetypal Chinese villain who disdained honest Anglo-Saxon guns and explosives, for snakes, poisonous fungi and spiders as his killing modus operandi, stroking his long beard and cackling as his victims died. In fact, this fear of the sinister Chinaman prevailed long after Jack London wrote his questionable book. When I was young, playground childhood physical punishment was always more malign if prefixed by the word 'Chinese'. Thus a Chinese fist was a mischievous punch with a knuckle extended and quite unlike an honest English assault (and perversely much more likely to do harm to the puncher than the punched). Pity the boy who received the Chinese burn on his wrist from the hands of another inspired by the Saturday morning Flash Gordon villainous Emperor Ming. As for Confucius; he was merely a man with a long moustache adept at dishing out profundities for use by giggling schoolboys in a fake and possibly racist Oriental voice; 'Man who pushes piano down mineshaft gets tone of A Flat minor'. 'Man who sneezes without tissue takes matter in own hands'.

The Germans brought their other great religion to China too. Qingdao is the centre of the Chinese beer industry, producing the internationally famous Tsing Tao beer because the colonists established a brewery here in 1903. The production plant claims great taste and aroma for their product, but it seems that the beer has political properties too. 'May the glowing dawn of the new century always shine on vigorous Tsing Tao beer', exalted the notice board at the brewery museum entrance. 'Our beer will lead the spirit of the times, devote to our society being keen on reform and create new resplendence in the 21st century'. So, beer as an agent of reform, national pride (though ironically 20% of the Tsing Tao beer company is owned by Japan) and creator of the zeitgeist rather than just as a means of getting pissed and generating sufficient false courage to approach the blonde girl at the bar. The museum is an interesting trawl through the beer making process, old-fashioned German wooden vats contrasting with the shiny, hermetic production floor where men in white overalls stare approvingly at the thousands of green bottles clinking their way along conveyor belts, jostling and pushing for position like so many Chinese commuters trying to board a train. Pleasingly, visitors get to sample a glass of the famous brew at the end of the tour and I happily joined other connoisseurs necking as much free beer as possible before being asked to leave. More sloganeering in the tasting room told me that the Tsing Tao Brewery has changed its strategy from 'first bigger then stronger' to 'first stronger than bigger', a distinction whose subtlety was lost on me as I downed my fourth glass and became increasingly keen on reform and resplendence. I was also pleased to be told by a Tsing Tao employee that beer has great nutritional value and health giving properties, as good as pork, eggs and milk, "rich in calories and easily digested" and this seemed like reason enough to have another glass.

The high point of German architecture in Qingdao is the old Governor's residence on a hill, squat and massive like some Bavarian hunting lodge on steroids. The house was home to four governors until Germany surrendered Qingdao in 1914 after a joint British/Japanese offensive at the beginning of World War I. German troops held out for two months of siege, though they were outnumbered 6 to 1 and the captive Governor Alfred Meyer-Waldeck stayed in a Japanese prisoner of war camp until 1920 while his predecessor Oskar von Trippel lamented the loss of the colony and warned his nation of the dangers of war with the US. (von Trippel possessed great foresight in this respect. He wrote 'A German - American war would injure German prospects more seriously than many believe' in the 5 July 1915 edition of Der

Tag at a time when most German militarists favoured unrestricted submarine warfare on American vessels).

The Governor's lodge is ostentatiously large with a delightful arboretum stuffed with plants from Europe to remind the residents of home and with a view across town to the churches and the Temple of beer. Mao stayed here on holiday in 1957 and visitors were queueing to take photos next to his bed as they had done at Yan'an (See Shaanxi chapter) though here they were not throwing cigarettes onto the counterpane in bizarre tribute to the great man. Mao slept in many rooms across China - a bit like Charles I or Mary Queen of Scots in white and black timbered properties across Britain. It must have been especially satisfying to Mao to sleep in the beds of China's old colonial oppressors, a clumsy allegory of the national revival he craved, like the new pack leader leaving his scent on the bedsheets and claiming his territory from the old.

Despite Mao's showboating, it's impossible not to admire the busy German colonists just a little and things didn't improve much after they left and Meyer-Waldeck had been carted off to Japan. The town was under Japanese control until 1922 when they graciously withdrew only to return again for a second go in 1938 until their defeat in the Pacific War in 1945. The interim years saw the whole of Shandong fall under the hand of warlord Zhang Zongchang. Zhang was known as the 'dog meat General' due to his fondness for the gambling game pai gow which is referred to as 'eating dogmeat' in China. During an era of lawlessness and reprehensible behaviour amongst China's ruling elites, Zhang stands out as a man particularly lacking in moral fibre, the very opposite of the virtuous leader that Confucius espoused.[10]

When not being compared to dog meat, Zhang was renowned as 'sanbuzhi' - the three don't knows - because he had no idea how many soldiers and concubines and how much money he had. Zhang smoked opium with the same alacrity as the equally nefarious Zhang Xueliang (see Liaoning chapter) and referred to his lovers by number instead of name. He was so profligate with his cash that he supplied his troops with insignia made from silver and gold cigarette papers and fled

---

10   Time magazine called him 'consciousless and avaricious' in a seventh of March 1927 article titled 'The basest warlord'.

bankrupt to Japan in 1928 where he shot and killed the cousin of the ex-Emperor Pu-Yi for meddling with one of his numbered ladies, receiving a $150 fine as a consequence before he was assassinated in turn in 1932. Such leadership makes the German rule seem benign and I wonder if the Chinese in Qingdao in the 1920s longed for the good old days when their masters had handlebar moustaches and spikes on their helmets and didn't smoke opium.

I left Qingdao on the morning train to Tai'an. The Germans built this line too (busy, busy, busy) but they cannot have imagined the sleek white bullet train that carried me to the foot of Mount Tai. The train left and arrived exactly on time and travelled at 198km/h through the Shandong countryside, a blur through the hermetically sealed windows of the air-conditioned cabin. Certainly the train didn't possess the romantic and epic qualities of traditional Chinese long-distance travel, but it was clean and comfortable and illustrated perfectly the sleek and efficient new China that is changing so fast. In China whenever I ask a local about the state of the economy, they would reply 'we are too poor' or 'too many people' and the notion that China was catching the West was usually met with a snort of derision; 'we are 50 years behind the USA'. Some of this is typical Chinese understatement, for didn't Confucius say that 'he who speaks without modesty will find it difficult to make his words good'. Some of it might be true. But this sleek high-speed efficient train ride through Shandong persuaded me that the 50 year difference is closing fast; at 198km/h in fact.

The tourist information centre at Tai'an was a comforting step back in time however. There is no place less helpful or less useful to a tourist in China than a tourist information centre. This one possessed all the standard attributes; an empty room with a scattering of dog-eared leaflets on wire racks and two chain-smoking middle-aged men, one with his feet up on the desk and the other playing computer games, their motorbikes parked in the middle of the floor denying access to the yellowing map of Shandong tacked to the wall. Neither man looked up or acknowledged my presence in any way when I entered, seeking some tourist information, so I walked back out to the train station car park and made my own way to a hotel.

Tai'an is a nondescript little place, but I came because of the huge and famous mountain called Tai Shan that looms behind, dominating the old town. However even these dusty streets were pleasant on this warm summers evening as I walked from the hotel and took in the sights. The buildings are only here because of the hill; so dominant is the mountain physically and culturally that often the whole town is simply referred to as 'Tai mountain'. Holy Buddhist and Taoist mountains pop up all over China, but when push comes to shove, this is the most famous one of all. 'If Mount Tai is stable, so is the whole country' goes the saying. Emperors have traditionally climbed (or been carried) to the summit - a successful ascent confirms a blessing from God and the mandate of Heaven, a failed summit attempt is a sign of trouble ahead. Qin Shi Huangdi, the first Emperor, ascended and so did Confucius who said 'the world is small' when he reached the top. Mao Zedong too climbed the 7000 steps, contradictory as ever; a revolutionary, a breaker of myths but a man prone to Imperial behaviour too.

The climb traditionally begins from Dai Miao Temple, where offerings can be made for an auspicious ascent to God or to Bixia Yuan Jun - the Princess of rosy clouds - who can give help to women struggling with conception, a sort of celestial IVF and whose temple on the summit is tiled with iron to resist the weather. The deity Shi Ganding is in the temple too, the representation of the mountain itself and requiring an offering before trampling all over his slopes. A stone from the mountain inscribed 'Tai Shan Shi Ganding' when placed in an alley or outside a house or better still as the cornerstone of a building is said to provide great protection, and all over town men implored me to purchase a boulder painted with the magic words, though how I was supposed to carry 20 kg of Tai Shan granite home was anybody's guess.

I couldn't enter the main hall of the 11th century temple until I had donned plastic shoe covers over my grimy sandals. I suggested I remove my footwear and go barefoot instead but this was not acceptable; clearly this was mostly about extracting money from me rather than respecting the deity. So I paid the cash, the covers split as soon as I put them on and I shuffled around the hall with shredded plastic trailing from my size tens.

The view of the mountain from the temple walls as the sun went down and the shadows lengthened was beautiful and I sat for a while looking down at the ancient trees and the venerable old stones. My reverie was broken by the temple attendant who was in the mood to talk; "Ni shi Shandong ren ma?" - "You are from Shandong?" I asked. No, he was from Henan, the neighbouring province to the west and he told me the name of his hometown. I'd never heard of it and he was incredulous, repeating the name several times before falling back on the age old last resort to explain something to a dumb foreigner by drawing the name of the town in characters in the air then on my arm. This was done on my thigh once, the length of the name so long that the sketching finger strayed dangerously close to my crotch, but regardless of how many times this technique is used to make the inexplicable clear, a finger squiggling in the air or close to my genitals possesses no discernible pattern and makes *absolutely no difference* to my understanding of what is being said.

Tai'an was a town of talkers and when I sat at a pavement cafe to eat jiaozi dumplings, a local professor of English pulled up a chair. He had just written a paper and wanted me to check if his title cut the mustard. Certainly it was grammatically correct but 'the study into the use of Internet research by students at a normal college environment with regard to the effectiveness of its use' was so wordy and convoluted that like a finger painting characters in the sky it ceased to have any meaning at all. He told me that 'normal' College is a euphemism for a place where students aren't very clever and lamented the overpopulation of the country which means that a degree or even a Masters is no guarantee of work in modern China. I suggested that the one child policy would sort this out; 'too late, too late' he said and popped another dumpling into his mouth.

Things had improved under Deng Xiaoping he said since at least now intellectuals were appreciated in China once more. Old Mao had taken time off from climbing mountains to sack the man's father who had also been a college professor in order to 'rusticate' him. This strange word means to send someone down to the country, to learn to be a peasant and to end their intellectual pretensions, since intellectuals were the 'stinking ninth category' in socialist China, below even reactionaries and landlords. So it was that millions of professors, doctors, engineers and teachers laboured under a hot sun in Xinjiang or in freezing snow in Qinghai and China's economy fell even further behind the USA.

I woke at 3am to climb the mountain, to avoid the heat and the 'ren shan ren hai' - the mountain of people and the sea of persons. Past the temples at the foot of the hill I walked where conquering emperors have recorded their visits and thoughts on stone tablets and past the stallholders asleep on a complicated arrangement of chairs in the dark hours before dawn. The sky was lightening as I passed the five pines pavilion where Qin Shi Huangdi had taken shelter from the storm and promoted the trees to ministers of the fifth grade as thanks (presumably the pines didn't have to take the Qufu examinations). It was nearly light as I panted up the near vertical steps of the shiba pan path of the 18 bends to the South Heaven Gate in my bare feet. I did this not as a pilgrim or from some sense of religious epiphany but because my sandals were hurting my feet; the old steps felt warm and smooth on my toes, a perfectly pleasant way to ascend though I had to be careful to avoid the occasional gobbit of spit on the stairs.

At South Heaven Gate the path flattens to a summit plateau lined with shops selling food and cards and Shi Ganding protective rocks. There's no sense of peace here, but further along and away from the main trail I was able to sit on a flat rock and to be alone watching the sun rise over the plains of Shandong, Qingdao and the coast to the east and Qufu's temples due south. Confucius said 'with coarse rice to eat, with water to drink and my crooked arm for a pillow - is not joy to be found therein?' I lay back on my rock on top of my mountain, examined my grubby feet, and considered how small the world was and the enduring wisdom of Confucius' words as the sun crested the horizon and warmed the rocks of this old and holy place.

HEILONGJIANG

黑龙江

463 730 km sq
Population 38.2 million

'In the depth of winter, I finally learned that within me there lay an invincible summer.'

Albert Camus 1913-60

It took me years to get to Heilongjiang. I had ignored it for rice fields and beaches, mountains and deserts in China's South and West though I always felt a yearning for the northern forests and the border with Russia. When I went, it had to be in winter. A summer trip would be a betrayal of China's sub-Arctic province where temperatures regularly drop to -30°C and on one famous occasion in 1956 fell to -52.3°C. Sure, the place would look good under fluffy summer clouds, the spruce forests green and regimented in military ranks, the Songhua River in Harbin luminous under a midnight sun hurrying fast to converge with the Amur River that forms the border between China and Russia and which the Chinese call Heilongjiang, Black Dragon River, since it coils through the north like a mighty serpent and is black with rich humus soil leached by the mighty forests. There would be Russians in shirt-sleeves by the river in July and the restaurants would move their tables onto cobbled Zhongyang Dajie to serve chilled vodka and marozhe-noiye ice cream.

But I wouldn't enjoy it. I would wonder how it all felt in a -30° refrigerator, the same river frozen under an uncompromising sheet of winter ice, the Russians wrapped in furs, frost crusting on their scarves from their warm gold teeth mouths, though I discovered that for Russians it is never too cold to eat ice cream.

I almost came to Heilongjiang years before, but it didn't seem safe. An explosion at the Number 101 petrochemical plant in Jilin City in November 2005 discharged an 80 km long slick of benzene into the Songhua River. Government agencies and scientists tracked the slow malevolent progress of the chemicals as they drifted down-stream through Harbin and onto Russia's Jewish autonomous oblast, Khabarovsk, the Russian Far East and into the Sea of Japan and the Pacific Ocean. Benzene levels reached over 100 times safe levels in Harbin, which led provincial leaders to shut off the city's water sup-plies, though in typically impenetrable Chinese government style the authorities refused to disclose the reason for the lack of water, claiming 'routine maintenance', which is a bit like telling someone whose house is burning down that there is a small problem with the heating.

This government obfuscation created wild rumours of earth-quakes and terrorism and panic buying of bottled water and foodstuffs. Meanwhile dead fish began to appear along the banks of the River. Flights and trains out of the area were soon booked out and it seemed contrary to be flying in the opposite direction at the same moment. So I didn't and I promised myself I would go soon, the moment the river wasn't filled with chemicals and water came out of the taps.

The benzene spill was a tragedy in a long line of environmental mishaps in China; all over the country I had seen the effluent of economic mismanagement and the sulphurous stink of get rich quick corruption. But the Jilin chemical spill at least had the positive outcome of some lively debate and some refreshingly honest condemnation of the event in the Chinese press. The dishonesty of Harbin officials was called 'an unjustifiable lie' and a 'terrible crime against society' by Beijing's newspapers[11] and Hong Kong's South China Morning Post said the incident raised fresh concerns about the willingness of mainland officials to break bad news.

The central government threatened to severely punish anyone who had covered up the severity of the incident, apologies were made by the Vice Governor of Jilin and the Deputy General Manager of the chemical works while the Vice Mayor of Jilin, Wang Wei, was found dead in his home two weeks after the spill. Yet local officials are just sacrificial lambs in Chinese politics. Beijing condemns local corruption and mismanagement with great solemnity and fanfare and turns misadventure into political gain. Local leaders often apologise, flagellate and go to prison. Sometimes they wind up as dead as Wang Wei, but just as often they are quietly forgiven and subtly reappointed to positions far away from their original misdemeanour in a grand game of musical chairs.

When I arrived in Harbin at last, the icy chill of mismanagement seemed more transient and easily ignored than the frigid air that blew across the Songhua River where the ice looked sparkling and benzene free under a bright winter sun. The weather is everything in wintry Heilongjiang but the problem with attempting to describe it is that when you're not there it becomes intangible and unreal and you're left only with questions. My journal is filled with superlatives - magnificent ice crystals and plunging temperatures feature on every page - but was it really that cold and how did it feel? How might I describe the relief of my feet thawing out in a café after walking in bright sunshine by the river turned to steel? What was that sensation when the Siberian air hit my lungs like needles and turned to crystals of ice in my nose?

---

11   Zhongguo Qingnian Bao and Jinji Shibao.

Was it really necessary to wear that furry hat with ear flaps that made me look like some demented Dr. Zhivago?

The weather makes obvious changes to the land. The river doesn't flow; the paths are coated with verglas necessitating a strange shuffling gait made worse on legs as thick as Heilongjiang spruce trees under layers of thermal underwear. The fields are cloaked in a layer of brittle snow, though it was a sparse covering in Harbin; mean, compact and begrudging and quite unlike the soft, voluminous and sugary Mae West curves of the Alps or Northern Japan.

The subtle changes wrought by the cold are more intangible and more delightful by far. In Harbin I liked to look from the window of a Russian cafe nursing a great steaming mug of Russian tea and gaze at the sun shining through charcoal sketches of trees in the sky that was always blue. When the weather is this improbably and delightfully cold, strange flurries of steam rise from the land and I could see everything with a dramatic clarity and intensity in the landscape devoid of humidity and washed clean of summer haze. Most dramatic of all was the hour before sunset - soon after 4pm - when the last vestige of winter sun warmth drained from the darkening sky and the land was blanketed by another night of glacial silence beneath a myriad of stars that pulsed and seemed brighter than normal stars.

I have never felt cold like this. In Liaoning and Jilin, those other frigid Manchurian provinces, I commented on the wintry chill as I rode trains with frosty windows and watched locals practice tai chi round a statue of Mao coated with ice. But I'd always been dismissed out of hand. "This isn't cold" people would laugh. "Go to Harbin if you want to feel the cold" they said. And they were right.

Harbin is the last big stop before Siberia. The cold could make it a forbidding town of exile; a gulag, the last place on earth. My tea steamed in my hand and I gazed through the window. A crow flapped across the sky and a breeze sent flurries of dusty snow spinning from the surface of the glacial river where prison inmate locals tramped head down stamping their feet and trying to keep warm. But across the same river came a twinkling of lights, phosphorescence smudging the sky like a neon aurora borealis, the source of which turns Harbin from a bleak end of the world town of frosty exile into a winter wonderland.

The Harbin ice festival has become big business and it's easy to see why. 15,000 workers carve great blocks of ice from the river and these are raised into massive frost-bound Russian churches, austere terracotta warriors, icy Pyramids and an enormous arctic Forbidden City. I finished my tea and walked across the river, the ice squeaking satisfyingly beneath my feet, towards the light, rejecting the offer of a horse-drawn sled since the walk kept me warm. I paid my money, entered through the enormous gates (made of ice of course), amazed at the scale of the ice city and the endeavour and energy of the workers (or were they artists?) - the men on top of cranes and scaffolds with curved knives and saws (and Lord, no gloves) putting the finishing touches to their creations.

Amidst the brute magnificence of the sculptures, there was artistry too and great attention to detail on the Warriors faces and lion head door knockers. There were artistic temperaments too from men who stood at the bottom of Thai temples and Japanese castles and berated their labourers in 'how can I work with these people?' frustration when they spotted a crooked cupola, an erroneous eave or some lackadaisical lighting.

For every sculpture had strands of neon buried like ice age fossils in the blocks of ice, which flickered garishly to life when the sun dropped. This was when crowds of tourists arrived and shrieked their way down the Great Wall glissade, slipping in summery high-heeled shoes or eating iced fruit and hot sweet potatoes from vendors crouched over their stoves to keep warm. But I preferred the place before the lights came on and the masses arrived. There was a sterile beauty then that shone in the afternoon sun, and the ice was astonishingly clear and translucent since the water of the Songhua is said to be particularly oxygenated and pure, notwithstanding the occasional mishap with benzene.

Harbin's council clearly know when it's onto a good thing and have built a Snow Sculpture Park too, full of snowy lions, dragons, temples and a huge historical frieze of freezing Han, Ming and Qing Dynasty figures that climaxed in gigantic glistening space rockets and a massive powdery image of Liu Xiang hurdling his way to Olympic gold. I could have studied the sculptures and taken pictures for hours if only it had not been so damnably cold, though the council had thought of this too and built cafes in which visitors like me could hunch over hot chocolate and mulled wine and nurse fingers and toes back to life. These prosaic steel huts were made romantic by a covering of snow or rustic wooden logs so I sat inside and imagined myself a Siberian peasant or an Inuit with his 20 words for snow and dreamt of 20 superlatives to describe the winter wonderland outside.

I had hardly begun when I met Andrei. He was from Chita in Russia's Far East and he grinned gold teeth at me in greeting as we spoke in faltering English about China. Andrei was gloveless and hatless and eating an ice cream. He wore a leather jacket and shook my hand in great powerful fists as he introduced his peroxide wife Elena whose teeth were also gold. Andrei ordered potent rice wine, swallowed it in one gulp and did not make the face that the Chinese do when they drink rice wine (I make the face too). He seemed for all the world like a gangster and was disparaging of the Chinese who came stamping blind into the cafe as their glasses instantly frosted up, screaming "Tai leung!" "Too cold! Too cold!"

Though I figured if I upset Andrei I would be sleeping with the fishes, it was refreshing to meet a cheerful and communicative Russian who smiled when he spoke. I had once traveled on the Trans-Siberian train where every stone faced Russian bureaucrat I'd met had been willfully unhelpful and as obscure as a Harbin politician in the face of a chemical spill, so I was pleased by this Russian's bonhomie. Andrei smiled and slapped me on the back and did not insist that I drink with him as the 7am buffet car vodka guzzlers on the train had done and who only left off their demands when I learned to say 'I am a recovering alcoholic' in Russian.

Harbin is still thick with the influence of Russia though most Russians have long since gone. My favourite cafe from the window of which I watched the sun hover low over Siberia and drop towards Moscow was covered with frosty ivy. The interior was a treasure trove of candles, icons and gilt edged mirrors where the waiter provided a little basket into which patrons dropped their hats and gloves. Dostoevsky and Anna Karenin would have recognised the menu of black bread, borscht and piroshki cabbage rolls (hearty food suited to subzero temperatures) though the chaotic service and the shouts from the tiny kitchen were reassuringly Chinese and the coffee was terrible, as it always is in China.

Harbin's relationship with Russia has been complicated. Originally a small fishing village, (Harbin means 'a place for drying fishing nets') the town became the largest Russian enclave outside Russia in 1918, known as 'the Moscow of the Orient', when thousands of white Russian emigres fled Bolshevik Marxism because they failed to see the benefits of Lenin's socialist utopia.

The Russians worked on the China Far East railway, established a Russian school system, published Russian language newspapers and journals and prospered. Their lives are preserved in aspic in a photo exhibition inside the huge St Sophia's Church in the town centre, the handsome red bricks and green onion domes of which might have been lifted straight out of the Kremlin and that looked most out of place amidst the Chinese tower blocks. The emigres dance and dress up for concerts in the photos in a determined recreation of home. They sit in swimsuits with picnics beside a bright summer Songhua River, devoid of chemicals and ice, but mostly they build wooden synagogues and churches and take solace in God so far from home, though the churches have all gone save for St Sophia itself whose survival was as random as the destruction of so much else in China during the whirlwind of the Cultural Revolution.

The emigres were far from home, though sometimes Russia reached out and pulled them back. In 1937 the Japanese army arrived in Harbin and thousands of Russians returned to their homeland. They were greeted by secret police order number 00593 of 20 September 1937 undersigned by Nikolai Yezhov[12] the perverted and cruel head of the NKVD which required arrest and persecution of the 'Harbinites'. The order stated that the returning Russians were members of emigre fascist spying organisations. Men faced immediate arrest, wives were subject to imprisonment in labour camps for 5 to 8 years while the 'socially

---

12 in a pantheon of 20th century monsters and sadists, Yezhov stands out as a uniquely odious character. The frenzied bloodlust of purges and murder in Russia in 1937 is known as the Yezhovschina and Russians still talk of the period with horror. Yezhov was later purged himself since his extremism was distasteful even to Stalin.

dangerous' children of Harbinites were to be placed in corrective labour colonies or special orphanages since their parents were soon dead.

There was little escape from Yezhov's net for the emigres from the place of drying fishing nets. Breast feeding women and ill children were initially spared but only until the milk was finished or their health was restored before they in turn were devoured. 48,133 Harbinites who had boated on the river, maintained the railway, built their churches, played their music, wrapped up warm in the Heilongjiang winter, loved their children and who stared out from the photos in St Sophia's Church were repressed - 30,992 of these were shot and thus spared at least the indignity and slow death of the camps. Harbin ceased to be known as the Moscow of the Orient.

But you wouldn't know it walking along the cobbled main street of town where the shops are filled with Stalin ashtrays[13], matryoshka dolls and huge fur hats that looked too warm even for -30°C. I bought a jar of caviar from a department store whose name was in Cyrillic script but returned to the shop when I noticed the sell by date had expired. The shop assistant tried to convince me that I had misunderstood since these were 'Russian numbers'. I laughed at this suggestion and in the end she laughed too and returned my money, shrugging her shoulders to explain that I could hardly blame her since the caviar had to be sold.

The Japanese occupation of Harbin in 1937 that drove the Russian emigres into the jaws of the Yezhovschina lasted until 1945. Accounts at the time are filled with the usual litany of heavy-handed police control, arbitrary arrests and the forced imposition of Japanese culture and language. Yet Harbin experienced a unique form of Japanese inhumanity during the long occupation and I took a draughty taxi through streets choked with traffic to the suburb of Pingfang to see this for myself.

The drive was a long one over rutted icy roads through ugly industrial suburbs. The low temperatures condensed the exhaust fumes of

---

13   Stalin is popular in Harbin -- the town is the only one left in China with a park named for the pipe smoking Soviet dictator. I resisted the chance to add a Sidalin memento to my Xitele doll (see Tianjin chapter) and thus increase my collection of 20th-century genocidal maniac ephemera.

whole minutes of unbridled carnal pleasure in 24 hours. Apparently, the colder the weather, the more inflamed the tigers libido; 100 cubs were born in the exceptionally cold winter of my Harbin trip - the park is easily the world's biggest tiger breeding facility and is single-handedly preserving the existence of this noble and beautiful beast.

A visit to the park should be an unashamedly positive occasion and while it is good to see so many tigers sauntering around and getting off with each other in the snow, a visit to a wildlife park in China can never be an entirely comfortable experience. I arrived at the ticket office and watched other tourists take photos by the huge fibreglass tiger outside - head inside mouth, pretend to scream, ready, click. I bought my ticket for the tiger bus and browsed the gift shop while I waited. Here were tiger toys and pictures and big tiger paw gloves, and though I had half expected tiger skins and medicine made from 10 second performance tiger penises, fortunately there were none.

So far so good and though the bus was distressingly unheated, we trundled happily through the park past tigers who looked content and well groomed and unfazed by the freezing cold. My fellow passengers were greatly exercised by the presence of tigers outside the bus as if they hadn't expected them to be there at all. Everyone left their seats the moment we entered the park, rushed from side to side to capture an impossible photo through the frost and protective metal grate on the windows or to run away shrieking when a tiger came too close, and I soon became more interested in watching this than the beasts outside. We left the bus to walk a freezing metal gantry above the tigers where I was glad to get a closer look at their massive heads and emotionless eyes that was not blocked by a mass of excited passenger heads.

It was here that the moral quandry in this valuable park, this preserver of species began. An old woman sat mummified in layers of coats and scarves and any scrap of material that had come to hand, with a box of chickens at her feet and a metal chute by her arm that funnelled down the fence and opened onto the yawning, scratching, fornicating tigers below.

The chickens sat fluffing their feathers against the cold and blinking stupidly, unaware that it would cost me just 40 yuan to have the old woman grab one from the cage and stuff it down the chute to the gaping Siberian jaws. This seemed cheap enough though the passengers were trying to bargain the price down and how much would it be for two chickens, or perhaps they were trying to negotiate a discount on some other tiger snack? This is understandable since a duck was a rather pricey 100 yuan, a sheep 600 yuan and anyone who wanted to throw a cow to the tigers would need to stump up a ruinous 1500 yuan, though I was unclear where the old lady was keeping her livestock and how they would be fitted into the chute.

There were no takers on this freezing day, presumably because the extraction of cash from wallet might have necessitated the removal of a glove, so I was left to wonder how tigers and crowd would react if a chicken was popped down the chute. A little simple research later back at home revealed videos of chickens being dropped with wild abandon and tigers ravenously feasting on hot summer days and a battered truck disgorging a cow from its back doors while tigers prowled expectantly. This showed me at least that the kill was quick since even captive tigers know to go straight for the throat - 1500 yuan of entertainment can be over in a flash.

As for the moral dimension; well, the tigers have got to eat and we would be poorer if the species disappeared from the world. But the sight of men, women and children cheering and applauding the death of the cow was unsettling and seemed Mediaeval, and I felt ashamed of the baying bloodlust.

China is beautiful and ugly at every turn and that night I ate at the five-star hotel on the Harbin Riverfront so that I could pretend I wasn't in China at all, since the wine was French and even the coffee was passable. Today was New Year's Eve and a lounge bar band was crooning their way through a strange and desperate medley of Britney Spears and 'Leaving on a jet plane' collection of tunes. At midnight a net of balloons was released onto the floor and pandemonium broke out as sophisticated diners left their cocktails and desserts to race to the floor and stamp on every balloon as quickly as possible.

I retreated to the ice bar where stools, lights, shelves and even piano were made of ice. It was so cold inside, despite the heavy fur coat I grabbed from the ice hook on the ice wall, that I knew I would be alone. I ordered a drink and listened to the popping of balloons and the band strike up Auld Lang Syne next door. Outside, the New Year was just as cold as the one just passed and I resolved to head south and end this icy Northern exile of tigers and Russians. I told myself that I would come back but doubted I would; there was so much of China still to see and I was possessed of a tigerish desire to feel the sun on my face and the sand between my toes.

HEBEI

河北

204 404 sq km
Population 60.4 million

`If you meet the Buddha on the road, kill the Buddha....the sacred
teachings are only lists of ghosts, sheets of paper fit for wiping the
pus from your boils`

Linji Yixuan, 9th Century.

Poor unappreciated, anonymous Shijiazhuang. This town that no one
has heard of earns just a page and a half in Lonely Planet's China guide
which in a place with 3 million people works out at about one word for
every 3000 citizens. Shijiazhuang is usually called 'gritty' or 'parochial'

or 'hard to love', though sometimes a making-the-best-of-it visitor will muse on how 'real' the place feels and how great it is to be off the tourist trail. But mostly this most functional of cities is just plain dull. There is no doubt that Hebei's provincial capital is thoroughly overshadowed by its Northern neighbour Beijing, and cultural metropolis or Paris of the East it is not. But Shijiazhuang has a special place in my personal journey of discovery in China, for it was here that I lived with a Chinese family for 2 weeks one summer, immersed myself in its gritty, parochial functionality and made a serious attempt to learn the Chinese language.

China's destiny as the world's 21st century economic powerhouse seems assured and it's taken for granted that soon the clothes we wear, food we eat and air we breathe will all be made there. Yet the world's workshop, the exporter of 800 billion dollars worth of manufactured goods every year speaks very little English outside the economic and political centres of Beijing, Shanghai and Hong Kong. And indeed, why should it? No more than 2 or 3 visits to the countryside was enough to convince me that pointing at photos on a menu, speaking *very slowly and loudly* in English and pretending to be a steam train for taxi drivers who I needed to drive me to the station simply wouldn't do. No, if I was really going to see this confusing, huge and capricious country, I would have to learn some Chinese.

Except even that term is no good, for the country has hundreds of dialects all quite different to each other. The Communist Party has tackled this as part of their great unifying campaign in which even the most far flung peasant village gets to feel the benefits of Socialism. So, along with one nation and one party comes one tongue with the introduction of Standard Mandarin or 'Putonghua' which translates as 'common language'. It hasn't worked of course and locals everywhere cling stubbornly to their local idiolects, but I came to Shijiazhuang because here there are no distracting dialects (or anything much else to distract me) and very little English is spoken. In this town my fledgling Mandarin would come on apace since 98% of the population speaks pure, clear, unadulterated and unaccented Putonghua.

I arrived by the new high speed and sleek rail link from Beijing, rehearsing the name of my Putonghua immersion school over and over in my head, since this would be an impossible destination to mime to a taxi driver. The train from the capital to Shijiazhuang epitomizes fast track, high speed 21st century China and carried me through the north Hebei countryside at a breathless 250 km/h and will soon be further upgraded to 350km/h so that the cabbage fields outside the windows can race by in even more of a blur. I knew sufficient Chinese characters to read that shi-jia-zhuang written above the huge entrance to the station, suitably grand for the receipt of 250km/h trains, means stone-family-village. Originally the 'shi' meant '10' since the village earned its name because it had been home to just 10 families. Such a backward and yokel appellation is not sufficiently go-ahead for this town struggling to emerge from the shadow of Beijing, so 'stone' which is also pronounced 'shi' it became.

This being China, my home stay did not run smoothly at first. I arrived at the school famished since I had risen from bed and left insufficient time to eat *and* catch my train. My tardiness caused me to tell my taxi driver to go faster, faster through Beijing, a novel experience indeed as I was much more used to asking Chinese taxis to slow down. By the time I arrived, even the dried cuttlefish and pig's feet on sale at the roadside stands looked tempting, but my endlessly patient teacher Mary who met me smilingly at the school told me that breakfast would not be possible because we had a 'very important job to do' and announced that we were going to the hospital. How sad that Mary should be ill on our first day I thought, but apparently it was I who needed a visit to the doctor. This is because every waiguoren or foreigner who stays in a Chinese household must be scrutinized and subjected to a battery of medical checks, since how else is the government to protect its citizens from the unedifying and unhealthy viruses of barbarians from who knows where?

Mary thrust a Flying Pigeon bicycle at me; "zi xing che – bicycle" and said we should go. China produces nearly a third of the world's bicycles, most of which are of the Flying Pigeon (Feige) or Forever (Yongjiu) brand. Both are 50 pounds of gearless iron with rod brakes and little stopping power. Most sport the benefits of chain guard and rear package carrier. The more sophisticated models have a bell. Mao's successor Deng Xiaoping once issued the Henry Fordian declaration that as China adopted 'Socialism with Chinese characteristics', there would soon be a Flying Pigeon in every household and the beast is traditionally available in any colour as long as it is black. The bikes seem to be uniformly assembled by workers with incredibly weak wrists since nothing is tightened properly and sure enough, despite my Flying Pigeon being fresh from the factory floor, before long a pedal had fallen to the floor. Such mishaps are clearly common place on the highways of Shijiazhuang because within seconds a man was at hand with wrench and hammer to put things right and for a couple of yuan I was on my way. Mary laughed and said that once everything had fallen off once and been properly retightened, the bike would last for years.

Those people who think that the Chinese no longer ride bikes should come to Shijiazhuang. At least half the city jumps on a bicycle every morning and the roads were a seething mass of furiously pedaling humanity. The rule of the road is that you must under no circumstances hesitate, deviate or show weakness of any kind no matter if the bike heading your way is laden with gas cylinders, water melons or live pigs. I soon became as stubborn and forthright as the other road users and used my bell with alacrity (mine was an up market Flying Pigeon), though in truth, hesitation was not really an option since my braking power was even less secure than my pedals.

We arrived at the hospital and left a full 3 hours later after my blood test, cardiogram, urine sample, eyesight exam and chest x-ray had pronounced me fit to stay with a Chinese family. The hospital queues were horrible since many Chinese labourers were getting examined before trying their luck on building sites in Thailand and Vietnam, but Mary played the waiguoren card without hesitation or remorse, explaining that my case was 'urgent' and so I shamelessly jumped the queues.

The workers were happy to delay their future prospects and there was much interested discussion and laughter as I had my blood taken and read the chart in the optician's room. This turned to an audible gasp as I removed my shirt in full view of the assembled throng for my cardiogram. The nurse was equally perplexed by my surfeit of body hair and after a few fumbled attempts to affix the pads to my chest she gave up and pronounced me fit anyway, though I would have thought this was self evident after I had cycled a Flying Pigeon through town.

Thank goodness she didn't send for a razor. My ordeal over, I asked Mary why it was necessary for me to have an eyesight test to stay with a Chinese family and she replied that this was because without it I could not stay with a family. This delightfully circular argument struck me as typical of the unquestioning acceptance by the average Chinese of the edicts of authority.

Back at the school, I fell on a bowl of vegetables and rice like a hungry wolf and then met with my hosts. Surprisingly, I was offered a choice of 2 beds for the night – my medical results must have been *really* good. My kind hosts were the sisters Liu, one of whom spoke good English and lived close to the school and the other who didn't and whose house was miles away and who would I like to stay with? I naturally chose the former but after much discussion was driven through the sprawling city to the other house.

There began a strange 2 hours where I sat on Ms Liu's leather sofa talking to a policeman who examined my passport and had been alerted to my presence by an alarmed neighbour, shocked by the appearance of a foreign devil in the flats and all the while a resident Chihuahua called Peony barked loudly and gripped my trouser leg in its tiny teeth and pulled hard as if encouraging me to leave. The policeman left satisfied that I had no criminal intent and no doubt reassured by my excellent eyesight and satisfactory urine results. But my trials did not finish there for no sooner had the officer left than Ms Liu burst into tears and said that her absent husband would be very unhappy if he knew I was here and so I couldn't possibly stay. And so it was that I shook the yapping Peony from my leg, drove back across town and arrived at the home of my new host family just 10 minutes from the school. I was shown to my room and the family proudly pointed out a Flying Pigeon standing shining and black in the hall which would be for my exclusive use during my 2 week stay.

Of all my experiences in China, some of my fondest memories are of staying with the Xu family in Shijiazhuang. Liu Jie, Dou Li and their son Jia Ming spoke little English though this was good since I was supposed to be speaking little English too, though they asked that I teach the basics of my mother tongue to Jia Ming or 'Ming Ming' as they affectionately called him, in the evening. My bed was comfortable and the food an unending parade of roast duck, rice, fresh vegetables, bean curd and prawns all of which Dou Li bought from the market on the street below their 3rd floor two bedroom government owned flat.

I soon learned that despite my protestations, I got the best of the chicken and the first glass of Hebei Billion Beer ('highly productive and conducive to good health') at every meal because I was an honoured guest. I learned also to be moderate in my praise of any single item since if I said that I liked something, it would appear at every meal thereafter. Thus mornings in the Xu household began with a bowl of red bean congee rice porridge made palatable only by the application of heaped teaspoons of sugar because I had been foolish enough to say how much I liked porridge on my first day. The same difficulty arose when I was taken on a night out to the local supermarket and caused uproar on the delicatessen counter by claiming that I was Dou Li's son. Here I quickly learned to say that I liked only the cheapest produce since it would instantly appear in the trolley and it was here that I saw Dou Li angry for the only time when she thrust my wallet back into my pocket with a scowl at the checkout when I had the temerity to suggest that I might pay. Our night in the grocery store ended in the tea section where we sampled cup after cup of cha and Dou Li produced ice cream and pistachios as we made a real meal of it. This was a regular event for family Xu and Liu Jie professed himself well satisfied since "the tea is fine and it's all for free" and the tea shop proprietor smiled wanly in return as he poured yet another cup of Pu`er. I bought a souvenir Chinese zodiac monkey made from tea to assuage my guilt and we wandered home through the Flying Pigeons satisfied with a good and thoroughly economical night out.

Ming Ming was a reluctant student and shy of speaking a difficult foreign tongue, but as his reserve broke down he made some progress. This was despite the attentions of his teacher called Valley who spoke worse English than Ming Ming by far. The boy's textbook was no great aid to learning either and was full of useless idioms like 'pride before a fall' and 'once bitten twice shy' and I returned from my own struggles with language in school one day to find that Ming Ming had neatly copied the phrase 'over the moon' 100 times into his thin notebook.

I asked Valley why she had chosen such an unusual name (I really wanted to ask if she was U shaped or V shaped and considered herself deep or shallow and whether she had siblings named after other geographical features) and she answered that she thought it sounded 'sweet'. Many Chinese choose an English name because it is fashionable to do so and base their choice on either a name that sounds similar to their Chinese name or something that is suggestive of desirable qualities. Thus, girls will often have pretty names and boys will choose names that profess strength and heroism. The Xus had not succumbed to this modern trend but introduced me at various points during my stay to their friends and neighbours 'Beautiful Bird', 'Beautiful Flower', 'I love the Army' and 'Generous'.

The family told me that they came originally from Shaanxi province, where Ming Ming's maternal grandmother still lives and takes her morning run every day on her bound feet through the streets of Xi'an. Liu Jie had been in the army for 15 years and served as a Major and showed me his pocket book certificate of service which seemed scant reward for a decade and a half of boot camp but which gave him free rides on Shijiazhuang's public transport. He showed me photos of a younger man with a buzz cut in uniform in the snow of Qinghai with Long March rockets in the background, huge and white with Chinese characters and the national flag painted on the side. Liu Jie spent four years in the remoteness of Western China on the edge of Tibet and saw his sweetheart Dou Li for only two months a year, but he had pictures of them together standing stiff and formal in the snow and of the young soldier doing a handstand, Dou Li laughing in the background. I expressed admiration for this gymnastic feat and was promptly treated to a repeat performance against the wall in the front room and Dou Li laughed and looked girlish just as she had in Qinghai all those years before.

And all the while my Chinese improved with Mary who said 'bu dui', 'not correct' a little less and 'hen hao', 'very good' a little more each day. As my language improved, so did my connection with the Xu family. Dou Li was anxious to apologize for the dirtiness of the city and thought I must find it a very dull place. I said that it really wasn't bad, though certainly the tall chimneys capped by red concentric circles pumped a lot of smoke into the air and vast swathes of the city had been razed to rubble. I wondered why this was the case and Dou Li agreed that these derelict sights were an eyesore but that "the government is very busy so the dirtiness can't be solved yet".This was a housewife's interpretation of the business of government. Jobs were being ticked off on a big list somewhere; they just hadn't got around to the cleaning yet. In fact there was a lot of sweeping in Shijiazhuang and on every street a worker was apathetically brushing dust from one street corner to the other. It's just that this made no discernible difference to anything much and the town was still grubby; travel writer Paul Theroux's assertion that the Chinese are 'sweepers not scrubbers' was certainly borne out in this town.

Others in Shijiazhuang were less circumspect than Dou Li and I was told that the town was a mess because Government policy there 'is like a child's face; three changes in an hour'. Shijiazhuang will probably look OK when it's finished; it's just that it never *will* be finished since there will always be something new to knock down. I was reminded of a popular joke in China in which a child asks his Dad what Communism is; "see the edge of the sky?" replies the gnomic father, "that's Communism; it exists, but we'll never reach it".

My 10 minute morning cycle past derelict sites and factory chimneys and an almost pretty canal path soon became a pleasant routine. Every day I passed the Shanghai beauty salon where the beauticians carried out a series of stiff, choreographed aerobic moves every morning to an ear piercing Chinese pop music backing. The girls in their identical uniforms and thickly made up faces would never give me a smile as they went through their routine though I grinned inanely at them every time I passed and stopped once, dismounted from my bike and pretended to join in.

Everyone rode their bike with the seat too low and their knees stuck out at right angles like so many circus monkeys and as the day warmed up, men would roll up one leg (and occasionally both) of their nylon slacks to reveal sheer nylon pop socks pulled up to pasty white knees. When it got really hot, they would take off their shirt and cycle in a white cotton vest.

One day school was delayed because the city was having an air raid drill practice, though I was unable to establish who these provincial Hebei townsfolk thought they might be bombed by. After the sirens had faded and the streets had refilled with cyclists and their monkey gait, I pedaled right down into the city to have a look and found that Shijiazhuang is not entirely devoid of cultural sights. Downtown is the Martyrs' Memorial dedicated to Norman Bethune the Canadian surgeon whose importance to China I also encountered at Yan'an in Shaanxi province (see Shaanxi chapter) and also to Eric Liddell and Dwarkanath Kotnis.

Liddell is the Olympic sprinter who wouldn't run on a Sunday commemorated in the film `Chariots of Fire` and served as a missionary in North East China throughout the 1930s. He was imprisoned by the Japanese in 1941 and by all accounts kept himself busy by helping the elderly, teaching children, arranging games and being an all round good guy before his untimely death in 1945. Kotnis is rather less well known in the West though he too has been celebrated in film by the Bollywood movie 'The Immortal Story of Doctor Kotnis'. He was one of a team of 5 Indian doctors who came to China in 1938 to treat soldiers wounded by the Japanese and served for 5 years in mobile clinics. His immortality in China was assured when he joined the Communist Party just before his death in 1942. His tomb records that 'The future will honour him even more than the present, because it was for the future that he struggled' and I wondered if the brave Indian doctor would have considered modern sprawling Shijiazhuang a future worth the fight.

Head filled with the heroism of foreigners whose deeds put to shame my feeble attempts to learn some Mandarin and integrate a little, I absentmindedly parked my Flying Pigeon along with hundreds of identical others outside the city swimming pool and wondered if I would ever find it again. The pool was a flailing soup of arms and legs and I was alarmed to see plastic urine buckets for children who might be caught short placed strategically on the edge of the water and in a place that seemed to maximise the chances of spillage. I retreated to the Jacuzzi which was also jammed with kids and old folks and became suddenly aware that this warm bubbling water was probably also full of pee so I left the pool, showered and got back on my bike.

The Xus were determined to give me a big send off so I spent my last day with my hosts hiking in the nearby countryside which they insisted was beautiful and remote, but which in reality was only a little less built up than the city proper. We ate Spam sandwiches on a hilltop overlooking China's biggest military training camp where tanks were hidden under green webbing, soldiers marched up and down in the hot sun and I wondered whether I might be arrested as a spy. We caught a taxi back to town and I made the driver laugh uproariously with my impersonation of a Hong Kong Cantonese accent. We ate hotpot that was so spicy with chilli grass that many diners in the restaurant took their shirts off and my lips began to vibrate and we cooled off with a red bean ice lolly outside the train station where my Shijiazhuang adventure had begun 2 weeks before.

And so it was that my time in this anonymous Chinese city came to an end. Though since 2008, Shijiazhuang has been anonymous no more and was thrust into the world's attention as the epicentre of China's milk scandal. The city is an important centre for the dairy trade and as I soared along the streets on my bike I had often been choked by the fumes of lorries owned by the Sanlu milk company emblazoned with their prancing 3 deers logo. Sanlu had the lion's share of the market before the scandal broke because its products were half the price of its competitors and in 2007, sales passed 10 billion yuan for the first time. The company's workforce surpassed 10 000 people by the end of that year and the government announced that a number of its products were exempt from inspection, having passed quality checks 3 times in succession. This might be where the rot set in for the 3 Deers Company and by early 2008 complaints were being made about the quality of its infant milk formula. Tests revealed that the formula was contaminated with melamine, a chemical designed to give artificially high protein content in the milk and which helps conceal its fraudulent dilution with water, but which causes kidney disease if swallowed. The Company and Hebei local administrators refused to sanction an official recall of Sanlu products and it took intervention from the New Zealand Prime Minister who alerted authorities in Beijing because

New Zealand was an importer of Sanlu products. Production was halted and tests carried out and all 11 samples from Sanlu were found to fail the melamine test which led to the arrest of Sanlu General Manager and Party Secretary, Tian Wenhua. The Vice mayor in charge of food and agriculture was sacked too and a week later, Shijiazhuang's Mayor Ji Chuntang resigned.

The crisis confirmed many of the International community's fears over the quality of produce and level of political corruption in China. The poisoning of babies milk was a particularly emotive issue and an orgy of criticism and reproach began in the world's press, to the acute embarrassment of Beijing. In late 2008, it was announced that the problem had spread to eggs and that six infants had died from kidney damage and a further 860 were hospitalized. Ghoulish details were released about the nature of melamine which is essentially a fire retardant plastic with carcinogenic properties. Arrests continued as it was announced that a lion cub and 2 baby orangutans in Hangzhou Zoo had died after eating Sanlu products. Meanwhile, countries around the world recalled all milk products imported from China including a chocolate body spread sold in sex shops in the UK that was found to be contaminated with melamine and no doubt dangerous to both spreader and recipient of the erotic confection.

China's Premier, Wen Jiabao announced that the government would punish those responsible; "None of those companies without professional ethics or social morals will be let off". Wen was certainly true to his word and early in 2009 the sentences were announced for those involved in the scandal that had caused so much injury to China's reputation. 2 dairy managers responsible for adding the chemical to milk were sentenced to death and the woman most widely blamed went to prison for life. Tian Wenhua was short, a little plump and 66 years old and cut a forlorn figure as she spoke in front of crowds in Shijiazhuang to apologize for her company's role in the scandal. I recognized on the pictures in the press the square near the town centre where she stood and felt a little sorry for her. But Tian had become a figure of hate in China and thousands of Chinese decried the life sentence she received, saying she deserved the death penalty too. 3000 comments were posted on news163.com; "even a 1000 cuts into myriad pieces can't make up for the deaths of the innocent children", a person in Shandong wrote, and from Shanghai a man demanded that she be forced to drink the tainted milk until she died.

The scandal rocked China but the death sentences and Tian's groveling apology change nothing since adulteration on such a scale is likely to reoccur in a country where a fast growing capitalist economy is coupled with a government unable or unwilling to regulate the food supply. In such get-rich-quick societies, the temptation to tamper in products where the margins are low is too great especially in a product like milk which the public have been taught to trust implicitly.

I waved the Xu family goodbye at the station and promised to keep in touch, but I love the excitement of a train journey and I was glad to leave Shijiazhuang's ordinariness behind. I was heading North and East, but stopped first at Zhengding just 20km outside the city. This small town is famous for its temples and pagodas and is pretty and full of history in a way that Shijiazhuang is not. The main temple dates from the 6th century and I entered the gates past a corpulent golden Buddha and between 4 scary Heavenly Kings who snarled and leered at me carrying huge Dao sabers and Qiang spears. The Pavilion of Great Mercy within is home to a colossal statue of Guanyin with 1000 arms (though I counted only 30) which at 21 metres high, is one of the largest wooden statues in the world.

This 1000 year old Guanyin shoulders the grief of the world and dispenses mercy and compassion rather like a Chinese Virgin Mary. I climbed the wooden steps, stared more closely into her benevolent, munificent face with its 3 eyes and saw 2 more eyes glinting in the half dark. These eyes belonged to a monk from the Temple who offered to read my fortune. So, I dipped my hand into his small velvet bag and extracted a piece of paper covered in tiny Chinese characters which the monk set to examining myopically and in great detail. He announced after some minutes that I would be lucky in work and love in the year ahead and that my daughters should be nurtured because they are worth '10 sons'. The whole process in the dark mustiness of the Temple beneath the serene gaze of a 1000 year old statue was all rather hypnotic, though the monk broke the spell when he clumsily concluded by attempting to sell me a lucky jade stone for 580 yuan.

Zhengding is the town of 9 towers, 4 pagodas, 8 great temples and 24 golden archways, though sadly all of the towers have long since disappeared. These apparently random numbers are all auspicious and reflect the Chinese obsession with digits, most of which are deemed to possess hidden secrets. Numbers are particularly linked with the sounds of their associative meaning, thus number eight is the luckiest of all because it is pronounced `ba` which sounds like 'fa', the Chinese word for the acquisition of wealth. Four is terribly unlucky because it is pronounced 'si' which is the same as 'death'. This explains why the 4th floor in apartment blocks is always the cheapest and usually occupied by some unsuspecting foreigner unaware of the mortal danger he faces every time he goes home. Chinese culture is a minefield of numerical mishaps. How is the unsuspecting visitor to know that courses in restaurants are best served in even numbers because the number two suggests harmonious existence and reproduction? But odd numbers can be lucky too, especially five which reflects the base colours and the elements of Feng Shui and seven which sounds like the word for wife or family.

One of the eight great temples in Zhengding is the Linji Temple named after the famous 9th century Buddhist teacher Linji Yixuan. This interesting character favoured harsh and abrupt dealings with his students in order to create enlightenment and could usually be found shouting at them or hitting them with a fly whisk. Linji was no respecter of doctrine which he described as "so much filth in the latrine" and promised that one's true Buddha nature could only be discovered if conventions and teachings are rejected outright, even to the extent of denying the Buddha himself.

Linji Temple is much less grand than the bigger Dafo temple and retains a quiet charm and lack of pretension of which the non-axiomatic Linji would have approved. There are several stele or large stone tablets covered in minute carved characters here and carried on the back of stone tortoises. Except these are not tortoises but `Bixi` - one of the dragon children who is renowned for carrying weight and can be found throughout China stoically and patiently bearing stone tablets of all sizes. I feel a great affinity for the quiet Bixi who uncomplainingly gets on with his quiet work, but this muscle bound tortoise is just one of several Dragon Children.

The others have similarly specific jobs and it became a hobby of mine to spot them whenever I was in China. Taotie who loves to eat and is found on cooking wares, Suanni who looks like a lion and loves smoke and can be seen on incense burners and the water lover Baxin who pops up on bridges are all easy enough to find. More spotter points are available for Chiwen who likes to see far and is always on the roof, Pulao who roars and is sometimes on the side of bells and Jiaotu who hates to be disturbed and is used on the front doors and thresholds of houses. Bi'an the powerful tiger and Yazi who likes to kill are found respectively on prison doors and knives and are the hardest to find of all. It's like train spotting for China travelers.

The journey north was a long one and the scenery an unending parade of small dusty towns and fields where I saw a man behind an ox ploughing a field wearing slip on leather shoes and a suit, though he was clearly not too hot since neither trouser leg was rolled up. I turned to a Chinese newspaper abandoned on the chair beside me in an attempt to relieve the boredom, but could make little sense of the densely typed characters and bold headlines. Fortunately a Hebei native called David (no heroic name like 'I love the army' for him) shared the journey with me and helped me to read.

It turned out that 2 hapless thieves called Ren Xiaofeng and Ma Xiangjing were making headlines in Hebei that day. Ma and Ren were bank employees and had spent 47 million yuan of the bank's money on lottery tickets. They had intended to pay back what they had borrowed the moment they scored a big win. "But we didn't win" wailed Ren. "It was then that we knew we were finished and that we had better escape, so we decided to steal some more money and flee". David also read me the story of a cat that had been murdered at Hebei University. "We turned around and saw a boy suspiciously looking right and left; that's when we realized that Garfield had been blown up", recalled a man who was privy to the event. The witness was sufficiently outraged to issue a sinister warning to the killer. "Garfield will find you", he warned. "He will go after you even if he becomes a ghost. Garfield with his head blown off will forever appear in your nightmares, that is my curse to you". I asked David if these were typical stories and he said they were since Hebei is `a little crazy`.

The temples at Zhengding pale into insignificance compared to those at Chengde. This was the summer retreat for the Manchu Dynasty built after the Emperor Kangxi discovered the area on one of his long hunting expeditions in 1703. These trips were an attempt to recreate the mythical hunting, outdoorsy existence of the Manchu people in days past, though the Qing Emperors rather spoiled the impression of bucolic charm and simple pleasures by marching forth from Beijing to Chengde with a retinue of 10 000 eunuchs, servants and concubines. Chengde was an escape from the intolerable summer heat of Beijing and the names of the buildings - 'Fleeing the heat mountain villa', 'The hall of refreshing mists and waves', 'the misty rain tower', reflect a determined effort to cool off. The Qing received visitors here as well. A mini Potala Palace called Putuozongcheng Temple was thrown up in 1786 for the reception of the Panchen Lama who mysteriously died before his return to Tibet. In 1783, the emissary Lord MacCartney visited from Britain to open trade discussions with the China. MacCartney arrived in a foul mood after learning that the boats he had used to sail up the river to Beijing had been painted with the characters 'Tribute bearers from the vassal King of England' and the situation deteriorated further when the affronted Englishman refused to kowtow to Emperor Qianlong. The meeting ended with no trade agreement and a letter from the Dragon Throne to King George III explaining that China had no use for trade since she already possessed all things, and ending 'O King, tremblingly obey and show no negligence'.

There is an even bigger and more elaborate Guanyin at Chengde inside the 18th Century Puning Temple with 42 arms and an eye on each palm. The Temple houses several dusty cabinets of religious exhibitions beside the Buddha gift shop where it is possible to buy a Buddha like bust of Chairman Mao. In one of these cabinets was a Kapala bowl made from the skull of a young girl and traditionally used in Tibetan religious ceremonies. Such bowls are carefully chosen from sky burial sites on the high plateau and are especially auspicious since the 'jiva' or spirit enters a body through the 10th hole at the top of the head. If it leaves by the same route, this is called a 'perfect exit', but the body has nine other holes, called golukas from which an escape can be made.

These are much less important to the Buddhist since no self respecting jiva would dash in or out of any old goluka.

Hebei is famous for its skulls. It was at nearby Zhoukoudian that the half million year old head and bones of 'Peking Man' were unearthed in the 1930s, giving temporary rise to the theory that all human life may have begun here. The bulk of the find was lost during the Japanese occupation and the whereabouts of this important archaeological discovery have remained a mystery ever since despite the best efforts of Officer Steve McGarrett in Hawaii Five-0 to solve the riddle in 1970s flared trousers in an episode delightfully called 'Bones of Contention'.

I continued east and was excited to see the sun reflected on the distant Bohai Gulf that separates China from Korea since two weeks in Shijiazhuang had left me somewhat starved of expansive ocean views. I disembarked at Shanhaiguan whose name means 'Mountain sea pass', because this is where the Great Wall of China meets the sea after its tortuous 6500 km journey from Gansu Province on the Silk Road much further West. For centuries this pass guarded the narrow defile between North-East and Central China and prevented the passage of the inferior Manchus and Mongols from the barbarian lands in the north. The pass was the scene of many battles before falling to the Manchus in the 17th Century, which heralded the end of Ming Dynasty rule in China.

The gatehouse here is called The First Pass Under Heaven. It's a colossal thing with walls 14 metres high and 7 metres thick and stands squat and impressive against the last fields in China before the sea. The scene was shrouded in a cloying and wet sea mist when I was there, but the photographers were still open for business and urged me to have my photo taken studded with the phrase 'Climb the Great Wall and be a true man'. I said it was too wet so instead they invited me into a tent covered in plastic where I could dress as a Red Guard and be a true man instead. Strangely, I was also able to dress as a Nationalist Guomindang soldier too, the uniform of Mao's enemies during the long civil war before the Communist ascension to power in 1949. I told the photographer that I was surprised to see this since the Nationalists are still in charge of Taiwan and the traditional enemy of China, but he understood this and that was why a photo dressed as a nationalist was five yuan cheaper.

The absolute terminus of the Great Wall juts out into the sea at a place called 'Laolongtou' or 'Old Dragon's Head' after the carved dragon's head that once stood in this place. Here was a cold choppy sea with seagulls buffeted on the wind and huge oil tankers offshore, though locals were still laughing and bathing and making the best of things. I strolled along the beach looking at the edge of the Manchurian Liaoning Peninsula in the distance and stopped at a restaurant where judging by the reaction of the waitresses, no foreigner had ever set foot before. I asked if I could eat and the manager replied yes, but did I have money to pay and no gas was lit or rice set to cook until I had opened my wallet and proved that it was indeed possible for a foreign devil to possess hard currency. The meal set me up for the climb along the Wall and up Jiao Shan Mountain – the first (or last) hill that the Wall traverses. The going was steep and warning signs mysteriously reminded me that there must be 'No Retrogradation'. I hoped I was not breaking this rule and continued to the top where the rain stopped, the sun came out from behind the most easterly clouds in Hebei and I was treated to glorious views over the coast, the old battlefields of the Pass and the Wall roller coasting west in a rare moment of solitude in the most populous nation on earth.

My final day in Hebei was spent further south at the seaside resort of Beidahe. This is one of the few real bucket and spade beaches in China and it was good to stroll along the prom, prom, prom here and watch the Chinese at play. The resort is a curious mixture of kitsch and politics. I had my photo taken in a cardboard speedboat on the beach and cycled out to see the Emerald Shell Tower, a truly ghastly hotel built in the shape of a giant conch shell. The beach out here was the exclusive preserve of couples having their wedding photos taken. (Couples have their photos taken before their wedding day in China so that their guests are not bored senseless). Dozens of brides were staggering around on the sand holding their powder puff dresses above their knees and sweating their make up off, while the grooms stood starched and mostly grim faced and held their shoes. The betrothed were waiting their turn to be photographed beside an intriguing collection of props on the sand; a couple rocked gently in a swing chair beneath an arch of plastic roses while another bride feigned rapt appreciation as her husband to be mimed a tune on a white grand piano, while other couples waited their turn, practiced expressions of enchantment and tried to ignore the sand blowing round their heads.

The beachfront gets more political further from the ice cream stalls and blushing brides. Along the coast, the sand is finer and the coves more secluded and these beaches were reserved for the use of high ranking cadres only. 'No stopping, No looking' said the signs but I stopped and looked anyway and machine gun toting guards in mirrored shades stared back. This was taking the Chinese regard for status and rank to new extremes and I wondered whether the party members here had first call on the candy floss too, yet Beidahe has a distinguished history of catering to China's communist elite and it is said that every member of the Politburo has a villa here. I remembered seeing black and white photos of Mao's Deputy Liu Shaoqi frolicking on the beach here with his wife and kids just a few years before he was denounced as a bourgeois right wing deviationist during the Cultural Revolution and left to a lonely death from cancer in prison. Mao spent some time at the nearby rocky outcrop called Pigeon Nest Park where he sat and contemplated the vastness of the ocean like some erstwhile King Cnut and penned a poem to Beidahe and the greatness of the Party. Mao's appointed successor Lin Biao was here too and supposedly plotted his escape from China in Beidahe after his failed coup in 1971, and although he officially died in a plane crash over Mongolia while fleeing to Russia, the tale that he was strangled in his seaside villa is infinitely more satisfying.

The resort is also a playground for China's workers who come for free holidays in the many sanatoriums for coal miners and factory workers and also for dozens of painfully sunburned tourists from Russia's Far East. All the street signs and café menus were displayed in both Chinese characters and the Cyrillic alphabet and I was asked if I cared for a drink in faltering Russian by a Chinese barman who assumed that I was also from Irkutsk or Vladivostok. How surprised he looked and then how delighted too when I replied that yes, I would like to sit with him and drink a cold beer, not in Russian or English but in my hard earned Putonghua from Shijiazhuang.

LIAONING

辽宁

151 295 sq km
Population 42.2 million

'Like spring I treat my comrades warmly,
Like summer I am full of ardor for my revolutionary work.
I eliminate my individualism as an autumn gale sweeps away
fallen leaves,
And to the class enemy I am cruel and ruthless like a harsh winter'

'The Four Seasons' by Lei Feng

Liaoning is in that part of China once called Manchuria, a place of history and romance, but which is now simply 'DongBei' or 'the North

East'. Such descriptive pragmatism is in keeping with many places I encountered in the country. Shanghai is simply 'above the sea' and the thousands of miles of ancient stone that winds through desert and over mountains is merely a 'Great Wall'. If London was in China it would be called 'Nanjing' or 'Southern capital'. The ancient sprawl of Cairo on the banks of the majestic Nile would be 'Shangjiang' – above the river - and Los Angeles would be 'Western town of narcissism and high crime' and not the City of Angels.

The province is named after the Liao dynasty that ruled China from 907-1125. 'Ning' means peacefulness but rarely can a region have been more inappropriately named. Liaoning is a victim of geography, a Far Eastern battleground for Russia, Japan, China and Korea that intensified in the last century after the discovery of abundant coal, iron and oil there (an estimated 146 billion barrels under the nearby Bohai Sea.) The sense of peace has further declined in the last 20 years; huge state industries became increasingly uneconomical and the province has seen labour unrest unprecedented in the People's Republic, as workers went unpaid or were laid off and factories were closed. Liaoning is now known as China's 'rust belt' which conjures images of disused dirt roads, barbed wire, abandoned smokestacks and desolate winding gear over disused mines, like a movie set in those films they make in the Western town of high crime.

I travelled from Shenzhen just over the border from Hong Kong where the check-in queues were interminable as a woman opened several Styrofoam boxes for inspection. She had been instructed to empty the pints of water that had collected inside as her frozen chicken wings and sausages being transported thawed out and I wondered where she could possibly be going where the shops had such an absence of meat.

I flew to Dandong, come to gaze voyeuristically into a country that is more exasperating and obscure to the west even than China. Dandong lies along the Yalu River and the town on the opposite bank to the People's Republic of China is in the Democratic People's Republic of Korea, a country that is neither democratic nor Republican though admittedly, the Nepotistic Hereditary Communist One-Party State of Korea doesn't have the same ring. The river here is not wide and I could clearly see the Korean border town of Sinuiju, though the place was deserted on this freezing December day and I saw no one in the park or on the Ferris wheel or walking to the factory gates or enjoying the fruits of democratic republicanism.

It's possible to get as close as 20 metres from the shore of North Korea in one of the speedboat or pleasure craft that line the river bank here but it was far too cold for that today. The metal gates were secured by padlock and chain and the boats sat inert in the freezing water, though neon lights plaited with barbed wire still flicked on and off as if someone had forgotten to hit the off switch when summer ended. There were pictures of married couples, orange life jackets over their wedding dresses and suits, enjoying the boats in bright sunshine with a North Korean backdrop. This seemed a strange choice of wedding location, but I thought about the newlywed photos I had seen in China - playing a white grand piano on a beach in Hebei, posing with teddy bears in front of Hong Kong high rises - and remembered that the most basic principle of recording a Chinese marriage is a divorce from reality.

There are two bridges over the Yalu at Dandong. One carries an occasional freight train or a minibus of middle-class Chinese gone abroad - it's easy for Chinese to cross into the DPRK - they don't even need to use a passport since the authorities can safely assume that tourists will definitely come back - and the other ends abruptly halfway across in a tangled nest of jagged metal. This is the old 1911 bridge constructed by the Japanese that was destroyed by US B-29 heavy bombers during the Korean War of 1950-53 despite the presence of Soviet fighters in nearby 'MIG Alley' as they attempted to cut off Chinese supplies to the North Koreans. The US claimed that the damage was all a terrible misunderstanding but from the end of the bridge, it looked like precision bombing to me.

I walked along the bridge, the border rushing cold and grey beneath, past black-and-white photos of war and with loudspeakers strapped to the massive iron trusses playing a spaghetti western version of Scarborough Fair. The route came to an abrupt full stop 100 metres from North Korea like an iron allegory of that nation's disconnection from the rest of the world. A man at the end stamped his feet against the -10° cold and breathed great vaporous clouds of smoke that froze on the collar of his coat pulled tight to his chin. Only commerce or prison can induce a man in China to endure such a level of discomfort, and this iceman's handwritten sign said 'travel abroad for five yuan' next to a pair of powerful binoculars.

I paid my money and looked through the lens, scanning the shore for signs of life. The Ferris wheel still didn't turn and no lights shone from blind windows. I began to wonder if this town existed at all though at last I spotted two soldiers who had laid their guns against an incongruous fibreglass camel to eat breakfast. Binocular man told me that business is not so good in the winter and he made little money. 'But at least I don't live over there' he said, prodding a mittened hand towards Korea; a classic piece of one-upmanship, essential to the self-esteem of all men. 'I may be freezing cold standing at the end of a broken bridge in an obscure provincial town trying desperately to recover the cost of a pair of binoculars, but at least I'm not as badly off as him'. I had the same feeling of thank-my-lucky-stars superiority to his uncomfortable job and no doubt others would have it in regard to me and my two star hotel, crowded train, cheap noodle, public bus tour of China.

The Democratic Republic is even closer outside town where a short stretch of Great Wall climbs steeply over Tiger Mountain and is the easternmost stretch of wall in all of China. I took a taxi to Tiger Montain and the window was broken through which a freezing Dong Bei wind whistled and turned my ears to glass from fields where crops and flowers were just a rumour. The driver apologised for the draught but reassured me that the weather was not so cold today. I tried to believe him as I watched patches of ice break off the not so cold river bank and float along the not so cold river border where small boats puttered in circles carrying men that might have been fishermen or soldiers. "The real cold is further north" he announced - he meant in Heilongjiang, the last province before Siberia. "Liaoning is okay for us Han, though the Manchus[14] suffer since they eat so little pork" he revealed, offering no further explanation for his inscrutable opinion, the authenticity of which I doubted I could ever check. The wall here was built to keep the Manchus out, but despite the clear disadvantage

---

14   nearly 10% of the population of Dong Bei is Manchu.

of minimal pork consumption, they crossed the impregnable, invaded China and established the Qing dynasty in the 17th century.

The taxi waited with idling engine and I walked past stallholders selling New Year socks and great hunks of frozen fish that might have been sturgeon, uphill to the entrance gates. No one was around to check my ticket and as I walked through, a red faced man came trotting towards me waving a broom and using a strange crouching gait designed to prevent a slip on the ice. He was angry and banged his broom on the door of a small hut which opened and issued a cloud of warm and musty air that smelt of electric heaters and dirty linen followed by a woman and child with sleepy hair. The man was outraged that tickets were not being checked but who could blame the woman and child for taking refuge from the cold? It was likely that I would be their only visitor today and I hoped that when my ticket was punched and the man had taken his broom elsewhere they would go back to bed.

The Hushan Wall here is very steep. I used my hands on the icy steps, worried that I might stick to the metal handrail and emerged panting at the top where I felt warm for the first time that day. There was North Korea; miles of frozen fields, a border village and on the horizon snowy crumpled nameless People's Republican Mountains over which American bombers once appeared finding bridges to bomb. The descent of Tiger Mountain brought me closer still to the border. The river here narrows to a stream 6 metres wide called Yibukua or 'one step across'. The water today was frozen to tarmac and it would have been easy to walk through one of the unmanned Chinese gates and skate the stream to the flimsy fence on the other side. The border sign warned me not to cross or 'converse or exchange objects with people on the other side', and I was desperate for someone with neither uniform nor gun to appear, so that I might converse and exchange objects with them. But North Korea was empty today and the chance of meeting anyone seemed slight indeed, though I resisted the temptation to proceed for fear of being grabbed by unseen hands, arrested and labeled a spy, though at least there might have been some warmth in a People's Republican jail.

Further along the fence, a child's pink woolly jumper matted with frost hung puzzlingly from the barbed wire - a symbol of desperate escape or mere garbage? Further still, rows of benches were lined up like US high school bleachers, empty now but on warm days available for the backsides of interested Chinese tourists. Conversing or exchanging objects might be unacceptable, but it was fine to just sit and look, to feel that life in a People's Republic could be tough but how much worse it was to live in a People's Democratic Republic.

All this skirting the border was fun, but I had been right into the hermit kingdom two years before. My visit was tightly controlled of course; I was guided at all times, visited only the places the authorities were happy for me to see and I had to ask permission every time I pressed the shutter on my camera. I saw astonishing pre pubescent musicians and gymnasts in the Palace of Culture, a breathtaking synchronised display of dance at the giant stadium in Pyong'yang and drank a cappuccino in the only coffee bar in the country. I took a trip to the de-militarised border with the South where US Marines stood eyeball to eyeball with North Korean soldiers in a pantomime that would be funny if it wasn't so stubbornly permanent, where I was told that I would be shot if I tried to cross the thin concrete strip that marks the boundary between freedom and oppression.

But meeting a person chips away at the mistrust of silence and I discovered that the citizens of the DPRK were just like me; they ate hot pot and drank too much imported Chinese beer and danced in the park. My soldier guide became confidential and good-humoured as soon as he had decided I was no threat to national security. We visited the fairground where holiday makers were scoring points by shooting cardboard Yankee soldiers and he winked and said that North Korea had to pretend to hate the Americans just a little. When a bee was trapped in our car, he shouted that it must be caught since it was a capitalist imperialist bee and would certainly sting us and when I wondered what to do with my garbage on our visit to the border he told me to throw it at a marine and start a war.

China pretends to hate America a little too at Dandong's memorial to remember the Korean War. There is a needle precisely 53 m high here to mark the end of the war in 1953 from which the view of Korea is less dramatic than at Yibukua, and a building next door that is called

'The Museum to commemorate aiding Korea against US aggression'. Outside a sign said 'no entry to the psychotic or disheveled'.

I was neither of these things so I entered heavy oak doors to see rhetoric in room after room of rusty rifles and photos of US prisoners of war holding pictures of Stalin and Mao and signs that said 'Hands off Korea' that was all so resolutely anti-American, while the Chinese conscripts who died in far greater numbers than American UN troops are always called volunteers since this emphasises the nobility of their cause. There are the remains of American germ warfare bombs with plague ridden locusts and pictures of civilians burning US flags since 'all over China publicity and educational activities to despise and hate US imperialists would develop widely. As a result the pro-American thinking, worship and fear of the US were done away with'. There is no mention that North Korea started the war.

The museum climaxes in a 65 metre diorama of burned-out tanks and painted battles where I failed to spot a single Chinese soldier who was dead or a single living American who wasn't begging for surrender, launching an unsporting blindside attack guns a-blazing like a cowboy or chewing with great redneck self satisfaction on a John Wayne cigar. There were some South Koreans in here trying on army uniforms for photos, the women wearing immaculate make up as Koreans often do. I wondered how they felt in this place that commemorated the formalisation of the division of their country, but they were joking and laughing for the camera as they tried on military hats. I recalled a conversation with a Korean soldier on the south of the demilitarised zone and realised that just as in the north, the hatred is more bluster and posture than reality. He had said that of course the South has to demand reunification and condemn the North, but in reality no one was bothered since the DPRK is so much poorer, and reunification would lead to huge subsidisation and tax bills for the South. At the same place, a US marine was wearing shades on a grey March day and called his men 'the best of the best'. He showed me where an American soldier had been killed by a North Korean axe as he tried to fell a tree that was obscuring his view of the North. 'Our soldiers returned the next day' he drawled 'and they cut down every tree and bush in the vicinity'. More posturing. More bluster. Never had a war come so close over a shrubbery.

I asked the curator why the museum was so hostile and didn't this make it rather dated at a time of 21st century China/America friendship and trade partnership when Yao Ming played basketball in the NBA and every Chinese city has a McDonald's and KFC? "Kuan mei yuan chao zhanzheng" said the curator- 'the war to resist US aggression'; these are Chairman Mao's words and they cannot be changed so easily. Also, Dandong is far from Beijing and few foreign guests visit here so it's not necessary to change the language. So Dandong's jingoism was down to its provincialism.

But I like small town China more than the big cities that are sprawling and unmanageable and with the exception of famous towns like Beijing, Shanghai and Xi'an, often look the same. Dandong's provincialism had been clear from the moment I boarded the plane with passengers carrying boxes of sausages instead of Louis Vuitton bags and whose behaviour on board had suggested they had never flown before. They had crowded round windows whenever there was something interesting to see, rang the bell and asked for extra food and stood up to retrieve their coats and plastic bags of vegetables from overhead bins as we came in to land on an icy runway at Dandong's tiny airport while hostesses shouted 'zuo xia', 'sit down, sit down'!

I'd seen it too on the taxi ride to town past dilapidated shacks and vegetable plots made barren by snow. There were cheaply constructed high-rises too and one of these was built right next to, and taller than, a tall factory chimney blowing clouds of yellow sulphurous smoke right against the windows. In all my travels in China I had never seen such a terrible house in which to live.

Public baths are a national institution in Korea and Japan where people relax, make business and get clean. I suppose it was the proximity to Korea that led to a bath being built in downtown Dandong and it seemed like the perfect place to get warm after the broken bridge and Tiger Mountain, though the presence of a foreign devil aroused a great deal of provincial curiosity here. Guests at such baths stow their clothes and stroll wearing not a stitch of clothing into a tiled and steamy refuge where men recline in tubs of various heat or perch on stools with soaps and brushes and scrub themselves clean. Dandong's bath seemed no different to the ritual of a Japanese onsen, but it soon became clear that this experience was novel in several important respects.

1, People stared openly and at great length at my hairy western body. Those who had not seen me through the clouds of steam were nudged by their friends who pointed me out. They also then stared. All of this led to me spending longer than I wanted up to my neck in a boiling 42°C bath. When I emerged feeling nauseous and scorched, I was bright pink *and* hairy so people stared even more.

2, Men were smoking in the bathhouse. Chinese males have an endless enthusiasm for cigarettes. They smoke on buses and in the gaps between carriages on trains. They smoke in restaurant and hotel rooms. They smoke at weddings and funerals. They smoke beneath no smoking signs. But smoking in a bathhouse takes planning and forethought; where did they keep their lighters?

3, Men were having the most astonishingly intimate legs apart raised in the air massages on hard tables from bare chested orderlies with wet flannels. I slunk lower into my 42° and now *I* tried not to stare.

All that steamy, soaked sensuality just made it feel even colder back outside, though at least I wouldn't have to shower in my hotel room where a sign above the toilet reminded me 'Please bathing in the bathtub'. Christmas was coming and the hotel had put a huge custom-made Santa hat on the giant boulder of seven colour jade that stood like a landslide in the lobby and the coffee shop was selling gingerbread houses and festive cigarettes.[15] I was more interested in the Kim Il Sung badges and Korean money on sale in the 9pm bitter cold from a man with a trolley by the river. He had the same brute determination as the fellow with the binoculars at the end of the bridge to make a sale regardless of hypothermia or frostbite and I was happy to buy memen-

---

15   These were the same as normal cigarettes but were sold by a girl in a sparkly hat.

tos of my past visit to the DPRK that I had been forbidden to buy when I was actually there.

Cold comfort, small profits, small town. Yet in one way, Dandong was the most international place in China that I have ever seen for the city was trilingual; it was there on the corner noodle shop, on the hardware store whose pots and pans were rimed with frost and on the Korean TV karaoke lounge where you could sing your way to ownership of prizes arraigned beneath bunting in the entrance hall; a case of beer, a monkey wrench or a pack of dishcloths which, soaked in water, would be perfect for an intimate massage. All had Chinese characters of course and many had English, or an approximation of English. The third script was hangul, the Korean alphabet that shares the artistry of Chinese characters, but unlike Chinese does not require you to sacrifice friends, family and mental health to learn.

Hangul was first developed in the 15th century by the 4th King of the Joseon Dynasty, Sejong the Great who believed that commoners could learn to read and write. Sejong claimed that even a stupid man could learn hangul in 10 days and since independence from Japan in 1945, hangul has become the sole official writing system in Korea. The script is an alphabet just like the Roman system in the West, though hangul blocks syllables together and has no lower case or capitalization.

For example;

ㅎ is h, ㅏ is a & ㄴ is n

ㄱ is g, ㅡ is u & ㄹ is l

You then combine syllables to form words, just as we do in English;

한 = h+a+n

글 = g+u+l

So; 한 + 글 = 한글, which says 'hangul'. Two syllables. Six characters.

With such a beautiful and simple script, anyone can learn to write essential phrases like;

'Democratic Peoples' Republic'

'I apologize for crossing the border; please don't send me to jail'

'This is a great massage but I would like you to stop rubbing me so hard with that flannel'.

In this weather I was relieved that the giant Mao statue outside Dandong train station was wearing a coat, though he could have used a hat too on that famously bald pate. The station shop was full of instant noodle and processed sausage sustenance but had a last reminder of Korea with a shelf filled with ginseng products. This famous plant is reputed to have miraculous medicinal properties in the curing of stress and for the treatment of male erectile dysfunction, though a wet flannel in the right hands could equally well cure this. American ginseng is said to promote cold, female yin properties while Korean plants are all hot, sunshiny yang. This is because things growing in cold places or on northern sides of mountains are strong in Yang and Korea and north-east China were the coldest areas known to most Koreans in traditional times. American ginseng was imported from tropical Guangzhou so doctors mistakenly believed it grew in tropical regions too.

The belief in the revitalising properties of ginseng is partly due to the shape of the root which resembles a human body. Dandong had been full of posters of ginseng roots twisted into the shape of a naked female form like some perverted parsnip or titillating turnip and it seems the more humanlike the root, the higher the price. The ginseng roots in Dandong's cold and deserted train station were poor specimens indeed, but I saw examples elsewhere like sexy vegetable ladies in presentation cases lined in velvet for 20,000 yuan.

I caught the train to Shenyang, Liaoning's provincial capital; a city that at first sight conforms to the faceless and bloated stereotype of the Chinese megalopolis. It was damn cold and I hunched in a taxi, the windows of which were thankfully intact, along bland boulevards in heavy evening traffic. Yet Shenyang has little treasures hidden amidst the rush to modernize, pollute and redesign and the first of these was my hotel. The Liaoning guest house was built by the Japanese in the 1920s and its heavy wooden revolving door, stained glass and chequered black-and-white tiled lobby were a stately reminder of a period that China would rather forget. Shenyang was called Mukden when the Liaoning Hotel was built. The Japanese defeated a Russian army here in 1905 and it was outside Mukden in 1931 that they blew up a section of their own Manchurian Railway and used this as a pretext for attacking the Chinese.

The Japanese commanders had built a 'swimming pool' at the officers club in Mukden that was actually a concrete bunker for two 9 inch artillery pieces and it was these that were used to shell the Chinese garrison and drive them out of the city. The Japanese Kwantung army proceeded to invade the whole of Manchuria which they renamed Manchukuo in a defiant statement of possession to the disapproving international community and installed the Qing emperor Pu-Yi as puppet ruler since he had been without a job following his unceremonious removal from the Forbidden City 10 years before (see Jilin chapter). By 1941 Japan had invaded the whole of the Chinese eastern seaboard including Peking, Shanghai, Nanjing and as far south as Hong Kong. Mukden was under Japanese occupation for 14 years.

The Chinese garrison that day was commanded by the 'Young Marshal', Zhang Xueliang who later kidnapped the leader of Nationalist China, Chiang Kai Shek in Xi'an in order to force him to join with the Communists and fight the Japanese (see Shaanxi chapter). Chiang never forgave the sleight of being held hostage in his pyjamas and took Zhang back to Taiwan in 1949 where he was placed under house arrest until 1990, which might make him the world's longest serving political prisoner. The Young Marshal chose sun kissed beaches instead of icy streets after his release and died of pneumonia aged 100 in Hawaii and not back in his Manchurian home.

My hotel window offered the most perfect view of Shenyang's Mao statue on Zhongshan Square; China's most histrionic and indulgent tribute to the Chairman built at the height of Cultural Revolutionary fervour in 1969. Mao stands massive and magisterial above a frenzied crowd of Red Guards, oil workers, peasants, soldiers, engineers and children all wildly exclaiming, marching, saluting, trampling symbols of the old and thrusting weapons, fists and Little Red Books into the sky. The figures all look very angry; you would too if your cap was fringed by long fingers of ice and your fists covered by a dusting of snow. Despite the brittle cold, locals surrounded the statute performing Tai Chi entombed in layers of clothes, one woman with a carpet wrapped around her shoulders and head, oblivious to the disapproving glares of Red Guards.

Mukden was the capital city of the Manchus and they built their own imperial palace here, like a Forbidden City in miniature. The Emperor Nurhaci launched an assault on China's Ming Dynasty from here in the 17th century, though China wasn't conquered and subdued until after the death of the great Manchu leader. It was Nurhaci's Aisin Gioro Manchu clan that ruled China until the end of emperors in 1911 and their Shenyang Palace is testament to their status before they took possession of Beijing. But it was a cold and lifeless place on this December morning. I wandered the empty halls and watched workers shovelling snow from Manchu court yards into wheelbarrows and could gain no sense of the concubines and servants who once walked these quiet and meditative grounds so at odds with the modern city outside.

I left the palace and searched in vain for the Women and Childrens' Centre whose recent opening the Shenyang government website had announced. The Centre contains a fighting room full of human sized rubber male figures and invites women to take out their anger and frustration by beating them without mercy. Counsellors are also on hand for some more sophisticated therapy, though they must under no circumstances be beaten.

China could use such an outlet for frustrated tourists that is full of rubber taxi drivers. I tried in vain to persuade a driver to use the meter or charge me a price that wasn't specially tailored to a foreigner, and wandered the cold street, the breath turning to ice in my nose. The drivers said that today was expensive because it was cold but this seemed an unlikely rationale in a city that is cold half of the year, so I jumped on a bus instead and was kept warm by a crush of Dong Bei bodies. I gazed through iced windows at grim suburbs and dozens of civic notices designed to improve Shenyang's driving – 'loving your wife, your family and your children amounts to nothing, if you disobey traffic regulations' said one. I was going to Fushun to pay tribute to Lei Feng.

Lei Feng is one of the most resilient icons of modern China; a 'hao bangyang', or good role model. At 20 he joined the People's Liberation Army and spent all his spare time and money helping the needy and reading the words of Mao Zedong. At 22 he died an unheroic death in Fushun when a telephone pole struck by an army truck hit him while he was directing the truck backing up. The Lei Feng Museum in Fushun is full of the evidence of his good deeds; Lei Feng polishing army trucks, Lei Feng washing his comrades' feet, Lei Feng helping old people across the road, and an abundance of relics; Lei Feng's simple clothes, the socks he darned as his friends slept and copies of his diary.

The diary is the essence of Lei Feng - 200,000 flowery words of self sacrifice and praise for Mao and the Communist party. Lei Feng became an expression of the notion of nobility and self-sacrifice during a period of great hardship in China. His enthusiasm for duty and wholehearted devotion to Mao knew no bounds. When Mao called the nation an engine and the citizen screws, Lei Feng took pride in being the shiniest screw of all. Whenever communist leaders get worried about the morale of the people, they breathe new life into Lei Feng. Mao Zedong told the nation to 'Learn from Lei Feng' at the end of the disastrous Great Leap Forward in 1963 and there was a big revival of his spirit following the crackdown on Tiananmen Square in 1989.

This individual anonymity, this cult of impersonality has no value in the West where we all want to be a someone and individual rights outweigh the collective. Who wants to be a machine, or far worse just a part of a machine? But in China Lei Feng's cheerful bob-a-jobbing altruism has more resonance and is more fun. The fifth of March has been designated official 'Learn from Lei Feng day' and I've seen people tidying up parks and cleaning Beijing's new metal street dividers on that date in tribute to the man that ex-pat Westerners in China affectionately refer to as 'The Fengster'. I've been called a 'Lei Feng ren' – a Lei Feng person - when I gave up my seat on a bus in Shanghai. I've listened to the popular song 'dongbei ren dou shi huo Lei Feng' (all north-easterners are living Lei Fengs) and I've received 100 thumbs up when I wore a Lei Feng T shirt in a Guangzhou street market.

Such is the affection for The Fengster that the government has submitted an application for 'Lei Feng spirit' to be accorded UNESCO intangible cultural heritage status. Lei Feng branded book bags and DVDs are available in the shops and best, most delightfully, gloriously of all is the video game 'Learn from Lei Feng'. In this, the player performs a variety of charitable acts, battles spies and learns famous Lei Feng quotes; 'A person's life is limited, but to serve the people is unlimited', 'For the party and the people I will plunge into the sea, march into mountains. Even if my head is smashed, my bones broken, my body will remain red, my heart crimson. Never will I change my mind'. Every time the player is promoted to a higher level, the clothes on his Lei Feng avatar become more average and lower class; the ultimate goal is to meet Chairman Mao and get his autograph.

So I sat on the cold bus for 20 miles, a rustless screw, a Lei Feng ren; if I had not spent the entire journey standing near the doors icy blasts, I would certainly have given up my seat. I hoped I might buy a copy of that diary, a video game or, oh yes, a pack of Lei Feng condoms[16], but when we finally rattled into Fushun the Lei Feng memorial museum was closed. A guard was on duty, with snow flecked woolly hat and army greatcoat - a fellow screw in the machine who might understand how far I'd come and let me in. But before I asked, I knew the answer was no; give a man a uniform in China and watch the inflexibility set in. 'Come back tomorrow, I can't help, go away'. Those were the rules, the machine said so. Screw you.

So I didn't get to see the telegraph pole that fell on Lei Feng's head or whatever else might have been inside. I spun on my heel and tried to smile, for as Lei Feng said 'if you are a ray of light, you have brightened a foot of darkness'. It was starting to snow and I had a bus to catch.

---

16   As produced by Wan Pi Tao Tao condom company in Zhejiang and emblazoned with the 'Learn from Lei Feng' slogan; a pack of three just 18 yuan - a bargain to keep your screw clean.

SHANXI

陕西

155 400 sq km
Population 38 million.

"I got everything I need right here with me. I got air in my lungs, a few blank sheets of paper. I mean, I love waking up in the morning not knowing what's gonna happen or, who I'm gonna meet, where I'm gonna wind up."

Jack Dawson, Titanic (1997). Dir James Cameron.

By 5am I had decided that you haven't lived until you've seen the sun rise over the smokestacks of Datong as I gazed from my hot and crowded train from Xi'an due at its dusty destination on the border with

Inner Mongolia at 5:30am. Sleeper trains in some parts of the world make a habit of pulling into a siding for a few hours to allow passengers some precious repose but alas, this rarely happens in China because most travelers want to end the agony of a journey on hard seats. I knew that my train would arrive before dawn and that I would emerge to blearily fend off the taxi drivers who lie in wait, whatever the hour, to squabble over my bags.

And so it was that I pressed my nose to the glass and watched the arid landscape of Northern Shanxi in the brightening dawn. I barely know how to describe the view from the window. Certainly I could mention the blood red sun breasting the horizon that was so flat I could see the curvature of the earth. I might also mention the crows, startled into life by the sound of the train and flapping uselessly between the parched trees or the timelessness of the small farms clinging to the railway embankment where a few goats wandered around looking tiny against the enormity of the landscape beyond. But none of this would do justice to the bleak emptiness of the North Eastern China view outside my window.

The Chinese have a fear of this country, which marks the end of their homeland and the start of something else; where the comfort of crowds is replaced by the unsettling loneliness of the grasslands. All on board were rousing themselves from sleep, sucking noodles noisily into mouths and combing hair made chaotic by a hot night on a hard sleeper bed. But all seemed to studiously ignore the brooding magnificence outside.

It was not the desert or the crows or the goats that really pulled on my sleeve demanding attention. As we inched closer to Datong, the view became a stubble of chimneys and factories. My copy of Hard Times lay on the crumpled bed and I determined that Datong would be my Coketown of 'red brick or brick that would have been red if the smoke and ashes had allowed it.... it was a town of machinery and tall chimneys, out of which interminable serpents of smoke trailed themselves for ever and ever and never got uncoiled'. Shanxi is the industrial heartland of China and Dickens' industrial town didn't have so many enormous concrete power stations or a bird's nest of wires running from place to place and besides, Coketown did not sit on the edge of a vast stony desert. Nevertheless, Dickens would have recognised the alley-ways of Datong where, even at this early hour, the streets were 'inhab-ited by people equally like one another, who all went in and out at the same hours, with the same sound upon the same pavements, to do the same work and to whom every day was the same as yesterday and to-morrow, and every year the counterpart of the last and the next'.

Coal is king in Datong and I had come because I wanted to know just how dirty one of the dirtiest cities in the filthiest province of the most polluted country on earth could be. I learned some time ago that there is no place for diffident good manners in China and that an end-less litany of 'after you' and 'no, you first' is thoroughly counterproduc-tive. Standing aside from the scrum provides a vague feeling of moral superiority that makes you last off the bus, last off the train and last to eat your lunch in the melee outside the noodle bar. I knew this, yet I lost the will to fight as our train pulled into the station, stood aside and was last through the gates and into the greying dawn of Datong town square.

Call it early morning lethargy or maybe my indolence was a result of having bought my ticket too late and ending on the cheapest bunk in hard sleeper - the one at the top which has 6 inches of head space and can be reached only by climbing over the beds of sleeping Chinese below and from which there is no escape once you're up, even if you re-ally need the toilet, and who would want to visit the foul toilet in hard sleeper anyway and I'm really thirsty because it's so hot in here but I can't reach my water because it's on the tiny table next to that man's pack of dried squid 6 feet below. Sometimes China just knocks the fight out of you.

It was cold and deserted once the last of the passengers had jumped into cars or onto the back of motorbikes and gone who knows where. I felt lonely and too far from home. Even the few hustling cab drivers were welcome company and I wandered over to a 5:30am end of the line noodle bar and disconsolately slurped noodles, chewed the meat and realised I was far enough north and close enough to Mongolia to be in mutton country.

The town had a fresh coat of grime, and within hours, I had a coat of grime too, but as the sun warmed the town and my energy returned I set out to explore.

Travel in China has its lows, and Datong at 5:30am was certainly one of these, though it's hard to remain down for long here. This is partly because the turn of every corner has a person labouring under a heavy load or coated in coal dust who is patently worse off than you, but mostly because the hospitality and resolute good cheer of the people is enough to drag the visitor from even the fiercest bout of self-pity.

I hailed a taxi, fixed a price and set off on a tour of town. My driver Chen was dressed for summer in a 'Wo ai Zhongguo' (I love China) T-shirt and asked me what I thought of Datong. This turned out to be a rhetorical question since Chen needed no answer or further invitation to extol the virtues of his hometown that was both ' hen mei' and ' hen you yisi'. (Very beautiful and very interesting).

First stop was Red Flag Square where there were no red flags and no statue of Mao but where parents were paying five yuan to let their kids beetle around on motorised pandas whose black patches were black and white patches were grey. We motored on to Huayuan Temple whose entrance faces east because its 10th century architects worshipped the sun, stopped for steamed jiaozi dumplings from a street side store (more mutton) before heading to the locomotive factory which switched to diesel only in 1988; then, north out of town towards the long line of crumpled hills on the skyline.

The pollution was getting worse by mid-morning and I became fascinated by this Shanxi oxygen that could be seen as well as breathed. I asked Chen what he thought about the pollution and he agreed that it was bad, but what could be done and weren't the dumplings good? The evidence of the nation's addiction to coal was everywhere. The floral tributes to the Beijing Olympics were covered in grime and with all the blooms dead, and all the while blue Dong Feng trucks loaded with big black lumps of fuel thundered past.

When we drove past our third mining village in five km I asked him to stop so I could have a look. Chen seemed a little perturbed by this and told me there was nothing to see. "The houses are too small" he said "and the people are dirty. Even their teeth are covered in coal dust". I could think of no better testimonial and wanted to go more than ever to meet the people with dusty teeth.

The corner of each track leading to the mining community was crowded with men between shifts who sat on motorbikes and waited for something to happen. They laughed and shouted at each other and were doing what the Chinese call 'chui niu' or 'blowing the bull'. The men can afford their motorbikes because the pay to mine coal is 3000 yuan a month, much higher than the national average, with a pension of 2100 yuan for retired long serving miners. The rewards are double for those in private mines which are staffed by migrant workers who move from mine to mine to find better salaries and conditions, but the 6000 yuan salaries come at a terrible price: 70% of all mining deaths in China happen in private mines. It's almost impossible for migrant workers to get jobs in government run mines.

The mining communities around Datong are self-sufficient and probably not unlike historic mining towns elsewhere with a sense of fierce pride and purpose to their work, though the white tiled buildings and clumsy slogans urging greater productivity have a sense of impermanence here compared to the stone built mining communities of industrial Britain. The miners on their bikes were happy to talk and said they were proud to do something good for their country. This seemed to me a return to the naive enthusiasm of the 1950s and 1960s. Those years were the halcyon days of Maoism when workers were encouraged to contribute to the great China machine. Lei Feng was the epitome of this spirit of sacrifice; a model worker who did extra shifts, read the works of Chairman Mao and died tragically young while doing his duty like a true 'homo sovieticus' (see Liaoning chapter for more details on Lei Feng).

We in the West are fed a diet of humanitarianism and liberty and don't want to be machines or parts of machines; certainly I would not want to work in a Chinese coal mine. China has five million coal miners and the annual death toll, mostly in smaller privately run mines, accounts for 80% of all mining deaths worldwide. An average of 10 miners dies every day; most of these deaths are in Shanxi, since a third of all China's coal is here. Safety standards have improved; compensation is given for injury and death and small mines producing less than

90,000 tonnes of coal a year have been ordered to close. The death rate fell from a high of 7000 in 2002 to less than 2000 in 2011. But dozens of smaller mines have reopened since coal supplies 70% of the energy needed for China's dramatic economic growth and the demand is high.

Private mines operate behind high walls and fences to deter prying eyes since safety standards are so low. A gas explosion at Chenjiashan mine at Tangchuan in November 2004 killed 166 miners. Though a fire broke out the week before and the miners had asked not to be sent down, the owners were eyeing a 400,000 yuan bonus for over fulfilling their quota and threatened their migrant workers with dismissal. In March 2003 72 miners were killed in a gas explosion at Meng Nanzhuang mine in Xiaoyi city. 70 more perished in a mine blast in December 2007 in Linfen city; the manager was arrested for the poor safety standards in the mine. At least 73 died in Gujiao City mine in February 2009, a further 30 at Wangjialing in April 2010 though authorities tried their best to shroud the tragedy in impenetrable political coal dust by trumpeting the miracle of the 115 miners who were rescued and by banning reporting of the uncomfortable truth that the mine was overcrowded, safety conditions were poor and that this was a government run not a private mine.

The environmental damage of mining in China is huge and produces 40% of all China's industrial waste. The slag heaps in Datong alone grow by 80 million tons every year. Coal is the single biggest factor in China's position as the world's largest producer of greenhouse gases and 75% of its carbon dioxide emissions come from the coal power stations that open at the rate of one every week. It's also the biggest reason why the towns of Shanxi are cloaked in a near permanent fog of pollutants.

The 10 most polluted cities in the world according to a recent World Bank study are all in China, and the real big hitters, the top of the list are in Shanxi. Datong is there, but Linfen, scene of the mining tragedy of 2007, has the ignominy of being number one. Coal is everything in Linfen and has created wealth, improved living standards, provided bigger houses, more cars, TVs and fridges. Yet the cabbages in the fields are coated in soot and no one hangs their washing out to dry. "If you hate someone and want to punish him", goes the saying in China "make him live in Linfen". The area is made worse because

China is exempt from Kyoto protocol's rules on emissions because it is a developing country. The government argues that they should have the same historical privileges that allowed industrial nations to develop their economies.

Yet even in Linfen, things have improved. The city had 163 bad air days in 2012, an improvement of 15 on the previous year and many factories have closed to improve air quality. China is also surprisingly a world leader in clean energy. A 2010 Australian report showed that China is second only to Britain in the value of its incentives to cut pollution and way ahead of the US or Japan. Her investment in clean energy topped $35 billion in 2009, compared to $18 billion in the US – significantly ahead of blue sky, fresh air Australia which is the world's worst per capita polluter because of her reliance on coal.

Change may have been driven largely by big business in Linfen rather than environmental concerns because the bad air has led to declining investment in the city, but there is more than one way to skin this Chinese cat. And anyway, who are we to preach since it is the Western nations who have moved their manufacturing base to China for reasons of economy and knowing full well that it is vastly more polluting than Japan, Europe or the US.

The miners at Datong weren't worried that they never saw the stars at night through the thick haze. "We know they are there" said one "and all of this will change". I decided that he was right when Chen announced we had arrived at the Yunggang, for the Buddhist caves here are reminders that Shanxi is not just coal, Datong is not all Dickensian. The province has a long history and coal is just the latest in a series of goods that have been traded from this strategic place. For hundreds of years, traders peddled salt, tea, grain and wool through here on their way from the Mongolian steppes and over the Taihung Mountains to the east. They brought their culture and religion too and Yunggang is a memorial to this trade.

UNESCO calls these fifth century caves 'a masterpiece of early Chinese Buddhist cave art', for they represent 'the successful fusion of Buddhist religious symbolic art from South and Central Asia with Chinese cultural traditions'. I'm no expert on fifth century caves but was struck by the mix of Persian lions, Indian gods and Hellenistic tridents dotted among the 50,000 statues in the 252 caves here which seemed like fusion enough.

The caves are busy, but complaining about crowds in China is rather self-defeating and anyway the combination of an early start thanks to my dawn train and Chen's advice "go to the last ones first; the Buddhas are best there" meant that I saw the carvings alone and unmolested. Chen was right. The 14th century Sakyamuni in cave 20 is the best Buddha in Yunggang; his ears reach almost down to his shoulders and his countenance is serene. The information board in front said he was smiling 'like he understood life', though he lacked the blue hair and red lips of the Buddha in cave five and I couldn't help noticing, even here, the Buddha's placid smile, his flowing robes and slender fingers were coated in a fine film of coal dust.

Up on the rocks, above the caves, the crowds disappear altogether. Up here are the crumbling remains of Ming Dynasty beacon towers; a signal system to protect the pass to Mongolia. The Great Wall is here on this barren cliff too though it's nothing like the sturdy and over restored wall north of Beijing. This wall of tamped earth is little preserved and can certainly not be seen from space as the daft rumour about the Beijing Great Wall goes. The soil here is loess, as it is across most of Shanxi. This thick layer of microscopic silt blown from Siberia during the Ice Age gives the province a timeworn and parched aspect, and above Yunggang the wall is made of loess too. For all its fame, the wall was a folly and an inadequate barrier to invasion of China. It speaks volumes about the defensive inward looking mentality of its builders, though in modern Shanxi this mindset like the wall itself is crumbling to dust.

Shanxi is an arid and mountainous place. 70% of the province is perched at 1000 metres above sea level or higher and the whole region teeters constantly on the edge of drought. Even the Yellow River cannot hope to irrigate this land or compensate for the feeble rainfall of 35 cm year. It takes 2 ½ tons of water to produce a single ton of coal; coal mining is sucking the moisture out of Shanxi. The Yellow is a mature river in Shanxi but has a midlife crisis at Hukou. The name Hukou means 'kettle spout', and the hiss of the falls can be heard from two km away as the 400 metres wide river is squeezed between the 20 metre gap at Jinshan Gorge. It's a mightily impressive sight but wildly off the beaten track and for all its brute magnificence I wanted to see a man plunge over the falls in a barrel at the very least after bouncing along on a creaky bus from Linfen for four excruciating hours.

But this is the China I love. The falls are called 'giant dragons fighting in a river' by locals who still wear button-down blue cotton Mao suits and walk their bicycles down arrow straight dirt roads between poplar trees. Children are snotty nosed and curious whilst old people's features are creased and cracked by days of sun and dust. They don't care too much for government since Beijing is 'over the mountains'. They drink sour Shanxi vinegar with their meals and they mostly live in caves.

Chinese cave dwellings are called yaodong and dot the hills all over rural Shanxi. 80 million Chinese live this troglodyte existence and the dwellings I saw were the very definition of cheerful functionality. These communal family spaces are centred around the kitchen and the 'kang' which serves as a daytime seat and a bed at night and under which the heat from the family fire keeps the occupant warm on cold Shanxi evenings. It's all too cosy for words and so popular is this yaodong Hobbiton existence that new apartments in northern China are sometimes built in imitation of caves.

Beijing seems resolved to leave the cave dwellers of Shanxi to their bucolic existence, though this wasn't always the case. Mao's great experiment in collectivisation and communization reached their zenith in Shanxi at the model commune of Dazhai. "Learn from Dazhai in agriculture" said Mao, and like all of his pronouncements great store was set by this. Dazhai was held up as the paradigm of all that was good and worthy in the Chinese countryside. The village mantra became 'change the sky and alter the land' and 'Move the Mountains to make farm fields'. Hundreds of millions of peasants visited the area to learn from Dazhai as Mao had instructed and the semiliterate village leader Chen Yanggui became vice premier of all China.

Mao loved to recount the traditional story of the foolish man who thought he could move a mountain. But the chairman's telling had a very socialist moral; Lo! With the aid of Mao Zedong thought and patriotic fervour, the mountain really could be moved. Dazhai, where peasants dug and toiled without respite, was evidence of this. This Maoist parable strikes me as ridiculous. Men cannot move mountains and even if they could, what would be the point? Leave the mountain alone you silly old fool and stop acting like a part of a machine. Dazhai is ridiculed as a symbol of socialist misadventure now that China has taken the capitalist road, though I had sensed an element of Dazhai fervour in the miners of Datong who took pride in their shift and saw a patriotic imperative in their digging.

Or maybe they just did it for the cash? I found evidence of the national respect for hard currency in the town of Pingyao which prospered on the back of the banking trade. The Rishenchang was China's first bank in this picture postcard perfect Qing Dynasty town. Opposite the bank lived Leilutai, the founder of the bank, whose residence is all lavish courtyards and gurgling fountains. Elsewhere in town, government offices, temples and pagodas are all preserved because the finances of China were transferred to Hong Kong and Shanghai and the fledgling banking centre of Pingyao was abandoned and preserved in aspic. Ironically, there is no bank at all here now.

I travelled to Pingyao on a bus that was smart and good and hurtled for six hours along Shanxi's new highway and over sinuous bridges that linked one loess escarpment pockmarked with yaodong with another. The bus was no smoking although naturally most passengers ignored this, and was fitted with TVs that showed the film 'Titanic' two and a half times. This movie is wildly popular with the Chinese and it's almost impossible to travel on a succession of buses or stay in three star hotels where the receptionist is usually glued to a TV, without seeing Rose and Jack battling the frigid waters of the North Atlantic at least once.

The drama on the Pingyao bus was dubbed into Chinese and I was struck by how much shouting there was. 'Lose, Lose' shouted Jack to Rose. 'Hold on', 'Wo ai ni' – 'I love you', hollered Rose even as the band played on and the last nut and bolt bubbled beneath the surface. We stopped for noodles and cha at a service station where the attendants were all dressed in purple and crowded around a soap opera on a portable set. I asked my fellow passengers what they thought of the movie. "Women hen xihuan zhege dianying", "We really like this movie", they all agreed and I wondered why. "Because it's exciting" said one "And the man with no money gets the rich man's wife". So that was it; the triumph of the underdog over privilege, the peasant over the landlord, the proletariat over the rightist bourgeois enemy of the working man. Mao's revolution was alive and kicking on the bus to Pingyao. "I think Lose is very sexy" breathed another passenger in English as he sidled up to me and thrust a forefinger of one hand through a thumb and finger circle made by the other. "She would make good fucking" he leered. And my illusions were shattered.

The bus was expensive and I not unreasonably expected to be dropped off in the centre of town. Instead, we roared past the Pingyao turnoff just as the Titanic thundered towards the iceberg for the third time on this interminable journey, and came to rest on the hard shoulder. 'Pingyao', shouted the driver and his assistant, muffled in pink woolly hat and scarf despite the summer heat, charged off the bus, tore open the luggage compartment and flung my bag onto the hot asphalt. This wasn't Pingyao and there were no Qing Dynasty roof tiles, cobbled streets and red lanterns fluttering in the breeze. I was standing near a road bridge beside a turnip field beside the middle of nowhere. The Chinese government has built thousands of roads that have little traffic on them and this artery was no different, so it was quite peaceful here beneath the warm sun and with the birds twittering in the trees. But where was I and how was I going to get to Pingyao?

I clambered up the embankment to where a sign beside an equally empty road said 'Pingyao 4 km'. A woman was breastfeeding her baby here and smiled demurely as I sweated past with my bag. This struck me as an unlikely location to suckle an infant, but I was too preoccupied with my dilemma of how to cover those 4 km to ask how this roadside had become her nursery.

My shiny armoured knight drove a two stroke three wheeled bike that belched clouds of black smoke into the air. 20 yuan and 15 minutes later I was uncurling myself at the door of my guesthouse and proffering effusive thanks, though I knew his presence on that country lane had been no coincidence and that bike and bus had been a team.

Pingyao is called 'Turtle City' because of the Ming Dynasty 14th century walls that surround the place. They're 12 metres high, six km long and the gates at North, South, East and West are the head, tail and legs of the turtle. The town was busy with Beijing and Shanghai crowds along the main drag but it took no time to escape the microphones and flags of the tour groups. The back streets of Pingyao are where it's at; here Shanxi families sluice cobbles with buckets of water, ride bicycles, corral chickens and chop vegetables and all with a film set perfect Qing Dynasty backdrop. There are no shops on the walls, so it was quiet there too. I took a hands in pockets stroll past the 72 watchtowers and circumambulated all 6 km of this temple to China's past that miraculously survived the wrecking ball.

Each tower on the wall is inscribed with a separate verse from Sun Tzu's military treatise 'The Art of War'. Sun's 13 chapters were written in the sixth century BC and taught that war cannot be predicted and anticipated. Rather, the great military leader must learn to respond quickly to unexpected and changing conditions. This all seems remarkably modern advice from a book that is 2500 years old and Sun would not be out of place as a keynote speaker at a modern sales convention.

The Towers told me 'all warfare is based on deception' and 'ponder and deliberate before you make a move', that 'there is no instance of a country having benefited from prolonged warfare' and 69 more pearls of wisdom. The walls of Pingyao are a special place with vegetable gardens on one side and a clutter of 200-year-old tiled roofs on the other. But I was forgetting that an army marches on its stomach and as night drew in, I descended heavy stone steps in search of food.

The cobbles of Pingyao had become a sea of lanterns. It's clear why Zhang Yimou filmed 'Raise the Red Lantern' here since the town had become almost a cliche; an achingly beautiful miasma of stone, timber, ceramic and light. Zhang's film is a melancholic 1920s tale of Songlian, a wife who drifted into madness like some oriental Ophelia, though she could hardly have chosen a more beautiful place in which to lose her mind. Later that evening, I borrowed a bicycle and could not have been happier as I pedalled the quiet streets, brushed the lanterns with my hands and felt the 200-year-old stone flags under my wheels.

The return of the crowds the next day felt like an anti-climax. I bought a 12 yuan ticket that entitled me to visit all 20 of Pingyao's famous buildings; this appealed to my tick box mentality and I set off to conquer them all. By noon my earnest and measured appreciation of studies, banks, courtyards, gardens and temples had deteriorated to almost a jog as I dashed from site to site and Qing fatigue set in. I abandoned my quest at 12 and recovered in the cool shade of a theatre where an impenetrable tale of lovers poisoned, then reborn, then dead once more was played out amid the clash of cymbals and banging drums.

I resolved to ride my bike again, but away from Pingyao through the Turtle walls and into the Shanxi countryside beyond. My destination would be Shuanglin Temple, seven km distant where 2000 painted statues grimace, leer and frown in 2000 different ways while others smile as if they understand life as the Buddha had at Datong. The statues were worth the ride and it was no surprise to see the red-faced black whiskered Guan Yu, the god of war there, since this third century general raised to celestial status, this ' Lord of the magnificent beard' is found all over China on doors and shops, in opera and video games.

But as impressive as the 2000 faces were, it was the round-trip on my nearly big enough bike that became the highlight of the journey. I bumped across the train line outside Pingyao and found myself almost immediately in the country. No sprawling suburbs here but buttercups on the verge, oxen at the plough and the occasional opencast mine and attendant slag heap to remind me that I was still in Shanxi. The sign said 'Linfen city 150 km' and I felt that I could have cycled all the way back to the city in the smog.

Luckless Linfen is always under a cloud of one sort or another. In September 2008 a mudslide there killed 254 people. The media blamed the rain but in fact this cataract was a mixture of mud and iron ore from a mine dam that had been overfilled by an illegal enterprise. A witch hunt ensued and the Governor of Shanxi resigned because he had failed to adequately insist on safety checks. This was Meng Xuenang who had been governor for only eight months after his previous sacking as mayor of Beijing following the SARS cover-up in 2003; it's probably time for Meng to consider retiring from politics.

But the sacking of officials is merely a ritual dance in China; a token gesture and a response to a hysterical outpouring of anger that alters very little. There are still 9000 waste dumps in China, 50% of which are without a safety permit. Such corruption is endemic and a plague to progress in China. Since the party ditched collective agriculture, smashed the safety net of the workers 'iron rice bowl' and embraced the free market, the nation has worshipped at the altar of getting rich. 30 years of economic reform have increased corruption and raised the stakes with cases involving ever larger amounts of money; it has been estimated that corruption accounts for 3% of the country's GNP. 120,000 people have been sentenced for corruption in the last five years and the number of officials ranked above county level and involved in corrupt practice has risen nearly 80%. The situation is no doubt compounded by a lack of free press and the mechanisms of investigative reporting.

It seems that China cannot resist excess in her politics. When Mao said 'its right to rebel', the Chinese people rebelled and launched the horrors of the Cultural Revolution. Mao's successor, Deng Xiaoping changed the course of China's revolution entirely when he said 'poverty is not socialism. Socialism means eliminating poverty' - an open invitation to get rich if ever there was one. Deng also said that it mattered not if the cat is black or white, as long as it catches mice. He meant that any path is acceptable as long as the ends are achieved, and Shanxi has embraced this philosophy like nowhere else in China. One need only visit Linfen or Datong to see this; the mouse is caught at the price of the air that is breathed and it seems to me that the miners of Shanxi are as trapped as the rodent.

Remarkably, Shanxi has an example of Deng's good cat theory more potent even than the polluted air, the private mines and overflowing waste dumps. The province is also the centre of the brick making industry and in 2007 it came to light that children as young as eight were being kidnapped and sold to these remote yards for 500 yuan each to work as slaves. The children worked 16 hour shifts guarded by dogs and were freed only after an Internet campaign by parents alerted authorities to this backyard slavery. Parents visited the yards in an attempt to locate their children since they had little faith in local officials who often colluded with brickyard owners and were obstructed by police, some of whom demanded bribes in return for finding the children. As international awareness mounted, the authorities acted. 570 slaves (including 69 children) were freed, local officials were sacked and brickyard owners sentenced to death. And so the dance goes on. In China, the mantra of economic progress has become a fig leaf masking every ugly social phenomenon. The economic imperative and the need for stability above all else has led to corruption and abuse on a grand scale. The cat is good so long as the mouse is caught.

So I didn't cycle to Linfen and was soon hoisting my bike back onto its stand amidst the pretty lanterns of Pingyao. I was leaving Shanxi on the evening train and had little idea what I felt about the place. Shanxi has its share of problems to be sure, but I thought of the walls of Pingyao and the Buddha's smile at Datong and remembered that there is beauty too and far more ancient than the province's current blight of smoke and corruption. I checked out of the hotel and the receptionist hoped I had enjoyed my stay. "Come back soon", he said "and when you do, bring some fresh air because we have none left in my province"! The people's resilience and optimism will endure. And their humour is blacker than the coal that they mine.

HENAN

河南

160 000 sq km
Population 98 million

*Tigress; It is said that the Dragon Warrior can go for months with-
out eating, surviving on the dew of a single ginko leaf and the energy of the universe.*
*Po: Then I guess my body doesn't know I'm the Dragon Warrior yet.
It's gonna take a lot more than dew, and, uh, universe juice.*

Kung Fu Panda 2008

China travel is exhilarating to be sure. Every encounter a source of interest, every day providing diversity and opportunity; the mountains

magnificent, the cities sprawling and ancient, deserts wild and untamed, the eternal Yangtze, misty bamboo forests, a grubby child mastering chopsticks in a Beijing hutong, the rhythmic thrum of bright red drums for a laughing couple at a country wedding, the spicy aroma of freshly prepared pork dumplings, the scratch of the venerable calligrapher's pen, the resonant 'hoooik' as a businessman clears his throat onto the pavement.

But it's also exhausting. So my six-hour train journey in an air-conditioned soft sleeper cabin to Kaifeng felt like blessed relief from the pell-mell pressure and overbearing interest of the crowds of Henan that had been superheated and saturated in humidity so that the air might have been decanted and drunk instead of breathed. Though the journey was during the day, I had long ago learned that soft sleeper berths aren't for night time only and stretched out in repose on crisp sheets as the countryside slipped by.

I intermittently dozed and chatted with my cabin companions who were surprisingly blonde haired and western and disabused me of the notion that I was the only Englishman in Henan. They were feeling the exhaustion of China too and although he was resolutely upbeat and claimed to have found everything 'fascinating', she wore the wide eyed startled 'get me out of here' look of the first-time visitor to China who would rather be on a beach in Thailand or eating fish and chips outside a B&B in Blackpool. And no wonder, for this couple's itinerary had been challenging in the extreme, through a succession of huge and rather nondescript cities in China's Northeast- Shenyang, Changchun, Dalian, Yantai, Jinan - that read like a roll call of 1950s heavy industrial centres; perfect for the tourist with a penchant for steel. These cities are made interesting by winter snow and ice but in summer offer only high-rises, chimneys, wide roads, choking pollution and people, people, people. The couple was determined to avoid China's tourist traps but in so doing were missing all the best bits and confining themselves to a dull hinterland. It was like going to New York and visiting a fish canning factory in Newark instead of the Statue of Liberty because there might be too many tourists there.

The couple got off the train at another anonymous town, my endorsements of Yunnan and Yangshuo and the Forbidden City in Beijing falling on deaf ears, and were replaced by an old Chinese couple who offered me grapes. The old man and his wife spent the rest of the journey working their way through a plastic bag of fruit and veg and though they must have been 70 at least, crunched every apple, carrot and stick of celery with the strong white teeth of 20-year-olds. This was the benefit of a low sugar peasant diet I suppose; a life of servitude and drudgery, Great Leaps Forward and Cultural Revolutions, oppression and uncertainty, but at least their molars were good. These sinewy old folks were from the generation where 30 million died of hunger and food was rationed; when a carrot was a blessing, an apple a benediction, in stark contrast to modern China where a quarter of the population is overweight, fattened on ice cream, ready meals and fast-food. I have seen the queues of podgy children and doting parents outside KFC all over China, though unlike the West, obesity is an urban middle-class issue rather than a problem for the poor since to be fat is a symbol of one's status.

I left the couple gnawing corncobs with their sturdy enamel when I disembarked the train into the humidity of Kaifeng, Henan's old Song Dynasty capital. You wouldn't know this was the capital of all China from 960 – 1126AD when by some estimates, it was the largest city in the world. The old city is completely buried beneath the accumulated silt of Yellow River floods[17] though the presence of such priceless remains beneath the ground at least meant a lack of high-rises in Kaifeng, since their deep piles might damage what lies below. A few reconstructed Qing Dynasty walls a beautiful city doth not make. Non high rise it might be, but Kaifeng is still a thoroughly modern and functional city and I wondered what archaeologists might discover here in another 1000 years apart from concrete, cars and white tiles. Even the famed night market was underwhelming, the cries of the hawkers half-hearted under persistent Tuesday evening rain. There were at least a few Hui Muslim food stalls selling sheeps eyes and what looked suspiciously like testicles next to kebabs and pistachio nuts to give

---

17   The river flooded 368 times from 1194 to 1938, destroying everything in its path with a combination of water and silt - one cubic metre of Yellow River water carries 37 kg of sediment.

the market a flavour of exoticism. The presence of Hui Chinese from the west was no surprise since Kaifeng was traditionally a great trading town and I knew that the opportunity for trade had also brought the first Jews to China here in the 11th century which makes the town more unique and exotic still. But this was all theoretical and failed to outshine the wet streets and the mundane office blocks and my diary that I wrote in a cheap hotel with dirty sheets says 'dull place, looking forward to moving on'.

The beauty of travel is that things change so fast. Of course this can also mean that disaster is just around the corner when things seem to be going well, but by morning the rain had washed Kaifeng (relatively) clean, the day dawned bright and clear and on a street corner by the Happy Hands massage parlour I met Jason.

I should say that Jason met me. He approached me with his rickshaw and ritual, a book of photos and affidavits from delighted passengers in hand and asked in perfect English if I would like to take a tour of town; how could I say no to who might be the only English-speaking rickshaw driver in Henan?

Jason was a marvel; a force of nature. He had taught himself English and kept a meticulous record of every foreign guest he'd shown his city to - I was number 605 - and had appeared on local TV shows and newspapers. He said his goal was to reach 1000 and appear on national TV, but this was "only a dream, only a silly dream."

We dodged traffic along Jiefang Lu which means 'Liberation Street', though Jason told me this name was due to the widening of the street and the liberation of the people from cramped conditions rather than any grand tribute to revolution, and onto the Iron Pagoda made from glazed tiles and whose name means indestructible. The Pagoda will celebrate its 1000th anniversary in 2049; a survivor of 38 earthquakes and Japanese shells and that used to be on a 20 metre hill reduced to nothing by Yellow River silt flood deposits; indestructible indeed.

We cycled to the two lakes in the centre of town called Yangjia and Panjia and Jason told me the Song Dynasty legend of brave General Yang and treacherous General Pan. He showed me the swimmers in Yang's Lake and sermonized on the absence of bathers in Pan's since the water there was as dirty as the old General's character. The fact that the lakes were joined and shared the same water was not mentioned by my guide since why should this be allowed to spoil a good story? Jason's tour finished at the old Guildhall where the Japanese had set up their headquarters in 1937 (the Japanese always chose the best building in town). I was hot and tired, but Jason's enthusiasm for the intricate wooden carvings all around the building re-energised me. There were pomegranates, grapes, sunflowers and spiders, each carving heavy with symbolism denoting wealth, plenty and the building of webs of business contacts. Better still were the scenes of Qing Dynasty village life with drunks, fortune tellers, musicians and blacksmiths going about their busy lives; Jason pointed them all out and though he had explained 604 times before, urged me with an enthusiasm that seemed misplaced in the midday heat, to look at the expressions, the movements of the figures. "Look at the man vomiting" he said. "Look at the dog barking at the beggar, look at the merchant on his horse; the peasant is pulling faces at him. Aren't they fine, aren't they fine?"

Jason told me of his life as his feet turned the pedals. He'd been born in distant Xinjiang after his parents were ordered there in 1963, but Kaifeng was their home, and the family had been permitted to return in 1987 when Jason was 20, though his ID card gave a false birthdate of 1969 so that he had been able to join the Army. Jason's soldierly career was a mundane life of cooking and administration and on leaving the Peoples Liberation Army, he got a job working in a glass syringe factory which he confirmed was as boring as it sounds. Most working-class Chinese are resigned to a life of career tedium, but Jason wanted more than this. He learned English and bought a rickshaw and 605 travellers later, here we were.

He was a serious man who took his role as ambassador for Kaifeng seriously too. His book was full of photos of Jason with foreign guests and in not one of these was he smiling. When he took a photo of us at the end of the tour, and despite my encouragement to grin, Jason remained frowningly serious again. He took his English seriously too, said he didn't smoke because 'it is bad for the memory' and practiced every morning and night, writing new words that he learned from foreigners in his book. My contribution to his lexicon was singularly useless; we passed a tacky gold Buddha outside a temple and Jason remarked that it was not ancient, though this was very obvious to me. "It is plastic" he said and I replied with nit-picking precision that in fact it was fibreglass. "Fibreglass", replied Jason who seized on the word and turned it over in his mouth, sa-vouring it like some new confection. So I got to scribble in his book too, on the first page just beneath where he'd written the Lord's prayer and what he called his codename - Golden Phoenix. I tried to explain that fibreglass wouldn't be a terribly useful word, but Jason was having none of it and we discussed the technical properties of construction materials as we snailed back along Jiefang Lu. "I have heard of Styrofoam" said Jason. "Is that a more hard wearing mate-rial than fibreglass?"

Our tour was done, but I complained that I had seen nothing of the old Jewish town. I knew that the synagogue had been destroyed by floods in the 1860s, but the Jews had an uninterrupted presence in Kaifeng for 700 years; surely there was something left that was more than a rumour? Jason of course knew where to go. He cycled into the grounds of the Number Four People's Hospital, past white gowned doctors smoking on the steps beside a door from which the bitter tang of traditional medicine floated to battle the fumes from an idling am-bulance that waited for an emergency. The men inside this door were dressed in green and crouched on their haunches in a modern day kow-tow in that way that men in China can for hours on end but that I am unable to do for more than 30 seconds before the onset of cramp. The men were tying shredded bamboo into medicine bundles. They told me this was for virility and to enable a man to have more than one child though Jason told me they were joking since how could bamboo make sperm swim faster and it is a truth universally knowledge in crowded modern China that a man should *never* be encouraged to impregnate a woman twice.

These perching purveyors of procreative placebos knew what we had come to see, and there in the darkened backroom beneath a con-crete slab, was a sunken well; the last remaining evidence of the syna-gogue in Kaifeng and the Jews in Henan. Just a well after all, but a snapshot of a people in a foreign land, tenacious in belief, surviving, prospering for nearly a millennia and then departing.

There was living evidence of the Jews in Kaifeng along 'Reading the Scriptures' hutong behind the hospital. Jason's rickshaw filled the narrow alley as he pedaled along just as I seemed to fill the tiny house of an 84-year-old woman who was also tiny and said she was descended from the Jews. She told me her niece was in Israel and showed me the Star of David and menorah above her bed, incongruous next to plastic Chinese ephemera – a lion, a dragon, a fan and a golden kitty with a paw raised to gather good luck and wealth. She told me that she observed the Sabbath and read the Torah at home since there is no synagogue in Kaifeng anymore. "I am the only Jew" she proclaimed and I felt the rare privilege of meeting living history, the last of her kind, a full stop to 700 years. "She's an old fraud" Jason said as we left the house, and shattered my illusions. "She does this for money and attention and is no more Jewish than me." Jewish or not, the old woman seemed convinced she was; I figured that at 84 years old she could believe whatever she needed to.

There is a painting in the National Palace Museum in Beijing called 'Riverside Scene at the Qingming Festival' that is so old and precious and iconic that it is only exhibited for a brief period every few years. It was painted by Zhang Zeduan during the Song dynasty of a town then called Bianjing but that exists now as modern Kaifeng. The painting is over 5 metres long and shows 12th century life in minute detail with hundreds of human figures going about their business; boats, buildings, sedan chairs, animals, vehicles and trees centred around the bustling Hong Qiao Rainbow Bridge outside the old city walls, though the bridge and walls have long gone.

The painting is called 'China's Mona Lisa', not because style or subject is the same but because like the painting behind bullet-proof glass in the Louvre that is smaller than you thought it was going to be, Zhang's painting is famous for *being* famous. Such is the painting's renown that Ming and Qing Dynasty copies were made that updated the scene and a 130 metre long animated version formed the centre piece of the China Pavilion in the 2010 Shanghai Expo. The picture is a grand statement of Chinese Mediaeval life and I can think of no European equivalent except for the Bayeux Tapestry. But like Norman arches and Saxon cavalry, the scene outside Kaifeng is utterly, irrevocably gone.

Though I went to the place where the picture was drawn, there is not a semblance or a ghost of a memory of Zhang's China where utilitarian concrete presents its blank grey expression and the blare of traffic drowns out the past.

The same is true of so much of Henan. This is the province where China feels most proud of herself - the cradle of civilisation along the Yellow River and the home of four ancient capitals. The past is glimpsed only fleetingly in Henan, in museums or a fragment of city wall that has survived the bulldozers. Bianjing has become Kaifeng and though the provincial capital Zhengzhou has retained its ancient name, it too has galloped into the future and buried its past.

There were hints and ghosts in the concrete pyramid of the Henan Provincial Museum, a dull and functional building already weather-worn and prematurely old like so much Chinese construction. Yet behind its plain facade the museum contains such a wealth of exhibits that are so very old that it's hard to make sense of them at all and perversely it's the greedy modern expansion of Zhengzhou that has unearthed so much ancient treasure as workmen chance upon buried caches of pots and bronzes on this avenue or that road as they tear up the countryside with mechanical claws.

The 20th-century Irish poet and historian Louis MacNeice was talking of ancient Greece when he wrote in 1939; 'And how one can imagine oneself among them I do not know, it was all so unimaginably different and all so long ago.' I felt the same in Zhengzhou amongst the 6000 year old pots. There are oracle bones in the museum too that offer a fraction more insight into the unimaginably different past. These are tortoise belly shells and ox shoulder blades that were heated and cracked during the Shang dynasty 3000 years ago then inscribed using a bronze pin with oracle bones script. These bones contain details of divination - the name of the person reading the bone, what questions were asked, the prediction made and whether this came true - and have been unearthed at several sites in Henan, but especially the ancient capital called Anyang in the north of the province. The bones were displayed in glass cases and largely ignored by visitors rushing to the frivolous and famous Han dynasty porcelain, though it was these shoulder blades and shells with their preoccupation with births, famine and Kings that brought the past a little closer and more imaginable for me.

The temperature outside the museum was touching 40°C and I couldn't get out of Zhengzhou fast enough, so I caught a taxi to the train station. The car was hot enough to crack an oracle bone so I opened the window to let in the air outside that was marginally cooler than that inside and which might stop me becoming for ever glued to my imitation leather seat. The driver was perturbed to see my discomfort and told me to sit up front and enjoy the air conditioning. He stopped dead in the middle of Zhengzhou's busiest main road and I climbed out and into the front seat amidst streaming traffic and much honking of horns, though I might not have bothered had I known what feeble breath of air huffed from the air conditioning unit, making no difference at all to my temperature that was by now high enough to threaten to send me into convulsions.

Though clambering to the front seat did nothing to cool me down, it did allow the driver to get better acquainted with me. He asked me how old I was and expressed great surprise when I told him, claiming that I looked half my age and spent the remainder of the trip praising my physical charms. "Such strong arms" he eulogized. "Good hair, a fine face, wonderful eyes" and so on to the point where I thought he might have fallen for me. Perhaps the heat had raised his libido or addled his brain; I just felt hot and bothered and wondered why every taxi ride in China has to be such an adventure.

Further west, Luoyang city was capital of 13 dynasties until the 10th century. China's first University was established here in 29 BC and her first Buddhist temple nearby in 68 AD called Baima Si or White Horse Temple where it is possible no doubt to sit on a white horse for a photo. Yet despite the effort to brighten the place up during the annual Peony Festival, Luoyang was hiding her colourful and ancient dynastic underwear well beneath skirts of concrete and an overcoat of grime and as I alighted the train I wondered if I'd even left Zhengzhou.

Luoyang does at least have the famous Longmen grottoes on the edge of town. 'Grotto' is suggestive of gnomes and fairy lights but these are grand Tang Dynasty UNESCO World Heritage caves full of carvings of Buddha and his disciples made sombre by decapitations and beheadings performed by Red Guards or trophy hunters from Metropolitan Museums of Art in New York, Tokyo and London.

I'd seen similar grand works of art at Datong, Mogao, Leshan and Dazu but how can one tire of gazing at a 17 m tall Buddha, perfectly executed in stone and placidly staring down on me as he had on all visitors for over 1000 years? The best feature of Longmen and the thing that makes the caves distinct from China's other ancient Buddhist sites is their position along the Yi River. It was as satisfying to gaze from a distance on the opposite bank through hanging willow trees at the Buddha as it was to be dwarfed by him close up. The sun made patterns on the water and modern China instantly felt ancient again; the eternal river flowing past the eternal rock.

The choked streets of Luoyang were dominated by billboards, one of which asked if I had 'Female health problems.' The same board offered a solution to the question posed; 'Please come to the procreation centre' in bold letters above two women whose relieved smiles suggested their wombs had been a barren place in which a man's seed could find no purchase, but for whom all such problems were solved in their joyful fecundity. I wondered if Kaifeng medicinal bamboo played any part in this miracle cure. Yet Henan doesn't seem to have a huge problem with procreation. It's China's most populous province and close to being the first to break the 100 million mark, up from half of this 50 years ago, though the experts are quick to reassure that the rate of growth is slowing down despite the best efforts of Luoyang's procreation centre.

The other advert I repeatedly saw on messy street corners and on flyovers and busy intersections was a government campaign that the people of Henan should 'together fight AIDS'. The efficacy of such wishful thinking non-specific strategising may be doubtful, but it is evident at least that Henan acknowledges it has a problem. In recent years the prevalence of blood selling among poor villages in Henan coupled with poor sterilisation techniques has created an HIV problem across the province. Local officials initially covered up the crisis that peasants called 'the nameless fever' and continued to trumpet the slogan that 'it is glorious to sell your blood' appealing to both patriotism and pockets by offering 40 yuan to anyone who did. Commercial blood collecting is now banned in China but AIDS campaigners believe there may be half a million cases in Henan alone and four million across China, most of whom enjoy little social support or adequate treatment.

AIDS is all part of the uncertainty of modern China that makes some yearn for the security of cradle to grave Maoist Communism. Henan clung longer than anywhere else to such notions, for it was in this province that the last Maoist collective existed in the village of Nanjie. Every day in the village would start with the collective song and celebration that 'united and strong, Mao Zedong's ideology shines on us' before the workers set off to their predetermined jobs in predetermined factories for life. Food, healthcare, schooling and accommodation were provided free in Nanjie and there were none of modern China's diverting and immoral influences; no karaoke bars, fancy restaurants and mahjong. Villagers studied Maoist quotations and participated in group weddings held once a year in front of a statue of the great leader. No one owned a vehicle, advertising was banned and only the village administrator Wang Hongbin earned money, a nominal $30 per month.

But uncertainty is everywhere in modern Henan; in the rampant growth of the cities, its high population, in the citizens' tainted blood. Nanjie socialist collective collapsed in huge debt and amidst allegations of corruption in 2008. In a late effort to save the village's struggling noodle factory and its livelihoods, the village committee bit the bullet of privatisation and turned its holdings into equities. Nanjie's ideologically puritanical party secretary Wang Hongbin gratefully accepted 9% of the company shares.

How Henan must long for the certainties of the past, the Longmen Buddha gazing passively over the River, safe behind Shang city walls, the reassuring bustle of commerce on the Rainbow Bridge over the Binjiang River, the future predicted and known on oracle bones. The only constant in the province seems to be the Yellow River that bisects Henan to the north of its ancient capitals. But in Henan even that which seems constant is not. The river that flooded so catastrophically through the centuries has been tamed by a series of giant dams and these have brought problems of their own. The Banqiao Dam in Southern Henan collapsed in 1975 after days of heavy rainfall, releasing 700,000,000 m³ of water that crashed over fields and through villages and drowned 230,000 people across several counties. 'The blare of the dam burst sounded like the sky was collapsing and the earth was cracking' recalled one survivor. 'Houses and trees disappeared in an instant. Numerous corpses and bodies of cattle floated in water amid people's wailing for help'.

The Sanmenxia Dam built in the 1950s in the extreme west of the province has not collapsed but has brought a different set of problems. When completed, the dam was hailed as a symbol of the new revolutionary China and its image printed on the country's banknotes. The phrase 'when the river is at peace, China is at peace' is writ large on the side of the dam, but this monument to socialism and Mao's determination to show the river who was boss is by any measure a failed project. The massive silt load of the Yellow River clogged the turbines of the dam so badly, that within four years of opening, 40% of its water storage capacity and energy production had been lost. Today the dam has less than 10% of its original storage and the 400,000 people who were evicted from their homes when the massive project was built must be wondering if it was worth it. Meanwhile the tamed river gets dirtier and dirtier. Over four billion tonnes of waste and sewage are discharged into the system each year; severe pollution has rendered up to a third of the river's water unfit even for agricultural and industrial use. These modern problems and the historic floods that washed through Henan towns, killed hundreds of thousands and destroyed the synagogue in Kaifeng suggest that the river will never be tamed and will always be China's sorrow.

The bus that took me south away from the river and into the Song Shan mountains was memorable and exasperating as journeys in China often are. For a while I searched fruitlessly amongst the revving engines in the Kaifeng parking lot, but finally there it was, decrepit and small, coughing and wheezing and throwing out plumes of acrid smoke; the aged uncle of the other sleek and youthful modern coaches. The air conditioner was non-existent of course and the temperature on board this mobile sauna was such that passengers might have been provided with towels and essential oils instead of tickets. And it was not just the passengers who overheated on this journey. The bus radiator clearly had a problem and the woman who collected the cash was required to multitask and regularly filled the steaming engine with water from a plastic barrel into an ingenious tube and funnel device behind the driver's seat in order to prevent the engine from glowing red hot.

This at least required regular stops to fetch more water which allowed everyone to get off for a few precious moments to cool their faces on the very faintest of breeze issuing from the slopes of the distant mountains. Back on board I was crushed thigh to thigh with a woman gripping a plastic bag of spring onions who sighed and raised her eyes every time the boiling radiator was thirstily refilled while I merely wished the conductor would stop pouring water into her plastic funnel and pour it on me. Spring onion woman's sighs became longer and louder when an old man wandered to the front of the bus and allowed his grandson to drop his trousers and pee down the bus steps though this was not unwelcome either since the driver helpfully opened the door to allow the shiny rivulets of urine to escape and declined to close it again when he felt a divine and cooling breeze rushing through the aperture.

The bus was full as they always are in China - so many people are *going* somewhere in this country. But two hours into our journey, the driver stopped by the side of the carriageway to pick up one more man who waved to us from the tall grass at the road's edge. The man grinned stumpy brown teeth, climbed aboard and whistled through those same teeth, whereupon his workmates leapt from the undergrowth like guerrilla soldiers and climbed aboard too. There were 12 bare chested labourers who needed to go to Dengfeng town and who threw their toolkits, yards of tarpaulin, coils of rope and wooden sticks onto the floor of the bus and sat down on them. This was too much for our aging thirsty bus that wheezed and refused to move and too much for the other passengers who were suffocating in their tiny space. So the driver ordered the workmen back onto the grass. Where moments before they were hollering and whooping as they climbed aboard, now they looked glumly disappointed as they debated their case and argued between themselves since the driver had decreed that just two of their number could stay on board.

And so we departed again, the two most senior labourers happily on the bus with vests on now, chatting and smoking, their stranded colleagues forgotten. We pulled into Dengfeng town at the foot of the mountains at last, the first natural beauty I'd seen since the Yi River at Longmen, for the panorama from the sweaty bus had been an unrelenting horror of cement yards, gas stations and broken houses. I was met by cheerful Lisa who took me to buy black plimsolls and baggy cotton trousers since I would need them to practice kung fu.

Shaolin Temple sits at the foot of the Song Shan mountains and is the epicentre of Chinese martial arts. The temple was founded in 492 A.D. when the emperor noticed that one of his favourite monks, an Indian named Batuo preferred to meditate in quiet and isolated places away from the imperial court which at that time was located in Luoyang. So the emperor built a temple in the mountains for Batuo and he was soon joined by other monks who preferred to get their heads together in the quiet of the hills rather than the in rush of the city.

This might have been the end of the story of Shaolin but for the arrival of another Buddhist meditator from India in 525 A.D. called Bodhidarma. This itinerant monk was rejected by the temple at first but like the labourers who tried to board our too full bus, he took himself away to try again. Undeterred, Bodhidarma simply built his own bus. He climbed the mountain to a tiny cave and vowed not to leave until he had achieved enlightenment. He is said to have stayed in his cave for nine years, meditating with such intensity that his image was burned into a rock on the wall (the shadowy stone can still be seen in the temple) and cutting off his eyelids so that he would not fall asleep while meditating.

When he had finished staring at the wall, Bodhidarma came down the mountain and became abbot of Shaolin. He taught the monks that meditation was the key to achieving enlightenment and rejected the idea that good deeds would help since they merely increase the ego and self pride of the do-gooder. Bodhidarma's dawn till dusk programme of introspection became the basis of Zen Buddhism but the Abbot stared in turn at his monks (he could do little else with no eyelids) and realised that all this sedentary meditation was ruining their bodies and turning their muscles to porridge. So he introduced a set of physical exercises which developed over time to the classic moves of kung fu.

The monks at Shaolin gradually established their own fighting system, which seems a bit contrary for a bunch of shaven headed enlightened pacifists, and over the next 1000 years the tales of monastic derring-do and brave combat became the stuff of legend. They battled against Mongol hordes and Japanese pirates, against the invading Manchus and became the first martial arts franchise when a second Shaolin Temple was established in Fujian province - the Henan Temple focuses on kicking; Fujian is more geared to boxing. As the saying goes; 'Nan Quan, Bei tu jiao' - South boxing, North legs. Now the temple would have to cope with me.

I have seen David Carradine in the 1970s series Kung Fu (Carradine's character Kwai Chang Caine was originally to be played by Bruce Lee, but Lee was rejected for looking 'too Chinese'.) I have seen Bruce Lee's swansong 'Enter the Dragon' in which he kicks a succession of men wearing ugly nylon 1970s clothes into submission. I was too old and sensible now to believe I could ever be the toughest mutha on the planet, and though my waistline is now more Kung Fu Panda than Bruce Lee, I thought it might be nice to learn a few moves, to retain some flexibility into middle age and because maybe, just maybe the opportunity to fight off all comers and impress a pretty girl in a bar might one day arrive.

Lisa introduced me to my Sifu (master) at a school on the edge of the temple grounds. The place was exactly what I had hoped for - a simple unadorned dirt square where young disciples were kicking and practising their movements, but the Sifu was not what I had expected. No wispy beard and venerable expression here, Sifu looked just like the small-time businessmen I've seen all over China; keys and mobile phone hanging from his belt and cigarette in hand. He liked that I called him 'Sifu' but this was almost the last time I saw my kung fu master who seemed incredulous that I would train for just one day and handed me over to the coach who was instructing the young students by barking orders and blowing a whistle.

My training did not start until the following day so Lisa kindly took me to the temple itself to show me around. China is full of people like this who will give up hours of their time for a guest and I wondered how many people in England would leave what they were doing to show a stranger round the Tower of London or Stonehenge. Lisa showed me a photo of her baby boy called Jiangdong - a portmanteau of Jiangsu and Shandong, the home provinces of wife and husband - who lived 300 miles away with his grandma. Lisa was the only person I met in China who regretted having a boy and not a girl. She would have tried for a girl as well but couldn't afford the 10,000 yuan fine; so she would content herself with little Jiangdong who she never saw but who would one day also come to Shaolin.

The temple is thoroughly geared up to exploiting its reputation and for all the fearsome weapons and high kicks I saw in Shaolin that day, the most frightening thing of all was the intensity of the slick marketing campaign. The road to the temple is lined with Wushu martial arts schools, where students in matching tracksuits went through a ritualised and synchronised series of moves. Very impressive it looked, but Lisa was the wife of a kung fu expert and scorned the student's efforts; "it takes more than a tracksuit to do kung fu" she said.

I discovered that practitioners of kung fu *loathe* wushu. When Mao Zedong banned kung fu in the 1950s he dreamed of ridding China completely of its feudal past. But banning kung fu was like trying to outlaw football in England; China is obsessed with kung fu from toddlers watching violent battles on TV to teenagers playing street fighter in video arcades to octogenarians practicing kung fu forms in ultra-slow motion everyday at sunrise in public parks across the nation. So the Chinese Communist party created two sports out of traditional kung fu; wushu and sanda kick boxing.

Self defence - the whole raison d'etre of kung fu - is irrelevant in wushu which concentrates on the art in martial arts. The emphasis is on speed, grace and acrobatics; a whole series of flips and handsprings that would be useless in a fight but look *so* pretty. Traditional kung fu masters see wushu as a political attack on their pursuit that has stripped away the central religious and martial aspects of their tradition. But the public loves wushu because it is so athletic and fast and consequently it is the style that is most often used in Hong Kong kung fu movies.

The economic high kicks and merchandising fist to the face continued past the entrance gate of Shaolin (100 yuan entrance fee). Stalls selling ice creams and illegal looking nun-chucks lined the route of the 'martial arts shopping centre', built on land previously occupied by dormitories for students and trainers, who like my chain-smoking Sifu had been moved out to purpose-built flats outside the grounds so that the temple looks uncluttered for the tourists.

Lisa and I played the game of trying to get a photo on the famous steps of the temple, but the crowds of kung fu disciples posing in tiger position, lunging with openhanded claws and waving Shaolin souvenir spears in the air made this impossible. There were some foreigners here too who had seen too many movies and were trying to discover themselves in the mountains of Henan. A bearded man dressed in black bounced on his toes and launched into kicks that looked likely to damage a hamstring or displace a hip, grunting and sweating from every pore as he did so. Two middle-aged women were practicing a ridiculous slow motion kung fu dance, circling each other and launching glacially slow attacks and watched by bemused Chinese tourists who seemed unsure whether to laugh or take photos. One of these women was wearing flesh coloured tights which at first glance suggested she was practicing a rare form of naked from the waist down kung fu; these were no doubt a comfortable and practical garment but left nothing to the imagination and were likely to drive a celibate Shaolin monk to renounce his vows.

Jason in Kaifeng had sympathised with me when I told him I didn't want to see the town's temple. "Oh, Chinese temples are all the same" he'd said and I was relieved to find someone who shared the view that I sometimes guiltily feel. Shaolin was the same style, the same layout as so many other temples I had seen and didn't even have the benefit of age since the original had been burned down by the warlord Shi Yousan in 1928. In fact Shaolin had an altogether bad time in the 20th century when the use of firearms rendered any amount of aggressive as a tiger, stepping like a dragon, fast as a lightning stroke, moving like a gust of wind iron kung fu irrelevant. In 1900 the Boxers believed they could use kung fu to harden their bodies and make them impervious to British bullets but discovered that Samuel Colt made all men equal. The Japanese continued the task of warlord destruction in the 1940s and in the 1960s the Red Guards tried to finish the job entirely, dragging the remaining Shaolin monks into the streets of Dengfeng for public humiliation and floggings.

But though Shaolin looked the same as most other temples it was saved by the movies and has turned its Bruce Lee fame into tourist dollars and survived. Not everything in the temple is new and there are remnants of its long past. There is a tree in the grounds that was full of holes where monks had stuck their fingers to develop iron hands, and depressions in the stone floor of the Pilu Pavilion where disciples practiced their moves and kicks over and over and over again. Lisa also showed me the temple where the monk Huike stood in the snow and pleaded to become Bodhidarma's disciple. The great lidless monk refused unless the snow turned red, so Huike chopped off his arm to spill his blood on the ground and show his devotion. (This is why monks traditionally greet with only one raised hand). I asked Lisa why Huike didn't just chop off a finger - surely this would have done the trick? She said she didn't know and sighed like the woman had done with the spring onions on the bus.

The climax of a visit to the Shaolin Temple is the display by monks of their martial skills. This involved an improbable series of kicks, flips and contortions (which looked suspiciously like wushu to me) and a monk throwing a pin through a sheet of glass. We applauded heartily and members of the audience were invited on stage to replicate some of the moves while I stared at the floor, humming my own kung fu mantra 'don't pick me, don't pick me' and exited past commemoratives DVDs, photos and strength giving Chinese medicine, I wondered if I would be able to throw a pin through a sheet of glass after my one-day training tomorrow.

I was woken by the shrill blasts of the coach's whistle at 5am. Kung fu requires fitness so I was off for an early-morning run with the other students. I stuck modestly to the rear while the 18-year-old trainees gamboled ahead, glancing back at the waiguoren who was puffing and blowing his way up the steps and round the Shaolin temple car park. On the third circuit one of the students sidled up and showed me how to cheat so we ran through bushes and arrived at the finish before anyone else; a triumph of brains over brawn. The 10 students at our school were a ragtag bunch in T-shirts, football shorts and plimsolls, running in a chaotic disorderly pack compared to the wushu groups who joined us on the early-morning tarmac in step, in tracksuits and waving flags in unison.

At breakfast, the young Shaolin disciples listened to tinny Chinese pop on cheap radios and asked if I liked it? "Do people in England listen to this one? Do you like that one?" The questioners were blissful in their ignorance that no one anywhere in the rest of the world would listen to music that bad. I began to wonder about the authenticity of my school; a Sifu who smoked, students in Manchester United shorts and shouldn't they be chanting Buddhist prayers instead of listening to Chinese pop?

My doubts were dispelled when the training began at 7.30am. We started with 30 minutes of stretching and I soon became aware that my feet wouldn't go as high on the brick wall as anyone else's nor my nose as close to my toes. These boys were *flexible* while I had all the suppleness of an ironing board. We moved on to the dusty training ground and began to jog slowly round, then into line to run one by one across the square. This I could do, my kung fu plimsolls slapping on the floor felt good and I was keeping up with the young bucks; maybe that stretching had done some good.

My fun stopped there. On the next pass the students jogged one by one and performed an outrageous high kick, foot cracking against their raised hand. I attempted to replicate this and fell over onto my baggy kung fu pyjamas. The next roundhouse kick was squatting low to the floor which at least had the benefit of having less far to fall so I tried again, my legs swinging in a parabola, knees cracking and crunching under the strain. Then things just got silly. Flying horizontal kicks, spinning lunges and somersaults accompanied by screams and pumped fists; I reverted to a sheepish jog around the square and sneaked off to continue my stretches since clearly I had not warmed up enough.

My coach wasn't sure what this stiff as a board foreigner could achieve in a day so we settled on some basic Shaolin boxing moves which were challenging enough. The more I practiced, the more my brain disengaged as I forgot to block or kick or shout or expel air correctly. Kung fu is a very specific art; the leg has to be positioned precisely, the fist clenched just so, but my coach was a smiling and generous man and told me 'good... better.... not bad' but always 'again... again... again'. Sifu made an occasional appearance to readjust my arm or demonstrate the deficiency of my defence by punching me in the solar plexus, and knocking the wind out of me. Due deference and respect prevented me from punching him back. I was also very scared of him.

But mostly he seemed pleased too and called over the old retired 80-year-old master who really looked the part with grey wispy beard and cotton pyjamas, but he just chuckled and shook his head and turned back to the young boys to show them a thing or two. Coach was less patient with his real students. Shaolin's pedagogical style is famously corporal and the Chinese have a saying – da shi teng, ma shi ai ; smacking is fondness, scolding is love. Though I did not see coach strike the students, he constantly struck the floor with his stave and moaned and shouted continuously; "too slow, no good, faster, slower, no, no, no."

Shaolin Kung Fu is based on several simple precepts. Arms and feet must coordinate in short powerful movements and the eyes, ears and heart must be in harmony. The requirements of the Shaolin monk are expressed in the form of sayings; aggressive as a tiger, shout like thunder, stay on the foot like a driven nail, be as heavy as a mountain but ready to act quickly; as light as goosedown, as hard as iron. The last of these is particularly revered in Shaolin. Monks train parts of their body to be especially resistant to force by the use of qi - vitality or energy that courses through the body - and by repetitive physical exercise that hardens the iron area and makes it impervious to pain. Thus, monks can possess iron hands or iron legs, iron heads, iron fingers and toes and even an iron crotch.

Like all truly civilised cultures, Shaolin had a siesta in the middle of the day when I chatted to the boys in basic Chinese before the afternoon workout. The boys adopted a strange mix of banter and horse play, launching kicks and headlocks on each other, the oldest bullying the youngest like boys everywhere. Most had been here two years and took the kung fu seriously but I wondered what the *point* of all the high kicking was; where would they go next when their training was done? I was thinking of career paths while the boys thought of qi and Bruce Lee. I wondered if the boys' education was as good as their kung fu and they laughed and said yes they could read and write and would join the army or maybe go to Shaolin Temple if they were wanted there. The quietest boy who was the best at kung fu spoke at last; "my job is not important. Kung Fu has given me life and self-respect" and I wondered if maybe it was I who had missed the point.

I could barely walk following the afternoon session when I continued stretching and practicing my simple moves while the boys swung lethal looking sticks and clubs and the coach shouted no, no, no and blew his whistle. Nevertheless, I hauled my aching body up the evening dusty road in the shade of ginkgo trees with Lisa to the main road where I could hail a bus. The vehicle was at least less crowded with labourers and urinating infants than the one from Luoyang. I slid the window open and watched the Song Shan mountains slide by and tried my best to look enigmatic. My eyes were narrowed, gazing far away in contemplation of the meaning of life. My body was a coiled spring like a kung fu master, my hands were clenched for combat and my crotch was like iron. But it was all pretence and I was thinking only of the future; dreaming of a warm shower and a soft bed and feeling as brittle and old as an oracle bone.

JIANGSU

江西

106 190 km sq
Population 75 million

Gardens... should be like lovely, well-shaped girls: all curves, secret corners, unexpected deviations, seductive surprises and then still more curves.

H. E Bates

The China Sex Museum, established in Tongli by two Shanghai professors is beautifully constructed in grey Qing Dynasty brick and set in pleasant formal gardens fringed by delicate bamboo; a haven from the busy boats that cruise the canals below pedestrians on the sensual curves of Song Dynasty bridges in Tongli. The place is intended as a rigorously intellectual examination of 2000 years of sexual habits in China though it was difficult initially to take it seriously.

I was greeted first by a ticket collector standing erect in his booth then by a statue with a 4 foot erection bursting through trousers and iron chains while the rest of the figure remained bound, to show that there is one part of a man at least that can never be fettered or subdued. Behind every blushing peony or shrubby bush lurked more statuesque statements of manhood, resting limply on thighs, inserted in recumbent concubines or bursting proudly tumescent through the leaves and pricks of rosebushes; a plethora of penises, a cornucopia of cocks.

The museum houses a collection of thousands of taboo items; teacups and fans, paintings and chastity belts, prostitute beds and most memorably, a saddle fixed to a chair sporting a wooden dildo used to punish licentious women. But Professors Liu and Hu's purpose in bringing together this eclectic group of objects is not to titillate but to enlighten. China can be prudish and puritanical about sex, notwithstanding the whores who ply their trade on the shopping streets of Shanghai or from cheap provincial hair salons across the nation, and Tongli is a haven of liberalism and progressive thought where anything goes and where behind every dahlia there lurks a sinister surprise.

'Any sexual phenomenon as long as it is voluntary should be allowed to exist' trumpeted the museum. 'Don't think that only your preferences are right and deny other's preference'. Every preference is catered for here, every position and predilection in delicate Qing dynasty porcelain much of which contradicted the museum's scientific analysis of how upright human walking changed the style of intercourse from 'insertion from the back to insertion from the front'. Every girth and texture is considered and entertained in dildos of pottery and wood and the museum is a reminder that buffalo and pigs were not mere beasts of burden or food in ancient China but could provide sustenance for more base appetites too.

But it was the presence of homosexuality not bestiality that I found most surprising in the museum. This was the only place I had seen in China that recognised an 'affliction' that officially exists only in the depraved and confused West. Here everything was out of the closet.

'Homosexuality is not a disease, much less a crime' said the information boards in the display of painted lesbians inspired by the frantic thrusting of Pekinese dogs. 'Discrimination against homosexuals is not scientific' it said, an argument more likely to persuade rational and empirical modern Communist China that does not look kindly on such 'deviant' behaviour.[18]

Despite the government's denial of the existence of this 'problem' the country has a long history of homosexuality and ancient Chinese held far more liberal views on the subject. Gay relationships seem to have been particularly commonplace among aristocrats and literary elites before the Han dynasty (206BC - 220AD), just as they were among their contemporaries in ancient Greece.

Chinese language has a special term to express homosexual love that dates from the Han dynasty. The phrase 'duan xiu' or 'cutting sleeves' is widely used as a euphemism for a gay relationship and refers to the story of Emperor Ai of the Han dynasty who fell for a handsome young man called Dong Xian. One day the lovers fell asleep together and when he awoke, the Emperor found that he was trapped because Dong Xian was sleeping on his sleeves, so rather than wake him from his slumbers, the Emperor cut off his own sleeves so that he could slip away unnoticed and the boy could dream on.

There are fewer records of transsexuals in China, and this subject is more taboo even than homosexuality. In literature there are the stories of Hua Mulan and Zhu Yingtai but they lived as men only temporarily which probably means that the Disney Mulan cartoons are not a deviant feast of transgender cross dressing, but simple wholesome family fun. Lou Cheng in the Southern Qi dynasty (479 – 503) lived for much longer as a male government official but was ordered from the imperial court when her ruse was discovered. She was labelled a 'renyao' or 'human goblin' for her deception, an offensive term that is still sometimes used in Hong Kong to refer to transsexuals.

Transsexuality was beyond the pale even for the Tongli Sex Museum and vestiges of restraint existed too in the museum gift shop which

---

18 Homosexuality was only removed from the official list of mental disorders in 2001

contained merely a selection of prim postcards showing views of Tongli rather than an assistant in basque and stockings selling reproduction punishment saddles or a selection of chastity belts as I had hoped. Heck, there wasn't even a DVD of Mulan on the shelves.

I was soon wandering the phallus filled forecourt again, out the gates and back into the China were the only public members are affiliated to the Chinese Communist Party and a girl will spread her legs only for gymnastic Olympic gold. The rest of Tongli felt a little mundane after the climaxes of the museum, though it was exceedingly pretty. There are a number of these gorgeous canal side villages in the countryside of Jiangsu with streets too small for cars and where cafe tables perch on cobbles overlooking the placid water of the canal with jasmine flowers and straw hatted women on flat bottomed barges drifting lazily by - a kind of Far Eastern and poverty afflicted version of straw boater privileged undergraduates punting on the waterways of Cambridge, but with chicken's feet not cucumber sandwiches in their lunch baskets. The houses are all the same in Tongli - squat, whitewashed buildings with grey roof tiles and double wooden doors, every one equal and the same in an infrastructure built many years before notions of communist equality, though I discovered as I searched the alleys and courtyards of Tongli, that some houses are more equal than others.

I met Mr Wang in the courtyard of his 350-year-old house and he bade me sit down on a bench polished smooth by centuries of buttocks in a garden where turtles brought luck by doing nothing more than sitting in the sunshine. Wang served me green tea in the traditional way, from a chipped teapot poured into porcelain cups little bigger than egg cups. This makes it difficult to drink because the cup is full of leaves and is too hot to hold and has to be constantly refilled. Eating with chopsticks and drinking tea is made willfully challenging in China; probably there is a moral message here, only those things difficult to attain are of worth. Imagine how dissolute and immoral the nation would become with the introduction of stout mugs with handles and knives and forks. Wang's house was similar to the Siheyuan I had seen in the Beijing hutong (See Beijing chapter), meticulously laid out with rooms positioned to maintain a sense of social order, the head of house in the best room, men separate to women and the whole positioned to catch morning sun, cooling breeze, feng shui, good luck, wealth, auspiciousness and curious passing foreigners who might want to drink tea.

I congratulated Wang on his lovely house and especially the 200-year-old canopied beds carved intricately with flowers and Qing Dynasty Tongli merchants that I saw through the wooden doors concertinaed open to the warm afternoon breeze. "But I have wi-fi too" explained Wang who was more concerned to demonstrate modernity than ancient timber and gave me a tour of his house pointing out kettle and TV and exclaiming "all mod cons" as he switched light bulbs on and off for my benefit so that I would understand that China was not stuck in the past.

These small Jiangsu towns were once workshops for the silk industry that was centred on the nearby town of Suzhou in the 14th and 15th centuries. As the trade declined, so did Tongli though this preserved the town from the ravages of concrete as it became a rural backwater. Jiangsu province remains an economic powerhouse in China despite the decline of silk (a third of all China's exports come from Jiangsu - the province's GDP is $450 billion) but Tongli has not shared in this, though the swelling appeal of Sex Museum garden statues may yet penetrate the growing tourist trade as thrusting urbanites from nearby Shanghai come to see how China once looked, but with all mod cons.

Suzhou has been almost swallowed up by tourism. This is a town of gardens, though there are only a handful left of the original 100 or more. The gardens are meticulously and deliberately laid out and filled with allegory and meaning though this is all rather meaning*less* when a space that was designed to be appreciated in solitude is filled with dozens of megaphone wielding tour guides and hundreds of tourists in matching hats, cigarettes stuck in mouths, screaming toddlers, a man listening to Peking Opera on a radio, visitors dropping biscuit wrappers on herbaceous borders and a cat gagging then vomiting on the stone tiles of a pagoda. The wealthy middle-aged American tourists I saw in the gardens were better behaved on the whole. They were on the standard Shanghai – Beijing – Xi'an China tourist trail and I wanted to tell them to break out of their five-star hotel prisons, to flee the beetling crowds of the Suzhou gardens and go west young man, to the mountains of Yunnan, the deserts of Gansu and the mysteries of Tibet.

The 16th century Humble Administrator's garden is the largest in Suzhou and I went here and to the 12th century Master of the Nets garden that once belonged to a retired official turned fisherman, and to the 14th century Lion's Grove garden too. Lion's Grove was constructed by a Buddhist monk called Tianru to commemorate his master who lived on Lion Cliff on Tianmu Mountain in nearby Zhejiang province. Chinese gardens don't attempt to improve on nature or even try to look natural and this garden is filled with rocks many of which represent wisdom and immortality because they were extracted from Tai Lake west of Suzhou. During the Song dynasty, these Taihu stones were among the most expensive objects in China; they are supposed to look like lions but were unrecognisable to me as dozens of Chinese tourists in baseball caps took photos and clambered all over them, puffing and panting as if they were scaling the Eiger's north face. Try as I might I could see no lions, only strange protuberances, smooth bulges and gaping limestone hollows. I think my mind was still on the Sex Museum in Tongli.

Though there were plenty of Western tourists attempting to appreciate the gardens, they are not easy places for Westerners to understand. The gardens are full of art, harmony and proportion - ideas that are bound to Chinese culture. Such concerns lead to rather cold and geometric spaces with ordered ranks of bamboo, plum blossom and peony bushes positioned just so; quite unlike the chaos and colour of a Victorian cottage garden or the greenhouses of Kew overflowing and abundantly green. Bamboo represents strength and upright morality in these gardens, peonies symbolise wealth and power. Plum blossom is one of the four 'junzi' flowers (the others are orchid, chrysanthemum and bamboo), that symbolise nobleness. The blossoms are beloved because they flower in winter when other plants have withered and died, thus they are seen as an example of resilience and perseverance in the face of adversity - a perfect metaphor for revolutionary struggle.

What was difficult to appreciate was made nearly impossible by the mass of people. My guidebook said that the Master of the Nets garden is best viewed on a summer's evening when the moon can be seen three times; in the sky, reflected in the lake and in a Mirror in the Moon Watching Pavilion, but I couldn't even get into the pavilion today and the reflections of the lake were shattered by the stones being thrown into the water by excitable tourists from Beijing.

Marco Polo visited Suzhou in the 13th century and reported '6000 bridges, clever merchants, cunning men of all crafts, very wise men called sages and natural physicians'. An old Chinese proverb says 'in heaven there is paradise, on earth there is Suzhou and Hangzhou' (a lakeside town in Zhejiang province). But I had seen little of Suzhou's delights - the bridges were crowded with people, wise men were at home enjoying peace and paradise had been drowned out by the microphones of tour guides who all turned up the volume to out shout each other but wouldn't have needed them at all if they would only multilaterally disarm and put their microphones away.

In fact these gardens were the most hopelessly crowded place I ever visited in China with the notable exception of Huangshan Mountain (see Anhui chapter) - a reflection of the booming domestic tourist market in China. My day was saved when I met Professor Huang in Lion Grove beside a rock that looked nothing like a lion. I was drawn to him because he was standing still and on his own, quietly contemplating the garden while everyone else rushed from rock to blossom to pond and followed their guide.

Huang had a roll of paper under his arm and a small leather bag in his hand. He had come to paint and ignore the tourists because the formality, regularity and fame of these gardens are the perfect subject for Chinese ink and wash painting known as shui-mo hua. This art form was developed in the Tang Dynasty (618 – 907) and uses a selection of precise tools that old Huang was happy to show me when I expressed interest in his art. The battered leather satchel contained an ink block and a variety of slender handled brushes - hsieh chao pi crab's claw brushes and hu ying pi Hunan sheep hair brushes, hua jan pi brushes for painting flowers and lan yu chupi brushes for orchids and bamboo, all of them worn and stained from years of use, the hairs smooth and sleek and tapering to a perfect point.

The trick with ink and wash painting is to capture the mood of the scene, the intangible quality and soul of a rock or a horse or a flower without actually painting the thing or merely reproducing its appearance. Huang set about effortlessly capturing the soul of the garden minus the tourists for my benefit. Clutching the brush lightly and at right angles to the paper, his strokes were sometimes broad and flat and sometimes the brush barely seemed to touch the page at all. He varied the amount of ink on the bristles to such perfection that every shadow and nuance of the garden was captured though those same strokes were mere blotches and smudges and not rocks and flowers at all.

The Ming Dynasty painter Wang Fu said shui-mo hua was about creating 'likeness through unlikeness' and the Qing Dynasty Master Qi Baishi who died in 1957 said that the subtlety of a good painting lies in it being 'alike and yet unlike the subject' (he lived long enough to see Mao's leadership that was alike and yet unlike Communism). To paint a horse, the artist should understand its temperament better than its muscles and bones and there is no need to accurately portray flower petals and stem - that is for scientists - but it *is* necessary to convey its vitality and fragrant simplicity.

Huang was adept at eliminating useless detail and produced astonishing variations in tonality as the same ink turned from deep black to silver to grey. He finished with a flourish by adding a red seal to the base of the painting - this is called 'adding the eye to the Dragon' - and then spoke the words that no incompetent amateur wishes to hear; 'now it is your turn'.

My overriding sensation was a reluctance to even let my brush touch the paper and spoil the pure white and absorbent virgin sheet that stared up at me like a reproach. What if I had too much ink? What if I had not enough? How hard should I press? Would the old man catch me if I made a run for it? Huang told me not to worry about the quality of my work as long as I conveyed the excitement of the painting.

"Be brave with your brushstrokes" he said. "Be elegant and incorporate your emotions into the brush - ignore your surroundings if they are inconvenient". This was sage advice and prevented me drawing a mass of people and megaphones and I let my emotions and brush run riot on a landscape of mountains, rivers and bamboo that bore no relation at all to where I sat. Huang continued to coach me over my shoulder and I found this off putting though not nearly as bad as the crowd who took leave of clambering over rocks to watch the foreigner paint.

My teacher's instructions became more abstract and inscrutable as I progressed; "show sturdy simplicity, avoid mountains with no qi, do not neglect the atmosphere and emotion of mist, ensure mountains and water are the yin and yang of your art, observe the rules faithfully but modify according to your own intelligence and ability".....and best, most wonderfully of all; "The end of all method is to seem to have no method".

The instructions reminded me of the imprecision and zen of kung fu that I learned at Shaolin (see Henan chapter) and just as my spinning kicks were more ostrich than hummingbird, so my brushstrokes were too heavy, my mountains absurd and my bamboo as lifeless and limp as a flaccid penis on a Tongli statue. But Huang was delighted with my efforts and congratulated me, though I suppose I *had* paid him the compliment of taking his advice to seem to have no method. As I stepped back to admire my classical Chinese landscape made real by delicate brush and ink, one of the numerous bystanders leapt forward and added some details of his own - some birds and bamboo - as if this was a free for all and not a complete and unimprovable work of art. I was outraged; his additions did not improve the piece and destroyed the wonderful sense of proportion I had created and also that sense of ownership and pride I had for my creation that now sits dusty and ne-glected in a kitchen drawer but which might otherwise be hanging on the wall of a Shanghai Art Gallery.

By evening the tour groups had left and soft rain was falling on the watercolour landscape of Suzhou's gardens and canals. I came to like the place without all those people, the antique market, high-street shops and the modern waterfront complex of theatre and restaurants on the edge of town. This had been built after a collaboration between Deng Xiaoping and Lee Kwan Yew had brought huge investment from Singapore. Lee Kwan Yew was the fastidious leader of Singapore from 1959-1990 who made rules on hair length and chewing gum and the waterfront was as clean, efficient and modern as he might have wished. This area felt as Western and generic (as Singaporean in fact) as any-where I had seen in China and was more like a waterfront in Melbourne or Perth than Jiangsu. But as I sat down to eat in one of the lakeside restaurants, the 'National Federation of industry and commerce auto parts chamber of commerce pick up gear and accessories committee' was enjoying its annual celebration of raised performance and high quotas next door. The air was thick with smoke, the floor with chicken bones, the room thick with the noise of laughter and karaoke. This was not sterile Singapore; all was as it should be and my world was once more reassuringly Chinese.

Suzhou may once have been the centre for Chinese silk, but the centre of Chinese politics was Nanjing. China says that history is not linear but that everything repeats and Nanjing has been the victim of repetitious violence, revolution and mayhem. The city's position has excellent feng shui since the qi energy that forms on the city's lake is kept from blowing away by the purple and gold mountains that rear up behind. So Nanjing, whose name means 'Southern Capital'[19] was the Ming Dynasty capital of China under Emperor Hongwu from 1356 to 1420, the Taiping capital from 1851 to 1864[20] and the Republican capital from 1928 to 1937 and 1945 to 1949, before Mao reasserted the claim of Beijing.

Yet the mountains are more adept at catching pollution than qi now and despite such propitious geography the city has suffered more than most in modern times. Nanjing was the site of the 1842 treaty that was signed to cede Hong Kong to Britain and that granted European concessions and trading rights in Canton (Guangzhou), Ningpo (Ningbo), Amoy (Xiamen), Foochow (Fuzhou) and Shanghai (the renaming of most of the cities is probably all part of China's cleansing process) and ordered China to pay $21 million in compensation for the costs of the Opium War with 5% interest charged on late payment.

Modern China calls this agreement and all others signed with Europe from this period 'unequal treaties' and a source of shame, though it is hardly Nanjing's fault that the humiliation took place in that city

---

19 Beijing means 'Northern Capital, Xi'an is 'western peace'. Dongjing or 'Eastern Capital' is Tokyo which perhaps tells us something about the territorial designs of ancient China.

20 For more details on the chaos and slaughter of the Taiping rebellion led by the self professed brother of Christ Hong Xiquan see Guangxi chapter.

aboard HMS Cornwallis. Yet the shame of 1842 Nanjing is as nothing compared to the righteous indignation and fury of 1937.

Shanghai fell to the Japanese onslaught of World War II in early December 1937 and as the Kwantung army swung westwards, it was obvious that Nanking would be next. The city was softened up by a series of heavy bombing raids before the Japanese arrived at the massive city walls and forced entry. This was no mean feat. The walls were constructed between 1366 and 1386 and are 12 m high and 7 m wide; the largest city walls ever built. They were cemented by 200,000 workers using super strong mortar made from glutinous rice; every brick is stamped with details of where it came from, who made it and sometimes the date. Two thirds of the walls survive - the only city walls to largely escape the destructive modernising of the Communists and a stark contrast to the tragedy of Beijing's walls (see Beijing chapter).

There ensued an incomprehensible six-week orgy of violence by Japanese troops when 200,000 Nanjing civilians were murdered and 20,000 women aged 11 to 76 were raped. The Chinese government had encouraged the citizens of Nanjing to stay and defend their city. "All those who have blood and breath in them must feel that they wish to be broken as jade rather than remain whole as tile" said the government who locked the gates and fled to their new wartime capital of Chongqing.

The massacre was frenzied and the killings indiscriminate. War changes man's behaviour and the very nature of war is a contradiction of all those things that society holds dear - the sanctity of life and property, justice and notions of civilisation and morality - yet the Japanese behaviour in Nanjing was bestial and contradicted even when judged by the rules of war. These pages are not the place to attempt to describe the massacre in great detail and anyway others have tried to capture the events of those appalling six weeks more thoroughly and movingly than I ever could. Chief amongst these is Iris Chang whose 1997 book 'The Rape of Nanking' was published on the 60th anniversary of the massacre and was motivated in part by her own grandparents' stories about their escape from the whirlwind of Nanking. Chang was one of the main advocates of a congressional resolution designed to force a full Japanese apology for the massacre and met Hillary Clinton in 1999 to discuss the issue. The author argued that Japanese apologies were too vague and she confronted the Japanese ambassador to the United States on TV to force the issue. Chang suffered a nervous breakdown in 2004 attributed to sleep deprivation and depression; she was apparently deeply disturbed by much of the subject matter of her research on Nanjing. Her suicide note read 'Each breath is becoming hard for me to take - the anxiety can be compared to drowning in an open sea' and in many ways Chang was another victim of the tragedy of Nanking nearly 70 years after the events.

Most Westerners escaped the massacre, including many on the USS Panoy that was bombed and sunk by the Japanese air force on the Yangtze River on 12 December 1937. The USA was outraged enough to receive over $2 million in compensation and the Universal newsreel of the time is stiff with outrage at the 'war mad Japanese machine gunners raining lead mercilessly on everything that moved' despite the flying of the US flag, the prominence of which the newsreels refer to over and over again. Some Westerners stayed in Nanjing, including the now celebrated John Rabe, a German businessman who despite his Nazi party membership headed an international committee that established a 4 km² safety zone in the centre of Nanking with 25 refugee camps around the US embassy. The Japanese troops did not completely respect the zone and carried off hundreds of refugees from there to be raped or killed; Rabe's diary is full of accounts of the horror, his helplessness and his naive faith in Hitler to whom he wrote in 1938 imploring him to help put an end to the slaughter. The safety zone sheltered 200,000 from the massacre and Rabe's grave now sits in Nanjing's massacre memorial site, a tribute to this Far Eastern Oscar Schindler who the Chinese call 'a living Buddha'.

Chinese museums are invariably dull as dishwater but this one is in turns gripping and appalling with its wealth of personal accounts and remains of war and of what the museum called '28 mass slaughters and 858 occasional slaughters'. Individual testimony hung from every wall, ceiling and pillar because there were too many to fit in; the sheer volume of tragedy had outstripped the museum space. There were accounts of the 18 December Straw String Gorge massacre when 57,000 Chinese prisoners of war were killed, their bodies dumped in the Yangtze. The 10,000 corpse ditch was commemorated too and the killing contest between two Japanese officers that was covered in Tokyo newspapers like a sporting event with regular updates on the score every few days was reported too.

The museum was overwhelming and this is no bad thing since it is good be a little overwhelmed by the enormity of historical events on occasion. But I was hoping for some reconciliation, some acknowledgement that it was all a long time ago and we need to move on. A man approached me outside the museum by a huge white peace statue at the exit of a curvaceous and curly haired woman who looked not in the least Chinese. He asked what I thought of the museum and 'didn't it make me hate the Japanese?' Well no, it didn't though I was appalled by the events. The museum information insisted that 'people can create a better future by looking back in the past' and this is true, though a better future can also be had by forgiving, and I felt a certain reluctance to be told to look back on the past and think of peace by a nation that refuses to acknowledge it's own troubled recent past and has the largest standing army in the world.

The man told me that Japan should apologise, but they have in various forms nearly 50 times, though certainly not in the way that China demands and without the compensation that Germany has paid out for her crimes in World War II. He was adamant that Japan hasn't apologised at all because Nanking has emerged as a fundamental keystone in the construction of modern Chinese national identity. It has become necessary for the people to hate Japan, to break into spontaneous riots against all things Japanese, to throw stones at the Japanese football team (see Jilin chapter), to fight over distant disputed offshore islands and in modern Nanjing to ban all Japanese companies because the enemy from outside reduces focus on the inadequacies and cruelty of the government at home. China is a great 21st century power, a key player on the world stage and needs to stop playing the victim.

There was little mention of reconciliation but plenty of retribution in the museum. The final rooms in the building contained a ticking clock and the sound of a drop of water that fell every 12 seconds to remind us that this is how often someone died in Nanking, though the impact of this exhibit was compromised by an incongruous gift shop next door selling candy floss, souvenirs and bright pink sausages turning on a heated grill. Last of all were the details of the 25 Japanese war criminals convicted at the post-war tribunal and executed for their crimes, though only two of these are connected directly to the rape of Nanking[21].

One of these was General Matsui, who the tribunal decreed had ultimate responsibility for the 'orgy of crime' at Nanking because 'he did nothing, or nothing effective, to abate these horrors'. Matsui's conviction was just. He did nothing to help though it seems that even he had become dismayed by the full extent of Japanese army atrocities in Nanking. His press release from the 18th of December said 'I personally feel very sorry for the tragedies to the people, but the army must continue unless China repents [of what he does not explain]. Now in the winter, the season gives us time to reflect. I offer my sympathy, with deep emotion, to 1,000,000 innocent people'. Nobel laureate Elie Wiesel has said that to forget the Holocaust is to kill twice. Matsui's crocodile tear conditional 'apology' was far too little too late and though reconciliation is long overdue, China is right to remember those six weeks in Nanjing.

It was good to be in the fresh air of Zijin Shan Mountain above Nanjing after hours of introspection and regret at the museum. Yuhuatai Memorial to communist fighters killed by the Nationalists is up here on the site of the Garden of a fifth century monk who gave sermons so moving that flowers rained from the sky. So too is the Jiangsu National Security Education centre, a museum of spying that is not open to non-Chinese residents for 'security reasons' though no one seemed to mind when I asked people exiting the museum what was inside. I was allowed at least to visit the King of Borneo's tomb who died on Zijin Shan on a 15th century visit and also the huge 14th century Ming Xiaolong tomb that contains the remains of the only Ming emperor buried outside Beijing.

---

21   14 of these 25 convicted war criminals are interned at the Yasukuni Shrine in Tokyo. Japanese leaders still visit this place to honour Japan's war dead which for the Chinese is further evidence of the insincerity of Japanese apologies.

It was the Ming in Nanjing who became more outward looking than previous dynasties and encouraged the building of a massive fleet of ships for the eunuch Admiral Zheng He to explore the world. Zheng's treasure fleet of 317 ships certainly travelled all over Asia and as far as East Africa though there is speculation that some of the ships travelled beyond the Cape of Good Hope. The best-known proponent of this theory is Gavin Menzies who in his book '1421 - the year China discovered the world' hypothesized that ships from the treasure fleet had visited the Americas 71 years before Columbus and had circumnavigated the globe a century before Magellan. There have been vehement rebuttals of Menzies work from historians who argue he has been careless with sources and research though the idea of a Chinese fleet built in Nanjing to discover the world is an intriguing one. This is particularly true in light of the hundreds of years of Great Wall insularity that followed and that is only drawing to a close now as China constructs a new armada to travel the world[22].

The big pull on Purple Mountain is the Sun Yat Sen mausoleum. Sun is the father of modern China, the radical who spoke of the three principles of nationalism, democracy and the people's livelihood, and who still unites mainland Communists and nationalists on Taiwan[23]. He died prematurely from cancer in 1925 and his body was moved with great ceremony to the newly built Nanking mausoleum in May 1929. It was an elaborate trip in a copper coffin with soldiers in attendance who traveled by train, boat, car and finally horse and carriage to the slopes of the mountain. I climbed the 392 steps to the huge building that represent the 392 million Chinese in 1929 - there are few finer illustrations of Mao's shortsighted population policy after 1949 than a realisation that they'd need 1300 steps now. There was a 20% discount for 'models of morality' to the mausoleum on production of a certificate and I wondered why such pillars of the community should still have to pay 80%. I might have argued that I am a moral person too, but I didn't have a certificate to prove it, so I paid the full fare.

---

22   United States figures estimated that the Chinese navy totaled 62 submarines, 26 destroyers, 48 frigates and 18 missile boats in 2010.

23   For more details on Sun, see Shanghai chapter

It's a surprise that the blue nationalist tiles and the Guomindang sun symbols are undamaged inside the mausoleum - a sign of the respect accorded to Sun Yat Sen that superseded even the ravages of Red Guards. Inside the mausoleum, signs said 'silence' and 'salute' and statues of the great man in western and Chinese dress showed how he had united traditionalists and modernists in the new Republic. The body itself was buried beneath the viewing gallery so that everyone had to bow to look at him and I left thinking that modern China could use a new Sun Yat Sen, a man universally respected who might properly implement the three principles that the great man espoused.

The view of the city was fantastic from Purple Mountain, made better for not actually being *in* the throb of the city, and I imagined 19th-century British colonists, Taiping rebels and 20th-century Japanese soldiers standing here and looking at the town they had subdued below. I had to descend eventually and before long I was back in the bustle of cars and fake stores - Nanjing is famous for its knockoff brands; I saw a Bucks Star Coffee Shop, a Pizza Huh restaurant, Adidos shoes and a McDnoalds burger bar in the city. I was drawn irrevocably to the great river since the Yangtze is fundamental to so many Chinese cities; its turbulent waters and eternal flow hold a strange fascination for me. There is a special bridge over the Yangtze in Nanjing that was only the second to span the river after the famous 1957 bridge in Wuhan (see Hubei chapter). Unlike the Wuhan Crossing however, this bridge was built by Chinese labour and without Russian help since the Soviets had packed their bags and blueprints following a fallout between Khrushchev and Mao, claiming the Chinese could never build a bridge on their own.[24] The Russians took their 'make yourself an A-Bomb' kit with them too. How satisfying it must have been for China to build both, though it puzzles me that bridge took longer than Bomb (China exploded her first A-Bomb in 1964).

The bridge was completed in 1968 at the very height of cultural revolutionary fervour so it's a statement of Communist triumph as

---

24   China had called the USSR 'big brother' and the USSR had called China 'little brother' before the argument. The split was probably a relief to Mao, for who wants to be patronised in such a way?

much as a means of transport. Cars are on top and trains below on this huge four and a half km long double-decker structure, but all passengers and drivers above and below can see the huge statues of workers and red guards celebrating with little red books the construction of a mighty bridge with toil, determination, bricks and mortar, Mao Zedong thought and without interference from those damned Russians.

The bridge is a vantage point as well as monument and while Chinese history might be circular, the linear history of Nanjing was laid before me. From the top I could see the ancient walls and the modern city turning neon as the sun set. There were the shipyards, and the muddy river sending coal barges east that sat so low in the water that it seemed they might join the USS Panay on the riverbed. In the distance was the Purple Mountain and though Sun Yat Sen is a mighty figure in China's past, his monument was invisible, dwarfed by the mountain's steep slopes. I could see the old town from here too where tragedy and triumph had walked arm in arm for hundreds of years. It was hemmed in now by busy roads and office blocks; a forest of shopping centres where armies of consumers were doing their bit for the modern Chinese economic miracle but where different armies with different ambitions for the Southern Capital had once prevailed. But Tongli was not visible; neither its sinuous waterways that carried silk to Suzhou nor the gardens with their rosebushes and erotic surprises to serve as reminder that there will always be a new generation created to forget the mistakes of the last.

PART 2

SOUTH OF THE YANGTZE

MACAU

澳门

27 sq km
Population 500 000

At the gambling table, there are no fathers and sons.

Chinese Proverb

I had never imagined that it was possible to travel slower than walking speed until I visited Macau. On an oppressively hot day outside the 600-year-old A-Ma Temple beneath Barra Hill I decided to flee from the sun on one of the curious contraptions called trishaws, lined up in three wheeled profusion by the Temple wall. Part tricycle and part rickshaw, there I could sit and drink and perspire in the shade and feel the breeze in my hair that sighed over the Gate of Understanding from the becalmed sea of the Porto Exterior.

Contrary it may have been, but I chose the oldest driver I could see who sat cross-legged by his bike in white vest, ankle socks and shorts pulled up beyond his midriff. He was more than half asleep and raising a wary eye lid as I approached and looked not unlike the unfortunate and massive turtle imprisoned in a box outside the temple as a symbol of luck and longevity, his shell half covered in the shiny wishes of Macanese Pataca coins.

I have since rationalised my choice in humanitarian terms; that no one would ever pick the old tortoise man over his younger sprightly rivals and that he would welcome the business. But the truth is I just wanted to see if those ancient, sun burnished and tinder dry legs were capable of turning the pedals and making the trishaw move.

They did after a fashion. We set off over the temple precinct cobbles at the speed of a glacier eroding its way from high plateau to valley. By the time we had circumscribed Sai Van Lake and approached the soaring Macau Tower, we had entered an altered universe where time and space have no meaning. Matter turned to antimatter as the Earth spun backwards and the great continents drifted inexorably apart. I seemed to see and hear everything with a new intensity; the beads of sweat on the old man's neck, the bright light reflecting on the lake, the slow rotation of knotted calves and metronome click of the trishaw's chain-set.

Such was my repose that I hardly noticed the pedestrians overtaking and the other trishaws racing along, peddled by men who might have been a quarter of my man's age. And then one of those pedestrians who sauntered past, peered lugubriously into my one mph sanctuary and laughed and suddenly I felt like a fool. Who was this lumbering, oversized and hairy westerner slurping a cream soda while an ancient and venerable old man toiled in front under a hot sun? Surely I had become an allegory for all that foreign oppression; a true white man's burden. Why didn't I just shout 'chop chop' at my coolie and be done with it?

So I called the trishaw to a halt, though there was precious little difference between this and the journey that had gone before. I gave the tortoise a sizeable tip, to assuage my guilt and his face lit up as he signaled he would wait for me to continue my tour. But as I looked back at the road we had traveled, the A-Ma Temple was clear in view, not 300 metres away. The trip had taken 20 minutes. So I declined his offer since I had a ferry to catch in three days and the terminal was a full 2 miles away; I stepped out of my chariot of fire and readjusted to the giddying pace of a gentle stroll.

It wouldn't take long to gently stroll over the whole of Macau, since this former Portuguese possession is only 27 km² in size. But what a wealth of history and interest is packed in. There's a seething mass of people packed in too - nearly 20,000 live in every square kilometre - so Macau could hardly fail to have human interest.

But the first people I went to see in Macau were all dead. Jesuits arrived here in the 1500s, but where there are Catholics, Protestants are never far behind and the old Protestant cemetery beside the Jardin Luis de Camoes stands as mute witness to their presence in Macau. Space is at such a premium that it's a wonder that this collection of deceased traders and adventurers still exists so close to the centre of town. Yet this quiet and shady spot has been restored and repaired so that we who haven't shuffled off this mortal coil can appreciate those who have.

The artist George Chinnery was buried here in 1852, who fled debt in England and India and wound up in Macau. His paintings are good though probably not great, but are one of the very few records of the people and landscape of the Pearl River Delta at that time. So they have a special interest for people familiar with Macau, Hong Kong and Guangdong; places that surround the Delta and which have changed irrevocably and impossibly in the last 150 years, so that Chinnery's pictures might be of a different planet rather than merely a different century.

Chinnery's most famous painting is of Doctor Colledge in 1838 re-storing the site of an almost blind Chinese woman. The doctor operated the first medical service run by Westerners for Chinese patients and has an almost messianic quality in Chinnery's picture. He lays his hand on the head of the woman who sits pale and submissive while her son, with an extraordinarily long pigtail known as a queue which mocks Colledge's bald pate, hands the doctor a note of thanks and kneels at his feet.

As a statement of Western compassion for and superiority over the natives, the Colledge picture is unsurpassed, but it's Chinnery's sketches of the back streets and port of Macau that I like best, where peddlers, porters, food sellers and fishermen go about their business in broad wicker-hatted daylight and in the shade of Catholic Church and Temple. They show an uncomplicated life that is utterly past, though the temples remain and isn't that my trishaw driver as a very young man crouched ready for business in the corner of one of his sketches?

Chinnery painted Dr. Morrison as well. This was no medical doctor, but a man of religious conviction who was healing souls. Morrison has a rather handsome face, gorgeous ringlets and full, sensual lips, though such earthly diversions will have been of little interest to the doctor who is translating the Bible in Chinnery's picture and whose mind was occupied with altogether loftier thoughts.

Morrison was the first Protestant missionary in China and produced the first Chinese version of Old and New Testament after years of lonely work. I don't have much truck with missionaries as a rule - all that saving the natives and man cannot enter heaven but through faith in Jesus Christ seems a trifle dismissive of the majority of the world's seven billion people whose gods don't walk on water or know the first thing about carpentry. But I can't help but admire the bloody-minded persistence of Mildred Cable, Gladys Aylward, Robert Morrison and 100 others whom God called to harvest Chinese souls.

Morrison faced resistance from Chinese officials who opposed proselytising and encouraged foreigner visitors only if they brought knowledge of useful arts like medicine and weaponry. Fierce resistance came too from entrenched Catholic interest in Macau which fought his right to preach as if the Reformation had never happened. But the doctor persevered. When asked on his arrival whether he expected to make any spiritual impact on the Chinese he answered 'No sir, but I expect God will'. Despite the ban on Christian books published in Chinese, he maintained a resolutely upbeat approach and utter conviction that he was performing God's work. Morrison learned to read and write Mandarin and Cantonese, despite the ban on teaching the celestial language to barbarian tongues and spent 16 years translating the Bible into Chinese. He was clearly not completely immune to carnal pleasure and a woman's soft touch; Morrison put his curly locks and sensual lips to good use and fathered nine children from two marriages. Yet his life seems to have been terribly lonely as he perched on hard boards in a dark study and wrestled with language and translation, the condemnation of Chinese and Catholics ringing in his ears. By 1834 his family had returned to England and his solitude was complete before his death in that same year and burial in Macau.

Chinnery's grave in the old Protestant cemetery is all lofty ostentation - a vertical slab of classically designed granite complete with Grecian urns. Morrison's grave is altogether harder to root out and sits in the corner of this quiet acre next to the miniature grave of his infant child. The tomb is littered with flowers that have fallen from the branches of the jasmine trees that flourish in this Protestant soil, and a profusion of blue dragonflies dart quickly around, disturbing the unquiet slumbers of the sleepers in that quiet earth and filling the languid space with their own missionary zeal.

Morrison's grave is a large horizontal slab with a long epitaph that carves out his achievements. I stared down at this with mixed feelings; a life well lived no doubt, but one defined by single-minded solitude and whose purpose and drive are somewhat discredited in a 21st century world that feels no such urge to convert and to save. 'Blessed are the dead' reads the slab 'that they may rest from their labours'. Amen to that.

Morrison would be appalled by modern Macau; the city has become a monument to avarice and greed, the gambling capital of the world, the city of 'if onlys' and pipe dreams, and I confess that I feel a little appalled too. Macau Island used to be the centre of this, and there are still some notable casinos here, but the gambling trade has recently shifted to the central island of Taipa. The casinos on Macau Island are old school and dominated by casino mogul Stanley Ho who had an absolute monopoly on gambling in Macau for 40 years.

Ho gambling is best exemplified by the Hotel Lisboa, a gaudy pineapple shaped structure that was the original Casino in Macau. Opened in 1962, the place reeks of that era; its gaudy carpets and ugly chandeliers have borne witness to a million broken dreams. In these rooms, Jackie Kennedy beehived women in capri pants or full skirted ballgowns with tight waist and low decolletage once leaned on the shoulders of single breasted narrow lapel Chelsea booted men while the roulette wheel span. I imagine Sammy Davis Jr or Dean Martin on the stage at the Lisboa and feel vaguely disappointed when I go outside and my taxi is a Toyota and not a Chevrolet or a Pontiac Firebird.

This is not to say that I'm a regular in the casinos of Macau. Frankly, I find the places a bit scary. All those gorgeous Chinese and Filipino girls taking my bets see my rabbit in headlights expression and know that I have very little idea what I'm doing and my careful wagers of 50 and 100 patacas look babyish next to the high roller stakes of the cigar chewing stereotypes next to me. Despite my timidity its amazing how fast my pathetically small pile of chips disappears, and when I make a bad bet and lose the last of my reserves, I instinctively know that there is no point in telling the croupier that I didn't mean it and can I have my money back?

Gambling is serious work in Macau and I'm struck by how little anyone seems to be enjoying themselves. Each bet is placed and received with a grim face and a barely perceptible nod of the head or tap on the baize in acknowledgement. No one talks and the only signs of energy are the great clouds of billowing tobacco smoke that fill the room. Mostly I don't like casinos because I don't know how to play though this can lead to a blithe and misguided cheerful optimism too. Pontoon I can manage, but all those tables of Fortune 8, Texas Hold 'em and craps are a mystery. I like to watch, but even an hour of voyeurism leaves me none the wiser. Bells ring, plastic chips are scattered across the table and claimed by the croupier in great greedy handfuls while I narrow my eyes and try to look like a hustler picking my moment to pounce and not someone who'd rather be at home playing Cluedo or Happy Families with my kids.

Even the slot machines are mean here; a mystery of spinning wheels and flashing lights that look nothing like the old James Bond fruit machine in my pub back home (Roger Moore era, max payout 10 quid). They call them 'hungry tigers' in Macau and they never get tired of fresh meat like me.

If the Hotel Lisboa will take the button down collar, vintage shirt off your back, this is nothing to its evil cousin behind. The Grand

Lisboa is the 261metre tall space age relative of the vintage hotel next door. It's Darth Vader to Captain Scarlet, Stealth bomber to Sopwith Camel, Black Sabbath to Frank Sinatra. This 2008 creation is Stanley Ho's old money response to the nouveau riche pretenders on Taipa. It's an extraordinary mirror glassed vertical monument to hedonism that looks as if it could come alive and destroy us all in a flaming Armageddon of blazing roulette wheels. Inside is the 218 carat 'Star of Stanley Ho' flawless diamond, the largest of its kind in the world. There are also 268 mass gaming tables, 786 hungry tigers and 430 Hotel rooms where luckless punters can sleep off their losses of the night before.

If there is a more vulgar and tasteless building in the world than the Grand Lisboa, then I haven't seen it yet. Bentleys are lined up outside in 'look what you could have' ranks and the visitor is piped in past rows of ATMs and through the great revolving door by the sort of lounge bar jazz that has no beginning or end, and no discernible tune. Inside, every conceivable surface is covered by every conceivable texture, shape and colour that speaks of luxury. Diamonds, crystal, jade, marble, seashell, animal skins, leather and ivory are shoehorned side-by-side without reference to taste or moderation. Great jade carvings and Golden Dragon boats sit expensively inside glass cases and the doormen smile ingratiatingly, dressed in ludicrous orange velvet.

For this is the palace of excess, the antithesis of the current European vogue for minimalism and discretion. Yet Europe is well represented in the casino mall by rows of jewellery and clothing boutiques, ideally placed for those lucky souls who leave the casino with money in their satin lined pockets. I wrote the names of the shops as I walked through the mall; Mont Blanc, Swiss Watch Co, Patek Philippe-Geneve, Chaumet-Paris, Stefano Ricci, Carates from Dominique France, Gerard Pervegaux, Van Cleef and Arpels, Titoni of Switzerland. The more European sounding the better and better still if the name Paris, Milan or Geneva was attached and even the daily cabaret in the casino concert Hall was 'from Paris'('a wild and sexy dance - not to be missed'). I'm not sure what conclusions to draw; a vogue in the Far East for all things European? An ironic, subtle and post-modern reaffirmation of Western control of China after the 20th century Communist rejection of foreign imperialism? Or maybe it's just shopping.

But despite Stanley's diamond edged hubris, he's been usurped by a newcomer on the block. For on Taipa is the mother of all gaming halls; a vast behemoth called The Venetian. This massive casino and hotel complex complete with gondola rides on a replica San Luca Canal is the largest hotel in Asia and the fourth largest building in the world by area. There are 800 gaming tables and 3400 slot machines here to spirit away your money more efficiently than ever before, though they try to be nice about it and in every room there is a sign that warns visitors to 'bet for fun only, not to make money', though neither option is a realistic choice for me.

The Venetian is built and owned by the US Sands Corporation, determined to make Macau the Las Vegas of the East. Over 50% of all revenue in Macau is now raised by gambling and 30 million visitors a year from Hong Kong and mainland China roll the dice here, so that Macau's annual gambling revenue of $7 billion a year is easily the highest in the world; not so much Las Vegas of the East, though Las Vegas might be the Macau of the West.

This mega-casino is another homage to Europe, though St Marks Square and the cobbled piazzas 'neath painted fluffy cumulus are a strangely listless affair and for all the authentic O Sole Mios and striped shirts of the gondoliers, the boats are electric powered and the San Luca Canal smelt of chlorine. 'This could be you' trumpeted signs by the canal with photos of cheerful Chinese, thumbs aloft in their gondolas, but on this sunny Saturday people were far too busy at the Red Dragon, Golden Fish, Phoenix and Imperial House gaming tables to be messing about in boats.

Shooting at the moon speculation has long defined Macau since licensed gambling was introduced in 1847 in an attempt to win back wealth that had recently been lost to the burgeoning British port of Hong Kong. Until Western style gambling was introduced in the 20th century, only Chinese games were played and it is still possible to see groups of Macanese locals hunched over folding tables in alleys playing Mahjong and Fan Tan in the hot afternoon and early evening as the lights flicker on at the Venetian and the Grand Lisboa.

For despite the pace of change, the old Macau can still be found amongst the baccarat. It is most likely to be seen on the island of Coloane, though this most southerly part of Macau is no longer an island at all since the hungry land reclamation of the Cotai Strip made necessary by the building of all those casinos has joined Coloane with Taipa like Siamese twins.

The Portuguese colony at Macau predates the British at Hong Kong by 200 years and on Coloane can be seen that curious hybrid of Portugal and southern China that has been all but consumed elsewhere. Coloane village, hemmed in by Cheoc Van (Bamboo) Beach and Hac Sa (Black Sand) Beach, is especially redolent of this. The village square here serves as an authentic juxtaposition to the artificiality of St Marks Square in nearby Venice and even the soaring Grand Lisboa can't be seen if you sit here by the sea with a Macau beer and a plate of bacalhau salted cod. The square is bounded by the 1928 Chapel of St Francis Xavier whose claustrophobic Catholic interior contains a relic of the venerated saint's arm bone. When I shuffled through, shafts of sunlight lit the chubby limbs of a cherubically baroque Jesus and two middle-aged Chinese men were knelt before the relic. They seemed unlikely Catholics with their aftershave, leather jackets and mobile phones and I wondered what their prayers were for. "Please O sainted Catholic apostle; make the numbers even on the roulette table".

There is a 1910 monument to the routing of local pirates at the opposite end of Coloane Square - a reminder of how Macau has changed in the last 100 years - though I was most interested in Lord Stow's cafe around the corner. This ramshackle place on the waterfront is the best spot in Macau to buy Pasteis de Nata egg tartlets hot from the oven, and to sit on the water's edge and talk to Sunday cyclists who, glistening with sweat, rest their carbon ultra lightweight bikes against the sea wall and take a break from hunting the Coloane Hills and their Tour de France dreams.

Great cyclists never had a pasteis de nata break or jostled for position in the peleton with crumbs of flaky pastry down their cycling vests and I venture to suggest that the abundance of pastry products is the most important reason why there has never been a Tour champion born in Macau. For the culinary temptations are too great. In Macau exists a melee of Portuguese and Chinese foods that gourmands would no doubt call a 'fusion'. Whenever I take the short hop by ferry from Hong Kong, I seem to spend my whole time eating. Chorizo sausage, casquinha stuffed crab, almonds and olives flavoured with too much olive oil and jaggery palm sugar are followed by serradura pudding made with crushed biscuits, cream and condensed milk (the sort of dessert a five-year-old would make if given free rein in a kitchen) and the ubiquitous nata egg tarts. Here also is the influence of other Portuguese colonies - curry from Goa, sweet potatoes from Brazil, chili shrimps and galinha d'Africana chicken flavoured by turmeric and cinnamon. As I waddle and burp around the casinos and pity those poor souls grim faced at the dice, I wonder if it's time for dinner and accept that every man has his addiction.

Macau still finds room for God amidst the hedonism and on the Alto de Coloane Hill stands a 19.99 metre white statue of A-Ma and the enormous Tian Hou Temple. Macau's name derives from the goddess A-Ma who elsewhere in China is called Tin Hau or Guanyin and A-Ma Gau means 'the bay of A-Ma'.

Legend says that A-Ma was refused passage on a rich merchants junk to Canton and hitched a ride on a poor fishing boat instead. A storm blew up and wrecked all of the grand ostentatious boats; only the old fishing boat remained - a parable indeed for all of Macau's vainglorious casinos. On her return A-Ma walked to the top of Barra Hill and in a glowing light ascended to heaven, though you'd have a job to see her glow in modern Macau what with all the neon light pollution.

I wandered down hill from the temple glowing too with the exertion of a walk in 90% humidity above a polluted panorama of reclamation, feverish construction, casinos and high-rises and wondered if I liked modern Macau at all. There is certainly a brute magnificence to what has happened here; a city cannot be preserved in aspic and I suppose construction of ancient Rome had its detractors and naysayers too when another green space was sacrificed for Forum, Coliseum and Pantheon.

Ancient Rome exists in Macau too and is nestled at Fishermans' Wharf next to Arabia, Tang Dynasty China and a mighty glass fibre volcano that 'erupts' at 5 PM every day. This monument to kitsch with bumper cars and war games is rather well done, but was as deserted as the canals and shops of Venice save for the Chinese centurion seated in the shade, his gladius and galea laid aside and lorica segmentata pulled open at the chest as he cooled off and smoked a cigarette with scant attention to period detail. Macau changes so fast that the next big thing becomes old hat in no time at all and of course every attraction above ground is in competition with the warren of activity elsewhere. I wondered how long it would be before the centurion put away his leg greaves for an orange velvet croupiers suit instead.

Young men in Macau don't just have Julius Caesar or Stanley Ho's army as a career choice. They can also be a triad. Macau is the strongest remaining bastion of this secret organisation, despite a marked improvement in public security and crime since the 1999 handover to China. The situation was so bad in the 1960s and 70s that when Portugal offered to hand back the colony to the mainland, China refused since they had no way of battling the gambling, prostitution and crime rife there.

The triad movement was started as a resistance to the Qing Dynasty in the 18th century when the Society of Heaven and Earth was formed to overthrow the Manchu emperor and restore Han Chinese rule. Triad members moved south to Hong Kong and Macau after the 1949 communist takeover and involvement in the murky underworld of casinos became an obvious attraction to them. The situation became particularly violent in the 1990s when the outgoing Portuguese all but gave up the fight against organised crime and the three main Triad societies - 14K, Shui Fong and Wo Shing Yee - battled for the criminal spoils from casinos, loansharking, prostitution and protection rackets. 30 people were killed in gun battles, fire bombings and knife fights. In 1999, gang boss Broken Tooth Koi was sentenced to 15 years in prison and sits there still behind razor wire beside the pretty egg tart village of Coloane.

Triad language and methods of operating are particularly grisly. The traditional weapon is a kitchen meat cleaver nicknamed 'chopping knife' and fingers go missing with alarming regularity when rival gangs have a disagreement. Koi cursed and shouted at his accusers in court and warned 'Bullets will have no eyes and knives will have no feelings' through the press, which almost amounts to gangster poetry.

Triad oaths are possessed of poetry too and those who join the organisation sign up to death by five thunderbolts or a myriad of swords if they betray the brotherhood. Yet modern revenues come mostly from a business called 'bate-ficha'; the selling of chips for commission through gaming promoters - a thoroughly prosaic, businesslike and bureaucratic arrangement that belies the ancient oaths, mystique and elaborate tattoos that the triads wear. A once noble and political society emasculated by greed.

Triads once controlled the brothels on Rua de Felicidade too. Now the cobbled avenue is lined with pastellorias selling pressed roast meat and cakes though I can't help but think that the name 'pressed roast meat' somehow evokes the more carnal past of this street whose name means `Street of Happiness`. The centre of Macau is a chequerboard of black-and-white cobbles and retains a Mediterranean air despite the massive casino Grand Lisboa rearing up and grabbing attention like a spoilt child behind colonnades and baroque churches. The old 17th-century Fortaleza de Monte fortress from where cannonballs scattered the invading Dutch is here and nearby a stubby lighthouse sits on Guia Hill, the oldest in Asia but now thoroughly dwarfed by all that is new. The town's centrepiece is the third in a trinity of squares after the brashness of St Marks and the egg tart square of Coloane.

Largo de Senado or Senate Square is the traditional heart of Macau framed by the Leal Senado Loyal Senate, whose interior courtyard high walls are decorated by Mediterranean blue tiles, and the 17th-century Sao Domingos Church. The cobblestones here form sinuous black and white waves and it was in the square at last that I found crowds who were not hunched over gaming tables. It wasn't always coffee shop tranquillity though; the square was the focus of cultural revolutionary riots in 1966 when students entered the Senate building to cite the quotations of Mao Zedong and sing revolutionary songs. They pulled down the statue of Colonel Vicente Nicolau de Mesquita, a 19th-century Portuguese general who had pacified the Chinese at nearby Baishaling Fort in 1849. In later years the poor Colonel was racked by depression and on March 3, 1880 murdered his wife and daughter at their fashionable home on Largo de Bica do Lilau in an almighty fit of pique before throwing himself in the river.

Such behaviour begs the question why the Colonel got a statue at all, or perhaps such stone commemoration is a natural consequence of do as you like colonialism and what's a little murder set against the subduing of so many natives? Yet the Colonel is an aberration, for much of what Portugal represented in Macau was benign and munificent. In Hong Kong the British ruled and imposed bureaucracy and cutthroat commercialism. The Portuguese in Macau integrated and ate egg tarts.

But they did Catholicise and up the cobbled hill past the pastellorias is Macau's most famous example of religious zeal. The massive church of Sao Paolo was ruined by fire in 1853 but the shell has been propped up and preserved and serves as an altar and a front door to the city. How appropriate that a facade should be the most famous landmark in all of Macau, for nothing is real in this Chinese city of gambling and illusion and of get rich quick happiness and pretence.

GUANGXI

广西

220 150 sq km
Population 49 million

'I often sent pictures of the hills of Guilin which I painted to friends back home, but few believed what they saw.'

Fan Chengda; Chinese Song Dynasty scholar.

Chinese provinces are like double-decker buses; you can travel for miles without a real glimpse of beauty unsullied by crowds and industry but sometimes two come along at once. Guangxi is like this. The north is all ravishing rice terraces and rustic minority villages built of aged timbers and further south is the karst scenery around Yangshuo that could well be China's most famous landscape of all.

The jumping off point for all this verdant loveliness, these Elysian Fields, is the city of Guilin whose very name is enough to send many Chinese into raptures. I mentioned my visit once to a shopkeeper in Beijing who congratulated me on my good taste and proclaimed it 'the finest place under the heavens', which seemed a rather archaic and poetic phrase from a man selling plasters, aspirins and condoms.

Guilin is the single most visited place in China, though many Chinese who come here get no further than the city, unaware that Guangxi's real charm lies elsewhere. I alighted the train, stunned and sleepless from 10 hours of Chinese songs piped into my ears; Ming Dynasty melodies had almost provided sweet repose, but there had always been a strident cultural revolutionary anthem just around the corner to startle me awake and test my socialist credentials. My salesmen companions had slept soundly enough and at times I was almost grateful for another rendition of 'The East is Red' since it drowned out the noise of the man whose toe poking through a hole in his sock and industrial snoring and wheezing are indelibly and irrevocably imprinted on my memory.

I had assumed that the music captive train audience was all part of that sinister broader plan, that indoctrination, that stubborn washing of brains that are a one-party state specialty. It was not until 7am the next morning that I discovered the rotating volume switch under the plastic peonies on the table that enabled me to turn the infernal music down, down and 'click' off entirely. My snoring companion in need of socks and his friends must have known of the switch. They were no doubt puzzled and probably infuriated by the foreigner who wanted to listen to that bloody music all night.

Guilin train station is a foretaste of the city beyond; quiet, manageable of size, modern and clean with some Qing Dynasty flourishes and attempts at greenery. No biblical Xi'an station crowds or Shanghai ruthlessness here; the sun shone, no driver tried to capture and condemn my bag to taxi servitude or shouted 'very cheap' with no idea where I wanted to go. Even the pigeons strutting the station forecourt looked content.

'Guilin' means 'forest of sweet osmanthus'. This might be overstating things slightly, though rows of these fragrant trees stand guard over the Li River along Binjian Lu. The river was a hive of activity today though not with industrial barges carrying coal to other riverside towns in China, but with tourist boats heading downstream into the twisted jumble of peaks in the Guangxi countryside.

Guilin has a taste of the strange, otherworldly limestone hills that dot the province in their tens of thousands. Wave Subduing Hill and Folded Brocade Hill swell improbably from the riverbank and across the River Li is the Seven Stars Park where hill after hill rises and falls and where each folds into another like a child's drawing of hills.

The karsts are a unique geological feature peculiar to this part of China. North of the city on the border of Guizhou, the hills are cone shaped with shallow sides called fengcong peak clusters. Guilin hills and countryside south are called fenglin or peak forest and grow isolated and vertical like massive old trees. Locals say the scenery is as pretty as a watercolour; a singularly appropriate idiom since it's these peaks and this scenery which feature in countless Chinese paintings that until this moment I had believed were a romanticised version of the Chinese countryside, since no hills could possibly look like that.

The Li River and the karsts also feature on the back of the Chinese twenty yuan banknote. Guilin is a town of tourists as much as sweet smelling osmanthus, and a local guide approached me and offered a special price on his 'Chinese banknote tour'. He had clearly judged me a man who liked to put a few miles under his legs since this was an extravagant trip on offer. We would visit the 20 yuan Li River naturally, but then needed to race to the one yuan West Lake near Shanghai, the five yuan Huangshan Mountains in Anhui, the distant 50 yuan Tibetan Potala Palace and storm north to the Great Hall of the People on Tiananmen Square that features on the 100 yuan note. Rampant forgery prevents China producing denominations higher than 100 yuan, though the guide would doubtless take me to any 500 or 1000 yuan destination I wanted, however improbably distant it might be.

I said no of course since I didn't have 6 months to spare but wonder how much he would have charged for this long march across hundreds of Chinese miles and how did he propose we travel our banknote tick box itinerary? A white Toyota saloon with a missing wing mirror was idling by the side of the road and I wondered if we would go to Lhasa in that? Unlikely of course, but it had go faster stripes and a magnetic compass sellotaped to the dashboard so we might just have made it. There was also a cassette player and a teetering pagoda of tapes piled on the passenger seat - more than enough Chinese music to recreate my train ride of the night before.

The decision to place Mao's face on the front of every banknote was a no-brainer for the bureaucrats, though the podgy and self-satisfied Mao they picked looks like he has chronic wind and seems an odd choice. The reverse side must have been much more complicated and could equally have featured such typical national scenes as Terracotta Warriors, Great Wall or foreign visitors looking bewildered and confused as locals shriek 'waiguoren' at them and ask for photos. The choice says a lot about the values of China and the things in which the nation takes pride; unsurpassed natural beauty (one, five, 10 and 20 yuan), national unity and control (50 yuan) and strong government (100 yuan). The other great national obsessions are food and military might. If ever a 500 yuan note is issued it should feature a soldier slurping a giant bowl of noodles on the reverse side of a flatulent Mao.

Seven Stars Park was deserted and rather lovely with views across the river to the bustle of Guilin crowded around the fenglin karsts that towered over houses and shops. The zoo at the exit of the park was a thoroughly depressing prison of concrete enclosures so I hurried past and stared at the floor instead of the pitiful parrots, the miserable monkeys, the sad snakes and the dangerously depressed ducks. The partially perky perching peacocks by the gift shop were being treated with little dignity, but at least they looked happy. Their gainful employ was to squat either side of romantic couples on a wicker swing chair, every inch of which was festooned in plastic roses of a red so gaudy it could only have come from a tin and which put me in mind of Alice in Wonderland playing card workers and off with their heads Chinese local officials.

Being alone and slightly grumpy after a sleepless night, I was immune to the charms of the brightly plumed birds and have no photographic record of my visit here. I stayed and watched some couples express their love instead and laughed at every soft focus photo that clunked from the grubby printer (price one Potala Palace), since every courting couple possessed the faint look of terror that comes from having a large bird perched close behind your head that could at any moment seize a soft ear in a sharp beak.

Such is the otherworldly freakiness of Guangxi's landscape, that when the Song Dynasty scholar Fan Chengda posted home his sketches of the hills, his friends thought that he had lost his mind or else invented surrealism centuries before Picasso painted both eyes on one side of a woman's head. More recently, George Lucas saw the potential of the place and used Guangxi as the planet Kashyyyk a long time ago in a galaxy far, far away. Lucas has fallen back here on the old sci-fi device of using at least two consecutive letters in a made up word to lend a planet or person mystique[25] though Guangxi is mysterious enough without hairy wookies battling a droid army or a little green man with a light sabre and confused syntax, because karst hills so many it has hmm. (this feeble Star Wars joke may only be intelligible to my male readers without girlfriends or wives).

It seems that almost every one of the 70,000 karsts in Guangxi has a name, and many caves created by the drip, drip, drip of water on limestone have monikers too. Wind Cave and Pearl Cave are famous in Guilin but their notoriety pales compared to Reed Flute Cave on the edge of town, at whose entrance clumps of grass once grew that were suitable for the making of whistles. There are no reeds today under the tramp of 10 000 tourist feet come to see the Crystal Palace of the Dragon King which was once used as an air raid shelter for some of the town's one million World War II refugees. It's a pity that the garish lights that festoon the cave today weren't there in the 1940s as they would have made escape from the marauding Japanese army and the privations of war so much more *festive*.

China has an unusual approach to speleology. What might look better in its original and ancient form is awash with coloured lights. When visiting a cave in China, it's advisable to wear sunglasses or hang

---

25   see Klaatu from 'The day the earth stood still', Zenn-la, the home of the Silver Surfer and the planet Aaamazzara from Star Trek.

behind the tour groups and wait for the lights to trip out so that you actually feel that you're in a cave rather than Las Vegas. Chinese caves are the campest in the world with their stalactites backlit in sky blue and water chutes glowing under a fiery pink. I've even seen escalators and a mirror ball in a Chinese cavern whose lights danced and played coquettishly on the limestone walls.

The journey back to the city seemed drab and grey after the technicolor of the cave, like returning to Kansas from Oz. They should light the Guilin karsts in rainbow hues too, though China might need several dams along the Li River to provide the power to do so. A select few *have* been illuminated including the Elephant Trunk Hill along the river who dips his nose in the water and is said to be the calcified remains of an imperial baggage pachyderm that turned to stone rather than rejoin the emperor's army. Lights also shone on the Dixiu San Solitary Beauty Peak in the centre of town - the king of all the Guilin hills within the walls of the Jiangjiang Princes' City.

This palace but not quite a palace was built in the 14th century for the Ming Prince Zhou Shouqian, 34 years before the Forbidden City in Beijing. 14 Jiangjiang princes of 12 generations lived in the walled compound which now serves as Guilin's University, but stone slabs at the entrance have clouds but no dragons - a reminder to the men inside to know the correct order of things and an indicator that this was a place of princes but not kings. Solitary Beauty Peak is the place where the poet Yan Yanzhi carved the first poem to praise the beauty of the local scenery over 800 years ago. 'Guilin's water and mountains are the best under the sky' proclaimed Yan, and the Song Dynasty tourist coach parties must have arrived in their droves.

There are caves inside Solitary Beauty Peak too, but these are far more sedate and understated than the acid trip at Reed Flute. These caverns contain carved poems, some Buddha Statuary and flowers planted at their approach. The curiously white stalactites inside are lit not by twinkling fairy lights but the shafts of dusty afternoon Guangxi winter sunlight through windows that have been hollowed out and give glimpses of the city beyond.

But the best views of Guilin are from the top of Solitary Beauty Peak. I panted up the 306 steps to the apex of the 'southern pillar of the sky' and watched the twinkling lights of the town spark to life from my solitary and beautiful perch. My attention was drawn not to the streets or the buses, the market or the Li River that snaked through it all. I had eyes only for the South; for the twisted fangs and crenellated ridges of 70,000 karst peaks - shadowy growths in the gathering gloom. There was the watercolour perfect China of Fan Chengda's countryside; there was the planet of Kashyyyk.

I teased and tantalized myself by heading North first, away from the other worldly hills and into a land of forests and rice terraces that claw out an existence from steep sided hills and reach their apogee near Longsheng on the Guizhou border. The journey here was pastoral through dappled sunlight and into burgeoning hills that were rounded and frankly normal compared to the jagged snarls I had seen from the top of Solitary Beauty Peak. The bus stopped so that passengers could pick Guangxi oranges from bushes that sagged under the weight of fruit by the roadside and as I crouched between leaf and branch, the scent of orange blossom became deliciously overpowering as it was stirred to life by the early spring sunshine.

This is Zhuang country, China's largest minority group who comprise 30% of Guangxi's population. Their religion is Daoist and animist which creates a rather appealing mix of tolerance and empathy for other living things. Dogs are especially venerated, but buffalo are also given birthdays in Zhuang villages, when on the 8th day of the 4th lunar month, these great beasts of the plough are washed and groomed and given the day off.

Daoism is based on the writings of Lao Tzu, the ancient Chinese monk who promoted non-competitiveness in all things and a refusal to compel events to happen; stubborn and inflexible things break easily and a Daoist should be modest and willing to overcome force with gentleness. Yet these gentle and fatalistic people have carved and manipulated their mountainous landscape and made it yield in a most dramatic and determined way.

The road to the mountainside Zhuang village of Ping'an is a dramatic sweep of hairpin bends that reveal unbroken panoramas of forest and hills and a sky today that was blue and speckled with ragged clouds such as it never is in Chinese cities. The hills are called The

Dragon's Backbone and are made geometric by a series of rice terraces that form uneven steps down to the valley floor. It is at Ping'an that this Herculean effort of agriculture becomes most dramatic and uniform and from the village the slopes assume the character of a 3D contour map of the countryside, a perfect visual representation of height above sea level that would cause a geography teacher to become very overexcited.

Villagers have gouged fields from every metre of land in order to cultivate rice on these hills by constructing terraces and changing what is vertical into horizontal. The hills are so steep that the fields are often very narrow; so narrow in fact that they are ploughed by humans not oxen since there is insufficient room for animals to turn around. "Small enough for a frog to hop over in 3 hops" one villager told me, "small enough to be covered by a coat" said another.

Deficiency in field size is compensated by size of hair in Ping'an. The women here wear their tresses very long and wrap them in shiny black coils like a turban or somnambulant serpent on top of their heads, the teeth of a bright plastic comb stuck in the top for safe keeping or perhaps to hold the whole towering structure in place. For a trifling sum, the women released the comb and allowed the edifice to come tumbling down to the floor from where they combed and wrapped and twisted and coiled it back into place while I took pictures, told them how beautiful it was and wondered if any would really like to cut it all off and run screaming from the village and it's tyranny of washing and brushing.

I slept in the village where red lanterns flickered on at night outside the wooden lodges and turned this remote corner of China into Bavaria, though as the village generator sputtered and stopped and plunged every house into darkness, I was reminded that this was no land of German efficiency. Still, the moon reflected on hundreds of wet, narrow paddy fields clinging to the mountain edge gave light enough and I fell asleep to the sound of croaking frogs as contented as a buffalo on his birthday.

I boarded a bus and travelled south the next morning but not before eating one of those curious meals that the Chinese call breakfast. I'm an 'eat anything, anywhere' sort of chap, but not at this most important meal of the day when I like to be no more adventurous and avant garde than occasionally slicing some fruit onto my cornflakes. China takes pride in her regional dishes and here on trestle bench, plastic tablecloth display were those of Guilin. So, breakfast was pickled tofu, local river snails and a generous dollop of lajiaojiang Guilin sauce; a sour and ferociously hot mélange of chili, garlic and fermented soy beans. The waiter invited me to enjoy and I wasn't sure if this was a suggestion, a challenge or an order. I gamely imagined the tofu as poached egg, declined a glass of sanhua jiu Guilin rice wine that could not pretend to be cappuccino and admitted defeat when one of the snails crunched in my mouth, since no boneless gastropod should have such a mouth feel at breakfast time or anytime.

So I bumped on the bus to Yangshuo burping chilli and watching farmers watching me watching their infant children watching the implausibly violent kung fu movie that masqueraded as entertainment on our journey. Old China hands will pooh-pooh my visit to this tourist town; too western, too full of backpackers, too clichéd they would remonstrate. But this was Chinese New Year and I could think of no place better than this party town of firecrackers and fun and scenery from another world to be on such an auspicious date.

Yangshuo meaning 'Bright Moon' is a country town ringed by karsts. The main drag is called Westerner Street and it has no doubt become an inauthentic parade of coffee shops, breakfast cafes and bars. But it's a beautiful place where stone flags are polished so shiny and smooth by the tread of centuries of shoes, that the red lantern shop fronts are faintly reflected at your feet. The town was taking the shou-sui tradition of staying up late on the night before the first day of the first lunar month very seriously, and the streets were thronged with merrymakers.

New Year is Christmas, Easter and birthday rolled into one and a tangled mass of complicated tradition and belief. The Chinese will cheerfully pour out their money on presents, decoration, material, food and clothing at New Year; a huge feast is held and family members move hell and high water to be present. The Spring Festival travel season in China is known as chunyun, when the number of passenger journeys exceeds two billion; since in modern China so many people have left home for work or university study. This is probably the largest migration in the world and makes those aerial shots of wildebeest on the African savanna look like small beer.

Old grudges are put aside, houses are swept clean of ill fortune and to make way for in coming good luck and hongbao red packets stuffed with crisp new Three Gorges or Li River notes are given to the unmarried and the young. Children have embraced this tradition and, following afternoon English breakfast in a western cafe that banished my tofu and snail remembrance, I wandered Westerner Street and was assailed by Oliver Twist ragamuffins with outstretched hands and hongbao imprecations. Graciously scattering a few West Lakes, I escaped their disappointed faces in a bar made pretty with narcissus for prosperity, chrysanthemums for longevity and dark green leaved kumquat bushes in tiny pots whose orange fruits represent gold.

The night brought chaos to Yangshuo. New Year is also a time of fireworks and firecrackers in China, the cheap and ready availability of which turned this town's eve of New Year into the Battle of the Somme. The bass throb of firework artillery rolled distantly around the hills while on the streets of town the staccato blast of machine-gun firecrackers rang deafeningly from shop fronts framed by blood red diamond shaped auspiciousness posters hung upside down to encourage the arrival of good luck. Residents made war with giant cones of gunpowder exploded in a phosphorescence of stars while others shot rockets from horizontal jars along the whole length of the street. The unpredictability of attack became quite wearing as I looked this way and that and wondered if somewhere out there a Roman Candle might have my name on it. I watched light after light blossom in the night sky, endured the shell shock of unexpected explosion to left and right, the repercussion of gunpowder salvos on ancient stone walls and saw clouds of smoke and gas drift across the Li River No Man's Land on the edge of town.

By morning, an uneasy truce had settled on Yangshuo. Blackened tubes of spent powder littered the streets; I watched an ethereal mist lift from the river and failed to buy a cup of coffee from the stay in bed morning after restaurateurs. Mist and baijiu spirit hangovers had lifted by mid-morning as shops threw up their steel shutters and a lion prepared to dance his way through the streets to the clang of cymbals from store to store.

Copyright is an alien concept to China and I went in one of those DVD stores where everything costs 10 yuan and the spelling or content of the movie cover can be hysterically wrong. I bought a copy of The Last Temptation of Christ since the critics comment on the front said it was 'absolutely hilarious' and listened to the argument raging at the pay counter as I queued. 'Bullshit!' yelled the American student who wanted his money back on a faulty box set of discs. The shop attendant was explaining that a refund to the first customer of the New Year was impossible since it would make the 12 months ahead hopelessly bad for business and render worthless all the cleaning, firecrackers, chrysanthemums and hongbao packets of the day before. The student was in no mood for cultural sensitivity - maybe he'd had a near miss with a firework the night before - and was sticking to his guns. 'Bullshit!' he repeated and looked at me with his most exasperated 'what can you do with these people?' expression.

New Year good luck was with the shopkeeper and I was able to explain that this wasn't bullshit but absolutely real. So I jumped the queue, made my purchase and appeased the deities by ensuring that her first transaction of the year was a positive one. Money could then be returned to parochial box set boy and all were content; I felt the warm glow of smug satisfaction at defusing a potentially damaging clash of cultures and restoring harmony between East and West. I would have been less pleased with myself had I known that on return to my home, my DVD wouldn't work either - absolutely hilarious!

There are so many rules attached to the lunar Festival that it would be too easy for a foreigner to get things wrong. Specific traditions are connected to specific days; my DVD diplomatic mission was on day one when the deities of heaven and earth are welcomed, Buddhists refuse all meat and many Chinese abstain from lighting fires or using knives (or giving money back on damaged DVD box sets). Married daughters visit their birth parents on day two which is also the time when the Chinese are extra kind to dogs and feed them well. The second day of Chinese New Year is the birthday of all hounds, though it's hard to believe that it felt like a special day to the flea bitten bags of bones that chased on the riverbank and fought over the remains of chickens or to the carcasses of dogs that hung on butchers hooks in Yangshuo's main market. (For more on China's canine culinary traditions, see Guangdong chapter).

Caution is exercised in the Chinese household on days three and four. This is considered an inappropriate time to visit relatives and friends since the exhaustion and the quantities of food eaten on days one and two are likely to lead to arguments. This is the Chinese equivalent of Christmas Day afternoon or Boxing Day when grandma has drunk too many snowballs, the batteries have run out in the kids' new toys, there's only toffees left in the tin of Quality Street and father is upset that he lost at Monopoly. So the Chinese go grave visiting instead, since to honour one's ancestors is an ancient tradition and the dead don't drink sherry and become obnoxious.

Yangshuo was a vibrant New Year's Day lantern and firecracker red, like a parody of China, since red is joy, prosperity, virtue and sincerity and the ancient beast called Nian that came on the first day to devour crops, livestock and villagers was scared away by a child wearing red. I wondered if this was just for the tourists, hired a bike and determined to set off into the countryside to find out; but which way to go? The bike shop owner had given me directions that were in equal parts enigmatic and useless. 'Ride with the sun at your back', he said 'and look for the mountain like a moon' as if I was searching for ancient treasure or the elixir of eternal youth. I pedaled round and round the town and was passing Westerner Street for the third time when Esther came to my aid.

Esther was riding a bicycle older than mine and should have been at home celebrating New Year or in a rocking chair in front of the fire dispensing wisdom, but any doubts I had that this old woman might not be up to the job were dispelled when another guy tried to muscle in on her fare. She turned to shout insults and threats unworthy of her years, bared her teeth like a lioness protecting her cubs and actually rammed his bike with hers. This scared the interloper away and Esther turned to me, benign and gentle once more. 'Let's go' she said.

My afternoon with Esther turned out to be the most fun you can have on a bicycle with an old Chinese woman. We turned off the main road down a ribbon of thin dirt track that I had already passed twice and we were instantly in a different kind of China; of buffaloes, pomelo trees, rice fields, rape seed and tiny cottages with flying eaves and of beetling crags on massive limestone hills that rose vertically in front of my wheel. We passed a karst that had a massive crescent shaped hole like a moon waning over the fields (so the bike shop owner's directions had been right), floated over an ancient footbridge whose sinuous curves seemed to grow like something organic on the riverbank and headed north while children in red ran behind shouting 'Xin nian kuaile', Happy New Year.

I discovered that firecrackers are not just for tourists. Every house was littered with the red paper remains of New Year ritual and I often heard the crackling of celebration rebounding from the valley walls. Sometimes we passed a house with perfect timing just as fuse was lit and demons were frightened away with such ear splitting intensity that I had to get off my bike, take my gloves off the handlebars and put them over my ears laughing at the unbridled joy and intensity of it.

We arrived with flushed cheeks in Esther's village, where more children swarmed around and for a while I jokingly swapped bike for buffalo and paraded along the road like a New Year deity or an offering brought to sacrifice. The buffalo's owners demanded a few yuan for the privilege of course, but it was worth it to smell the rankness of the beast's back, feel its stomach bubbling and protesting between my legs and to hold the gnarled horns like fossils in my hands.

Esther's house was basic in the extreme with a pig running in the tiny backyard and to my shame I entered the front door in trepidation at the food I might be offered. I wondered if it would be polite to refuse but was served plates of delicious fresh vegetables; the pig had no cause to be worried since meat would be given only to honoured guests and I was hardly that. Rice flour noodles sprinkled with coriander followed radishes and cucumber in sour ginger, lotus root and green beans, and all from the prim garden that ran down the side of Esther's house. We finished with candied plums and little cups of weak jasmine tea with leaves floating sparsely on top that I had to sieve through my teeth.

Esther had lived in this house for the whole of her life and sent her children away to university in Guilin and Nanning so they could be educated and spared a life in such a place. This redoubtable old woman had subsequently learned English that brought my pathetic attempts at Chinese into painfully sharp contrast, so that she could visit Yangshuo and return with curious foreigners to cycle the lanes between fields that she knew too well. Business was good and Esther had an A4 exercise book to prove it. She proudly showed me eulogies from Kevins and Johns, Sues and Michelles from Canada, Britain, Australia and France who loved their China guide and recommended her to others without reservation. I was happy to add a testament of my own for this matriarch who had cycled, cooked and fought off the competition so ably; ' a real firecracker of a New Year guide'.

After lunch we cycled to the river instead of back to Yangshuo where Esther loaded my bike onto a trailer pulled by a two wheeled tractor and promised to meet me further downstream. I swapped pedal power for a bamboo raft that floated serenely down this tributary of the Li, my head shielded from the bright early spring sunshine by an incongruous McDonald's brolly. We sometimes hit small rapids where the clear waters narrowed between the fenglin peaks and burbled over rocks and in between reeds. This was disconcerting on such a flimsy craft but my pilot dressed in suit and brogues seemed to know what he was doing and before long I could see Esther waving cheerfully on the riverbank and pointing at my bike which I had momentarily believed I would never see again.

Soon we were freewheeling along the bank of the river to the outskirts of Yangshuo, me with that cheerful ruddy winter complexion and warm glow of a day well spent, Esther wondering if she could fit one more client in before nightfall. The river here is broad and flat and heads south west towards Guangdong, though most Guangxi water flows east to the border with Vietnam where the beautiful Detian Falls drop 40 metres in three stages right along the boundary of two nations and on which the use of a bamboo raft with or without McDonald's umbrella would be ill-advised. The falls sit on the Youyi Guan friendship pass though this is a rather unfriendly border that was at war in 1979 and where officious border guards confiscate tourist guidebooks if the map of Taiwan is a different colour (and therefore a separate country) to the mainland. China's borders are naturally porous since it's near impossible to police so many thousands of kilometres, but guards at the official crossing points can be excessively bureaucratic and picky, checking paperwork and stamping forms with the anal exactitude of a man who really does have all day. Yet there is a bumbling incompetence to their officiousness too; a soldier checking my passport as I entered Tibet clearly couldn't read - a skill that might be considered a prerequisite for such a task - and I once saw a dangerously overcrowded bus entering China from Nepal disgorge fully half its passengers who walked over the border and clambered back aboard as soon as the bus was through and all this in full view of the police. It seems the overloading of vehicles is only illegal as the checkpoint is crossed. Before and after is fine.

We were close to Yangshuo now and as much as I was anticipating a warm cafe and hot noodles, I rather missed the simplicity of Esther's vegetable garden and pig. We passed the theatrical protuberance that juts into the river where Zhang Yimou's folk musical 'Impression Liu Sanjie' is performed, though not tonight as the hundreds of fishermen and maidens who take part were at home celebrating New Year and getting ready to be kind to dogs.

The show is undoubtably impressive, but the story of its director is more impressive still. Zhang survived labour as a farm hand during the Cultural Revolution and reputedly sold his blood to buy his first camera when he was 18. Such sacrifice did not go unrewarded; Zhang took his remaining platelets to the Beijing Film Academy and became an internationally acclaimed director and designer of the opening ceremony of the 2008 Olympics. A true rags to riches tale; there was hope for Esther yet.

We turned into Westerner Street where I dismounted to bid farewell to my guide. I'd enjoyed her company and admired her tenacity, but this was an unsentimental farewell; Esther was soon walking away down the street, pushing her bike and looking for a tourist to commit to tomorrow's trip so that she could ride home and sleep well.

Yangshuo was still dressed for a party and the night market was in full swing. There was the usual jumble of Qing Dynasty teapots and those strange metal spheres that relieve stress when rotated in one hand. I was attracted to the Han warrior chess sets with archers, emperor and concubine ready for battle but as usual finished with a bag full of cultural revolutionary miscellany. I can't resist a good lantern jawed peasant marching shoulder to shoulder with a soldier to a new socialist world and bought posters and stickers that I supposed said 'Follow the thoughts of Chairman Mao' or ' Down with the Imperialist running dogs'.

How the receptionist at my hotel laughed as she explained what the Chinese characters really meant. 'Don't even bother if you're not drop dead gorgeous', 'Even Chairman Mao thinks I am supermodel handsome' and (rather more primly) 'I am not the type of guy who jumps into bed with any woman' said the words below handsome soldiers and generals on badges and posters. 'Free dinner for a one night stand please' trumpeted the text beside a man grinning cheerfully astride a tractor, while the characters beneath the Buddhist monk kneeling head bowed at the feet of the Red Guard said 'nonsmoking, non-alcohol, non-woman (sic). What a tragic life!'

Things became stranger still when after dinner I ambled through the gloom of early evening as red lanterns flared into life and I agreed to accompany a local fisherman down to the river to see a good shag - imagine my disappointment when I realised he meant a bunch of old seabirds. Cormorant fishing has a long and distinguished history in Guangxi, though now it's all much more to do with tourism than sustenance. My fisherman friend took me out on a boat onto the black river and lit fires inside two metal baskets for light and to attract fish, the warmth from which was welcome as this was February and the night had turned cold since the sun had dropped behind the limestone karsts. The cormorants plunged from the front of the boat into the inky water on the end of a leash attached to a small metal ring around the base of the neck. Every time a bird caught his quarry, he disgorged it onto the floor of the boat since the metal ring made it impossible to swallow any fish that was large enough to be of use to the fisherman.

There is an art to all this and it is said that in years past the cormorant would be treated like a relation since one good bird could feed a whole family. But crouching on a clapped-out boat, the cold river rushing beneath my feet in the pitch black night, watching seabirds vomiting fish wasn't really my idea of fun and I was glad to be back on dry land.

Guangxi was once thoroughly remote and the people here have always had their own way of doing things. Fishing with birds is just one example of this; in 1955 the province officially became the Zhuang autonomous region. And at times it feels that the people of Guangxi hardly want to be part of China at all. It was in Guiping town in Guangxi that the Taiping Rebellion began, when a schoolteacher called Hong Xiuquan declared himself the brother of Jesus Christ and led an army of one million against the ruling Qing Dynasty. The uprising began over resentment that Han immigration had put pressure on Guangxi's scant arable resources and by 1860 Hong's army controlled the capital Nanjing and large swathes of eastern China. The Qing defeated the Taiping with the aid of Queen Victoria's favourite general, Charles 'Chinese' Gordon who later popped up to Peking to sack the Summer Palace and scatter precious Qing artefacts to museums and private collections across the world (a practice known as Elginism after the cultural vandalism of the Earl of Elgin, another Victorian superman, at the Acropolis in Athens). By the time the dust had settled and Hong had been sent to heaven to join his brother, the rebellion had cost 20 million lives - the deadliest civil war in history.

China has misappropriated the independence of the Taiping just as Guangxi's cormorants and karsts have become quintessentially Chinese too. Hong was Christian but his battle against ancient dynasticism is seen as good Communism. The Taiping fanatical rejection of Confucianism and wild destruction of historic sites and buildings are a precursor to the Red Guard mayhem of the 1960s when to rebel was good and millions more lives were ruined or lost.

If fishing with birds in the dead of night felt risky, this was as nothing to the next bright and still morning when I rose serenely above Guangxi's hills in the basket of a hot air balloon. It had all been a bit of a spur of the moment decision based on recall of how much I had enjoyed ballooning years before above the Australian outback; so why did I feel so nervous now? As we ascended with another bright orange blast of flame high above the fields scattered like mahjong tiles between the peaks, I realised why. This basket was budget sized, Lilliputian, diminutive, designed for a homunculus, like they'd run out of wicker when it was built. The edge barely reached my waist and I gripped on with umbilical determination to my refuge, torn between cowering low on the floor and a weird vertiginous desire to throw myself over the edge.

I settled for a strange half crouch primitive man squat and gaped with Neanderthal slack-jaw at Guangxi floating below, like a dream or a wide angle Peter Jackson Middle Earth movie shot. Crescendos of peaks corrugated into the distance as if the whole world was covered in karst. I took the best photographs I have ever shot when I dared to take my hand off my cradle, though it was impossible to truly capture the luminosity of that view as the early morning sun lent contrast and purple luster to the land. You really had to be there, though without crowding me or taking any of my space in that tiny basket you understand, and although we were aloft for barely an hour it took days to come back to earth from that unworldly flight and accept that not all China can be like Guangxi.

GUANGDONG

广东

196 891 sq km
Population 110 million

`To secure a husband, a woman needs first to cook good soups'

Cantonese saying.

Guangdong is a province that lacks restraint. For a start, there are too many people. Guangdong has 80 million permanent residence and a further 30 million migrant workers, which makes this a most populous place in a most populous of countries. The migrants come because once where there was an impoverished and backward region, Guangdong is now an economic powerhouse. The province's $522 billion economy is roughly the same as Sweden's and Guandong has benefited more than any other part of China from ex-Premier Deng Xiaoping's open door policy of low taxation and special economic zones where unfettered capitalism has been allowed to develop, free of the irritating constraints of fairness and welfare that communism so inconveniently promotes.

The motto of the Guangdong tourist board is 'Look to the future', though the Chinese word for future sounds like 'money' which is much more appropriate for this go ahead, materialistic and high energy place. So it was that I arrived in the provincial capital Guangzhou with low expectations indeed. Arrival at the East station is a sterile and comfortable experience; air-conditioners hummed, a woman slopped water on the already glassy floor of the arrival hall and this felt just like the modern station I had left in Hong Kong. But as I walked through the automatic doors I entered the Guangzhou I had been expecting.

Steamy, chaotic, filthy Guangzhou. The city once called Canton is the third biggest in China and my bus traveled a high-level roller coaster route over a dozen flyovers above identikit houses, rusty air conditioning units clinging to the side, stretching into the distance and hardly a patch of green in sight.

I was heading to the *real* train station in Guangzhou. Hardened China train travellers have been known to shudder or burst into tears at the mention of Guangzhou. These people might have tackled desert stations in Gansu, the frozen north beyond the Great Wall in Heilongjiang and ridden the express over the Tanggula Pass to Tibet. Yet Guangzhou central train station holds a special fear for all travelers on the China train network.

The station is old and confusing with stairs and corridors tempting unwary passengers onto the wrong train. It has dark and sinister cupboards in corners where who know what lurks. Above all, it is crowded; insanely, continuously, endlessly crowded with a surging sea of Cantonese and migrant passengers sitting on boxes, sprawled on the floor like casualties of war or pushing, shoving and madly sprinting to get on a train.

Today was easy though. The weather was good, the trains were running, the crowd had enough instant noodles and cuttlefish flavoured potato snacks. There was almost a holiday atmosphere here and I saw one woman dancing around her cardboard boxes, though it was clear that this had more to do with rice wine than joy at waiting for a train. She wouldn't have been dancing here in January 2008 when Guangzhou central train station faced the mother of all queues.

An unusual weather system and abnormal atmospheric circulation blew freezing weather from the North in the middle of that month. Unprecedented snowfall was dumped on the central and southern Chinese provinces of Hunan, Hubei and Jiangxi. Guangdong was cold and miserable but largely unaffected by snow but such was the severity of China's worst storms in 50 years in those provinces further north that electricity supplies were disrupted and 223,000 houses were toppled by snow and ice. Worst affected was the city of Chenzhou on the border of Hunan and Guangdong whose three and a half million people were without electricity or water for nearly 2 weeks.

The absence of electricity meant that trains stopped running on the main Guangzhou – Beijing and Shanghai lines. The timing of this could hardly have been worse, just two weeks before the Chinese New Year holiday when most of Guangdong's 30 million migrant workers leave the drudgery of their factories and return home. It's like Christmas in the West but without the three-month run up and with an even greater spiritual and cultural importance. The Chinese simply *have* to return to their families at New Year to feast and celebrate and to create an auspicious year ahead. It is estimated that 180 million Chinese ride the trains at this time of year.

So the factories were closed and the workers trudged through wet streets in cold drizzle, clutching food and family gifts to catch their train. Tickets were issued on a first-come first-served basis, so although the queues were growing, people persevered ate their food and stamped their feet to keep warm. By the last week of January there were 260,000 at the station waiting to board and some estimates suggest that this number swelled to 800,000 at its peak. 800,000! I stood on the station forecourt and tried to imagine this vast crowd surging and swaying and trying to board non-existent trains but the number was inconceivable to me. 12,000 police were drafted in to keep order and the seriousness of the situation can be measured by the appearance of Premier Wen

Jiabao who braved the cold and the crowds, put on his winter mac and came to the station to pacify the multitudes. "All the works are proceeding expeditiously" announced Wen through a tiny hand-held megaphone, "the number of trains that resume services is increasing everyday".

By early February the power was on and 400 trains a day pulled out of Guangzhou. It was too late to prevent a stampede to board on 1st February when a migrant watchmaker called Li Hongxia was trampled to death, but by the middle of February the Chinese New Year hordes had dispersed and Guangzhou station had returned to its normal confusing state of mere overcrowding.

China was caught out by the storms that hit southern regions unused to coping with snow. It's a bit like England where schools close and transport grinds to a shuddering halt at the merest hint of frost, whereas Canada and Scandinavia hardly count snow as bad weather at all until every surface is covered by at least a foot of the white stuff. Countries that sent aid to help China included Mongolia who rather touchingly gave $43,000 for disaster relief and the army distributed nearly half a million quilts in what they called "the war on wintry weather". How typical of China to give the emergency a military connotation though I think 'the battle against reactionary snow and ice from anti-Communist cloud formations' has more of a martial ring to it.

A bright socialist sun was shining and I searched out Guangzhou's green spaces. Yuexiu Park is China's biggest and in the centre stands a statue of a bunch of Billy goats. This is a reference to the city's fabled founding by five immortals riding goats, each of whom planted a sheaf of grain to symbolise that the inhabitants would never know famine. The city is often known as 'Yangcheng' or 'Ram City' and ornamental lions outside banks, offices and homes often sprout horns from their heads in ovine tribute.

The park has a big red Ming Dynasty gate tower called Zhenhai Lou and Guangzhou looked almost lovely from up here, with the sun splashing off the Zhu Jiang Pearl River and the unedifying detail of the city lost in the splendour of scale. But back on the streets in the chaos of traffic and jumble of inglorious tumbledown buildings I just wanted to be somewhere else.

There were no motorbikes at least, rasping between cars and sending two stroke blue smoke into the soupy air. They'd been banned from the city in 2006 to reduce pollution and congestion and also because of the preponderance of motorbike thieves, some of whom like the infamous 'Hand Choppers' had taken to removing with a surgical slash of a blade the hands of anyone foolish enough to cling onto credit card or purse.

Tourist sites featuring Guangzhou had told me that there is much of interest here for the visitor who is prepared to search. Never has a town of eight and a half million people been damned by such faint praise; the statesmanlike Ming Dynasty beauty of Beijing doesn't take 'searching out' and the colonial grandeur of Shanghai is obvious to even the most blinkered tourist. So, that was my challenge; to find something to like in Guangzhou.

Western imperialists seemed to like the place and set up shop in Canton for 200 years of trade before the 20th century Communists removed all such pernicious barbarianism. The city occupies an unrivalled position at the head of the Pearl River Delta and close to Hong Kong, and every adventurer keen on making a fast buck in Cathay passed through here.

The fastest buck of all was to be made from opium and it was at nearby Humen that the Chinese official and modern day hero Lin Zexu destroyed 1200 tons of opium stocks in protest at these imports that made money for Barbarians and misery for the Chinese. The British response to the destruction of the precious crop was rapid and gloriously hypocritical (see Fujian chapter.) The first Opium War began and at the Nanking Treaty of 1842, China humiliatingly climbed down and handed control of five treaty ports to the Brits.

In Canton the British and the French took possession of Shamian Island and I was headed there in my attempts to find beauty amidst the pollution and the crowds. The island was really just a sandbank but land reclamation increased its size and solidity and by 1859 The Lady of Lourdes Church and a prim collection of European style houses were built. The island is an oasis now just as it was when residents were insulated from the chaotic Cantonese world outside by high gates that were locked by 10pm and guarded by Sikhs at the British end and Annamite troops where the French traders lived. There's no traffic on the island now and old couples sit and play mahjong in the shade of spreading Banyan trees with an incongruous backdrop of buildings that could be Regency England or Renaissance France. It's all very lovely and peaceful and still a favourite spot for European tourists who stay at the luxurious White Swan Hotel on the riverfront or take refuge here while waiting to adopt Chinese babies who are mostly orphaned and female.

But Shamian is about the most atypical place in the whole of Guangzhou so it doesn't really count. The island is preserved and protected and no doubt one of the 'hidden delights' that the tourist board were trumpeting, though the locals weren't always so enamoured with this enclave of European eliteness.

An anti-British movement at nearby Sanyuan Li in 1841 was led by a local farmer called Wei Shaoguang. Rebels attacked the British camp and killed around 200 with simple farm tools that are now on rusty display in Guangzhou's Temple Museum. Liu Er San Lu runs through the heart of town and means 623 Road (23rd of June) in commemoration of a march by 100,000 Chinese who demanded the return of Shamian in the 1920s. British and French troops fired on the crowd and killed 52, though perhaps the troops overreacted and the crowd was simply queueing for a train.

It's not just inquisitive Europeans who were drawn to Canton. Huaisheng mosque was established by Abu Waqas, the uncle of Muhammad in the seventh century who died in town and is buried in the Islamic cemetery. The mosque possesses that quiet and calming assurance of ancient stones, immune to the noise of traffic on streets nearby. An inscription above the door reads 'Beneath white clouds and where the mountain turns, there stands a brilliant stone pagoda in the style of the western regions, handed down by Emperor Gaozu of the Tang Dynasty' but it's the Guangta Tower minaret that seems more brilliant than the mosque itself. Rebuilt in the 11th century, this is the world's oldest minaret outside Mecca whose name means smooth since it's so plain and unadorned. I loved the simplicity and functionality of this vertical antiquity that was so out of keeping with the rest of modern Guangzhou whose god is Mammon and where a Tower of Babel might be more appropriate than a minaret.

Everything of beauty that I had seen in Guangzhou had been introduced from outside. I needed to see some Chinese loveliness and wandered to the banks of the Zhu Jiang since the river at least was a permanent feature of the city that had been harnessed by the Chinese and looked so pretty from the top of Zhenhai Lou. Guangta Tower had originally served as a lighthouse for ships on the river at the start of the maritime Silk Road and a walk along Yangjiang Lou, Guangzhou's waterfront boulevard was fine indeed. Not as fine as the Bund at Shanghai to be sure, and the wind off the notoriously filthy river had a curious sulphurous smell, but I'm a sucker for a riverside view and who could deny that the muscular barges, kite flying locals, vendors selling youtiao dough sticks and swooping Cantonese gulls had a vibrant and energetic beauty?

Walking inland to Guangzhou's famous Qingping Market, close to a region of town occupied by African immigrants that locals call 'Chocolate City', I sensed with the dawning realisation that the city's beauty lies not in conventional quiet places, historic buildings and wonders of nature but in its cheek by jowl vibrancy, in its train station crowds, frenetic pace and in the cheerful optimism and hospitality of its people. Not a conventional beauty to be sure, but a rough and ready charm and a cheerful juxtaposition to the classical gardens and formality to be found elsewhere in China.

Qingping means 'peaceful', a delightful juxtaposition too for a place where a maelstrom of buying and selling assaults the senses. But it's not the crowds and the typically boisterous sellers that make the market famous, but the goods that they sell. Qingping is the centre of the exotic food trade in Guangzhou and provides most of the produce of the euphemistically named 'Wild Flavour' restaurants around town.

There is a Chinese saying that the Cantonese will eat 'anything with legs that isn't a table and anything with wings that isn't an aeroplane'. Cages of flying foxes, giant toads, civet cats and snakes can be found in Qingping. Here too, are tortoises, dog carcasses, owls, tiger paws, badgers, an occasional monkey and those strange prehistoric armoured beasts called pangolins that are native to southern China. All are destined for the dinner table.

The 2003 SARS outbreak was blamed on the civet cat consumption and the selling and eating of some animals has been banned. Cleanliness and health have been newly prioritised and I saw posters here demanding 'Everyone should honour the policy of paying attention to product safety'.

But the Cantonese taste for exotica is insatiable and a black market trade in rare meat continues to thrive. In Guangdong more than anywhere else in China there is an uncommon willfulness to try something new. As I strolled the city, restaurants tempted me in with uncooked deer blood, raw muscle and jiaozi dumplings stuffed with crab ovaries, though I wouldn't have thought you'd get much meat off a crab's reproductive system. There is a determined culinary imagination at play in Guangdong where health authorities recently put a stop to restaurants serving chickens that have been bitten to death by poisonous snakes and cooked up for a supposedly detoxing meal.

Snake bite chicken may be off the menu but locals still ascribe powerful qualities to animal parts that are said to strengthen their human equivalent. Thus ox tongue gives the diner eloquence, duck or monkey brains make him clever and bull's testicles..... well, you get the idea.

This is all thoroughly repugnant to the average Westerner of course, but Guangdong's conspicuously exotic consumption has to be seen in the wider context of the Chinese relationship with food. Cantonese is just one of the four major cooking styles in China and places particular emphasis on the use of fresh ingredients, hence all those live beasts on sale at Qingping, and the use of a minimum of seasoning so that food tastes as close to original as possible. For the Chinese, food is a divine pleasure. The average Cantonese spends a third of his income on meals and the common local greeting 'sik jor farn mei?' literally means 'Have you eaten yet?'

But with one fifth of the world's population and only 10% of the world's arable land, the Chinese palate has had to be particularly innovative and efficient. A famine cuisine developed in China; wild plants, bamboo, lotus roots, seaweed, fungi and insects are commonly consumed and the Chinese have long been accustomed to eating *every* part of an animal. The need to preserve firewood has led to lots of flash and stir frying in superheated woks.

China's first Master of gastronomy Yi Yin cooked for the Shang Emperor in the 16th century BC and Chinese cookbooks dating from the sixth century are the oldest in the world and make modern celebrity chefs seem like Johnny-come-latelys. Confucius knew that philosophical thought begins with the stomach when he said "food can never be too refined, meat can never be sliced too thin" and the Song Dynasty poet Su Dongpo wrote an ode to pork, possibly the only time that a nice bit of bacon or pork scratching has been eulogised;

> Pork in Huangzhou is plenty
> There it costs utterly lowly
> The rich detest it; the poor fluff it,
> Slow the fire, hold the water,
> It comes alive when the time is right.

Not the best poem I've ever read, maybe his verses on chicken or beef are better.

In China, the principles of yin and yang are applied to food. All meals must have 'hot' yang masculine meat and spice and 'cool' yin moist and soft vegetables and fruit. Fish is favoured because the Chinese word 'yu' sounds like 'abundance' and noodles are a long, sinuous symbol of longevity. Rice is the great unifier of the table however, setting off the texture of all other food and revealing multifaceted and complex flavours by its simplicity. But pity the poor vegetarian in China since the non-consumption of meat there is a symbol of poverty rather than an environmental gesture or a sympathetic nod to the fate of doe eyed cattle, cheerful pigs or cute civet cats.

The hottest and most yang food of all is dog and the munching of Fido is where western confusion at Chinese culinary tastes turns to outrage. I saw rows of roasted dogs hanging on hooks in Qingping and their faces, frozen into perpetual snarls, were the stuff of nightmares. But gou rou has been a source of food in China for over 2000 years and is thought to have medicinal properties that are especially beneficial in the cold winter months.

Most Chinese don't eat dog and there is a slight taboo attached to it even here where it is often euphemistically referred to as 'xiang rou' or 'fragrant meat' and sometimes arithmetically as '3 + 6 meat' since the word for nine and dog are homophones, both pronounced as gau in Cantonese. Chinese animal protection networks have been established and there are now 40 societies to campaign against the consumption of dog, though it's the inhumane killing rather than the eating of canines that they are particularly exercised about.

But these grinning hounds in a butcher's doorway were quite up-front and I asked the shopkeeper how a dog should be cooked. She said it is best stewed in thick gravy or by roasting but that it is not so popular any more. She told me that consumption of cats had declined too since the banning of snake eating which put paid to the popular Guangdong dish called Longhudou or 'dragon fights tiger' whose name derives from the use of snake and cat meat. "Actually cat meat is not as delicious as dog" she said "the chefs cook it for fun to see if they can make it taste nice", though this sounded like the argument of a dog meat retailer.

The ban on Longhudou was really a response to protest about the eating of cats, but in a classic piece of Chinese Confucian political thinking, snake eating was banned instead so that the government was not seen to be responding to pressure which could lead to a perception of governmental weakness and possible civil disobedience. Whatever the logic, and even though cats are now less likely to lose their ninth life in a Guangdong cooking pot, the West can get quite emotional about all this scoffing of pets.

Animal rights activist and dog lover Brigitte Bardot was talking about Korea when she said on a radio interview that dogs "are friends not animals" and that "cows are grown to be eaten but dogs are not; a cultured country does not allow its people to eat dogs", though her views could be equally applied to Guangdong.

This illogical and somewhat blinkered argument presupposes that the Chinese see dogs as 'friends' and anyway dogs *are* grown to be eaten in China. Every roasted body swinging in front of me was of a uniform type and size and bred for the table; even a Cantonese gourmand would not dream of sampling a Dalmatian or a Pekinese if he fancied just a light snack. And anyway, dogs and cats have been eaten in the West too. Roast cat was a favourite in Mediaeval Europe and during wartime rationing in the UK, cats found their way into stews and pies and earned themselves the nickname 'roof rabbit'. In the words of the 1940s rhyme;

> Oh kittens in our hours of ease
> Uncertain toys and full of fleas
> When pain and anguish hang o'er men
> We turn you into sausage then.

I stopped by a Cantonese restaurant for lunch where boisterous diners at plastic tables shouted, laughed and spat bones on the floor since a good restaurant should be 'renao' or noisy and lively. I spurned the crabs' ovaries for a serving of the most famous Southern dish of all. The Cantonese call dim sum 'yum cha' which means 'with tea' and these delicate parcels of minced meat and vegetables are a cultural institution in Guangdong and Hong Kong. Some of these were good though I got bored with the blandness of texture and taste, declined the steamed chickens' feet and longed for some spicy Sichuanese hotpot or crispy Peking duck. I tried the rice porridge congee which tasted of nothing at all and fell like a wild beast upon the custard tarts, a Portuguese import from nearby Macau.

So it came back to imports again. I don't want to belittle China's creation of modern, frenetic Guangzhou, but it had been the peaceful leafy European streets of Shamian and the ancient Muslim minaret that had moved me most. Even the Portuguese egg tarts had been tastier than the dim sum.

But Guangdong is not just Guangzhou. I took a boat through the straits where the Pearl River meets the sea and flows all the way to Lantau Island in Hong Kong, sporting huge cathedral like power stations on the shore where we surprised pink dolphins surfing the wake of the boat, indigenous to these waters but more at risk from pollution and propellers with each year. I took a train to Zhaoqing where the famous Qixing Yan seven star crags and Dinghu Shan nature reserves offer a respite from the 110 million people. The reserves reflect the

Chinese obsession with the personifying of natural features. I saw the Chuanchu Toad Rock and the Shizang Stone Hand and ambled past the Leaping Dragon pool, the Immortal riding a crane, the Dragon mother borrowing a vessel, the Black Dragon playing with pearls and the White clouds embracing trees. It was all rather pretty though they just looked like rocks to me.

The Jesuit priest Matteo Ricci lived in Zhaoqing in the 16th century, published the first maps of China available in the West and introduced the Chinese to trigonometry. He was embraced in China because he used Buddhist and Taoist parallels to make his teaching appealing, dressed as a Chinese scholar and learned the language. Further around the coast at Cuiheng and almost in Macau, I saw the Portuguese style house of Sun Yat Sen, the great revolutionary hero of China, who was born here in 1866 and introduced the thoroughly foreign principles of nationalism, democracy and socialism to China that Mao and the Communists adopted and subverted in the 20th century.

Foreign influence is everywhere in Guangdong just as thousands of Cantonese have left the province to live elsewhere. It was the Cantonese who helped connect the Pacific and Atlantic by railroad in the embryonic United States and almost any Chinese community abroad is likely to be Cantonese. The food that a foreigner eats in a restaurant in Chinatown is likely to be Cantonese too, though it's a pale imitation of the real thing with barely a toad, a duck brain or a fluffy kitten in sight.

All this import and export of culture means that Guangdong is a most untypical Chinese province. I didn't like it much, but perhaps this just meant that I couldn't warm to a place that, for all its 110 million Chinese people, was so un-Chinese. The Han Chinese are in a minority here, just as they are in distant Xinjiang and Tibet and the lingua franca is not Mandarin Chinese just as it is not in the distant west too. By these criteria, the province should hardly be in China at all. Forget Tibetan independence, free Guangdong!

Anyway, to like or not like 'Guangdong' is a futile expression since the mountains are so different to the coast, the villages to the towns and Guangzhou is unlike anywhere else at all, so which bit to not like?

The most untypical place in Guangdong and possibly the whole of China, is Shenzhen. I've been to Shenzhen a dozen times or more since it's the first town in China from my home in Hong Kong and the shopping is cheap there. Shenzhen has not developed over the years in the normal way but has been pumped with cash since 1980 like some bodybuilder on steroids and has become showy, developed some health problems and is out of proportion as a result. The city might be grotesque but I can't resist sneaking back for another look.

Before 1980, Shenzhen was Baoan, a tiny rural fishing community, but by 1990 the place was turning over $26 billion a year. China's first McDonald's was built here and a nuclear power plant had to be erected to service the city's energy needs.

The reason for such rapid change is that Shenzhen won the Deng Xiaoping economic jackpot. The area was chosen as the first of Deng's special economic zones and given unrestrained access to investment, trade and the temptations of the free market capitalist economy over the border at Hong Kong. The resulting boom created jobs and wealth but its fair share of problems too as poor workers flocked to its golden streets from provinces further north; it is estimated now that 50% of Shenzhen's population are illegal immigrants.

The city has an air of desperation away from the shopping malls and is the only place in China that I have felt truly threatened and at risk. Back street alleys are filthy and rat infested where limbless beggars wheel past on home-made carts demanding money and tired prostitutes in cheap clothes shout 'I love you long time'.

Shenzhen has a drug problem too. China's long history of drug addiction was ended by the Communist Party who were quick to control every aspect of people's lives; their jobs, their marriages and sex. But as China loosens its hold on the economy and society, people are making their own choices again. The number of arrests for drug crime has risen fourfold in China in the last 10 years and independent sources claim 7 to 12 million addicts nationwide of whom 80% are under 35.

The Chinese economy is freest of all in Shenzhen, so the drug problem is worse there too and exacerbated by the thousands of jobless migrants who found the streets were not paved with gold after all. How China would benefit from a modern day Lin Zexu to cleanse the streets of that 'foreign mud'.

Shenzhen is a shopping town too. It's the epicentre of the Chinese counterfeit trade and I took a taxi to Dafen artist village to see some of the counterfeiting for myself. 'Artist Village' suggests some bucolic retreat where lovelorn ascetics search for inspiration, though in reality it's just another dreary modern suburb surrounded by the jackhammers bent on Shenzhen's improvement, no different to the rest of the city save for a giant bronze hand holding a paintbrush outside.

There are 5000 artists here and they'll paint anything, any size. I strolled past Van Gogh's sunflowers and stars, plump Rubens cherubs and more smirking Mona Lisas than I care to remember, before settling on some modern Chinese art fresh painted on huge canvas for the price of an IKEA clip frame.

Back at the border, the Luo Wu shopping centre is a cornucopia of Prada bags, Tiffany jewels and Chanel scents. Every shopkeeper wanted me to 'come in - just looking' and I eventually settled on a Shanghainese tailor who measured my inside leg and knocked up a dinner suit with satin lapels for 800 yuan. Movies are big business here too and seemingly the only product that makes local police hot under the collar. So, when I entered a DVD shop to select the latest blockbusters for 10 yuan each, a steel shutter was pulled down behind me, and the movies were passed down from a hole in the ceiling by a disembodied hand. 'Good quality' the shopkeeper pronounced, but when I got them home found they had been filmed at the back of a movie theatre and I could hear every cough and fart from the audience and see every head bobbing past the screen as a customer risked missing the best bit on his way to the toilet.

Shenzhen is also home to the most eclectic set of tourist attractions I've ever seen. There is an underwhelming overseas livestock farm with milk cows and a half hearted pigeon display, though at least the animals here are well tended and not about to be eaten. It is wise to give most wildlife parks and zoos in China a very wide berth. Even though China has laws that forbid the poaching and hunting of endangered species (much to the disappointment of Guangdong food fanatics) it has no legislation to prevent cruelty and abuse to animals. As a consequence, wildlife parks can be an appalling experience where it is not uncommon to see live goats and cows fed to tigers and animals pacing mindlessly in blood smeared tiny concrete prisons. At the biannual Shanghai Animal Olympics, monkeys pedal bikes, bears fight and ride motorbikes on the high wire cables and humans box with kangaroos. I'm ambivalent about the consumption of dog but wouldn't go within 500 yards of the average Chinese zoo.

Shenzhen's 'Windows of the World' is much more acceptable. Here the banners by the multicoloured fountain boast 'give us a day and we will show you the world'. Delighted visitors can travel by foot or golf cart to scale models of every iconic structure around the globe from Sydney Opera House to the great Pyramids of Giza to the Houses of Parliament to the Taj Mahal. I went because it sounded so kitsch but this budget world tour is really rather well done and I joined in with Chinese tourists who were racing from Indonesian temple to Aztec tomb for photograph after photograph on their journey around the world, which must be quite useful for a nation where many are still not granted a passport.

It is interesting to watch the average Chinese tourist at play. First, women get quite excited and laugh and shriek a lot. The men smoke and dress in the same cheap suits that are worn for all activities (I have even seen locals jogging in suits and farmers ploughing the field in fetching two pieces). Sometimes they take their jackets off. They take lots of photos. All of these must feature at least one person in order to have interest. Landscape photography alone is never acceptable. All people in the photo must raise two fingers in a victory salute, particularly if they are from Southern China or Hong Kong. All no entrance signs on the exhibits are to be ignored and I saw dozens of tourists clambering on the Tower of Pisa, Ayres rock and the Manhattan skyline with its twin towers intact. Above all, orderly queueing for rides is never encouraged.

The Park's centrepiece is a giant Niagara Falls - the brochure was as gushing about this as the water rushing over the falls itself 'with the force of thunderbolts'. I was told to ' drink in the beauty of Shenzhen' from the 108m high Eiffel Tower and though the view wasn't great at least I couldn't see the beggars and whores from up there.

The Grand Canyon log flume was fun though. Everyone wore a free plastic mac and I wondered why until the final 50 metres after the plunging drop when I was hit full in the face by a water cannon hidden in the dahlias. I clambered away from the Grand Canyon, went to inspect the artillery that had so injured my pride and was delighted to find Chinese tourists pushing one yuan coins into a box that controlled the cannon's switch, at the push of a button soaking the unsuspecting thrill seekers who thought that the ride was over. This was fun, and I pushed in some coins and did some soaking too but reflected that the same system in the UK would probably result in physical violence being done to the squirter.

I strolled past Mount Rushmore and the Colosseum, out of the park and into a taxi for more water-based thrills. I was going to 'Minsk world', a huge decommissioned Russian aircraft carrier and formerly part of the Soviet Pacific fleet that is permanently moored at Dapeng Bay. You'd have thought that such a unique and bizarre attraction would always have appeal but remarkably in 2006, the company that owned the Minsk went bust. The giant carrier was put up for sale, a snip at 128 million yuan, and a new owner was found who has renamed the whole area ' Merry Military Harbour', and revamped and rebranded the whole thing.

I was able to pass through Minsk Square whose 'Turn Swords into Ploughshares' sign sits rather incongruously next to the naval battle simulation (once every hour, extra fee applies) over a gun metal grey bridge and onto the ship itself. It seems redundant to say the carrier is big, but my God it *is* big. I walked up and down stairs through the bridge and past missile silos and sleeping fighter jets and tried to imagine life on the high seas defending the Soviet system against evil dollar diplomacy at the height of Cold War politics. But I liked the dancing best.

Merry Military Harbour had imported dancers from Russia, who dressed as sailors, kicked and pirouetted their way through a musical that apparently told the tale of a seaman's life traveling the world on board the Minsk. It was all very enjoyable and slightly camp though I wondered if these excellent dancers who might be classically trained in the Bolshoi and St Petersburg, ever wondered how they wound up frolicking like the Pirates of Penzance on a ship in Shenzhen.

So, I'd finished where I started in a Guangdong immersed in foreign influence and defined by its migrants. It was a short journey across the border but orderly and efficient Hong Kong might have been another world. As I exited the train the summer humidity broke, sheets of rain poured down, and I imagined how pleased the dinnertime crowds in Guandong would be that it was raining cats and dogs.

.

HUNAN

湖南

207,254 sq km
Population 67 million

*"China's people are poor and blank...on a blank sheet of paper free
from any mark, the freshest and most beautiful characters can be
written, the freshest and most beautiful picture can be painted"*

Mao Zedong

Chairman Mao's trunks are big. Voluminous even, with one of those
belts attached like a 1960s catalogue model or Ursula Andress emerging
from aquamarine water onto a paradise beach in Dr No. Michael Phelps
and other swimmers in their NASA designed shaped-to-the-body

fast-skin suits should try breaking records in the Chairman's pants. Now there's an Olympic event I'd pay to see.

I'm gazing at Mao's swimmers through protective bullet proof glass in the Mao museum at Shaoshan, a rather untypical slice of rural China in the heart of Hunan. For it is here in 1893 that Mao first cast his socialist gaze, kicked his anti-rightist left and right legs, drank the honest and untainted milk of the Chinese peasantry, expelled undesirable foreign influence into his nappy and bawled his little revolutionary lungs out. From 1966 to his death in 1976, an average of three million Chinese came here every year to pay respects and breathe the anti imperialist air that inspired Mao. Things became quieter after his death when the cult of Mao was reassessed and the party declared he had been 70% right and 30% wrong – a remarkably precise and scientific average. These random numbers have become an immutable law in China and my attempts everywhere to flatter the Chinese by suggesting that maybe 50-50 or 60-40 might be closer to the mark or even that Mao was right eight times out of ten were met with patient denial. No, 70-30 had been decreed and this was irrefutable. Such criticism doesn't seem too bad of course; 70% right surely qualifies Mao as an A grade demagogue. I'd settle for being wrong only 30% of the time.

No matter, the village has enjoyed something of a renaissance in recent years. The museum with the trunks was built in 1991 and a big new bronze statue of Mao was erected two years later. When I arrive, the air is not so much rarified and revolutionary as a bit misty and drizzly. My journey here from the provincial capital Changsha on a broken–hearted old bus had tested my revolutionary credentials on a number of levels. Firstly, the farmer next to me insisted on pulling the hair on my hirsute Anglo-Saxon arms and giving me the thumbs up. 'Hen Hao', 'Very Good' he told me, like it had been a conscious decision on my part to grow body hair. Most people smoked for most of the journey despite some new 'no smoking' signs above the driver's poster of kittens in a basket and after two hours of this fug, like the predicted 80 million Chinese predicted to die from smoking related diseases over the next 25 years, I could almost sense my life shortening.

China smokes 1.7 *trillion* cigarettes a year and most of these are of the class D tobacco lung busting blue acrid haze variety. There is nothing too romantic or sophisticated about these Hongtashan (Red Pagoda Hill) or Double Happiness brands and while they're cheap, my hair pulling buddy told me that he smoked 30 a day and spent 150 yuan of his 550 yuan monthly salary on fags -so not *that* cheap. To add to my general discomfort, a woman was resting her feet on a goat that complained vociferously and banged his bound cloven hooves on my chair throughout the trip, though to be fair the goat neither smoked nor touched my arm hair.

On arrival, I made straight for the statue where groups of men were posing with flags and fags and giving the victory V sign. On most of the hundreds of statues across China, Mao is striding purposefully forward, coat ruffled by an imaginary and divine breeze and hand raised as if hailing a taxi, but in Shaoshan, Mao stands bronze, diffident and rather avuncular with his hands behind his back. Perhaps this is the new image of Mao - a kindly uncle and old friend who knows what is best for his flock, even if for only 70% of the time.

I paid respects but didn't remove my hat - Hunanese winters are far too cold for that - and trotted up the steps to the museum and onto the exhibition hall. Lots of grand revolutionary statements here, lots of firearms that fought in the hands of justice and equality against the paper tigers of imperialism and lots of video of baying crowds and weeping Red Guards waving their Little Red Books on 1960s Tiananmen Square while their contemporaries in the West listened to the Rolling Stones and grew their hair. Also, there were some rather good waxworks of Mao on the 1935 Long March (youthful, handsome, energetic) and meeting heads of state in his later years (wise, benevolent, authoritative) sitting on ugly 1970s furniture. But it was the mundane items in the collection that interested me most and made the man seem human rather than some blue suited, hand waving cartoon. Here is Mao's comb and toothbrush[26] and here also his huge bed where he spent hours issuing directives and reading classical Chinese literature. His old grey knitted cardigan and green slippers – a sure way to shatter that

---

26   though by all accounts oral hygiene wasn't high on the Great Helmsman's priorities - Mao's personal physician Liu Zhi-Sui maintains Mao *never* brushed his teeth but preferred a quick rinse with green tea.

revolutionary mystique – are here too, right next to those swimming trunks with a belt.

For Mao, swimming represented an opportunity for self promotion and the triumph of the human spirit over the brute forces of nature; a recurring sentiment in recent Chinese history – see gigantic dam on Yangtze River, extraction of coal from implausibly deep mines in Shanxi, and the carrying of the Olympic torch to the summit of Everest. But apart from such crashing symbolism and the political benefits of displays of such virility, I think Mao just loved swimming.

Mao's first public swim was in the Pearl River in the south of the country, near to Hong Kong. This 1956 bathe took place at a time when Maoism seemed to be running out of steam and it seemed necessary to remind the people that this was no intellectual or bureaucratic revolution (as Mao believed the Russian one had become), but one based upon the heroism and physicality of the Long March and war with the Japanese. The Pearl River is a modest but extraordinarily dirty stretch of water and witnesses have described the leader floating past turds and chemical waste, which slightly detracts from the inspirational nature of Mao's breaststroke, but the Chairman climbed from the fetid water, toweled himself off and pronounced " if you put a fish in distilled water, how long do you think it will live?", though this profoundly irrelevant statement ignores the fact that a fish thrown in a tank with the remains of human bowel content wouldn't last too long either. Such wisdom will have been little consolation to the bodyguards who were obliged to accompany their Boss in their underpants, so precipitate was his decision to take the plunge and drift through the detritus, float through the faeces and paddle with the poo.

But it was the swims in the Yangtze of 1956 and 1966 that are most famous, when Mao defied conventional wisdom that the Mother River could never be tackled due to its treacherous currents, whirlpools, poisonous snakes and disease ridden snails. Yet the boy from Hunan did it and felt equipped and vindicated in launching China into the equally treacherous currents of the Great Leap Forward and Cultural Revolution. It seems churlish to point out that Mao didn't actually *swim* but sort of floated on his back like so much flotsam for miles downstream but no other political leader can boast of such sparkling feats of heroism. Ronald Reagan might have shared screen time with a mischievous chimpanzee (in the execrable film 'Bedtime for Bonzo') and Arnold Schwarzenegger has battled drugs barons, cyborgs and aliens but Mao Zedong's heroism belongs in the real world.

I slept in Shaoshan's grand new hotel, built to accommodate new middle class red tourists with disposable income and a bourgeois desire to visit the proletarian home of the Father of the Nation. The place was almost empty when I arrived and I was treated to overwhelming attention in the restaurant from a total of six giggling waitresses. The menu was written in Chinese characters and their ears, accustomed to the guttural accent of Hunan, could make no sense of my standard and rather basic Chinese as I attempted to order meat with my steamed rice. "Shenme? Ni yao shenme?" "You want what?", they asked. No problem; I could fall back on the linguistically challenged routine of making the noise of the animal I decided to devour. Now, Chinese is a very different language to English in terms of tonal requirements, sentence construction and excessive use of the letters q, z and z but it seems that not only do the Chinese have a centuries old culture and language based on Confucianist philosophy that is quite different to my own, but their animals make completely different noises too. 'Oink Oink' and 'Baa Baa' were quite indecipherable to my charming hosts who by this time were in paroxysms of laughter and had called the Head Chef to look at the crazy foreigner making noises.

In the end I got a strange gulping noise at the back of the throat animal that may have been duck. It was of course cooked in the Hunanese xiangcai style; that is with enough chili to cause temporary paralysis of the face. Mao said it was this fiery food that made the Hunanese people so 'red' and by the end of the meal my face had turned a shade of crimson sufficient to make any socialist proud.

The next morning dawned bright but with a bitter wind blowing off Shaoshan's pine clad hills. It was time to visit the centerpiece of the whole village: China's answer to Washington's birthplace in Westmoreland County Virginia or Churchill's Blenheim Palace. Mao's birthplace is an unprepossessing place built of local pine and tamped earth and entrance is very deliberately free since even the lowliest peasant should be able to pay respects here. The rooms, furniture and grounds confirm that here is the home of a real peasant (albeit a fairly well to do one) who experienced some real hardship. And this might be the appeal of Mao, that despite all his faults, he was pretty genuine; a real peasant, a real revolutionary and soldier, a great poet, writer and calligrapher. And boy, could he swim too.

The information boards in the house eulogize and describe life chez Mao. I learn that Mao's Dad was a 'thrifty, hardworking and crackajack (sic)' man and that the teenage Mao spent time in the kitchen urging his nearest and dearest to give up family bonds for the 'Big Family' of China. Frankly, this must have been irritating for the Mao clan and I can just hear his old Mum now...'yes, dear, I really will give up family bonds if you don't go and tidy your room'. Meanwhile, his younger brothers Ze-Min and Ze-Tan must have tired of games of 'Revolutionary uprising of the masses against the suppression of the landed classes' in the backyard where they always had to be servants of the old regime, while Mao played the young revolutionary who gets to hit his brothers with a big stick.

As I strolled back to the village past cabbage fields, I stopped at a tiny store where the owner had hung a photo of Mao when he called on her family during a visit to Shaoshan in 1959. She tells me that Mao 'saved' China and recalls that during the Cultural Revolution, so many Red Guards visited, that they slept on her floor. "They were very nice though...very disciplined and polite and they helped me carry water from my pond and gathered firewood. They had red books and shouted 'Long Live Chairman Mao'!"

I decided more fresh air was in order before the suffocating bus ride back to Changsha and took a walk in the countryside, imagining Mao hiking these hills too, a copy of Marx's *Das Kapital* and some lemon squash and Kendal mint cake in his rucksack. Progress on my own Long March was accompanied by martial music piped from speakers cunningly disguised as rocks, and I soon arrived at the prosaically named 'Building #1' which Mao visited on another trip to Shaoshan. Complete with bomb shelter and cinema, Mao came here to contemplate the launch of the violence and mayhem of the Cultural Revolution and stayed for a grand total of 11 days, which doesn't seem a terribly good return on a place built solely for his visit. He also swam/floated in the nearby reservoir which must have seemed like child's play after the floaters and whirlpools of the Pearl and Yangtze. Shaoshan saved its kitsch for last however when I turned a corner and for 10 yuan was given the opportunity to dress as a Red Guard, complete with imitation firearm, and pose with a spectacularly unconvincing cardboard cutout of Mao reclining in rattan chair and clutching a tiny cardboard Double Happiness cigarette. This caused a great deal of interest and photo taking from my fellow Shaoshan pilgrims, and no little laughter too. It must have been my hairy arms protruding from my too-short Socialist sleeves that amused them

Arrival back in Changsha was a shock after the mountains and forests of Shaoshan. This is one of those huge and anonymous cities that no-one outside China has ever heard of but with a population as big as London. I said goodbye to my fellow passengers and disembarked next to the Xiang Jiang. This River is protected by 2 goddesses, Erhung and Nuying who committed suicide here after the death of their husband; the characteristic spots on Xiang Jiang bamboo are said to be the teardrops of the women. Changsha means 'Long sand' and it is the river that gives the city its name because of the narrow midstream bar there. Now called Orange Island, the bar was once off limits to Chinese and home to ostentatious European architecture built to represent permanence and with a sense of superiority since Changsha was a treaty port from 1903 with 'special trading rights' for Europeans. No wonder the locals had a revolution.

The island is home now to a new gesture of superiority and permanence. Work has finished here on the largest statue of Mao in China. The Chinese Tourist Board reported that the marble statue 'will cover a floor space of 2300 sq m and will tower 32 metres high'. Further, the project will include a memorial hall in which 'Mao's written works and possessions giving insight into his extraordinary life will go on display. The statue will become a main tourist attraction'. I love the certainty of this last sentence- its almost an order- but they're probably right because 32 metres is pretty damn big and the tallest statue in China. This big marble Mao went straight in at #49 in the biggest statues in the world league, tucked in between such gilded luminaries as the Memorial to the Virgin in rural Bulgaria and the Monkey king at Maharashtra in India. Naturally everyone assumed the new statue would fit the familiar pattern of Mao statues found on traffic circles and town squares all across China – Mao standing middle aged and overweight with hand aloft wearing dour overcoat, but this statue is different and depicts a 32 year old Mao looking cool with long, wind-swept unkempt hair like the wheels have just stopped spinning on his revolutionary skateboard.

Impressive indeed, but read this press release from the China Daily newspaper in 2005; 'The Hunan provincial government has decided to build a statue of the great leader Mao. This statue will be made of marble and will be *183 metres* high, since Mao's height was 1.83m'. Now that would have been some statue. Forget 49th place, this Maozilla would have been comfortably #1, beating the Spring temple Buddha at Leshan in Sichuan province into a cocked hat. Let's get some perspective here; that other colossus at Rhodes was reputedly a paltry 30 metres in height, the Great pyramid at Giza is 137 metres and the dome of St Paul's cathedral a piddling 111 metres. It's like laying 15 and a quarter double Decker buses or nearly 80 Yao Ming's (China's most famous basketball player and carrier of the flag at the Beijing Olympics) end to end. What happened to such a grandiose plan and why did The Chairman shrink to a paltry 32 metres? I think we should be told. On questioning, several locals professed ignorance of such ambition and were quite satisfied with the 32 metres they were given, though I couldn't help feeling that my questions had sowed some seeds of disappointment about what might have been.

They were however able to tell me that Mao had swum between Orange Island and the shore on the occasion of his 65th birthday. I registered this with barely a flicker of surprise since it was becoming obvious that, much like a Labrador I once owned, you couldn't hold the Chairman back when he got a sniff of water...'No Mao, come back, stop it, come back I say...Oh Jeez, he's gone. Whose turn is it to dry him off?'

Mao's old school, the Hunan #1 teacher training school, stands on the banks of the Xiang Jiang. He studied here from 1913-18 and despite failing his Art exam by drawing a circle and calling it an egg, was named student of the year in 1917. He returned as a teacher in

1920 and became Principal in 1922 which is a meteoric rise by any standards and probably a sign of things to come. Perhaps this success in his teaching career was due to his use of the school's open air well for his morning baths. Mao tells us that the freezing water was good to cultivate 'fortitude, courage and boldness' though goodness knows what the students must have made of it. Still, I bet he didn't make that involuntary noise the rest of us make when his testicles entered the freezing water; maybe the insulating properties of those trunks with the belt had a point after all.

The only thing to rival Mao's fame in Changsha lies in the Hunan Provincial Museum. Inside the Museum's dimly lit rooms are the remains of 3 Han Dynasty tombs excavated in 1972. Now, I like History as much as the next man but there are only so many bronzes, sculptures and lacquer work bowls I can gaze at thoughtfully before I start heading for the 'I Love Hunan' commemorative erasers and bookmarks in the gift shop, even if the exhibits *are* 2100 years old. But wait, hold the 'My dad went to Changsha and all he bought me was this T-shirt' shirt; this museum is also home to the mummified corpse of the Marquess of Dai. This 2000 year old toff is remarkably well preserved after her burial in a lead sealed coffin and 80 litres of preserving fluid. Scientists have been able to determine the diseases she had (gall stones and bilharzia in case you're interested) and food she ate and have taken the time to extract her internal organs and store them in jars in the same room. This was all rather startling though my squeamish expression was nothing compared to the twisted snarl frozen on the face of the mummy.

Yet in the 21st century, Changsha has an altogether different kind of notoriety and fame. Yes, there are the near perfect remains of 2000 year old Han dynasty royalty (and her kidneys) in the museum here and yes, one of the most infamous dictators of the 20th century whose economic policies and extravagant designs for the revolutionizing of the Chinese peasantry affected the lives of millions was born close to this otherwise unremarkable inland city, but Changsha today is best known across the most populous nation on earth because of TV.

Most Chinese provinces have their own TV stations and are remarkable only for the banality of their programming. Viewers across China subsist on a diet of political meetings, military parades, dodgy Kung-Fu movies, Ming Dynasty costume dramas in a cardboard Forbidden City and the occasional space launch. But Hunan province TV changed all that. Hunan gave China 'SuperGirls'.

Viewers of 'Pop Idol' will recognise the format of SuperGirls, or 'Mongolian cow sour yoghurt Supergirl contest', to give it its full appellation, where hundreds of hopeful girls audition for an opportunity to sing and show off on the telly. But that's where the similarities end.

I took a bus out to a drab suburb of Changsha on a cold afternoon to see the unprepossessing TV studios which sit behind ornate but rather untidy gates. A sign warns visitors that the concrete slope should be negotiated with care since it is 'crafty and slippy', yet here in 2005, 120 000 hopefuls braved the artful incline to audition for the show. They came from all over the Middle Kingdom and were aged 4-89. The participation of arthritic, croaking old hags persuaded the organizers to put an age limit on the following series of 18-40, though I think the 89 year olds should have been given another chance. There followed a weekly knockout competition in Changsha where the weakest two performers had to face off in a 'PK' or 'Playerkill' and this is where things got really interesting.

First off, the Chinese People's Political Consultative Conference, a political advisory body that meets once a year and previously chaired by such luminaries as Mao Zedong and Deng Xiaoping, issued a strongly worded condemnation of the show. Maybe it was the glittery stage set or the hot pants worn by some competitors that got this august body all hot under the collar, or maybe they objected because some of the Supergirls' singing really wasn't so super. Liu Zhongde, a delegate from the conference, decried the competition as 'poison' for the nation's youth, and which 'distorted mentality'. Liu opined that he wasn't against openness but that "if you open the doors and windows to let in fresh air, flies and mosquitoes are bound to come in too". China Daily added to this chorus of disapproval when they said that Supergirls is "like Western fast food". I'm not entirely sure whether this implies that the show is unsubstantial, undesirable and unhealthy or whether they meant that Supergirls is a convenient stopgap; no replacement for really nutritious culture of course, but delicious in its own way.

Regardless of such disapproval, China loved the show. The final was watched by 400 million people; that's more than the population of Western Europe and easily the most people who have watched a single TV show anywhere ever. Even the final episode of 'Dallas' or the trial of OJ Simpson didn't get that many viewers. More impressive still is that viewers were required to vote in the Playerkill by text and 800 million obliged throughout the series - part of the overall income of 766 million yuan (nearly $100 million) generated by the show. Except the votes weren't called 'votes' since this word was deemed too politically charged, so 800 million viewers texted in officially sanctioned 'messages of support' instead.

Regardless of the niceties of nomenclature, this is by any measure an astonishing level of interest and the largest expression of democracy that has ever happened in China. No matter that it was for women singing beneath a glitter ball rather than for a democratic and representative legislative government body. Sadly, the vote was not without scandal and whispers of corruption when the 2005 final was won by the girl who was universally regarded as having the weakest singing voice of the three girls who had survived the rigours of the Playerkill. Vote rigging and multi texting have been rumoured and the China Daily gleefully ruminated on this 'imitation of a democratic system which ends up selecting the singer who has the least ability to carry a tune', as if the Supergirls debacle negated the whole political process of the Western world since the French Revolution.

The winner who couldn't sing was 21 year old Li Yuchuan. Except she could sing and is actually rather good and anyway, locals told me that she won because of her unorthodox style and her 'aggression'. I think this means that she is tomboyish and speaks her mind, which runs counter to the traditional Chinese view of the pretty, demure and rather subservient female so this can be no bad thing. No bound feet for Li, but chunky boots, orange hair, a couple of huge concerts in Shanghai, 5 million yuan donated to leukaemia charities and the cover of Time magazine in October 2005. As I left Changsha, I couldn't help feeling that Li, the most popularly elected person in Chinese History, is 21st century Hunan's new revolutionary. No wonder the Peoples Consultative Conference was upset.

Hunan province slides into Hubei about 150km north of Changsha in a patchwork of water around Dongting Hu, or Lake Dongting. The provinces here are named after their proximity to this massive expanse of water; Hunan means 'south of the lake' and Hubei is 'north of the lake'. The lake is China's second largest and is normally about 3000 sq km which is quite impressive in itself, but during the July-September floods this can increase to 20 000 sq km. Such bald statistics hardly do justice to the inconvenience this growth spurt must bring to the local population, though the wetness and the sediment that the four rivers feeding the lake bring create excellent alluvial farmland. During my winter visit, farmers were temporary squatters on fertile land on the shores of the lake, knowing that they would have to surrender their neatly tended plots to the water when the summer rains came.

The lake is home to the finless porpoise; so called because of its lack of dorsal fin, though locals call it 'jiangzhu' or 'River Pig'. Environmentalists believe there are only 1400 river pigs left of which perhaps 300 are rooting for truffles or rolling in the mud or whatever river pigs do, beneath the waters of Dongting. China Daily announced in 2007 that the Dongting lake area will be restored to a sustainable biodiversity environment within 5-10 years, which sounded like a sufficiently vague time estimate to ensure that a far longer time will elapse before real progress is made, and predictably enough little has been done to improve the environment of the area. Further delay could prove fatal since finless dolphin numbers are declining by 8% per year; the River pig may yet follow the Baiji or Yangtze dolphin into extinction.

Hunan mice are rather less endangered. I was interested to find out how a 10 fold increase in the lake's size affected life in this part of rural Hunan and asked a few villagers about this annual inundation. They all seemed remarkably sanguine about something that was unstoppable and inevitable; after all, why worry about things that can't be changed? However, several locals also mentioned that the floods in June 2007 were especially bad 'because of the mice'. It seems that during this flood, mice were driven from the islands of the lake and invaded dozens of local communities. This of course damaged crops and dykes and has led to a general distrust of small rodents in the vicinity. No chance of a local Hunan branch of Disneyland as Mickey would be chased from the premises by an angry mob with pitchforks. But how many is 'many'? All agreed that there were hundreds of the little critters running wild that murine summer of 2007, but in fact it seems likely that *millions* swam ashore and ran around in some kind of crazy rodent biathlon before locals, armed mainly with shovels hit them on their tiny whiskery heads in an orgy of bloodletting. No surprise then that the creation of 'sustainable biodiversity' doesn't figure highly on the priorities of local families who are far too busy tidying up billions of tiny corpses and moving their farms back and forth to escape the floods or to worry too much about the river pig.

The lake is also home to one more creature. In the year 278 BC, a Chinese poet and official called Qu Yuan waded into Dongting Hu holding a large rock and disappeared forever like some ancient dynastic Ophelia into the cold and icy depths beneath. This act of quiet desperation, a protest against government nepotism and corruption has been commemorated across China almost ever since. Legend says that locals rowed out to save poor Qu Yuan, beating drums and splashing paddles to scare the marine life and throwing rice and dumplings into the water to keep the fish (river pigs among them presumably) away from the submerged body. And so was born the Tuen Ng or Dragon Boat festival, where teams of paddlers race across the water beating drums, and villagers throw gifts of rice wrapped in three cornered silk packages into the water every May across China from Hong Kong to Beijing to Shanghai to Sichuan.

The social idealism and unbending patriotism of Qu Yuan have long served as models for Chinese officialdom. Mao expressed his admiration for such sacrifice and selfless devotion to public duty in the 1950s and sanctioned the publication of a stamp bearing the drowned Mandarin's likeness. There is however no record of Mao having taking part in the festival either by throwing rice packages into the water or putting his back into paddling a boat, but then after all, who needs to row when you can swim?

HAINAN

海南

33 940sq km
Population 8.3 million

Everyone is born a king and most people die in exile.

Oscar Wilde.

I remember the 1970s like a cliché. Nylon flares tucked in socks I'd ride my Chopper bike to the corner shop where Mungo Jerry played on the radio to buy cream soda. It was *always* blazing hot in the 70s so I'd stop on the way home and take greedy gulps from the bottle (five pence back on return), burp my way up our front drive past my Dad's Ford Capri and push aside the coloured plastic strips that hung in the frame of the kitchen door. My mum would be mixing Angel Delight and we'd go and sit in the front room beneath a picture of a crying clown because Miss World was on the telly.

Nothing screams 1970s like Miss World. The pageant recorded monumental TV audiences throughout the decade, when beautiful ladies with Farrah Fawcett flick hairstyles in American tan tights strutted in high cut swimwear past wide lapel black-tie judges. Bob Hope left off entertaining the troops in Saigon to laugh in the face of feminism[27], Bruce Forsyth married Miss Puerto Rico and a litany of beautiful women promised to use their fame to travel, to help children and puppies, to make the world peaceful.

By the 1980s it all seemed a bit old hat. Organisers tried to update the show by introducing personality and intelligence into the evaluation of beauty and vital statistics were no longer deemed vital. But the show was past its prime, just like a faded beauty queen. Interest was sagging and the changes were mere face paint on a show that had become flabby and unattractive. I had grown up and didn't much care for cream soda. The Sex Pistols were on the radio and soap operas were on the TV.

But in Hainan it is still the 1970s. 'China's tropical Hawaiian paradise island'™ hosted Miss World in 2003, 2004, 2005, 2007 and 2010, during which time, with crashing inevitability, China had its first winner.[28] In this new, revamped and politically correct Miss World, contestants were joined on stage by the daughter and grandson of Nelson Mandela to sing for World AIDS Day - Mandela gave a televised speech too, a Miss World away from his Robben Island freedom fighting revolutionism. A special 'Beauty with a purpose' category was created for contestants most inclined to use their physical perfection to help others and in the pursuit of world peace, though reassuringly there was still a beach beauty prize too for those less inclined to altruism but who looked damn good in a bikini. In 2004 Maria Montilla arrived on the island, won the crown and ticked all the boxes. She is ravishingly

---

27   In 1970 he said "Anyone who would try and break up an affair as wonderful as this has got to be some kind of dope".

28   Zhang Zilin in 2007. China won again in 2010 and 2012

beautiful, a professional triathlete and the founder of a programme in her Peruvian homeland to give breakfast to hundreds of children in poor areas. When I checked her website, she claimed she had organised many other charitable initiatives but that 'she doesn't care currently' (she is probably too busy with her professional 'Marinera' dancing career). Maria inherited the title from the daughter of Middle of the Road, Lady in Red crooner Chris DeBurgh who claims on *her* website that she is 'a girly girl who lurrrrrves her clothes and shoes' and whose favourite books are 1984 and Animal Farm. You couldn't make this stuff up.

In 2007, Hainan hosted Mr World too. Juan Garcia Postigo from Spain beat 56 other contestants to the crown, all of whom had to build rafts, run up hills and learn Kung Fu in addition to looking gorgeous. Postigo was overjoyed with his win and said "I love food and making people happy". Beauty with a purpose indeed.

It's not just Mr. and Miss World that recalls the 1970s on Hainan. My visit coincided with a big Chinese holiday and hundreds of mainland tourists were dressed in flowery shorts and matching shirts (and Lord, socks with sandals) as if they were auditioning for a part in Hawaii Five-0. This was the Chinese middle class abroad, ostentatiously and slightly self-consciously enjoying a little sun, sea and sand on China's tropical island and getting burned pink into the bargain.

It had been clear that Hainan would be different when I flew low over palm trees and wooden huts on the descent to Sanya Phoenix International airport. This was Thailand or Vietnam below our wing; we were after all much closer to Hanoi and Bangkok than Beijing. The airport terminal was built like a native house from tropical wood; a fan, shaped like palm leaves, lazily stirred the air and the roof was crowned by giant pineapples. The immigration staff smiled and urged me to have a nice day instead of refusing to look up or speak at all which is the behaviour I have come to expect from a person in a uniform in China.

Outside the terminal at least, I was in China again. Taxi drivers were demanding ridiculous money for the trip into town and I had to employ my injured 'you're overcharging me because I'm a foreigner' voice and walk disconsolately towards the bus before the price came down; a technique I had employed usefully on taxi ranks all over China.

Sanya is Hainan's tourist town with miles of golden sand beaches and though it was holiday week I had not booked ahead since there is always *somewhere* to stay and I like to look at my room first and choose the one which has the fewest number of cigarette burns on the carpet. My attempt to catch a train to Hainan should have warned me that my turn up and pick a room approach wouldn't work this time. The train to Hainan from China has to cross water and since 2003 has been loaded onto a railway ferry at the end of the Leizhou Peninsula in Guangdong province to make the one-hour trip to the north of the island. I was intrigued by this train on a boat solution to a problem and determined to buy a ticket in Hong Kong. But I couldn't. Everyone was going to Hainan to frolic on the beach like Mr. and Miss World and though I smiled sweetly and tried to use my beauty with a purpose on the ticket seller, there were no tickets to be had and I flew instead.

It's not that there were no rooms available, I just couldn't afford them. Prices were inflated by 500% during holiday week and I couldn't bring myself to hand over 4000 yuan for a three star room where the bath didn't drain, the light gave off a brightness equivalent to a stuttering candle at the bottom of a well and a prostitute would ring me at some unearthly hour to tell me I am very handsome and to ask if I wanted 'masagee' - presumably the price for this service would be vastly inflated in holiday week too.

The reason for all this hyperinflation is that Hainan is hot. This is a boon in wintertime when the rest of China, even the southernmost states and Hong Kong, are perishing cold; so wealthy Chinese come to Hainan to enjoy the sun and to wear Hawaiian shirts. These sun-seekers are seriously rich and I saw them all over Sanya displaying their wealth on their wrists and around their necks, driving massive black cars like gangsters and standing on the beach with their Armani suit trouser legs rolled up to the knee. Such well-heeled travelers could afford to go abroad of course, but the securing of a visa is still a tricky business for all Chinese, no matter how much bling they possess and anyway most are quite insular and prefer to holiday in their own country. (they are like Americans in this respect, only 20% of whom own a passport).

Visitors to Hainan are from all over China, but especially the freezing North. I spoke with many on my visit who said their homes were in Gansu, Liaoning, Hebei or Jilin and their voices became the ghosts of my travels, a summation of all those distant provinces where I had battled snow and deserts and interminable queues in train stations. It's the willingness of these northerners to spend, to splash the cash, that made Sanya's hotel rooms so ruinously expensive. It means property on Hainan is booming too; luxury villas and golf courses are springing up all over the island to cater to these people that the Chinese call 'migratory birds' come to warm their feathers in the winter and to fly home when the North finally warms up.

I soon downsized my expectations and like a migratory bird directed my taxi driver to the beach at Dadonghai as I knew Sanya's budget accommodation was packed into narrow alleys here, where hawkers sold all kinds of tropical fruit from wooden stalls. But even here, prices had been trebled and though I was resigned to paying up, there was not a room to be had.

A youth hostel manager saved me. He pointed to a pile of tents in a grubby outhouse where a mongrel dog was extravagantly licking his balls and said I could use one of these for 100 yuan. He offered me the choice of pitching in his concrete yard beside some large green bins above which clouds of flies buzzed and where more dogs licked themselves and each other in a frantic display of hygiene or foreplay. "Or", he said, "You can take a tent and camp on the beach". And so it came to pass that I sat outside my fabric room beneath coconut trees and watched the waves crashing onto the sand at Dadonghai. An on shore breeze from the South China sea ruffled my hair, the fat pink children of wealthy northerners splashed in the shallows; my tent was in front of the most exclusive (and madly expensive) beachfront properties in Sanya and I was the King of Hainan.

But this wasn't Florida or Benidorm so I was something of a foreign curiosity and the migratory birds often approached to ask me where I was from and why was I in a tent and didn't I know there was an excellent hotel not far away? A security guard from the luxury villas behind told me to go away but I informed him this was a public beach so I wouldn't and remarkably, thrillingly *he* went away. (This bureaucratic retreat was perhaps the single most surprising -and un-Chinese - thing that happened to me on Hainan).

But mostly people were friendly and just wanted to chat, like all people on holiday who are relaxed and have time to kill. People were keen to tell me how wonderful Hainan was and weren't these the best beaches in the world? One man explained to me that the Chinese on Hainan are in paradise since "we ate the snake and not the apple because the Chinese always prefer meat to fruit", though the impact of this proverb was lost because he had to explain it to me four times.

Their view was very insular of course - the opinion of people who had never seen the beaches of Thailand or Australia - and by mid-afternoon, though the sand may have been like icing sugar, I could hardly see it at all beneath the crush of sunbathing tourists. The sea too, was no doubt pellucid and aquamarine but was a soup of bobbing bodies wrapped in inflatable rings. I took a dip with them and have never chatted to so many adults who couldn't swim, though I suppose if you come from China's frozen North there's not much chance to practice.

"Isn't it fine?!" "China's Hawaii!" smiled the bobbing corks and actually it *was* rather fine to see the Chinese letting their hair down and giddily enjoying the beach. It felt like a bright vision of the future, though I also thought of the contrast between so much wealth and the grim poverty of the countryside and guessed the future might not seem so bright and sun kissed for all Chinese.

At the edge of the beach the migratory birds were eating and banging their plates on wooden boards while businessmen sang karaoke very badly though it didn't matter since everyone was here to have fun. Dozens of kites were fluttering above China's 'cleanest ocean' in China's 'cleanest air' (both claims made by Hainan's official website) and the more adventurous migratory birds were trying their hand at scuba-diving, though like most activities in China this was excessively regimented; don ill fitting wetsuit, join lengthy queue, ride in groups of 20 in clapped-out speed boat, dive for 15 minutes, return in boat, hand back wetsuit, proceed to next activity. It would've been good to have longer to enjoy the dive just as it would have been good to have more than one square metre of beach to yourself, but there were just too many people – a phrase I had often recited on my China travels.

By sunset, the karaoke stands had turned to bars where Russian teenagers were paid to dance on stage by lecherous businessmen who clapped and cheered, their glasses askew and eyes screwed against the smoke that curled from the cigarette which never left their mouths. Kites continued to fly, but now they had neon lights framing their shape and strung along their tails. They flew incredibly high like blinking satellites in the night sky held by serious men who clung to hundreds of metres of string wound round elaborate spools. Perhaps these men were coal mine managers from the North come to relax and exchange one winding gear for another.

The kites were reeled in when the fireworks began. I stayed on Hainan for four nights, and for every one of them the sky was filled with the mayhem of exploding rockets. This might have been inconvenient if I had wanted to sleep, lights flashing through the walls of my paper thin tent, but I was happy to sit on the beach and watch the show until the last rocket exploded, the last whizz bang popped and the last sparkler fizzed and died after midnight.

The explosives were set by bravado men who used their cigarettes to light the fuse while young girls ran screaming from them just as they had run hysterically hours earlier from the waves that splashed on their feet. Indulgent parents let their children light the fuses: I saw toddlers wandering around with fiery sparklers and couldn't decide if the Chinese approach to fireworks is careless or carefree. Other revellers were lighting fuel bricks beneath paper lanterns and letting them drift into the night sky. There were dozens of these drifting over the headland like a flotilla at the end of the beach and I liked them so much that I tried my hand at a launch too but found they had to be coaxed and cajoled into flight. My first effort collapsed unceremoniously into the sea, but with the enthusiastic support and advice of local experts, my second floated serenely away like all the rest. It felt good to see its red light so far away and out of reach that had been in my hand moments before, like a captive thing set free in the wild.

The blackened remains of gunpowder littered the sand the next day, like the beaches of Normandy after D-Day. I woke to find another tent pitched not more than 2 metres from mine, though there was an empty half mile of sand upon which to sleep. My neighbours had not disturbed me in the night, though that they had chosen to sleep so cheek by jowl was a perfect reminder of what the Western traveler in

China cannot understand. The concept of personal space is a non-starter in this country not so much because of the crowds, but because the Chinese have so little concept or need of it. It simply doesn't figure in their psyche at all and the moment I accepted this was the moment I began to really enjoy journeying in this land of jostling elbows, of pushing and shoving and shouted-too-close-to- the-face conversations.

I bade a cheery good morning to my conjoined twin and wandered to the extreme end of the beach to see some naked people. The eastern edge of Dadonghai beach is, to my knowledge, the only place in the whole of this prurient country where China's 1.3 billion people can take their clothes off in public and let their pubic hair down. In other countries, nudist beaches are hidden coyly behind gates and trees, but Sanya's naturists were separated from the masses only by a few rusty barriers that looked as if they had been purloined from the side of a dual carriageway.

The area was populated exclusively by men of a certain age standing skinny and hairless save for a scrubby patch of black pubic hair with hands on hips in the crashing surf gazing enigmatically into the distance. It might have been quieter to camp here, further from the fireworks and with less chance of waking to find another tent inches from mine. But it would have been disturbing to rise in the morning and unzip my fly sheet to gaze on the naked form of a Han Chinese businessmen come south from Shandong to enjoy the warm sun and invigorating sea breeze of China's Hawaii. There was not a single woman amongst them and I should know because I watched for long enough in the interests of research until one of the lithe Greek gods padded over and beckoned for me to join him. I declined and hurried away not because I'm prudish but because I get stared at enough in China when I have my clothes *on* thank you very much. And anyway, it was time for lunch.

There is a great tradition of grammatically imprecise English menus in China, though I have never seen such a collection of mistranslation as I encountered at the cafes on Dadonghai beach. I spurned the hot dog stands since the memory of the nudist beach was too fresh and I was left with a startling and tempting choice of dishes such as ' the sheet iron pig digs up', 'unwearied effort however beefsteak' and 'explodes the potato strip' washed down with some 'fried fresh orange juice'. All of which reminded me of a friend who visited a western restaurant in Shanghai and chose fishcakes from the menu. The waitress returned sometime later with an expression on her face that radiated doubt but also a defiant 'well this is what you asked for' expression, and placed a plate in front of her that contained a piece of fish and a slice of Black Forest gateau; fish – cake. I don't recall whether my friend ate her lunch.

I ambled back to my accommodation, resolved to pack up and see more of Hainan than just the beach, and found the door of my tent zipped open. The hostel had warned me of the dangers of theft and that thieves on the beach often resorted to complicated tricks to lay hands on the valuables of their unsuspecting victims. This seemed an elaborate ruse indeed - arrange for dozens of naked men to stroll around one end of the beach to distract me, and then slip into the unguarded tent to steal my tube of toothpaste, since I had left nothing more valuable inside, though in fact nothing had gone and I decided that I must have left the tent open in my rush to get onto the beach that morning.

I went back to the hostel past wedding photo couples standing in the silty water with abandoned concrete monstrosities behind them whose purpose was unfathomable to me. The bride and groom were passively obeying every instruction from the photographer behind the huge lens who barked out jump, embrace, lift her up, put her down orders. And why *wouldn't* they obey, since the side of the photographers van trumpeted that he was from 'Golden Lady p-hotogenic (sic) experts. We know everything; even plain ladies will look good'.

I rode a bicycle to the heart of old Sanya past the street markets whose stalls tottered under the weight of giant tropical fruits -- mangoes, bananas and pineapples, delicious custard apples, sweet lychees and enormous durian and jackfruit[29]. The stall holder told me that Hainan's fruit is better than anywhere else (by 'anywhere' he meant the rest of China) because it's not picked until it's ripe. He had a point because supermarkets in China transport their food before it is ready and

---

29   the jackfruit here were enormous - three foot tall and weighing 20 kg. Must be all that Hainan sunshine and fresh air.

ripen it off the tree or sometimes with the aid of chemicals; certainly his mangoes were fat and juicy and delicious.

The rest of Sanya city was rather less picturesque and sweet. There were fishing boats jammed so tightly into the wharf that I wondered how they could get out to do any fishing, though this is a moot point since the waters around Hainan have been so over fished that they have become the marine equivalent of China's Gobi desert. The boats looked rustic and pretty enough, especially when some firecrackers were set off on board one, though there were so many boats that I couldn't tell on which one and I wondered at the wisdom of setting off gunpowder on the wooden decks of this tinder dry armada on a hot Hainan day.

Sanya's main market was neither rustic nor pretty. It was a depressing place of cheap plastic toys and even cheaper clothes where I could have searched all day and found nothing to buy. There was a wet market too, full of smelly fish imported from more abundant waters and with floors so wet that I feared I would fall over and sit in some rancid effluent or fish heads that would never scrub clean. There were grinning sheep heads and disemboweled dogs for sale too, their faces frozen into the permanent snarl of the dead and at last, clean and fragrant piles of herbs and vegetables, verdant and heavenly after I had walked the valley of the shadow of death of fish, sheep and dogs.

All those corpses and innards and bulging eyes seemed the stuff of nightmares, but were just meals and sustenance for locals; a link in the food chain. But back in the main drag of the markets I saw something that felt harder to rationalise than any abuse of animals I had encountered in China. I had seen dogs and cats in Guangdong soups and chickens fed to tigers in Heilongjiang, seahorses skewered on sticks in Beijing and fish bludgeoned to death in Hong Kong. Yet all of it felt justifiable on some level; as food or as an intrinsic part of an alien culture. But here in Sanya I saw an animal sorely misused, that I could not justify and that for all my travel in China left me as confused and baffled as if I'd never been to the country in my life.

The animal that caused such bewilderment was a rat. A woman had set up stall on a wooden table to sell plugs, though these were no ordinary plugs. They were inset with coloured lights that flickered on when the woman plugged one into a circuit board to prove that they worked and were worth parting with 10 yuan for. That the lights came on didn't seem to be enough for the woman who needed some other way to demonstrate the efficacy of her plugs. So she had connected the circuit board to a wire cage on her table, inside which a brown rat hopped with pain whenever she completed the circuit and made the cage live.

Aside from the moral issues connected to this lab rat, I couldn't see the point of her sales pitch - why would it be useful to buy a plug that can electrocute vermin? Still, the plugs were selling well and no one seemed to mind the squeaking and dancing of the rat, in fact the whole enterprise raised laughter from the passing shoppers. I mounted my bike, marveled how different this country is to home and drew a mental list of pros and cons as I cycled back along the river to decide whether there was more to admire about China than to dislike.

I pedaled past the boats and steeply uphill to Luhuitou Park whose expansive views across the whole of Sanya went into my pros column, especially because I couldn't see or hear the rat from up here. Luhuitou means 'deer turns its head' after a Li minority legend of a deer that transformed into a beautiful girl as it turned to face a young hunter. There's a rather dull statue of the deer at the top of the park where tourists were having photos taken, two fingers raised in victory or chomping ice creams or possibly fingering hand in pocket the plug they'd bought from the market below and which they knew was in full working order.

Despite the Li legend, there was no evidence of Li culture here; I knew I would need to go elsewhere on Hainan Island for that. The Li are Hainan's original inhabitants who populated the central highlands of the island long before the Han Chinese came here on holiday in Hawaiian shirts. They arrived from Guangxi province in the third century BC and traditionally looked quite different than the incoming Han; men wore their hair in top knots from which the Li take their name and women had elaborate Maori style facial tattoos intended to make them undesirable to raiders and rival clans.

The Highlands are remote and the Li still lived a basic hunter gatherer existence there as late as the 1930s. I was braced for a tortuous journey on a rattling public bus to get there but as I returned my tent to the hostel after a second firework and lantern night on the beach, I noticed a row of three motorbikes lined up in the hostel forecourt. It's

261

nearly impossible for a foreigner to hire a vehicle in China though this cannot be a reflection of a desire to keep China's roads safe since the country has easily the worst traffic accident record in the world. There are 90,000 deaths on China's roads every year and hardly a week passes without some report of a 10 vehicle pile up on the fast highways outside Shanghai or a bus fallen into a ravine on the mountain passes of Sichuan. I've eaten dodgy food in China, climbed high mountains and met nefarious characters but I've always felt it's the roads that will get me in the end. On reflection, perhaps the refusal to allow foreigners on the roads is designed for *our* protection since how could I possibly know the strategies for dealing with marauding taxi drivers, buzzing scooters and lumbering Dongfeng trucks?

But on Hainan everything is different. I asked the manager about the motorbikes, the Chinese name for which is pronounced exactly like 'more torture' and he said I could ride one away for just 100 yuan per day - this was one thing on Hainan that had not been hit by galloping holiday inflation. But I didn't have my license. "No problem" said the manager, "your big nose and white skin are your license". So it was that I fired up my red (which added to my lingering sense of danger since red vehicles are of course faster than all other colours) Da Yang more torture (made with pride in Guangzhou); 125 cc of precision Chinese engineering, feeling worried that the hostel had no helmet to give me - the hostel manager said the Chinese don't believe in helmets 'since men's heads are like coconuts' - and pulled nervously into the streaming Sanya traffic.

It was a long ride to the Li homeland, but once I turned off the main road and began to climb into the hills, there was less traffic and the ride began to be fun, though an unexpected tunnel made me feel horribly vulnerable as coaches and lorries roared past me, horns blaring in the dark. It was good to be on a road trip in China where I could stop and look whenever I wanted and though my head is not a coconut, it was fun to feel the warm tropical island breeze blowing through my hair.

My first stop was at Yalong Bay where entrance to the beach also granted access to the shell museum whose deathly dull exhibits promoted ocean conservation - Save the Oceans! Save our Shells! — but whose souvenir shop sold all manner of gifts made from shells, special offer for today only on shell clocks. But I was done with beaches and felt the call of the hills. The beauty of independent transport is that you can pause whenever you like and when I saw a sign for Nantian Hot Springs, I pulled off the road to soak my bones. This was opportune since the more torture was living up to its name and I was beginning to ache all over. Everything rattled and shook on my Da Yang bike – is it possible to have vibration white knuckle in your feet and your arse? In fact the only thing that worked *really* well on my motorbike was the horn, a sure indication of the priorities of the average Chinese road user. Also I wanted a wash; I had slept for 2 nights on a beach and had sand in places where sand does not belong.

The hot springs were as full of tourists as the sea had been at Dadonghai, though here no one wore a rubber ring and everyone was sweating and red not because of the sun but because they had been boiled pink like prawns. There were hot springs and very hot springs and springs with bags of spices at the bottom that leached a brown effluent of herbs into the water and made me feel as if I was infusing in a giant pot of chamomile tea. But I spent most of my time in the fish therapy pool where I luxuriated with a dozen others while hundreds of tiny fish nibbled dead skin from our feet. This was unbearably ticklish for a while but soon became weirdly soothing and pleasant, at least until a little fish swam up the leg of my shorts and got to work painfully with its little mouth.

There were more wealthy Chinese from the distant north being poached in the springs and we talked as the fish munched. All said they were 'businessmen' though I'm not sure what this meant - politicians, cadres, soldiers, mine owners, the controllers of lives, the exploiters of the workforce? But they were friendly enough and their children, the future of China, were polite and cheerful though why wouldn't they be since sitting in a warm pool being masticated by tiny fish was infinitely preferable to being exfoliated by coruscating winter winds north of the Yellow River.

My motorbike puttered further uphill and over the watershed to Wuzhishan. China's smallest city is a nondescript place surrounded by verdant hills and tidy countryside where Li village potbellied pigs snort and fuss amongst tidy rows of Li village cabbages. It's all too pastoral and verdant and though everything was well tended, I could see no one out in the fields or hard at work. Palm fronds fluttered in the breeze and buffalo wandered on the streets determined to make roadkill of me and my Da Yang bike and in a somnambulant midday heat, these highlands seemed as far from the industry of Shanghai, the mines of Shanxi, the ice of Manchuria and the politics of Beijing as it was possible to get. And therein lays the charm of China; a whole world in one state and I was enraptured enough to forgive the sight of the poor electrocuted rat in Sanya and to have a good opinion of China again. This lasted right through to lunchtime in Wuzhishan when the cheap plastic stool I was sitting on outside a dumpling restaurant collapsed. As I sprawled on the pavement none of my fellow diners laughed, but equally no one helped. They all just stared in silence, presumably wondering why foreigners choose to eat their dumplings lying down.

Wuzhishan was the capital of the Li autonomous government until 1987 when the central authorities reasserted close control over the area. The reason for the attack on federalism was that the local leaders had spent their 4.5 billion yuan road grant on importing luxury goods and cars from Hong Kong and Vietnam with the help of local naval units and were selling them on to the mainland at a profit of 150%. Politicians in Beijing became suspicious when 90,000 cars were imported to Hainan in two years (only 10,000 had been imported in the previous 30 years) along with three million TV sets which seemed an excessive obsession with driving and game shows for an island with a population of eight million.

Wuzhishan city is named after the hill nearby whose name means 'five finger mountain' and which at 1867m is Hainan's biggest. The five spikes of rock at the summit are said to be the fossilised fingers of a dying Li clan chieftain, though from where I stood on the hill by the extravagant city offices built on the ill gotten gains of cars and TVs, I could see only two and the hill looked more like a camel's hoof than a chieftains hand.

I rode to Qizhi Shan, the Da Yang still vibrating and trembling between my legs. The seven spikes on this hill are the seven Li immortals and are less lofty than the five fingers though I could at least see all seven. Most people visiting the area are introduced to these stories but they felt like myths that are petrified and fossilised, like the rocks on top of the hills. The whole Li culture felt the same; preserved and stereotyped for the tourists. I may have been wrong on my fleeting visit and perhaps the Li lifestyle is as alive and buoyant as ever, though on my trip to the mountains I didn't see a single topknot or a facial tattoo.

It was like this at Binglanggu Primitive Culture Tourist Centre too where coach loads of Han tourists arrived and shouted down mobile phones as they paid to see the totem worship area, the rattan and bamboo workshop, the ancient folk instrument demonstrations and the medicinal herb garden. All this sounded like an old cliche - the sort of stuff the Queen and Prince Philip are obliged to see whenever they go abroad - though I was a little more interested in the Longgui Li boudoir and was disappointed that the climbing knife ladder and walking on red hot metal bars exhibitions were not running today. No wonder Li culture is on the decline if that's how they spend their leisure time.

Vegetation has been reduced to a cliché in Hainan's highlands too. Near to Binglanggu, authorities were extracting more tourist dollars at Yanoda Rainforest Cultural Tourism Zone where visitors could pay to see a portion of China's tropical rainforest though there was 100km^2 of the stuff they could see for free. Ah, but this was a 'diamond class attraction' though I was unsure where this put it on the pantheon of precious gems and it seemed to leave little room to manoeuvre. Where would this place the Forbidden City and the Great Wall - gold class, triple platinum, kryptonite?

Ya-no-da means 1-2-3 in the local Hainanese dialect where according to the literature with its diamond class claims, I could escape 'far from the madding crowd'. But despite the Thomas Hardy imprecations and the prospect of eating tropical fruits, the waterfall rope bridge and riding the American shuttle bus in straw sandals to the river adventure in Fantasy Valley, I gave Ya-no-da 1-2-3 a miss, though the 'huge magic fungus' sounded more interesting - I would only need this and a cheap bottle of cider to recreate my misspent teenage years. There's plenty of this cultural misappropriation in China. The nation is proud of its 56 nationalities, but sometimes they are reduced to triviality as they dress up, smile, climb knife ladders and above all dance, dance, dance for the tourists.

China is not averse to a little geographical appropriation too. Most Chinese think Taiwan is part of their nation, and I've noticed too that on Chinese maps the southern border that girdles Hainan makes an extravagant loop south from the island through 1500 km of ocean almost to the island of Borneo. This is because China lays claim to the tiny islands that make up this archipelago for reasons of pride, tradition and because oil was discovered here in 1968. They're called the Spratly and Paracel Islands and account for a few square kilometres of land in over 500,000 km² of ocean and it seems nonsensical for China to claim them (though no more so than British control over the Falklands I suppose), though at least they are uninhabited and there are no natives that can be encouraged to dance for the tourists. Ancient Chinese maps refer to the Qianli Changsha – the 10000 li[30] stretch of sand and the Wanli Shitang – the 10000 li of stone pools which China claims refers to the Spratly and Paracels. Yuan, Ming and Qing Dynasty records refer to the tiny specks of land with a clear assumption that they are Chinese.

However, Vietnam, Thailand, Malaysia and Brunei think they have a stronger claim. In 1998 China sank two Vietnamese gunboats as part of the ongoing dispute and despite a 2002 agreement granting access for all, the Taiwanese president visited the islands in 2008 and reasserted sovereignty. China has begun to station small numbers of troops on the islands to reinforce her claim though I can't imagine what life is like for these men on their barren lumps of rock so far from Beijing dumplings, Shandong beer, the bustling markets of Guangzhou and the pretty xiaojie misses of Shanghai.

I like the Philippines claim to the islands best. It is based upon the adventurism of Thomas Cloma, a fishing magnate who on 11 May 1956 took formal possession of the islands with 40 men and renamed them Freedomland. Cloma intended to open a cannery and develop guano deposits in ways that are unclear to me but his 'Notice to the

---

30   a 'li' is a Chinese unit of measurement roughly equivalent to 500 metres and still in common use today. The word for li combines the characters for field and earth since it was considered to be the length of a single village.

whole world' that claimed an unchallengeable requisition of the rocks and their bird poo met a violent reaction from China and Taiwan who reclaimed the islands forcibly three months later. So Freedomland was short lived and Cloma finished in a Ferdinand Marcos jail, though the nation's claim that the islands are theirs is based on the rather dubious assertion that Cloma sold the territory to the Philippine government for one peso before he was incarcerated.

That they weren't his to sell hasn't deterred the Philippines and the argument rages on. The Chinese maps are unequivocal enough - the islands are China's; look, the border loops right round and so it must be true. If it *is* true, then Hainan is no longer the 'tail of the dragon', a full stop to the Empire, since it no longer sits at the furthest point south of the most populous nation on earth. It would be a shame if this was no longer true because part of Hainan's romance lies in its position at the extremity of everything.

These thoughts floated through my helmet less head (I really should have been concentrating on the road) as I putt putted my bike back to the coast at Tianya Haijiao - 'the ends of the earth'. My bike had a puncture on the way but as I pushed it disconsolately on the outskirts of Sanya my problems were soon solved. This being China, a man leapt from a side road and offered to fix it. This being China he overcharged me. This being China he offered to change money, sell me other things, arrange a ride in his brother's taxi, introduce me to his mother, insist I eat noodles and offered me a cigarette. So I was soon on my way - another credit in my mental 'I like China' column.

So it was that I parked two good wheels by the beach and had photos taken by the giant sweetheart stones and limit of the sky, edge of the sea boulders that grew out of the sand as if one of the Li immortals had dropped them there. Hainan was once a place of exile and known as the gate of hell, since nowhere could be further from the court of the Emperor and the centre of the Empire. Qing records state that only 18 people came to Hainan voluntarily during the whole Song, Yuan and Ming period – an interval of 700 years. Those who did, came because of punishment and exile, like the famous official Hai Rui who has a memorial dedicated to him in the northern Hainan capital of Haikou. A play celebrating this bright and honest official's treatment by a corrupt emperor was written in the 1960s and sparked the Great Proletarian Cultural Revolution since Mao took the criticism of the despotic emperor to be a comment on his own rule (if the cap fits, Chairman Mao).

So Hainan was the tropical equivalent of Jiayuguan fort in distant Gansu, another place on the edge of the world beyond which there are only bandits and barbarians. I remembered the scratched desperate messages of exiled officials on the Gate of Sighs at the edge of the Gobi desert at Jiayuguan; 'Who is not afraid of the vast desert, should the scorching heat of Heaven make him frightened?' (see Gansu chapter) These giant pebbles on the beach near Sanya are Hainan's equivalent of that gate.

How different Hainan is now. Not a place of exile, but a place of migration for wealthy Chinese who want to be warm. I would have lingered on the beach at the end of the Earth but dusk was on its way and though my horn worked perfectly on my more torture motorbike, the headlight did not. It was not yet quite dark but I could see fireworks and lanterns already decorating the sky over Hainan, exploding in a profusion of colours above the crowds on the beachfront and celebrating the end of another perfect day in paradise.

HONG KONG

香港

1092 sq km
Population 7 million

"A barren island with hardly a house upon it."

British Foreign Secretary Lord Palmerston on Hong Kong, 1842

Some teenagers in Hong Kong ride bicycles. Except they don't really ride, they wobble and totter in giggling crowds along bike paths and crash into walls and fences. Many are defeated by gravity and surrender to huge training wheels on the side of their bike which ensure that they don't fall but make them look like ridiculous oversized toddlers.

RIDING THE DRAGON

I once saw a woman in Hong Kong racing down a slope on a bike into a road tunnel. She paid scant attention to the most basic principles of steering and brakes and slammed headfirst into a wall. I leapt a barrier to ask if she was all right and she laughed awkwardly, saddled up and rode away, her front wheel buckled and demented like a bike that a circus clown or Salvador Dali might have ridden. And in that moment, two of the most basic tenets of Hong Kong were laid bare.

1, People spend little time outdoors so they don't know how to ride a bike. Blistering summer heat, pollution, high-rise living (so people usually don't even *own* a bike) and lack of time cause this since children are far too busy cramming and becoming high achievers to have fun, making air-conditioned shopping malls a more attractive leisure proposition.

2, No one likes to show embarrassment and thus lose face in Hong Kong, even if they bang their head and buckle their wheel on a brick wall.

However, basic tenet number one is not completely true. There are groups of teenage boys in Hong Kong who *can* ride bicycles. Only these are unlike any bikes you've ever seen. They have tiny wheels and undersized frames that are hardly big enough to accommodate a battery like a breeze block that is tied to there to power a riot of twinkling and flashing lights and two enormous speakers that hang either side of the back wheel and blare out Cantopop at deafening volume. This unaccountably popular synthetic music, unique to Hong Kong, is an appalling mix of electronic dance and saccharine sweet love ballads sung by pretty boys dressed in white staring disconsolately in front of an open window whose net curtains billow tragically behind, though no matter how they sing and clench their fists in despair, nothing can mend a broken heart.

And so the cycling Cantopop fans ride round and round of an evening so that others may benefit from their sensational transport. There is no malice in these boys though and if you ask them to turn the music down they say doi m'jew (sorry) and do as they are told.

This is because they are subject to Hong Kong tenet number three, that it takes ages for young kids to grow up and become worldly wise (and for some this never happens). You can see it in the girls starched white school uniforms and knee-high socks - no cigarette puffing, shirt out teenaged angst here - their Hello Kitty bags and hair grips and the boys cheerfully strolling the streets in Cub and Scout uniforms and indulging in the kind of excitable behaviour that would get them beaten up and strangled by the woggle on the streets of Manchester or London. Certainly their canto pop dream machines would be thrown into a canal.

It's all very different to mainland China where millions ride confidently to work on sturdy Flying Pigeon bikes, where there is not a training wheel in sight and no one crashes into fences or walls. I've lived and worked in Hong Kong for years and call it 'China-lite'; I'm in China but this is a sanitised and westernised version of the full cream, slightly unhealthy and rather addictive version across the border.

This is because the region only became part of The People's Republic in the 1997 miracle of unification following British Prime Minister Margaret Thatcher's change of heart (another miracle) and handing over of the whole colony, lock, stock, barrel and thriving capitalist economy to the largest communist state in the world. Prince Charles popped over and ended 156 years of British rule by lowering the Union Jack in the stifling heat and torrential rain of a July Hong Kong night. A perfunctory handshake with Chinese Premier Zhang Zemin who spoke of the ending of 100 years of vicissitudes for Hong Kong, and the ceremony was over in less time than it takes to say ' Her Majesty's dominions, on which the sun never sets'.

The partying in China was not so short lived. It's difficult to over-estimate the happiness, the sheer unbridled joy of the Chinese at the return of Hong Kong, and the removal of this perennial thorn that had pricked away and reminded them of their own century of vicissitudes, of colonial control, Japanese invasion and civil war. Hong Kongers were generally less pleased. Those who hadn't fled the city in anticipation of the Chinese takeover, watched as Chinese troops poured across the border, wondered what would happen next and tried hard not to think of the massacre at Tiananmen Square eight years before.

They needn't have worried. Life and unfettered frenzied neon lit capitalism has continued and prospered under rule from Beijing since even the control freak, schoolma'am authoritarianism of the Chinese government is reluctant to kill this cash cow. Deng Xiaoping had promised 'one country two systems' for Hong Kong, and that's exactly what it got. Hong Kong Basic Law article five reads;

'The socialist system and policies shall not be practised in Hong Kong and the previous capitalist system and way of life shall remain unchanged for 50 years,' ...though no one seems to know what'll happen at the end of 50 years in 2047.

So the Communist Party remains illegal in Hong Kong which must make it the only place in the world where the ruling political group has no legal existence in the country that it rules. But despite a nominally independent government, free trade, booming dog eat dog capitalism, all those foreign gweilo (white ghost) faces and the 8000 skyscrapers (more than anywhere else in the world), if you scratch the surface of this on the edge of China but not really part of China place, it begins to look very Chinese indeed.

You can see it in the Temple at Wong Tai Sin where supplicants bow to statues of Buddha and Tin Hau clutching great handfuls of incense sticks and where every year a holy man pulls a fortune stick from a bamboo pot and the city's destiny for the next 12 months is decreed. You can see it in the narrow lanes of Kowloon where the street hawkers in white vests are just the same as in Shanghai and Beijing except they shout 'Buy buy' in Cantonese not Mandarin. The smell in these alleys is more pungent than that of their mainland counterparts and remain one of my first memories of arrival in Hong Kong, an olfactory assault that still transports me back to my bewildered, sweaty, what have I done arrival in the Far East.

The smell is chiau deo fu or stinky fermented tofu hanging in the window of dai pai dong cafes. It would be a gifted writer indeed who could properly describe the odour of this evil cousin of innocent soy bean curd known locally as poor man's meat; think of your overweight uncle's nylon socks that have been worn for a week in a heatwave then sealed in a bin liner with a piece of ripe camembert and you're somewhere close.

I've never had the courage nor the inclination to put rancid tofu into my mouth since even walking past a shop where it is for sale can make me retch, despite the fines that are occasionally levied on dai pai dongs if they allow their chiau deo fu to smell too much, which is a bit like punishing a man with a big bass drum if he makes too much noise.

But Hong Kong has plenty of other foods and stinks for the more adventurous palate. I've tried 100 year old eggs that are really only 100 days old but look indescribably ancient when they turn black and grey after preservation in salt and potash. Also the flesh of the durian fruit, a large spiky brute like some Mediaeval torture device and whose stink is so bad that the fruit is banned from most hotels in Hong Kong.

Hong Kong's most famous delicacy is dim sum, little sweet or savoury parcels whose name means 'to touch the heart lightly' the consumption of which is a citywide obsession especially on Sunday mornings when generations of a family sit down to yum cha. I can take or leave dim sum and when my teacher at a Cantonese lesson told me that we would learn how to order Hong Kong's favourite dish, I asked if we could do something else since the lesson would be wasted, I rarely ate dim sum and thought it vastly overrated. My teacher's shocked expression was such that I thought she would terminate the lesson there and then, for surely she had not realised that she was spending an hour a week with a man who was such an uncultured barbarian. I stammered that perhaps I just hadn't tasted good dim sum yet and of course we should go ahead with the lesson since how could a gweilo live in Hong Kong without having his heart touched lightly? My lessons ended two weeks later due to my teacher's 'other commitments', though surely this was just coincidence?

If the Hong Kong Chinese love of obscure foodstuffs is redolent of the province over the border (see Guangdong chapter), their respect for officialdom and pettifogging rules is similar to that of people all over China. This helps create a remarkably law-abiding and harmonious society where few are subject to fear of threat or physical harm, even if they are 17 years old, expose their knees and dress like Baden Powell in broad daylight.

Such compliance is based upon Confucianist precepts of respect and justice that are over 2000 years old, but to the average liberal, I know my rights product of the French Revolution Westerner, all this order and obedience can be cloying at times. I've learned that doing as I'm told by modern day Mandarins is best for a quiet life but I'm still amazed by the sheer bloody-minded inflexibility of bureaucracy in Hong Kong. This has been demonstrated to me many times such as when once returning to my car after a theatre performance at midnight in the downtown city. My vehicle was the only one in the car park and about 50 metres distant from the attendant who sat sentinel and listened to Cantopop in his box by the gate. I stopped to pay the fee to this man who no doubt derived little joy from his poorly paid late night shift except perhaps through the exertion of a little peaked cap authority. He said no, I had to be in my car to make the payment. So I returned to my lonely vehicle, drove the 50 metres back, had the same money accepted by the same man through the same window of the same box and I went on my way.

There are just certain ways that things must be done in Hong Kong. When I applied for a driving licence, the woman behind the glass screen (officials are nearly *always* behind glass screens) took my application, placed it on a tray and told me to come back in two weeks. I dutifully returned and queued again when I met the same woman behind the same screen who took my untouched application from the same tray and printed a license there and then. The process took all of five minutes and the two-week delay served no discernible purpose except to prove that this is the way it was always done.

When my water supply was cut off at home, I phoned the water board who told me it would be fixed at 9:27 PM - a remarkably specific time, though accurate to the minute when six hours after my call water came gushing from the taps. I was woken with a start at 2am the next morning by a man from the same office checking off his list of jobs which no doubt read;

1, give weirdly specific time for repair

2, make repair at time specified and not before even if fault can be rectified several hours earlier

3, phone client 4 to 5 hours later to confirm efficacy of repair

4, ensure minimal application of common sense and maximum adherence to the rules.

Yet Hong Kong can also be wildly spontaneous and chaotic too. She lets her hair down for numerous festivals every year and chief amongst these is the lunar New Year whose importance is so great that some of the shops actually *close* - an otherwise unheard of event. New Year has a host of traditions attached. Whole houses are cleaned from top to bottom, children stay up late and wear new clothes and red packets of money called lai see are distributed, though the money must be new and never in multiples of four, since the number four is so unlucky.

New Year is also a time for dragon and lion dancing when acrobatic troupes parade the streets followed by musicians who bang drums, symbols and gongs in a cacophony of noise loud enough to drive demons away, though this is nothing to the explosive snap of firecrackers - an act of subversion indeed since they are banned as too dangerous in safe and orderly Hong Kong. There's something reliably exciting about these high energy dances. It's so exhausting that members of the dance troupe in their little black 1950s plimsolls swap in and out of character in order to have a rest and there's no doubt that the lions earn their right to the strings of hundred dollar bills that hang from shopfronts and bring the business another year of good luck as they are gobbled down by the wildly gyrating beast.

The clanging and crashing reaches deafening levels at performances of New Year Cantonese opera, an ancient art form but one that suggests the performers may be in actual physical pain as they wail for three hours to the accompaniment of music that sounds like a box of pots and pans being dropped down a flight of concrete stairs. Such is the popularity of opera that it appears three or four times a year in my local village when a special arena is constructed to accommodate the crowds and traffic is diverted. The concert hall (called a matshed) is a work of art in itself; 100 feet of intricately latticed bamboo poles constructed by men in white vests who crawl up and down the bamboo under a hot sun for a week tying the structure together with plastic strips. They labour for a further week to disassemble the monster before life and traffic in the village returns to normal, and all this for just two or three days of shows. I sometimes wonder that they make such an effort when there is a perfectly adequate Town Hall made of brick and stone not 300 yards away, but when I see the massive edifice with its colourful flags and painted stage backdrops take shape and the crowds of locals in their brand-new lunar clothes filing in I'm glad that they do. In a city that's aware of the value of everything and where spontaneity is often found wanting, it's refreshing to see something happen that makes so little economic sense.

There are no operas or parades in the Tang Dynasty Qing Ming festival in spring. On this red letter day, families visit the graves of their ancestors to sweep and clean, to offer food and wine as gifts to the dead and burn counterfeit ghost money worth hundreds of millions of dollars to ensure a comfortable existence in the afterlife. Graves are usually positioned in scenic spots with a view of the sea and bones which are kept in large earthenware jars are often lifted out to share in the feast.

This might seem macabre, though I have often walked past remote graves with their view of the sea and their chunky brown pots and been tempted to peek inside at thigh bones and grinning skulls. It must be comforting to be one of those shuffling Cantonese grannies, climbing bamboo steps to the wailing opera to know that when you go, you'll not be forgotten; your bones will never be lonely, you'll always have a view of the crashing ocean and your grave will be kept clean.

My favourite festival of all in Hong Kong is in October. The mid Autumn Festival is derived from the tradition of worshipping the moon, without whose constant changes to reflect the seasons it would be impossible to have a bumper harvest of the five grains. In Chinese legend the Sun is yang and the Moon yin and the deity who lives in the moon is a yin female fairy called Chang-e who flew from Earth and has lived up there ever since, presumably surviving on the bountiful supply of cheese.

Hong Kong celebrates the festival with lanterns and mooncakes which date from the Song dynasty when Chinese defenders hid messages in round buns to plan a revolt against Mongol invaders. Today's mooncakes go on sale at least a month before the event and in true

Hong Kong entrepreneurial spirit are available in any combination of flavours and fruits. My local Starbucks offers a cappuccino version.

Traditional mooncakes are made of red bean and lotus paste and are so rich and sweet that to finish a whole one in a single sitting is quite impossible. Just like the original Song dynasty mooncakes, these have an unexpected surprise hidden within - a boiled egg - which is enough to induce nausea in the unexpected celebrant gamely battling through red bean paste misery.

I like the Moon Festival best not because of its sickly cakes or fairy in the full moon but because it signals the end of stifling, sweaty summer and the start of months of blue sky, crisp air winter when you can actually sit outside without your eyeballs and teeth sweating. Summer in Hong Kong is astonishingly hot. Mind blowingly, gobsmackingly, three showers a day humid, when air-conditioners become your best friend and it is polite to ignore the sweat stains spreading across strangers shirts from underarm to back and on to chest, until the happy moment is reached when the whole shirt becomes a uniformly dark colour and people become unaware of the amount of fluid leaking from your body. Local Chinese hardly seem to sweat at all and begin to wear jumpers and coats while I'm still perspiring and fighting fungal infections. When I look at grainy photos of colonials in white suits, crinoline and tweeds and starched and flounced muslin petticoats, I wonder that the British didn't focus on colonisation of countries that are less stifling. And I have a feeling that they had no split window, ductless or packaged terminal air-conditioners in the 19th century, which makes me feel more ill than if I'd eaten a whole mooncake, boiled egg and all.

Hong Kong is the city of grand statements, from the massive skyscrapers that surround the harbour, to the hugely expensive steel and glass $20 billion Chek Lap Kok airport built in 1998 by demolishing a mountain and creating a new island in the South China Sea. The new airport replaced the old city centre Kai Tak runway where arriving passengers looked into the kitchens and bathrooms of high-rise residents as their 747s weaved between tower blocks.

Property is one of Hong Kong's grandest of all statements and is given fittingly grandiose names like Giverny, Symphony Terrace, Bellevue and Fortunate Villas though residents are often far from fortunate since the names belie the reality of the tiny 400 square foot apartments that lie within. The more ornate ironwork, crystal and marble the better in these ostentatious tributes to an Italian renaissance that exists only in the minds of developers and Hong Kong fei tzai, a Cantonese term that can loosely be translated as 'chav' or 'bogan'.

But the residents of Emerald Gardens and Diamond Plaza are devoid only of taste and not cash, since such properties sell for anything from 10 to a hundred million Hong Kong dollars (about £1-£10 million). Adverts for such properties are preposterous and usually feature white grand pianos and periwigged footmen, and make absurd claims of views and vistas that bear no relation to reality; I read of a new tower block advertised recently which stood a modest 30 floors high but the top two levels were numbered 66 and 88 since both these numbers are lucky in Chinese numerology and I suppose give the block a sense of elevated style and import. My favourite recent example of ostentatious economical with the truth advertising though was from The Palazzo, a new group of tower blocks beside the Shing Mun River in Fo Tan. The adverts for these flats in a nondescript New Territories suburb trumpeted a building that towered aloof and alone beside a sparkling river and adjacent to bucolic pastures that stretched into an infinite patchwork of fields that could be rural Herefordshire or New England. Gone were the train station and surrounding tower blocks, the sewage works and main roads and I've never seen the notoriously polluted river looking so blue.

There is another typically grand Hong Kong statement on the hills of Lantau Island above the swanky new airport. The Tian Tan Buddha (so called because its base is a model of the Tian Tan altar of heaven in Beijing) is 34 m high, weighs 250 tons and is the largest seated Buddha in the world. Impressive indeed, though I have long since discovered that there is a biggest, heaviest, serenest, tallest and oldest category for every conceivable Buddha statue in China. The Buddha *is* impressive though and sits in remote and mountainous isolation the like of which most people are unaware even exists away from the concrete of downtown Hong Kong, though on public holidays, festivals and weekends, it is as crowded here as in the bright lights of Central, Wanchai or Causeway Bay.

In fact 80% of Hong Kong's countryside is unspoiled national park, saved from the construction hammers by precipitous slopes that make building a chore. Former Governor Murray MacLehose enshrined the protection of these wild places in the 1970s and created the MacLehose Trail that connects footpaths from east to west right across the territory.

I've staggered across most of this trail and can tell you it's brutally steep and tough in places, a series of switchback ridges and precipitous ascents interspersed with forests of bamboo, sandy beaches and views to distant high-rises on Hong Kong Island. For almost all of the 100km, it's hard to believe that this is Hong Kong at all. This is especially true on the slopes of Beacon Hill where notices warn the unwary hiker to take care near the wild monkeys. 'Don't feed them or annoy them' they advise since the monkeys have big teeth and are likely to bite. Also, do not tempt them with plastic carrier bags because these avaricious troublemakers will help themselves to the food that they assume is contained therein.

All of this advice seemed reasonable and achievable but I had more trouble with the final instruction that said I must not look the monkeys in the eye because this would be interpreted as a challenge, particularly by the males who no doubt would assume that I was coming on strong to their red arsed harem. So I walk along with food and plastic tucked safely inside my rucksack, gazing at the floor and trying my best to avoid eye contact with monkeys that swing from trees above or chase around my feet on the floor. I always prepare my best 'don't mind me, I'm not looking for any trouble' expression on these occasions last used when entering any pub in the east end of London, and have so far escaped unscathed from the jungle, the sounds of mocking simian laughter and derision ringing in my ears.

It's not just monkeys that hikers have to watch out for. Wildcats and hairy pigs lurk in these jungles too and I've been confronted by an angry porcupine rattling his quills on a number of occasions - why do these beasties always have to be so *cross*? - but I avoid meeting their eyes too and scuttle safely away. There are sometimes huge webs knitted across the path with big black and yellow spiders lurking malevolently at their centre and I'm filled with blind panic whenever I walk through one of these and desperately pull sticky strands of web from my face and wait for its creator to run down my shorts.

Worst of all are the snakes. Hong Kong has a bewildering variety of snakes, some of which are extravagantly poisonous and I don't care how many times I'm told that they're more scared than me, when I see one it's enough to send me running pell-mell into the nearest spiders web or crashing into a troop of monkeys where I'm bound to catch the eye of at least one. Hong Kong snakes are squeezes or biters and the advice from government agencies that if bitten you should both stay as still as possible and seek immediate medical attention has always seemed singularly contradictory and unhelpful. The biggest squeezers are long, muscular and terrifying pythons who don't even have the decency to leave when you see one since if you're that big you don't need to run or slide away from anyone.

I've had two encounters with pythons, once when I drove along a quiet country lane in the small hours of the morning and felt my tyres bounce over one that was lying across the full width of the road. The bump felt like driving over a fire hose or some traffic calming measure, but when I returned the snake had slithered off into the undergrowth in a supreme gesture of indifference.

The second encounter wasn't really mine but that of a near neighbour who had been walking her Siberian Husky and watched while a python grabbed the dog and squeezed it to death in front of her very eyes while she threw stones at it and shouted 'Go away!' and presumably tried to look like a mongoose. Since hearing this tale, I've always carried a penknife when I hike, though what I would achieve with this in the event of an attack is anyone's guess. I could certainly remove a stone if the python had one stuck in his hoof. And anyway, don't pythons look you in the eye and hypnotise you like the snake in Jungle book? It seems eye contact with any wild Hong Kong beast is best avoided.

The trees, vines, bushes and bamboo on the hills around Hong Kong are astonishingly dense and to stray off the path is to invite many hours of exhausting bushwhacking from which the foolish adventurer emerges dehydrated and covered in scratches, having possibly encountered a Japanese soldier who doesn't know that the war is over. The jungle on the hills above Kowloon hides other surprises too. I found the tunnels, marker posts and gun emplacements where British and Allied forces dug in and died on the Gin Drinkers Line as they attempted to withstand the Japanese onslaught. The line was supposed to be impenetrable, but it took the invaders next to no time to overwhelm the defences, scamper down to the city and cross Victoria Harbour to Hong Kong Island where the ragtag remains of British, Indian and Canadian troops surrendered on Christmas Day 1941.

No doubt being outnumbered ten to one was the main factor in the British defeat, but there seems to have been a certain underestimation of the Japanese too. The attacking Kwantung Army had been battle hardened by five years of warfare in China and were alerted to the position of the Gin Drinkers Line by British washing hanging out to dry. Even the name of the defensive line is suggestive of the complacency of the ruling elite whose superiority had been unquestioned for so long. No doubt they would rather have been enjoying a cool drink in the afternoon shade beneath a lazy fan in their mahogany and cigar smoke whites only officers clubs than dealing with the impertinent Japanese.

Hong Kong Island itself should have been more defensible and the British seemed shocked that simply announcing that Hong Kong would never fall didn't make it so. Furthermore, there was a belief that the Japanese eye shape precluded a night-time attack since they would not be able to see properly and that the crossing of Victoria Harbour would be terribly problematic for the invaders who were racially prone to seasickness (really!). When the attack came, it was after dark which seems damned unsporting of the Japanese.

The subsequent occupation of Hong Kong, like that of Singapore and Shanghai, was an inglorious chapter for the colonial powers in Asia and a salutary lesson for locals who recognised that European superiority was a myth, and so began the path to independence. The British fought gamely enough at the high pass that links the north of Hong Kong Island with the South called Wong Nai Chung Gap, but after the surrender it was the local Chinese East River Brigade guerrilla army who blew up trains and attacked garrisons and the locals who bore the brunt of Japanese aggression, rationing and brutality in Hong Kong and all across China.

Those Westerners who didn't escape the occupation mostly wound up in Stanley internment camp on the south of Hong Kong Island. About 2800 men, women and children were held at this non-segregated camp for 44 months from early January 1942 to August 1945. Records show that 121 internees died in the camp, though 14 of these were killed by a bomb dropped by a US plane on 16 January 1945.

I first became aware of the camp on a visit to the Imperial War Museum in London where the Day Joyce sheet was on show. It's impossible to take in the thousands of displays in the museum and make the obligatory stop in the museum gift shop for your commemorative 'We'll Meet Again and other wartime hits' CD and reproduction poster of Lord Kitchener with his pointy finger and extravagant moustache. But this display really caught my eye - a bed sheet embroidered and appliquéd with the names of 1100 internees and a coded diary.

Individuals get lost in the enormity of World Wars, but here was a reminder of the Johns, Jacks and Joyces who suffered in the camp for nearly four years. A reminder that we shouldn't lose sight of the impact of war in a welter of statistics, and that conflict doesn't just ruin millions of lives but ruins one life, and then another and then another. It's the individuals who really stand out at the War Graves Cemetery in Stanley today, a quiet and tidy patch of green shaded by Jasmine trees and made more poignant by the proximity of the hawkers in Stanley market and the games on the Stanley beach just five minutes stroll away. The uniform simplicity of Commonwealth War Graves never fails to move me. They have an austere dignity and if the serried ranks and manicured lawns don't get you, the graves have a sucker punch too in the eulogy carved to respect a grieving relative's sense of loss.

Still, there was compensation in misfortune. In 1948 the War Claims Act set a confusingly precise sum of $60 for every month spent in internment plus one dollar a day for missed meals, so that an individual who spent the whole war in the camp could clear a tidy profit of $2684. The Chinese who suffered under Japanese occupation received nothing of course and such were the conditions and shortages in Hong Kong during the war that many simply left when they could and the population of the city fell from 1.6 million to 600,000 during wartime.

But Hong Kong has that same stoic resilience that exists all over China and a population that has quietly got on with life no matter how many long marches, invasions, civil wars, five-year plans, great leap forwards, famines, floods, droughts and cultural revolutions are thrown at them. The population recovered quickly, business boomed and eight months after the Japanese surrender, the Territory's British civilian administration was restored. Britain realised however that she couldn't run her colonies as she had done in the past. The mystique of colonial rule was broken; greater equality had to be granted and as a consequence local Chinese were no longer restricted from certain beaches or from owning assets on the prestigious Victoria Peak.

Thousands of Chinese fled into Hong Kong after the communist takeover of China in 1949 which created an economic boom and made the region more Chinese and less like an anomaly. The influx also led to greater overcrowding especially in the shantytowns that crept up the slopes of the eight hills that surround Kowloon and give it its name.[31] A huge fire destroyed the homes of over 50,000 people in 1953 and the government commenced a programme of mass public house building to provide affordable homes for those on low incomes.

The first estate at Shek Kip Mei was ready by 1954, though these brutalist and functional housing units were small in the extreme; 2.2 m² were allocated for each adult and less than half that for a child under the age of 12 and sanitation was rudimentary to say the least. Yet 50% of all Hong Kong residents live in public-housing today and new high-rises constantly sprout up and bristle into the sky, the reason why Hong Kong is considered to have the highest population density in the world for all its national parks, mountains, jungles, spiders and pythons.

Nowhere was more crowded than Kowloon Walled City, an anomaly in the heart of urban Hong Kong. The British takeover of the New Territories in 1898 had not included this six acre site and so it remained outside the law until the 1980s. The police had no right of entry and as a result the walled city became a notoriously overcrowded nest of criminals, tax evaders, triads, unqualified doctors and general

---

31   Kowloon actually means nine Dragons, eight of which are Mountains. The ninth is the boy Emperor Zhao Bing who drowned in the harbour during the Song Dynasty.

ne'er-do-wells. By 1980, there were 50,000 crowded inside, the authorities could stand it no more and sent in police to clear the place before demolishing it in 1993.

Kowloon walled city is now a pleasant parkland with a bicycle track where people can wobble and crash their bikes with impunity. Yet locals bemoan the loss of the old city since it had personality and a unique Hong Kong charm. Ignore the rats and the violent triads and there might be something in this, since Hong Kong is after all filled with people who fled the claustrophobic control of Communist China to live in a place where individual freedom (especially to make money) is a basic and inalienable right. Unadorned market capitalism is joined by nationalist sentiment too since the citizens of Kowloon Walled City were like modern-day Robin Hoods delivering a sharp poke in the eye to the British Sheriff of Nottingham.

But there is no doubt that British rule has brought benefits to Hong Kong. The corruption that is so rife in mainland China is largely missing here since Governor MacLehose founded the Independent commission against corruption (ICAC) in 1974. The same Governor who established walking trails across Hong Kong created an enduring legacy, certainly more than the final Governor Chris Patten who seems best known for eating too many egg tarts.

MacLehose inherited a city and particularly a police force notorious for corruption, but the new law gave power to investigate any civil servant who appeared to be 'living beyond his means', an accusation I lay myself open to every time I go for a drink down in the upmarket gweilo enclave of Lan Kwai Fong where each bottle of beer in every achingly trendy bar is ostentatiously expensive.

Corruption is no longer a career choice for Hong Kongers, but there is still a way to get rich quick. Hong Kong loves to gamble, though there are only three legitimate ways to do so. Betting on football, horse racing and the Mark six lottery are fine, but gambling on mahjong and cards, illegal gatherings in warehouses to bet on fighting crickets and a myriad other ways of making a bet are not. Presumably, betting on how many seconds it would take to start sweating on leaving the house in midsummer or how many times a cyclist can fall off his bike each hundred metres are also outlawed.

The Mark six lottery is a Hong Kong obsession to rival shopping and has raised over $HK20 billion for government and charities since its inception in 1975. But this is as nothing compared to horse racing which raises $HK10 billion a year in gambling profit. This might be only third highest in the world after the USA and Japan, but Japan has 24,000 races year and the USA has 55,000. Hong Kong has just 700 races per annum, so the amount gambled on each race is infinitely higher than in Tokyo or Kentucky. The races are great fun whether you go for the high in the stands shirt and tie, dim sum and champagne option or the trackside, plastic beakers of beer, running to place bets, shouting and screaming, feeling the rush of air as a ton of galloping horseflesh races past a metre from your nose option. And it's satisfying to remember that I too am making a contribution to Hong Kong charitable causes with my extravagant $HK5 and $HK10 each way bets.

The government has a remarkably pragmatic attitude to gambling. The less generous might call it hypocritical. Placing a bet is banned because of the social evils that attend this vice; because money given to a bookmaker is money taken from the mouths of children and because it can lead to debt, corruption and crime. Because a Hong Kong gambler just doesn't know when to stop. Yet the authorities have learned to be flexible with their concerns where horse racing is involved since it's so damn profitable. Illegal gambling on British premiership football became so popular in the 1990s, that the government simply legalised it under their control so that they garnered a share of the profits. As a consequence the crowds (almost exclusively male) in and outside Hong Kong Jockey club betting shops on weekend Hong Kong streets are thousands strong and sway back and forth in triumph and despair as the race begins or the result comes in of a game between two British Northern industrial towns where none of these gamblers will ever go.

This pragmatic if you can't beat them join them attitude is typical of this town. Hong Kongers can be fiercely practical and chameleon like in adapting to their surroundings, whether moving from traditional boat dwellings into public flats, escaping over the border from Chinese Communist control or leaving Hong Kong altogether as so many did after the Tiananmen massacre and before the handover to China. Most

Chinese communities across the world are likely to be Cantonese and this willingness to blend and adapt is apparent even in their names.

There are by tradition only 100 names in China and all Chinese can be traced back to and have some connection with 'old 100 names', the original surnames from Chinese history, Chinese names are written surname first, so Bei Mei Ling is Miss Bei and Tang Le Ying is Mr Tang. Surnames often have no real meaning but first names do. Girls names reflect good and gentle qualities; Ming is bright, Yan is kindness and Mei is beautiful, while male names are of course more associated with strength and virility.

But in true Hong Kong adaptive style, many locals choose Western names to replace their Chinese ones, since for businessmen the West is vital to trade and to the young the West is cool and trendy. This explains the unfathomable western slogans on T-shirts in Hong Kong which are misunderstood by the wearer or are just plain nonsense. I've seen some first-rate examples over the years and among my favourites has been 'Say no to hard drugs' worn by a tiny ancient woman bent over with arthritic back as she did her shopping. I've also sent earnest, bespectacled and oh so innocent students home from school to change, whose shirts have announced 'I like to do it doggie style' and 'Do you like my fluffy pussy?', but accompanied by an undeniably cute puppy or kitten.

When choosing Western names, Hong Kongers go one of three ways. The safest choice is the closest approximation of their Chinese name, so Sai-Man becomes Simon and Wing-Me Winnie. More risky is to plump for a fantasy name; meet Ferrari, Coke, Apple, Purple and Gandalf. The riskiest strategy of all is the most popular, that is the choice of a name that represents good character qualities. Sometimes this just about works; I have met Scholar, Bright, Radical, Dominant and the twins Healthy and Hearty (who ironically enough were both sickly specimens). Sometimes the choice is poorly conceived and on a recent trip to the bank I was served by a bright and attractive woman whose pin on badge told me she had picked the name Concrete; firm and dependable no doubt and a good foundation for financial investment, though her pallor was a little grey.

Nothing is predictable in Hong Kong and in a city of thrusting modernity gone mad, traditions still prevail. Many of those bold high-rises and shopping malls have been built with the demands of feng shui in mind; that centuries-old belief in good luck and providence based on positioning and place whose name means wind and water.

The huge and high end shopping centre on Hong Kong Island called Pacific Place came in $HK3 million over budget since feng shui experts had insisted that a 130-year-old banyan tree on the site had to be preserved. A swanky new hotel at glamorous Repulse Bay is built with a big gap in the middle so that the dragon's flight from sea to mountain is not impeded. The award-winning HSBC bank in the financial district is built in the shape of a laughing Buddha with a clear view to the harbour, since water is essential to financial prosperity. Inside is filled with mirrors since water reflected will bring extra wealth which is why most financial institutions in Hong Kong sport a fountain or a pond in which a few miserable koi carp swim languidly around. Hexagonal mirrors called bat gwa are especially beneficial because they bring wealth but also reflect bad luck away to its source. Indeed the whole of the central financial district is said to be prosperous since it is built on a dragon's vein.

Numerology is important too and it's rare to find a fourth floor or any multiple of four in a Hong Kong building since the word for four is 'sei' and that sounds like death. Eight is 'baat' which is similar to prosperity, so multiples of eight can be found everywhere. But it doesn't stop there; sapsaam (13) means sure life, 24 is easy to die, 28 easy prosperity, 138 prosperity all your life, and 168 is everlasting prosperity.

That so many lucky numbers are associated with material wealth speaks volumes about what is important to Hong Kong. China has embraced this go-ahead materialism since the takeover in 1997 though in other ways they attack the principles and limited self-governance upon which this is based. My favourite building in all of Hong Kong is the Bank of China Tower, 305 metres of angular and triangular modernism that is beautiful in its simplicity, especially at night when it is lit by a calm white light in contrast to the luminous greens and garish reds that surround it. The building, designed by IM Pei, flies in the face of feng shui where triangles are bad because of all those disturbing sharp corners. What's more, the corners point directly to government office house in a direct challenge to the rule of the Hong Kong administration. The masts on top of the building are thrust skyward like two incense sticks or chopsticks in a bowl of rice, the classic symbols of death.

It's like China is trying to reclaim Hong Kong as her own in a cultural as well as a merely geographical sense, by removing those anachronisms and 'olds' that were attacked so vigorously during the time of Mao. But these beliefs are creeping back into Chinese society too - did they ever go away? - and in 2008 the Chinese government reinstated the Qing Ming Festival across the whole of China. This policy was as pragmatic as the Hong Kong approach to gambling since the people of China had never given up sweeping their ancestors tombs.

So Hong Kong remains a delightful mix of tradition and modernity. It's different to China proper since Hong Kong is not really a place - it's a state of mind rather than a state; a conduit through which ideas, goods and people travel. It didn't grow in the normal way and certainly not in the way that Beijing did from its humble beginnings thousands of years ago. Hong Kong is an invention, an apparition, a contradiction.

But it *is* China, and increasingly so since the British left. On reflection their 156 year rule feels like an interlude, a pause in a much longer story. Certainly it's possible to remain resolutely aloof from all the Chinese-ness of the city as an ex-pat in swimming pooled luxury behind iron gates and shopping in stores for Vegemite and baked bean reminders of home. But the thousands of enthusiasts who lined the streets in 2008 when the Olympic torch went past were all waving Chinese flags - an unthinkable proposition just 10 years before. The streets and especially the alleyways of the city are the Hutongs of Beijing filled with the shouts of the Cantonese language of Fujian and Guangdong. The rush to buy and sell, the headlong flight to the future is the same as in the whole of eastern China. The elaborate temple roofs and incense burning of the followers of the Buddha look the same as in Hunan or Hubei, Guangdong or Gansu though the temples in Hong Kong are completely surrounded by high rise flats.

But in Hong Kong the unexpected can also happen - a game of rugby on Kings Park, a whiff of chiau deo fu, the Star Ferry chugging across the harbour towards the scintillating, astonishing high-rise view and suddenly it doesn't seem like China or anywhere else, but more like the most surprising and unique city on earth, no sweat.

JIANGXI

江西

170 940 sq km
Population 43 million

'Politics is the art of looking for trouble, finding it, misdiagnosing it and then misapplying the wrong remedies'

Groucho Marx

There was a perfectly acceptable expressway through the mountains on the eastern border of Jiangxi but our bus spurned ease and comfort for a long-winded journey through the drizzly rain on winding roads plunging down and climbing tortuously, the bus engine whining in first gear as we crossed a succession of valleys.

I was frustrated by the tedium of the bus metronome wipers at first but really I was in no rush and decided to appreciate the view through wet windows of the bamboo forests, the tinkling waterfalls that plunged down the steep hillsides and the small villages by the side of the river. No one tended the fields yet they were meticulously laid out in rows of cabbages and rice and the only splash of colour that was not green were children in red neckerchiefs who stopped their games by the roadside to wave at the bus as we drove past.

We did finally leave the valleys and the vegetables and climbed one last time onto the highway suspended on great stilts of concrete, the village toy houses far below. Progress was fast now as tunnels took us through and not over the hills and gave shelter from the grey monotony of misty rain and as we burst out of the last of these we entered unexpected bright sunshine and a sign announced that we were in Jiangxi at last.

Another 'Welcome to Jiangxi' sign followed minutes later to dispel any lingering doubts that I had crossed the border and then another and another. This looked like a tactic of overcompensation for a province that is no one's favourite, that few have heard of, that contains nothing un-missable; no buried Emperors or great cuisine here and in Jiangxi the hills are not mountains and the rivers are not Yellow or Yangtze (though the Yangtze does form the northern border of Jiangxi with Hubei) . Even the rain had decided to give the province a miss.

I would discover for myself whether the province really was dull. For now, I was busy watching the television at the front of the bus that was tuned to CCTV, China's government-controlled network of news, sport, current affairs and what passes for 'entertainment'. I have spent many a lonely hour lying on a hard-as-a-board Chinese hotel bed flicking through CCTV channels, looking for something, *anything* to watch and finding only poorly acted soap operas and Ming Dynasty dramas where the characters spend a great proportion of their time banging fists theatrically on tables or adopting over surprised (or is it constipated?) expressions. I've watched low-budget army dramas where heroic, humourless Red Army soldiers, mouths set in grim determination, repeatedly evade capture by nationalist or Japanese forces that are theatrically evil and who also bang their fists on tables and look over surprised that they have been outwitted yet again. Sometimes the tense drama of war and revenge is relieved and CCTV becomes giddy and irreverent when young men in green trousers and pretty girls with bunches dressed like 10-year-olds in knee-high socks and dungarees host hilarious slapstick game shows during which cheap graphics – Ouch! Oops! Crash! - swirl on screen lest the viewer miss any bucket of water, custard pie or pratfall.

CCTV's xinwen lianbo, 'news simulcast' is on air every day at 7pm to report on government policy and successes to its 500 million viewers; everything is carefully scripted and prepared and even the few English language news and current affairs channels on CCTV are filled with over earnest and wide eyed presenters who failed to get a job on proper TV networks elsewhere where they might be required to probe or question or deal with the unpredictability of events.

Nothing spontaneous happens on CCTV[32] and those events that are unpalatable or unexpected are usually ignored. This includes the 9th February 2009 fire that caused 4 billion yuan of damage to the Beijing TV cultural centre and Mandarin Hotel that are adjacent to the CCTV headquarters. The blaze was caused by an illegal Chinese New Year firework display that had been authorised by CCTV officials who smuggled the pyrotechnics past police checkpoints and ignored warnings to cancel the display. The iconic 230 metre high CCTV building is a radical steel and glass loop of vertical and horizontal sections in a contorted arch and nicknamed 'the giant underpants' by young, educated Beijingers who will take any opportunity to ridicule the stodgy network whose low production values and propaganda they despise. Insults soon appeared on the Internet when CCTV refused to report on or acknowledge their part in the conflagration or mention the fireman who died. 'Liar, liar, pants on fire' went the criticism, though it wasn't actually the giant underpants that burned. There has been other internet mockery of the overblown and over budget CCTV vanity project that has been compared to a figure seated on a toilet and to the female

---

32   The CCTV channel 5 sports broadcast of the Beijing Olympic opening ceremony when broadcaster Hu Ziwei accused her co-presenter husband Zhang Bin of adultery on air is a notable exception to this.

genitalia counterpart to the phallic but sadly charred TVCC annex next door. It is said that even the Dutch architect Rem Koolhaas was in on the joke when he designed the procreative buildings.

'Babystars' was showing on the bus today - lots of little girl infant Madonnas doing sexy dancing in tiny dresses and lip syncing 'like a virgin'; a programme that is perhaps naïvely and joyfully innocent but seemed to me more offensive and injurious to the nation's well-being even than illegal fireworks. The miles flew past as I gazed at Jiangxi fields and hillside shrines in the company of those talented Shirley Temples though regrettably the coach pulled into Wuyuan town bus station before I had the chance to discover who was more talented than the rest and would go through to gyrate in the regional finals.

Wuyuan is hardly a beautiful town though every house and apartment, government office, bridge and public toilet was built in the squat, white Huizhou style so typical of this region (see Anhui chapter), which lent the place a certain pleasing uniformity. My connecting bus wouldn't leave for five hours so I took the opportunity to ride into the surrounding countryside on the back of the motorbike of a local man who instantly declared himself an expert on the region and had nothing better to do than drive around a foreigner who had time on his hands.

I hoisted my leg over the bike and we putt-putted 12 km to Little Likeng village along a raised road with views of rapeseed fields and a chalky escarpment where more Huizhou white homes sat bleached and bright in the afternoon sun. Little Likeng clung tenaciously to the riverbank, looking beautiful and ancient with its jumble of buildings, the house fronts ensnared by tendrils of vine and wisteria and buffalo ponderously working the fields. But the village is small and I was surprised to be confronted by an electronic ticket entrance gate when I gave 60 yuan to enter and where I had my thumb print scanned to create a computerised ticket as if I was entering the Pentagon. The Forbidden City in Beijing has a less sophisticated ticket system than this small Ming Dynasty village by the river in rural Jiangxi.

Many of the village houses had delightful carvings around door lintels and window frames – 'we can't help expressing admires on the exquisite workshop of the buildings' (sic) trumpeted a sign carved by a proud local who, try as he might, simply couldn't resist pointing out such artistry to thumb printed visitors. I wandered through the village and up the small hill behind for a glorious view of all those complicated grey tile rooftops and the motorbike rider followed me since he was my self-appointed guide, though he spoke not a word of English and seemed to know nothing about Little Likeng. He did however make a point of stating the obvious whenever he could. 'River', he said. 'Vegetables' and 'Hill' as if I had never seen such wonders before. His guiding criteria was based upon shoehorning the few words of English he knew into the conversation rather than on telling me what I didn't already know, though I might have regretted missing Likeng's 'Road' if it had not been pointed out.

"Ni zai motuoche keyi deng" I suggested, but he refused to go and wait by his motorbike when there were 'fields', 'trees' and 'clouds' to be pointed out. We stopped for lunch in a garden of giant marrows and gourds and sat like Gullivers in Brobdingnag under massive three foot winter melons that hung from the trellis like swords of Damocles above our bowls of rice. Naturally I bought the driver his lunch - this was the least I could do after the valuable lesson in common nouns he had given me - and he was incredulous as I spat out the heads of the dozens of tiny river fish cooked in flakes of chilli that we were served. He regarded this as waste but though I was willing to crunch the fish bones and swallow their scales, I couldn't bring myself to eat their wide surprised CCTV soap opera actor eyes.

We dawdled back on the motorbike to Wuyuan past more villages that were almost the equal of Little Likeng in beauty and I wondered if the residents of these hamlets felt envy or relief that it was their neighbours who had hit the tourist jackpot, for although lots of money would be made at Little Likeng, peaceful and productive village life must be impossible there with all those tourists leaving prints from feet as well as thumbs.

The long bus journey to Jiangxi's provincial capital Nanchang would have been tortuous a few years ago before the construction of the main road, but back on the empty highway the miles flashed by and the journey was improved immeasurably by the absence of glammed up toddlers pouting and thrusting their hips on the TV. We roared past the town of Jingdezhen, the traditional home of Chinese porcelain where factory chimneys smudged the blue Jiangxi sky with their ceramic smoke. It is from Jingdezhen that the name kaolin (which is what the English call china clay) derived because it is at nearby Gaoling that the clay and feldspar used for making pots is extracted.

And what pots they are. The town turned to making porcelain statues of Mao during the Cultural Revolution and quality in mass-producing 21st-century Jingdezhen has become more variable still. But from the 14th century Qinghua blue and white porcelain produced in this town became internationally renowned for being 'white as Jade, as thin as paper, as bright as a mirror, as tuneful as a bell'. A Yuan Dynasty porcelain jar produced in Jingdezhen was auctioned for 230 million yuan (14 million pounds) in London in July 2005 - the highest price ever paid for a bit of old China. There are only 300 specimens of Yuan Qinghua in existence today so it's no wonder they're so valuable. By comparison, there is enough Ming and Qing Dynasty Qinghua that you might one day come across a piece in an attic sale or antique fair, retire from your job, leave your spouse for a topless model and buy a sports car. Numbers of more recent Qinghua were boosted by the 1986 discovery of the 1752 Dutch wreck Geldermalsen with its cargo of 240,000 pieces of Jingdezhen porcelain that were auctioned for $12 million in the same year. Nearly 200,000 pieces had survived at the bottom of the sea[33] and were in excellent condition because they had been packed in tea. Most of the crew died because they weren't.

As the bus left the freedom of the highway for the repressive clogged arteries of Nanchang town, my lack of enthusiasm for the town was confirmed. Here was another traffic choked, polluted and oversized Chinese city; Nanchang might be a great place to live but to an outsider it seemed entirely anonymous and dull and I couldn't leave fast enough. The city is famous across China however as the place where the People's Liberation Army was born. There was a Communist uprising here on 1 August 1927 led by Zhou En-Lai the old revolutionary hero turned

---

33   Oh go on, since you asked;18 complete dinner services, 2263 cups and saucers for hot chocolate, 63,623 tea cups and saucers, 522 teapots, 19,535 coffee cups and saucers, 495 chamber pots, 681 beer mugs and 606 vomit pots.

statesman and Foreign Minister who met Richard Nixon on his visit to China in 1972 when Mao was too old and frail, and who is regarded as the man who curbed the excesses of the Cultural Revolution.[34]

Zhou's uprising was a failure and he was driven from town with his ragtag band of soldiers to the south of Jiangxi where he met up with Mao Zedong and his 900 men and established a guerrilla base in the remote mountains of Jinggang Shan from where they plotted and schemed, regrouped, set off on their long march in 1934 and made history.

But the defeat at Nanchang is only a matter of perspective. References to '8-1', 1st August, exist all over the town; on the PLA flags that flew from the brutalist modern army headquarters outside which soldiers stood like statues in the smog wearing shiny boots, in shop fronts and government office windows and on the huge monument in the town square, though like Nanchang itself this seemed rundown and rather dull. The men who led the uprising with Zhou and who re-organised at Jinggang Shan with Mao are the stuff of legend in China, and known as the 'Eight immortals'[35]; an allusion to Taoist deities of old. The stories of their heroism and derring-do read more like myth and wishful thinking than reality, but this merely adds to their renown since like ancient tales such as Journey to the West, The Water Margin, and the legend of Shaolin Kung Fu (each of these famous Chinese stories is discussed elsewhere in this other, less famous book about China), the tale of the eight immortals is romantic and does not need to be entirely true to resonate across China since such stories represent almost everything that the nation admires in its heroes, its citizens, its leaders.

The eight immortals were regrettably mortal after all and the last of China's great revolutionary leaders passed away in 2007. But such is the power of the legend that their descendants still exercise a great deal

---

34 For more details on Zhou see Tianjin chapter.

35 The 'immortals' are; Deng Xiaoping, Chen Yun, Peng Zhen, Yang Shangkun, Bo Yibo, Li Xiannian, Wang Zhen and Song Renqiong. Their Headquarters in the mountains was the village of Ciping that was destroyed by artillery fire in 1930 but has been rebuilt as a shrine where dewy eyed revolutionaries still visit to pay tribute at the vainglorious Martyrs' Tomb.

of influence in modern China. They're known as 'the Princelings'; a rather disrespectful term for the sons and grandsons of heroes. Although they do not form a political party, the Princelings lobby and use their parents' privileges to hold senior positions, though many are only in their 30s and 40s, for which ordinary cadres would struggle for decades. Such cronyism has led to enmity and resentment of the arrogance of the Princelings whose power has been reduced by the emergence of a new wealthy elite that has sprung from China's 21st century economic miracle, though this new elite is not averse either to using privilege, corruption and cronyism to promote their cause.

I was desperate to leave Nanchang but at the impossibly crowded train station I fell victim to a bureaucratic frustration that I had seen others suffer but which up to that point I had escaped. I queued dutifully and in the usual way; that delightful mix of jostling and elbowing and jealous guarding of space lest someone jump in front that exists wherever there is a crowd in China. I reached the front after a mere 25 minutes and mentally prepared my 'I am a foreigner, I don't speak Chinese well' speech so that the woman behind the glass in the battered hat of a Chinese Railway servant would not speak too quickly and would take pity on me and not get *cross*. But as I stepped forward to the counter to take my turn I could see no woman there. Or rather I could see the backside of a woman disappearing towards her tea break and a sign that said 'window closed' where she should have been. I stood in infuriated silence for only a moment before I collected myself, dealt with the frustration of wasted time and turned to join another queue. But in the few seconds that I had been staring angry and powerless at my disappearing persecutor, *every single person* behind me had jumped to other queues so that not only did I have to bump and jostle and queue all over again but I had to do so behind dozens of people who should have been behind me. I could understand at that moment what drives people to violence or to madness and imagined a Kafkaesque train station hall where every line I joined ended with a closed sign and hoots of laughter from railway staff and where I spent the rest of my days queueing, queueing on my knees with wild hair and bloodshot vacant staring eyes.....

But I got my ticket in the end and rode the line north to Jiujiang where Jiangxi turns to water around the border with Hubei and massive Poyang Hu Lake[36] disgorges its maze of streams into the Yangtze. I meant to stay a while in Jiujiang to look at the 16th century pagoda by the river and at Stone Bell Hill where the restless water of the Yangtze converges with the calm of the lake, but the taxi drivers who crowded outside the train station wouldn't let me. "Go straight to Lushan" they said. "The weather is good on the mountain" they said. "Don't delay" they said. "I will take you" they said. "Very cheap" they said. So I didn't see the Yangtze at Jiujiang and went up the mountain instead.

Lushan has a long history as the home of the 12th century White Deer Grotto Confucian Academy founded by Zhu Xi and the pre-eminent intellectual centre of its day, but it is as a 19th century colonial settlement that the mountain is now best known. Nearly 1500 metres above the insufferable summer heat of the Yangtze River plain, the Europeans constructed stone villas and churches, concert halls and libraries here and called their village on the mountain Kuling.

The driver who coaxed me into his cab and drove the switchback road to the top of the hill turned out to be as unhinged as he had been remorselessly persistent on the train station forecourt. He was incapable of sitting still and spent every moment of the blind corner, plunging drop by the side of the road journey shouting into his mobile phone, smoking cigarettes or retuning the radio from clanking Peking Opera, to saccharine Chinese ballots to staccato and shouty Chinese comedians whose audience shrieks and howls and applause I feared would be the last sound I heard as we plunged through the barrier and down the hill back to the Yangtze River. My driver evidently had a problem with his trousers and fiddled and groped at his crotch throughout the trip, lifting his backside from the seat and sometimes gripping the steering wheel between his knees so he could grapple with the radio and whatever was troubling him inside his underpants simultaneously.

The stars were shimmering in the clear cold mountain air by the time we reached the barrier on the road at the village entrance that

---

36 Poyang Hu is China's largest freshwater lake during Jiangxi's wet summer months with a surface area of over three and a half thousand square kilometers.

prevents any visitor from ascending the mountain top without making payment of 180 yuan. The long queue of idling cars was no impediment to my restless driver who swerved onto the wrong side of the road and drove to the front of the queue, shouting 'Laowai, waiguoren - I have a foreigner, let me pass' through his open window while his Laowai passenger cringed in his seat wearing a facial expression that was a curious mix of embarrassment and relief at not having to queue.

The driver dropped me at an old stone built hotel and followed me into the draughty entrance where he began his war of attrition again, insisting that I would need his services tomorrow. He laughed outright when I told him I planned to hike through the village and onto the rim of the high plateau from where Jiangxi and Yangtze would be visible a mile below. "It is too far, too far" he explained, but the forecast was for sunshine and I wanted the exercise and no matter how tiring, the walk would be preferable to more hours captive in his taxi with his itchy pants. So this time I really insisted and the driver got back in his car and drove slowly away searching for someone on the top of the mountain who could be persuaded they needed to be at the bottom.

I woke early in my wood panelled colonial Victorian room and the promised sunshine was pouring through the panes of the oak window and illuminating swirling clouds of dust that spun and swerved like my taxi driver of the night before. The market outside was in full swing despite the chill early morning and though the sun was high in the sky I could feel little warmth from it yet. Vegetables were piled onto the open backs of lorries, dark green cabbages and orange carrots vying for attention next to other trucks where ducks and chickens squabbled, oblivious to their cooking pot destiny, and nearby a wheelbarrow of rubbery pink pigs heads with their eyes closed and whose mouths seem to be smiling at the fussing of the birds.

Lushan is famous for its scenery (the presence of European villas was assurance of that because the colonists always chose the nicest places for themselves) but also for its politics. Chang Kai-shek, the leader of the Nationalists appropriated a sturdy villa on the hill and planned the defeat of the Communists from up here before he was defeated in his turn by Mao who took Chiang's villa for himself. The house is called Meilu Villa after Chiang's wife and is a carefully preserved replica of

China's tumultuous civil war and growing pains as she struggled slowly towards freedom; a signboard inside the house says the villa witnessed 'the glory and decay of Chiang Kai-shek'. The name 'Meilu' is inscribed on a rock in the carefully landscaped garden, dense and green in the temperate mountain air. The stone is an unlikely survivor of revolution because it is carved in Chiang's own hand and the story goes that when Mao found workers attempting to chisel the words away when he stayed in the villa in 1959, he stopped them saying 'this is history; even if you chisel away the words, Meilu Villa is still here'.

When I visited Meilu I understood that Mao chose to stay here not simply for the symbolic resonance of sleeping in a house once owned by his enemy. China's leader must have stayed here too because the villa is beautiful, spacious and well-proportioned with massive bedrooms, handsome oak floors and a sun-kissed terrace where Mao was once iconically photographed in a wicker chair gazing across the garden imagining a bright future for China. Or maybe he was simply admiring the flower beds?

Now it was possible for visitors to have a photo in the same chair on the balcony overlooking the same herbaceous borders, and also to walk through the bomb shelter and stare at the swimming pool that was constructed especially for Mao's visit, though the small rectangle of water was hardly big enough to satisfy the Chairman's heroic aquatic feats.[37]

There were no such trappings and none of the crowds at Premier Zhou En-Lai's villa on the other side of the tinkling stream that ran by the old Protestant church. Meilu had been crammed with tour groups but this villa was empty - a testament to the enduring appeal of Mao whose cult of personality is as strong as ever. When Zhou first came here, his neighbour was still Chiang. He came in 1937 to negotiate with the Nationalists with 'an elegant and smart demeanour.... regardless of the danger to himself', according to the information boards.

By 1959, Zhou was amongst friends as all the Communist bigwigs arrived together for the eighth Plenum of the eighth Central committee of the Communist Party of China. They came by boat along the

---

37 See Hunan chapter for more details of Mao's love of swimming.

Yangtze; an information film in the villa showed the leaders on board ship waving at the camera and swimming - Mao floating contentedly, Zhu De the leader of the Army looking mildly panicked in a rubber ring. The film might have been a record of some geriatric pleasure cruise. But this visit to the mountain was not for pleasure. The 1959 Lushan conference happened at a critical juncture in Chinese history. The Great Leap Forward had patently failed; collective farms were not producing enough food, peasants were frantically creating useless steel in backyard furnaces, the weather had been awful and China was soon to endure the most terrible man-made famine in history. (Some estimates suggest that 30 or 40 million starved in the 'three bitter years' of 1959 to 1961). The conference took place in another sturdy building of European design a gentle one kilometre walk downhill from Meilu Villa through the dappled shade of cedar trees. I wondered if Mao and the other delegates strolled down the hill every morning to talk economics and ideology in the conference hall, though Mao was a swimmer not a hiker and would have preferred a bullet-proof black Red Flag limousine.

Another film was showing in the conference hall, this time of the 1970 Central Committee, all garish technicolour green uniforms and red flags, red tablecloths and Little Red Books in the hands of chanting idealistic delegates. Mao's big swollen face was red too, though this cannot have been through physical exertion since he was entirely motionless throughout the movie; the video preferred to call his countenance 'amiable, kindly and tolerant'.

The leaders face might have been called enigmatic and aloof but I think the Chairman looked merely confused since by the 1970s Mao was increasingly infirm and incapable; two years later China's strongman was too frail even to greet President Nixon on his historic visit; a job that fell to his old Lushan neighbor Zhou En-Lai. Nevertheless the audience watching the movie was in pantomime mood; they cheered whenever Mao came on screen and booed his wife Jiang Qing who has been blamed for all the excesses of the Cultural Revolution so that red faced Mao can be exonerated.

The main conference hall was upstairs and there was a real sense of history here where the fate of millions was decided, standing amongst the rows of tables with place names marking who sat where, each with a teacup and an ashtray decorated with heroic images of revolution, Mao's teacup and ashtray bigger than anyone else's. The 1959 conference was a particularly stormy affair, teacups or not. Before the meeting at Lushan it was still possible to question and criticise Mao whereas by 1970 it was all acquiescence, applause, Little Red Books and a big red face. During the conference Peng Dehuai, China's Defence Minister wrote a private letter to Mao criticising some elements of the Great Leap Forward. Peng was one of Mao's oldest colleagues and one of the dwindling few who could still speak his mind to his old comrade in arms. But Mao's reaction to the mild criticism was such that no one seriously questioned him again and China's collective leadership was replaced by the dictatorship, cult and paranoia of one man.

Mao extended the conference by 10 days when he read Peng's letter but rather than providing opportunity to enjoy the cool clear Lushan summer air, the delegates were ensnared in the conference centre to hear Peng attacked, denounced and expelled from the Party - he was replaced by the slavishly obedient Lin Biao who waved the Little Red Book harder and faster than anyone else in the 1960s. Mao's speech of 23rd of July 1959 is extraordinarily passionate and bellicose and provides a better understanding of the man than almost anything else he said. Oversensitive and injured, Mao enlisted the sympathy of his audience before going for the kill - the whole sounds like nothing more than the cant of a devious and truculent demagogue, a dangerous man, an unpredictable man, a man used to having his own way.

'I have taken sleeping pills three times' said Mao 'but I can't get to sleep' as if we should feel sorry for him. He justifies the mistakes and the shortages caused by the creaking economy; 'just because there were too few vegetables, too few hair grips, no soap.... everyone became tense'. 'If people don't attack me, I won't attack them' he said, though he admitted there had been 'chaos on a grand scale' and in a display of mock humility he admits to being 'ignorant about economic matters' since his concern is only revolution.

Peng was crucified for daring to speak his mind, though Mao urged people to speak up if they have something to say. 'If you have to shit, shit! If you have to fart, fart!' though everyone knew by now that the stench of criticism and personal opinion was unwelcome to Mao. It's a plain talking and earthy speech by the old Hunanese peasant who was never one for refinement or airs and graces. But it's an ugly intolerant speech too and a clear indicator of where China was headed for the next 15 years - it's this that makes the Conference Hall at Lushan so important.

The fresh air of Lushan's woodlands smelt good after the oppression of the conference hall and the thoughts of Mao's stinky speech. I traced the edge of the plateau past the old movie house that has shown the same film, 'Lushan Lian' since 1980 (this is a world record but how the villagers of Guling must long for a change), a story of love on the mountain that is said to be so powerful, it transcends political divides. Further still I passed the holiday villa of Pearl S Buck the American author who spent her childhood summers on Lushan. Buck's 1931 novel 'The Good Earth' earned her the Nobel Prize for literature (the first American woman to win this award) and describes life in a poor Chinese village before the 1949 revolution. The book has been credited with doing more than any other to foster understanding of China in the US and to prepare the nation psychologically to be an ally of China in the upcoming war against Japan. As such it might be an even more powerful story than the tale of requited love being shown over and over in the movie theatre down the road.

Two hours of walking took me away from the honey coloured stone colonial buildings altogether and into dense forests on well- worn paths past water cascading over rocks into deep pools where I'd seen 19th century Western missionaries over dressed in white suits dangle their feet in old sepia photographs.I passed Mao's new villa by Leilu Lake constructed because Meilu was no longer considered suitable for China's autocrat and was insufficiently large to contain his ego. The villa had none of the homeliness and worn down character of Meilu with its huge and impersonal rooms - a reflection of the huge and impersonal man that Mao had become, though the enormous bathrooms did at least give Mao the opportunity to fart if he needed to fart.

Yesterday's driver had been right; Lushan was a big hill and the walk was long but I loved this route away from the crowds striding out and swinging my arms on the Brocade path, the very edge of the escarpment where the summit plateau ended abruptly in cliffs and black crows cawed their protest and spoke their minds as they wheeled on the breeze below my feet. I climbed steeply uphill finally to Guling and ate lunch in a restaurant where huge frogs in a glass tank labelled as 'river chicken' stared balefully up at me, trying to establish if I was the kind of man who liked to eat amphibians.

A driver was waiting outside of course, because wherever there is a gullible foreigner in China, a taxi is always lurking on the off chance, not far away. And so I descended to the real world through the tall trees on the steep hairpin roads and past 'Beware of rear end collusion' road signs which sounded more like a sexual act than a traffic warning. 'You are leaving the beautiful area' said another sign at the bottom of the hill. Lushan *had* been beautiful but this seemed a bit tough on the rest of Jiangxi where there was beauty too, though it might not be China's most exciting place, and where everything seemed to be defined by politics, which in China and anywhere can sometimes be really, truly ugly.

Crowds on Huangshan mountain - Anhui

Mr Zhang cooking in the desert - Ningxia

Jason the rickshaw driver - Henan

Beach wedding - Hebei

Primary school children - Shanxi

The author with Mao - Hunan

Pool players - Gansu

Maoist memorabilia - Shanghai

The road from Tibet to Nepal

Old man glasses - Ningxia

Author at Tongli sex museum - Jiangsu

Young Red Guard - Shaanxi

Shaolin Kung Fu school – Henan

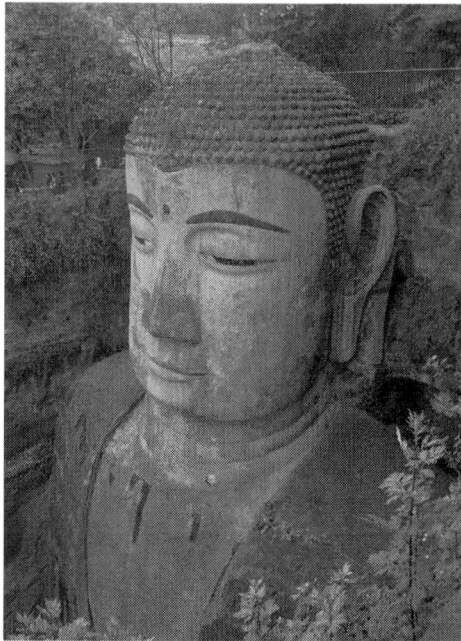

Giant Buddha at Leshan – Sichuan

Ice sculpture in Harbin – Heilongjiang

Tulou houses in Fujian

karst landscape from a balloon – Guangxi

My trusty Dayang motorbike – Hainan

The path along Tiger Leaping Gorge - Yunnan

FUJIAN

福建

124 342 sq km
Population 35.3 million

"Without stirring abroad one can know the whole world. Without looking out of the window, one can see the way of heaven. The farther one travels the less one knows."

Lao Tzu

The man behind me in an Olympic T-shirt is blowing a plastic horn like a vuvuzela that makes a noise out of all proportion to its size and I'm just debating whether to ask him to stop or risk damaging Anglo-Sino relations by forcibly removing the thing when the athletes walk

317

onto the track and a hush descends as we await the start of the race. The runners glance nervously across at their rivals, then with the crack of the pistol they're off, leaping gracefully onto a three wheel bike and pedaling furiously to the first sack of grain which is hauled onto the back of the bike before speeding off to the next.

For this is the 60 metre 'snatch the grain and get it into storage' race at the 6th National Peasant Games in the new Peoples Stadium in Quanzhou, Fujian Province and not the 100 metre final at the Olympics in Beijing despite my neighbour's T-shirt, parping horn and unbridled enthusiasm.

Quanzhou city has great historical significance as the terminus of the 'Silk Road on the Sea' and is said to have been rivaled in scale only by Alexandria in Egypt 800 years ago when it was the busiest port in Tang Dynasty China. Echoes of the old China remain here along the quay crowded with boats or in the shabby old mosque that is one of the oldest in the country. It's hard to escape the incongruity of Moslems walking the streets of a town in this Far Eastern, Han Buddhist corner of China, but these are the men and women whose descendants came here to trade and who secreted away the mysteries of gunpowder, printing and the compass to the West.

The city has rushed to modernize and lost much of its character to the high rise and the wrecking ball and the stadium built to host the Peasant games is just one more addition to the steel and glass skyline. It would be good to report that the Games are a seething mass of peasant ethnic diversity from the four corners of China, come to celebrate the unity of a nation and the athletic prowess of their kinsfolk in a vibrant mix of costumes, ethnicity and Babel of minority tongues. But they're not. Barely a tenth of the seats are occupied, though the man with the horn is making enough noise for ten, and a man in the fourth row is not watching the race at all but elaborately excavating his nose with the fingernail on his pinky. The nail is extraordinarily long and perfectly designed to get to those hard to reach places. Chinese men sometimes grow their nails in such a way in order to celebrate and announce a rise in social status – no more back breaking or nail splitting work in the fields for them. The enhanced ability to root deeply in the nasal cavity is just a happy bonus.

He's probably come to watch these men loading sacks onto a tricycle to remind himself of his life in those distant pre-manicured peasant days and the next event must surely also be a trip down memory lane since it is the 60 metre 'transplant the rice' race. This time competitors race with bundles of rice and plant them into artificial paddies on the track before racing back to the start. There is much controversy and the man blows his horn even louder when one unfortunate competitor is disqualified for missing a hole with a seedling, but things calm down when attention is taken by a close finish in the agricultural throwing event – like shot putt but with bundles of rice.

There are 180 events in total and many of these are more traditional sports such as table tennis, shooting and basketball, though the Games are essentially a celebration of the lives of China's 750 million peasants. So, the throwing, carrying and planting of rice is followed by tyre pushing (like the 100 metre dash but much, much slower), kite flying, folk dancing and Chinese Chess, though the last is certainly one of the less enthralling events for spectators at the Games. It's like having Backgammon at the Olympics.

A pity the stands aren't full since this is a rare public celebration of China's noble and long suffering poor. It is of course horribly sentimentalized and I can't help thinking that the organizers might find a place for other traditional peasant sports. 'Competitors line up please for the half mile sprint as local official bulldozers knock down your homes to make way for a lucrative four lane highway, followed by the race for compensation' – a terribly tedious event since it goes on for so long and has no definite outcome. Or how about some old fashioned 1950s style sparrow-scaring, as peasants were required to do during the catastrophic Great Leap Forward, to really get the crowd on their feet? (Prizes awarded for the most sparrows killed). This would be followed in subsequent years by the great locust invasion and crop destruction caused by the lack of insect predators. It's difficult to know how to award prizes for that one.

But it's too easy to be cynical and the promotional brochure tells me that the games are a true celebration of the ethnic diversity and labours of China's peasants. However I'm hot and hungry and there's no food or drink out here in the bleachers and I wonder why. A stadium bureaucrat reports that there are insufficient people here to warrant the provision of basic life necessities and anyway "these are just peasants and they would litter the food everywhere" and this seems a more honest indication of the view of China's underclass amongst Chinese officialdom.

The Peasant Games hog the back pages in Quanzhou but Fujian is really most famous for brewing a jolly good cup of tea. Traveling North from Quanzhou and into the interior of Fujian takes me through Hui'an territory where the women dress in an approximation of a 12th century Song Dynasty costume. The women in this fishing community are said to have a feudal head, democratic belly, economical shirt and generous trousers, since they wear elaborate hair ornaments, flared trousers and a short shirt that exposes their midriff. This is not necessarily a good thing on a 70 year old toothless peasant woman as she guts fish.

Further into the interior, Fujian becomes increasingly mountainous and far flung. This is tea country and these remote lands are where the South China Tiger is said to still roam. The first rail line didn't prod into these hills until the 1950s and the Red Army who arrived here mob handed in the 1960s reported that some communities were unaware that the Qing Dynasty had been overthrown 50 years before. I wonder how they missed the small matter of the Japanese invasion in the 1930s; maybe they thought they were tourists come to sample the tea.

Nowhere is more famous for its tea than China and only Hangzhou Longjing tea in Zhejiang province is more renowned than the crop from Fujian (see Zhejiang chapter). This makes the hills here with their perfect mix of soil and climate very famous indeed. The Chinese claim that a taste for tea cannot be taught or trained but is in one's heart and I would endorse this since I enjoy a nice mug of milky Tetley's with 2 sugars as much as the next man. I am a philistine regarding the finer points of tea drinking however and Fujian's famous Oolong tea would be wasted on me. I was nevertheless keen to sample a particular brew called Da Hong Pao to see if my palette could be refined. The name of this tea means 'Big Red Robe' after an Imperial official who hung his red robe up six centuries ago, rolled up his broad dynastic sleeves and helped with the picking, though China rarely satisfies herself with a single legend and an alternative tale has monkeys in little red robes swinging from bush to bush and picking the best leaves like some kind of ancient Chinese version of the PG Tips chimps.

Whatever the origins of Da Hong Pao, I didn't get to try it because I'm not a millionaire. There are only 3 bushes of original Red Robe tea left, constituting a 1000 year old copse which perches precipitously on the side of Wuyi Shan Mountain. The bushes slid part way down the hill a few years ago but are now fenced and protected and cosseted with 'No Smoking' and 'No Touching' signs so that they can't slip or burn or be picked by unscrupulous hands. Second grade Da Hong Pao is available in the inevitable tea shop down the road at just 100 yuan a pot but this is from bushes that have been transplanted from the originals. The waitress told me that each pot contains one leaf of Da Hong Pao though the utter improvability of this dissuaded me from reaching for my wallet.

Tea from the originals is much, much more expensive; Big Red Robe tea sells for 400 000 US Dollars per pound. Actually, if some more money than sense billionaire coughed up this much cash, he'd own all the Da Hong Pao produced in a whole year, for the annual yield of these 1000 year old bushes is just one imperial pound. Flavour varies, depending on the weather since the bushes are never watered. The guide tells me that the taste is sometimes floral like sweet scented osmanthus and sometimes more earthy, depending on how dry the year has been. Either way, the fragrance lingers on your tongue for a long time; though I'm not convinced this would be a good thing in an 'earthy' year. Presumably there would be a slightly bitter lingering after taste too, having spent so much on a cup of tea.

I would certainly fail to recognize the floral tones of Da Hong Pao, just as I failed to appreciate the finer points of the world's most expensive coffee when I tried it in Yunnan province. This is called civet coffee since it is made from beans that have been ingested and passed through the back passage of a weasel like creature called a civet cat. This thick and extremely bitter beverage would have been rendered drinkable only by the addition of several heaped spoonfuls of sugar or by handing it over to a coffee shop and asking them to turn it into a double whipped cream Frappucino. I still can't help wondering how civet cat coffee was first discovered; some people just have too much time on their hands.

I returned from the remote tiger infested, tea covered Fujian hills to the provincial capital Fuzhou via Zhouming village where 800 years ago, the lifeless bodies of carp floating on the local stream gave warning that the water had been poisoned by enemies. Carp are still worshipped here as divine and the village has a little carp cemetery with tiny little graves; 'Here lays Colin the fish, gone to the great pond in the sky. May his scales remain undimmed by time'.

Fuzhou is a boom town, a huge sprawling and rather soulless place, though not without interest hidden among the sky scrapers and shopping malls. For it was here that the Baochuan was built in the 15th century; in its day, the largest ship in the world and sailed by Admiral Zheng He to parts of Asia, Africa and possibly the New World, depending on who you believe and this at a time when the rest of the world was floating around in tubs barely a quarter of the size. It remains a huge missed opportunity that the Ming Dynasty abandoned the possibilities of sea exploration and grounded its fleet at a time when a less insular approach might have led to the world domination that modern China seems closer than ever to today.

Also in Fuzhou, just down the road from the 1969 Mao statue built to commemorate the ratification of Maoism as state religion, is the museum of Lin Zexu. This 19th century Chinese official is forgotten in the West though once he had his own waxwork in Madame Tussauds and Manhattan's Chinatown has a statue of him still. The contrast with China could hardly be greater, for here Lin is remembered as an heroic Qing official with an unusually strong moral code and one of a very rare breed in 19th century China – a man who stood up to the British.

Lin took his stand against the opium trade, or 'foreign mud' as he called it. In 1839 after being sent to neighbouring Guangdong province, Lin arrested 1700 opium dealers and confiscated 70 000 opium pipes. He also, and most famously, burned 1.2 million kg of the drug before dumping it into the sea. Reports that local marine life spent the next decade blissed out on the sea bed or swimming frantically in circles in search of their next fix remain unconfirmed.

All of this may seem like admirable behaviour and should help to establish Lin's reputation as an opiate-busting anti drugs Tsar, but the British Government were enraged. Lin's letter to Queen Victoria (who may have enjoyed a little drug use herself) was published in The Times and asked "where is your conscience?" This of course, made the assumption that 19th century Empire builders possessed such an unnecessary conceit, indeed British politicians remained particularly unencumbered by anything as inconvenient as a moral code around the time of the Opium Wars in China. Pounds, shillings and pence surely had a great deal to do with this since the Government made a 2000% profit on each 130 pound chest shipped to China from India and Afghanistan. In 1790, 3000 chests were delivered to the opium dens of the Middle Kingdom, but by 1836 this had risen tenfold. No wonder Britain went to war with China twice to preserve this trade. British liberal responses to all this are remarkable for their hypocrisy; opium was banned in the UK but considered suitable and necessary to the Chinese constitution and a blessing to them and at 2000% profit per barrel, the thoughtful Brits were happy to shower China with such blessings. Poor Lin was exiled to distant Xinjiang and died there in 1850. The import of opium continued and Lin's waxwork in Tussauds was no doubt converted to Gladstone, Livingstone or some other 19th century luminary just as soon as Londoners lost interest in viewing the effigy of this unscrupulous Chinaman who had caused Britain to go to war.

If Fuzhou is the typical could-be-anywhere amorphous Chinese city, Xiamen is the shape of Chinese cities to come. This city by the sea is smaller, cleaner and far more attractive than its big provincial brother further north. The city is famous for a number of reasons, though first among these is its food, especially Fotiaoqiang; literally 'Buddha jumps over the wall' – a soup containing fin, sea cucumber, abalone and shaoxing wine, though I was more interested in the local huashengtang or peanut soup served from huge bubbling, Dickensian, please-can-I-have–some-more vats all over town at two yuan a bowl.

The town is also famed for its Minju Fujianese Opera and Dog Kung Fu whose rules require participants to fight on hands and knees, though bum sniffing, territory marking and licking one's own private parts are sadly missing from the sport. This fighting style was traditionally practiced by women whose feet were bound and therefore could hardly be expected to stand and kick; tough on the knees though.

There also seemed to be an excessive number of hair salons in Xiamen catering to a local population who clearly have a passion for fashion. These places are an education in how to tease and prune straight black hair into any number of styles. The stylists whose window posters claim to be able to make a Brad Pitt or an Angelina Jolie out of anyone lounge on the steps outside their shops since no one ever seems to go in. They shout 'Hello!' in a vaguely intrusive way since they have less interest in greeting the foreigner than in making their extravagantly coiffured fellow stylists laugh. The hairstyles they sport, which in no way would tempt you into the salon for a quick makeover, are ludicrous; coloured and lifted and permed and spiked, they're desperate to look different to a billion of their countrymen. 'Hello, Hello!' they shout and I want to shout back, 'Your hair looks really, really bad', though in essence I suppose their desire for non-conformity is no different to the democratic bellies of the Hui'an women.

Xiamen has a glorious Tang dynasty temple called Nanputuo, though like the farmer who has had the same broom all his life and has only had to change the handle and bristles twice, to claim such antiquity is to ignore that the whole place has been restored timber by timber over the years. It's a busy working temple where everyday hundreds of locals and students from the nearby university come to pray for health, happiness and the blessings of a son or success in their exams. The Heavenly King Hall here has an image of Wei Tuo, the protector of Buddhist doctrine who is holding his staff pointing down to signal that the temple will provide lodgings to weary travelers and if I hadn't already checked into my guesthouse I'd have been tempted to ask for a bed to see if the offer was really genuine. A horizontal staff means 'clear off, go and stay somewhere else, just because we're Buddhists doesn't mean you can roll up and expect a free bed you cheapskate'.

The temple also has a magnificent 1000 square metre captive fish pond filled with silver and golden carp and where dozens of luck bringing reptiles stand on top of each other in tottering towers of turtles on the few rocks scattered around the lake. Good Buddhists can gain merit by buying fish from local vendors and freeing them here, though considering this practice has been going on for hundreds of years, the lake should be completely rammed with happy saved-from-the-wok fish. The absence of fish and the prosperity of local fish sellers suggest that something fishy is going on here and as the carp swam in lazy circles, I mused that they must be dizzy from being captured and released over and over again. Still, what's a little carp scam between Buddhists; the temple gives free lodgings after all.

Fish are not the only creatures escaping their destiny in Xiamen since the city has long been a point of disembarkation to points around the globe. Fujianese are traditionally driven to emigrate by economic hardship but also by tradition and a spirit of adventure and the chances are that many of the Chinese in your local high street hail originally from this part of South-Eastern China. The lack of social welfare in modern China also no doubt plays a part, since in the poor mountainous interior of the province; the government gives a poverty alleviation allowance of only 50 yuan per child per month.

The loss of young, educated people from Fujian became so great during the 18th Century that the Qing government placed a ban on emigration, but even the Dragon Emperor couldn't cool his subjects' itchy feet and today over two million Fujianese live abroad in Malaysia, Singapore, the Philippines and the USA and 80% of the population of Taiwan can trace their heritage back to the mountains and coast of Fujian.

Not all emigrants find streets paved with gold. The 23 men and women aged 18-45 killed searching for cockles on Morecambe Bay in the North West of England in February 2004 were from Fujian. These people from Xiamen, Fuzhou and the tea mountains in the North were swept to their deaths in icy waters having paid 10 000 yuan each to snakehead gangs to smuggle them into the UK and whose families are now burdened with this impossible debt charged at 10% interest per annum which is many times their income. The Gangmaster of the cocklers, Lin Liangren was convicted of manslaughter and sentenced to 14 years in prison for his greed and exploitation of his fellow countrymen, though blaming one man for this tragedy is an oversimplification and does nothing to alleviate the suffering of the destitute families back in Fujian who are not entitled to compensation since their dead relatives were law breaking illegal immigrants.

Few emigrants come home to Fujian but the most famous returnee is Tan Kah Kee. This Xiamen native made his money from rubber plantations in Malay and returned in the 1950s to contribute 100 million dollars for the building of Xiamen University and Jimei school village on the outskirts of town. The school is a beautiful stone built edifice that calls to mind Evelyn Waugh and the crack of leather on willow. Surrounded by mature trees and grass land, this place is a real escape from the frenzy of modern China. The rubber millionaire lived like a pauper and there is a poignant display of his worn out umbrella, shoes and suitcase at the school; this is the kind of man who probably released dozens of fish into the lake at Nanputuo. Such was his altruism that Tan was given a state funeral in Beijing; a remarkably brave and open minded gesture by Mao and the Politburo, since millionaire businessmen and radical Communists usually make uneasy bedfellows.

There is a mad scramble to board the ferry from Xiamen waterfront across to the island of Gulang Yu. This is because crowds on all forms of public transport in China have a life of their own and rushing and pushing is just how these things are done. Actually, there's no need to rush at all because the boat is big and I've paid an extra one yuan to stand on the top deck which is no more luxurious but has more room and an electric fan which lazily and pointlessly stirs the hot air.

The crossing traces a delicate arc across the harbour and gives a brief and lovely view of the historic island. Straight ahead are the mish mash of colonial buildings and the bouldery peak of Sunlight Rock and over to the left the giant statue of Koxinga and the open water to Taiwan beyond. Such colonial enclaves have a history rooted in deplorable exclusivity of course, but with its traffic free cobbled streets, stout old buildings and handsome banyan trees, it's hard not to infinitely prefer Gulang Yu to the frenzy and pollution of Fuzhou. It's certainly the preferred location for young local couples since it seems there is a bride and groom lurking behind every stuccoed corner and gabled end. They're having wedding photos taken; she dressed as an Edwardian virgin and he cravated and aesthetic like Oscar Wilde or an extra from a Gilbert and Sullivan show, though Wilde was seldom seen in Nike trainers. I think he was more of an Adidas man.

The privileged ex-residents here seem to have lived a bucolic existence in their country clubs and tinkling their pianos (the island still has more pianos per capita than anywhere else in China). History and great events disturbed their idyll only fleetingly such as when 7000 US sailors visited on shore leave in 1908; an event sure to have shaken the tea and scones routines of the daughters of respectable gentlemen. The US fleet returned in 1938 when the USS Asheville saved 60 000 Chinese interred by Japanese on the island with no food and water. These interruptions aside, the colonials sipped their pink gin, played tennis and took mass at the Catholic Tianzhujiao Tang Church, until the colony slipped quietly into history and everyone went reluctantly home to the austerity of Europe at the end of the war.

Nowadays the island is a holiday destination where locals can ride electric cars, paddle in the sea and watch dolphins do tricks at the aquarium. Gulang Yu has been further reclaimed by the Chinese by the erection of a huge statue on Fuding Rock. The Chinese say that Fujian is eight parts mountain, one part water and one part farmland, but the province must be at least half a part statue since the construction of this huge monument which is impressive from the Xiamen ferry but overwhelming up close, its 41.2 metre height accentuated by its position on top of a giant boulder from where it gazes symbolically across the Taiwan straits towards China's 'lost province'.

The steely gaze belongs to General Zheng Chenggang or Koxinga perched above Bright Moon Garden which is named for a poem written by the great man. 'I miss you so much', wrote Koxinga, 'I can't sleep while the moonlight seeps through the curtains'. This sounds horribly like a Celine Dion power ballad or a Cantonese pop song; clearly the General was a better fighter than a poet. Perhaps, like most Chinese poems, it sounds better in its original language.

Koxinga was a great soldier from his leadership of a rebel army in 17th century Fujian against invasion from the Manchus; 'Resist the Qing, restore the Ming' was his rallying cry, which scans better than that poem about the curtains. More famously, he freed Taiwan or Formosa as it was then known, from Dutch control. This war of liberation provides an interesting insight into the 17th century European sense of superiority since Frederic Coyott the Dutch Governor of the island believed he could defend the island from attack from 25 000 of Koxinga's soldiers with barely 300 men. Coyett writes in his diary that the Chinese 'had no liking for the smell of powder' and that '25 Chinese are not the equal of one Dutch soldier since they are insignificant and effeminate men.' Even by this reckoning Coyett had insufficient numbers and one week later on 27 January 1662 the mathematically challenged Governor lay dead, his blind confidence revealed as ignorance and hubris.

Koxinga died in turn, just 5 months after the liberation of Taiwan, apparently from 'overwork', which is gratifying for all us indolent types who will never liberate anywhere. He is remembered in tribute across China and Taiwan alone has a total of 63 statues dedicated to the all work and no play General, which makes the stonemasons there pretty overworked too. For the Chinese, the General has become a symbol of reunification with Taiwan, hence his determined gaze across the ocean from Gulang Yu. Taiwan has become a source of frustration and a symbol of humiliation in China since the defeated Nationalists fled there in 1949 and established an independent nation under the tutelage of the US. The certainty that Taiwan, like Tibet, is an historic and inalienable part of China and will come home one day is mostly a quiet sort of resentment, though occasionally these claims have broken out into open hostility and interference such as during the 1996 Taiwanese Presidential elections when China held large scale military exercises off the Fujian coast to encourage the Taiwanese to vote for non-separatist candidates.

Nowhere has the hostility been more pronounced than in Xiamen, the closest mainland city to Taiwan and from where Taiwanese outlying islands are barely 20 km offshore. The island of Jinmen, formerly known as Quemoy can be seen when standing by the billowing granite robes of Koxinga and it looks an inoffensive enough place from up here. Yet this is the Nationalist front line and almost precipitated war in 1958 and again in 1966 when China became convinced that it was being used for Taiwanese military exercises and began to drop high explosive shells on it. A major diplomatic incident ensued and for a while it seemed that war between China and the USA would start here, though the Peoples Liberation Army soon silenced their guns and like Koxinga resumed their suspicious and eternal vigil from Fujian.

Xiamen has long been a place from which to resist attack or conquer new land. Further along the coast is the Qing Dynasty fortress of Huli Shan where a 14 metre long, 49 ton German made cannon still keeps guard. Locals were forbidden to enter this militarily sensitive area until 1984, but now Huli Shan and its surrounding beaches are full of tourists and families swimming, eating and getting thumbs aloft photos next to the big gun.

I arrived here in the middle of a Qing Dynasty reconstruction of the firing of a cannon, performed with much gusto by soldiers dressed in 19th century uniforms in the searing heat. The show climaxed in a bang sufficiently loud to make everyone in the crowd scream, babies to start crying and every dog in a two mile radius to begin barking, though this must be nothing to how the big German gun must have sounded when it gave voice.

Departing delightful Xiamen and Gulang Yu with a heavy heart, my mood was brightened by the prospect of a train journey which in China is never dull. I chanced my luck in the station waiting room 'for soldiers and mothers' fully aware that I am neither, and was later shocked to discover that my hard sleeper car was kitted out with TVs. Other things were more familiar; it was reassuring to have the fruit seller on board who as usual traversed up and down the narrow corridor every 10 minutes for almost the whole journey; I guessed her enthusiasm was commission based so that every orange sold was vital.

The distance to the mountains in North-West Fujian is not far, but the journey is long because the train has to describe a huge loop to skirt the hundreds of mountains that make up those eight tenths of the province. This leaves time for some more fruit from the enthusiastic seller and also some peanut soup which is passed to me in a bowl with a pair of chopsticks. I puzzle over this for a while and eventually slurp the hot soup from the bowl like everyone else.

I got off the train in Yongding because it's the closest town to a famous and unique site 50 miles away, but Yongding itself is very far from being a tourist town. It's a grubby place where a few half-hearted strings of neon lights do nothing to brighten the cheap and hasty buildings and where locals sit around on motorbikes and pass the day. I was so at a loss for something to do in Yongding that I spent my time there in a local bakery sampling their cakes.

There are of course worse ways to spend a couple of hours and I eventually waddled out with cream around my mouth to take a taxi to the heartland of the Hakka people in Yongding County. The journey through the hills was on a fast road that inexplicably ended and deteriorated into a rough track every mile or so before transforming into smooth asphalt for a while before my taxi slammed on the brakes and bumped across stones again. This continued for most of the 50 miles so that the driver became increasingly less inclined to slow down and we bumped and crashed along as I clung on with white knuckles and Yongding cakes regurgitating in my mouth.

The Hakka people have lived in these remote hills since they were driven from Northern China by war centuries ago. Scarred by their experiences and subsequent flight, they have taken a highly defensive approach to home building and it was these homes that I had come to see. These fortress houses or 'tulou' were discovered by the West in the 1980s when CIA analysts spotted them on aerial photographs and alerted Ronald Reagan to the construction of 'missile silos' so close to Taiwan.

It's tempting to lampoon Reagan for this error, though I suppose it's an easy enough mistake to make since the Tulou are so big and round. The first sighting of a cluster of Tulou is mightily impressive and makes the long journey over the hills and along the road that isn't quite a road worthwhile. There are 20 000 of these communal homes scattered across Fujian and all take the same approximate form. Huge circular or sometimes square fortresses, the Tulou are built from rammed earth and glutinous rice with five feet thick walls and tiny windows way up high. They are usually built on three or four floors with a central courtyard where ceremonies, cooking and socializing take place. Old people tend to live on the first floor to avoid wheezing up too many steps and in my first Tulou I met a 99 year old Hakka grandmother firmly positioned on the ground floor who grinned toothlessly and told me that the Tulou were 'very good, very good'.

Nowadays the Hakka supplement their income with tourist dollars and in some of the bigger Tulou such as Zhencheng Lou built in 1912 and with 222 rooms, it's possible to buy Hakka dolls, pictures and musical instruments or to stay the night. Agriculture is still king though and everywhere were blackberries and persimmons drying in the autumn sun. The Hakka were conspicuous by their absence and the Tulou deathly quiet apart from a few tourists because I visited during the day and the people were out in the fields just as their ancestors would have been in years past, though I suspected that some might be in Quanzhou running the snatch the grain race.

The Tulou are a remarkable solution to the needs of a community and have been around for hundreds of years. The oldest Tulou, in Hu Le town was built over 1200 years ago but I also noticed circular houses built as late as the 1960s for it seems that the Hakka believe that the design can hardly be improved upon. In Hukeng village, which is the center of the Hakka tourist trade, even the public toilets are built in the Tulou style. Never have I felt such a sense of tradition when relieving myself.

The Tulou are designed to accommodate the extended Hakka family so that they can eat, play and worship together since many Tulou have an ancestral hall or temple in the central compound. In Hukeng, I met a tiny number of the millions of Fujian exiles who had returned from their homes in Singapore on holiday to recall how their ancestors lived. I wondered what this communal life was like and imagined that they would see only the benefits of shared happiness and hardships, but their view was of how difficult it must be to lack privacy and to share every aspect of life with relatives who you might not even like. I thought of the 99 year old woman sitting in her Tulou doorway and arranging persimmons in the dappled sunlight and decided that she would probably disagree. For one's life could hardly be better than to live in a round house far from the Emperor and drinking a cup of fine Fujian tea.

HUBEI

河北

569 800 sq km
Population 60.31 million

On and on the Great River rolls, racing east.
Of proud and gallant heroes its white-tops leave no trace,
As right and wrong, pride and fall turn all at once unreal.
Yet ever the green hills stay
To blaze in the west-waning day.

Luo Guanzhong- 'Romance of the 3 Kingdoms'-14th Century

There is poetry in the rivers and hills that connect Chongqing prefecture to Hubei province. This is a land of battles and heroes, of betrayal and men with unfeasibly long beards, as told in the classic 14th century book 'Romance of the three kingdoms' by Luo Guanzhong.

China's population is immersed in the history of the events of this book and to have no knowledge of the Three Kingdoms is to hardly understand China at all. Life was simpler in the second and third century kingdoms of Shu, Wei and Wu where heroes stood tall and villains met sticky ends. The long story of the three kingdoms was retold in 84 episodes on Chinese TV in the 1990s and tells the tale of three warriors Liu Bei, Guan Yu and Zhang Fei and the villainous Cao Cao. The Warriors take a fraternal oath in a peach garden to defend the kingdom of China from her enemies and though not born in the same month or year , hope to die on the same day - an oath that is still used by Triad groups in China today.

I pondered all of this as I sat on the deck of our boat from Wanzhou long after everyone else had returned to the warmth of their cabins. I enjoy these solitary moments in China when there is no one tugging my sleeve to take me on a ride in his taxi or to sell me a genuine Ming Dynasty pot or is shouting 'Hello Waiguoren' to the foreign curiosity. Lights twinkled on the black hills that reared into the curtain of night, but mostly there was nothing to see or hear through my shroud of blankets but the pulsing of the engine that turned the props of the boat deep in their Yangtze soup.

At midnight the vessel swung to starboard and pulled into shore by the Zhang Fei Temple, and as the boat slept, I shrugged off my blankets and disembarked with my guide called Snow White who emerged bleary eyed from our cabin (a male with an effecting girly name – see Chongqing chapter). The Three Gorges Dam further east has raised the water level so much here that the whole temple has been moved brick by brick from its previous location. This devoured 40 million yuan of government funds and now the structure was covered in ribbons of red fairy lights that we'd seen for miles upstream and that lent the ancient building the budget look of a 1980s youth club discotheque.

The steps to the temple were lined with hawkers who even at this early hour offered us busts of Mao, Three Kingdoms scrolls, Chinese tea sets and other items essential to a three day river cruise traveler on a dark 1am hillside. I entered the large dark wooden embossed gates and decided that this was 40 million yuan well spent if you like those dioramas that feature life-size dummies retelling historical events. Zhang Fei didn't die on the same day as his sworn brothers but was murdered by his own soldiers who he had treated with cruelty. A low budget shop dummy re-creation shows the men creeping treacherously upon their commander who sleeps with his sword beside him like a great powerful bear and with his eyes open as a defence against the fate that was about to befall him.

This was no kind of death for the warrior Zhang who had turned back an army of 10,000 by brandishing his spear and challenging them all to a fight to the death, like some drunken Geordie with his shirt off outside a pub on a Saturday night. Zhang's bravado scared the leader of Cao Cao's army so much that he fell down dead on the spot. But the warrior could be a sensitive soul too. Quick to anger, he was fiercely loyal to his friends and fretted over the safety of his daughter who as a moody teenager was probably like, totally embarrassed by her father showing off in front of her friends.

One can research Zhang Fei's semi mythical life further by immersion in Luo Guanzhong's long book. Far easier though to read the numerous Japanese Zhang Fei manga cartoons or play video games where by pressing the correct combination of buttons, the player makes the warrior spin 360° and bring his spear crashing to the ground hard enough to cause an earthquake. No wonder Cao Cao's general died of fright.

Guan Yu was even scarier. Chapter one of 120 in the book describes Zhang Fei's sworn brother as excessively tall with a long beard, 'a face and lips the colour of red jujube fruit, eyes like a Phoenix and eyebrows that resembled silkworms'. Despite his 50 kg Green Dragon Crescent blade, Guan Yu was betrayed and murdered - this is the reason why Zhang Fei was so grumpy. Guan's head was delivered to Cao Cao who fell into a faint when the box was opened and the fallen hero's beard stood on end, his eyes opened and he probably wiggled his silkworm brows.

The legend of the three kingdoms permeates Chinese society so thoroughly that many modern Chinese proverbs are derived from the story. It is said that a wife can be changed like laundry, but friendship like the brothers can never be replaced.

'Speaking of Cao Cao' is the Chinese equivalent of 'speak of the devil' and the Chinese also say that the young shouldn't read the 12th century adventures of Song Jiang in The Water Margin and the old should resist The Three Kingdoms. The former has too many pages of brawls and machismo which might have a bad influence on impressionable males while the latter is full of deception and fraud. Old people are supposed to 'know the will of the heavens' according to Confucius and shouldn't fill their heads with Cao Cao's trickery and if they tried to emulate Zhang Fei's spinning earthquake Kung Fu, would just put their back out.

There was territory and deception aplenty at Baidicheng further downstream. Our cabin was too hot and I woke with a Guan Yu red face at dawn by the river town of Fengjie where the concrete and rust view through my grubby porthole was so terribly ugly that I began to wonder if the inundation of many Yangtze towns by the giant dam might not be such a bad thing. Baidicheng is a short coach ride from Fengjie and was full of golden week holiday Chinese tourists. You can't blame the residents of ugly Fengjie for earning a few dollars, but Baidicheng is a tourist trap par excellence.

We were led on a mazelike route that took in every conceivable shop at the ferry pier before we paid to board our bus. The guide grabbed our cash and seemed to miss the point of her megaphone by shouting as loudly as she could all the way there. Down the steps and another maze of shops where other megaphone grannies bellowed at us, brought us to the temple gates. Here we paid some more cash, pushed through the turnstiles and a man in trousers that were too short asked for a contribution for the souvenir photo that his friend in three kingdoms fancy dress had just taken of me. The photo was rubbish; me, some turnstiles, a huge sign announcing Baidicheng as 'the number one tourist destination in the world' and a crowd of people looking understandably depressed at spending so much money.

I declined the photo but consumer opportunities did not end there. For just 50 yuan bare chested porters were ready to whisk me up 400 steps to the temple summit on a 'sedan chair' that was really a piece of garden furniture tied to a couple of bamboo poles. I declined and walked breezily up past unhappy tourists clutching souvenir snaps who had been turfed out of their chairs by bearers who insisted that 50 yuan gets you only *halfway* up.

The temple itself is utterly mundane (100 yuan to make a wish inside). Much of the old structure was submerged by the rising water of the Yangtze and I wandered the courtyards and past the shop dummy tableau of the death of Liu Bei in 265 AD in awe of the commercial acumen of the local Chinese, rather than with any sense of history or antiquity.

The Chinese call Baidicheng the city of verse since so many poets have written about it. Li Bai is the most famous Chinese poet of all, and as long ago as the 8th Century, he realised just as I had that the best part of Baidicheng is leaving it behind;

> *This morning, I depart the town of Baidi, engulfed by vibrant clouds.*
> *I return to far away Jiangling within a single day.*
> *From both banks, the steady sound of shrieking monkeys fills the air.*
> *Our little boat has already carried me past thousands of hilltops.*

We were amongst the same thousand hilltops in little time after I had paid the bus mama who hollered thanks through her megaphone in my face and I had battled once more the attrition of shops. Baidicheng is where the Yangtze bursts into the Three Gorges and though we were in Chongqing still, by the time our boat had left the claustrophobic and vertical rock behind, we would have crossed into Hubei.

Li Bai described Qutang Gorge as 'a 1000 seas in one teacup' since here the Yangtze squeezes into a gap called Kuimen Gate that is little more than 100 metres wide and boils and rolls through 8 km of vertiginous rock. I had become quite used to handing over crumpled Chinese banknotes by now and gave over more money that entitled me to a VIP seat at the front of the boat where I might catch a glimpse of the old Han dynasty plank road on the cliffs above or the square holes of Meng Liang's staircase which leads to the platform where General Yang Jiye was killed by traitors. Yang's faithful bodyguard had climbed at night to retrieve the body but was deceived by a monk who crowed like a rooster to signal daybreak. The bodyguard retreated, though I had no idea how as I gazed at the perfectly vertical granite wall by the side of the boat, but returned later to punish the deceptive monk who crowed no more when he was hung by his feet from the cliff.

Everyone was a VIP on board today and though there was room for but 30 seats, the enterprising crew had arranged for at least 150 people to pay for first-class treatment. So in the end no one could really see and the megaphones of 10 tour guides commenced battle that was as merciless and cutthroat as that of the generals of ancient times.

I asked a fellow VIP why we didn't complain at the overcrowding but he said that there was no point since no one would listen. He was possessed of that defeatist and conformist manner of the small Chinese man whose fatalism precludes protest but became more animated on seeing me reach for pen and notebook and forgot all about the view of the Gorge. "Don't write only bad things about China" he said. "Most foreigners only say bad things and there are good people in China too." I added insecurity to passivity in his list of faults, but that conversation stayed with me as a reproach for the rest of the day and whenever it became too easy to criticise or laugh at this nation so different to home.

I retreated from the megaphones and VIP crowds and soon had a much better view from the balcony outside my room with Snow White. We could see the caves high on the cliff face where wooden coffins from the 2000 year old Ba Kingdom are found. No one seems quite sure how these ancient people put the coffins there, nor how their ingenious civilisation came to an end. But as Luo Guangzhong said in the very first sentence of his extravagantly long three kingdoms book; 'The Empire long divided must unite, long united must divide. Thus it has ever been'. No rest for China then.

The Gorge ended suddenly, the boat was bathed in sunlight once more and our scenery flattened out into monotonous rolling hills. Life on board had become rather pleasant. I played cards and talked with Snow White and tried to avoid the lonely middle aged woman who had taken a liking to me. The three kingdoms is not the only romance that many Chinese are searching for on these river cruises that double as a floating dating agency. The woman had taken to blocking the passage with her chair so that I couldn't get past and offered me a tangerine every time she saw me as if I was vitamin C deprived. So I stayed out of her way and sat on deck watching the hills rolling by and counting evidence of abandoned fields and villages as we drew closer to China's great dam.

Sometimes too, I lay on my bed in my tiny cabin and watched the antennae of armour plated cockroaches as they felt the air and climbed the wall, and listened to the monotony of the pulsing engines. The cabins were cramped with hardly room for vermin at all, but the crew had still managed to shoehorn an enormous TV in for those passengers who wanted to watch Chinese game shows instead of the famous and dramatic scenery outside.

When I tired of watching insects, I read the diary of Captain Glenn F Howell who had travelled the Yangtze on the gunboat USS Palos in 1920 and 1921. The river was quite different in Howell's day when colonial boats operated with impunity. The water flowed faster then, as if rushing China to change and passage through the Gorges was a difficult business indeed.

The first unaided steam vessel to make the trip upstream in 1900 from Yichang to Chongqing had been the predictably named 'Pioneer'. Captained by Cornell Plant, the trip took 73 hours and the captain wrote a guide to every rock, cliff and whirlpool through the dangerous Gorges and received that rare accolade in China - a memorial of thanks to a foreigner. An obelisk was built on the bank overlooking the most treacherous part of the third Gorge called Xiling, where a huge and dangerous submerged rock had sunk many ships and which Plant brilliantly named 'Come to Me Rock'. There is a gravestone in Hong Kong where the great navigator died on his way home in 1921 but the Yangtze Memorial is now submerged. Come to Me was destroyed by explosive charge many years ago and what remains is now far beneath the new surface of this much deeper Yangtze.

Before Plant's successful voyage, boats had to be pulled and manhandled upstream by gangs of men. Captain Howell is especially admiring of these trackers, of whom there were 200,000 working when his gunboat was on the river. The trackers earned just three dollars and their food for each trip and every journey would take two months giving a maximum annual income of $12. The work was incredibly, improbably, outrageously tough, pulling and heaving boats against the powerful flow of the river. The men died of illness, injury and drowning and were naked beasts of burden for eight months of the year since clothes were superfluous to such work. Yet Howell marvels at the spirit of the men; 'In spite of the unending toil, the few years of life…. they are an extraordinarily happy group of human beings. Carefree, never thinking of the morrow, today's chow and tonight's sleep register the limits of their desire".

Or maybe Howell is being terribly patronising about the jolly natives whose lives surely can't have been much fun. There are still trackers at work today on some of the Yangtze side streams, but these are just for laughing tourists and none work with an absence of clothes. I disembarked and took a small boat up a tributary called Daning He and through the Xiaosanxia little three Gorges where the scenery was the most magnificent of the whole trip but where I saw no trackers at all, naked or otherwise.

Daning He has lost much of its power and the advertising hording photos of wildly excited tourists tearing down rapids on inflatable boats that are barely seaworthy are now redundant. We transferred to a tiny wooden boat instead where a fisherman sang songs and we drifted past his friend who sat artfully on the cliff side playing a reed flute whose warm notes bounced and echoed off the valley walls. The man gave us a toothless tour of the history of his remote valley and I asked Snow White what he was telling us. But my guide was a city boy and could make no more sense than me of the old man's heavy Sichuan accent.

Back on the boat, my girlfriend gave me another orange and a wink and we meandered downstream in golden evening light. I turned my face to the sun, tossed some more peel into the choppy waters and decided that for once Chinese tourist hyperbole was not unwarranted in this beautiful place.

We were in Wu or Witch Gorge, the second of the 3 Gorges and passing into Hubei province, when my reverie was broken by the metallic clang of the ship's loudspeakers. The Chinese are inordinately fond of personifying and naming natural features and here in Wu every rock and cliff has a name and a story attached and the ship guide had decided that these needed to be pointed out. Here then were the Goddess Yao Ji and her 11 sisters, Congregated Immortals Peak, Flying Phoenix Peak, Rising Cloud Peak and a dozen more. When the peaks were exhausted, our announcer didn't hesitate to remind us that 3 Gorges stamps and coins were available on the first deck, and in case we had missed that message here it was again. And again. And again.

The 8th Century poet Du Fu went head to head with his contemporary Li Bai and offered his own thoughts on the Gorges in his elegy to Wu called Autumn Thought;

Jade dew withers and wounds the groves of maple trees,
On Wu mountain, in Wu gorge, the air is dull and drear.
On the river surging waves rise to meet the sky,
Above the pass wind and cloud join the earth with darkness.
Chrysanthemum bushes open twice, weeping for their days,
A lonely boat, a single line, my heart is full of home.
Winter clothes everywhere are urgently cut and measured,
Baidicheng above, the evening's driven by beating on stones.

If I had cried tears, they would have been not for chrysanthemums, but for the turgid tinny repetition of that woman's loudspeaker voice.

The end of Wu Gorge was once called Huoyan Shi or Flint Rapid, where limestone rocks jutted from the water and bit chunks from boats with stone teeth. These were blown up in the 1950s with many others in the last of the gorges called Xiling that was notorious as the most dangerous stretch of water along the whole river.

When the water was low in Xiling, junks would unload their cargo and be hauled by teams of 100 trackers or more past Ox Liver, Horses Lung and Yellow Ox Gorges, Come to Me rock and the White Bone Pagoda whose giant pile of bleached bones was all that survived of the many thousands who lost their lives in this frightening place. Du Fu was less lyrical about Xiling;

Three dawns shine upon the Yellow Ox
Three sunsets and we go slowly
Three dawns again and three sunsets
And we do not notice that our hair is white as silk.

But the water has risen 135 metres and Xiling is placid now. I slept as deeply as the river beneath and dreamt of tangerines not thrashing water and come-to–get–me rocks and started awake to crashing cymbals and banging drums at the riverside town of Jiuwan. Snow White hadn't heard a thing and I began to believe that I had dreamt it until we disembarked and walked past locals eating bowls of congee rice porridge besides still trembling massive drums. Other locals were brushing flies off hunks of meat and offering them to passengers while more still had rows of silver fish laid out to dry on trestles. I asked if the fish were good and the seller in his thick plastic apron and cut off rubber boots answered "of course" with some incredulity. He meant they were from the Yangtze and couldn't be anything other than good since as he reminded me, the water in that mighty river is "especially clean and pure."

Now, I had been traveling downstream for two days and had seen all manner of detritus floating on the river, from the contents of passenger ship toilets, to oil slicks and small flotillas of Styrofoam and on one occasion a dead pig which had caused such excitement amongst my fellow passengers that they rushed to the rail to take photographs. Even my lady friend had left her corridor barricade unmanned to have a look. I had as much cause as anyone to doubt the fishmonger's veracity; clearly he wanted to make a sale, but I don't think he was telling a conscious lie in order to do so. Such is the Chinese veneration of the Yangtze that this man wanted to believe the water to be fine, even when his eyes told him it was not.

I wouldn't want to fall into the Yangtze and take great gulps of its crystal clear water, but at Jiuwan I came close. We walked past the drums, the meat and the fish and tiptoed into slender dragon boats that whisked us further upstream. All of us had been issued with oars but didn't need them as the guide beat out a tattoo on a small drum and cranked up an outboard motor that sputtered out a pother of smoke and made oars and drum entirely redundant.

So we raced along Jiuwan stream past chattering monkeys in trees right down at the water's edge and my fellow dragon boaters tried to row and stand up and see the monkeys better all at once. The boat bucked and reared and I thought of the Yangtze's poisonous bilharzia snails, its river snakes and its filth and clung to the sides, closed my eyes and thought of England.

In fact the water was much cleaner in this side stream away from the riverside towns and the fish seller's claims started to have more veracity. We arrived at a floating stage and watched a badly acted Three Kingdoms show where the performers dressed in budget 14th century nylons and the amplification was so cheap and tinny that the shrieked entreaties of females to Zhang Fei were almost enough to make my ears bleed.

I had to change seats because the stench of the public toilets at the back of the bleachers was overpowering, but reflected that in a few short years toilets, stage, microphones and all will be at the bottom of the river when the Three Gorges Dam is complete and the water level is raised by a final 40 metres.

My Yangtze trip was all about the dam; its presence had loomed inescapably since we had boarded our boat two nights before. It had been in the abandoned shacks and deserted fields on the river bank and in the new settlements and houses and the occasional marker posts that had triumphantly proclaimed where the river would finally reach. As I shouldered my bag, squeezed past the giant telly, locked my cabin and left the boat at Yichang, I was finally going to see this monumental project, this tamer of rivers of which China is so proud.

Visiting this ground breaking and monumental structure was one of the dullest afternoons imaginable. I'm not sure what I was expecting, but the dam is just a big lump of functional concrete and today's filthy grey air had merged with the grey of the dam and my photos look like they've been taken through tupperware. It's an undeniably important big lump of concrete of course as evidenced by the level of security I had to cross before I could even get close. Bags were checked and re-checked and the whole area was crawling with Peoples Liberation Army guards whose excruciatingly boring task it was to stand guard in case something exciting happened. There would be respite from the tedium perhaps by watching the dam through the changing seasons. How beautiful this huge lump of concrete might look under mellow fruitful mists of autumn, beneath glittering crystals of winter ice, as a perch for songbirds 'neath the pattering of spring rains or baking under the furnace of a white Hubei summer sun.

It took the government half a century to choose a site for the dam, and part of the reason for the delay and the bored soldiers is that the location had to be defensible from attack. The carefully tended flower beds were laughably called a viewing area though today I couldn't see a thing, but somewhere on the hills above were anti-aircraft guns, Brigade Headquarters and emergency response units. I'm unclear who the authorities consider most likely to attack but the government knows there's nothing so unifying as a common enemy though it would take a really big bang to damage this dam.

I really don't want to get statistical on you but damn it, this dam is big. 610 feet high, 6864 feet long; 26 million tons of concrete were poured to create a reservoir of 40 million cubic metres of water. The project has cost 180 billion yuan ($30 billion) and it would be a shame to lose it to a terrorist attack after going to all that trouble and expense. The soldiers are also no doubt prepared to protect the dam from other threats and a 15 year old dressed as a soldier was determined to avert the threat of my picture taking. "Bu keyi", "you can't" he said and placed his hand over my lens though a Chinese tourist was making the dullest and mistiest home movie ever right next to me. You see, the Chinese are a little sensitive about their dam. The purpose of this new Great Wall is the provision of electricity and the prevention of floods, though it has been suggested that because so many tributaries join the Yangtze *after* the dam and because the turbines will soon become blocked by the 530 million tons of silt washed down by the river every year, it will do neither very satisfactorily. Add to this the risk of earthquake and landslide and China's long history of dam collapse[38] and it becomes clear why the international community withdrew all funding for a project that was deemed too expensive, too inefficient and too likely to end in tears.

So the Chinese did what they do best; they defied international opinion, mobilized the masses and built the thing themselves. There's a whole load of politics tied up with this dam. Sun Yat Sen suggested building it as early as 1919, Premier Li Peng hastened the project as a

---

38 Such as the Banqiao Dam in Henan Province that fell down in August 1975 after heavy rain with the loss of thousands of lives (see Henan chapter)

source of distraction after the Tiananmen Square massacre of 1989 and in the Hubei tradition of Li Bai and Du Fu, Mao wrote a poem about it;

Great plans are afoot:
A bridge will fly to span the north and south,
Turning a deep chasm into a thoroughfare,
Walls of stone will stand upstream to the west
To hold back Wushan's clouds and rain
Till a smooth lake rises in the narrow gorges
The mountain goddess if she is still there
Will marvel at a world so changed.

The dam has assumed almost mystical properties. I tore myself away from the panorama of mist and concrete to peruse the 3D model of the project in the gift shop where Three Gorges clocks, keyrings and T shirts do their bit to alleviate that 180 billion yuan cost. A Three Gorges commemorative video was playing in here too that talked of the 1931 flood when 140 thousand died. Such tragedy will happen no more; the video trumpeted that the dam will be 'a patron saint to protect people's lives' and like a beacon in the heavens will 'accompany the great illumination of the Chinese nation'. Meanwhile an orchestra played sweeping and triumphant melodies that were as grand and pompous as the dam itself.

It's the social and environmental impact of the dam that most exercises the international community. Over a million people have been uprooted, 13 cities, 140 towns and 1352 villages have been submerged. Often these settlements were of great antiquity, though oftener still they were of great ugliness. It is feared that the huge reservoir into which the industrial and human waste of Chongqing, Wanzhou and a dozen other Yangtze towns is poured, will in time become a great fetid cesspool. There's fear too for the future of rare nesting birds like the Siberian crane, for the Yangtze's 361 species of fish and for the diminishing of the wonderful scenery of the Three Gorges.

But the video had an answer for this too. The river is no doubt more placid and flows more freely than before, but this was 'like listening to a leisurely melody after a rhapsody. The river that has flowed violently for thousands of years is now gentle and agreeable'; a masterful political spin that turns the alteration of China's great river into an unequivocally good thing. The taming of nature is a recurrent theme in Chinese history and the dam was built partly to show God who is boss.

The crowds at the visitor centre couldn't have been more proud of the dam if they had mixed the concrete and installed the turbines themselves. Snow White was in raptures too; "Isn't it fine?" he breathed, and as an expression of single mindedness, of the sheer force of will of China, I had to agree. Also, China might have no choice. Over a billion people consume a lot of energy and I noted that if the air was polluted here in Hubei, it was not nearly as bad as above the towns of Shanxi where coal is king.

We ate extravagantly at the dam side city of Yichang where the mountain rearing above town for once really does look like that which it is compared to. No dubious horse's lung or congregated immortals here but silhouetted in rock, a fully visible and perfectly formed recumbent Mao Zedong (though the more I study my photos, the more it looks like Homer Simpson).

There's another dam in Yichang that has been rather forgotten amidst all the hoopla that surrounds it's Three Gorges big brother. Called Gezhouba, it's as concretey and dull as a dam should be and was a dry run for the massive structure nearby. But the building of Gezhouba is a salutary warning for how things can go wrong. This dam was begun on Mao's birthday on 26th December 1970 as a tribute to China's leader, but was not completed until over 10 years later since the quality of construction was so poor and had to be repeatedly started again. My mind turned to the 40,000,000 m³ of water pressing against China's new dam and I fervently hoped that they'd got it right this time.

We took a bus through the evening on the five-hour journey from Yichang to Hubei's provincial capital Wuhan. Our bus guide had the usual Chinese sense of civic pride and told us over the microphone that the traffic flow in Yichang is excellent and superior to Wuhan since Yichang is a small city of only three million. She also claimed that the citizens of Yichang are unusually fit since they always exercise, though I saw not a single person jogging, cycling or practicing tai chi from the window of the bus as we took an endless series of lefts and rights through the city streets, carried along with Yichang's exemplary traffic flow.

More than anywhere else in China I had expected to see locals practising the slow and deliberate moves of tai chi here, for Hubei is the home of this ancient form of kung fu. Zhang San Feng was disillusioned with the violent, hard movements of traditional kung fu and sat outside a temple in the Wudang Hills in the north of Hubei 1000 years ago. He watched the sinuous movements of a viper fighting a magpie and established the soft, low impact philosophy of taijiquan meaning 'supreme ultimate fist'. The bird and the reptile helped him to discover the internal force called 'neijia' which helps to focus the mind and bring a state of mental calm and clarity. How different Zhang's philosophy might have been if two dogs humping had passed his way that morning.

The techniques of taijiquan were soon recorded and thousands of practitioners began to enjoy the secrets of internal circulation and the ability to repel the yang of violent force with the softness of yin. So respected was the art that by the 15th century 300,000 labourers spent 10 years building the temples that are scattered across Wudang Shan. Where better to practise the ancient art than in a sun dappled glade outside one of these venerable buildings, the birds gently warbling in the trees as I crouched like a viper or a magpie and felt the presence of old Zhang San Feng?

Unfortunately, I was tearing along a Chinese highway in the dark, the bus windscreen wipers doing battle in vain with the rain that came down in sheets outside and obscured Hubei entirely. So I would practise a little tai chi on a wide public square by a busy road in Wuhan next morning rather than in the bucolic hills of Wudang. Having joined in gamely with a crowd of old women practitioners in pyjamas who moved to amplified music so loud it would have scared a viper or magpie away, I can report that my internal circulation and mental clarity are not good. I know tai chi is not a competitive sport, but I felt compelled to do better than old Hilda and Ethel alongside me, but as they moved consummately in slow motion from one foot to the next and held a position of spring-loaded alertness ready to attack with effortless ease, I felt rivulets of sweat pouring down my back and sharp pangs of cramp in both my yin and my yang.

I waited for a break in the cacophonous music, gave thanks to the ladies who had let me join in and left in the nick of time since they were about to complicate their moves with swords tied around with ribbons and I was in danger of doing myself a mischief. This was no way to spend an early pre-breakfast hour and I found the rest of Wuhan equally exhausting.

This is a city of eight million and Miss Yichang was right when she spoke disparagingly of Wuhan's traffic. The roads are packed for despite all those people there is no subway in Wuhan, though the furious noise and chaos in town is made worse by the frenzied construction to remedy this including on most of the square where I had failed to be as supple as those old women. The People's Square was pulverised and cordoned off with great cranes hunched over yawning subway holes. The Mao statue in the centre was smothered in builders dust but intact and untouched, though the chairman seemed to have no intention of catching one of the new trains since he was standing in arm aloft revolutionary pose looking for all the world like he was hailing a taxi.

Arising from the merging of three boroughs; Wuchang, Hankou and Hanyang, this portmanteau mega city hub of dozens of railways roads and expressways is known as the thoroughfare of nine provinces. China is shaped like a chicken[39] and Wuhan is the heart. My guide explained the city is very convenient for all parts of the chicken since it is only 1000 km from Shanghai, Beijing and Guangzhou. Officials are very proud of their town and praise its size, energy and industrial prowess. Wuhan is sometimes compared to Detroit though even better than its American cousin since on the Wuhan website we are told that 'while Wuhan is a booming city with the car industry that has since 1970 been growing stronger and stronger but at the same timeline (sic) we are sorry to say, Detroit is a city that has been declining'. At least they are sorry about it.

---

39 Seriously, check it out on the map at the front of this book. Manchuria is the head, Xinjiang the wing and Korea the beak. Hainan Island looks like an egg.

Wuhan might be producing more cars than Detroit but I wondered if the people who lauded the city and called it home had ever been anywhere else and discovered the quality of life on offer there. For Wuhan seemed almost unliveable to me; polluted, overcrowded and chaotically sprawling, the city is by far the hottest of the three furnace towns that include Chongqing and Nanjing along the Yangtze. I imagined wandering the streets in summer temperatures of 40°C in 100% humidity while traffic belched fumes and jackhammers pounded the ground and wondered if the old women would still be out practising tai chi.

The city's most famous site is the Yellow Crane Tower perched upon Snake Hill above the Yangtze and I dutifully climbed the steps past red lanterns and ponds full of terrapins to appreciate its beauty and the fine views of the city that can be had from the top. But of course, the pollution rendered the city invisible and the third century pagoda has been destroyed and reconstructed so many times that the present incarnation and its internal elevator are younger than me.

Chinese poets have waxed excessively lyrical about the tower and the legends attached to this place. Li Bai bade a sad farewell to his friend in Wuhan;

My old friend had said goodbye to the west, here at Yellow Crane Tower.
In the third month's cloud of willow blossoms, he's going down to Yangzhou.
The lonely sail is a distant shadow on the edge of a blue emptiness,
All I see is the Yangtze River flow to the far horizon.

Cui Hao eulogised in the eighth century and sounded depressed;

Long ago a man rode off on a yellow crane,
All that remains here is Yellow Crane Tower.
Once the yellow crane left it never returned,
For 1000 years the clouds wandered without care.
The clear river reflects each Hanyang tree,
Fragrant grasses lushly grow on Parrot Island.
At sunset, which direction lies my hometown?
The mist covered river causes one to feel distressed.

Old Mao liked Wuhan and had one of his extravagant bombproof villas built here. Unlike other such hideaways scattered across China, the chairman actually used this one and came to Wuhan for extended breaks from the politics of Beijing, a city he disliked, almost every year in the 1950s and 1960s. I can understand why Mao liked the city since it is as uncompromising, earthy and belligerent as the man himself. Close to his home province of Hunan, Mao could eat glutinous rice pies, re-gan mian hot and dry noodles, Mianwo salty doughnuts and Hunanese fish here. He could swim in the river too and it was in Wuhan that Mao defied logic, demonstrated his virility and relaunched his political career with well-publicised Yangtze paddles in 1956 and 1966.

Wuhan commemorates the swim still and every 16th of July hundreds of enthusiastic paddlers splash and thrash their way across and remember Mao's words that the river's 'swift flow may train the body and temper willpower'. It's all very revolutionary and good and entirely in keeping with the city's socialist traditions. It was in Wuhan that China's 20th-century revolution was born when an uprising was launched in 1911, spread across the nation and led to the abdication of Emperor Pu-Yi ensconced in the Forbidden City in distant Beijing. Revolution returned to Wuhan in 1967 when at the height of the Cultural Revolution the Wuhan Workers Red Guards battled the 'Million Heroes' for control of hearts and minds and to prove their devotion to Chairman Mao. Over 1000 people died.

Gritty, polluted, crowded, steamy, revolutionary Wuhan. I strolled pavements past grey apartment blocks streaked with rust and branches of HFC Hubei Fried Chicken whose bold red shopfronts represent a different kind of revolution, and searched for something that was ancient or lovely. This was a tough mission but I found it at last in the Hubei Provincial Museum beside Wuhan's enormous East Lake. There are 200,000 artefacts here but on most museum visits I see a tiny fraction of the displays before taking my equally tiny attention span to the gift store and coffee shop. This museum was different because 15,000 of the items come from the fifth century BC tomb of the Marquis of Yi that was found and excavated in 1978. I don't want to go overboard here but the two and a half thousand-year-old artefacts are mesmerising. This is partly because of their great antiquity; only a Philistine would fail to be impressed by something so old, but the variety is dazzling too. There is lacquer work, weapons and coffins here, decorative rings and tiny jade animals that were placed inside mouths and other orifices of the marquis and the 21 women and one dog that were buried with him.

Best of all are the Marquis' bells. These enormous 65 bronze chimes weigh two and a half tons and the museum has recreated them for a daily concert. They took five years to reconstruct, since each bell is surprisingly sophisticated and can make two notes depending on where it is struck. The concert's sombre resonance sounded ancient and ponderous and gave a delightful glimpse into this barely perceptible intangible world so old and utterly unlike anything I know. It was certainly the most relaxing 20 minutes I spent in the chaos of Wuhan.

I tried to remember the calm of those bells as I traveled across town to Hankou. But it was impossible in the bustle and vivacity of this town and I did what all visitors to China must do - relax, enjoy the frenetic pace and go with the flow. I passed again the murky waters were Mao had floated downstream and came to the 1957 Yangtze River Bridge, known as 'first bridge'. This colossal Soviet inspired construction must have made a huge difference to the town and its link to the world ended the tedium and danger of river crossings when every railcar, citizen and lump of coal had to be floated across.

The people of Wuhan were very pleased with their new bridge and many children born in the city in the late 1950s were named 'qiao' which is Chinese for bridge.[40] It was this bridge that Mao referred to when he eulogized 'a rainbow of iron and steel' in his poem that promoted a great dam. The best views of city and river are from this great arc of socialist realism and not the Yellow Crane Tower, which provides a fitting allegory for the triumph of old over new, though all such comparisons are mostly irrelevant in foggy, polluted Wuhan.

Further along the riverbank is the old colonial concession era district of Hankou, opened as a treaty port in 1861. The British, French, German, Japanese and Russian concessions were very unwelcome to Chinese locals who stoned foreigners as they walked the streets, but the main Zhongshan Dadao High Street classical buildings are now filled with the modern concessions of foreign clothes stores and bars selling

---

40   A similar thing happened in 1930s Russia where many children were burdened with the name 'tractor'.

foreign beers. The buildings here are grandiose and designed to give a sense of permanence just as much as those of the concessions in Tianjin and Shanghai, but Hankou's foreign heyday was already over by the early 1900s. Before this, chazi tea buyers arrived here from all over the world and drank champagne at the Hankow club before racing their cargo of black and green tea to London. The first leg from Hankou to the red buoy at Wusong near Shanghai could take as little as 36 hours if the ship did not run aground, then down the South China Sea to Singapore for stockpiling coal and the last leg to London. Brokers would rush to meet the vessels as they docked after a 30 or 40 day voyage, break open the chests in high excitement and test samples of Chinese tea. Yet the rise of Indian tea production put paid to the China market and ended Hankou's role as a viable port forever.

I walked the streets of Hankou and looked for echoes of the trade in the old buildings that now fly red flags and found it not in the granite classicism or the heavy oak doors but back on the riverbank. The timeless Yangtze flowed past and it was possible to imagine steamships and the hoisting of tea chests here since the river is still busy with a confusion of boats.

There is a statue here in Binjiang Park by the riverbank to commemorate flood control measures introduced by the Communists even before the building of the first bridge. A Mao portrait is attached to the obelisk above his poem about swimming;

I have just drunk the waters of Changsha and come to eat the fish of Wuchang.

Now I am swimming across the great Yangtze, looking afar to the open sky of Chu.

Let the wind blow and waves beat, better far than idly strolling in a courtyard.

Today I am at ease. It was by a stream that the Master said; 'Thus do things flow away!'

Floods were always a big deal in Wuhan and it seems the government was a little premature in celebrating the ending of the problem since parts of the city flooded again as late as 1998. I guess the giant dam will sort this out once and for all. My Yichang guide had told me of this inundation and that her brother had made a joke when their house flooded. 'At least now we can go fishing' he had announced, which may not rate as top-class banter but shows admirable optimism at the sight of his front room converted to a pond.

There's another statue less than half a mile from the unwarranted celebration of flood control, a tableau of leaping dolphins that seems more at home in Hawaii than Hubei. These are Baiji freshwater dolphins that are found only in Yangtze River. Make this *were* found in the River since a 2006 expedition to find river dolphins by world scientists and conservationists spotted a grand total of none and the species has been declared functionally extinct - the first aquatic mammal to achieve this unwelcome status in half a century. It's tempting to blame the dam for this just as it gets the blame for every environmental illness in modern China, but the real fault lies with the 1950s Great Leap Forward. Traditional veneration of the Baiji was renounced at this time as an old-fashioned and backward superstition that had no place in modern, rational empirical China. Farmers were encouraged to hunt the dolphins for meat; they needed no second invitation at a time of chronic food shortage and chased the baiji to the edge of extinction. So the statue in the old colonial town that celebrates the diversity of life in the great river might just as well commemorate a woolly mammoth or a dodo for all its relevance to modern China.

There's a similarly rare beast in the Shennonjia Mountains north of Wuhan. Golden monkeys with blue faces and no noses (How do they smell? Terrible!) swing in the trees and giant salamanders swim in the rivers of this Jurassic Park. I especially admire the ridiculous salamanders - giant amphibians that grow to nearly 6 feet long, breathe through their skin and wear a permanently bloated, self-satisfied and frankly unnerving smile. Basking in the shallows, the salamander looks not unlike Chairman Mao floating in the Yangtze at Wuhan.

Shennonjia is best known not for nose less monkeys or Maoist salamanders but for the reclusive Chinese yeti called the Yeren. A group of cadres caught a two metre tall creature covered in reddish fur in the glare of their headlights in 1976 and since then nearly a dozen sightings, the discovery of coarse hair, faeces and giant footprints suggest that there might be something out there in the wilds of Shennonjia.

The New York Times took up the cry in 1980 with the headline 'It's tall, it has wavy hair and Chinese keep hunting for it' but if the Yeren exists, it's been around for far longer than this. One story holds that the primitive hominid is descended from men who escaped into the forests to avoid work on constructing the Great Wall. Qing Dynasty poet Yuan Mei spoke of the existence of a creature 'monkey-like yet not a monkey' and Qu Yuan, the Grandaddy of all Chinese poets who wrote in the fourth century BC might also have heard of beasts with human speech. Qu's poems are all dragons and mountain ogres and sound like an early 1970s prog rock band;

Is there any place at all
Where the sun's rays never fall?
In that realm of pitchy night
Does the dragon shed his light?
Ere the rising of the sun
By what tree is brightness spun?
Where does winter seem to blaze,
Summer show but chilly days?
Stony Forest how to reach,
Or the beasts with human speech?

But my chances of spotting a beast with human speech were slim indeed. Most of Shennonjia is off-limits to foreigners and my visit was a fleeting drive on the forest outskirts, though I peered from the bus window between the ancient trees and saw an occasional tell-tale rustle of leaves or heard the crack of a branch that was no doubt caused by the giant footfall of an ape, or else some Golden Monkeys and salamanders frolicking at play.

The truth is I had as much chance of seeing a Yeren striding down the high street of Wuhan. It was back to the city that I traveled to take one of the nine thoroughfares away from Hubei, the heart of the chicken, though it was to the river that I returned once more. The eternal Yangtze flowed past me, tamed by giant dams, but carrying the silt of Tibet and rushing on; on to Shanghai and the sea.

The clouds depart and sunlight's beam, reflect upon this mighty stream.
Hubei had made me a poet too.

354

SHANGHAI

上海

6341 sq km
Population 23.1 million

'The higher the buildings, the lower the morals.'

Noel Coward.

I knew that if I got up early enough in Shanghai and beat the traffic congested streets, I would see old folks foxtrotting on the Bund; skipping lithely across the pavement. Clouds of steamy breath left their lungs on this freezing morning as they waltzed, the massive towers of Pudong looming improbably behind.

I was resolved to experience Shanghai municipality in an offbeat way, maybe go to the suburbs of this enormous city of 13 million people or visit the outlying towns of Songjian, Sheshan and Jiading. Songjian has the obvious temptation of 'Thamestown', a middle-class commuter belt built in imitation of an English Home Counties idyll, complete with mock Tudor houses, church and village green: a kind of turn-of-the-century cliche where the church clock says it's ten to three and there is honey still for tea, but with Chinese characteristics. There is a Swedish, Spanish, Italian, Dutch, German and American town too. Yet everything comes back to these few square miles in the heart of this most atypical Chinese city and to the river that has shaped the history of Shanghai.

Shanghai means 'above the sea' which befits its role as a major port and centre of commerce. The vital strategic position of the place can be best appreciated by approaching from the east and into the gaping jaws of the Yangtze River. Here boats slide past the massive Gateway buoy and Middle Sand Light (Zhongsha) which marks the point where Yangtze River meets East China Sea. The water moves fast here and has travelled 6000 km from the high Tibetan plateau, arriving at the rate of 1.2 million ft³ per second, bringing with it enough silt to form 25 yards of new land every year; it seems the Pacific ocean is being filled with the Himalayas.

Boats sailing past Zhongsha aren't in Shanghai yet. They first sail 50 miles past Chongming Dao, China's second largest island that is called the tongue of the Yangtze as it lolls and slobbers in the river's mouth. The island was once a place of banishment but is now home to one million people and is slated as the likely location for China's Disneyland, when the bleak muddiness and screeching of wading birds on the tongue will become all fairy castles and oversized mice. Past Chongming and the wrecks, sandbanks and traffic on the approach considered to be the most dangerous in the world, boats turn to port to Shanghai, where the Huangpu tributary meets the Yangtze.

This is the site of an ancient accumulation of silt created whenever one body of water meets another and called the Woosong Bar. The Bar was an historic impediment to traffic since it made the water only 12 feet deep; no problem for old Chinese junks, but a really big problem for 19th century European vessels keen to develop trade with Shanghai and which often drew 20 feet or more. There were no technical difficulties in removing the bar but the Chinese Manchu authorities of the late 19th century haughtily refused to countenance such measures, much to the frustration of pragmatic European traders.

Such was the terror and infamy of Woosong that Tennyson wrote a poem about it;

> Sunset and evening Star,
> And one clear call for me!
> And may there be no moaning of the bar
> When I put out to sea.

Well, there was certainly a lot of moaning *about* the bar from the European traders, who finally prevailed upon the Manchus to agree to have the sandy inconvenience removed, though it was not until 1937 that the Bar was completely dredged to 28 feet.

This bit of shovelling instantly brought Shanghai a ticket to the lottery as a major international trading centre, though European enjoyment of this was short lived indeed, what with the small matter of World War and the Communist takeover of China. Maybe this is what the Manchu intransigence was about all along, since the bar blocked European access to Shanghai and thus to the Yangtze and the interior of China. A big pile of sand on the riverbed may have been the most cost-effective coastal defence strategy in history.

Forget New York, Shanghai is so good they named it six times. SongHu, Shen (after a locally revered hero), Shencheng, Haisheng, the Paris of the East and the Pearl (or sometimes the whore) of the Orient, lies 30 km upstream along the Huangpu. The city was both pearl and whore during the period of Western dominance in the 1920s and 1930s. In truth, it was this period that drew me to Shanghai and was my motivation for standing on the Bund watching quickstepping middle-aged Chinese in the freezing early morning cold.

Bund is an Anglo-Indian term for an embankment by a muddy waterfront and the British lost no time in creating a little piece of England here. The waterfront is lined with solid, Victorian municipal edifices that are quite out of character with much of the rest of Shanghai and certainly with most of China. It's like travelling to the Cotswolds and finding teahouses, pagodas and Chinese lanterns. A stroll along the Bund would make a British person homesick, though I wondered what the ballroom dancing couples thought of it all. "The buildings are very grand" they all agreed as they paused their waltzes, though I suppose persons learning Western dances are unlikely to disapprove of Western architecture.

The road is called Zhongshan Lu now but it's still a monument to Western financial might and interference in Shanghai. I strolled past the 1911 Shanghai club, that bastion of male moneyed exclusivity that boasted the longest bar in the world in its day and may have been a place to drown one's sorrows regarding the more troublesome bar at Woosong. The club was exclusive though in a rather less contentious manner than the sign ordering 'No dogs or Chinese' that supposedly existed in Huangpu Park at the opposite end of the Bund at the same time.

Next up is the sixth floor neoclassical monster that was the Hong Kong and Shanghai bank and considered (probably by the British) to be the finest building east of the Suez. Outside are two huge bronze lions, copies of the originals freed from Japanese imprisonment, though already with paws and noses rubbed shiny by Shanghaiers eager for a dose of good luck. The interior is an outrageous statement in marble and wood and with eight ceiling mosaics saved from the ravages of the Cultural Revolution, when Red Guards were persuaded that covering the tiles with stucco and paint would be less troublesome than chipping every last one off.

Next door's customs house sports the largest clock in Asia, modelled on Big Ben and which played the same Westminster Quarters until the 1960s when Red Guards changed it to 'The East is Red', that voguish paean to Mao and China's unofficial anthem at that time (see Yunnan chapter). Best of all on the Bund is the Peace Hotel, its triangular copper roof pointing rakishly to the sky. This was the most prestigious hotel in town where Noel Coward wrote 'Private lives' and the famous jazz band played every night. Here Shanghai's plutocracy smoked opium and counted their money on the rooftop terrace in Art Deco opulence.

The hotel was built by Victor Sassoon, a famous hotelier from a famous Jewish family and who owned a further 2000 buildings in Shanghai. Sassoon once said that 'There is only one race greater than the Jews, and that is the Derby', and it's tempting to agree with him when one studies the history of the Jews in Shanghai. Before and during World War II, some of Shanghai's richest men conspired to save tens of thousands of Jews - probably more were saved in this decadent and sybaritic town than in all Commonwealth countries combined. Wealthy Jewish families like the Sassoons and the Kadoories had arrived in Shanghai to make a fast buck since the early 19th century. They were followed by White Russian Jews and non-Jews fleeing the revolution who settled in the old French quarter around Huaihai Lu (then called Avenue Joffre). Many of these wealthy Russians were reduced to penury and the most unfortunate to prostitution in Gracie's brothel on Jiangsu Lu. Their presence is commemorated by the synagogues and Orthodox Saint Nicholas Church, named for the murdered Tsar and which still sports an icon of Mao painted above the door that saved it from Red Guard destruction.

The biggest influx of Jews was between 1937 and 1939 when 20,000 poured into the city to escape Nazi persecution. This group were confined to the three-quarter square mile Hongkou ghetto by the Japanese where they lived in crowded and insanitary conditions though not in fear of their lives like the ghettoised Jews of Europe. Late in the war, Nazi Germany put pressure on the Japanese army to devise a plan to eliminate Shanghai's Jewish population. A delegation visited Hongkou and the Japanese Governor asked the Rabbi Shimon Kalish "Why do the Germans hate you so much?" Kalish replied in Yiddish "Zugim weil mir senen orientalim" - 'the Germans hate us because we are oriental'. The governor smiled and the Jews were left unharmed since the Japanese were oriental too.

The community vanished rapidly after the war and by the 1950s the synagogues were shuttered and Shanghai's Jewish community was gone. Yet to walk through Hongkou is to surround oneself with ghosts. The area is remarkably untouched in this most modern of cities, though it is poor Shanghainese who lounge outside the synagogue, cycle along lanes that could be Eastern European and hang their washing from windows whose lintels are engraved with the Star of David.

The Jews came to Shanghai because as the rest of the world closed its doors, the city remained one of the rare free transit ports. The entry was facilitated by Ho Feng Shan, the Chinese Consul-General in Vienna who defied orders and issued thousands of visas on humanitarian grounds. Ho received a black mark in his personnel file, but was recognised posthumously by Yad Vashem when he was awarded the title 'Righteous among the Nations.'

Hongkou is on the north side of Suzhou Creek and separate from the main part of the city. It's amazing to think that the creek once provided Shanghai's drinking water because it's now a black and foul smelling soup of industrial and human waste. The water has been cleaned in recent years and is now deemed pure enough to host rowing competitions, though the participants must live in dread of capsizing.

I walked towards Wiabedu Bridge which crosses back to the Bund through Lu Xun Park. Lu Xun was an early 20th century writer who made books intelligible to the common man by breaking from the impenetrable Chinese classical traditions and who loved the city so much he named his son 'Haiying' or ' son of Shanghai'. His most famous book 'The true story of Ah Q', concerns a worthless peasant who stumbles from disaster to disaster but who, like Doctor Pangloss, believes each one to be a triumph and who dreams of revolution but is executed instead. Lu Xun satirises the Chinese character but has great affection for his country and I hope that when I write about this confusing country that I remain more affectionate and admiring than exasperated too.

Famous Chinese are commemorated all over Shanghai as if to compensate for the humiliation of the Bund whose buildings are hardly Chinese at all. A big bronze statue stands at the end of the Bund - this appears to be Mao but is in fact Chen Yi, the first Communist mayor of the town and Vice Premier before his purging in 1967. It's not only Chen's hair and collarless suit that are the same as his boss, his policies were slavishly devoted to Mao too. Bourgeois, middle-class 'foreign' Shanghai was viewed with suspicion by the earthy peasant Communist Party and the city set about overcompensating for years in an attempt to prove its loyalty to the revolution. The Cultural Revolution was more extreme and more devoted here - even the traffic lights were changed to associate socialist red with progress instead of signaling a reactionary stop. This must have caused a deal of confusion on Shanghai's roads, though the multi vehicle pile ups that would have ensued as people tried to remember which was stop and which go would at least have involved only bicycles since cars belonged only to bourgeois imperialists, capitalist running dogs and party leaders in the 1960s.

The Cultural Revolution was planned and implemented in Shanghai by the Gang of Four. Mao's wife Jiang Qing was one of these and became an irresistible scapegoat after Mao's death for the wild excesses of the time, though at her trial Jiang argued that she was ' Mao's dog; whoever he told me to bite, I bit'.

Jiang committed suicide in 1991 and remains a reviled figure in China, but like the best Shanghai missies, she started out in the theatre. The high living beautiful young Shanghai girl of the 1930s can still be seen in the antique markets of the city on endless Western tobacco adverts. Her hair is usually short and she's wearing a cheongsam dress - a racier version of the traditional high necked Chinese qipao with high cut sleeves and a daring side slit revealing a shapely leg. By the 1940s cheongsams came in transparent black, beaded bodices and velvet; sufficient to turn the head of a British banker, Jewish immigrant or Japanese soldier. Even during the Cultural Revolution, the Shanghai missy found ways to express her style with a tailored Red Guard jacket or a curl in the hair beneath her military cap.

Little is known of Jiang's life as a Shanghai movie star in the 1930s, but other leading ladies became famous throughout China. Ruan Lingyu was known as 'China's Garbo' after playing a virtuous prostitute in 'Shennu' (Goddess) but committed suicide aged 24. More famous still is Zhou Xuan whose name means 'beautiful jade'. Her nickname was 'Golden Voice' and in her best known movie 'Street Angel' her frail and beautiful voice enraptured the city. Zhou lived a messy and complicated life of failed marriages, suicide attempts and illegitimate children and died in an asylum for the insane aged 38. Her life seems to mirror that of the city in those turbulent years; beautiful and entrancing but out of control and always likely to come to a sticky end.

Shanghai's sticky end came in 1949 when Mao stood on Tiananmen gate and announced that China had 'stood up'. The clubs, bars and opium dens were closed and the 70,000 prostitutes who worked the city, mainly around Hui He Lu (Seeking Happiness Lane - where houses had names like 'sweet dew' and ' lingering smile'), were given more gainful employment. The racecourse was closed and converted to a People's Square. Even the famous gangster Big Eared Du fled the city and died a millionaire in Hong Kong in 1951.

The city that had China's first banks in 1848, telephones in 1881, streetlights in 1882, running water in 1884, autos in 1901 and trams in 1908 was deliberately run down and allowed to decay since it represented the foreign control that the new China deplored and because the party had a strong puritanical streak that condemned all that Shanghai had been.

Forgiveness was granted in 1991. In that year the government announced that Shanghai would be rebuilt and reinvented as a modern metropolis - the financial and commercial heart of China - and the jackhammers and wrecking balls have hardly paused since. Even the no holds barred culture of the 1930s has returned; new clubs and bars are springing up across Shanghai and one of the city's most famous dancers now is Jingxing, a former army colonel who had a sex change in 1995 - a story straight out of 1939 if ever there was one.

Since the mid-1990s, five new businesses have opened every hour in Shanghai and from 1992 to 1997 the city achieved an annual growth rate of 13%. 20 million square meters of buildings have been levelled so far in the rush to construct a new Shanghai. This figure is rising all the time and in my time in Shanghai I was woken and rocked to sleep in my hotel bed by the sound of construction all day and every night.

This rush to modernise is most clearly seen at Pudong on the opposite side of the river to the Bund. Over here, the buildings have become as iconic as the Peace Hotel but on a much larger scale. The area was nothing but marshy farmland until 1990 and is now host to a forest of skyscrapers and three of the tallest buildings in the world. Impressive indeed, though I question the wisdom of building them on a bog.

The best of these is the Jin Mao Tower, 420 metres of art deco steel and glass with a tasteful hotel bar at the summit. I gazed down on the river traffic from here with a sense of sophistication and pleasure that modern architecture can make a dramatic statement yet retain elements of Chinese culture and form, though my complacent musings were shattered when I saw the size of the drinks bill. The Shanghai world finance centre next door is even bigger at 492 metres. It is China's tallest building and is also a dynamic statement in steel and glass though it looks like a giant bottle opener. This is because it contains a huge aperture at its peak to reduce the stress of wind pressure and to serve as a subtext for Chinese mythology that represents the earth with a square and the sky with a circle. But the hole was neither the sky nor a moon gate in the eyes of the Mayor of Shanghai who saw only the rising sun of the Japanese flag. So the circle was flattened on one side and a bottle opener was born.

Most notable of the three mega structures that are possibly sinking into the bog is the 457 metre tall Oriental Pearl Tower. I went inside this too on the principle that it's good to explore since inside the Pearl Tower is the only place in Shanghai that you can't *see* the Pearl Tower. The information told me that the building is based on a verse of the Tang Dynasty poem 'Pipa song' by Bai Juyi about the delicate sound of a pipa instrument whose music sounds like pearls falling onto a jade plate.

> The bold strings rattled like splatters of sudden rain,
> The fine strings hummed like lovers whispers,
> Chattering and pattering, pattering and chattering,
> as pearls, large and small, on a jade plate fall.

The information boards also told me that the Yangpu and Nanpu bridges 'seem like two Chinese dragons frolicking with the pearls of the tower'.

The building is very ugly. The 11 giant pearls are red, swollen and bloody protuberances and the whole structure looks like nothing so much as a giant syringe or a huge rocket ready to launch into the sky and for the sake of the aesthetics of the Shanghai skyline, it might be better if it did. I prefer the old town of Puxi and walked there through the garish tunnel beneath the Huangpu whose multicoloured lights were almost as tacky as the building I just left.

The old town is centred around Yuyuan Gardens - the epitome of a classical Chinese Garden and wrapped around the famous tea house of Huxinting, reached by a zigzag bridge since evil spirits can't go round corners. An added benefit is that the Oriental Pearl Tower is almost invisible on every zag, though it pops right back into view on the zigs. Yuyuan was spared during the Cultural Revolution because it had been headquarters of the Little Sword Society; an anti-imperialist offshoot of the Taiping uprising of 1853. There is no better illustration of the Western ignorance of China than this rebellion that killed at least 20 million and is the bloodiest civil war in history. The revolt was led by the enigmatic Hong Xiquan who claimed to have ascended to heaven and returned to Earth with a new set of internal organs and whose followers believed he was the younger brother of Jesus Christ (See Guangxi chapter for further details of the Taiping rebellion).

Hong's failure to take Shanghai was the beginning of the end for the rebellion and he died of food poisoning in 1864 in Nanjing. The victorious Qing dynasty blasted his remains from a cannon to ensure that he would have no resting place in the afterlife. The Small Swords Society (Xiao Dao Hui) held the old town of Shanghai for 18 months, an impertinence that ended in much bloodshed and heads on spikes.

The West might be ignorant of this massive event but so too are many Chinese except in the very broadest terms. Generally I found the Chinese to have great knowledge and appreciation of ancient and often mythical tales that illustrate the greatness and antiquity of the Middle Kingdom. They also have a pretty comprehensive knowledge of modern events and of China shaped by Communism; the in between is a great void as if nothing of note happened then. This despite the respect paid to the Taiping by the modern party who emphasise the anti-imperialist sentiments of Hong. His magic internal organs and celestial big brother get less of a mention.

Hong's policies were certainly enlightened and progressive. Private property, foot binding, opium, gambling, slavery, prostitution and polygamy were all to be banned in Taiping China; sentiments that would have met the approval of Mao. Hong's implementation of these policies was often brutal and his focus was on urban China and neglect of the countryside and this is not unlike modern Communism too. As for Hong's godlike status; one need only observe the adulation of Mao to draw further comparisons still.

I became very fond of Shanghai cuisine while I was in the city and especially of breakfast served on the street from hand drawn carts in the old town. Food is exceptionally important to the Shanghainese and their greeting of 'how are you' is 'Ni chi fan le mei you?' literally means 'have you eaten yet?' These breakfasts were cheap and sociable at the best of the day before the streets began to hustle and bustle and by 9am the stalls had gone just like the ballroom dancers on the Bund. But it was so cold that I was reluctant to take off my gloves to eat the jiaolongbao dumplings and sometimes nuzzled them into my mouth straight from the paper bag and wondered if my fellow diners decided that this was how all barbarian foreigners ate their breakfast.

The Yangtze is the great cultural demarcation line in China like the Mississippi or the Mason-Dixie line in America, the European Alps or the Scottish-English border in the UK. There is a great deal of suspicion and a marked sense of superiority from both sides and I was told many times in China by someone in the North that the Yellow River was the cradle of Chinese civilisation and that the people in the South were interested only in money and must be mistrusted all costs. Southerners meanwhile were enthusiastic in their condemnation of the northern 'peasants'. The river is also a line of temperature demarcation and traditionally no house south of the great river was endowed with a system of heating. This might be fine in steamy Hong Kong or Guangdong but struck me as peculiarly unkind in Shanghai which sits only fractionally south of the Yangtze and whose winters are very cold indeed.

Shanghai's greatest culinary contribution to the world is the hairy crab and this is served in a variety of soups and as a whole beast, hairy legs resting on a bed of beansprouts and chilies, up and down the restaurants on Nanjing Lu. This is the premier shopping street in the whole of China where anything can be bought and where I wandered beneath the signs flashing neon and into the 11th floor 'number one department store' which claims to receive 100,000 customers every day. I continued south along Yunnan Lu and onto Huaihai Lu in the French concession. This part of Shanghai was claimed by France five years after the Brits got the best bits along the Bund and they spent the next 100 years turning it into a leafy, sophisticated, wide boulevard approximation of home.

The father of modern Chinese republicanism, Sun Yatsen, lived here on Rue Moliere (now Sun Zhongshan Guju) before his death from liver cancer in 1925. Sun was a remarkable man and the only nationalist leader still revered by the Communists. There are memorials to Sun all across China and most notably on a huge scale in Nanjing (see Jiangsu chapter). His sturdy villa surrounded by mature gardens is a memorial to domesticity and tranquillity and it's possible to imagine the great fighter for freedom pruning his roses here and being called in to dinner by his wife Soong Qingling.

Perhaps Sun's popularity has declined for I was the only visitor to the house that day and as I turned the Bakelite door handle and entered the spacious hall, the woman inside was most alarmed to see me. She showed me into the dressing room and told me the tour of the house was to begin in 20 minutes so I sat in a leather armchair that did a passable impression of flatulence whenever I moved and beneath a ticking clock as the traffic droned distantly outside along the leafy boulevard.

I asked if it might be possible to have my tour immediately since I was the only visitor and no more were expected, but was answered 'No; the scheduled start was in 20 minutes', with that same intransigence that had refused to shift the Woosong Bar. Eventually my solo tour began; here were Sun's reading glasses and here his writing desk where presumably he plotted revolution between bouts of deadheading the petunias. But the house didn't feel radical at all and could have been the residence of a country vicar from the Home Counties or a magistrate in provincial France.

There is more revolution to be had further east along Huaihai Lu at the site of the first National Congress of the Chinese Communist Party. Here is no end of 'radical struggle' and 'heroic anti-feudal resistance' where Mao and 12 other original delegates met in 1921 to discuss their path to power and are commemorated by waxworks and revolutionary songs. This gathering of firebrands was discovered by the French police so the radicals fled to Zhejiang and continued their discussions on a boat on Nan Hu Lake.

The site is one of the sturdy shi-ku-men (literally, stone framed doorway) houses that have been wonderfully preserved and restored in recent years and now form the heart of Shanghai's dining and coffee culture around the Xintiandi quarter. The stocky buildings are a mix of English style terraced housing with Chinese courtyards arranged in straight alleys called longtang and it's possible to sip an overpriced cappuccino or order a lightly toasted olive panini with French brie and avocado on a bed of rocket leaves in the cafes next door to where Mao and his buddies plotted the overthrow of all such bourgeois indulgence.

Yet despite their rhetoric, there was always something slightly bourgeois about the Chinese revolutionary leadership too. Mao was a peasant but wealthier than most, Zhou an old school intellectual in the mandarin tradition and Sun Yat Sen a Hawaii and Hong Kong educated medical doctor who married into the wealthy Soong family without bothering with the triviality of divorcing his first wife.

The Soongs wielded more influence over 20th-century China than perhaps any other family. Qingling married Sun (who was 30 years her senior), Meiling became the third wife of Nationalist leader Chiang Kai-shek, Ailing married the head of the bank of China (and was said to be the first girl in Shanghai to own a bicycle) while TV Soong became Chiang Kai-shek's foreign minister and the richest man in China. It is said that of the three sisters, Ailing loved money, Meiling loved power but Qingling loved her country. Sun's widow stayed in the quiet house with a ticking clock on Rue Moliere until 1937 and then lived elsewhere in Shanghai and Beijing until her death in 1981. Two weeks before she passed to the great socialist utopia in the sky, Qingling was admitted to the communist party and given the honorary title of President of the People's Republic of China. Her sister Meiling declined to attend Qingling's funeral and died in America in 2003 aged 105 after what might be called a full and interesting life.

I spent the whole day wandering the streets of the French concession fortified against the cold by coffee and xiaolongbao as the sun dropped and the Oriental Pearl Tower over the River lit up and became more ridiculous still. The tower was a pulsing rocket of neon as the tree-lined streets gave way to the crowds and alleyways of the old town on Dongtang Lu. This is Shanghai's premier antiques market, though antique is a misnomer in this place of mass produced Ming dynasty pottery and Qing painted scrolls. Here I found a 1920s pidgin English dictionary for use by colonials in the city when 'can-do'. 'savvy', 'chop-chop', 'look-see' and 'chow' give an insight into the pecking order for Chinese and foreign in those times and in which I discovered a live fish was a 'walkee walkee fish' and a brain a 'savvy box'.

Mao's Little red book is ubiquitous on Dongtang Lu, though many of these *are* original and no wonder since one billion of these collected quotations from Chairman Mao were printed during his lifetime. Red Guards were expected to know his book by heart and it's the Little Red Book that is being waved by one million hands and its quotations shouted by one million voices during the mass demonstrations on Tiananmen square in 1966 in adulation of Mao. Not the younger brother of Jesus Christ to be sure, but something pretty close.

Even more common in the market are the Mao badges that many Chinese pinned to their flesh to show their devotion to the great man, though I liked the watches better. These fall into two categories and I bought one of each. The first was an original from the Shanghai watch company, the timepiece of choice for all respectable revolutionaries since because of the limited supply, a Shanghai watch meant power. The company has produced 120 million watches and is still in Shanghai, but refuses to depart from the plain functionality of the original design; digital is anathema in this preserve of handmade precision. My other watch was a modern bright red one on which Mao's right arm, clutching a little red book, waved with every ticking second. These are cheaply made and no doubt make the doyens of the Shanghai watch company shudder; within two days the minute hand had ground to a halt over Mao's broad forehead and his waving left-arm had swung down so that the red book was held inappropriately over his groin.

Dongtang Lu is a cornucopia of Cultural Revolutionary delights. There are badges and books here, posters of socialist ballet dancers, Red Guard uniforms, armbands and statues of Mao. These are a particular favourite of mine and I can rarely walk away from a good ceramic revolutionary replica. I picked up one of Mao in his dressing gown and surrounded by admirers after his heroic swim in the Yangtze in 1966 (see Hunan chapter). If I could only find a glazed scale model of the Oriental Pearl Tower I would be a happy man indeed.

I left Shanghai by the magnetic levitation train or Maglev, the German designed fastest train in the world, which whisked me with Germanic efficiency from the city suburbs to the airport at 400 km an hour. At this speed, we quickly left the outskirts of the city and I was soon magnetically levitating through cabbagey fields that could have been anywhere in China. The train was smooth and impressive and unlike any train I had ever caught and if I closed my eyes, I hardly felt that I was in China at all. But that was okay, since I had just left a town that hardly felt like China either.

ZHEJIANG

浙江

103 600 km sq
Population 47 million

'Tea is drunk to forget the din of the world'

T'ien Yiheng

Mister Wong sat in his front room on a chair surrounded by green leaves and told me to call him uncle. My new friend served tea[41] from the bushes that queued up in rows over the hillside outside his window,

---

41   He told me to 'chi cha' - to eat tea rather than 'he cha' drink tea, because people in Zhejiang believe that eating the leaves is good for digestion.

lines of orderly precision edged by a deciduous forest of chaotic silver trees that looked more European than Chinese. I'd walked along country lanes past prosperously comfortable villas to arrive at uncle's house. It was a pleasant walk in dappled sunlight; wood pigeons cooed in the branches and always the hills that rose and fell in gentle curves were covered in stubby tea bushes, thick with dark green precious leaves. It was a long walk but worth it because Wong lives in Longjing and Longjing serves very special tea.

The village is ground zero for all the tea in China, the single most famous and important tea production centre in the whole country. Longjing means 'Dragon Well' and is named after a nearby well that contains relatively dense water. After rainfall, the lighter rain water floating on the surface is supposed to resemble the swirling tail and flashing scales of a traditional Chinese dragon, and it is this water that should be used to infuse the local green leaves to create the holy grail of green tea.

Uncle Wong was using tap water not dragon water for my cup of tea. He served tea in a glass which made holding the cuppa a little tricky (though not excruciating since in a good cup of green tea the water is never fully boiled) but is vital so that I could see the beauty of the leaves rising and falling in the water through the transparent glass; "like orchids" said Uncle Wong, "opening and closing and extending their waists gently and slowly."

Longjing tea was granted the status of 'gongcha', or imperial tea, during the Qing Dynasty by Emperor Kangxi. It was Kangxi's grandson Qianlong who visited the area and, enamoured by the tea pickers, plucked some leaves himself in imitation of their graceful movements. Legend says that Qianlong received a message that his mother was ill so he hastened back to Beijing with such speed that he simply shoved the leaves into his sleeves (there's a pun on tea leaves and tea sleeves in there somewhere). Upon his return and like a dutiful son, Qianlong immediately visited his mother who noticed the fragrant smell of the leaves inside her son's robe. Qianlong had the leaves brewed for his old Mum and....well you know the rest. Health was restored and the fame of Longjing green tea was assured. Qianlong conferred Imperial status on the 18 bushes in front of the Hu Gong Temple on Shi Feng Shan

(Lion Peak Mountain) and the tea that these 18 produce is auctioned annually for more money per gram than gold.

Wong's tea was not *that* special though he told me that even his brew sold for 1000 yuan per half kilogram as he showed me his occupational qualification certificate to prove he had been tested and accredited to produce good tea worthy of such a price. "My tea tastes as good as Emperor tea" he said, "it's just not as famous", before pouring more water into my glass, though never to the brim because this is a sign that you want a guest to leave. It was essential for me to have several glasses of tea since each one has unique qualities. "The first is rather bitter" said uncle, "and the second is best - more sweet and mellow", though by the fifth and sixth glass I was having trouble differentiating the taste and thinking only of my exit strategy to the toilet.

There is distinction between glasses and also between harvests in the complicated business of tea. Most tea plants across the world are harvested four or five times a year, but in Longjing there is usually only one harvest period of six weeks in spring. Tea shoots grow quickly in springtime and absorb nutrients from the soil which makes spring tea the tastiest but also the *healthiest* tea of the year; every glass of green tea I drank in Uncle Wong's parlour would be adding years to my life.

Qianlong's aged mother was saved by green tea and drinkers across the world are still enjoying its anti heart disease, anti cancer, pro digestion calming effects. Green tea is good for fighting acne, losing weight, promoting bowel regularity, stabilising diabetes and preventing stress. A glass of green leaves swirling and drifting like orchids in a glass of hot water will make us happy and healthy, calm and benign. It will heal our wounds, restore our souls, save the world.

The most renowned property of green tea is as an anti ageing product which is why Hangzhou close to Longjing is known across China as 'longevity city'. Research suggests that the antioxidant properties found only in green tea reduce free radical damage to the skin, keeping it more elastic and firm - green tea drinkers can wave goodbye to crow's feet, sagging breasts and bingo wings. There are three Japanese in the list of the 10 humans who have the longest recorded life which seems to bear out the research, since Japan consumes green tea in quantities similar to China. Yet the top 10 also contains four Americans and number one is a woman from France, which suggests popcorn, hamburgers and red wine might be just as efficacious.[42]

Longjing is naturally the most potent, life-giving, restorative tea of all but Uncle Wong was preoccupied with charlatans, tricksters and fakes. Only the leaves picked within a designated 168 km² zone around Hangzhou's West Lake can be considered true Longjing tea, but the brew is produced and marketed all over China. "Zhejiang, Fujian and Yunnan tea might be good tea" explained Uncle Wong, who was becoming agitated thus undoing the calming effects of his tea, "but it's not true Longjing tea and they should not be able to call themselves Longjing." This was a convincing sales patter and probably true, but China is the land of the counterfeit, the kingdom of fakes, so why should tea be any more immune to repackaging and re branding than DVDs, wrist watches and basketball shoes? Uncle's tea was the real deal however - it said so on the packets - and he cheerfully showed me through to another room after I had drunk my fill, where his wife was waiting with more tea, encouraging me to buy and 'take a memory of Longjing home'.

Longjing village is part of a wider area in Zhejiang at the centre of which is West Lake, a body of water that is worshipped, venerated and adored like no other in China. Hangzhou town sits on the edge of the lake and I had rarely seen a more prosperous and satisfied place in the whole country. There is a Ferrari and Rolls-Royce garage in Hangzhou (though no one was ever inside choosing a car when I passed) and a free bicycle service for tourists and locals - I tried to imagine such a thing in distant poverty stricken Guizhou or Gansu where the bicycles would be dismantled for spares in an instant. There were coffee shops that really were Starbucks and not Buckstars as I had seen Jiangsu, real diamonds on wrists poking from expensively tailored suits, real iPods in manicured hands and real wealth in Hangzhou so that the real problems and poverty of rural China felt really, really far away.

'Be born in Suzhou, live in Hangzhou, eat in Guangzhou, die in Liuzhou' goes an old Chinese saying, for Suzhou is famed for the quality

---

42   The longest lived human on record is Jeanne Calment, a woman born in France on 21 February 1875 and who died 122 years and 164 days later on 4 August 1997.

of its education, Guangzhou its food (though not if you don't like weird stuff – see Guangdong chapter) and Liuzhou is a town in Guangxi province famous for nanmu wood coffins that are supposed to halt the decay of the body.

Hangzhou is famous for everything which is why every Chinese should aspire to live there; the scenery, the fresh air, the women, the water are all exceptionally fine and now I suppose the Ferraris are the best in China too. Most of all, Hangzhou has its Lake. Marco Polo called Hangzhou 'the city of heaven, the most beautiful and magnificent in the world' and said that a voyage on the lake 'offers more refreshment and pleasure than any other experience on earth' (what *anything*? It's not often one can say that a well traveled explorer should get out more).

The lake is certainly pretty. But the sunlight bouncing on any lake and rolling hills covered in woodland can be reflected in any body of water. I lost count of the number of times that locals approached me and congratulated themselves on the quality of their lake. 'It is fine' they said - a statement rather than a question - and the claims they made knew no geographical or emotional bounds. West Lake was the finest in China, in Asia, in the world - I'm relieved the claims went no further than this, for the Sea of Tranquillity on the moon is scenically unique too, though devoid of water and thus not ideal for boating.

I wanted to tell them that there are lakes in Europe and America, Africa and Russia that are infinitely grander and wilder, more remote and spectacular and which are not lined with souvenir stalls or choked with pleasure boats, but that would have been ungracious so I simply agreed that West Lake was very fine indeed.

The Chinese like to categorise and list and impose order when none otherwise exists. Spontaneous exploration of West Lake is not encouraged - indeed it is hardly possible since some parts of the lake shore have been turned over to private ownership where entry is possible only with payment of a fee or has been forbidden altogether, this despite the constitution of the People's Republic demanding that natural resources belong to the masses. Those who know best have decreed there are 10 best known and worthy scenic spots around West Lake each marked by a stone column written in the calligraphy of Emperor Qianlong, the man with the sickly mother. This means that 10 spots are hopelessly overcrowded while the rest of the lake that is no less scenic remains relatively uncluttered and unspoiled and a far nicer place to be.

The 10 spots are largely man-made additions to the lake - a pagoda, a causeway, a fish pond in a private garden, a bridge, a courtyard, an Imperial Pleasure Park, a man-made island and a temple bell; the beauty of the lake and the hills is only an adjunct to these, in combination with the moon on a clear night or the remnants of snow, that which is natural is there merely to enhance what is man-made. This is entirely consistent with the Chinese approach to taming nature and I'd seen it at the Three Gorges on the Yangtze River and all over the country. Natural beauty is wonderful, but the hand of man makes it more wonderful by far.

Man's hand is evident in Hangzhou's waterways too. The main 'river' in town is not really a river at all, but a huge canal that snakes its way through the eastern Chinese countryside all the way north to Beijing. Like the Great Wall, there are plenty of superlatives applied to the Grand Canal (though no one claims to have seen it from space) though deservedly so since the canal is the longest man-made waterway in the world by miles (it runs 1776 km from Beijing to Hangzhou) and was constructed over centuries by a total of five million labourers.

The first section of this mammoth waterway was dug in the fifth century BC and the Yellow and Yangtze rivers were linked (this was the purpose of the canal all along) during the seventh century Sui dynasty. The canal soon became a vital source of transportation but suffered grievously after the development of sea routes and especially the invention of the steam train. It languished and by the early 20th century much of its course was overgrown, collapsed and unnavigable though work in recent years has begun on restoring the canal to its former usefulness, as the demands of China's burgeoning economy and the overloading of her roads and trains has become more acute.

The canal comes to a full stop in Hangzhou though not with any dramatic sense of finality. Rather, it peters out and becomes smaller until fading away into countryside south of the town after its long journey. It's a singularly undramatic sight in proportion to its dramatic importance - just a muddy tract of water, wider and flatter than a normal river, with a succession of barges terminating their walking pace journey or heading north (but not to Beijing since the full length of the canal is far from restored yet). Frankly though, what was I expecting? The waterway has only an economic imperative and this makes humans and canals dull no matter how important, though a riot of commerce on wooden Sui dynasty boats or an army of bare-chested conscripted labour toiling under a midday sun beneath the crack of an overseers whip would have been nice.

Despite its dull pragmatism I liked the canal very much, not because it looks pretty but because it represents something that runs quite contrary to the norm in China. Apart from a brief period of Ming Dynasty exploration, when the Admiral Zheng He explored the seas around Asia, and possibly further depending on who you believe (see Jiangsu chapter), China has been a terribly insular country for many hundreds of years. The keep-'em-out Great Wall is the physical embodiment of this insularity, but the real walls existed in people's minds and reached their height during the reign of Mao when China cut herself off entirely from the rest of the world until a group of US table tennis players introduced the ping of 1970s western capitalism to the pong of cultural revolutionary dogma.[43]

The Grand Canal is the antithesis of traditional introversion. It was built to facilitate communication and contact rather than to stop it and helped to shift political power from the Yellow to the Yangtze River basin. This is a good thing. It seems to me that the ancient dynastic capitals along the Yellow River that have mostly been levelled and modernized (see Henan chapter) were so mired in antiquity and holier-than-thou conservative and complacent cradle-of-civilisation-superiority that China would never change. The rice eating entrepreneurial south was far more go ahead and it's no coincidence that when the Grand Canal changed China's geographical focus, her mindset changed too as the country entered upon a new golden era that is arguably being revived again now.

I wanted to see more of Hangzhou's water, her canal and lake, but the whole town was awash in water because of the persistent afternoon

---

43   Sino American ping-pong diplomacy prepared the way for Richard Nixon's visit to China in 1972.

rain and as the lake and sky were the same single grey sheet of wetness so I took refuge indoors. If West Lake is the spiritual heart of Hangzhou, then the economic centre is Qinghefang shopping street. I wandered the reproduction Qing Dynasty shop fronts for a while and admired the elaborate cigarette smoking device on sale that enabled the addict to put a lit cigarette into a pocket and that caught all the ash - never had lung cancer been so convenient. But it was too wet even for shopping so I ducked into a restaurant and ordered the local salted duck. This dish is traditionally served by a daughter's parents to her prospective partner. If the parents don't like the look of the suitor, they would serve him wings or legs to suggest that he fly away. Serving the duck's nether regions means the boy's luck is in for if he will eat the worst part of the duck, he might be willing to go to any lengths to please their daughter.

The duck tasted fine but the restaurant was under renovation and smelt of industrial strength adhesive so that I began to feel like a spotty faced teenager crouched under a darkened underpass trying to get a high with a paper bag of glue. I complained to the waitress that salted duck and solvent abuse were an unwelcome combination and she returned with a huge can of perfumed aerosol that she proceeded to spray all around my head, onto my face and as a garnish on my food. So now the room smelt of glue and cheap perfume. The mega-pack aerosol is the standard response to all manner of Chinese malodorous scenarios; cigarette smoke so dense that visibility is reduced to three foot, toddler vomiting on bus, toilet backing up in train station waiting room, dead dog in lobby of hotel, maggot-infested putrefying headless corpse in wardrobe? Get out the aerosol.

The aerosol was almost as ineffective as a bowl of potpourri I once saw on the floor of the gentlemen's toilets in a massive city centre Chinese train station. In a hellish environment that had never been properly cleaned where 10,000 men defecated and emptied their bladders every day, that bowl of rose petals, lavender and star anais was the very essence of futility, the definition of a battle lost.

China is full of battles lost and won. The Lingyin Temple has stood on the shores of West Lake for 1700 years and been destroyed and rebuilt 16 times. 3000 monks once worshipped in this place whose name means 'Temple of the soul's retreat' but there are a fraction of that number now and the vast majority of people walking the temple steps and lighting incense today had cameras and tour guides not saffron robes or sutras.

The tourists were kneeling in front of an enormous wooden Sakyamuni Buddha on cushions marked with the wrong day of the week. I was puzzled by this lack of attention to detail and a monk told me that they said tomorrow's day because Buddhists prepare their souls and thoughts for the next day before the sun has set on the current one. "Anyway every day is the same for Buddhists" he said. "Measurement of time and days is meaningless to us who are concerned with the very nature of existence" which made me wonder why they bothered with the day of the week cushions at all.

The best part of Lingyin is scattered over the steep rocks by the side of the temple that is called Feilai Feng – 'the hill that flew here'. This strange name is attributed to a Buddhist monk who thought he recognised the hill as one from his home in India and asked if it had traveled here through the sky. There are pagodas and statues dotted over the hillside, hidden amongst rocks and trees like an elaborate garden of gnomes on Feilai Feng, devilish spirits, austere Buddhas, warriors and great corpulent bare-chested gods sitting cross legged and laughing joyously though really that degree of obesity and high cholesterol is no laughing matter.

A pagoda marks the spot on the hill where the founder of the temple is buried. This was the original purpose of pagodas in China - as an elaborate gravestone - though they have come to mean something entirely different and developed into ornamental towers long ago; an essential part of the landscape of any self-respecting Ming and Qing Dynasty Chinese town. Some of these pagodas have become the symbols of whole cities and districts, the iron pagoda in Kaifeng, the leaning pagodas in Dali, the Wild Goose pagoda in Xi'an and the Yan'an pagoda are fine examples and stood like marker posts on my journey through China. (See Henan, Yunnan and Shaanxi chapters). Though traditionally designed to house Buddhist relics, many were built not with any religious or spiritual meaning attached at all but simply to embellish the landscape; because they look pretty.

The pagoda on the hill that flew here was certainly not pretty though it had a sort of grizzled, moss covered rugged charm. There is a mausoleum close to Lingyin Temple that commemorates an ancient warrior who was similarly grizzled and rugged - a famous Song Dynasty patriot who has evolved into the standard model of loyalty in Chinese culture. Such was Yue Fei's devotion to his country that he had the four Chinese characters 'jin zhong bao guo' tattooed onto his back which means 'serve the country with the utmost loyalty'. Yue Fei was a great warrior who trained his eyes to spot black cicadas in a tree from 100 paces away by staring for long hours directly at the sun - don't try this at home - and then became a Kung Fu expert and master of the 18 weapons of war - the hammer, spear, talon, stick, sabre and 12 others that may or may not include the candlestick, rope, revolver and lead piping. Yue Fei was betrayed by the Prime Minister Qin Hui (the farsighted warrior didn't see *that* coming) and charged with treason though the tattoo across his back was used as evidence that this could not be so.'Though it isn't sure whether there is something he did to betray his Dynasty, maybe there is' (sic) said Qin Hui and the phrase 'maybe there is' has entered the Chinese language as an expression to refer to a spurious accusation or a fabricated charge.

For their part in Yue Fei's execution, iron statues were cast of Qin Hui, his wife Lady Wang and two of his subordinates to kneel forever at the grave of the wronged patriot in supplication. It was traditional for centuries for visitors to spit or urinate on the four statues to show contempt for such villainy, though now the statues are protected, clean and dry and free from phlegm, and thus one of the few places in China where people are actually discouraged from spitting. This was a pity because though Chinese spitting drives me to distraction, it would have been fascinatingly obscure to see people spitting contempt at centuries old iron, though no more arcane I suppose than burning Catholic plotters on bonfires every fifth of November.

The Chinese saying advises people to 'be born in Suzhou' because of the quality of education there. But as I walked through the wrought iron gates and into the leafy gardens of the city Qing dynasty high school, I reflected that Hangzhou has some quite impressive educational provision too. The school was founded in 1899 and the English teacher there was delighted to give me a tour of the three floor Museum that told the story of the school that he explained was 'a model school for the construction of spiritual civilisation in China'.

2000 students attend Hangzhou high school and they're no doubt proud of their seat of learning that has survived war, invasion and revolution. The school has a turbulent history but provided uninterrupted education to Zhejiang's intellectual elite though for a while they were shifted to humble alternative premises when the Japanese commandeered the buildings to wage war.

The teacher proudly showed me details of the school's famous alumni – the author Lu Xun, Li Shutong a bearded Chinese professor who stood next to Mao on Tian'anmen Gate when he pronounced the establishment of the People's Republic of China in 1949 and a host of other, no doubt eminent Chinese, but whose names regrettably meant nothing to me. (Four other students from the school had helped to form the Chinese Communist Party in 1921 - the middle-class East Coast wealthy intellectual antithesis of Mao's earthy Hunanese peasant radicalism).

But I hadn't come to the school to see the museum. I was itching to meet some students; I'd seen corporally punished juniors and kids on playground parade who sang to me and stared at me in rural Shaanxi and Guizhou, but what would the highly educated and motivated children of Hangzhou's Ferrari driving, coffee drinking middle-class look like?

The first thing I noticed was that the classrooms were hardly less crowded in this elite school than they had been in the rural north and west. The students were better dressed in matching tracksuit tops, but they still sat beside piles of drab looking textbooks in tightly packed economy class rows each ready for educational take off but brought to earth by the drab monologue and rote learning didacticism of the teacher. Perhaps it wasn't always like this, but the permanent rows of desks and the dense chalked script on old-fashioned blackboards suggested otherwise, and for all that this was an elite school, the student washroom that I passed on my way to the top floor gave off an eye watering odour that was comparable to that of the ammonia stench of a train station toilet, with or without a basket of potpourri. I suppose the stink would at least prevent students from popping in for a crafty cigarette break when they should have been a geography class, since no one of sound judgement would want to spend longer in these toilets than was absolutely necessary.

Hangzhou high school's top floor was more impressive. This was the home of the school's observatory club where the brightest and most confident of students were wheeled out to meet me to talk of their passion for education and the stars. There was a huge telescope beneath sliding roof doors up here and though the students were willing to let me place my eye to the lens there was no point; they told me that Hangzhou has only two or three viewing days a month, and today was one of the other 27 when thick Zhejiang clouds and pollution drifting west from thousands of Shanghai factory suburbs made the universe invisible.

The students up here in the clouds were delightful and welcoming but very intense. All had a clear focus on what they called 'their dream', of Qinghua University and Ivy Leagues. They loved astronomy (naturally), psychology, language, music and maths but never TV or pop music or hanging out with friends and all had glassy eyes that had nothing to do with Yue Fei sun staring and everything to do with ambition. But ambition is as much to do with who you know as what you know, and most students wore red Young Pioneer badges; access passes to the bottom rung of the Communist Party that might open doors which would otherwise remain closed. Life for these pioneers was a steady mix of stargazing and exams. "What happens if you fail?" I asked. The students replied they would be upset but more worrying by far was the thought of disappointing their parents. The President of the astronomy club, eloquent in English with short cropped hair and crisp knee length socks had no such concerns. "I will not fail" she said and looked rather confused by the question, as if the idea of anything other than success was as distant as the planets beyond the clouds.

The other students on the school paths and courtyards wheeling their bicycles in the late afternoon gloom were less steely eyed than the astronomers but they were ambitious too. They also wore Pioneer badges and talked of work and success when I stopped them to chat, though some were more shy and seemed ambitious only to escape this strange foreigner and his daft questions. These giggling teenagers were the embodiment of change in China, their breezy confidence and willingness to talk so different to their introspective parents and grandparents who even in this prosperous corner of China knew hardship and whose ambitions often went no further than a factory job and the next meal.

These educated ambitious open minds are China's future. Their children will see a very different country where the wealth of Zhejiang is felt in the vast hinterland and mountains of the West, a country that is less insular and insecure. As I shook hands with the students and they pedaled slowly away through the school grounds and out into the Hangzhou traffic I reflected that political change in China will be slow too since it is best to work hard and not to question, to make your parents proud and to be loyal, like the tattoo on Yue Fei's back. Travel, the Internet, the global community and students like these who look not inward but outward to the stars will make the change, though the pace is painfully slow and I may not be around to see it unless I start to drink more green tea.

.

PART 3

THE WILD WEST

.

SICHUAN

四川

570 000sq km
Population 87.5 million

*There are many paths to the top of the mountain, but the view is
always the same*

Chinese proverb

Sichuan's provincial capital Chengdu was voted the nation's fourth most
liveable city in China Daily's annual survey of 2010[44] but this might be
more of a comment on the frenetic, polluted awfulness of many Chinese

---

44   Dalian in Liaoning province was #1

towns than the sylvan and stimulating charms of Chengdu. The survey draws on a host of criteria; cost of living, standard of housing, density of traffic and quality of air and in all of these, Chengdu seemed not unlike Guangzhou or Changsha or Wuhan or Chongqing or a dozen other provincial cities where I caught trains, negotiated taxis, choked on fumes, jostled with crowds and searched for the quickest way out to the countryside.

Chengdu means 'perfect metropolis' which is a bit of wishful thinking, but the place turned out to possess some hidden calm and character that was not immediately obvious as I crossed Yihuan Lu, Erhuan Lu, Sanhuan Lu, Ring Roads 1, 2 & 3 on my way to town from the airport, my standard Chinese entirely unable to cope with the shouted, slurred, garbled Sichuanese of my driver.

China calls the Sichuan dialect 'tuhua' or earth speak, a reflection of the informal, levelheaded and unpretentious nature of its citizens, though there is also an element of Beijing disdain in this term for their callow and unrefined country cousins. But after a few days in Chengdu I began to feel a part of the place and to appreciate its subtle charms in a way that I never did in theatrical, self regarding Beijing, and if only the China Daily survey had used the insouciant, laid-back, easy-going, jovial nature of a city's citizenry as the base measure of livability, then Chengdu would surely come out on top.

Chengdu's affability is best reflected in her social life. The city outdoes Shanghai in its number of tea houses and bars though it has barely half the population (though Chengdu is still *big* - China's fifth largest city with 13 million people) and it struck me as I wandered the dowdy backstreets of town past thickets of bamboo that life here is less frenetic than in the cities of the East where a man with three hours to spare would use it to hustle and make money. In Chengdu, he would spend it drinking tea. Chengdu has dozens of these oases of calm, where people sit on bamboo chairs and chew the fat; the really famous ones are in a public park and in the grounds of the 17th century Wenshu Temple so I went to both, slurped tea and imagined myself Sichuanese.

The Temple tea garden is enclosed by four stout and venerable grey brick walls accessed through two heavy lacquered wooden doors that together formed a circle like a magic portal between the serenity within and the crowds outside who burned houses, mobile phones, clothes, DVDs and ghost money (face value 88 000 000 000 000 yuan) all made of paper, so that their departed friends would be comfortable in heaven. I paid 10 yuan to the attendant who passed the gaiwancha handleless cup with lid and saucer carpeted with a sprinkling of parched and rust coloured leaves through her tiny window and indicated that I should sit down. A white coated ancient man shuffled over and extravagantly poured boiling water from a long spouted kettle into my cup and did so again and again whenever the gaiwancha became more than half empty. I would be there still, receiving refills if my brimful bladder had not caused me to spring from my chair and leave the garden with a sense of energy and purpose entirely out of keeping with everyone else who was placidly sipping their tea.

People were reading newspapers, or posing with the pretence of reading the newspaper or giving up entirely and making themselves comfortable with a newspaper blanket. Others were slapping playing cards on the tables with great exaggerated swipes, or playing mahjong or practicing the slow deliberate moves of tai chi. Old men hung caged birds from the branches of ginkgo trees and gazed admiringly at them or commented appreciatively on the song or the plumage of the caged birds of other old men. Almost everyone methodically chewed sunflower seeds and peanuts and the stone flags beneath the bamboo seat legs were littered with the carapace detritus of the ruminants. Everything was done at half speed or sometimes even quarter speed, with great deliberation and the scene put me in mind of a giant tortoise enclosure I had seen once in a zoo or a Mexican town in a spaghetti western before a gunfight when nobody moves but the air is pregnant with the possibility that something could happen as a bundle of tumbleweed blows across the street.

But in Wenshu tea garden nothing *was* going to happen. The old men's birds chirruped, mahjong tiles tapped on tables and a People's Daily newspaper lifted just a little from the face of a wheezing snorer as he breathed out, oblivious to the dyspeptic tea pourer limping wordlessly from cup to cup. All this repose, this passing the time of day disinclination and easy sociability was so delightfully out of keeping with much of pell-mell, get-rich-quick modern China, that the tea houses became my refuge in Chengdu and soon I was a giant tortoise too, gazing into space, dozing with hands laced on stomach, noisily slurping 10 yuan tea that became weaker with each cup.

Renmin Gongyuan Peoples' Park teahouse was a different proposition to the inertia of Wenshu. I went on a Sunday and saw Chengdu at play; the teahouse here was as garrulous as Wenshu had been tranquil, where families gossiped and joked and flew kites and extracted full value from their 10 yuan gaiwancha by slurping greedily and calling the attendant with a snap of fingers so that he trotted from table to table, hot water sloshing from his kettle and making tiny boats of peanut shells.

The entire park was like this, a cacophony of noise and a tribute to the persistent sociability of the Chinese, for why would you want to play cards, practice an instrument, paint, learn to waltz or indulge an unhealthy passion for karaoke at home, when you can do it in public in the company of hundreds of others? I moved around the park and as the noise of one activity faded, another rose to take its place as loudspeakers competed with each other and stern dance mistresses shouted instructions at their students, demonstrating foxtrots with unnatural jerky movements, a swivel of the hips, palms raised, jet black ponytail hair swinging from shoulder to shoulder.

China has an astonishing capacity for noise. TV sets and karaoke machines are turned up loud and the constant dissonance of car horns in the cities sets my nerves jangling to the point where I want to jump in next to the driver who is leaning on his horn and bang his head on the steering wheel, shouting 'you're not making the traffic go any faster you idiot'. But most Chinese genuinely, truly seem to have no awareness of the racket filling the air around them. Though there is a reverence for peaceful places and Buddha-like calm, most do nothing to achieve any degree of serenity in their lives and spend their days surrounded by tumult.

I took a trip to a Sichuanese Opera in Chengdu and the local resilience to noise was in evidence here too. Chuanxi Opera is a provincial derivation of its more famous cousin in Peking with the same elaborate costumes and the same caterwauling voices on stage. The stories they tell are apparently rooted in Sichuan myth and history though I have never been to an opera anywhere in China at which the storyline has been even the slightest bit intelligible to me.

The show at the Qing Dynasty Shu Feng Ya Yung teahouse was an abbreviated, dumbed down form of entertainment, but all the better for that, and the crowd were treated to short digestible passages of opera interspersed with hand shadow puppets that were astonishing and lifelike; a delicate songbird perched on a branch, a plump blinking owl and horses galloping across a prairie. The performance reached a fascinating climax when a cute and fluffy bunny nibbling on grass was attacked, savaged and devoured by a fierce shadow puppet dog. There was juggling and a knockabout comedy routine as well that made little sense to me but was rendered comical by the grotesque facial expressions of a poor persecuted husband as he was cuckolded by a domineering wife. (I was reminded of the fearsome reputation of Sichuanese women that I had heard about in Chongqing).

There were solos on traditional Chinese instruments too, on gongs and drums, a stubby brass trumpet called the suona and an upright violin called gaohu. These ancient instruments are made more complex by their simplicity. There are no valves on the suona and only two strings on the gaohu but the musicians somehow contrived to squeeze an amazing variety of sounds from something so basic; a classical Chinese composition based on a love story in which the strings soared and swept and were bent into ellipses until I thought they would snap and a thunderous, rollicking tune called 'galloping horses' that sounded like a Chinese version of The Shadows. The suona player puffed his cheeks, turned crimson red and seemed to have no need for inhalation as his trumpet imitated bird calls and what the programme described as 'the intimate words between lovers', though I couldn't imagine a scenario where a woman would squawk like a prehistoric bird into my ear on a hot date.

The climax of these greatest hits of Sichuanese music was a madcap collection of men dressed as demons, dragons and monsters, breathing fire and presenting the curious phenomenon unique to Chuanxi Opera called Bianlian or 'face changing' where, by sleight of hand, the performers change their face masks dozens of times from green to blue to black and gold to show off or 'to show the rapid diversification of the gut and the roles innermost being', according to the information at the door.

Yet through all of the birdsong, and the galloping horses and the billowing flame, the audience talked. Or rather they laughed and shouted and hailed each other across the room and cracked seeds with their teeth, yelled into their phones and summoned the men in Qing Dynasty outfits so they would walk across the front of the stage and pour more tea. It was chaotic and informal; the antithesis of the hushed respect of theatre in the West where mobile phones are silenced and the audience glare in reproach at a raised voice or - God forbid - someone shuffling through seats with 'excuse me' whispered repeatedly as they arrive late. The noise had simply been transplanted to theatre from People's Park and the streets outside but wasn't an irritant at all. Sometimes I watched the groups of people laughing and talking instead of the performance - a show within a show.

Chengdu was covered in dust. I was unsure if this had blown south from the arid deserts of Gansu and Mongolia or whether it had been stirred up and blown onto every surface by the knock it down and build it up construction in progress across the city. Yet the Chinese mania for construction was less frenzied here than elsewhere and the city planners had partly adhered to the most basic principle designed to make life bearable for the people who live in a huge building site: try to finish one major project before starting the next.

Some parts of town were mercifully complete and positively sophisticated. Songxiangjiao antique market ran alongside the canal where the pavement artists and paperback books on sale reminded me of the streets around the Pont Neuf in Paris, though there were more cultural revolutionary badges and ceramic models of Mao, fist raised defiantly in the air like some prizefighter, than along the River Seine. An area of Qing Dynasty hutong buildings had been preserved in the centre of town where urbane restaurants jostled for space with refined coffee shops. There was no construction or desert dust here, where the flagstones had been washed and polished to such a high sheen that I stood on a street corner and watched three motorbikes slide over in a slow motion crash, their riders unhurt but grinning sheepishly and juggling bike and spilt shopping as they hurried away.

I settled on Western food for respite from the unending parade of noodles and rice and chose a restaurant with a long menu of Belgian beer which appeared to be based more on hope than reality as each one I pointed to was out of stock and I settled for Qingdao beer from Shandong instead. Kuan Xiangzi is a tourist area so massages with inflated prices were available in many shops, though ear cleaning was most widely available of all. This is an elaborate performance of tiny brushes, fluids, wax and flames that is announced by the chimes of large tuning forks struck together. The whole procedure is probably highly efficacious but I did not take part since my Mum always warned me to put nothing in my ear that is smaller than my elbow, though perhaps if I had, I would have heard the honking traffic or the delicate tinkling of cups and slurps of tea at Wenshu with new clarity and intensity.

Almost every store in Kuan Xiangzi had panda bear key rings, toys, mugs and T-shirts for sale. Sichuan is the world centre of panda habitat and Chengdu has cashed in on this cute, familiar, terribly endangered and eminently marketable beast. I tried to take a bus to Chengdu's Giant Panda Research Centre but was defeated by the lack of any systematic numbering or naming of roads in the city - some addresses have four or five different numbers - so I caught a cab instead.

It was atmospheric and misty amidst the swathes of bamboo at the Panda centre, making it difficult at times to see the approach of hundreds of children on day trips from local schools, come to appreciate China's most famous animal, the survival and breeding of which has become a source of nationalism and a diplomatic tool as bears are handed over to the zoos of friends and trading partners and withheld from everyone else. The children could be heard well enough through the mist, running and laughing and tumbling in their red communist youth neck ties and paper plate panda masks, made at school the day before. Signs around the enclosure said 'Quiet' and 'Sssh!' and 'Pandas asleep' but there was little prospect of 40 winks while the teachers battled numerical inferiority with microphones and the children waved and shouted 'Hello Panda'; a perfectly futile exercise since everyone knows pandas are Chinese animals and don't speak a word of English.

The blur of excitement reached its apogee at the infant panda enclosure. The rosy faced children scoffing their sandwiches were cute, but they had nothing on the bundle of fluff, black-and-white teddy bears that tumbled over each other and blinked at us with bright and black eyes from behind the glass and who, unlike the big lazy adult pandas who eat up to 30 kg of food per day, were interested in more than just sleeping and chewing bamboo.

The centre was aware of the appeal of their babies too. Only the infant pandas were kept behind glass so they couldn't be seen properly, but no matter, for the trifling sum of 1000 yuan the public could go inside, have a proper look and a photo with a cute, adorable little cherub. It was tempting of course, for where else in the world could one get to sit on a bench and put your arm around the shoulder of a panda? But those people who had succumbed and returned from the inner chamber of cuteness, the fluffy fiefdom clutching a photo, wore the expression of the exploited as they tried to convince themselves that the photo had been worth every cent even though the panda resolutely refused to look at the camera or respect the visitor's financial outlay.

Everything was calmer and quieter in the new buildings on the edge of the park where an abundance of pandas sat around and did nothing as pandas are wont to do. I counted 15 bears in one enclosure; there are only 1500 pandas left on the planet so this was 1% of the world's population, like seeing 60 million humans in one place. There is insufficient room for pandas and almost 100 million Chinese in Sichuan and it's the fault of humans that there are so few pandas left. 50% of Sichuan's panda habitat was destroyed by logging in the 1970s and 1980s. The bamboo that is left flowers and dies every 25 years so the bears have to move to new feeding areas, the unavailability of which leads to starvation or inbreeding since the remaining reserves are isolated from each other which prevents a healthy exchange of panda genes.

Yet honestly, the pandas hardly help themselves. They breed only once a year and are notoriously fickle in their choice of partners; someone should introduce them to the phrase 'beggars can't be choosers'. Pandas need only screw to save their species; surely this is not too much to ask? Bamboo is a panda's only food source and provides barely enough protein and nutrients to sustain such a large animal and this explains why they sleep and eat all day. Frankly, the species as a whole should reassess their lifestyle choices.

Authorities in China are belatedly doing their bit to help panda survival and increase their libido. Hunting and tree felling are forbidden and punishable by death in panda breeding habitats and a peasant can be given a reward equivalent to twice his annual salary if he saves a starving panda. The centre has established a relatively successful breeding programme (124 pandas born and counting, of which 88 survived) and most encouragingly of all, the gift shop has developed a dung-for-profit scheme that turns panda droppings into odour free bookmarks and statues at a price far less inflated than that of having a photo with a cute and cuddly baby.

There was a bigger and more famous panda centre to the northwest of Chengdu at Wolong until 2008. On 12 May that year, Sichuan was hit by a massive earthquake that destroyed the facility and killed one of its 64 residents, Mao Mao, a nine-year-old panda that was buried under tons of rubble. The loss of Mao Mao was particularly keenly felt because she had been brought in from the wild and was thus genetically unique, though her five cubs survived and have good genes and excellent breeding potential too. The quake was a calamity and its effect continues to resonate today. At least 70,000 people were killed and five million made homeless, two million of whom were still without permanent shelter a year later. There were photos and displays in my guesthouse and across Chengdu of the collapsed towns and tented communities in remote mountainous regions of Sichuan that border Tibet.

The government was initially praised for its handling of the catastrophe. Response was swift when it became apparent just how severe the quake was and international aid and support was sought; a stark contrast to the even bigger quake in Tangshan in 1976 when China closed her communications and pretended nothing had happened at all (see Tianjin chapter). Hundreds of billions of dollars have been spent on reconstruction and Premier Wen Jiabao visited the disaster zone and announced that the destroyed town of Beichuan would not be rebuilt but preserved as a reminder of the disaster for future generations. Thousands of tourists have been to the site to pay their respects and no doubt to pose in front of the rubble, two fingers raised aloft.

I took Wen's visit to be a positive thing, like King George VI and Princess Elizabeth clambering over the rubble of blitzed London in

World War II, but as I looked at a display of pictures on a downtown Chengdu noticeboard, a man sidled up to me clearly keen to practice his English. "Crocodile tears" he said; this was fine idiomatic English indeed. "Whenever there is a problem, Premier Wen is there, with his megaphone and his tears, and then he goes back to Beijing and does nothing to help the people or to change China." It is true that there had been a degree of political outrage in the days following the quake because of the disproportionately high numbers of schools that had collapsed. The government tried to downplay this uncomfortable truth and eventually suppressed criticism that 20,000 schoolchildren died because of the shoddy construction of schools - grieving parents called them 'tofu schools' built as cheaply as possible while corrupt officials pocketed the cost savings. Protests were finally silenced by the threat of arrest and the withholding of monetary compensation that these poor and powerless and now childless parents could not afford to forgo on a point of principle.

All of this does make Wen's tears seem a tad insincere. But the Premier was popular across China precisely because he displayed a humanity and level of emotion that is in stark contrast to most stony faced Chinese politicians. Wen is a cheerful, avuncular character and the most likeable and three dimensional Chinese leader since Deng Xiaoping, the Sichuan native[45] who the people chummily referred to as just plain 'Xiaoping' since he was mentor and brother to all Chinese, though such cosy fraternity was rather spoiled by the crackdown that he led at Tiananmen Square in 1989.

The stranger's crocodile tear criticism of Wen was entirely typical of the contrariness and independent thought of the Sichuanese. Sichuan's Red Basin with its three harvests a year has long been China's biggest provider of agricultural produce and the sheer numbers who

---

45 Deng was born in Guang'an in Sichuan in 1904 but did not return to his hometown after leaving it to make revolution in order to avoid the development of a cult of personality. Such egotism would have been at odds with his pragmatic, down to earth tuhua Sichuan character. This is in stark contrast with Mao whose cult reached an almost godlike status in the 1960s and whose hometown of Shaoshan is a place of pilgrimage and a monument to his immortality (see Hunan chapter).

live in the province along the banks of the Yangtze River make the region an alternative power base to Beijing. Chengdu was the last city to hold out against the Communists in 1949 and the first to show the independence of thought to break away from the cloying constraints of the communist command economy that prevented modernisation across China and caused 10% of the population of Sichuan to starve to death in the famine of 1960-61.

Recovery was instigated after 1975 by Governor Zhao Ziyang - the man who fell from grace because he showed sympathy for protesting students in 1989 (see Beijing chapter). Zhao implemented the household responsibility system whereby plots of land were let out to individual farmers. This sowed the seeds of recovery and encouraged the green shoots of market reform that flowered into full-blown rampant capitalism with the blessing of Xiaoping and his pragmatic cat theory (see Shanxi chapter).

The influence of Sichuan is felt all over China. The people have migrated and responded to economic opportunity without hesitation and I had met Sichuanese and heard their mangled approximation of Chinese in almost every province that I had visited. Sichuanese women are regarded as good wives because they are strong and work hard, and men are monkeys or mice, inclined to mischief and high spirits and found everywhere; indomitable and ubiquitous.

They are renowned as being especially able to 'eat bitterness' that is to persevere and endure any level of discomfort and hardship - a trait that is especially admired in China. It was Sichuanese that I met working in dangerous coal mines of Northern Shanxi, enduring the monotony of Shenzhen factories and who were living in appalling conditions, mending and re-mending the plummeting high-altitude road from the Tibetan plateau to Nepal.

The famous eighth century Tang Dynasty poet Du Fu who lived in Chengdu and wrote 200 poems there and whose thatched cottage has been recreated like a gingerbread house in the city park said; 'brooding on what I have lived through, if even I know suffering, the common man must surely be rattled by the winds'. Du Fu knew how the people suffer and stoically abide and this is truer now even than in the eighth century. Through famine, corruption, migration and earthquake the

people of this province patiently endure and prosper, though they have
been truly rattled by the wind.

Even the food in Sichuan is defiantly different and reflects the province's fiery lust for life. They like their food 'mala' - numbing and hot
- with plenty of huajiao Sichuan pepper. They dry fry and sauté, season
everything with chili and favour an oily red broth that sets the eyes
stinging and turned my tongue to wood, a thing that no longer belonged to me. I ate spicy Gong Bao chicken and chilli fried snails and
fish, fragrant pork slivers and huoguo fire pot in Chengdu and soothed
my mouth with fragrant Sichuan tea. When I tired of spice, I asked
for mild dishes but this was anathema to cooks who couldn't understand why I might want my food without chili and dropped peppers
in anyway.

Much of the best food in Sichuan has its origins in street food,
what the locals call 'xiaochi' or 'little food'. Dumplings, 'ants climbing
a tree' (bean thread noodles laced with chili paste and sprinkled with
pork) and DanDan noodles, named after the bamboo poles that street
vendors traditionally used to carry around condiments, abound on every street corner and my visit soon descended into a parade from xiaochi
to tea house and back again. And just like the people, and even with the
diversity of cookery across China, Sichuanese restaurants have found a
niche in every city. China is the place of food, goes an old saying, but
Sichuan is the place for flavour.

Of course Sichuan is more than Chengdu and I resolved to leave
the city despite its superabundance of noodles and tea. My departure
was delayed by a counterfeit 100 yuan note that I returned to the bank
from whose ATM it had come. The note was confiscated and stamped
and I was told to return for a replacement in three days. But I could not
because I was moving on - but you must - I can't - you must and so on
in a painful display of wilful bureaucratic obstructionism. This has persuaded me that in the (likely) event of receiving any further counterfeit
notes on a visit to China, I'll pass them off to other unsuspecting fools
and go nowhere near a bank, though to be fair I did receive a delightful 'receipt for the seizure of counterfeit money', signed in triplicate by
the manager as a souvenir for my trouble. So I left Chengdu with 100
yuan less in my wallet pondering with regret how much xiaochi this

could have bought and rode the bus to the county town of Anren for two hours which cost barely a tenth of what I'd lost. This seemed a long way to come for a museum, though this was no ordinary exhibition.

Fan Jianchuan is a multimillionaire property developer who looks not unlike any other successful late middle-aged businessmen in China, made rich from the fruits of socialism with Chinese characteristics, with his buzz cut, black dress shoes and mobile phone pouch clamped to his belt. But Fan has spent his money on art and the creation of what might be the world's biggest museum complex to house it. The museum is self regardingly called the Jianchuan Museum Cluster, but this is no hubristic flight of fancy. It brings together an impressive collection of art and tackles issues that China is normally thoroughly uncomfortable with. Fan's particular interests are what he calls 'the two great disasters of our century' - the anti-Japanese war and the Cultural Revolution - and the museum complex is largely devoted to these. The Cultural Revolution is usually too sensitive a topic to be tackled in this way, but Fan has gone for it on a grand scale with rooms full of Mao statues, posters, badges, 30,000 cultural revolutionary mirrors and 10,000 cultural revolutionary clocks. Fittingly in a province of tea drinkers, there are cultural revolutionary teapots too, though fewer of these were made since the ardent energetic passions of revolution are at odds with the peaceful repose of drinking tea. The gallery information board next to the red pots and jugs, painted with the faces of Mao and his wife Jiang Qing explained 'the red contents painted on the teapots during the Cultural Revolution only prevailed 10 years. The teapots that had lived the peaceful and quiet life for thousands of years, regained their former peace after the 10 years uproar of the insurrectionists'. The choice of language is interesting here - the Maoists are 'insurrectionists' and teapots are imbued with human characteristics; like the ordinary people of China, they want only to live in peace.

The anti-Japanese war is more standard fodder for the communist government but here too, Fan has taken a challenging and brave perspective by considering the sensitive role of Chinese traitors or 'hanjian' (up to one million Chinese fought for Japan in the war). The collection shows photos of Chinese laughing with Japanese officers; such scenes are taboo in other Chinese museums. The theme of war spills into the museum grounds where set into one of the many plaza squares are huge perspex walls of red handprints provided by the old combatants of the war, many of whom were close to 100 years old when they were invited by Fan to make an imprint.

There is the 'crowd statues of 200 heroes' too; larger-than-life bronze figures of the war each attired in uniform and each a re-creation of a real soldier from the anti-Japanese war with an individual expression and set of equipment like a modern day set of Qin Dynasty terracotta warriors but more satisfying by far because of the absence of crowds and permission to get up close and really study the figures instead of viewing them through a long lens.

Fan has also created a 'gallery of women's tiny shoes' to commemorate that most unique Chinese tradition of foot binding. The history of this strange practice is shrouded in story and myth but legend says that a 10th century royal concubine called Yao Niang had her feet bound to appear more feminine and graceful at the Royal Court. The practice filtered down from royalty to the wealthy to the masses and evolved into a system concerned not with mere beauty but the control of women's freedom, power and independence.

The shoes in Fan's collection are beautiful embroidered works of art, but don't look like shoes at all since it seems improbable that any foot could fit inside. Yet the ideal length of a bound foot was three inches or under - only a foot with this measurement could be called a 'golden lily'; feet that did not achieve this tiny size were known as silver or iron lilies, terms that would have been highly insulting to the girl.

The golden lily was achieved by wrapping the feet of a girl as young as four in 10 foot long silk bandages, removing and rebinding every two days. It was the mother's job to bind the feet and the process usually started in the late autumn when the onset of cold weather would numb the foot and make the process a little less painful, since the four smallest toes had to be broken so they could be folded beneath the arch of the foot. Men reputedly found the golden lily erotically stimulating but they were not permitted to see the naked foot; rather they saw it wrapped in silk and embroidered slipper - a sort of early shoe fetish. Fan had managed to acquire a 'sex chair' for his collection, designed to create full and easy access to the desirable feet and thus heighten the sexual pleasure of the man. The chair was carved from wood and had a high, slanting back and long broad arms that extended far beyond the seat. This design enabled the woman to sit and place her legs along the arms of the chair, providing easy passage to her lilies, be they gold, silver or iron.

There is apparently no end to the energy and ingenuity of Fan Jianchuan. Not content with tackling sexual and cultural revolutionary taboos, he has created a hall to commemorate the 2008 earthquake containing wrecked cars, boulders, a clock stuck at 2:28 PM when the quake struck and Wen Jiabao's loudhailer that the premier used to address the dazed survivors at Wenchuan and Beichuan to ensure his crocodile tears could be properly heard by everyone. The museum is home to a huge pig called Piggy Resolute that was rescued from the rubble after 36 days - a celebrity and a beacon of hope after the tragedy, Piggy Resolute even has a pop song written about her.

Astonishingly, Fan's next museum hall is intended to tackle the issue of corruption in China. This tireless Chinese businessman has asked for nominations from the public so that he can name and commemorate China's 100 most corrupt officials based on the criteria of seniority, amounts involved and impact on society. Fan has said that he hopes this exhibition will have a positive impact and become a kind of anti corruption education centre, though many local political leaders with their big houses and fancy cars must be praying that they don't get voted in.

It's appropriate that the defeat of the Japanese and the glorious rise of communism should be so thoroughly commemorated in the Jianchuan Museum Cluster since a further two hours west where the Red Basin begins to ripple and fold into the foothills of the Himalayas is the town that is most celebrated in communist mythology, the genesis of the super heroism of the party, the lodestone of the cult of leadership and the excesses of revolution.

And yet on arrival, the small town of Luding is a nondescript and under whelming place with the usual mongrels wandering the usual decrepit bus station where everything is covered in dirt and nothing seems quite finished. Luding is the centre of the world for the Chinese Communist Party, where the heroic Long March to evade capture by the Nationalists nearly came to a halt at the crashing, thundering Dadu River. There were insufficient boats to cross the Dadu, so the communist army was forced to use the 18th century Luding suspension bridge. On the morning of 28 May 1935 Lin Biao's second division were ordered to take the bridge, so they marched 120 km in 20 hours, defeating numerous nationalist forces who blocked their path on the way, and arrived at the Bridge on 29 May, only to find most of the planks had been removed and that Luding city on the opposite bank had been occupied by enemy troops.

Lin's brave soldiers responded by clambering monkey like along the chains of the bridge under withering machine gun fire. They defeated the Nationalist garrison, secured safe crossing for the entire communist army by 2nd June and prevented the collapse and the failure of the entire Long March. 'Victory was life' proclaimed army chief Peng DeHuai and Edgar Snow, the Western journalist who visited the communist base at Yan'an (see Shaanxi chapter) restated the importance of Luding when he wrote that 'defeat was certain death' in his famous book 'Red Star over China'. The bridge is perfectly peaceful today and apart from a squat memorial cairn, there is little to suggest that such feats of heroism could have happened here once. Hand-over-hand bridge climbing courage has been a staple of elementary school education in China for decades, but this is just the communist story and it's questionable whether such indomitability occurred at all.

Jung Chang doesn't think so. She is the author of the fabulously successful (and fabulous) 'Wild Swans', the 20th century tale of three generations of Chinese women and their experience of revolution and catastrophe during modern China's difficult birth. Chang had been a devotee of Mao, a Red Guard cheering the godlike presence of China's great leader on Tiananmen Square in 1966, but she has turned on her erstwhile hero and like all reformed addicts is passionate and tireless in her condemnation of what she once found so irresistible.

Chang argues there was no battle at Luding Bridge and tales of a heroic crossing are mere propaganda. She uses a witness called Li Xiuzhen in her biography Mao – The Unknown Story (2005) to debunk the cult of the Great Helmsman and the party; Li says there was no battle, no machine guns, and no soldiers gamely swinging from the bridge above the torrent of the Dadu at all. It also seems likely that the defending Nationalists were poorly armed with old bolt action single shot rifles and ancient ammunition compared to the Communists' modern submachine guns, a claim that further undermines the image of communist derring-do. It is certainly likely that some kind of battle occurred and the crossing of the bridge was no cakewalk, but even Deng Xiaoping, with typical Sichuan straight talking honesty admitted in a conversation with US national security adviser Zbigniew Brzezinski that the traditional view of the battle is mere propaganda. 'We needed that to express the fighting spirit of our forces', said Deng. 'In fact it was a very easy military operation'.

There is so much that is obscure in Chinese history, so many half truths and so many walls that make the grasping of reality unobtainable. These walls take physical form in China – the walls around cities, in courtyard homes and above all the Great Wall in the North which might be China's biggest myth of all that failed to keep barbarians out but encouraged the Chinese to stay at home. While Europeans were sailing to discover new ideas and new lands, the Chinese cowered behind stone and mortar just as the myth of the Yellow River cradle of civilisation discouraged sea trade and the myth of the Dragon Emperor prevented (and still prevents) parliamentarianism, debate and democracy.

Jung Chang's book has not been released in China and the Luding story, of gunfire and the greatness of a party forged in blood goes unchallenged, though it is arguable that a nation needs a few myths to sustain itself and garner self-respect; for every Luding Bridge, there's a miracle on the beaches of Dunkirk, a liberation of prisoners from the Bastille and a Che Guevera poster, all languid revolutionary chic.

There is another myth 100 km south of Chengdu at the town of Leshan, though as fantasies go, this one is quite impressive. Sichuan is a big province and despite the Chinese frenzy of road building, it's still a tough place to get around, especially in the far west where switch back roads through earthquake country are covered in ice for much of the year and take desperately long and dangerous routes over remote hills. The trip to Leshan was rather easier and I soon found myself on a broad highway through the agricultural lands of southern Sichuan. This is where so much of China's food is grown, the economic powerhouse of western China, though I failed to see much of it since the mist that lent atmosphere and a romantic quality to my sighting of pandas, had returned and blotted out the view. There might have been a Thomas Hardy pastoral scene of tinkling brooks, squat stone houses, sheaves of wheat in tidy neat lines and hedgerows alive with the sound of larks ascending outside my bus window, though in reality the mist probably hid dull and efficient farms on an industrial scale. My world was reduced to the motorway verge where workers swept in a futile attempt to make China clean and risked their lives as trucks went thundering past, though even this view was preferable to the karaoke TV at the front of the bus where Chinese pop blared out to an incongruous backing of lions in the Serengeti and windsurfers in Hawaii.

It was market day in Leshan and a portion of Sichuan's produce was on display on teetering trestle tables; fat watermelons and enormous carrots weighed on handheld scales and sold for prices that were improbably cheap. But Leshan hardly needs vegetables since most of the town's income is in tourist dollars because of the gigantic stone myth that exists by the side of the river on the town's outskirts.

There is a Buddha built here at the confluence of the Dadu, Min and Qingyi rivers that is the biggest in the world. A monk called Haitong started construction in 713 AD in order to calm the dangerous currents of the water, which promptly happened due to the sheer volume of stone that was excavated from the cliff face and dropped into the river. Haitong of course attributed this happy event to the power of the Buddha and the myth of Haitong's tenacious piety was given further credence when funds for the construction of his great tribute to God dried up and he gouged out his eyes in protest; blind devotion indeed.

But the Buddha is real enough. I got off the bus at the edge of the park and the top of the cliff so that I would have to walk for an hour or so before I could see Dafo, and when I did I would emerge from the trees at the top of the Buddha's head. I liked the prospect of this drama, gazing at the enormous figure square in the face, at his 7 m long ears and down the full 71 m length of his body to his eight and a half metre long big toes.

How could I not be impressed by this Buddha? 'The mountain is a Buddha and the Buddha is a mountain' goes the local saying; my first glimpse was astonishing and I couldn't take my eyes from his robes, his heavy lidded eyes, his calm smile and enormous hands resting on knees as I walked the steps cut into the mountain that descended from his head to the river that the Buddha calmed below. The mist had cleared though it was cold, but this improved my view by keeping the crowds away since this is a *popular* Buddha. Everyone wants a glimpse of Dafo and on weekends and holidays the Army has been called in to keep order as thousands crowd the steps, threatening to plunge to their death at the Buddha's feet, or rush to the side of boats that beetle on the river, desperately trying to get hands outstretched 'holding the Buddha' trick photos, oblivious to the possibility of a capsize that would throw passengers, cameras and incense into the cold river.

I met Tibetan monks at the Buddha's feet who sought me out to take a photo of their group at this sacred site. There were plenty of others around but they clearly didn't want to ask them, for the Han Chinese had invaded their homeland, so how could they possibly trust them to frame and focus a photo satisfactorily? The monks were enormously grateful and hung a prayer scarf around my neck, shaking my hands effusively and chanting Om Mani Padme Hum as they prostrated to the statue. Their devotion was touching, the climax of a long arduous journey from home and testament to the continuing power of the Buddha to heal and inspire, and who was I after all, to suggest that it wasn't Dafo who had calmed the river waters?

I took a van from Leshan for the drive that took me further west because I couldn't stomach more karaoke and because the van driver offered - where else in the world would someone be prepared to stop planting cabbages and drive a stranger 50 miles for 100 yuan? I was glad the bank in Chengdu had removed the temptation to pass off a counterfeit note as payment for my bargain trip and my driver maximised her profits further by avoiding the highway toll. This was achieved by following 30 cm behind a bus as it drove through the gate, though even this couldn't prevent the barrier from slamming onto the roof of her van before we were through. The driver ignored the bang, but 500 yuan of damage seemed a poor return for avoiding a five yuan toll.

The fresh air and countryside of southern Sichuan was a relief after the smoke and noise of Chengdu, though I was missing the teahouses, and the real life birds twittering in the trees were a poor substitute for an imitation of birdsong on a trumpet. Sichuan is a picture book of deserts and huge ancient forests, isolated villages and lakes. But I'm most drawn to the brute magnificence of mountain scenery; the province is crumpled with the evidence of tectonic upheaval rising to the massive bulk of Gongga Shan in the South West that at 7556 metres is Sichuan's highest peak. There are so many hills here that if you ironed the province out flat it would double in size, but there is one hill of modest size that is head and shoulders above all others in Sichuan.

Emei Shan is a sacred Buddhist mountain and inscribed on UNESCO's list of world treasures because of its exceptional cultural significance since Emei is the place where Buddhism first became established in China and spread throughout the East. UNESCO's justification for this inscription says it is also an area of 'natural beauty into which the human element has been integrated... underlining the importance of the link between the tangible and intangible, the natural and cultural'.

A good Buddhist would walk to the top of Emei Shan but I took a bus and hoped that I would receive at least some degree of blessing for walking down. The town at the foot of the mountain is called Baoguo and has been converted into a kind of one-stop Buddhist lifestyle centre to cater to the crowds who combine a visit here with Leshan to receive the double blessing of pilgrimage and swallowing some fresh mountain air. There are vegetarian restaurants serving tofu that looked suspiciously like meat where rows of vegetables and herbs were arranged outside in a pleasing palette of brown and green, though the restaurants with live birds and enormous toads in cages on the pavement outside appeared to be doing better business. Delicate white irises that the Chinese call 'little ducks' and stone icons lined the river bank and incense and candle shops led to the temple where cans of coke were arranged in neat pyramidal offerings to the gold Buddha statue. Baoguo Temple marks the end of town and the beginning of the mountain, though even here, Buddhist commerce thrived in the 'spiritual gift shop' where zhuye qing cha, bamboo leaf tea was stacked high on the shelves.

I stayed a night in Baoguo since I liked the serenity of the place out of season and loved the view of the huge mass of the mountain that rose in folds behind the town before disappearing into the mist. I ate a meal in my hostel of crisp fresh vegetables, tofu and chewy meat that I hoped wasn't toad, after which the owner appeared with a threadbare basketball wondering if I wanted to shoot some hoops. We played on a large square, book-ended by a covered stage that was surmounted by a red communist star, the strident sharp edges of which seemed out of step with the contemplative Buddhist town. Andy the manager had lived in Baoguo for his whole life and explained that films had once been shown weekly on the stage when 10,000 people crammed into the square to watch Japanese soldiers fleeing the onslaught of the brave Chinese, reports of splendid agricultural productivity and, no doubt, heroic soldiers clambering hand over hand, immune to gunfire on Luding Bridge.

As we walked back to Baoguo through the University Gardens, Andy showed me where his childhood house had been 'when all this was paddy fields', and where he had caught fish from the river that ran past the gift shops. The modern version of Baoguo is by no means an unattractive place but still the fields had been replaced by roads, the river channeled and subdued. I reflected that my travels in China had probably come 30 years too late; how I would love to have seen the country untouched by so much modernisation, before Deng said to be rich is glorious and before so much of China was spoiled because people got what they wished for.

There was no need to book my seat on the bus to the mountain summit the following day since the sign that hung on the wall of the bus station announced this was the 'tourist dead season'. The thick forested vegetation thinned out as we climbed circuitously around the back of the mountain and for once I was glad of a little modernization; the bus chugged away and the mountain was *steep*. By the time we reached the forlorn car park at 3000 metres, there were hardly any trees at all and banks of mist blew across the landscape turning the sky to cotton wool, though occasionally lifting to remind me that there was still life and greenery and trees far below. The car park and slate steps at the beginning of the trail were precarious with the accumulation of last winter's snow, though there was too little to make use of the Emei Shan ski ground on the other side of the hill, a facility that didn't seem very spiritual or Buddhist, though I suppose hurtling down this steep mountain in the mist on a couple of pieces of wood might bring one closer to God.

I shouldered my pack, and thought of Lao Tzu who said that a journey of 1000 miles begins with a single step and began to walk. It was 30 km back to Baoguo, but all downhill and I would break the journey with a night in one of the venerable and ancient monasteries that lined the route all the way down the mountain. This would be a delight of old timber, slate floors and chanting monks and I had heard in Baoguo that some of the temples provided electric blankets which on this cold and snowy mountainside had more appeal even than 1000 years of monastic history. Damn that modernisation!

I walked 20 km on the first day to Hongchunping monastery and though my calves protested at the unyielding thud, thud, thud of tens of thousands of stone steps, that walk on Emei Shan was one of the most delightful days I spent in Sichuan, in the mountains, in the whole of China. Mist and snow cleared as I descended into forest so varied and lush that I understood why UNESCO was so excited about this place. There are 3200 plant species on Emei, which is 10% of China's total; Nanmu trees - tall, straight and flawless, perfect for temple pillars - gingko trees with their crescent leaves and medicinal properties that have been so close to extinction and, above all, bamboo in great dense swathes across the hillside, strands as thin as my finger and as thick as my leg and that grow so fast that I felt I could watch it become bigger if only I stood still for long enough.

But standing still wasn't an option. I'd eaten a hearty breakfast and set off late from Andy's hostel and the ascent had taken *forever* as the bus wheezed up the hill and stopped for two shopping breaks that were disguised as an opportunity to use the toilet, though there were only four of us on the bus and no one had the least inclination to shop or to urinate. I had no torch and imagined all that bamboo would suck every atom of ambient twilight from the sky and I did not want to be stuck on this mountain in the dark, no matter how beautiful it was, not with all those evil monkeys out there in the forest.

Emei Shan is renowned for its monkeys. Such is the popularity of the mountain that these big hairy Tibetan macaques have lost all fear of humans and will attack and rob anyone who seems likely to be in possession of food or looks at them in the wrong way. I saw no monkeys for 19 ½ of the 20 km I walked on my first day, but finally encountered some babies sitting playfully on a fence close to Hongchunping. They were cute and mischievous of course, though I didn't like their ears that looked as if they belonged to an old man, but I knew that where there were infant monkeys, adult monkeys could not be far away. I turned the corner, and there they were. Every monkey stopped picking fleas from other monkeys, fixed his yellow eyes that seemed too small for his big baboon head onto me, opened his mouth and snarled great ivory defiant fangs. Worse still, the monkeys were sitting on a suspension bridge barring my way and there on the other side was the monastery, a pot of rice on the boil, electric blanket warming my bed.

I had no choice; firmly, resolutely and raising my bamboo walking stick above my head, I advanced. A monkey jumped on my back and grabbed a bottle from my rucksack, grinning malevolently as he sat on the bridge iron chains with his trophy. But my blood was up; I quickened my pace and opened my throat shouting a war cry as I banged the stick on the bridge - death or glory. Miraculously, mercifully the monkeys scattered into the trees, staring resentfully down at me and I was able to continue my Long March. This had been my Luding Bridge. Against unlikely odds I had defeated the enemy. Victory was sweet, heroism had triumphed and children would be taught of this day for generations to come.

I vomited all night in the monastery. Sickness is an occupational hazard of travel, especially in a country like China, but I'd been lucky until now and not once had I found myself leaning over a Chinese toilet and minutely inspecting its inadequate plumbing. I had a strategy for sickness which involved checking into an expensive hotel, sleeping between crisp cotton sheets and watching sport on cable TV while I recovered with sips of mineral water. But the long dark night of the soul that I experienced at Hongchunping could not have been further removed from this ideal. Sure, the electric blanket was warm as toast, but I spent much of the night traipsing squeaky wooden floors to the most primitive squat toilets I have ever seen and fully 100 metres up the hillside behind the monastery to evacuate the contents of my stomach over and over again. On the plus side, the night gave me an insight into the inner workings of a monastery; monks were awake in shifts for most of the night chanting in low voices and ringing bells, but I had eyes only for the outhouse and their quiet worship cannot have been enhanced by the sound of my retching.

Dawn was a blessing, a benediction. I had been worried at first that I might die in the night, though by 3am I was worried that I might not; perhaps the chanting monks had been asking God to spare me? I passed on breakfast and set off down more steps in a daze and daring any monkey to come near me so I could vomit on him. But the fresh mountain air was reviving and I was able to stop for a pancake and a cup of coffee at the Hard Wok Café where the view across a wide valley carpeted in trees was so lovely that I began to forget the trials of the previous night and feel glad once more that I was still alive.

There were more monkeys lining the final 10km of my walk, but they held no fear for me now and I strode through oblivious to their snarls, past more temples and the pool where Puxian the Bodhisattva of Universal Benevolence rested with his six tusked elephant on an ascent of the mountain in the 6th century. I bet he wasn't harassed by monkeys.

The final part of the path is called the venerable trees terrace and is the most touristed part of the mountain. I began at last to see other living creatures that were not monks or monkeys, a sprinkling of shops appeared and the trail became more *organized* and *structured* - just how Chinese tourist groups like it. 'Here is the best place to take a picture' said one sign, 'monkeys are our friends' said another. I had to take issue with that, though stalls were selling tomatoes and cubes of tofu to feed to our simian chums in an attempt at bribery and rapprochement. I was not yet ready to make peace and continued down, past the wooden signs listing 'Socialist principles for the benefit of hikers' and 'Socialist viewpoints about honour and disgrace'. 'Take hard work as an honour, regard loving ease as a disgrace, take advocating science as an honour, regard being benighted as a disgrace', they said. Also, 'be honest, tolerant and law abiding and don't jack up or beat down prices.'

Loving ease didn't seem so disgraceful to me now as I trudged finally, achingly into Baoguo. I rode the bus back to Chengdu where flames still roared under street corner woks and tea was being poured by ancient tea garden attendants whose shuffling gait I was now imitating. But my heart wasn't in it anymore since the rolling mountains and vast spaces of Sichuan had become more appealing by far than her cities.

But the mountain had taken its toll; I had been sick and bullied by monkeys and the damp mountain mist felt like it had entered my bones. I luxuriated in a hotel bathtub and dozed. I was tired; my legs would take days to recover from those steps and the high altitude sun that had sometimes forced its way through the fog had scorched my face. The mountain had transformed me into a temporary tribute to this huge and charismatic province. I wanted only to lounge on my hotel bed, to eat my favourite food and to use as little energy as possible. The dark lack-of-sleep rings around my eyes had completed the change; for the next few days at least I would be more Giant Panda than man.

SHAANXI

陕西

200 000 sq km
Population 37.5 million

'Don't wait for problems to pile up and cause a lot of trouble before trying to solve them. Leaders must march ahead of the movement not lag behind it'

Mao Zedong

In China conversations are shouted, TVs are set at a volume so loud that speech distorts and throats are cleared with great hacking gusto across the nation at all times of day, though especially at dawn. Every writer who has ever tried to encapsulate this huge and confusing nation has something to say about spitting, so a long diatribe against the extraordinary national hobby of expectoration would be old hat. All I would say is that it's a rather disappointing affair; for all the gurgling and rasping, that which is expelled is rather insignificant and small and is dribbled from the mouth instead of launched like a projectile. If you're gonna spit, then do it properly! I feel offended not by the fact that the Chinese spit, but because they don't know *how* to spit.

It was in Shaanxi that I saw a man use his heel to grind his phlegm into a hotel carpet and I reflected on all my travels to China, I had never seen anyone spit on a carpet before. I wondered if this was an indication that Shaanxi would be uniquely challenging and that the carpets across the province would be slick with sputum.

Yet in many respects, Shaanxi is the most typically Chinese province of all. It is situated close to the centre of the country with the classic too hot in the summer, too cold in the winter Northern Chinese climate and with the Yellow River, that most iconic symbol of Chinese civilisation, crashing squarely through.

The provincial capital Xi'an, with its walls and Warriors is of course altogether less typical. Tell any Chinese that you're touring the country and he'll straight away ask if you've been to Xi'an, since to not visit the ancient capital is to not visit China at all. I did as was expected and arrived by rail at the train station at Xi'an that was like a work of art; here there are crowds of workers in grey clothes and scuffed shoes shuffling in lines, the station buildings as dark and soot covered as Lowry Salford factories. There are glimpses of Breughal and Bosch too in filthy satanic corners where peasants squabble over bundles of food and shout at each other in rage as they buy tickets or climb aboard trains, while I wandered Da Vinci-like, trying to retain the serenity and the wry smile of a Mona Lisa.

I've caught a train three times at Xi'an at all times of day and night and understand that there is no way of arriving early or late enough to avoid the crowds. The station is always busy. This should be no surprise in a city of five million in which this is the only way in and out for a population who rarely owns a car, but makes the purchase of tickets and boarding of trains a Herculean task. Yet how could so many people need to buy a ticket at 5am? The queues were two hours long and

I knew that if I ever reached the front the seller would speak through a tinny microphone, making her instructions unintelligible to me and causing everyone to become enraged as I held the queue up even more.

Except queue is hardly the correct word at all. People desire a ticket above all and will do all that is necessary to procure it. This is survival of the fittest in its purest form and I knew that even as I reached the holy grail of the ticket window, if I left so much as ¼ of an inch gap or a three second pause in my conversation with the clerk, some Darwinian alpha male would be spitting at my feet, pushing in and taking my turn. So I cheated. For 40 yuan, a tout queued in my stead, met me hours after at a prearranged place in the station beside the huddled masses crouched like refugees beside their parcels tied with string and handed over my precious ticket. Meanwhile I explored the town.

If it wasn't for the intact Ming Dynasty walls, Xi'an would be like most other Chinese cities; badly planned with too many ugly modern buildings and witch broom women who sweep the roads clean, sending clouds of dust into the air to settle on other surfaces where it is swept clear by other women. The Xi'an city walls are very special indeed and it is possible to walk or cycle right round their 14 km length. They're restored of course but this hardly matters in a country whose ancient city walls have been torn down elsewhere and most notably in Beijing by officials who believe only in 'progress'. There's a drum and bell tower in Xi'an too possessing a pleasing geometric thin at the top, wide at the bottom Ming style which mirrors that of the walls - the chunky grey brick solidity of which looks capable of really defending a city.

I descended the walls to plunge into the old chaotic Muslim quarter of town. Modern Xi'an is encroaching on this district and I was soon buying raisins, walnuts and fresh flatbread from a street vendor and considering whether there can be any less appetising food than sheep hooves simmering in a vat of chili, just 50 yards from pavement cappuccinos outside Starbucks. Muslim Xi'an and its mosques and narrow alleys where limping dogs barked as I walked past the gaudy wall posters of Mecca peeling from the walls, reminded me of nothing so much as the far north-west of China in Xinjiang and Gansu. This is unsurprising since the great trade route that the 19th century German explorer

Richthofen called 'The Silk Road' winds its way over mountains and through deserts all the way from the distant west and ends here.

Xi'an was called Chang'an (Eternal Peace) in those days; the terminus or beginning of what was then the greatest trading route in the world. The itinerant monk Xuan Zang returned to Chang'an in the seventh century from the far west and India and was immortalised in the Chinese classic 'Journey to the West'. Xuan had departed without the emperor's permission but returned as a hero, his arms laden like some robber librarian with ancient Buddhist texts. The symbol of Xi'an, The Big Goose Pagoda was built to house all those boxes of books. But commerce was more important than theology to Chang'an and the cloth, spice, animals and food that traveled up and down the Silk Road made the city the biggest in the world during the Tang dynasty seventh century China.

Chang'an 900 years before this was more important still, since it was the capital of the first emperor of China, Qin Shi Huangdi. Qin unified the country, began construction of the Great Wall and gave his name to China, but it is in death rather than life that he is best remembered. The emperor craved immortality but hubris overcame him when the poisonous mercury pills that he demanded his physicians produce to prolong his life had entirely the opposite effect. He died in eastern China and ministers disguised the smell of his untimely demise with rotten fish while he was returned to Xi'an. But despite his desire to live forever, Qin was well-prepared for death too and had an elaborate tomb guarded by thousands of terracotta warriors constructed 40 km east of the town.

This is what people come to see in Xi'an and this is the staple of all the antiques stalls and shops around the Muslim quarter where replica warriors of all sizes are bartered and sold. I considered avoiding the warriors altogether since what was the point of going? Reproduced in thousands of models and photos and so boringly familiar, there seemed no reason to join the hundreds of others who go there, take their photos and leave.

Yet here I was boarding a bus with the guide rattling off all those details that everyone seems to know already. "The warriors are the eighth wonder of the world" he droned. "They are over two thousand years old; they were built to protect the tomb of Emperor Qin . Here are eight thousand warriors, every face is different" and so on, until the drone of his voice seemed hardly different to the sound of the traffic outside.

Our first stop wasn't at the warriors at all but at a shop selling models of the warriors. China is one of the few countries where tours take their victims to see the merchandise before tackling the main event. I grumbled that I didn't want to buy stuff, but the shop triggered a surprising change in my mood since it was so darn interesting. Apart from anything else, they had full-size warriors made from Jade and retailing at US$10,000. The owner claimed that they were the only shop licensed to produce reproductions of Emperor Qin though this proud claim to copyright seemed hollow in a country where anything can be reproduced for a price, and Xi'an was absolutely heaving with terracotta reproductions; every street side store groaning under the weight of archers, generals and horses. The warriors in this store were probably more finely crafted than elsewhere. We saw women patiently carving the figures from clay before they were fired in 900° ovens for days. Elsewhere were huge and detailed lacquerware screens and tables showing Ming Dynasty hunting parties and banquets, workers endlessly smoothing down and painting on layer after layer of paint; so much effort to make something so hideous.

Outside, terracotta warriors stood to attention missing their heads. This was so that dumb tourists like me could stand behind them and pretend to be a soldier. My guide seemed crestfallen when I chose to do this instead of buying some lacquerware but gamely took my picture while I tried to look anciently Chinese. In the end I relented and picked a kneeling soldier from amongst the ranks of hundreds to stand on my sideboard at home just as every visitor to Xi'an surely must do.

The warriors were discovered in 1974 by a farmer digging a well and that self same yokel was signing the book of his life changing event inside the enormous aircraft hangar where the warriors are housed. No photos were allowed unless the book was bought and I'm sure he could not have imagined such a life of indolence before his shovel clanged against a terracotta head all those years ago. Visitors were funneled into a 360° movie show telling the story of Qin and his warriors. We were reminded that the great Emperor - tyrant wasn't just about ter- racotta but created a unified currency and language in China and built 6400 km of highways which makes him almost as road crazed as the current government. The movie was very cheaply produced and I have rarely seen less convincing fight scenes, where ancient Chinese sol- diers screamed and threw extravagant back flips and somersaults at the slightest touch from the enemy.

The main event was more impressive. The 40 km journey, shopping break, autographing farmer and dodgy film had raised anticipation to such a level that no one could fail to be excited as they entered the doors onto the raised platform and saw all those dusty ranks of troops below. There are three pits, of which number one is the most impres- sive with seven hundred warriors excavated and another five thousand still underground (what a sight it will be when they're all unearthed). I was genuinely ready to be disappointed and unmoved, but it's all far too overwhelming for weary cynicism, though it would be wonderful to get closer to the warriors and see all those individual expressions and hairstyles up close.

The rule that visitors must not photograph the warriors has been re- scinded and now everyone reels off dozens of shots to bore their friends and neighbours with at home. There's a separate 'actual site special photo service' where for 150 yuan a visitor may leave the throng, get a little closer to the warriors and have a photo at the exact spot where the farmer made his discovery. There's also a terracotta photo souvenir booth where I took the opportunity to have my photo spliced onto the body of a warrior and where I could stand amidst a phalanx of repro- duction soldiers and pretend I was in Qin's army too. Tourism is life through a lens and the mad scramble to photograph rather than *look* at the warriors is replicated at the Taj Mahal, the Grand Canyon and the Eiffel Tower. The phenomenon is made worse by digital technology which removes the worry about wasting film and by the belief in China that no photograph has any worth unless it features a person in it, pref- erably with two fingers raised in a victory salute.

Emperor Qin was a man of grand gestures. He is celebrated in China as a great and strong leader, though he was also intolerant of dis- sent and had all those books that hinted at criticism burned and buried alive 460 scholars who had dared to speak out against his rule. 'What was so remarkable about Qin Shi Huangdi?' asked Mao in 1969. 'He executed 460 scholars. We executed 46,000 of them.' Such rib cracking gaity! Mao had truly lost all sense of proportion and reality by this stage of his life. It's no wonder that Mao Zedong is often compared to China's first emperor. Nationalist, ambitious, dictatorial and resistant to criticism, the two men are one and the same. It's just that Mao's victims were buried by the Cultural Revolution rather than beneath the foundations of the Great Wall.

Qin's grandest gesture of all was saved for his mausoleum, a couple of miles from the Warriors. The tomb hosts untold riches according to the ancient Chinese historian Sima Qian. He wrote that the mausoleum took 700,000 workers 38 years to build and is filled with 'models of palaces, pavilions and offices as well as fine vessels and precious stones.' The tomb supposedly contains mercury replicas of China's great rivers flowing to the sea through hills and mountains of bronze. Pearls represent the sun, moon and stars.

But now, the tomb is just a grassy mound. Steps lead to the summit from where a good view of the plains is spread out and where the inevitable hawkers thrust statues in my face. 'Ming, Qing' they shout, though each statue is identical to that of all the other sellers. The Chinese are rightly proud of all their Qin Dynasty history, though this doesn't stop occasional looting of tombs and attempts to sell the history to foreign dealers such as when a warriors head was offered in June 1987 for US$81,000. The salesman was executed; another victim of China's first emperor.

Most of the warriors haven't been unearthed and the tomb hasn't been opened because the authorities don't want to spoil things. All of the warriors were originally painted in bright colours and these fade within hours when exposed to the air. So, the response has been to leave them underground until a technique has been developed to preserve the bright blues and reds. The same is true of Qin's tomb. How to open the door and not destroy all those fragile silks, jewels, paintings and mercury? Remote sensing technology has revealed chambers, stairs, terracotta dancers and acrobats but the ancient writer Sima Qian warns us that all is protected by booby-traps and crossbows. This sounds more

Indiana Jones than a reason to stay out of the tomb, but the Chinese restraint is admirable. All those riches, all that fame and they're waiting so that the contents of the tomb are best preserved for future generations. Such patience is slightly surprising in a country that is racing towards industrialisation with scant regard for the quality-of-life of its citizens or the pollution of its rivers and air. So, an anonymous and rather uninteresting grassy mound it remains whose contents are tantalisingly out of reach. Surely it wouldn't hurt to have one little peek?

Qin may have built miles of roads in China, but those of the Wei Valley around Xi'an are tiresomely busy. So I followed the good example of the ancient Taoist sages who took refuge from the corruption of the capital in the Qingling Mountains. I soon passed the Huaqing hot springs, the scene of the 1936 Xi'an incident when the Nationalist leader Chiang Kai-shek was kidnapped by Zhang Xueliang, a leading general in his own army. Chiang was refusing to stand up to the invading Japanese and was chased through the Li Shan Woods in his pyjamas and found shivering beneath a rock, though his teeth can't have been chattering since he had no time to put them in due to the haste of his departure. Chiang was forced to meet with his enemy Mao and together they signed a united front against Japan though this marriage of convenience collapsed soon after the Japanese surrender and the two sides were soon tearing lumps out of each other again. The photo of Chiang and Mao's meeting is priceless; all smiles, green tea, comfy chairs and cheerful Bonhomie. But Chang is reviled in China now and Huaqing revels in the idea of him running away like a baby. 'This is the window that Chiang Kai-shek jumped out of' trumpets one sign, while the place he was captured is marked by an incongruous Neo Grecian pavilion. I was surprised to see no Chiang Kai-shek pyjamas on sale.

I arrived at Hua Shan in the Qingling Mountains where Lao Tzu, the most famous sage of all lived for a while and contemplated life before writing the Taoist masterpiece Tao Te Ching. Lao was conceived when his mother gazed on a falling star, stayed in the womb for 62 years and was born when his mum leaned against a plum tree. I would have needed to lean against something too if I'd been pregnant for six decades. The legend states that the Tao was written when Lao Tzu returned to Xi'an and was challenged by a sentry who asked him to produce evidence of his wisdom. But modern historians have no poetry or romance in their souls and say that the book is merely a compilation of Taoist sayings from many sources in the fourth century.

The Tao Te Ching says that people have a habit of behaving unnaturally and upsetting the balance of the Tao and my ascent of Hua Shan mountain outside Xi'an felt like an unnatural act during which my balance might be upset at any moment. The mountain is a mass of vertical granite and as I marched up steps cut into Green Dragon Ridge (Canglong Ling) the views to either side were dizzying and vertiginous to the valley floor 1000 metres below. I kept to the easiest path wherever possible but Chinese hikers in slip on shoes and flip-flops were on the difficult route and taking to heart the Chinese saying 'there is one path and one path only to the top of Hua Shan', meaning that sometimes the hardest path in life is the best.

The difficult route on Hua Shan is insane. The steps here are cut into vertical rock and at times a series of wooden planks are bolted to the rock face with nothing but space below. Locals call this 'Changkong Zhandao', 'the walking on air road' and hikers shuffle along and giggle and shriek, though unlike years past they do have the option of clipping onto a safety rail, a compromise of which Lao Tzu would surely have disapproved.

A photographer had set up shop near to one of the summits. He was charging customers 50 yuan to put on a belt, clip to a fence and sit on a rock that protruded into the yawning chasm below. The resulting thumbs aloft pose could then be printed and laminated in double quick time. The man said that business was good and no one had died by falling off the rock yet. Here was the new China encapsulated; an individual making money in a free-market economy from tourists with surplus cash and leisure opportunities that had never existed in the past and providing an opportunity for the obligatory Chinese photo of yourself without which the splendid mountainous backdrop would be of less worth.

The summit of Hua Shan is extraordinarily airy and beautiful and might lead even the most jaded traveler into Taoist meditation. From up here it's easy to see why the peak is named 'Flower Mountain' since it has five peaks arranged like the petals of a flower. Each is crowned by a temple where Taoists and hermits still congregate today in the search for something nobler than all that Mammon on the plains far below. There are five great Taoist Mountains in China said to originate from the limbs and head of Pangu. This primitive hairy giant burst from a cosmic egg after 18,000 years and set about creating the world. With a swing of his giant axe he separated the murky yin of Earth from the clear yang of the sky and to keep them separate, the mighty Pangu pushed up the sky. This took him another 18,000 years (get on with it Pangu!) During which time the Earth grew 10 feet wider, the sky 10 feet higher and Pangu 10 feet tall everyday. His job complete, Pangu was laid to rest; his breath became the wind, his voice the thunder, his eyes the sun and moon, his blood the rivers, his body the mountains, his facial hair the Milky Way, his fur the forests and his bones the precious minerals of the Earth.

I love the attention to detail of the Chinese creationist story. Even Pangu's bone marrow is accounted for (it becomes diamonds), his sweat falls as rain and the fleas on his fur are carried by the wind to become the fish and animals of the world. We humans are not Pangu's dandruff or the contents of his nose, but are shaped from river mud by the goddess Nuwa. The goddess crafted us individually and lovingly just like Qin's Warriors, but Nuwa was a goddess in a hurry and came up with the time-saving method of dipping a rope in the water. The drops of mud that fell from it became new humans; not as intricately carved or as beautiful as Nuwa's first efforts, and rather clumsy and ugly, but humans nonetheless. Delightfully, wonderfully the story says that Nuwa's original creations are the Chinese, while the rest of us are just blobs of mud. When I first heard this, I felt I understood as never before the intense nationalism and prejudice that is sometimes so ugly in China and also the depths of shame and resentment that must have existed in the years before the Communist takeover when China was so patronised and abused by muddy foreign devils.

If I felt a sense of serenity after my reverie in the warm sunshine on the top of Hua Shan, this soon dissipated on my journey back to Xi'an. The coach was suspiciously cheap and the reason soon became clear as we made our third stop at a souvenir shop on the way to the city. I was hot and tired and didn't feel Taoist at all and to my shame and showing a complete lack of cultural sensitivity, I had my first proper argument in Chinese. "I don't want to shop" I shouted pathetically "I want to go home!" and turned to see every pair of eyes on the bus glued on me. Those at the back had stood up to get a better view and while no one joined in or offered an opinion, it was clear that the waiguoren losing his rag was very interesting indeed.

Another opportunity to observe the Chinese propensity to wordlessly stare when things get interesting was soon to present itself. Two miles after my outburst we had a crash. Not a great big screeching tyres, driver through the windscreen kind of incident, but a crash nevertheless. It was more of a bump really with no damage done, but bus and car stayed resolutely stationary instead of moving out of the way, while the traffic backed up and edged its way around the two vehicles that sat pressed against each other in embrace in the middle of the street. Meanwhile the drivers argued about culpability. This was a full veins bulging shouting match with flecks of spit landing on each other's faces and very soon the staring began.

Every passenger got off the bus and stared. Passing traffic stopped and the drivers exited their vehicles to stare. Cyclists and pedestrians stared. The white sun in a cloudless sky stared. No one intervened, they just stared. Meanwhile the pantomime continued and then just as it seemed I might spend the rest of my life staring and shopping on the way to Xi'an, the shouting stopped, the drivers got back in their vehicles and we were on our way. I had seen nothing to settle the argument; no exchange of money or shake of hands but clearly some essential criteria have been met. No one had lost face, both had won and we could leave.

As if this endless journey hadn't offered enough, another event disturbed my air-conditioned reverie before we reached Xi'an. As we sped along the carriageway, there was a middle-aged man lying flat on the hard shoulder beside a car whose doors were wide open while another man pumped his chest. No one staring, but here witness that other strange Chinese social phenomenon - the reluctance to get involved and help someone in distress. I have travelled far and wide in China and I suppose have gained a little understanding of the culture and norms of the Chinese in doing so. Yet this determined unwillingness to lend a hand baffles me. The Chinese are a reserved people and have a fear of standing out from the crowd and this might go some way to explaining this behaviour (and could account for the mass hysteria of the Cultural Revolution too). Yet I have a suspicion that there is an ingrained dog eat dog selfishness about the Chinese psyche too. 'If it's not affecting me or my immediate family or friends, it's not my concern, so why should I help that man I don't know and what difference does it make to me if I push in front of you in the queue, even if you've been waiting for your train ticket for two hours?' It's a strange paradox in a culture that is so community minded and who's Buddhist, Taoist and Confucian philosophy preaches concern for each other and the diminution of the self. Maybe it wasn't always like this, it's just that China has gotten too damn crowded and it's impossible to care about anyone much when you're fighting for the same space.

Finally, we were driving past Xuan's books in the Big Goose pagoda and inside the crenellated Ming Dynasty walls though my relief was tempered since I knew the trials of the journey were merely foretastes of another stern test at the hopelessly crowded train station. For tonight I was traveling 300 km north to Yan'an.

I decided to fortify myself with some Shaanxi food at a restaurant near to the station and wandered along to find something traditional and local. One of the stores here had a woman sitting in the window on a swing. She was excessively made up and manicured and grinned at me coquettishly in her lacy tutu, though the effect was rather spoiled by a large cold sore on her lip. Her name was Tanya and she was from Russia but spoke no English so I couldn't ask how she felt about sitting on display like a nymph on a swing. So I asked the shopkeeper instead who naturally told me she was very happy and enjoyed her work. He told me that Tanya was only there at weekends since there weren't enough customers during the week to run to the expense of a beautiful Russian model. The shop was a glamour emporium full of make-up and sparkly garments and I noticed that some of the clothes were displayed on shop dummies whose heads were those of terracotta warriors. I liked these and showed my appreciation by buying some hair slides for my daughters and hoped that in some small way I was making a contribution to Tanya's wages.

But it was food and not hair slides that I craved and here at last was what I wanted. Shaanxi restaurants are easily spotted by the strings of chilis that hang outside. The hot pepper of Shaanxi is red, long and has a sharp head and is added to most dishes as hot pepper oil. It is best avoided before an overnight trip with stinky Chinese train toilets. I was tempted by a dish of Paomo stew of steamed bread noodles and cooked in lamb broth which is traditionally served in a big porcelain bowl. I've had Paomo before and know that however hard you try, it's nearly impossible to finish more than a quarter of the bowl and this always recommends it to me, but the weather was too hot for a huge steaming bowl of stew so I grabbed a Guokui wok cake of wheat flour dough for the journey. These are the size of the lead or iron wok in which they are baked, a plain and simple snack that is supposed to represent the lack of sophistication and big-heartedness of the Shaanxi people themselves, (tell that to the heart attack man on the highway). I had this with biang biang noodles which are extraordinarily thick and can be up to a metre long and wound like coiled serpents on my plate, next to the huge bready mound of Guokui. Noodles and bread; a real taste of Shaanxi and I would be suitably sustained for the long journey ahead, though less adventurous and exciting perhaps than the spicy sheep's feet or the goats brains available in the Moslem quarter close by.

The most fascinating and exciting thing about my noodles was that the character for biang is the most complicated in the whole Chinese dictionary. Chinese characters are drawn by a series of strokes of the brush or pen from the most simple which have just one stroke to the more complicated that can be 10 strokes or more. It's a beautiful but amazingly complicated and regimented system of writing that must be the curse of every Chinese schoolchild's life since all have to be learned and in precisely the right stroke order. Thus the name for China is 'Zhongguo' which means 'Middle country' and is written like this;

中 国

'Zhong' is five strokes of the pen and 'guo' is nine.

I spent a year learning about 200 Chinese characters but my efforts slackened off because;

a) I discovered you need to know at least two thousand in order to be able to read a newspaper

b) if I missed even a day's practice, I began to forget everything I had learned

c) I was spending so much time rehearsing characters that I began to lose contact with my friends and family.

So, like a true pampered middle-class Western I gave up. This is not an option for one billion Chinese and I'm sure that the sheer bloody-minded perseverance and discipline needed to learn to write in China contributes to the rote learning, unimaginative style of teaching that is often the norm here. This in turn might lead to a sometimes blinkered approach to life, lacking in spontaneity. So political repression, lack of personal freedom, mass conformity and self-discipline is all down to those pesky characters. The leadership recognised that character learning might be a contributory factor in high levels of illiteracy in China and considered romanising and abandoning the system in the 1950s but in the end, for better or worse, the traditionalists won out.

The character for biang is 57 strokes. And the word is written twice so that's 114 strokes for a bowl of noodles which seems a lot, even if they are a metre long. Characters are not the only confusing factor in the language of course. Foreigners who choose only to speak and not write and thus don't have to wrestle with 57 stroke characters still have tones to contend with. Standard Putonghua Chinese has five basic tones; rising, high-level, falling, neutral and the uniquely complicated and confusing falling then rising tone. Thus every word has potentially five meanings depending on how you say it. The classic example to illustrate this to foreigners embarking on an attempt to learn Chinese is enough to kill their nascent enthusiasm stone dead.

It goes like this; 'mama ma man ma ma', which means; mother scolds the slow horse? Each 'ma' has a different tone and therefore a different meaning. Or there is 'si shi si, shi shi shi, shi si shi shi si, si shi si shi si shi si' which means 'four is four, 10 is 10, 14 is 14, 44 is 44'; a uniquely confusing and altogether useless phrase.

The same tongue tying principles are true of Shaanxi province whose name means 'West of the Mountains'. But neighbouring Shanxi province means 'west of the Mountains' too, but because tone marks are not written when Chinese is translated into Romanised pinyin script, the names have to be written differently because their tones are different. Shaanxi is a falling/rising tone so it gets two letter A's, while flat level Shanxi gets just one. It's all very confusing and gives me a heaadaache.

My departure from Xi'an station was the most chaotic yet. I had a precious soft sleeper ticket thanks to the queuing skills of my hired hand but decided that if I paid someone to buy my ticket and waited in the soft sleeper lounge, I was hardly experiencing the real China at all; I might as well be carried through the streets in a palanquin, wearing a pith helmet and grumbling about the bloody natives.

So I queued with the hard seat passengers and by the time I was having regrets and looking longingly at the sofas in the lounge, it was too late and I was being carried along with the surging crowd as the guards flung open the gates. This was worrying and yet wildly exhilarating. Passengers threw their bags, boxes of dried noodles and children over the fence and trampled over and called each other in the wild and desperate response to the Chinese command 'all aboard'.

I put aside my British 'after you' reserve and trampled and crawled with them. Using an old Shaanxi granny for purchase, I launched into the sanctity of the crisp white sheets and lace curtains of soft sleeper. This carriage was unique in my experience since it was coupled to a hard seat one and this was the first time I'd seen the full horror of a Chinese train's lowest fare. Most passengers weren't seated at all but were crammed into the passageway and the more unfortunate actually had their face and hands pressed to the glass at the door separating me from them. No wonder they ran for the train if the penalty for tardiness was standing like this 12 hours. I went to bed with a dull sense of guilt but was soon sleeping the clickety-clack slumber of a blameless child.

By the morning everything had changed. The sun streamed through the window onto my sleeper class vase of plastic flowers and outside the raggedy suburbs and Ming walls of Xi'an were replaced by the dry and primitive loess plateau of Northern Shaanxi. These low hills with dry gullies are the consistency of crumbly cheese and must be the same hills that Gladys Aylward led her happy band of orphans over in 1940 on her way from the Inn of the Sixth Happiness to Xi'an in order to escape the advancing Japanese. Such heroism must have felt like child's play to Gladys after she had mastered the tones and characters of Chinese in the years before.

Conquering Japanese aren't the only disaster to have befallen this part of China. On 23 November 1556 the most deadly earthquake in history hit Shaanxi. The quake supposedly killed 830,000 people which is way, way in excess of its nearest rival for deadliness, the 1976 Chinese earthquake at Tangshan where a mere 250,000 perished (see Tianjin chapter). We have quite detailed accounts of the quake from the scholar Qin Keda who describes mountains shifting and rivers changing course. Qin concludes that lives are best saved in an earthquake if people stay indoors and crouch in a safe place, rather than run outside to be swallowed by chasms or hit by debris. This prescient advice is still followed today, though in some parts of Shaanxi where 60% of the population died, there was little hope of escaping death at all.

Yan'an has a new and very expensive train station that was empty and forlorn on the day that I arrived. I don't know what the Chinese expression for 'white elephant' is but this station seemed excessively large for a town that has probably had its day. Yan'an is one of the key revolutionary sites in China along with Mao's birthplace. Millions flooded here during the 1960s but the number has reduced to a trickle as the Chinese economy has grown and interest in the austerity and heroism of the revolution has waned.

There is a strong puritanical streak to Mao's revolt and nowhere is that spirit of self-sacrifice and self regard more evident than in the story of the Long March. This was an epic communist journey in 1934 and 1935 of 25,000 li or eight thousand miles from their base in Jiangxi in the south of China to the relative safety of Yan'an in the North. The communists were fleeing their nationalist enemy Chang Kai-shek who tidied away his pyjamas and put in his false teeth and harassed them all the way over the mountains and torrents of Guizhou and Sichuan and through the deserts and grasslands of Gansu to Shaanxi.

Only 10,000 of the 100,000 communists who began the march made it to Yan'an, but no matter a legend had been born and no communist could hope to achieve high office in China after the revolution unless he had been part of this monumental hike. Mao called the march 'a manifesto' since it 'proclaimed to the world that the Red Army is an army of heroes, while the imperialists and their running dogs Chiang Kai-shek and his like are impotent'. He's probably right when he claims that the march did more than anything to spread the message of communism, since 200 million saw the marchers go past and had contact with this army who were deliberately polite, civil and kind. They helped with the harvest, fetched water and left pictures of Karl Marx behind.

Yet Mao had a complicated march. He was carried for much of it but still got very ill. He abandoned his infant child in Yunnan province, met a new wife (the notorious Jiang Qing who went on to terrorise China during the Cultural Revolution) and hugely overstated the length of the march which was actually more like four thousand miles than eight thousand.

Nevertheless it remains an impressive achievement and is certainly a more romantic route to power than that taken by baby kissing, vote grubbing, modern Western democratic politicians. The town that the bedraggled and exhausted remnants of the communist army shuffled into must have been a shock to the survivors of the march. Yan'an is a dusty and nondescript place with an end of the world feel and must have seemed very different to the lush greenery, gushing streams and verdant hills of Jiangxi from where they had departed a year before.

But the Red Army made the best of it, settled down to life in local yaodong caves and plotted their return to Jiangxi, Beijing and every other part of China. There are three main revolutionary sites in Yan'an and it's possible to see in these a gradual settling in, slippers under the bed approach to life for the communists here. The first, in the centre of town called Fenghuangshan is the most basic. The wooden beds and draughty caves here seem small comfort after marching so far, but the gang soon moved out of town to Yangjialing where the caves are more spacious and finally to Wangjiaping to live in relative luxury in real houses with bathrooms and not a cave in sight.

Yangjialing is the key revolutionary site because the Red Army spent the most time here and it was here also that Mao was anointed the official, undisputed leader of the party. I really liked the place and unlike many historical remains it took little effort to imagine what had happened here. The hall where the seventh national plenum met to elect Mao as party leader is built of plain stone and sits squarely in the centre of the complex. Inside, rows of wooden benches are lined up in front of the stage where a wooden lectern is framed by badly drawn pictures of Marx, Lenin and Stalin next to black-and-white photos of Mao preaching from the very same lectern in the very same hall in front of the massed ranks of hand clapping cadres who are seated on the very same benches.

Thrillingly, I was able to recreate this picture and for an outlay of 10 yuan I was given a Red Guard uniform and a wooden gun and the opportunity to be Chairman Mao. This caused a remarkable degree of excitement amongst the few other visitors at Yangjialing that day who ran to stand next to me while their friends took photo after photo. I asked one man to explain this degree of interest and he replied that everyone thought it was funny since I didn't look like Chairman Mao at all. I liked the idea of these tourists laughing at my picture as they showed friends in living rooms in Shaanxi, Beijing and Shanghai.

Mao lived for years in Yangjialing in a traditional yaodong cave, a short walk from the assembly Hall. The rest of the communist leadership were his neighbours in caves of their own and they might have lived a rather convivial and bucolic existence here if they didn't have the Japanese to fight and a revolution to win. Myth and legend surrounds Yan'an almost as much as the Long March. It was here that the party was retrained and re-equipped and here the successful revolution of 1949 was made possible. The Chinese view Yan'an as something noble and pure; a community based on fraternity and equality. Here women's feet were unbound and peasants toiled for the community rather than for a landlord. Here Mao wrote poetry and inspiring revolutionary texts that were compiled into the Little Red Book 25 years later.

It's not just Chinese writers who have created this golden view of Yan'an. An American journalist called Edgar Snow was here too and his 500 page book 'Red Star over China' played a vital role in swaying western and Chinese opinion in favour of Mao. Snow perfectly captures the enthusiasm of the early revolutionaries on the Long March and at Yan'an and was particularly enamoured with the leadership of Mao who he conversed with on a number of occasions. But Snow's glasses are excessively rose tinted. In fact Yan'an was a microcosm of what the whole of China later became; a closely controlled and policed state with a powerful leadership whose revolutionary credentials were not to be questioned. It was at Yan'an that Mao launched his rectification movement, a campaign that killed 10,000 people accused of being 'intellectuals', though Mao didn't bury them alive as Qin Shi Huangdi had.

It is questionable whether Yan'an was a communist utopia, just as it is doubtful that the Long March was as far or heroic as the communists claim. But the reality hardly matters at all and the romantic perception and brave story of remote Yan'an has become an integral part of the mythology of the ruling party. I was not immune and romanticism is probably the reason why I had taken the long journey from Xi'an the day before.

The caves where the leadership lived, cut into the hillside above Yan'an are austere just as communist homes should be. There were a few people milling around and spitting on the floor outside the yaodong of the future Premier and Deputy Party Leader Zhou Enlai and Liu Shaoqi but it was Mao's cave that was drawing the crowds. I wandered reverently where the great man had sat at his desk and written his obscure political polemics and past the window seat where he had written more. Mao's literary output was so prodigious at Yan'an that it seems he must never have slept, yet the huge bed in the next room was evidence enough that even revolutionary messiahs need their shuteye. The bed was cordoned off, presumably to deny tourists the ultimate souvenir snapshot. Visitors had endeavoured to pay tribute to Mao by throwing cigarettes onto the bed and there was a generous pile of fags on pillow and counterpane. Mao was a heavy smoker and I'm sure this is what he would have wanted.

The very act of being in dusty and distant Yan'an had encouraged me to feel that I deserved lunch in the town's swankiest hotel. The bean sprouts and mutton were good but here I was subjected to more furious Chinese staring from my waitress who stood close to my elbow and watched every mouthful as I crunched self-consciously and smiled weakly at her. Back outside the sun was crushingly hot and a group of children followed me openmouthed down the street. Yan'an was wearing me down because I was such a novelty here, though I felt certain that more Western tourists would surely come when they heard of the opportunity to dress as a Red Guard and fling cigarettes on to Mao's mattress.

How much more difficult it must have been for the early Western visitors to the town. Notable among these was the Canadian surgeon Norman Bethune who arrived at Yan'an with his mobile blood transfusion unit in 1938 and saved communist and Japanese lives on the battlefield before he succumbed to blood poisoning in 1939. Mao turned his prodigious pen to the life of the doctor in his essay 'In memory of Norman Bethune' which became required reading in Chinese elementary schools during the Cultural Revolution. 'We must all learn the spirit of absolute selflessness from him' wrote Mao 'with this spirit everyone can be helpful to each other. Bethune became one of the few Westerners commemorated in China and buried at the Revolutionary Martyrs' Cemetery in Shijiazhuang (see Hebei chapter). In 2006 the socialist doctor completed his journey from Ontario Canada to national Chinese hero when a 20 part drama series about his life aired on Chinese TV made with a budget of 30 million yuan, the most expensive Chinese TV series to date.

My pre-teen following lost interest in the foreigner and veered off into a small primary school and I decided to follow them. Class had begun and they were late but tailing a Westerner was probably excuse enough and they ran laughing to their seats as I followed them in. Of course wandering into a lesson would be an unwelcome intrusion in some countries but rural China is nothing if not welcoming and hospitable to guests and I was soon adding value to the lesson by conducting the kids in an English rendition of 'two little dickie birds sitting on a wall' (with actions). So many students in one class, the children were crammed in behind small wooden desks with snotty noses and the teacher looked worn down by their exuberance.

The teacher in the next classroom seemed to be running a tighter ship and here the children were silent and attentive as she paced the room. A pigtailed girl was singled out to write some characters on the board but she stumbled over the complexities of all those strokes. Whack! The stern mistress had improvised a length of plastic tubing as a memory aid and brought it down sharply on the girl's shoulder as penance for her mistake. I gave a start and turned away but didn't feel appalled as perhaps I should, for why should a child centred, group work Western liberal teaching and learning environment be applicable to remote and rural Northern Shanxi, especially when there are all those characters to be learned?

I finished in Yan'an by taking a taxi up the shattered and dusty loess hill to the Song Dynasty pagoda that has become a symbol of the revolution. The wheezing vehicle inspired little confidence and after three failed attempts at the steep road, the driver reluctantly gave up the fare and left me to walk to the summit alone.

The view was hardly inspiring from here and Yan'an looked dusty and decrepit, the Yan River a non event through the centre of town. To the north there was more dust and hills all the way to Inner Mongolia, the view peppered with cave dwellings. Bleak and brown to be sure, but I liked Yan'an for its remoteness and lack of pretension and as I scanned the horizon, there was a patch of colour at last; a crimson square of revolutionary flag flapping in a hot desert breeze over this distant town where modern China began.

CHONGQING

重庆

82 400 km sq
Population 32 Million

*'Eating highly seasoned food is unhealthful, because it stimulates
too much, provokes the appetite too much, and often is indigestible.'*

'Miss Beecher's Domestic Recipe-Book' (1846)

Chongqing was covered in bright red Chinese flags when I arrived,
though they did not flutter in the azure firmament of a downtown
Yangtze River sky but hung limp and dirty in the dish cloth air of this
notoriously polluted and fogbound town.

There were certainly a *lot* of flags though. Big bold statements of loyalty outside factories and offices, flags hanging from broom handles tied to air conditioning units and railings, flags fluttering behind taxis and bikes and tiny scraps of red, barely visible behind grimy tenement windows or plastered to roadside trolleys where giant superheated woks made breakfast for Communists hurrying ravenously to work.

Chongqing feels especially pleased with herself since this strategic place confined to the peninsula of land between the Yangtze and Jialing rivers played an important role in recent Chinese history. Mao and his great Nationalist rival Chiang Kai-Shek met here in 1945 to discuss the division of spoils after the defeat of Japan; the communists had done the bulk of the fighting and Chiang's Nationalists had cowered while the Japanese dropped bombs 218 times on the river junction of their remote wartime capital. But Chiang had no desire for compromise and Mao returned to the mountains grumbling that he had won the war but his rival wanted to return and harvest peaches. He massed his troops, drew up a plan of campaign and launched a civil war for which Chinese flag manufacturers are forever grateful.

I arrived in the city with 23 bright and eager students in tow and as a consequence had the services of a coach and driver and two guides, which grated terribly against my usual go where I want when I want free-spirited self-reliance. In China I can pull out a book and sit by a stream or eat food with a stranger outside a noodle bar with suspect health and safety certification whenever I like. I can jump on a clapped-out bus with locals going home from market and watch dusty villages slide past the window and wave to children playing with car tyres in cabbage fields. I'm a traveler not a tourist and wherever I lay my hat, that's my home. I'm Willy Loman. I'm Marco Polo. I'm Jack Kerouac. I'm Genghis Khan.

Except having a guide turned out to be rather nice. In Chongqing I didn't fight the queues in a hopelessly overcrowded train station, or walk the hard shoulder of a busy main road where my bus had un-expectedly turfed me out. I didn't get scalped by taxi drivers whose meters were perpetually broken. I didn't get turned away from a hotel because I wasn't Chinese. Above all, with a guide I was able to meet the people of China and have a conversation with them that amounted to more than a discussion of the weather and an apology that my Chinese is so bad.

The response to this is always 'No, you speak Chinese very well' to which I say 'No really it is very bad, but you are very kind'. But my guide who met us at the airport didn't take part in this traditional social dance when I told him his English was very good. "I know" he grinned and hurried us across the road to the waiting coach.

When we left Hong Kong the sky was brilliant blue and for a while I believed that we would see Chongqing in sunshine. We watched the in-flight information on the prevention of swine flu but the hard-hitting message regarding correct disposal of tissues and the social morality of covering your face when sneezing was somewhat undermined by a badly drawn cartoon pig whose thoroughly immoral coughing and sneezing caused no end of amusement to everyone on board. By the time Pigsy had finished his polemic, the clouds outside were as thick and impenetrable as the 'strong nasal mucus flow' that he had cautioned us against.

Our guide introduced himself as Steven, though his Chinese name translated as White Snow Forest, so he was inevitably known as Snow White. The other guide was from Chongqing since the local accent is so strong that even Snow White would struggle to understand it. His name was Jade King, but told us to call him Eric.

Eric swayed and tottered at the front of the coach as we drove into town and told us everything he thought we needed to know about Chongqing. The city's name was given by the 12th century Emperor Zhaodian and means 'double celebration'. The city is surrounded by high mountains which is why it has so much fog. The city is known as 'Mountain City'. The city is known as 'Fog City'. The city has 42 bridges across its rivers. The city is known as 'Bridge City'. Summer temperatures in the city are regularly over 40°C. The city is known as 'Oven City'.

I had heard this last one before. Chongqing is one of three 'furnaces' in China along with Wuhan and Nanjing further east on the Yangtze, where high temperatures and crashing humidity make them the worst places on earth to take a summer vacation. Yet Eric was phlegmatic about all this, since people from Chongqing were 'born to climb mountains' which I took to be a comment on their spiritual as well as geographical prowess. The fog lent the city drama and what are baking summers and freezing winters to people who have such fine cuisine?

He handed me a moon cake as he explained, that sickly sweet and barely edible Chinese autumn delicacy that became the second one I had surreptitiously binned in a single day after I had bitten into one presented during Porky pig's swine flu prevention advice and concluded they taste no better at 20,000 feet than sea level.

Eric saved his trump card for last, and what ample compensation it was for the citizens of a town whose weather, pollution and brute ugliness might otherwise make it a singularly unpleasant place to live. For Chongqing has the most beautiful girls in China. This, Eric opined, is down to the health giving properties of the local spicy food and from walking up and down all those hills, which presumably gives them pert bosoms, flat tummies and buns of steel.

Such declarations exist all over China. Every city, province and municipality lays claim to girls that are best because the water is pure, the air clear, the hills steeper, the rice good or because they dance, sing, farm, cook, make revolution or love better than anywhere else. Such postulations are utterly unquantifiable of course but it's boundlessly interesting that across China this was one of the first things I was regularly told.

Eric's eulogy was tempered with caution. "The local girls are very fierce", he warned. This was also a consequence of the spicy food and meant that men did all the housework in Chongqing and obey their wives who twist the ears of husbands who refuse to submit, which is why Chongqing men are known as 'soft ears' elsewhere in China.

Eric was unmarried which explained why his ears were so straight, but should he ever decide to throw his lot in with a hill climbing, chili chomping, angry Chongqing girl he would be spoiled for choice. The town's population since becoming the fourth city to achieve independent prefecture status in 1997 is 32 million. By some reckoning this makes Chongqing the largest city in the world, spread over an area that is the size of Belgium - a lowland country that has become the standard unit of measurement for all such useless facts. China is full of such sprawling towns - there are 90 cities spread across the country with a population that exceeds one million and almost every provincial capital has a population that is bigger than London or Paris. Yet who outside China has heard of Chongqing, Changsha, Shijiazhuang, Kunming, Wuhan or Chengdu? Unfortunately the average Chinese megalopolis has been modernised and transformed and polluted to a depressing degree of bland uniformity and as I journeyed from province to province it sometimes became difficult to distinguish one city from another.

Not only does Chongqing have beautiful girls, it has the Yangtze River. By the time we reached the centre the fog had become more dense and turned to light drizzle and I was congratulating myself on how good it was to see the city in proper Chongqing weather and pretending that I was glad it wasn't sunny. There, below one of Chongqing's 42 bridges, unmistakable through the fog, were the wide waters of the river. Polluted no doubt and tamed by the dam hundreds of kilometres downstream, the river looked sluggish and grey. But this was still the Yangtze; the water that the Chinese call The Long River or just The River, that flows over six thousand kilometres through the heart of China and I felt an irrepressible thrill as it slid below.

We had come to this town because of this river. This is the same for all visitors to the city and everywhere we went in Chongqing, making- the- best-of-it-foreigners wandered foggy streets and through vast crowds marveling at the colossal ugliness of the place, as they killed time and wondered why they had come and waited for their Yangtze cruise to begin.

The city is not without interest; you just have to dig a bit deeper than in Beijing or Shanghai. Eric warned that Chongqing would be a 'sea of people' on this holiday week and the town centre was filled with Chinese tourists who followed tour guide flags, poked my face with umbrellas and laughed uproariously, enjoying themselves in the way that only people who get scant time off from work each year can. These families had come to see the river too, though their boats were rusty and workmanlike and not the huge white floating hotels that foreigners were ready to drift away on.

We dived into the urban planning centre; a rather prosaic name for an exhibit of massive scale models of the city that are really rather good, especially when a man flicked a switch and hundreds of tiny lights came on in flats and offices and on the tiny boats that travel up and down stream. They should rename this place and the crowds would roll in, especially those who spent their holidays at British seaside resorts in the 1950s and enjoy a nice model village, though for added authenticity staff could pump in fog to obscure most of the model for two thirds of the year and in summer transfer the whole exhibit to a local steam bath.

The museum attendant insisted that the displays were an 'urban picture scroll' and not a model village and on hearing I'm from England told me that Chongqing is twinned with Leicester in the Midlands, though he pronounced it as Lye-chester. "I think Lye-chester's traffic is extremely convenient" he declared; traffic flow is another great conversation starter across China and right up there with the relative attraction of females.

The information board by the urban picture scroll said that Chongqing has 'great cohesion and radiation force'. I don't know if this is true, but gazing at the model and trying to guess when the lights would go on and off, it was possible to see just how strategically important the city is. Chongqing is built on a narrow finger of land where the Jialing River - a massive waterway in its own right - joins the third largest river in the world. This river junction must have made an easy target for those Japanese wartime raids and now serves as a vital point for Yangtze trade and tourism. Dozens of boats were moored or circled the steps down to Chaotianmen docks, and if anywhere can be said to be the cultural and geographical centre of a city of 32 million people, this is it.

The steps down to the riverside are shallow, but there are a lot of them which is why Chongqing is famous for its Bang Bang army. There are 100,000 of these men with few skills and minimal education, who have picked up the cheapest of tools - a bamboo pole or 'bang bang' and some rope - and hang around the city's docks, markets and bus stations ready to carry a load.

Similar jobs involving brute strength have disappeared from China, banned by the Communists as demeaning feudal practice. Only tourists ride rickshaws and the drivers snigger at the price they charge, but

Bang Bang men are still considered a necessity in Chongqing. This is because there are so many goods arriving and disembarking in this river town and so many hills and stairs which make it difficult to transport anything, even over a very short distance.

So Chongqing is one of the few Chinese cities where I saw no bicycles and where men with bamboo poles lurk on street corners as beasts of burden. A Bang Bang soldier will carry anything and charges between five and 20 yuan for a load, depending on size and distance traveled. I saw a few baskets of eggs, bundles of newspaper five yuan loads, some live pig, and TV set 10 yuan loads and a fridge freezer 20 yuan load that was not carried by pole at all but slung on the back of a Bang Bang man while another soldier helped balance the weight.

This is no way to scratch a living and rather than looking muscular and powerful from their bamboo exertions, the Bang Bang soldiers look worn out. They're all underfed, bedraggled skin and bones under cheap clothes - how could they be anything else on five to 20 yuan a load? They're mostly economic migrants and I wondered how poor their previous existence must have been to drive them to the fog and the rain and the furnace of Chongqing where the eternal muddy river brings endless goods to be carried up endless stairs. But like so many of China's oppressed and disadvantaged, the Bang Bang soldiers retain a cheerful optimism and treat their bamboo calloused shoulders as a badge of honour, for what would be the point of carrying the weight of the world aswell as their bang bang pole?

The life of a Chongqing porter has improved since the government introduced free primary school education for their children and free skill training for their wives. He is also unlikely to go hungry since the street food that can be found all over China is especially cheap in Chongqing. There's the usual selection of youtiao fried bread sticks and noodles and some shrimp dumplings, limp and incongruous so far from the sea. But in Chongqing, hot pot is king.

I've eaten hot pot on a hot summer evening in Hebei where diners took their shirts off and encouraged me to do the same. I've also eaten it in Xinjiang where a sheep's head bubbled in a voodoo cauldron and looked at me with lidless eyes and grinning teeth, but Chongqing is the ultimate hot pot challenge. To say Chongqing huoguo is spicy is to do it a disservice. Spicy is the pepperoni on a pizza in front of a Sunday afternoon football game or the hottest house curry on a trying to impress the new receptionist Friday night out from work. Chongqing hotpot is death-defyingly, supernaturally hot. Medical emergency hot. Armageddon hot. The first symptoms are quite normal but quickly develop into a physical discomfort unlike anything I have felt before or since.

I was soon sweating and wondering why my tongue felt so big and why I could hear a strange rushing sound like water in my ears as I spooned more napalm into my mouth, though I experienced a sort of relief as my lips and even my teeth turned numb and the pain subsided. By the time I'd finished, my face was buzzing and vibrating and felt like it no longer belonged to me.

This all begs the question why locals want their food so hot that their mouth feels disembodied from their head and even at this early stage I was already concerned how the hot pot would interact with another of my orifices at a later stage. Eric explained with ineffable logic that huoguo was a cooling food, especially in the hot summer months when it was good to sweat and that next time I should really try hotpot made from buffalo stomach which was certainly the best.

I didn't tell Eric, but there wasn't going to be a next time. Huoguo is probably a ritual; an ordeal by fire that a true Chongqing local must negotiate. Or maybe it's a definition of the uniqueness, the resilience and the endurance of a people who tamed the river and sit at a crossroads in the heart of China and who count themselves as from neither north or south, east or west. Or it could be still that you get used to it, just as you get used to the fog and 32 million people and to a city that has so little beauty but is your home.

Actually I did eat hotpot again but in a sadly compromised form. Away from the chaotic food carts on waterfront steps where Bang Bang soldiers fill their bellies and numb their pain, it is possible to buy a bastardized dish called yuanyang that is divided like a yin and yang symbol into spicy and mild. But even this became too much for me and I was soon telling vendors or anyone who cared to listen that I was 'pa la', literally 'scared of spice' and dreaming of a nice bowl of chicken soup.

We left central Chongqing for the nearby district of Ciqikou where our hostel was perched on the riverside and I could sit on the balcony trying to spot the other river bank through the mist. I wanted to stay longer, count the boats on the river and watch the Bang Bang men whose feet slapped on stone steps as they shouldered their loads. I wanted to ask Eric to ask them what their lives were like and could I hold a pole for a moment and feel how smooth and worn it had become under those gnarled fingers. But our driver was gunning his engine and sending more clouds into a sky that already smelled of diesel, so I wouldn't even have time to see the city at night. The municipal government website raves about Chongqing after dark when 'myriad twinkling lights greet the eyes.... like bright pearls forming another Milky Way', a hotpot of mixed metaphors damning with faint praise a city that is best seen after dark.

Chongqing was charming once and Ciqikou or 'porcelain city', where pots and vases were produced and sent down river, is the only reminder of the Qing dynasty town that once surrounded Chaotianmen. We drove there past diao jiao lou houses that stood on stilts by the riverside and had miraculously escaped the re-planning of the city that races on at such a rapid, face numbing pace. Ciqikou was busy with crowds and the cries of shopkeepers who were trying to out shout each other and banging drums or blowing horns to get my attention. But there were Qing Dynasty flagstones beneath my feet and the squat wood and stone buildings rose no higher than two floors above my head. As I gazed into the inky blackness of the river after dark, Ciqikou had its own myriad of twinkling lights as locals sucked the last vestiges of enjoyment from their holiday and launched red candle lit paper lanterns into the night sky.

Eric went home for the night and the students retired to bed, presumably exhausted by spicy food and the sight of beautiful women marching up and down hills clutching their husbands' ears. So I sat up late with the receptionist and Snow White and drank Chongqing beer whose claim to be 'made from pure and fresh Yangtze water' seemed a contradiction in terms. Snow White was from Beijing and Chongqing must have felt like a foreign country to him too, but the fuwuyuan in charge of the lobby was a typically feisty and rather beautiful local.

Miss Yang also failed to conform to the usual Chinese pleasantries and told me my language was not so good. I remarked that she must be one of those angry Chongqing women that I had heard about. 'Yes' she replied 'and I smoke and drink and I'm a lesbian too', as if this was further evidence of her rage.

Snow White was excessively proud of China and showed me pictures of the National Day Parade that had celebrated 60 years of Communist rule. His pictures were rooftop shots of distant aerial military hardware and not the parade itself since attendance had been by invitation only. Ordinary Beijingers were invited only to stay at home and given the veiled threat that their presence on the streets would constitute a security risk.

So Snow White had watched it all on TV, like hundreds of millions of other Chinese and told me the sight of all those rocket launchers, tanks, goose-stepping soldiers and cheering children had made him shed tears of pride. It's very tempting to mock this fervour with a jaundiced western eye, and certainly goose-stepping soldiers have a very different connotation for me. But it's also refreshing to connect with enthusiastic and popular patriotism since in England, flag waving and love of country have long since been appropriated by football hooligans and the far right. Such nationalistic fervour can easily spill into territorial aggression and blinkered superiority - ask any Tibetan about this - but Snow White is an educated and literate adult, a representative of a new generation of Chinese not unlike the middle classes in the West. It's just that, like most of his peers, he had retained an exuberant faith in the merits of his own country.

But he could be sceptical too. Snow White told me a joke that night in the bar that seemed almost subversive;

There were four men - one from England, one from Africa, one from China and one from the USA. A reporter asked them a question;

'What is your opinion about the food shortages in the rest of the world?'

'What are shortages?' replied the Englishman

'What is food?' replied the African

'What is opinion?' asked the man from China

'What is the rest of the world?' wondered the American

What a punchline! Snow White knew his country's shortcomings, yet in the next moment grabbed my pen as I drew a map of China on the back of a coaster, to sketch in the province I had missed. For to him and every Chinese, Taiwan is indisputably and irrevocably part of China, and its continued separation from mainland control is no laughing matter.

An acceptance of the party line seems unshakeable in most Chinese, for who would question a government that in 60 years has changed the nation so completely? From a failed state in 1949, China's transformation has been breathtaking. Total GDP has risen to 30,000 billion yuan, per capita totals from 216 to 19,000. Life expectancy has risen, illiteracy has fallen. China has to be understood in the context of these overwhelming numbers; the marching soldiers and celebrations are for the Chinese people, why should foreigners understand? For all its problems, the revolution has succeeded. The people are proud. China has stood up.

Ciqikou is surrounded by evidence of past humiliations that make China's current progress and strength more pleasing still. The porcelain port is bounded by the river and surrounded by small mountains that are said to provide perfect feng shui. But Chongqing was the wartime capital where the Nationalists retreated and left Beijing, Shanghai and Nanjing to the ravages of the Japanese Kwantung army. It was in these hills called Gele Mountain that the government imprisoned 300 Communists and tortured and killed all but 20 of them during the war. The nearby Stilwell Museum commemorates American involvement and assistance in the war, though no doubt it's gratifying to be reminded by the marching National Day military that China craves assistance from no one in modern day conflicts.

The suburbs of Chongqing stretched interminably but after three hours of road, the hills were stripped of high-rises and we were in the countryside where blue sky, forgotten like a rumour in Chongqing, broke the monotony of grey. Larks ascended over leafy ginkgo trees, the fruit of which is a cure for cancer. It was all achingly verdant and bucolic after the grind of the city, though the sign as we approached Dazu - 'Legal laws promote countryside, depend on law to preserve harmony' - reminded us that this pleasantness and this concord would not be possible without rigorous application of the rule of law.

Dazu is an ancient town in the west of Chongqing near the border of Sichuan, that massive and populous province from which Chongqing was ripped in 1997. There are 50,000 rock carvings here dating back to the seventh century Tang Dynasty, though most were created during the 12th century under the stewardship of a local monk called Zhao Zifeng.

Our coach was an aberration in this small town and we left it by the edge of an escarpment where the land plunged away and rose up again in a series of hills that rolled away for dozens of miles to the malignant smog of Chongqing. The town was alive with the bustle of market. Cages of innocent wide eyed beasts lined the pavement unaware of their cooking pot destiny. There were rabbits and chickens here and plump guinea fowl, spherical and ridiculous; my students cooed and sighed over them and declared it a shame that they had to die.

We later ate at one of these restaurants where we were fed huge quantities of delicious meat and boiled rice in a wooden pot bound by metal rings like an old ship's barrel. Meals were always plentiful and delicious on this guided tour (another inconvenience I didn't have to trouble myself with), though two problems occurred at every sitting. The first were the technical difficulties of eating food that was too big/ slimy/bony/tough to grab with a pair of slender bamboo chopsticks. Today's challenge was roasted pigs legs, trotter intact, covered in thick gravy which could be neither stabbed or ripped or lifted with any degree of success.

The second problem was the vegetarians in the party, whose number had increased out of solidarity for the rabbits outside. Waitresses respond with equanimity to such a request though vegetarianism is a puzzle to most Chinese; why wouldn't you eat meat when you can afford to?

So the chef acted like we must have been mistaken, the vegetarian dishes appeared and as a matter of course I tested them to see if there really was no meat in the bubbling soupy broth. As usual in this Dazu restaurant I tasted chicken or pork or beef and told the waitress that this really wasn't a vegetarian dish at all. As usual she was puzzled by my objection since it surely was vegetarian since it contained only a *little* bit of meat but she would take it away and laugh with the chef at the fussiness of foreigners who ate animals' food and had not even *touched* their pigs legs.

The carvings at Dazu are less ancient and formal than other more famous Chinese statues at Mogao and Datong in Gansu and Shanxi. There are impassive and grand Buddhas and Bodhisattvas here but there is everyday life and colours and comedy too. Stone cats chase petrified mice and an ancient buffalo that is led through the nose by a Buddhist shepherd is an allegory of man's inability to find his own way to redemption.

My students made appreciative noises about the art, the antiquity and the magnificence of the sculptures, though they looked puzzled when I pointed at a carving of a lorry and told them that this was Tang Dynasty too; the truck was actually added in the 1950s to celebrate China's industrial advance. Strange to think of visitors coming here and looking around then; surely they were all busy with making revolution on collective farms or forging backyard steel?

Everyone brightened up when we reached the huge carving for which Dazu is most famous. This is a Song Dynasty stone version of a Hieronymous Bosch painting - a vision of hell with a grizzly variety of punishments that serves as a warning to all those tempted to stray from the path of righteousness. Punishment is especially far reaching in Dazu's Hell. Drunkards are punished for sure, but so are those who persuade others to drink. Meat eaters suffer torment but so does the woman feeding chickens for market. The carving is unfinished so that people can wonder why, just as they should puzzle over the very meaning of Buddhism.

I revisited Buddhist torments in the vision of hell exhibition next to the restaurant while the meat eaters tried to pick up pigs legs with chopsticks and the vegetarians ate steamed rice. There are 18 layers of hell where sinners are boiled in oil, eaten by dogs and chopped at the knees and in this spectacularly bad exhibition I walked across the river to hell and from cobwebbed room to dungeon where jerky dummies performed unspeakable acts on each other and the air was filled with the screams of purgatory and coloured lights flashed on and off. Snow

447

White and Eric came with me and we marveled at the upside down dummy being sawn in half along his groin by a grinning demon and counted the devils that were missing their heads. We emerged blinking into sunlight, resolved to lead a better life and returned to the restaurant to try again with the pig and to drink Dazu beer.

Our hotel in Dazu was typically three star. The lobby was grand and contained all those items essential to the comfort of the Chinese traveller. Here was the business room with improbably slow internet connection, and electronic price board where rates bore no relation to reality. The rooms were predictably dreary and even the presidential suite listed at 6998 yuan per night will have had cigarette burns on the carpet. The ornamental fountain outside the revolving front door that no longer revolved was covered with a rusty brown algae growth.

I avoid bland provincial Chinese hotels at all costs and prefer the homely and cheaper surrounds of a hostel, but on this trip everything was booked and paid for. Three star breakfasts are a particularly distressing experience and contain a variety of chilies, vegetables and cuts of meat that are singularly unappealing at seven am. Limp fried eggs are another chopstick challenge and China can surely not claim to be a fully developed and sophisticated member of the family of nations until she is able to produce a hotel cup of coffee that doesn't taste like mud.

We left Dazu on one of those pointless three lane Chinese highways that has no cars and goes nowhere. Many of these rural strips have been re appropriated by locals and on this one, a farmer was leading his animals while others strolled along in the middle lane and were startled by the honk of our horn. This road was framed by a row of fancy solar lights in the shape of a delicate hand holding a lotus flower. The road didn't need these lights that stood only two metres apart and Eric asked me how much I thought they cost with one of those 'you're not gonna believe this' questions that are impossible to answer. "50 thousand yuan each" he exclaimed before I had chance to think of a sensible response. Clearly the civil servant responsible for these white elephants was getting a kickback from the company who provided the lights. The same back scratching system works all over China where roads like the one we were on are built and then dug up to provide money for construction firms, the very opposite of a free market economy.

The bureaucrats sometimes took the system of 'guanxi' a little too far; Chongqing was embroiled in a wave of corruption, gangsterism and arrests during my visit. The provincial governor was under investigation for taking 100 million yuan in bribes. Taxis, construction and markets were apparently all under the control of organised gangs though at least the Bang Bang soldiers were still free of corruption. Wen Qiang had been police chief of Chongqing for 16 years but he too was under arrest after he confessed to sex with underage girls and his enraged wife led investigators to his carefully wrapped stash of 20 million yuan hidden in a fish pond beside the new Chongqing airport express way. New police chief Wang Lijun was apparently incorruptible and local triads had put a 12 million yuan price on his head, though he joked that this was far more than his head was worth.

So the lotus flower solar lights were small fry indeed, though Snow White's patriotism rendered him uncomfortable discussing even this small scale dishonesty. Yet he was always able to temper his views with a moment of humour, a joke or a dash of cynicism. I asked him why such things happened and he replied 'T.I.C' - 'This is China'. He was right, for the normal rules and my Western preconceptions don't apply here. And 'T.I.C' became our set phrase, our rationalisation, our justification for all that was bizarre or unexpected on the rest of the trip.

Our dead end, million yuan asphalt stuttered to a halt by a small field. We clambered over drainage ditch and dry clods of earth to a tiny collection of stone dwellings less than half a mile from the road for which the village had no practical use at all. We had plunged into rural China where arrangements had been made to help on the farm and the students spent a couple of hours weeding and poking pathetically at the ground with a hoe, like city dwellers sent down to the country for re-education during the Great Leap Forward. Our task was to plant saplings which would be grown and sold to local governments furiously planting trees after years of deforestation all over China had led to catastrophic soil erosion and massive dust storms. Many of these trees had been lost to the furnaces that had sprung up across the nation when peasants had abandoned their fields and responded to Mao's call to make backyard steel. The making of metal was an act of revolution and many women sacrificed even their hair to the flames. But much of the steel was useless, the untended crops failed and China was plunged into a dark famine that may have killed 40 million people.

The men and women who chuckled at our feeble efforts in the field were true Chinese peasants for whom three star hotels and solar lights are an irrelevance and who might one day leave the labour of the land to carry loads from a bamboo pole in faraway Chongqing. They drank watery soup and enjoyed a break from routine, but stared with bemusement at these workers who giggled and farmed ineffectually and who chopped at the soil in sunglasses.

Two hours of manual labour was more than enough for us all and we strolled pleasantly through the village to an old house that stood alone by a bamboo grove and a gravestone for a departed pooch that read 'the first dog in all of China'. This was the home of Yang Yong Feng whose name means 'Forever Peak' and who greeted us in Zhongshan Mao jacket and slippers. He thought that he might be 79 years old and had been married to his wife for 60 years who now sat in the bare bones kitchen of the house. I'd said hello to Mrs Yang who had ignored me, but the old man explained this was because she was thoroughly deaf. Yang himself could only communicate with her now by cupping his mouth to her ear and bellowing loudly, so mostly they existed in a comfortable silence.

The house was basic in the extreme with outside squat toilet and the main room filled with a random collection of furniture, bicycle and a poster of Mao lopsided on the wall. The old man was eager to show his prize possession; an enormous pig in an outhouse that grunted and snuffled a wet nose and stank extravagantly, though these pig's legs were unlikely to land on a dinner table soon because he was Yang's sole asset, if you didn't count the Mao poster, and the old couple's existence balanced precariously on a guaranteed income pension of just one thousand yuan a month.

Here was a perfect opportunity at last to use the language skills of Eric and Snow White and I could barely contain my excitement at asking questions of this living relic of 20th century Chinese history. Yang was toothless and old but remarkably lucid on the experiences of his life. He answered my questions cheerfully, frequently bursting into gales of laughter as his wife sat on a stool and stared and wondered what we must be talking about.

Civil war and Cultural Revolution had passed by his village but such cataclysms had little interest to a poor man who had continued to farm while a nation was born. Mao's economic experiments of the late 1950s had been much more difficult. The Great Helmsman had announced his 'Great Leap Forward' in 1957, whose policies driven by wild urban ideology instead of peasant commonsense, had contributed to the terrible famine.

The old man told me that he had avoided the fate of 40 million of his countrymen and survived by eating bark off the trees and local clay that they called 'Goddess of Mercy earth'. This merciful mud had been too hard to digest for most, but Yang understood that if he ate only a very little he would gain some nourishment without his digestive tract and bowels seizing up. This is the context by which modern China must be judged. If things are still imperfect, they are at least better than they were and why wouldn't economic progress and security be important to a nation that was eating earth 50 years ago?

We waved goodbye to Yang who returned to his farm and to shouting at his wife after this brief day of difference in his long life. His four daughters and son had escaped their parents' primitive rural life many years before; Yang and his wife would soon die and their house would be swallowed up by urban sprawl and I wondered what would happen to their pig.

In less than five minutes easy stroll we were back amongst white tile, blue glass high-rises, motorbike showrooms and an inexplicable row of shops selling only mahjong tables and tiles - how many mahjong emporiums does a small town need?

We had a long drive to Wanzhou city, further east along the Yangtze River, with a stop at ancient Longxing village which turned out to be not ancient at all but almost entirely reproduced; an approximation of what the Chinese tourist board thought a Qing village should look like. This was where some of those Dazu mahjong tables finished up. Whole rooms of old men shouted and clattered tiles in the way that the Chinese call 'the twittering of sparrows' or played the quiet and to me utterly mysterious game called Sichuan poker with lollipop stick playing cards.

Back on the bus, Snow White told me that this had been a most unusual tour and quite unlike his usual trips to the Great Wall or Shanghai. These glimpses of rural China had been an eye-opener for a Beijing boy too and he explained that normally he deals with only two types of tourists - dabizi big nose foreigners and dabing big pancake locals, so-called because these tourists bring along their own cheap snacks to save money.

Snow White explained that dabizi and dabing require very different things from their tours; the Chinese desire structure and large groups and leaders with flags while foreigners prefer informality and small groups and to feel that they are at least attempting to see the 'real China' whatever that might mean. This dabizi tour of Bang Bang soldiers, old farmers, tree planting and Chongqing smog was rather difficult to categorise.

We stopped again at services outside Wanzhou and were approached by four soldiers who offered military grade binoculars to Snow White for the bargain price of two hundred yuan. We asked to see their ID but regretfully they couldn't show this to a foreigner because of the highly sensitive military information it contained and I wondered how many details of uranium tipped rockets and secret underwater tunnels to Taiwan could fit onto a small square of laminated plastic. But the binoculars were good and even had a crosshair with plane, helicopter and battleship on to confirm their authenticity, so Snow White handed over the cash.

We boarded the bus and Eric who was wise to this Chongqing chicanery laughed long and hard at Snow White's city boy naivete. Eric explained that these were no soldiers but a bunch of guys dressed in military fatigues out to make a fast buck from idiots like us on binoculars that were worth barely half the amount that Snow White had paid. How terrible to be deceived in this way, though as I thought of all the scams and the half-truths I had fallen for across a nation where a wealthy foreigner was usually seen as fair game, I was secretly pleased that for once it was the other guy who had been suckered by a Chinese deception.

Wanzhou was another sprawling and ugly town clinging to the banks of the Yangtze, like Chongqing in miniature. The city is closer to the huge and infamous Three Gorges Dam and the Yangtze here has doubled in size and looks more like a lake than a river. The riverside was probably once the most interesting part of town but all that was old has been submerged or ripped down and the only building of any antiquity that I could see was a 1920s clock tower close to the port where Yangtze passenger cruises depart.

We were going to catch one of these boats but not before circling the town several times in search of our restaurant. The driver grew increasingly frustrated by the directions given down the phone and was especially confused when he asked if we needed to cross the river. 'No, just the bridge' replied the helpful restaurateur. The restaurant was called 999 and I hoped that we wouldn't need emergency services after eating here, but the noodles, the duck and the tofu were delicious and things were becoming less spicy as we moved downstream. There were no cumbersome pig's legs here either, though the vegetarian dishes still contained thin slices of meat.

My students groaned with disappointment as I led them along the quay and past the luxury liners to our grubby Chinese vessel. I extolled the virtues of an authentic Chinese experience with real Chinese people but also looked longingly at the gleaming white ships and their white gloved waiters holding inauthentic trays of sundowner cocktails.

Our boat was packed to the gunnels with dabing tourists and we entered past a heaving and throbbing diesel engine that sweating men in white vests coaxed and cajoled with spanners and grease guns. The crew had been washing and we had to duck between waitress dresses and mechanic pants hanging from pipes and cables to find our sparse and utilitarian cabins. As leader of the tour I had been assigned a twin bed first class cabin all to myself; I threw down my bag and lay on the bed, luxuriating in the space and trying to ignore the strange fungal growth on the wall of the bathroom. Eric had left us and returned to Chongqing smog, but where was Snow White? I found him laying out a blanket on the deck with the other guides and was immediately thrown onto the horns of a moral dilemma as I thought of the empty bed in my first class room.

Reader, I did the right thing. But Snow White laughed when I removed my shirt and called me 'houzi' or monkey since I am hairier than the average Westerner and certainly more than any man from China, so I threatened to send him back to the deck where he belonged. I explained that hairy shoulders are a sign of great virility and strength of character and despite this shaky beginning, sharing turned out to be very pleasant. Snow White and I talked into the night and ended up back on deck, drinking beer and wrapped in jumper and hat against the cold air as a huge and yellow full moon rose above Wanzhou and the engines pulsed into life.

Just like Chongqing, Wanzhou looks better at night. Neon flickered on all over the hills and as we caught the Yangtze flow in midstream, the chaos of port and town seemed distant indeed. We rounded a bend, floating towards the Three Gorges and Hubei and as we passed under a high and sinuous bridge, a farewell writ large in neon reminded us we were leaving 'di yi chang', the first and best city in all of China. This is quite a claim for a dirty and nondescript port, whose main purpose was to hasten departure to somewhere better. Snow White glanced at me in the cold night air and laughed. 'T.I.C' he said, and passed me another beer.

XINJIANG

新疆

1 650 257 sq km
Population 19.63 million

`I have not told half of what I saw`

Marco Polo

Xinjiang is a land of superlatives. The hottest temperature ever recorded in China, the highest road in the world running south into Tibet and the second highest mountain in the world on the border with Kashmir[46] are all here and whilst in this land of extremes, I set my own

---

46   49.6 degrees centigrade, five thousand metres above sea level & K2

world record of most pistachio nuts consumed by one man in a single week.

It's also over one and a half million square km in size. This is about the same size as the whole of Western Europe where over 400 million Germans, French, Spanish, Italians and the rest drink beer, do unspeakable things to bulls, ride mopeds in expensive shoes with beautiful women down cobbled streets and beat the English at football. In Xinjiang province there are less than 20 million human beings which makes for a whole lot of emptiness; though here even the barrenness has a melancholy charm, even the bleakness has beauty.

'Province' is the wrong word of course. Xinjiang is an 'autonomous region' for the Moslem Uighur minority group and on arrival in the provincial capital Urumqi, I feel like Alice down the rabbit hole; mosques, madrasahs, minarets and mutton – I'm in China but it doesn't *feel* like China. Curiouser and curiouser.

There's a simple enough explanation for this; it's all down to rhubarb. Any self respecting adventurous traveler in China no longer ends their journey at the Great Wall in Beijing or the warriors in Xi`an, for today the Silk Road is where it's at; for this artery of trade through Xinjiang, where camels once padded across deserts and past oasis towns, through Persia and onto the Mediterranean at Antioch has a winning combination of drama, romance and excitement.

There's no doubt that silk has its place in history; Greeks and Romans talk of China as 'Seres' or 'the kingdom of silk' from the 4th century BC and there is rumour of the well drilled and battle hardened legions of Marcus Crassus running away like big girls from the battlefield of Carrhae in 53 BC, so startled were they by the bright silk banners of the enemy Parthian troops as they fluttered in the breeze. (Get a grip Marcus!) China jealously guarded its sericultural secrets and barbarian theories abounded regarding the mysterious production of this luxurious and clearly rather-frightening-when-caught-in-a-cross-wind merchandise. The Romans imagined that it grew on trees, the Indians called it 'woven wind' but the Europeans outdid them all in wild conjecture and concluded that it might be spun by fairies. Silk became so valuable that it was used as currency in Rome and the wearing of silk togas as a status symbol drove the philosopher Seneca to distraction.

He deplored silken clothes "If one can call them clothes at all ...clad in which no woman could honestly swear she is not naked", as he no doubt attended another feast of bacchanalian excess in a fever of puritanical condemnation with young girls in silken garments, just to check that everything was as deplorable as he believed.

Yet the Europeans discovered that there really was no such things as silk fairies as early as the 6ᵗʰ century and were planting mulberry trees and making silk from cocoons smuggled from China in the robes of Nestorian monks shortly after. Furthermore, it was German Explorer Ferdinand von Richtofen, uncle of the World War One flying ace the Red Baron who first used the term 'seidenstrasse' in 1877, so there never really *was* an ancient `Silk Road`.

The exchange of goods has always been important in Xinjiang. It gave form to all the major towns in the region and transplanted Buddhism and then Islam from India and Persia; but it was along a vast network of trails rather than a single road and involved an astonishing array of products of which silk was just one. Eastbound caravans brought gold, precious metals, textiles, ivory and coral while furs, ceramics, rhubarb and cinnamon traveled west. At first glance, precious stones for rhubarb seem a poor trade by the west, until you realize the importance of rhubarb. The abundant qualities of this mundane plant are as a cure for indigestion, dysentery, period pains and skin diseases. Rhubarb became so valued in Europe that Marco Polo left a bag of it in his will and in the 1500s the price of rhubarb in the markets of France was four times that of saffron. Such were the renowned laxative qualities of Rheum Rhubarbarum that in retaliation for Britain's deplorable behaviour in the Opium Wars, a Chinese official in the 1850s threatened to ban the export of the relieving crop, thus condemning the unsuspecting British public to chronic and eternal constipation. On top of all this, it tastes jolly nice when coated in crumble and custard.

So enough of this talk of silk; this ancient and important series of commercial routes through the heart of Xinjiang linking continents and civilizations, transposing language and culture and breaking down ethnic and racial divides should be called the Rhubarb Road.

Nowadays, rhubarb is no longer center stage for ketchup is king in modern day Xinjiang. As red sauce is often a palliative for grim food, so the production of ketchup is a dressing for the town's failings; for despite its name, which means 'beautiful pastures', a beautiful city Urumqi is not. The place is a long way from anywhere and in addition to producing gallons of condiment is 2250km from the sea (though I still spotted fish for sale in the market), which makes it the most land-locked city in the world. Despite this, in 1992 the Chinese government declared Urumqi a port, a triumph of necessity over logic since this appellation has brought trade and tax benefits to the ailing economy of this most un-port like town. North of Urumqi is remoter still, for here in the tongue twistingly isolated Dzoosotoyn Elisen desert is the point on earth that is most distant from the sea. This was pinpointed by British explorer Nicholas Crane as recently as June 1986 who applied the splendid name 'The Eurasian pole of inaccessibility' to this doubt-lessly impressively lonely but probably under whelming spot. It feels strangely reassuring that British explorers should still be making such eccentrically Victorian and frankly pointless discoveries as late as the mid eighties; there is life in Britannia yet.

I'm sure that a guided tour of the local sauce producing factories would be worthwhile, but it seems to me that the only really interest-ing part of Urumqi is the Moslem quarter where I arrived on a day when sand blown from the Tarim basin had put paid to the prospect of invigorating blue skies. Moslems in Urumqi and across Xinjiang are called Uighurs and are of Turkic rather than Chinese descent. They speak little Han Chinese and have long campaigned, and occasion-ally won, separation from China and the creation of their own East Turkmenistan state, though this prospect has grown ever more remote since the Han population of Xinjiang is now seven and a half million, risen from just 300 000 in 1949. In Urumqi, the Uighurs are getting muscled out and the Moslem quarter too is crowded by gleaming high rises and billboards advertising Nike and Chinese petroleum.

Vestiges of the old life remain however and when the call to prayer sounded or I sat beneath a photo of Mecca and ate mutton kebabs in a restaurant filled with the hubbub of the Uighur dialect, I hardly felt I was in China at all. The center of the Moslem quarter at Erdaoqiao is a pale imitation of what once was. This market, whose name meaning 'bridge of two roads' tells of its key location along old trade routes, was once a dusty and chaotic place but has been sanitized and 'improved' by the opening of a new covered emporium in 2002. Sure, you can still buy Uighur embroidered hats, local silk, Yengisar daggers and dried fruit here, but it's a sadly sterile version of a Central Asian bazaar where statues of Uighur traders outside wear minority dress and lead donkeys in a Han approximation of local autonomous regional culture. Such themes are repeated again and again across Urumqi where smiling Moslems on billboards and in shop windows offer baskets bursting with walnuts and grapes and are always dancing, dancing, dancing in spontaneous regional minority outbreaks of joy at life in the Chinese People's Republic.

I headed out of the city to find the real Xinjiang, whatever that might mean, and think that I discovered it at Heavenly Lake. This mountain idyll, perched at two thousand metres above sea level and surrounded by the Tian Shan mountains, is sublimely beautiful in winter when covered in a thick sheet of ice or in summer when the glacial clear waters sparkle and nomadic Kazakhs settle in their yurts and put their horses to pasture at waters edge. The West Queen was certainly entranced by the lake when she entertained King Mu of the Zhou dynasty there in the 8th century BC. Like a lovelorn teenager she wrote 'the white clouds drift while the mountains reach the blue sky. Passing thousands of mountains, crossing ten thousands of rivers, you come to us from a faraway place. If you are strong and fine, would you like to come back to us again?' The King answered 'I will come again', but he never did. Too busy I suppose.

I checked into a non-descript hotel by the train station in Urumqi since I had a ticket to buy the following morning. The receptionist had made her self comfortable on an iron bedstead beneath a Barbie duvet and was understandably reluctant to leave this cozy sanctuary for something as trivial as a customer. Nevertheless and with the weariest of sighs, she threw back her grimy cover, took my money, handed over change from an unpleasantly warm bundle of Yuan shoved into her nylon socks and gave me a key and a laminated set of hotel rules which must be observed at all times. I discovered with magnanimity that there would be 'no prostitution or going whoring' in this establishment and tried to remain unconcerned as I read a price list of every

459

item in the room with details of what must be paid in the event of theft or breakage- an elaborate version of the 'nice to see, nice to hold, but if it breaks consider it sold' notices in fastidious gift shops. Thus, if I smashed a light bulb I had to stump up a single US dollar, but if I chose to make off with the toilet, I would be stung for a full $150 cash, no questions asked.

Not unreasonable I surmised, and after all an improvement on the Urumqian hospitality of ex Governor Yang Zengxin who in 1916 invited all whom he suspected of disloyalty to a fine banquet whereupon he beheaded his guests one by one. Yang lost his head in turn at a Russian banquet in 1928 and it's to be hoped that he at least scoffed some caviar or perhaps downed some good Russian vodka before he got the chop.

Next morning was train ticket buying day. This would be a straight forward and painless process, hardly worthy of comment in most countries. Not so in China; a Communist country and utopian society where all men are equal and the Proletariat have thrown off their chains. But for the reality of the disparity of wealth and position in a nation that exercises a weird kind of 'socialism with Chinese characteristics', look no further than the train system. China has four classes of ticket; ying zuo or Hard seat is cheap but can be loosely translated as sharing a wooden bench with your buttocks pressed hard against those of your fellow passenger, whose baby screams in your ear for most of the journey while the man opposite makes more noise with his noodles than you thought humanly possible and spits chicken bones onto the floor between your feet. Interesting certainly and no doubt a deeply valid anthropological investigation of the mores and reality of life for China's poor, though not the very poorest for whom train travel remains as distant a prospect as paying for a damaged toilet bowl in a Chinese hotel. People have emerged traumatized from hard seat carriages and sworn never to ride a Chinese train again after a long distance ying zuo experience which is a pity because the other classes are rather nice.

Ruan zuo or soft seat is essentially the same experience but with a cushion on your bench, but the China train system also offers ying wor or hard sleeper and finally, the decadent and thoroughly bourgeois ruan wor or soft sleeper. Ying wor is definitely the way to go; a comfortable bed in a six berth cabin but still sociable and affordable for most locals and with a greasy dining car attached where you can set the world to rights with a local farmer or mobile phone salesman over a bottle of Tsing Tao beer. It feels authentic but with the edges knocked off for an Englishman softened by a lifetime of indulgent capitalism.

There was no queue at all in the station as usual, but a wild, thrashing melee of humanity fighting to be first to the single grubby window open in a row of 20 behind which a bored clerk files her nails. Urumqi station at 6.30am was no different but here I had the assistance of a friendly local policemen who after laughing at my pronunciation and asking how much I earn (most Chinese get this formality out of the way early on in a conversation) helped me to the front of the 'queue'. He did this by shoving others out of the way, blowing his whistle loud and often and occasionally giving legs a little tickle with his big stick. My liberal upbringing screamed disapproval of such boorishness and I felt vaguely ashamed that my foreignness had granted me line jumping privileges; but the queue was very long and I really needed that ticket. My new friend even made the purchase for me and handed me a soft sleeper ticket since he naturally assumed such a soft lad would need a soft bed. So, I would have a lockable door, a vase of plastic flowers on the table, a small steel pedal bin to encourage me to keep my chicken bones off the carpet and would share my cabin with three members of China's nouveau riche. Hardly the authentic and earthy experience of a real traveler but then I needed some comfort as my journey was for 24 hours to the very edge of China. I was going to Kashgar.

Half the fun of Kashgar is getting there and the journey is magnificent. The train snakes its way for a whole day and night through remoteness the like of which I had never seen before. From one window, the view was all vertical and jagged as the Tian Shan Mountains merged into the mighty Pamirs separating China from all those countries ending in -stan, once part of the Soviet Union but now exercising fierce independence from Russia. Turn my head and the view is horizontal across the Taklamakan Desert. This wilderness whose Uighur name means 'go in and never come out' was the most feared obstacle on the Rhubarb Road and stories abound from early travelers of the ghosts and evil spirits that reside there. Furiously hot in the summer, Taklamakan is the paradigm of a cold desert and given its relative proximity to the frigid air masses of Siberia, regularly reaches minus 20 degrees centigrade in wintertime. During storms in 2008, the desert became a winter wonderland when it was reported that the entire quarter million square kilometres were covered in a four centimetre dusting of snow for the first time.

The train ploughed on past wind farms and an occasional group of the nomadic tents called yurts huddled in the lee of a hill, their occupants galloping on horses like they'd just ridden away from Genghis Khan's cavalry. I spent the journey playing cards with Peter - we also tried scrabble but realised that in China ten points for Q and eight for X makes no sense. Peter enquired about my income then shared an inexhaustible supply of dried fruit and pistachios with me. These are a staple food of the inhabitants of Xinjiang whose longevity is often attributed to their consumption of an average of 100kg per person of dried fruit and melons every year. No wonder so much Chinese rhubarb was sent west since there is no need for its laxative qualities here.

A brusque policeman checked my passport barely 10 miles out of Urumqi and returned to paw through every page later in the journey. I asked Peter why and he said " Because he can" and I think of the pushing, whistling policeman in Urumqi station and muse on the development of a nation where officialdom has so much arbitrary power and individual rights matter so little. This separates China from many countries in the west, though I decide that if you give a young man a uniform, a big stick and little accountability he'll behave the same anywhere in the world.

These interruptions aside, I soon settled into the delightful rhythms of a long train journey and watched the scenery meander past in a wilderness of beige as we passed somewhere close to the Eurasian point of inaccessibility. I drifted off to sleep in the sanctum of my ruan wor carriage and dreamt that a policeman had sentenced me to 10 years in a hard seat carriage on a diet of dried fruit while he eternally demanded to inspect my passport in a Sisyphean world of red tape.

I woke in the same province but another world. Defined by its remoteness and at heart a Medieval city, 70% of Kashgar's population of 350 000 are Uighur, though a Babel of negotiation – Kazakh, Urdu,

Tajik, Uzbek and more - can be heard on the train platform. The city is precisely 3380km from the capital though like all of China, exists on Beijing time. This means that offices and shops open at 10am and close for sunset at 8pm. Workers in Government offices are not allowed time off to pray, which effectively rules the Moslem population out of government related employment. Such clumsy attempts at government control are mirrored in the Central square of Kashgar where the 18 metre statue of Mao is one of the largest in all China and looms arm aloft in an allegory of the power and presence of Chinese control. The Chairman gazes beatifically down on the Peoples' Park where locals fly kites and a sign announces preferential treatment for Kashgar residents over the age of 65 who can enjoy free park and zoo admission, while also boldly announcing a free annual health check for all those over 100.

Many locals do live extravagantly long lives (must be all that dried fruit) but despite the prospect of good health and endless zoo visits, Beijing's control over this remote outpost has often been shaky. Following Mongol control, Turkestan was fully reclaimed by China in the mid 18th century but lost again when Kashgaria was briefly taken from the protective wing of Peking by the infamous boy dancer–cum soldier Yakub Beg who established a court here in 1866. This extravagant and charismatic Uzbek with 300 wives ruled with great violence before his overthrow by an advancing Qing Dynasty army and death by poisoning in Kashgar in 1877.

The city continued to misbehave and from 1933-44 was ruled by Sheng Shicai. Nominally a governor for nationalist China, Sheng danced to Russia's tune and became a card carrying member of the Communist party of the Soviet Union in 1938, though he was rather less enthusiastic about China's brand of Marxism and executed many Han Chinese suspected of communist leanings in 1942, including Mao's little brother Mao Ze-Min. Sheng wisely fled to Taiwan in 1949 and the East Turkmenistan Republic came to an end in 1950 when the Peoples Liberation Army entered Kashgar. The leaders of the independence movement died mysteriously and conveniently in a plane crash whilst on their way to parley in Beijing and when the Kazakh Osman, the last of the separatist leaders was executed in 1951 that should have been that.

Except it wasn't and Kashgaria continues to challenge the authority of a government nearly four thousand kilometres away. In 1997 alone, 48 Uighurs were executed by the police for 'separatist acts' including five men who hung the east Turkmenistan flag on Mao's statue on 5th June. That event followed the Ghuljia incident and Urumqi bus bombs in February 1997 which killed 20 and left 70 injured and a Chinese raid on a terrorist training camp in the Pamirs in January 2007 when according to police '18 terrorists were killed, 17 captured and over 1500 hand grenades were seized'. Separatism just won't go away and on 4th August 2008, just four days before the Olympic opening ceremony in Beijing, at least 16 police officers were killed by what Chinese officials called 'a terrorist group', though the New York Times described a muddled and confused battle in which it seems policemen were fighting other policemen with machetes. Curiouser and curiouser indeed.

Human Rights Watch claims that the Chinese authorities are manipulating the situation for their own ends. They say that when China wants to attract foreign investment in Xinjiang, authorities claim that only a tiny number of 'bad elements' are engaged in separatism. On the other hand, when it desires international support for its crackdowns on the local population, the government raises the spectre of international Islamic terrorism; a recourse given extra impetus by US support since 9/11. Such crackdowns mirror the earlier ferocity of Yakub Beg and Sheng Shicai and seem thoroughly counter productive since repression will surely lead to radicalization of the local population. As it stands, the Uighur population seems to have settled for a brand of wary cynicism; they refused to answer any of my questions on the merits of Chinese rule and remarked only that 'some like it' when asked about the huge statue of Mao looming over their central square. The West remains largely ignorant of the situation in Xinjiang though this is probably because Xinjiang, unlike Tibet, has no Dalai Lama to bring its cause to the world's attention and because the West is enchanted by Buddhism and suspicious of Islam.

Id-Kah Mosque, built in 1442, is the geographical and spiritual heart of Kashgar. Here, 10,000 worshippers assemble on Friday afternoons dressed in traditional chapan three-quarter length coats, embroidered dopas and knee length leather boots to worship their God. Veiled women and young children stand outside the mosque, holding teapots of water and Nan breads wrapped in cloth to sell to worshippers as they stream from the building. The sign erected inside the gates announces that the mosque became a specially protected historical relic in 2001 which 'shows fully that the Chinese government always pays special attentions to the another (sic) and historical cultures of the ethnic groups, and that all ethnic groups warmly welcome the Party's religious policy'. Quite a claim and I decided to try to find out for myself if 'all ethnic groups live friendly together here and cooperate to build a beautiful homeland' as the endlessly optimistic sign claimed.

I slept at the former Russian Embassy on Seman Street near the middle of town because of its history and place at the centre of the 'Great Game'. This phrase was first used by Captain Arthur Connolly of the East India Company before he was beheaded in Bukhara for spying in 1842 and describes a period of intrigues between Britain and Russia as they quarreled over control of Afghanistan and Britain aimed to secure access to India. Relations became so bad that the respective ambassadors in Kashgar refused even to speak to each other for years, which sounds more like an unhappy suburban marriage than the basis for Great Power diplomacy and control over a vast area of Central Asia.

The hotel was all faded grandeur – gilded mirrors, stuccoed ceilings and candelabra, but no electricity after 8pm and a faintly brown tinge to the water that sputtered intermittently from gold taps. But despite the declining standards, I met the Imam of Id-Kah mosque here. He sat on my lumpy four poster bed, since even this was less uncomfortable than meeting a Westerner in full public view, and I tried to get some impression of a life that could hardly be more different to my own. He was remarkably young to be head of the biggest mosque in China but was clearly a devout man with a quiet thoughtfulness beyond his years. As our conversation progressed, the Imam defied Western preconceptions of Moslem holy men and the exclusivity of their faith and professed a universal love of all religions. "We are all the same" he said, "for the central message of the Koran and the Bible is love and toleration of others", though his qualification that if a man injures you its forgivable to injure him back in equal measure was rather more Old Testament than New.

The Imam was entirely happy with Chinese rule which "gives complete freedom of worship", though this view came as little surprise since I was not foolish enough to suppose that a staunch opponent of the government would be granted such a lofty position in the community of Kashgar. More surprising was his parochialism and lack of awareness of the rest of the world. Uighurs are Sunni Moslems and the Imam had no idea who the Shias are since "none of them live in Kashgar". He also wanted to know what the Pope was and was puzzled why I didn't have a beard.

Yet I was glad that the Imam's interest and knowledge lay only in his home town and that he measured his wisdom only in devotion to his God. In an age of globalisation, internationalism and the internet, it was refreshing to meet a man of great local standing whose life centered on his community. He was unaware of western hostility and suspicion of his religion and unaware too that he might refuse to meet an infidel such as myself. Naivety it might be, but I was simply a fellow creature in the likeness of God (despite my lack of beard) whose interest in his life made me worthy of his time which in this busy Moslem town was no doubt precious. And anyway, I think he was as interested in me as I in him.

His parochialism was due most of all to Kashgar; glorious, remote, inaccessible Kashgar, surrounded by snowy mountains and deserts filled with demons, where the rest of the world is so far away that it seems profoundly irrelevant. 'Es salaam Aleikum', 'peace be with you'; we shook hands and made ready to depart, but there was one more question. "How much is a donkey in your country?" the Imam asked, and this may have been the most wonderfully parochial and disingenuous question of all.

The question needs some context though, for donkeys are big business in Kashgar, especially on a Sunday. I swung past the government information signs on the outskirts of town ('stabilize and control the birth rate to solve population problems and promote comprehensive development') and the number of cars grew less as the donkey carts increased. For on Sunday, at sunrise, here at the Yengi bazaar, a gazillion sheep, donkeys, horses and the occasional camel invade the sleepy town and the haggling begins. Tens of thousands of Uighurs, shepherds, nomads, farmers and interested observers converge on the market in a dusty, chaotic and lovely madness. Deals are struck extravagantly with a sense of theatre; no quiet handshakes and murmured assent here, but rather a general shouting and slapping of backs, feigned indifference and outraged retreat before a deal is struck by a middleman and an animal finally changes hands. There is much road testing of horses and donkeys which are ridden at breakneck speed by potential buyers who shout 'Boish, Boish!' which can be loosely translated as 'get out of my way you crazy tourist or you will be trampled to death by the little cloven hoofs of my donkey'. The jingle of bells and dust kicked up by hoofs add to the assault on the senses. Behind me, a rough temporary shack sells snacks of steamed sheep intestines, and next to this, farmers prod and pinch every inch of sheep tied in neat little rows. A wispy-bearded man pushes roughly past pulling a bellowing Bactrian camel (Boish, Boish!') and a farmer jokingly asks if I have some daughters who might marry his sons since boys are too much trouble. I gazed at the tall cypress trees and at the sun already hot despite the earliness of the hour as it lit up a dusting of snow on the distant Pamirs and it seemed that save for the occasional truck disgorging its load of cattle, the wonderfully chaotic scene must be unchanged for centuries.

Trade in beasts has always been important in Kashgar, indeed China's control of the region ironically long rested on barter with the nomadic barbarian tribes that presented the most serious threat to Chinese rule. Horses were traditionally the most sought after commodity and the Han Emperor Wu-Di once sent sixty thousand troops to capture three thousand of the mystical 'blood sweating' horses renowned for their speed and stamina from far off Ferghana in modern day Uzbekistan. These horses did indeed appear to sweat blood, though this was apparently caused by mundane skin bacteria, and were transported through Xinjiang on the Rhubarb Road along with peacocks, parrots and lions. The 'camel bird' or Ostrich is said to have caused the biggest stir, though this might have been surpassed by the later sighting of a giraffe in Beijing in the 15th century which caused considerable alarm as it loped along by the Forbidden City and was mistaken for the hoofed Qilin of Chinese mythology.

Neither ostrich or giraffe were at the market, though the nearby wedding ceremony where the men span round and clapped a rhythm to the dap drum and hammered dulcimers was far more interesting than some flea bitten camel bird or long necked even toed ungulate ruminant. Akbar the groom approached me here and passed over his mobile phone number, telling me it was 'most important' that his wife has an unbroken hymen.

I rode a donkey cart back to Kashgar and stopped at a village of baked earth terracotta houses where a family invited me in to share their Sunday lunch. Here I sat on a woven rug and dined on Uighur kebabs of mutton, liver and fat, the ubiquitous mutton stir fry called laghman and goats head soup and marveled at the generosity of people who have so little but happily give so much (though mutton for every meal might be too much of a good thing). My last stop was at the Aba Khoja mausoleum, a delicate 17th century structure shimmering with translucent celadon-green tiles. Here amongst the conical graves, each with a small hole to allow the soul of the dead to travel, are the remains of Yakub Beg and here also is the tomb of Iparhan, a beautiful Uighur woman who Emperor Qianlong took as a wife. She was called 'Xiang Fei' or 'Fragrant Concubine' since she was said to give off a natural scent (which doesn't sound altogether pleasant) and died as a faithful partner of the Emperor or from a broken heart as a prisoner far from her homeland depending if you believe the Han Chinese or Uighur versions of this tale.

As I departed Xinjiang it seemed to me that opinion on this vast and fractured region, just like the story of Xiang Fei is all down to perspective. The Uighur often sees China's presence in Xinjiang as interference designed to destroy their ancient culture and identity. As Chinese from distant coastal cities in the east emigrate to this new frontier in large numbers, test nuclear weapons in the wilderness south of Urumqi, dig for oil and build roads across the vast Taklamakan desert, the government in Beijing has a different perspective entirely. Along with disruption and coercion, it's clear that China is bringing the 21st century and all its attendant benefits to the Wild West and in this way at least the imperialism of China's modern Communist dynasty is little different to two thousand years of dynasties from Han to Qing who benefited Xinjiang with the advantages of silk and rhubarb in centuries past.

GANSU

甘肃

365 284 sq km.
Population 26 million.

'God provides the men and women needed for each generation.'

Mildred Cable.

Gansu is traditionally described as having `three too manys and three too fews`. The items in superabundance are sand, rock and wind which are rather less useful than the rain, grass and soil that are in such short supply.

All of this rock under foot and sand blown around the head makes this oddly shaped province on the edge of the Gobi Desert a uniquely challenging place to get around. No lush rice fields, cosy cafes, frequent buses or department stores out in the countryside here. Instead, the vast horizontal expanse of the desert, the frozen sentient mountain peaks in the distance beneath an azure sky, the plaintive call of the sand plover, the inscrutable face of the camel and all that wind, sand and rock are enough to drive a man to torment.

So, I imagined myself a latter day Marco Polo and felt rather pleased with myself as I traveled through Gansu and battled climate and terrain. But then I heard about 'The Trio' and the smug smile of satisfaction, the serene countenance of superiority were wiped from my face. The Trio were three travelers just like me who toured through Gansu over a 13 year period and visited the same places that I had been. Except these tourists were middle aged women from the British Home Counties, who explored between 1923-36 when the absence of a train line or good roads in the province meant that they voyaged everywhere on the back of a cart pulled by a donkey.

Their names were Mildred Cable and the sisters Francesca and Eva French. These petticoated peregrinators met bandits, generals, princes, refugees, nomads, monks and prostitutes and fought scorpions, heat, dust storms, thirst and exhaustion like Gladys Aylward in triplicate as they roamed the province and crossed the Gobi five times to evangelise and give alms. Oh, and they took a deaf mute ex-slave girl called 'Topsy' with them wherever they went.

I have an instinctive dislike of the notion of evangelising and 'saving the natives', but these old girls were different and the account of their travels in their book 'Gobi Desert' is devoid of proselytising or the desire to convert the reader. Eva describes herself as 'the fervid nihilist, the incipient Communist, the embryonic Bolshevik known to the world as Eva French', which doesn't sound like your typical Salvation Army-floral print-church fete-more tea vicar middle aged disciple of the Lord.

The friends rescued Topsy from bondage for 10 cents in 1928 and describe how the little seven year old arrived at their door with legs covered in dog bites since she couldn't hear their warning barks. Their book is imbued with a sense of fun as they traveled to the remotest corners of the province with bags of Bibles and Topsy in tow, teaching her sign language and approaching every new encounter and challenge with a sense of wide-eyed wonder and matronly enthusiasm that perhaps only people with a very real sense of vocation can achieve. And all of this in those ridiculous and voluminous skirts that women born in the age of Victoria felt compelled to wear.

The Trio were expelled from Gansu by the advancing Communists in 1936 and returned with Topsy to what must have felt like a life of quiet desperation in pre-war England, where their tales of hidden Buddhist treasures and fluent Chinese will have had little currency. Mildred died in 1952 and the sisters within three weeks of each other in 1960 in one of those tear jerking can't live without you filial moments and Topsy has joined her Missionary Mothers in Heaven too. Someone in Hollywood should really make a movie of it.

So, my trip through Gansu felt a bit tame in comparison. If I'd known of the Trio I would have worn a Victorian apron style tablier top layer half skirt over bustle and a cuirasse bodice in a cross dressing tribute to the experiences of those brave ladies. As it was, I alighted from my train at Liuyuan in jacket and scarf as protection against the early morning chill of the desert.

This seemed like hardship enough since despite The Trio's best evangelical efforts, Liuyuan is a God-forsaken spot. There is nothing but sand, stone and wind here for miles around and I was glad enough to squeeze into a taxi with my new friend David to be whisked off to Dunhuang 130km distant. I met David on the overnight train from Xinjiang and he'd told me that he was a Christian in the way that people who have newly acquired a faith feel compelled to do, though David was not peddling his God but had turned to selling hearing aids after failing a teaching qualification. We were joined in the cab by Mr Yang who had snored impressively all night on his bunk wearing shirt and tie (though he did take his jacket off) and I considered how useful one of David's hearing aids would have been as we tried to make conversation while roaring across the desert.

For the road was straight and flat and there were no other cars in sight and no self-respecting Chinese taxi driver would resist such an opportunity to put his foot down and 'see what this baby's got'. The journey was the single most terrifying taxi ride I endured in a nation of hair-raisingly bad driving. As I gazed out at the flat and lifeless expanse of the desert, images of record attempts on the Salt Flats of Utah came to mind and I tried not to think about Donald Campbell on the flatness of Coniston Water as his vehicle lifted gracefully into the air and somersaulted him to his maker. Only David seemed at ease since he knew he might soon be in the bosom of the Lord.

Finally, oh so very finally, we arrived in Dunhuang. This town, whose name means 'Blazing Beacon' is a legendary oasis town on the old Silk Road and well worth enduring a white knuckle taxi ride to see.

The desert in North-West China is mostly a disappointing affair. Yes, the Gobi is over half a million square km in size and receives only 7 inches of rainfall a year and is the second least populated place on earth behind the Polar ice caps. But its name means 'gravel covered plain' and this pretty much sums up this flat and stony wasteland that separates China from Mongolia. I've seen Peter O'Toole in Lawrence of Arabia on the TV at Christmas and I want sweeping dunes, dramatic string orchestras, armadas of camels silhouetted against the setting sun and Omar Sharif in my deserts.

Dunhuang has got all this (though the orchestra and Omar Sharif were sadly lacking) at the Mingsha Shan just outside town. Here the dunes soar up to 1715 metres and tourists come to enjoy a true Arabian experience. The name means 'singing sand mountain' since two Han Dynasty armies are said to be buried beneath the sand here, and when the wind blows, the roll of their war drums can be heard. The dunes do indeed make a strange drumming sound when the wind blows up here, though my heart beating hard from that taxi ride and not long dead Han armies might have been responsible for this.

Local authorities in China have a habit of fencing in natural wonders and charging people to have a look and Mingsha was no exception to this, though frustratingly for the money grubbing bureaucrats, the vastness of the dunes is unfenceable and a 300 metre walk to either side of the gate gave access for free. Once inside there was plenty more to spend money on since sand sliding, paragliding and the inevitable camel rides are on offer and as tourists shrieked and posed for pictures by the burping, ruminating camels, Mingsha Shan seemed more Blackpool Pleasure Beach than Lawrence of Arabia.

A climb to the top of the dunes changed all that. My ascent was a murderously difficult two steps forward one step back climb on loose sand, and after an hour of this I realised how quickly and feebly I would die if let loose in a desert for real. The summit was an outrageously trigonometrical delight where four razor sharp edges converged in a perfect and tiny pyramid and I squashed the apex with my buttocks knowing that the edges would be blown to reformation as soon as I left.

It's not often in a country of a billion people that the traveler has opportunity for repose; for real solitary and delicious reflection, but my half hour on top of a pointy dune at dusk in Gansu province was one such moment. The descending sun, gigantic and red as it dropped behind other more distant dunes, the vastness and sense of history of the place, the gentle kiss of the breeze as the wind scoured across the desert, the hollow drum of the Han army sand made my sunset perch so beautiful.

Descending along the razor edge, the sand plunging away on either side of me, I spotted a beetle scrabbling over the sand. I considered philosophizing on this tiny scrap of life in such a void of lifelessness but judged that sliding down the dune was far more pressing, so down I sped. I was of course removing sand from my ears for days after and also realised that the application of sun cream in the desert simply leads to a shot blasted face and a complexion like sandpaper, but as I lay panting and exhilarated at the bottom of the dune, I felt I'd really achieved something. I have learned since that Mildred, Francesca and Eva beat me to it and their book describes the screams of delight as they raced down in the 1930s. I bet they got sand in their stockings.

It was dark by the time I approached the entrance gate, but the man with the camels was still touting for business. "Come ride" he said but I pointed out that it was too dark. "My camels like the dark" was the reply and he offered me a trip to distant Kashgar which he said would take no more than 70 days. Although the hardships of such a trip would give some measure of parity with the intrepid Trio, I declined and made conversation by his camp fire as he stroked his camels and they grunted at me. "Do you like your job?" I asked. "Yes", the man with the nocturnal beasts replied, "I love camels and they love me". It was good to see someone so happy in his work.

The camels in the Gobi are of the two humped Bactrian variety and these are pretty remarkable beasts. The Camelius Bactrianus can run at 60 miles per hour, store up to 180 litres of water and live without fluid for days, even when carrying a load of 250kg. Its long woolly fur keeps the camel cool in the heat of the day and warm at night when the temperature in the Gobi can drop to as low as minus 40 degrees in the winter, while its wide feet, closeable nostrils and long eyelashes are all perfectly suited to desert life. No wonder the camel man at Mingsha loved and admired them so much.

I checked into the local four star hotel to empty the sand from my pants and was given a choice of double bed without bath or single bed with. I chose double and expressed regret at the lack of bath but was delighted when a knock at the door revealed two smiling attendants carrying a bath which they promptly plumbed into my room. The offer of some sliced camels foot on room service was tempting but instead I wandered onto the roof. Up here, the dunes were framed by stars, the sand was drumming and presumably the camel loving attendant was still offering his nocturnal Bactrians, feet intact, to likely customers below.

But really, no one goes to Dunhuang for the sand or the camels, regardless of their closeable noses. The big draw here is the caves at Mogao. There are 492 of these Buddhist caves built into a low mountain ridge and they date from 366 AD when monks and travelers began to build statues and shrines to pray or give thanks for safe passage through the feared Taklamakan Desert to the West. So far, so good and not terribly unlike many other famous religious remains the world over. The difference with Mogao is that sometime in the 11th Century all 492 caves were sealed to protect the manuscripts, pictures and frescoes inside.

The priceless treasure trove of ancient Buddhist art and culture remained undiscovered until the early 1900s when an itinerant Chinese Taoist called Wang Yuanlu wandered in and appointed himself guardian of the temples. Wild rumours spread about these treasure houses in the remote deserts of China and European explorers soon resolved to go and see for themselves. The first of these was the German Albert von le Coq who in 1905 tossed a coin to decide whether to check out the rumoured caves at Dunhuang or travel 1000km in the opposite direction to Kashgar near the border with Afghanistan. Kashgar came up heads and Le Coq became the explorer who nearly was; like the man who nearly drummed for The Beatles or the astronaut who missed out on that trip because Neil Armstrong was chosen instead; a footnote in History.

The glory of discovery was left to the British explorer Aural Stein two years later, though le Coq did get there eventually and spirited books and frescoes back to Germany (though all the best ones were gone), most of which were destroyed by Allied bombing in World War II. Stein trekked for 17 days through the wastes of the desert covering 380 miles and reported that his party saw 'not another soul' in all this time. His journals claim that 'an air of hopeless decay hung over the place' and certainly the caves even today seem impossibly remote and desolate.

Yet any feelings that that those 380 miles might have been wasted were dispelled when Stein met Wang Yuanlu who agreed to show him around. The explorer's journals are business like and informative and not given to unnecessary flourishes or purple prose, but one can sense Stein's lip smacking excitement as he surveyed the treasures inside Wang's caves, though he doesn't truly break his stiff upper lip Edwardian reserve until Wang showed him Cave 17.

This tiny adjunct off a bigger cave is today known as the Library Cave and had been discovered by Wang some years before. Inside here were thousands of ancient manuscripts, military reports, music scores and Confucian and Taoist classics all in near perfect condition. Here too, in true Indiana Jones style, was the world's oldest printed book from 868 AD, the Diamond Sutra, so called because according to Buddhist teaching, it is 'sharp like a diamond that cuts away all unnecessary conceptualization and brings one to the further shore of enlightenment'.

There began a period of fevered negotiation between Stein and Wang where one tried not to sound too excited and desperate and the other adopted an 'I shouldn't really, but go on then you've twisted my arm' approach, until the men shook hands on a price of 170 pounds and the best of this unique collection was hurried away at dead of night to the British Museum in London. The French explorer, Paul Pelliot finished the job a few years later for a further 50 quid and in all, 40 000 manuscripts and relics are now under lock and key in London and Paris.

The Chinese are understandably a bit miffed by all this, though it's unclear whether it's the loss of these ancient relics or that Stein and Pelliot got them so cheap that annoys them the most. Either way, and like the Greeks who want their Elgin marbles back, requests for the return of the treasure have been given short shrift by the British Museum despite a 1980s UN resolution calling for the return of all artefacts to their country of origin.

The irony is that Stein's collection can't actually be viewed at the museum since it is too delicate to be displayed, though the digitisation of artefacts in progress means that it can all be viewed on line. This seems to be a poor substitute for looking at the stuff, though viewing the Diamond Sutra through reinforced glass in an air conditioned room in London wouldn't be too satisfying either, for it is only in the caves that the real power of the artefacts is revealed, since the antiquity and remoteness of Mogao lends the remains enormous resonance and dynamism.

My guide at this 'great art gallery in the desert' according to Mildred Cable (for naturally the Trio went here on their donkey cart too) was knowledgeable and enthusiastic about what the Foreign Devils left. The oldest caves are Wei Dynasty and Indian in style, with peacocks on the walls and statues with long noses, curly hair and large breasts like some ancient Jayne Mansfield. I was told that the later Sui Dynasty caves from the 6th Century are more Chinese in style. In here the figures are stiffer and more inflexible and I resisted the temptation to point out that this is like modern Chinese government officials.

The real glory of the caves are in those from the 7th and 8th Century Tang Dynasty, where Apsaras fly on the walls and picture stories of the Good Prince who gave his body to a tigress to feed her hungry cubs are told in colours that are still remarkably bold. In these caves, Guanyin the female bodhisattva of compassion has changed from male to female to become the patron of motherhood and the most worshipped figure in China, as the Chinese adapted Buddhism to their needs. Cave 96 has a magnificent 34 and a half metre Buddha modeled on Empress Wu

Zetian that is the 3rd largest Buddha statue in the world and too big even for Aural Stein to cart off.

My guide was fiercely proud of the caves and the greatness of China she saw reflected there. "In this cave is the statue whose smile is like Mona Lisa, but 1000 years older than yours, No sir, these statues are not in the Japanese style since everything they do is copied from us. This Buddha has the most beautiful hand in China and this is the 9th biggest Buddha in the world and more beautiful than all the rest".

So many superlatives and I was beginning to dread the tongue lashing I would receive at Cave 17 where my ancestors escaped with so much Chinese history like thieves in the night. Yet here, the guide's patriotism softened and she became more circumspect and philosophical. "It was for the best" was her unexpected response to my question how she felt about Stein, "since if the treasures had stayed in China, they would only have been destroyed".

And she might just be right since White Russians fleeing the Bolshevik revolution took refuge in the caves in 1920 and authorities are still clearing up the unholy mess they made. It was only the intervention of Premier Zhou En-Lai in the 1960s that prevented Red Guards from destroying the caves entirely during the Cultural Revolution, since at that time, all forms of old culture, habits and customs were unacceptable to the young revolutionaries.

I declined the opportunity to pay extra and see Cave 465 where Tantric Art portrays sexual union creating the ultimate state of enlightenment since despite the magnificence of the caves, I agree with Rudyard Kipling who said that a Buddha a week is enough for any man. But now I wish I had and I'm consumed with regret and curiosity at just what the cave is like. I wonder if Mildred and the girls went to see this chasm of copulation with its fornicating frescoes? I bet they did.

I missed the Jade Gate Pass too. This is because it is a ruined Han dynasty gate over 100km from Dunhuang in the middle of absolute nothingness and I couldn't face the prospect of a 200km round trip with a speeding driver who would use this as an opportunity to terrify me witless. I can appreciate the importance of the gate since it traditionally marked the absolute end of China (and therefore all civilization) and the beginning of the route west where barbarians and desert demons lurked; they just shouldn't have put it so far away.

The gate marks the route taken by Xuan Zang in the 7th century on his way to India. This most famous of Chinese monks was forbidden to travel by the Tang Emperor, but he went anyway and sneaked past the blazing beacon towers of Dunhuang in the dead of night on his pilgrimage. He returned 16 years later with armfuls of texts which are now stored in the Big Wild Goose Pagoda in Xi'an, and in doing so did more than anyone to convert China to Buddhism. The story of Xuan Zang is interesting enough, but it is the imagined tales of his adventures written by Wu Cheng'en in his 16th century 'Journey to the west' that are best known. Every child in China knows these stories where Xuan Zang becomes Tripitaka and is accompanied by Monkey, Pigsy and Sandy on a quest to defeat endless demons and ghosts and discover enlightenment. Many middle aged Westerners know it too from the 1970s Japanese series 'Monkey Magic!' where, despite being dubbed *really* badly into English, the Monkey (born from an egg on a mountaintop) was able to ride a cloud, summon monkey warriors by plucking hairs from his chest and can only be defeated by Tripitaka's disabling 'headache mantra'.

Xuan Zang founded the Fa Xiang school of Buddhism which claims that things exist only as far as they exist in our minds and where Buddha hood is achievable only by the very few. This seems a strangely exclusive form of Buddhism in which only a select few can join the club, but it is just one of the many ideas to spread down Gansu's Hexi Corridor.

The Hexi Corridor is a singular geographical feature that accounts for Gansu's elongated shape. Stretching from Dunhuang in the west to the provincial capital Lanzhou in the east, the corridor is a 1000km stretch of flat land, 15km wide at its narrowest point and bordered by the Tenggeli and Badain Jaran deserts in the north and the Qilian Shan Mountains in the south. With its string of fertile oases, the corridor has long been vital as a trade link between East and West and the only way through otherwise strikingly inhospitable land. Access to the corridor was of course jealously guarded by the Chinese and nowhere is this more evident than at the place called Jiayuguan or 'Barrier of the pleasant valley'.

As I approached the self styled 'smallest city in China', the train tannoy was issuing a long and very important sounding announcement. Such speakers are expertly designed to ensure that poor souls who are grappling with the complexities of language have almost no chance of identifying even the key words so I wondered what the problem could be. Was it engine failure perhaps or Bactrian camels on the line? Mongol hordes stampeding across the Gobi Desert determined to recreate the glories of yesteryear and on a direct collision course with the train? The tannoy quietened and guards began to traverse the corridors selling jewellery and it became clear that the announcement was merely a sales pitch designed to crank up fevered anticipation amongst the bored passengers as the train staff boosted their incomes.

I had a hotel in mind in Jiayuguan but the taxi driver knew better and told me in hushed tones that he knew a 'good one'. This is the moment in China when alarm bells should ring and you attempt to exit the vehicle before the driver whisks you off to a rat infested place 20km out of town where he gets a 10% commission. But no, my driver reassured me "you can trust me; I am an honest man because I come from Northern China. It's only the people from the South who are sneaky and dishonest".

I had no comment on this heart-warming display of national solidarity, having discerned no noticeable difference in levels of honesty between the good citizens of Canton or Manchuria, so I sat back in the VW Santana and enjoyed the ride. Inevitably we arrived at a hotel called 'Chang Cheng'. This means 'Great Wall' and there are at least three such hotels in any self-respecting Chinese town, since the name I suppose is suggestive of permanence, stability and reliability. Or perhaps it simply means that foreigners aren't really welcome. Or maybe this hotel could be seen from space.

The driver lifted out my bag and assured me that anything in China called Chang Cheng is 'bound to be good' and this was especially true in Jiayuguan where even the public toilets at the train station had been shaped with casements, parapets and battlements as if to keep out those who had been caught short. In fact the driver was an honest northerner after all and the Great Wall hotel, though strangely deserted was perfectly fine. This despite the room in the lobby called 'male sex toilet' inside which a disabled cubicle was for 'deformed man' and one broken urinal was labeled as 'out of control'. I settled comfortably into my room and took the advice to 'buckle up the chain on the door before you go to roost', since I don't think its chicken to be cautious and wanted to be egg-stra rested for Jiayuguan Fort the next day. (Apologies for this egg-stremely bad joke.)

The Fort is certainly the most famous site on the Hexi Corridor and has become an icon for the Chinese. Built in 1372 with such precision it is said that just one brick was left over from the 100 000 used, the Fort is described as being the mouth of China with the Hexi Corridor as the throat. For many years it was the 'impregnable defile under heaven' as the Ming architects claimed, since all traffic from east to west had to pass through here between the Qilian Shan and Black Mountains of the Mazong Shan range.

More than anywhere, this is the ancient end of China before the badlands of the West. The purpose of this massive fortification with 10 metre high walls and double gates seems to me to be as much to do with symbolism and reassurance as with meaningful defence and is just like the Great Wall itself in this respect. The massive walls are connected by three huge gates; Easternmost of these is called Enlightenment and the middle gate is known as Conciliation. The Western Gate looks over the vast and terrifying expanse of the desert and mountains and is called the Gate of Sighs and from here, corrupt officials, criminals and traitors would be exiled to a life outside China, and thus to a fate worse than death. The gate is still a repository for the graffiti of desperate men. 'Who is not afraid of the vast desert?' writes one cursed exile, 'should the scorching heat of Heaven make him frightened?' I must say that Ming Dynasty graffiti of the condemned man is much superior to modern attempts which rarely stretch to more than 'Jim woz 'ere' or 'Terry loves Julie'. Mildred, Eva and Francesca woz 'ere too of course and wrote 'the scene is desolate beyond words and if ever human sorrow has left an impress on the atmosphere of a place, it is surely at Jiayuguan'. I could hardly have put it better myself.

Near to the Fort is the very end of the Great Wall, the western terminus of this most famous symbol of Chinese insularity. It was said that travelers should throw a stone at the Wall here; if it rebounded they would return home and if not death amongst strangers was one's fate. If the stone echoed, the trip would be prosperous. My stone was a little too large and hit the ancient wall with a dull thud and damaged the tamped earth masonry. I think this means 'you're an insensitive vandal who doesn't think things through properly. Please don't come back'.

It felt strange to be standing atop the most western portion of this iconic structure staring at the desert, just as I had stood at the point furthest east looking at the sea towards Japan (see Hebei chapter). It was cold and made me think how miserable the soldiers must have been to serve here near the desert demons when they could have had a cushy posting and a couple of concubines in Peking, just as Roman soldiers must have hated serving at Hadrian's Wall on the border with Scotland. The wall had been restored and repaired (and would need further work after my stone throwing) and was no doubt lacking in authenticity. But the view of the desert was the same, the mountains were still dusted in snow and the camels were crouched by the impregnable defile of heaven in the lee of the wind just as they would have been 500 years ago.

The Fort was built not as a ceremonial place to dump China's unwanted into the Wild West, but to keep invaders out. This was a centuries old problem along the Hexi Corridor and even as late as the 1870s, a Moslem rebellion spread through Gansu and threatened to destabilize the whole Middle Kingdom. This spot of bother was orchestrated by the Gansu Moslem Ma Huolong who was defeated under siege by the Qing General Zuo Zuotang at the town of Jiuquan in 1871. The siege lasting 16 months was described by Zuo as 'the most perfect feat of my military career' and was followed by the death of over a million Chinese Moslems and the virtual elimination of the religion in Gansu.

Ma and 80 of his officials were sentenced to death by slicing. This uniquely Chinese form of execution is better known as 'death by 1000 cuts' and was used from about 900 AD until its abolition in 1905 where the condemned person would have portions of his flesh and limbs methodically removed by knives over an extended period of time. The delightfully poetic Chinese euphemism for this gruesome practice is

'Lingchi', which derives from a classical description of ascending a mountain slowly and systematically until the goal is achieved.

Such barbarism fuelled anti-Chinese sentiment prevalent in Europe at the time. The travel writer and photographer Sir Henry Norman returned gleefully to Britain with tales and photos of this terrifying practice in 1895. He wrote that 'the executioner grasping handfuls from the fleshy parts of the body such as the thighs and breasts slices them away....the limbs are cut off piecemeal at the wrists and ankles, the elbows and knees, shoulders and hips. Finally the condemned man is stabbed to the heart and the head is cut off'. Further reports suggest that opium was often given to the victims, though it is not clear if this was too alleviate or worsen the agony, and that the torturer usually began by putting out the eyes, rendering the unfortunate victim incapable of seeing the remainder of the procedure and thus adding to the psychological terror of the ordeal which lasted three days and involved a total of 3600 cuts.

I hate to spoil a good story but all of this seems unlikely to me. While the punishment certainly existed, the actual process cannot have lasted too long since the victim would not have remained conscious after the first two or three severe cuts. Just as with Medieval beheadings, the executioner would have been bribed by friends or family to apply the coup de grace quickly and minimise suffering. Such prosaic details have not detracted from a good bit of Victorian xenophobia however and many other late 19th century writers joined Norman in salaciously recording and cataloguing the details of the uncivilized Chinese whose lands were being occupied by Europeans as their attention was taken by the grasping of handfuls from the fleshy parts of the body.

Western attacks on China were nothing new of course and further down the Hexi Corridor towards Eastern Gansu there is remarkable evidence of Western interference in China from long before the days of Victorian land grabbing in Hong Kong, Peking and Shanghai. Here in remote and poverty stricken Yongching prefecture is the small village of Liqian whose population is said to be descended from the Roman legions of Crassus. Oxford sinologist Homer Dubbs ignited this debate in the 1950s by positing that 145 survivors of Crassus' legions defeated at the Battle of Carrhae in 54 BC were taken to China. These men were used in the Chinese attack on Yongching in 36 BC where accounts record foot soldiers 'in a fish scale formation' which may have been the Roman testudo, or tortoise of interlocking shields that was otherwise unheard of in China. Dubbs suggests the legionaries dismantled their tortoise, settled in Yongching and in 5 AD established the town of Liqian, whose name is the Chinese word for the Eastern Roman Empire. These soldiers far from home married local girls and it is their descendants who inhabit modern Liqian.

The most compelling evidence for all of this are the locals in Liqian, now renamed Zhelaizhai, some of whom really do look different from your average Chinese. Here can be found Chinese with blonde hair and green eyes and here also a 1.8 metre skeleton was unearthed from a 2000 year old tomb in 2003, which added further credence to the Roman walls discovered in 1993.

There are of course myriad reasons why a rogue gene may surface and create hazel eyes or sandy hair in a sea of Chinese, but the villagers of Zhelaizhai are clinging fast to their heritage in the wreckage of their lives. For the village is desperately poor and the people make barely a living from a small field of barley or a few unhappy sheep. The link to Rome is a way out of poverty, for surely tourists will come to gaze at the result of communion between East and West, between the dusty fields of Gansu and the Eternal City? A Doric column has been erected in the village beside the remains of the wall that has been hacked away by farmers in need of building materials to provide visitors with a focus for their visit. Yet the column is cracked and dirty and no one seems to come. Even in nearby Yongching town the Caesar Karaoke Bar on Imperial Entertainment Street is empty and so the ancestors of Crassus continue to labour in the fields as they have always done, harvesting the barley that is the colour of their hair.

My journey east by train continued through the Hexi Corridor between mountains and desert to its terminus at Lanzhou. This unprepossessing city is the provincial capital of Gansu and was listed as the world's most polluted city in the 1990s. Its ranking has slipped to the mid twenties since then and Linfen City in Shaanxi is now the world's filthiest. This slide could easily be arrested if a few more factories spilling smoke into the sky above Lanzhou and waste into the Yellow River were built and if locals would only leave their car engines idling more often, their city could yet recover the coveted top spot.

Marco Polo spent a year in Lanzhou in the 13th century but 'with no experiences worth recording', though this is a little tough on the place since it does possess a certain gritty charm. Chief among Lanzhou's attractions is the Gansu Provincial Museum. I inadvertently visited on the first day of free opening and the place was mobbed. A brass band wheezed and puffed their way through a series of tunes that wouldn't have been out of place at an English summer garden fete and local officials took turns to make drab speeches under an arch made of balloons that looked as deflated as their listeners. The doors opened and a mad rush ensued as the crowd hurried to see the exhibits they'd probably seen several times before, but had to be seen again since this time to look was free.

The museum is home to a 2nd century BC silver plate inscribed with Bacchus the Roman god of wine found hereabouts and which gives credence to the claims of the villagers of Zhelaizhai, and also the complete skeleton of a woolly mammoth dug from the Yellow River in 1973 which lends weight to those Chinese who claim that the river is the cradle of all civilization whether human or hairy with tusks.

The most famous exhibit here is the Flying Horse of Gansu. This 34cm high statue dating from the 3rd century was unearthed in nearby Wuwei in 1969 and has so entranced China that it has been adopted as the official symbol of tourism for the entire country. As a consequence, Lanzhou sports endless Flying Horse saloons, craft shops, housing estates, public parks and statues, the most notable of which greets visitors to the city from its pedestal outside the train station.

The bronze original in its glass case depicts a horse running at full tilt with three legs high in the air and one rear hoof standing on a swallow as a symbol of speed and whose head is turned upwards in understandable surprise. After all, who wants to be galloped upon by a horse? Except the horse I'm looking at might not be the original at all since the one on display is usually a copy and the original on tour or in storage so that it doesn't get worn out by staring eyes. The horse is accompanied by 99 bronze horses and chariots forming a guard of honour that are magnificent and as impressive as the Terracotta guard of honour in Xi'an in their own way. I can't work out why they're not more famous.

I was keen to see the Long March exhibition in the museum too which was advertised as being on the 3rd floor. I could find no sign of the heroic deeds of Mao and his beleaguered Communist troops in 1935 and asked an attendant if such an exhibition existed. "Long March?" He said. "No, that finished 70 years ago." I suppose he meant the March itself; if he was referring to the exhibition then they should really think about taking the signs down.

Lanzhou didn't look like even one of the top 100 most polluted places in the world on the day I was there. The city is hemmed in by mountains and I hiked to the top of Lanzhou gongyuan from where everything was bathed in sunlight and looked dynamic and full of vitality rather than grey, forlorn and overcrowded as I had been warned. The surrounding hills were covered in orchards and fruit trees which accounted for the dozens of fruit sellers on the streets of the town. Most common of these are the Xigua or melon carts where customers noisily consume the fruit and spit the seeds onto the floor from where they are retrieved by the stallholder who collects, dries and resells them.

But it's the Huang He or Yellow River that is most impressive from this lofty perch. Coiling snakelike through the centre of Lanzhou, this is China's mother river. Few waterways capture the soul of a nation more deeply than the Yellow. It is to China what the Nile is to Egypt; the cradle of civilization and a symbol of unending glory.

Today the river was benign and children were flying kites beside Zhongshan Bridge, the 'first crossing' that was preceded by rafts made of inflated sheep stomachs as a method of crossing from one side to the other. Yet the Yellow is not called 'China's sorrow' for nothing, since it has flooded over 1500 times in the last 3000 years and sometimes catastrophically such as in 1887 when two million died on the North China Plain and in 1931 when an incredible four million were drowned.

The name Yellow refers to the perennial ochre of the muddy water in the lower course of the River due to the volume of loess earth suspended there. Other particles now cause most concern since the River is stained with pollution and sewage and over exploited to such an extent that barely a trickle reaches the sea at the Bohai Gulf many miles to the East. 50% of the River is biologically dead and birth defects and waterborne diseases are increasingly common along its banks. The government has made the cleaning of the River a priority over the next few years, though today the river sparkled and looked almost beautiful and the residents of Lanzhou were playing happily beneath an untypically blue sky by the cradle of civilization where their ancestors first learned to till and irrigate.

I walked hands in pockets back down the dry hillside to the city past young men in leather jackets playing snooker on tables that sat lop sided and perched on bricks by the roadside and who grinned through missing teeth and shouted hello. I declined their offer to join in and crack some balls with bent cues on baize discoloured by desert sun since I had a train to catch but reflected that on my journey through deserts and villages, past forts and caves that I had come to appreciate the stones, sand and wind and even the grubby cities and rivers of Gansu. Mildred, Francesca and Eva would have been proud of me.

GUIZHOU

贵州

170 940 sq km
Population 39.5 million

'Minorities are the stars of the firmament; majorities the darkness in which they float.'

Martin H Fischer (b1920 Shanghai)
US Biochemist, Nobel prize winner

I arrived in Guizhou on a bright and blustery blow-away-the-cobwebs day. The wind was blowing dry the sheets and towels attached to poles from windows so that the drab old-before-their-time high rise blocks looked like sailboats, though I worried that a stray sock would be sent spinning onto the honking traffic below.

This was certainly an untypical day in Guiyang whose name means 'precious sun'; a reflection of how little fair weather the city enjoys. Perhaps the name is no mere meteorological appellation, for this province is so poor, so down at heel, so out on its luck, that the sun's golden disc is precious comfort in people's stormy lives and the most important currency they have.

There is a saying that in Guizhou there are no three days without rain, no three hectares without a mountain and no three coins in any pocket. The province is China's poorest; poorer even than the deserts of Gansu and the high altitude plateaus of Qinghai and Tibet, though in those places the sun is scorching and withering and not precious.[47]

I stayed less than a day in Guiyang but this was enough to see the grinding poverty of the place where gangs of men crowded around the train station and on street corners with hoes and hammers and boxes of tools like some labourer army ready to make war. They were looking only for work, but there is none since, ironically for a place of precious sun, Guizhou was suffering under a drought that has drained the province's rivers of water and made dust of its fields.

I saw monkeys in the park who looked poor and bedraggled too but who, unlike the people of Guiyang, address their shortages by sneaking into the adjacent hospital when they can to steal the food of patients too weak to resist. And there were dogs everywhere, licking at scabrous wounds and yawning extravagantly on piles of bricks. One mutt whose bloody tail had been stripped of fur sat and watched a child squatting for a shit and was watched in turn by the infant as he devoured it.

Guiyang is well off the tourist trail and it is good that I had not expected much of the place since this saved any lingering sense of disappointment. I was soon on the train due east to Kaili through tunnels cut into the limestone hills, watching the scenery slowly improve and

---

47   Guizhou's GDP per capita is around $1200 per annum. Gansu is $1700, Tibet $2000 and Qinghai $2500. Shanghai is over $10,000 per annum. The poverty of Guizhou is accentuated by its proximity to far wealthier places like Guangdong and Hong Kong whose per capita GDP is four times higher even than Shanghai.

the sun disappear behind clouds. There was no restaurant car on this train and I declined the food on offer from the buffet trolley that was as functional as the province itself; hocks of meat floating in spicy soup and served in a plastic bag, knotted at the top like goldfish won at a fair and noodles over which boiling water was poured through an improvised funnel fashioned from the top of a two litre bleach bottle.

I was meeting a guide in Kaili who would take me on the 500 km journey through the south east of the province to Guilin in Guangxi. It is rare for me to rely on company in China, though made necessary now because the roads and the buses to Guilin would be terrible and because my scant schoolboy Chinese would be even less use than usual in a region that speaks little Mandarin. This is minority country, dominated by Miao and Dong Chinese. Billy was from the Miao minority and met me smilingly at his office as he tapped out a receipt for guide, driver and car on a computer below a large portrait of Mao Zedong. We sealed the deal with a game of tennis on the court next door whose lumps and bumps provided perfect excuse as I ballooned yet another ball into the net and we agreed to meet the following morning to explore Kaili since it would be market day.

The doormat of the hotel reminded me that this was indeed the eve of market. 'Xingqi san' - Saturday - was writ large there, a common feature of Chinese hotels that are sometimes dilapidated and dirty with sinks that don't drain and toilets that don't flush, but whose entrance mats always accurately keep record of the day. I slept and the mat said Sunday when I walked back through the lobby the next morning. Billy was there again and we walked downhill to the bustling market that had taken over the main road where buses and low-budget Toyotas had been jostling for space the day before. We had steamed pork five yuan dumplings from a stall that also sold fried serrated pink pieces of meat that were the combs from atop the heads of chickens. I admired the stocky white dogs in Kaili, like Tintin's Snowy, more attractive than the gloomy curs that fed on the bowel contents of babies in Guiyang. Billy told me they were called 'Xiasi', that they were expensive and had short front legs designed for chasing wild animals up hills. I wondered if my guide was pulling *my* leg and if there might be another Kaili dog with short legs on one side ideal for running in circles but Billy assured me he would not lie on our first day together so I trusted him, though I watched every xiasi dog carefully in the hope that it might run up an incline and prove the efficacy of its stumpy front legs.

Animals feature strongly in rural Chinese markets. Sometimes there are just *pieces* of animals and there were some ghoulish sights in Kaili as there had been elsewhere; sheep heads gazing dolefully from trestle tables and shin bones on hooks, though fortunately nothing to rival the poor tortured rat I had seen in Sanya (see Hainan chapter). The rats in Kaili were all dead since the poison on sale was '100% guaranteed to kill'. Stiff rat bodies were lined up as evidence of this claim, some of which had been posed in kung fu stances, others had cigarettes dangling from their dead mouths in a surreal gesture that rather muddied the water; did the little chaps die from the effects of the wonder poison on sale, or had they merely smoked themselves to death?

One stall holder who had a blue budgie tied to a string called us over. The advantages of having a guide were already becoming apparent - perhaps I would hire one more often, since Billy made budgie man's purpose clear to me where normally I might have been puzzled and wondered just how much meat you can get off a budgie, and why did the man have only one for sale? The bird would tell my fortune if I gave five yuan to the man with a thin face, looking not unlike one of the rats with a cigarette hanging limply from his mouth. I paid the trifling sum and the budgie was grabbed roughly, thrust onto a row of envelopes, one of which it seized in his beak, before being shoved into a cage.

The envelope of course contained my fortune and quite a crowd gathered to hear the vague collection of aphorisms that the budgie had deemed my lot in life. I wanted specifics; when would I die, how much money would make me happy, would I ever eat a chewy comb from the head of a chicken, would the hotel ever get its day of the week doormat wrong? Instead I was told I would be happy, though sometimes I would have bad days. Did I have children? Yes, then they would be happy too and successful in life, though as rat faced man explained, this could only be categorically, incontrovertibly assured if I handed over another six yuan and 80 jiao; a surprisingly specific sum. Maybe he wanted to expand the business and buy a new budgie.

It wasn't all livestock (or deadstock) in Kaili market. There were haircuts in the street and I took a photo of one old man who posed with his scissors but whose friend behind twisted his flat cap sideways just as I pressed the shutter. My shot has the man half turned in outrage, hat on aslant and looking for the entire world like Norman Wisdom. This part of Guizhou is populated by the Miao and it was market day for them too. They had descended on Kaili in their hundreds from tiny villages of wooden houses to buy and sell, to haggle and trade; for where else were they to purchase an elaborate silver nickel headdress, the six metres of cloth needed to make a traditional Miao pleated skirt or have their fortunes told by a small blue bird?

The Miao came to China's south west from the Yellow River region two thousand years ago, driven out by war. Their number today is estimated at about 10 million with a further million and a half in Vietnam, Thailand and Laos where they are known as Hmong, which makes them one of the largest stateless groups in the world today. The Hmong in Laos fought with the Americans in the Secret War in Laos in the early 1970s and were singled out for retribution when the Communist Pathet Lao regime took control in 1975; as a consequence, a further quarter of a million fled Laos and have settled in USA. Most of these are in the Upper Mid-West or California and I like to imagine them surfing in their elaborate tribal headdresses or practicing shamanistic rituals in the snow in Minnesota and Wisconsin.

Miao rituals really set them apart from other minority groups in China. Their clothing is an extraordinary mix of symbolism and impracticality; silver headdresses, thick hammered necklaces and yards of indigo dyed cloth serve as ethnic and social denominator as much as decoration. Just as the Miao are a sub group of the Hmong, so they are divided into sub groups in their turn. So in Guizhou, there are Changjiao Long Horned Miao who wear their ancestors' hair in great piles on their heads, Flowery Miao, Red, White, Green and Black Miao and all with their distinct customs, rituals and superstitions.

Billy knew them all. My guide became indispensable on the long road to Guangxi in explaining what we saw and more than once he listened in on conversations of locals who assumed he was Han Chinese and who jumped in surprise when he joined in. The Miao are a mountain people with a long history of independence and rebellion against Chinese interference and as we drove across the misty mountains of South East Guizhou, it became clear how the ruling Han found it hard to subdue the Miao and why they have maintained their unique self-reliance; for these mountains are remote and wild and the forests are still filled with demons and the ghosts of ancestors and with wild boar and snakes. The danger from demons may be exaggerated but that from snakes is not. Snake bite is such a danger to Miao hunters and farmers that they swathe their legs in strips of cloth like First World War soldiers puttees, only more colourful.

Billy told me there are few Chinese visitors to Guizhou because 'they like the crowded famous places'. There are few foreign visitors either. In every village we walked into, with its cluster of wooden houses, picturesque on a hillside around a cobbled dancing square, we were greeted with great interest and a little shock. In one hamlet a woman left off plucking handfuls of feathers from the limp body of a chicken to ask what I ate to become so tall, and in another a crying baby was admonished with the threat that the strange, lanky visitor would eat her if she did not.

When I wasn't the bogeyman, the Miao women were welcoming and hospitable - always women because the men were out in the fields or on long hunting trips looking for birds and boar with a short legged dog running faster uphill than down. Old women seemed to be most quick to adapt to the idea of a giant baby devouring monster in the village since I was first and foremost a commercial opportunity to them. They emerged from their dark houses bent double by a lifetime of hard labour and poor diet and offered up trinkets of silver and intricately stitched embroidery while Billy told me what was good and what every needlepoint bird and silvered crescent moon meant. I suppose they'd had a lifetime of adapting to change - the coming of the soldiers on the Long March, self-important officials after revolution, a road from the town and cable TV. I was puzzled that so many of these remote shacks had an incongruous satellite dish perched on its eaves and in one case on a ramshackle shed inside which black and white blotched pigs grunted and fussed. Satellite TV is banned in China, but in rural Guizhou it is permissible since the government figures that no one here speaks

English, therefore the inflammatory and perfidious message of foreign broadcasts are wasted on the people.

The Miao houses were all on three floors and Billy explained this was for animals at ground level, people above and rice on top, though this was one part of local culture that I didn't need interpreting because I had learned it at school in History lessons when the teacher told us about castles and knights and the feudal system. That was what rural Guizhou reminded me of; it was Medieval England with all the back breaking out in all weathers hard work, a distant, incomprehensible and rather irrelevant King, the fear of illness and acceptance of death and the desperate attempt to make sense of a world that could be so arbitrary, where food could run short, a crop could fail and where rice was given better accommodation than people. Except Medieval peasants didn't have satellite.

We walked between villages on a thin strip stone path beside a stream and Billy showed me which plants are good to eat and pointed out hundreds of squirming tadpoles in a mossy pond as we munched on pink azaleas from a hedgerow. There were chicken feathers and blood on some of the trees that grew on the bank of the stream; shamanistic remnants of villagers eager to ward off misfortune and prevent the return of angry ghosts. The Miao are animists and ancestor worshippers and believe the sky is propped by twelve silver pillars. Superstition and pernicious spirits called 'tian' permeate every part of their lives; if a bird roosts in a house it is time to move, wiping a crossbow or rifle with the blood of animals prevents injury while hunting, pregnant women must not enter a house's front door, cotton string wound round the wrist will ward off evil.

Part time priests, shamans and diviners operate in every village, don special clothes and employ chants and prayers to cleanse a place of evil and bring back lost souls. They are paid in food; sometimes an animal is sacrificed - 80% of pigs in an average Miao household are consumed at spirit ceremonies - especially when rice is being planted or at a funeral since the Miao believe that the spirit divides into three after death and the part that remains in the house must be placated by food and gifts and by the placenta from the dead person's birth that was buried beneath the house years before.

This all seemed a long way from the provincial capital Guiyang with its fast food stores and monkey thieves just a few hours away and though Guizhou is not China's most geographically remote province, it felt very remote indeed. Some Miao are Christian due to the efforts of the missionary Samuel Pollard who founded churches amongst the Miao until his death from typhoid in 1915. Pollard's main achievement was in developing a written script for the Miao using the same system of syllabics that missionaries had used amongst Cree Indians in North America, but the evidence of Pollard's work to save souls in Guizhou is scant indeed. The belief system here seemed more native American than Protestant and the Miao are as spiritually remote as ever.

Changes that have occurred seem entirely superficial. Satellite dishes have sprung up on roofs so that the Miao can watch programmes they don't understand, some wear jackets over their indigo clothes so that the colours don't run in the rain and many Miao have substituted mass produced Chinese towels in horrible colours for their traditional headdresses. This has not happened in the very remote village of Basha, where villagers go into the forest to cry and wake up the ghosts and the women sit at ancient looms that are another reminder of my high school spinning jenny, flying shuttle history classes. The drought was so bad here that some men were not in the fields but sat on shady porches and smoked pipes; their hair was long and tied in a top knot like the terracotta warrior statues in Xi'an.

The relentless Chinese appetite for road building is making the valleys of Guizhou more accessible and will yet bring change that is more profound. When I saw a new concrete bridge or a giant yellow earth mover by the side of a road, the Miao felt like a culture on the brink that would soon be swallowed and digitized as the crowds arrived and Guizhou became one of those 'famous places' that Billy said the Chinese loved so much. Even in Basha there was evidence of contact with modern life. A young girl dressed in all her leg wrapped, indigo, silver necklace, head scarfed finery wouldn't let me take her picture until she had combed her hair and made it just so. When her grandmother posed for a photo, she grabbed my digital camera in her gnarled hands and deftly pressed the play button to see how she looked. Throughout my trip the Miao were perfectly happy to have their photo taken - no stealing of the soul, white man speak with forked tongue here - though they always insisted on seeing the picture and shrieking with laughter as they crowded round the screen.

Billy was ambivalent about the encroaching Han Chinese; his views were as contradictory and inconsistent as I sometimes think mine are. When I asked if he considered himself Miao or Chinese, he answered 'Miao' without hesitation. He said China does nothing for the Miao and repeated the old line about the mountains being high and the Emperor far away. Yet he had that Mao poster in his office and said that the Chairman was a great man. Billy also peddled the old line about Taiwan being an unarguable and immutable part of Communist China - some issues are just not open to debate, regardless of cultural background. The Communists were at least better in their treatment of the Miao than the Nationalists had been. Mao and Miao had mutual respect because the mountain people of Guizhou had given assistance to the Communists on their Long March; the nationalists had been cruel and killed thousands of Miao across south eastern China and as far away as Hainan.

In Billy's opinion, the majority Chinese simply don't understand Guizhou. Most write the province off as too poor and too remote and would not entertain the prospect of a visit when there are shops and Great Walls and terracotta warriors and river cruises elsewhere. He told me that when he went to University in Beijing, the urbane and sophisticated students from Shanghai and the capital wondered where he was from and were amazed when he replied Guizhou. 'How did you get here?' they wondered. Billy replied that he had set off six months ago and ridden a donkey and the students nodded and gasped and believed him.

When Mao's Long March passed through Guizhou, the women didn't emerge from their huts to watch because they were naked, unable to afford clothes. Girls wore a string and a rag when they reached puberty and many died in their early twenties from TB, childbirth and the opium pipe. In some ways Billy's life had been typical of Guizhou. His website (toguizhou.com) describes eating rats dressed with salt and ginger, picking gravel from tofu that had been dropped on the floor and dreaming of a taste of milk. But Billy has an education and a website since his father said 'if you don't study hard, you are going to make friends with the water buffaloes'. So Billy had left his village where he said the teachers were only good at drinking rice wine to study English and become a thoroughly modern Miao, quite different from his peers in rural Guizhou. He is fluent in languages, a regular visitor to the big towns of Kaili and Guiyang and has flown in a plane, though he still loved the countryside best and when I asked him his birthday, he hadn't a clue.

Billy is a modern man in another important respect. It is still very rare for Miao to marry non Miao, indeed it was illegal to do so until the 1950s, but my guide was married to a Dong. It had been a complicated marriage, Billy explained, that lasted two days so that one day could be given over to Dong ceremony and the other to Miao, though this was nothing compared to the forthcoming celebration of the birth of the couple's first child who would be named and raised and immersed in both cultures; a Mong or Diao perhaps?

It's a wonder that Billy got married at all, since Miao courtship rituals are elaborate and take ages beating around the bush. It is impolite to be too forward in boy meets girl Miao culture; the idea of saying 'I love you' or 'I think you've got a face like a bulldog chewing a wasp and wouldn't marry you if you were the last man on earth' is unthinkable. It's far better to say 'I am a bird with a broken wing, can I rest in your branches?' Such avian advances can be rejected with a delicate 'my branches are too small since I am just a sapling', or 'my roots are too shallow'. Or perhaps, 'I'm waiting for a nightingale and you look like an old crow', or maybe 'I have Dutch elm disease, you'd best stay away'.

A sung courtship is even better than words and at the spring time Sister's Meal Festival near to Guiyang, hundreds of suitors visit eligible girls dressed in kilograms of silver headdress, jewelry and embroidered finery to transmit their feelings through song and through rice. The girl responds to the advances of a boy who wants to sit in her branches with a ball of sticky rice containing a message; two chopsticks for yes, a maple leaf for maybe and chilies for no way, not in a thousand years. Courtship pleasantries completed, the Sisters Meal transforms into a jubilee of drumming, bonfires, bull fighting, horse racing and fireworks before everyone gets pissed on rice wine and staggers home.

Our journey had taken us over the mountains of the Miao country and we were entering the marginal, riverside land of the Dong. Houses became less elaborate and clothing less colourful and it became clear that to the Dong, the river is everything just as to the Miao the mountains are home. Houses were built along the riverbank and sometimes on stilts in the river; water wheels turned and scooped the stream onto rice fields. The Miao eat chickens and pigs but the Dong prefer ducks, geese, fish and toads; the fruit of the river.

The Dong villages were simple clusters of wooden buildings blackened by wood smoke and there were less songbirds in cages hanging from pine trees now (songbirds are a sign of wealth since a good one can be more expensive than a buffalo, though they're less good at pulling a plough). I couldn't decide if the Dong are poorer or merely less ostentatious than the Miao or perhaps this was merely the difference between an introverted and an extroverted culture. The two groups are certainly aware of their differences; the Dong traditionally claim that the Miao are dirty and primitive; the Miao accuse the Dong of dishonesty, though such views clearly had not been an impediment to Billy's marriage. In the main however, and to my untutored eye life looked largely the same here as up in the mountains. It was equally tough with long days in the field, old women carrying massive bundles of sticks and bamboo on their backs and the sucking noise of farmers' legs behind a plough and buffalo as they walked up and down the paddy fields.

We stopped to eat at tiny restaurants, the cook sweating behind a massive wok like one of the satellite dishes on the Miao wooden houses, underneath which flames roared with blue and orange intensity. These restaurants displayed fresh vegetables outside the front and I simply pointed to what I wanted; the chef would throw it in with pork or beef and chili and coriander, the flames would roar, and we would eat. Sour soup ladled from stone pickling jars, jiao jiao river fish, bamboo and jueca dragons claw mountain vegetables were served too - the most basic and functional food and a reflection of a region that has often suffered shortage and hardship and turned to the plants of the forests and hills for sustenance.

Yet these simple meals were amongst the best I ever ate in China (and the cheapest). Every meal was finished with sticky rice wine.

The most famous brand of this potent beverage is called Maotai and this comes from Guizhou too. Maotai provides relief from hardship and comfort to the poor and dispossessed. As the Guizhou saying goes 'if we didn't have maotai, we wouldn't know how happy we were'. Remarkably for such powerful liquor, Maotai is renowned for its health giving properties. Just a little of this vigorous intoxicant can contribute to the retention of youthful good looks and is remarkably efficacious in preserving the liver, though even with such affidavits, there was never a time at the end of a meal when my heart didn't sink when a bottle of rice wine was produced.

Everything in a Dong village is made of wood and locals are understandably twitchy at the prospect of a fire. Information notices blazed across the hillside and on walls so that a fire would not. 'Fire safety is everyone's responsibility', declared one, 'be careful to make not one mistake' said another. Each village had strategically placed drums of water beside the chicken coops and tool sheds to fight flames. There were serious faced fire officers in some villages, unsmiling with the weight of responsibility, whose job it was to spot and fight fire if one should start. With the men out at work and the women busy around the village, this job was often left to an ancient old man dozing in the spring sunshine who seemed ill-equipped to deal with a massive sheet of flame roaring down the hillside and consuming everything in its way. Most Dong villages have a tower, a tall wooden pyramidal structure from which a drum can be beaten in case of fire or enemy attack, but more commonly used now as a kind of village hall, a meeting place and the centre of the village where old folk sit and smoke or snooze or play mahjong.

It was fun to spot these squat ancient looking structures, though none were very old; fires had seen to that. Most villages had just one, but Zhaoxing has five. This Dong Village is a picture perfect place of Drum Towers and bridges hidden deep in the mountains. It is made more dramatic since the approach through ugly, joyless concrete towns over roads rutted by heavy lorries on their way to Sichuan, makes this wooden idyll so unexpected. Zhaoxing is a village on the turn. A large entrance gate is being constructed and new sewage pipes laid so that hotels can be built and an entrance fee charged, but for now the place is all timber shacks and weaving looms, clouds of wood smoke drifting across the market, skinny dogs with puppies hanging from their teats, waddling ducks and the thump, thump, thump of wooden mallets as women beat the indigo cloth they have dyed in order to bring out the shine.[48]

Zhaoxing was the perfect place to pause and take stock on my journey. I sat on the balcony of my guesthouse and looked out over the five Drum Towers (one for each clan) and the decoration on each rooftop that is shaped like an old Chinese coin, designed to bring luck and wealth to every household. I felt lucky to be here, though slightly less so when Billy appeared with a bottle of rice wine. We played cards with locals that night and the village was almost pitch black by 10 o'clock - more mediaevalism to accompany the pigs on the first floor, the rice on the third and the women washing clothes in the river. I taught pontoon to Dong and Miao and they taught me an absurdly complicated game called 'Beat the Ghost'; maybe it was the rice wine that made it seem so confusing. I didn't get close to understanding this game and every time I played a good card, another rule was introduced; 'no, you can't play the Queen unless a seven hasn't been turned over' explained Billy. 'Remember to collect suits - what's that, you have a run?' whereupon he would look and declare my success invalid because clubs can't be counted as a run when hearts are trumps and the 10 of diamonds is still in play, unless it's a Tuesday but only if the night is cloudy and it's not a full moon.

I woke with a sore head, all that trying to beat the ghost I expect and nothing to do with the maotai, but was revived by a walk through fields and forests until we had views of the wooden village below. We strolled past the school where children were lined up on parade in great solemnity, though one boy grinned shyly as I pulled a face. The school was brightened with a painted quote from Deng Xiaoping regarding the importance of education, below which the rules told the students to be true to their country and to socialism and only later, right at the bottom, to work hard and study well.

---

48   The shiny surface of the cloth is highly prized and created by the use of egg white. Other cloth has a duller, red tone due to the application of buffalo blood.

We went past other children who weren't at school at all, but sat by the path and amused themselves whittling and shaping wood with a rusty machete. Children are less cosseted here than in the West where a machete would be considered an inappropriate plaything, though on the other hand every baby I had seen in a Dong village was wrapped and carried at all times by an old matriarch called a za who fussed and preened their rosy cheeked grand children who gurgled and smiled with contentment at never having to walk or make any effort at all. We meandered past farmworkers and I watched a woman walking a buffalo up and down her field - more of that sucking noise as each foot left and re-entered the mud. The work looked desperately hard and monotonous, though every time the woman reached the end of her small paddy and caught my eye, she smiled and said hello, and I may be mistaken, but I think her buffalo smiled too.

There were grave stones covered in incense and offerings on the hills above Zhaoxing. The Dong cremate their dead only if they die young. Children are sometimes beaten first by their parents in mock outrage at their offspring's lack of consideration in dying before their time and before they ever had opportunity to support the family, and in order to prevent their spirits from returning to haunt the ancestral home. This was an altogether different and even more confusing game of 'beat the ghost'. But most Dong are buried in a coffin made from the pine tree that was planted when they were born. Up here on the hillside the graves had a clear view of the village, the clouds scudding across the sky and some rare Guizhou sunshine glinting on the wet fields where women and buffalo went about their work, so the spirits and ghosts were content and calm.

Zhaoxing is famous for bridges but the best example of a Dong bridge is further south and just over the border into Guangxi at Chengyang. The bridges here are called fengyuqiao - wind and rain bridges - since they are elaborate covered structures that give shelter from bad weather and the one at Chengyang is bigger and better and older than any other. The drive was slow even by the standards of Guizhou since the road was rough and a lorry had careened off the road and ditched itself in a paddy field; a crane had arrived which blocked our way while it pulled out the poor half submerged truck. The vehicle made a sucking noise as it left the rice field that was louder and more satisfying still than a farmworker's legs ploughing with a buffalo and it was entertaining to watch as the crane strained under its load and to wonder if it would be pulled over and submerged with the lorry. More interesting still was the choice of clothing of the crane driver. This was dirty, difficult work and what better outfit to wear than a white jacket and white dress shoes with no socks? Perhaps he was off to a wedding after saving the lorry.

Lunch was at another tiny restaurant with an abundance of fresh vegetables where the cook's wife was boiling and removing the fur from a rat so large that I thought at first it was a cat. Billy looked at me and raised his eyebrows expectantly but I declined the opportunity to recreate a formative experience of his childhood and stuck to pork. At least I *think* it was pork.

The bridge that links Guizhou to Guangxi was in such bad condition that goal posts of metal tubing had been erected on one side to prevent access for lorries whose weight might cause the bridge to collapse, creating more work for the white suited and booted crane driver who at this rate, would *never* get to that wedding. Yet Chinese lorry drivers are undeterred by mere notions of safety or death and were simply levering up the barrier and squeezing their lorries through and over the bridge that shuddered and groaned alarmingly under their wheels.

We were in Guangxi now and China's poorest province was behind us. But provincial boundaries are arbitrary divisions and we were still in Dong country. The bridge at Chengyang was magnificent; a study in proportion and form with its five pavilions and not a single nail used in its 78 metre long wooden length. It seemed eternal and indestructible though this is a replacement built in 1916 after the old one burned to the ground, and although there are dark alcoves for shrines all along the bridge, these are empty of worship and incense due to the fear that this bridge might suffer the same fate.

Chengyang has a drum tower too, handsome and sturdy as they all are, and full of old men who sat there all day in blue zhongshan jackets and slippers, in comfortable silence as they smoked their pipes. The men looked ancient, browned by the sun and gnarled like they were part of the fabric of the tower. I asked their age - the oldest was 84 but might have been 150 - and what they remembered of old Chengyang. One said life was a hundred times better since the reform and opening instigated by Deng Xiaoping in 1978. Before that, the years were bitter and food was scarce and the leadership bad, though here too in this remote tower of wood was a poster of Mao; a homage to the man whose policies had caused so many Dong and Miao and Tibetans and Muslims and Manchus and Mongolians and Han Chinese to starve.

I complimented the men on their good health and failed in my refusal of rice wine that was offered to me. "It is good to drink and smoke a little" said one. "Mao Zedong smoked but didn't drink and died at 83" he said, "but Deng Xiaoping did a little of both and lived to 93" he continued. And then came the trump card; "Zhang Xueliang[49] smoked and drank and took drugs and slept with many women and lived to 103" he opined and sat back into his cosy cat like reverie, pleased with his homespun philosophy while he smoked his pipe.

Meanwhile the womenfolk of the village danced. This was for tourists but nevertheless it was in a real Dong Square outside a real Dong Drum Tower and the whole effect was authentic and pleasing. Men blew into the instrument made from bamboo called pipa while others bashed drums. I was struck by the same thought that usually occurs to me when I see minorities put on their dancing shoes and shake a leg in China, that is, how easy and basic the dance was. Even I could do this gentle sashaying from side to side, one foot out, one back, clap your hands and circle round perambulation that reminded me of the thoroughly genteel dancing in a BBC adaptation of a Jane Austen novel; not for Chinese minorities the whirling maniacal spins and leaps of African tribal dance, the gyrating hips of the Turkish belly dance or the tumbles and thigh busting kicks of a Russian Cossack.

The old women with crooked backs poured out of doorways with their trinkets on completion of the performance and showed more speed and dexterity than many of the dancers. They were remarkably persistent and grabbed me with their swollen jointed fingers, especially after I had bought a trifle from one thinking this would excuse me from

---

49   The Young Marshal who opposed Chiang Kai-shek and was placed under house arrest for 41 years in Taiwan – see Liaoning chapter.

further attention, but which actually offered a green light to all the others who saw the prospect of a foreigner who was easily parted from his cash.

Billy helped me of course, as he had since we had left Kaili, with words in local dialect that seemed to satisfy the old crones who took their right angled backs and baskets of goods elsewhere. Billy and I talked about the dance and I said the girls were pretty, especially the one on the right who had looked at me and smiled and offered me rice wine at the end and who I assumed, with every ounce of male vanity I could muster, must have fallen in love with me. My guide disagreed. Billy pointed out the girl that he found most agreeable, who he would most like to do the two-step Dong cha-cha with, to take round the back of a Drum Tower, to canoodle with in a quiet corner of a wind and rain bridge. His choice had danced very nicely thank you, but was far from the epitome of classic beauty in my eyes and I said so. Ah, but beauty is culturally bound and ethnically specific just as shamanism and ancestor worship are too. Billy explained that the girl's round face was auspicious because it would hold more thoughts to help people, she was short and this would make her a sturdy worker in the fields, and anyway a tall girl would need extra headroom in the house and this would mean extra wood, extra labour, extra costs. Above all, Billy was drawn to her Dong derriere, since a big bottom meant healthy babies.

I parted from Billy in Guilin, shook his hand and pitied him the 500 km, 20 hour journey back to Kaili. He seemed unfazed and said he would soon be back playing tennis on the lumpy court; after all what was such a journey to a man who had known real hardship? It was a beautiful spring day by now, Guilin's osmanthus trees were bursting into leaf, the women in the villages would be walking behind their buffalo in the thick cloying mud of a paddy field and the sky was alive with birdsong. The Miao people believe that the song of the swallows guides them to their homes; Billy raised his face to the sky, closed his eyes as he felt the precious sun on his face. He spotted his swallow, climbed into the car and drove back to Guizhou.

NINGXIA

宁夏

66 400 sq km
Population 5.9 million

'I have always loved the desert. One sits down on a desert sand dune, sees nothing, hears nothing. Yet through the silence something throbs, and gleams...'

Antoine de Saint-Exupery, The Little Prince

Ningxia is a tiny jigsaw puzzle piece province in the north-west of China, crisscrossed by crumbling fragments of the Great Wall and sandwiched between the grasslands of Mongolia and the low mountains of the Quwu Shan that bubble from the desert of Gansu and continue to swell to the high plateaus of Qinghai and Tibet. No one at home had even heard of Ningxia and many people in China have not either, yet the province holds a unique position in Chinese history. It is also the place where I came closest to abandoning all sense of wonderment and appreciation of the history and culture of this great nation in favour of violence.

For Ningxia is particularly remote and far-flung. To say the province has places off the tourist trail would be a misnomer for there *is* no tourist trail in the mountains and the deserts here nor in the provincial capital Yinchuan. As a consequence I received look-at-the-foreigner attention like never before; people stared and hooted and shouted at me as if they'd never seen a real standing, walking, breathing waiguoren and perhaps they hadn't. Sometimes the attention became threatening, and this had never happened to me in China before either, where outside of worldly wise Beijing and Shanghai, people have always been interested but retain a degree of reticence, shyness even, wary of the laowai who could do something strange and foreign at any moment. I was threatened by a man outside a fast-food restaurant in Yinchuan, whose gaggle of friends sat on mopeds, their hair bouffanted and teased into spikes like a tribute to the hardy clumps of grass on the edge of the desert outside town. I didn't want to shake his hand because I knew he was laughing at me, at my size, at my clothes, above all at my big nose, so he shoved me and shouted while his spiky friends looked on. "Laowai" he said. "Waiguoren, big nose [something, something], my town, [something], don't like" and then a long and impassioned diatribe that I didn't understand at all, full of posturing and for the benefit of his ludicrously coiffured fiends.

This gave me a chance at last to use the Chinese insults I had painstakingly learned on my travels. I avoided the more extreme curses that involve a sexual act performed on various members of your enemy's family; mother of course, but also Dad, older brother, father's older brother, Dad's father, Dad's father's brothers and sons, Dad's brother's nephew's cousin's livestock; in fact anything with the requisite number of limbs and holes and a pulse. Such insults would only lead to more trouble so I stuck to the lower-level Chinese curses which revolve around dogs and eggs; running dog, stupid egg, though here too I avoided the most extreme variant, turtle's egg which is highly offensive and likely to lead to a fight, though no one has ever really been able to explain to me why.

But this teenage miscreant was the exception rather than the rule. Most people just stared. There were several types of stare in Ningxia. These included the 'glance away when our eyes meet' stare, the full unabashed, no blinking, mouth agape stare, the 'walk over for a closer look' stare, the 'stare, turn to friends, burst into gales of laughter, stare again' stare (this one was particularly favoured by young people), the 'stare and shout combination' stare[50], the 'walk past in street, pretend not to stare, glance back over shoulder to stare' stare and a dozen variants thereon.

Despite the stares, Yinchuan was an interesting town and devoid of the pollution and the frenzied pace of cities further east, though still with the uniform town centre where all that was old and interesting had been bulldozed, replaced by office blocks, anonymous hotels and cheap clothes shops outside which huge speakers throbbed and pulsed with Chinese dance music played at a volume more suited to an illegal rave in a field than the high street in a provincial town. Most stores in China have one of these speakers and they compete with each other, turning the road to a disco and I often wonder what the old ladies trailing bags of vegetables must make of it as they count the pennies and do their daily shop.

The real action in Yinchuan when I arrived was at Nanmen Square where people bought cheap T-shirts sporting nonsensical English phrases (Time makes an alien, land your homeland! Carnival is my the plesure (sic) - Everybody likes to be freedom!) and played the temporary games that had been set up on the concrete. Chief among these was the old favourite shoot the balloon with an air rifle, but stand on the scales to have your weight reported was also popular as was my personal favourite, roll a hoop across the floor to land over and win a packet of cigarettes. I wondered what price this game must have been since cigarettes are so cheap in China. Perhaps it was more about the thrill

---

50 The shout is always 'waiguoren' - foreign person - to which my reply was invariably 'zhongguoren' - Chinese person!

of the chase, like on British fairgrounds where the prizes are usually gigantic luminous stuffed Loony Tunes characters that no one in their right mind could possibly *want*.

There is a half size replica of Beijing's Tiananmen gate on the edge of Nanmen Square, complete with flagpole and portrait of Chairman Mao and where even the underpass is designed to look like a station on the Beijing underground. I had my photo taken here then checked into a grubby two star hotel, plain and unadorned, but with a remarkable collection of bathroom products designed to maximise the sexual pleasure of anyone choosing a night of passion in a room with a threadbare carpet and no windows. Here were vibrating condoms in 'dream sea soft song strawberry flavour' and packets of 'sanitary lotion', though I was unclear if these were for application to genitals, hand washing or to clean around the U bend.

The hotel may have been un-salubrious but I slept well and dreamt the sea soft strawberry song dreams of a man tired by the long journey to Ningxia. When I woke, the cigarette packets and hoops had been cleared away from Nanmen, the gangs of threatening youths had ridden their mopeds home and I had the good fortune to meet a man who spoke English and didn't stare at me at all.

Jim was a student at Ningxia Normal University and over coffee he said that his friend had a car, he would like to practise his English, so would I like him to guide me to places of interest outside town? I accepted with enthusiasm since I wanted to see more of Ningxia than the shopping malls of Yinchuan and this happy arrangement would avoid dealing with bus timetables and taxi drivers who invariably overcharge, drive too fast, smoke too much and behave like turtle eggs. So as we drove out of town towards the distant Helan Shan Mountains, and though the sky was filled with rolling un-desert like grey clouds, I felt a lightness of being and pleased at last to be in Ningxia.

The roads on the outskirts of Yinchuan are nonsensically wide and over engineered. China's road building projects are legion and often more related to lining the pockets of local officials and contracted firms than to public convenience. Here the girth of the roads was more akin to airport runways than the suburban arteries of a provincial town. These were eight lane behemoths that cut a swathe through the parched horizontal land and ended uselessly where they condensed into two lane bumpy tracks between orange trees 10 miles outside of town.

The roads had been a gift to the people of Yinchuan from the previous Governor, to celebrate the 50th anniversary of the creation of the Hui autonomous region of Ningxia by a benign and generous Chairman Mao in 1958. The Hui Chinese Muslims are the descendants of Arab traders who were keen to exchange fluids with local women in addition to silk and spice. There are 10 million Hui in China, conspicuous in their white hats and selling mutton and sesame flatbread called dah bing from restaurants and on the night market street stalls. Mao chose to recognise their unique culture and position in China by creating the Hui autonomous region[51] which appears a magnanimous gesture, though it seems incongruous that a communist government would choose religion to define a group's ethnicity.

Mao was also aware that the Hui are thoroughly assimilated into Chinese culture, unlike those troublesome Tibetans, so he had little to lose by the gesture. This is well illustrated by the life of Zhang Chengzhi, a Hui boy raised as an atheist who is credited by People's Daily as being the very first Red Guard when he used this term as a pen name in 1966. Zhang convinced other senior level students to use the collective name Red Guards and together they issued a big character poster on 29 May 1966 promising to 'resolutely carry out the Great Proletarian Cultural Revolution to its end'. And so the murderous and destructive Red Guards were born; soon students all over Beijing followed the lead of Zhang, though the boy himself renounced his past and converted to Islam in the 1980s.

The Hui were probably grateful for the establishment of their homeland but 80% of Hui people continue to live elsewhere, which means that only a third of the population of the Ningxia Autonomous Region is actually Hui. This seems a bit ungrateful, but then why would one choose to live in distant, barren Ningxia when you could

---

51   Tibetans, Uyghurs and Miao also have their own autonomous regions though all such places are autonomous from the cloying attention of central government rule in name only.

be selling goats head soup in Xi'an, reciting the Koran in Beijing or skewering mutton in Shanghai?

Jim was a political animal and thoroughly approved of the Governor's gift though acres of the old town had been flattened to make way for the dictatorship of tarmac. My guide was a fully paid-up member of the Communist Party with all the unquestioning approval this entails. He described the complicated application procedure for party membership and how he still had to sit a monthly interview with a local party bigwig who would ask him to explain his ideals, how they matched the teachings of Mao and Deng Xiaoping and how he had usefully spent the previous 30 days serving the nation. (Showing a foreigner the heroic socialist utopia of freshly tarmac'd Yinchuan would no doubt get a mention this month).

This all seemed sanctimonious; exactly the sort of nannying attention that a teenage boy making his way in the world would not enjoy and I wondered why Jim bothered with party membership. "Because it brings great benefits" he replied. I had hoped for a more idealistic response; 'because I believe in the fundamental dictates of Socialist equality and the radical Marxist thought that we can all shake off the shackles of the oppressor, to free ourselves from bondage, to create a new and just reality'. But no, Jim was more motivated by earning a few extra yuan.

The realpolitik of my guide's party membership; the access to foodstuffs, promotion and better housing it brought was symptomatic of how the party has become an agent of inequality across China, the very opposite of its ideal. Yet as Jim told me the story of his life as we trundled across the countryside on now narrow roads, I became less judgmental. He had grown up in Hebei in desperate poverty since his parents were peasants and needed to work but were often too ill to do so. Electricity and running water were a rumour in Jim's childhood home and when he left to serve for three years on an anti-aircraft battery in the People's Liberation Army and though he earned an insignificant 80 yuan a month, Jim at least tasted meat and white rice every day. He left the Army to build roads in Ningxia, toiling in scorching summers and winter blizzards for 1500 yuan a month though he missed the fun of the great socialist 50th anniversary unnecessary suburban eight lane highway construction project of 2008. He did however build many other roads in the countryside around Yinchuan and told me several times through the day 'I built this road' or 'I am proud of the quality of this street' as we skirted the Helan Shan Mountains, crossed the bridge over the Yellow River or thundered home arrow straight on a flat road towards Yinchuan.

In the context of Jim's struggles, his pragmatic party membership took on a different complexion. It became a sensible response to hardship, an insurance policy, an attempt to get ahead, no worse than wearing an old school tie or a golf club membership that is supposed to be about improving one's handicap and mastering the tricky approach shot on the ninth, but is really more concerned with face time with the boss, though of course the Communist Party was always supposed to be more world changing, so much *better* than all that - the Chinese Communist party as a giant golf and country club? There's a new thought.

Jim and I were on our way to the site of the Xixia Mausoleum where the Xia Emperor Weiming Yuan Hao had established an independent kingdom in 1038 against the wishes of the Song Dynasty Emperor that flourished but collapsed and was utterly wiped out under the charging hooves of Genghis Khan's cavalry less than 200 years later. Very little is known about the Xia kingdom now since the Great Khan's thoroughness was compounded by the robbery of Russian and British archaeologists in the early 20th century who came to this remote place and spirited away 90% of Xia artefacts to museums in Moscow and London.

They couldn't take the Emperor's cone shaped tombs though and they sit inviolate like giant dollops of ice cream melting in the sun into the flat landscape. A museum has been built here that tells the story of Xia's nine emperors using tableaux and dummies and the occasional carved stone that the greedy Russian and British eyes missed. In retrospect, it seems that the kingdom was doomed the moment Weiming died, for he was succeeded by a progressively weaker and more dissolute bunch. The Weiming shop dummies looked a fierce bunch, but Jim told me that the founder of Xixia had regrettably been killed by his son because he had 'occupied' his son's wife after which the uncle killed the son and nephew killed the uncle in a squabble that makes my family

Christmas arguments over which TV channel to watch look like small beer.

The Xixia kingdom was beautifully placed between the Yellow River to the east and the Helan Shan Mountains that rear up and buckle the landscape to the west, though even this strategic position was no defence against Genghis Khan. The grey clouds had settled on top of these same mountains and were depositing their load so that our drive along another of Jim's roads at the foot of the hills reminded me of travelling across Rannoch Moor in the Scottish Highlands, the hills of Glencoe surrounded in mist on a dreich spring day. By the time we pulled into the car park at the mouth of the Helankou pass that cleaves its way in a narrow defile through the granite, the sun had come out and the hills didn't look Scottish at all but more like the jagged brown mountains from death and destruction news reports in Afghanistan.

The ancient inhabitants of Ningxia carved thousands of images into the walls of the canyons here as they traversed between the river plain and the deserts of Mongolia. We trod the same route beside the clear stream that descends from the gullies on the mountainside and where signs pointed out the more notable carvings on the rocks above, marked by blobs of red and yellow paint that were not in keeping with the ancient stone, though they made the pictures easier to spot.

The carvings are between three thousand and ten thousand years old. They deal with the time-honoured themes of rock art worldwide; namely wildlife, domestic animals and scary faces and the attached museum deals with the equally time-honoured Chinese theme of dusty exhibits in glass cases beneath dense swathes of information in badly phrased English, though the site feels suitably ancient and wild and desolate with its high cliffs, plunging waterfalls and simple line drawings that predate Xixia, Genghis Khan and Chairman Mao. The most famous carved scary face here is that of the sun god who looks not unlike a Rastafarian and featured on the promotional literature for the place. These leaflets proclaimed the Helan Shan Mountains 'one of the 50 must see places for foreigners in China... evaluated as the most influential tourist scenic area in China' – an extravagant claim and evaluated by whom?

On the way back to Yinchuan with Jim ('I built this road'), we stopped for lunch where my guide and driver promptly changed their order to the most expensive item on the menu when I announced that I would pay. Just outside Yinchuan we passed a huge twenty thousand seat sports stadium under construction that seemed oversized for such a small town -- an example of gigantomania and hubris just like the roads here. Close by were gleaming five-star hotels that Jim told me were for the exclusive use of party officials and their guests.

I felt mischievous so I began to prod my card-carrying Communist party friend; "Why should party members only have access to these hotels? Isn't communism supposed to be about equality?" But Jim was well drilled; "For now inequality is the reality in China but we are moving towards equality and freedom for everyone which is our ideal".

Yet China seems further from her ideal than ever; the poor poorer, the rich richer, the wealth gap wider. Socialism with Chinese characteristics has created an economic powerhouse, but mere lip service is paid to communism, the ideals espoused by Lenin and Marx as dated, indistinct and quaint as the grainy footage of Mao announcing freedom and revolution from atop Tiananmen Gate in 1949.

I did my bit for equality by sleeping in the cheapest hotel I could find in Yinchuan. The receptionist announced that her rooms were en-suite and when I opened the door I discovered 'en-suite' meant that a toilet had been plumbed into the corner of the room, which coupled with the absence of a window, gave the impression of a prison cell. I slept fitfully on dirty sheets dreaming of escape and hoping the door would not open as another inmate was thrust in who wanted me to comfort him in this dark and dreary place. Yinchuan gets only 186 mm of rain a year and by the morning the grey clouds of yesterday had been replaced by a characteristically blue sky. I rode the train south to Zhongwei town where the flat stony dry landscape dotted with patchy grass and coal power stations around Yinchuan turns into proper desert; all rolling dunes - an infinity of sand and men with headscarves and camels.

The train to Zhongwei had come from Beijing and was packed with migrant workers escaping China's decrepit industry in the Northeast to find work in Lanzhou, the city strung along the Yellow River in

Gansu. Yinchuan was near the end of the journey for this train that had trundled for hundreds of miles past the great Buddhist statues with their covering of coal dust in Datong, then through the steppes and the steel city Baotou in Inner Mongolia. As a result there was not to seat to be had.

There can be no more uncomfortable journey for a foreigner in a province of stares than through the hard seat carriages of a Chinese train. I counted seven carriages before I reached the sanctuary of the buffet car, plonked down my bag and ordered breakfast. All the way, people stared and nudged awake their travelling companions to stare and refused to acknowledge me or muttered 'you ren' - 'have person' when I enquired about the availability of a seat that seemed to be spare. For a while I squeezed next to a man because he said I could but I met more Ningxia hostility from him who poked and prodded and said my nose was 'tai da', too big, so I told him I would sit elsewhere before I was tempted to call him an egg or a dog or tell him I'd occupied his Mother. Hard seat carriages are a step back in time in modern China, crowded with peasants who carry hessian sacks instead of suitcases, the men in old army uniform stripped of insignia and buttons though they were discharged years before, since the green military jacket is the best item of clothing that they own.

I sat with migrant workers from Liaoning at a greasy buffet car table and ate fried eggs with chopsticks. We talked about where they were going and where they had come from. I remarked on how cold Liaoning was in wintertime which must be how *every* casual conversation about China's north-east goes but they still complimented me on my Chinese. I answered 'mama huhu' which is a phrase that means 'so-so' and that I regularly use in reply to the compliment because in China it's good to be self-effacing (just as it's good to dish out compliments) and because the phrase never fails to raise a laugh. I wondered at first if this was because I was using mama huhu in the wrong context, but my Chinese teacher assured me I was not; it's just strange and incongruous to hear a waiguoren with limited Chinese speaking an idiomatic phrase, like a second language speaker in England saying 'it's just not my cup of tea' when he doesn't like something.

The Liaoning migrant chuckled over my phrase all the way to Zhongwei, repeating 'mama huhu' under his breath as he crushed cigarette butts into the remains of his fried egg. When I got off the train, he was still pleased and he waved and shouted 'mama huhu' from the buffet car window as the train creaked and regained momentum on its journey to Lanzhou.

I could tell Zhongwei was a small unsophisticated provincial town because the view from the train had taken so little time to turn from desert to town centre and because many old men wanted to shake my hand when I sat in the shade of a tree on the town square. This was the prettiest place I'd seen in Ningxia and I wanted to just sit and listen to the old folks play Chinese chess under the trees while I pondered my next move. The games were strictly segregated; poker under that tree, chess under another while under further trees, old folks were handing their ill-fitting dentures to a man whose white coat afforded him an air of professional expertise as he attacked the teeth with a big iron file.

Yet another tree gave shade to a group of amateur musicians who warbled tunelessly through a series of Chinese folk songs, while others sawed at two stringed erhus, an ancient Chinese instrument whose sound is either atmospheric or painful depending on the skill of the player. I wanted to sit quietly in the cool air of the shade, the trees filtering stripes of desert sun from the sky uncluttered by clouds, but the locals wouldn't let me. The old men favour large circular glasses attached to elaborate hinges in this part of China and their eyes were fish-like and magnified as they stared and then sat down beside me. "Where are you from?" "Your Chinese is good". "Mama huhu, mama huhu" I replied and they chuckled appreciatively. The only way I could get the old men to go away was by sitting perfectly still, staring straight ahead and making myself as uninteresting as possible. If I were to extract a drink from my bag, read a book or write in my diary, a ripple of excitement passed through the small group which would grow to a crowd as people joined who might be less impressed by the presence of a waiguoren in town but who thought something might be happening and naturally didn't want to miss it.

'Look at the foreigner writing', the old men would say and peer over my shoulder, giving me the thumbs up as I wrote 'the old men are looking over my shoulder'. The scene lacked only a man throwing me peanuts and a young boy rattling a stick along the bars of my cage.

I tried to escape attention once by listening to music on my iPod but this was a terrible mistake and led only to the men taking in turns to listen, nodding appreciatively and tapping their feet to the Beatles and Jimi Hendrix, though no doubt they thought their own music superior and considered Hey Jude mama huhu at best - a song that might be improved by the addition of a little erhu or the sound of teeth being filed.

Zhongwei's temple is called Gao Miao, an eclectic and riotous mix of Taoist, Buddhist and Hindu themes; a relief from Chinese temple fatigue and one of the most interesting temples I saw in the whole country. This is partly because of its location - there are not so many temples in China from where the view is of the sluggish Yellow River framed by rolling desert dunes - and partly because of the strange impact of the Cultural Revolution on this place.

A dazzlingly white statue of Mao stands outside the temple, a reminder of how Red Guards were ordered to destroy and dismantle all that was old in the name of progress. I had to screw up my eyes to look at Mao in the glare of the sun, this time in a jaunty cap, his overcoat ruffled by the wind (Mao's overcoat is usually being wafted around in statues - it always seems to have been blowing a gale in the 1960s, though I suppose that to the sculptors these were the winds of change; the result of revolutionary pressure not barometric pressure). The Chairman looked as smugly pleased as ever but at Gao Miao his revolutionary disciples built up instead of knocked down. The Red Guards dug a series of bomb shelters and tunnels beneath the temple in the late 1960s in case of attack from the USSR, a fellow socialist country but one that had betrayed its revolution by adopting capitalist elements to her economy, criticising the previous leadership and building a threateningly large number of offensive weapons, all of which is exactly like China today.

The USSR didn't attack and the tunnels were never used. Today they've been converted to a dark and cold depiction of Buddhist hell where unfortunate papier-mâché sinners are sawn in half and boiled alive by fiendish beasts presided over by impassive and unsympathetic judges. The tunnels are filled with the anguished loudspeaker cries of the poor tortured souls though I was distracted by the smooth walls of the tunnels themselves. It would have taken months of digging to build the shelter and I wondered at the arbitrary nature of Cultural Revolutionary destruction. I'd seen it before; here things were knocked down, there they were preserved. Some places of exceptional cultural and historic value were saved on the whim of the leadership, but this exception applies to the Forbidden City or the Potala Palace, not a dusty little temple in Zhongwei. The preservation of smaller sites probably comes down to the attitude and influence of local officials and the distance from revolutionary Beijing, though distance had been no impediment to the destruction of the Rongphu Monastery, 5200 metres above sea level at the foot of Everest, and revolutionary propaganda had been sent on a satellite into space in 1970 (See Yunnan chapter).

The sun seemed brighter than ever, the sky more brilliantly blue after the tunnels of Gao Miao since the darkness of Buddhist hell was alleviated only by the flames beneath cooking pots or limbs torn from anguished sinners painted luminous lest they be missed. The streets and parkland were utterly dry. The clouds of dust were kept from swirling around the heads of shoppers by the use of a truck that trundled up and down the High Street spraying water and chiming Happy Birthday on a loudspeaker system that drowned out the erhus in the park like some demented ice cream van.

The Yellow River flows right past Yinchuan and is bordered by green lush grass in a town where everything else is parched and brown. Like the Nile in Egypt, the Yellow River in Ningxia is a ribbon of fertility, moist and fecund, though on reflection that phrase belongs in the bathroom of a two star Yinchuan Hotel next to the vibrating condoms and the sanitary lotion.

The river is water and irrigation and food and transport and trade in Ningxia. Motorboats drift down stream now, pumping diesel fumes into the sediment of the river, but traditional transport in Ningxia was on yangpi fazi boats, made from the skins of sheep inflated and lashed together as a primitive raft. Now the yangpi fazi are for tourists and I rode in a van 10 km upstream on a bumpy dirt track then sat astride a raft back following the current to Zhongwei with a group of Chinese who screamed at every splash and rolled up their trouser legs but left their shoes and socks on. Despite their screams, the raft was surprisingly stable, the inflated sheep riding every wave and eddy with ease. I trailed my feet in the Yellow River which was surprisingly cold and spat dust into the water, imagining my phlegm travelling hundreds of miles west through Shaanxi and Henan and into the sea at Shandong. My feet disappeared as soon as I had lowered them more than two inches into the water, such is the level of sediment the river picks up from the crumbling dry landscape of north-west China and which makes the Yellow River truly yellow.

It seemed inappropriate to be amongst all this sand and not encounter a camel. Yet riding a camel is like dating Miss World. Fun and exciting for a while, you feel on top of the world and pleased that everyone notices you, though they're more interested in your striking partner than you. But it soon becomes dull, monotonous and slightly uncomfortable and you quickly run out of conversation though the long blonde hair and flashing teeth of the camel never *really* lose their appeal.

I knew all this having been persuaded to get the hump with a camel before, but when Mr Zhang approached me on the outskirts of Zhongwei with two leggy beasts and asked if I wanted to sleep with a camel in the desert, the prospect of a night away from two star gurgling pipes and basket-by-the-toilet Chinese hotel hospitality was so appealing that I agreed to go.

We set off from the Shapatou Desert research centre that was established in 1956 in an attempt to stem the creeping tide of desertification in northern China that contributes to food shortage and the huge dust storms that engulf Beijing each spring. Old Zhang told me the camel ride would be two hours, but like Chinese bus journeys, it seems that Chinese camel rides always take longer than advertised and it was fully three and a half hours before we dismounted to pitch the tents, the camels collapsing onto their stomachs, knees bending in the wrong direction and almost hurtling me into the desert.

The ride was on flawless fine grains of sand, over ridge after ridge of dunes though always with a distant telegraph pole or discarded piece of plastic in view to remind me that this was not the Sahara and we were never too far from town. My camel was very well behaved on the trek, plodding dutifully on and tied to Zhang's camel by a rope attached to a nose peg. Zhang's camel however stopped often to grab greedy mouthfuls from stubby bushes, farted hard and copiously and tried to sit down at any opportunity while Zhang made unintelligible guttural sounds of disapproval; so much for inexhaustible ship of the desert.

The scenery was magnificent; there is something appealing about virgin terrain, the sand smooth and sculpted, sometimes rippled and ridged by the wind and blown into sharp edges that were scattered and rearranged by the large flat feet of our camels.I appreciated the scenery that was so unlike China when my mind wasn't drawn back to the discomfort of my mount. Legs splayed a little too wide, seat a little too hard, riding on the flat was bearable enough, but whenever Clive (for that is what I'd named my camel) crested a dune he would break into a jog trot down the other side, my testicles smacking on his hump and making me relieved both that I hadn't taken up Zhang's offer of a three-day trek and that my child rearing years are behind me.

Our red tents were stark against all this yellow and like true adventurers we built a fire, placed a smoke blackened pot on top and cooked dinner. I never did find out Zhang's first name and our conversation was limited by his lack of English and strange Ningxia approximation of Chinese. My guide did have command of a limited range of desert specific English though, so we sat in the sand as twilight engulfed the desert like the first men on earth and muttered like Neanderthals to each other; 'food good', 'sun hot', 'sand many', 'camel tired'.

The last wasn't strictly true. Zhang had left the camels untethered and they wandered off who knew where in search of tasty leaves, though the bushes close to the camp seemed perfectly fine. I expected no better from Zhang's errant camel who clearly had an attitude problem, but I was disappointed in such behaviour from Clive. I was concerned that the camels were gone for good and we would have to carry our own cooking pot out of the desert, but Zhang knew they weren't and sure enough an hour or so later they returned, stomachs gurgling from their meal, their faces haughty and supercilious as camels always are.

When the fire was extinguished, the camels had settled down and Zhang was snoring outside his tent, I walked onto the steep dune that towered above our campsite. I wanted to get closer to the curtain of stars and lay there for two hours, my face lit by the bright moon, body in a silent & lifeless reverie like the desert all around me. I was barely able to tear myself away; for when was I likely to see stars like this again in China?

Dawn broke pale and cold but by the time Zhang had slowly and deliberately packed tents and pots onto the backs of the camels, the sun was high in the sky and the sand was sticking to the sweat on my face as we plodded home. His camel continued to fart and misbehave but Clive was good even when Zhang untied him and gave the rope to me so that I could steer my ship of the desert home with little tugs on his nose. "Ta xihuan ni" - "He likes you" said Zhang; "you are very good!" "Mama huhu", I replied and for the first time Zhang's weather beaten old face creased into smiles, his laughter ringing out into the clear air of the Ningxia desert.

YUNNAN

云南

380 000 sq km
Population 45 million

*"The scenery here is overwhelming grand. Probably it's like can-
not be found elsewhere in the world. For centuries it may remain
a closed land, save for such privileged few as care to crawl like ants
through its canyons of tropical heat and up its glaciers and passes
in blinding snow..."*

Joseph Rock describing Yunnan in 1929.

The Chinese Tourist Board is only too aware of the specialness of this
region and if I could only go back to one province, Yunnan would be

it. Its name means `South of the Clouds`, but officials have christened it `plant kingdom`, `animal kingdom' and most intriguingly, `non-ferrous metal kingdom` and if that doesn't open the tourist floodgates, I don't know what will.

The good men at the Tourist Board have also helpfully drawn up a list of the 18 wonders of Yunnan to instruct and inform the wide-eyed visitor here. So here can be found bamboo hats used as cooking lids, mosquitoes so large that it is said that three are sufficient for a meal, young girls who carry tobacco pouches referred to as old ladies, locusts eaten as a delicacy and 14 other such marvels. Yet the real wonder of Yunnan is in the quiet town of Shigu.

Shigu is a place hard on the banks of the Yangtze River. Here the River is called 'Jinsha Jiang' or 'Golden Sands', but it's also variously referred to as 'Chiang Jiang'; the Long River or simply `Jiang`; The River. For despite the historic claims of the Yellow River in the North, the Yangtze is *the* Chinese River. Fully one twelfth of the world's population and a huge proportion of China's trade, agriculture and industry are centred along this prodigious stream. China without the Yangtze is unthinkable.

And yet the River almost bypassed China completely. Its origins lie high in The Himalayas and like the Irrawaddy, the Salween and the Mekong, the Yangtze thrashes and tumbles its parallel way due south toward South East Asia to disgorge into the sea. But at Shigu, something remarkable happens. Here the river does an alarming about turn and heads north, tries desperately to wriggle its way back south again and settles into an easterly journey before slipping into the East China Sea at Shanghai some 5000km distant.

Simon Winchester in his wonderful homily to the Yangtze called 'River at the Centre of the World' urges us to not underestimate the importance of this turn, since without the Yangtze China would be different indeed. This is no indecipherable kink in the river at Shigu, but an amazing 180 degree hairpin bend, volte face, observable in any atlas by even the most cartographically challenged. It's all caused by Cloud Mountain, a rather unprepossessing lump of limestone which the river understandably decided to go round rather than through in distant Miocene times in a process technically known as `river capture`.

The mountain fails to conform to the North-South trend of the local Heng Duan Shan or Horizon-splitting range, but instead lies at right angles to the prevailing topography and fully in the path of the river, thus diverting its course.

The Chinese explanation for such a profound geological occurrence is rather less prosaic and who would not prefer the tale of Emperor Da-Yu who, with the aid of a brigade of dragons, placed Cloud Mountain square in the path of the on-rushing Yangtze in order to divert the river into China like some pre-historical mystical engineer.

Shigu town is small and little visited though the Tourist Board enthusiastically extols the area as 'like a wonderful landscape painting that never ends.' But this is not strictly true, since Cloud Mountain is an unremarkable peak and the town is lifeless, with the usual share of hasty shoddy buildings constructed in white tiles that enjoy the benefit of economy but little else. The town is remote and isolated and possesses a certain charm in consequence, though the streets are dusty and dull and even the local dogs open a lazy eye on my approach and decline to bark or sniff my crotch as any self-respecting village mutt in China should do.

Yet remarkably, Da-Yu's refusal to allow even a drop of precious Yangtze water to escape the Middle Kingdom is not Shigu's only claim to fame. The name Shigu means 'stone drum' and commemorates the defeat of Tibetan invaders in 1548. The drum in question, which is really a marble tablet, sits forlornly beneath a ramshackle wooden pagoda and describes 'heads heaped like grave mounds, blood like rain and dykes choked with armour' as the invaders from the west were bloodily repulsed. It's possible to see the remnants of a fissure in the drum (just between the words 'blood' and 'rain') and it is said that the split reopens in time of war but is sealed when peace reigns. Clearly the drum is unaware that the world remains far from peaceful yet.

Mao's Red Army came here too in 1935, when 18 thousand men were ferried across the river over four days and nights, the enemy nationalist soldiers in hot pursuit. The Communist troops destroyed the boats once they were safely across and reportedly called to the Nationalist vanguard standing impotently on the other bank to 'come across; the swimming is fine'. They may well have stuck out their tongues and blown raspberries too.

The crossing was a key moment in the 10 000km retreat to safety of the self-styled Peoples Liberation Army, though not as famous as their other river crossing at Luding Bridge later in the March (see Sichuan chapter). Like so much of Chinese history, the March is shrouded in rumour and myth and may have been neither as long nor as heroic as the Communist party claim. Indeed Mao's experience of the Long March was more of a long carry since he was saved the rigours of much of the route from his perch on a palanquin supported by four sturdy porters. No matter, the march is the cornerstone of Communist mythology and like Britain's evacuation at Dunkirk, is a prime example of how a hasty retreat can still be covered in glory.

Mao's chair bound passage through Shigu is commemorated by a cement monument crowned by a red star beneath chestnut trees high above the river. From here the Jinsha Jiang's about turn, the unexpected prominence of Cloud Mountain, the hazy sunshine on the broiling ferment of the water below first southbound and then north, are all visible. It seems appropriate that the Chairman's calligraphy reproduced on the cement in his characteristically expansive brush strokes are not a diatribe about revolution and the march, but a paean to the river; the lifeblood of a nation that China almost missed.

Yunnan possesses strength in diversity, from steamy tropical jungles in the south to jagged snowy mountains on the border with Tibet in the north. Of the 30 000 species of plant in China, 18 000 can be found here. The province has less than 4% of the land in China, yet contains about half of all China's bird and mammal species including the Yunnan snub nose monkey, a giant forest dwelling ox, China's last remaining tigers and the Asian elephant. The elephants are a particular favourite of camera wielding shrieking tourists, some of whom have been attacked and injured in recent years. The local view is that the beasts are angry with people and this might be right since their natural habitat has been stripped to such an extent that only 300 elephants remain.

Yunnan's human population is diverse too and some 38% of the province's population is a member of a minority tribe. I came across my first of these in the picturesque lakeside town of Dali where I spent a happy hour dancing around a fire with a group of local Bai people. Dressed in their traditional costumes of blue with details of white, a colour they hold in high esteem, they offered me glass after glass of fermented rice wine. And this was my kind of dancing – no need for rhythm with the Bai; an apologetic shuffle, step forward step back that is my standard hokey cokey on dance floors across the world more than sufficed, though I'm convinced that I became more expressive, more in tune with the spirit of the piece, the more wine I drank.

Dali is the kind of ancient and weathered stone town that should exist all over China but rarely does. Hardened travelers and grizzled backpackers pass scorn on the town that has been spoilt by tourists and commercialization but they can still be seen on the main Huguo Lu or Westerner Street sipping their lattes and buying pirate CDs. Despite the influx of tourists, the town is beautiful, nestled as it is between the 4100 metre Cangshan Mountains and the 250 square km Erhai Lake and beside which ancient fishing villages and Bai markets thrive, unspoiled enough to satisfy even the most demanding of travelers jaded by the spoiling effects of tourism of which they are a part.

Yunnan's famous Three Pagodas are in Dali and I took a coughing and wheezing mule cart part way there, before deciding that walking beside the poor beast and making encouraging noises was an infinitely kinder and faster choice. The 9th century pagodas form the corners of a symmetrical triangle and are visible from miles around since the tallest is nearly 70 metres high. During repair work here in 1978, 700 Buddhist antiques were found inside the walls, though it seems incredible that these sculptures and documents can have lain unfound for 1000 years; rather like discovering a lost Rembrandt under the sofa while vacuuming the floor.

The pagodas were built to deter dragons that bred in the nearby swamp and seem to be fulfilling their role admirably since I saw not a single dragon on my visit there. The left most pagoda leans alarmingly to one side since an earthquake that hit Dali in 1925 but this only adds to its charm just as with that famous tower in Pisa, and makes the pagodas more popular and famous still.

The extent and variety of minority culture in Yunnan is astonishing and it's impossible to travel far in this province without encountering a new dialect or a new form of elaborate headgear. The Black Lisu on Yunnan's western frontier with their fearsome reputation and rope and pulley crossings of the Salween River and the Nu who drink water dripping from stalactites as the symbolic milk of fairies are within striking distance of Dali; but I was most interested in the Yi.

The Yi are Yunnan's largest ethnic group and can be found from Kunming to Lugu Lake in the north. Traditionally disparaged by the majority Han Chinese, the former name of the Yi is the Lolo and this is now a derogatory term in modern China. The Yi have been historically divided into Black Yi nobles and White Yi commoners, the lowest of which are called 'xiaxi' whose name means 'talking tools'. The Communist takeover of China has not been without its faults but has at least put paid to a caste system where one group were no better regarded than the equipment with which they tilled the land.

The Government has also ended the physical isolation of the Yi by a prodigious building of roads. There are now nearly eight thousand kilometres of roads in Yi territory compared to a grand total of seven kilometres at the time of the Communist ascension to power in 1949. Yet the building of roads has by no means eradicated the separateness of the Yi who famously worship fire in an elaborate torch festival every sixth lunar month. The Axi are a smaller branch of the Yi and celebrate a more elaborate festival still on the second day of the third month with a grand carnival of body paint and nudity. This ritual commemorates a local wizard called Mu Deng who saved the Axi during a freezing rain storm by starting a fire. The villagers parade barely clothed around a huge fire and in a sudden frenzy hack a pig to death before slicing off its head. Then the Bimo, or village Shaman, all feathers, beads and elaborate headgear, gives thanks to the gods for having given the knowledge to make fire.

The festival is now a great tourist attraction and no doubt lacking some authenticity, but is typical of the strangely syncretic nature of many of the beliefs of Yunnan's minorities. Even though most of the Axi attend church in nearby villagers, they have remained animists and cling to the old traditions. And all this in a nation of godless Communism.

But China is anything but simple and religion has long been at the centre of confusion, disturbance and revolt across the country. The Dungan revolt is the most famous of China's religious rebellions, when between 1648 and 1878; around 12 million Hui Muslims and Han Chinese were killed in 10 unsuccessful uprisings in Shaanxi, Ningxia, Gansu and Xinjiang. The revolt spread to Yunnan as well and here is called the Panthay Rebellion after the Burmese name for Chinese Muslims. It was led by Du Wenxiu based in Dali who established the Pingnan Guo or pacified Southern Nation and besieged the provincial capital four times. Dali was recaptured by the Qing army in 1873 at the cost 20 000 lives and poor Du's head finished on a carriage to Peking preserved in honey, which is not a sweet way to treat anyone.

Massacres of around one million Yunnanese Muslims followed but despite this the provincial capital Kunming still retains a traditional Muslim quarter amidst the gleaming high rises. I explored the quarter and ate local kebabs, but my best memory of the Spring City, so called because of its temperate climate, is riding the dodgems at the tiny fairground in Cuihu Park. The very purpose, the raison d'être of dodgems is to bump the living daylights out of other unfortunate souls, but here we found ourselves alone and driving round in forlorn circles. Nevertheless, the sight of a waiguoren and his children driving a purple bumper car in the park was hot news in Kunming that sunny April day and we soon drew a sizeable crowd of onlookers. The crowd cheered every time we passed and took photos since without these, how would anyone believe that such an event had ever occurred?

This all naturally led to a degree of self-consciousness on my part and I excused myself by shouting "wo de haizi xihuan", or "my children like it". Only much later did I learn that in Yunnanese dialect, 'haizi' means shoes and not children. Thus as I sat in my tiny purple car with my knees beneath my chin, I had cheerfully been announcing to the assembled masses that my footwear was having the time of its life.

The existence of a separate dialect emphasizes the separateness of Kunming and here too one fifth of the residents are from minority groups, including the smallest tribe of all, the Dulong of whom only

75 remain. Yet in other ways, this is just another big and booming Chinese city racing to be modern and nowhere is the incursion of modern China with all its attendant problems more pronounced than at Dian Chi Lake, north of Kunming.

The lake's nickname, the 'Sparkling Pearl embedded in the Highlands' is excessive even by the standards of Chinese hyperbole regarding their natural wonders, though this body of water, China's sixth largest, is a picturesque place around which families and honeymooners flock. Kunming's emblem are a golden horse and green rooster and the Lake here is encircled by golden horse and green rooster hills, the horse born of the sun and the rooster the moon and bringing lush trees, flowers and prosperity when they appear. The more scientific name for this range of hills is the Xi Shan, or Western Mountains, though they possess a third name since physical features are usually personified in China to lend them more worth.

And so it was I found myself hiking up Sleeping Beauty Hills, whose name reflects the undulating contours said to resemble a reclining woman with tresses of hair flowing into the sea. I paused on what may have been the woman's pelvis to consider the legend that says a couple from a local village spent two years here building a Dragon Gate but before the Gate was done, the young man leapt to his death after breaking off the tip of a calligraphy brush. I might have been inclined to see this as an overreaction and an indication that the man was not a suitable choice for a life partner, but instead of blessing her good fortune and finding a less hysterical guy to settle down with, the girl filled the lake with her tears and turned to stone, forming the mountain range whose contours bear her shape.

Modern China has encroached on Dian Chi and the lake is not full of a girl's tears. Rather, this body of water would be inclined to drive one *to* tears since it is so notoriously polluted. The lake has shrunk to a third of its original size and silted up, 55% of all marine life within is dead and on my visit, luminescent green algae was being washed onto the shore and was collecting on the hulls of the pleasure boats shaped like swans. The proposed dam at Tiger Leaping Gorge further north is designed to provide water to Kunming and to irrigate the Lake, though this seems rather like destroying one ecosystem in order to save another.

More comforting is the bike lane that was under construction when I visited and which will completely encircle the lake when complete. This is a beacon of hope since the willingness of local government to spend millions of yuan on a project that does not involve cars or high rise apartments feels like a turning point. A bicycle path is non-essential, gives little appreciable boost to local economic growth and is a frivolous nod to quality of life and recreation. How refreshing this is and I demonstrated my approval by hiring a 10 yuan clapped out bike and setting out along the new path until my pedal fell off.

Back in Cuihu Park I spurned the dodgems and ate a bowl of 'Across the Bridge Noodles', Kunming's most famous culinary offering and named for a woman who after becoming frustrated by taking food to a scholar in a cottage on an island and finding the meal cold by the time she had crossed the bridge, decided to take the broth, add meat and vegetables and heat the soup on arrival. This delicious and famous dish might never have been invented if the scholar had the good grace to break off his studies and fetch the food himself. Thank goodness for male chauvinism.

I slurped my still deliciously hot broth beneath the statue of Nie Er who set music to Tian Han's strident martial song with a surfeit of exclamation marks in the 1920s, and which became the national anthem in 1950.

> Arise! All who refuse to be slaves!
> Let our flesh and blood become our new Great Wall!
> As the Chinese nation faces its greatest peril
> All forcefully expend their last cries
> Arise! Arise! Arise!
> Our million hearts beat as one
> Brave the enemy's fire, March on!
> March on! March on! March on!

Nie marched on to a boy's own adventure of a life that puts my humdrum existence to shame and then ended when he drowned in Japan aged 23 in 1935 while fleeing to the USSR to escape Chinese

Nationalist persecution, though rumours persist that he was murdered by right wing Japanese radicals.

Tian met his fate at the hands of his friends when he was tortured and killed along with the Mayor of Kunming in the Cultural Revolution. This was at a time when 'The East is Red', an ode to the magnificence of Chairman Mao, was adopted as a new anthem for modern China;

> The East is Red, the sun is rising.
> China has brought forth a Mao Zedong
> He amasses fortune for the people
> Hurrah! He is the people's saviour
> Chairman Mao loves the people
> He is our guide, to build a new China.
> Hurrah! He leads us forward!
> The Communist Party is like the sun,
> Wherever it shines, it is bright.
> Wherever there is a Communist Party,
> Hurrah! There the people are liberated!

There are lots of Hurrahs and exclamation marks here too, though my favourite bit is the word 'a' before Mao Zedong which serves to add to the munificence of his presence and the sheer good luck of the people of China that he came. This ditty was ubiquitous in 1960s China when people were encouraged to not only sing but to perform a daily dance in honour of the great man. Even extra-terrestrial beings were given their dose of redness when in 1970, China's first satellite carried a radio transmitter that broadcast The East is Red for all 26 days of its orbit. That'll be why they haven't bothered making contact then.

There are two ways of leaving Kunming. I chose the train North and watched Yunnan's countryside roll past on the way to Lijiang, though the first rail from the city headed due South into Vietnam in 1910. This connection with another country before Kunming had any link with the rest of China is one of the Tourist Board's 18 wonders of the province, though the real transportation wonder in these parts is the Burma Road that heads due West.

This 717 mile highway links Kunming with Assam in India through outrageously fickle, remote and inhospitable terrain. There have been roads and trails through these highlands for centuries but the name 'Burma Road' really resonates because of events of the Second World War. For this was the furthest extent of the Japanese advance when it seemed that the whole of Asia might fall to the relentless Kwantung Army, when Japanese submarines had been spotted in Sydney harbour and Northern Australia was reeling from the bombardment of the Japanese air force.

America sent Joseph Stilwell to command the defence of Burma and coordinate operations with the Chinese Nationalist leader Chiang Kai-Shek. But the US General was so acerbic in his dealings with all, that he earned the sobriquet 'Vinegar Joe' and fell out continually with the de facto leader of China who he regarded as corrupt and useless and referred to as 'Peanut' for reasons that are quite unfathomable to me.

Vinegar Joe was turfed out of Burma by the Japanese in 1943 and walked into India using the 'Stilwell stride' of 105 paces per minute. I tried to replicate this outside my house and gave it up as a bad job after 210 paces. The cutting of the Burma Road necessitated the supply of China by air and there followed the establishment of the 'Flying Tigers' under the guidance of US Air Captain Claire Chennault. He proceeded to organize the flight of hundreds of missions across the five thousand metre high Western Himalayan range which the pilots referred to as 'The Hump' with typical soldierly understatement. 607 planes were lost flying the Hump but the Chinese Army were supplied and rendered capable of offering some resistance to the Japanese invasion of their homeland.

Chennault may have had a girl's name but he was cut from the same military cloth as Vinegar Joe with a face that might have been hewn from granite. Unlike Stilwell, he's a great hero in the Far East and commemorated by statues in China and Taiwan. He's also highly regarded in the US where he was inducted into the 'Society of Red Tape Cutters' in 1942 by Theodor Geisel who is better known as Dr Seuss, and whose polemic that Chennault defended Burma long before others changed their tune about the invulnerability of US to Japanese attack is a long way from green eggs and ham or the Cat in the Hat.

Chennault divorced his first wife and married Chen Xiangmen in China. She was 32 years his junior and a journalist, writer and politician in her own right, but Vinegar Joe was not to be outdone by Chennault's vigour and dashing good looks. Stilwell decided that if the Burma Road was cut, he would simply build another and in 1943, construction began on the 1736km Ledo Road. Churchill expressed his reservations about this 'immense laborious task unlikely to be finished until the need for it has passed', but Stilwell persevered. 15 000 US soldiers and 35 000 locals were engaged on this brute task and the road was finished in two years, though it provided only a fraction of the supplies humped over the Hump by the Flying Tigers.

The great Asian US military testosterone battle didn't finish there since Detachment 101 of the Office of Strategic Services was also based in Kunming to coordinate the resistance fighters of Northern Burma. The office oversaw the formation of the Kachin Rangers who were placed under the command of Carl F Eifler and were dropped behind enemy lines. Tales of these gung ho, we can do anything ass-kicking all American heroes are legion, though my favourite is how they attacked enemy positions with the seat cut out of their pants since their dysentery was so bad it was necessary for them to fight and defecate simultaneously. No doubt the troops played merry hell in the bars of Kunming, trousers intact, on their return from the jungle after the Japanese surrender, though only 150 out of the original three thousand Kachin Rangers survived the war.

It's a wonder how the survivors adjusted to their regular lives after the intensity of their experiences in the highlands of Burma, yet China is a country where everyone has to evolve or perish. This is abundantly true in Lijiang, a beautiful Ming Dynasty gem of a town beneath the snow bound beetling crags of Jade Dragon Snow Mountain. I took a public bus here from Dali and it became one of those inexplicable why have we stopped here, what's going on journeys so typical of China where the driver is inclined to take a break at every opportunity and pull over to talk to the drivers of dusty lorries about who knows what? Moreover, like all public buses in China, this one steadfastly refused to leave the confines of town until every seat and space between the seats was filled with the backside of a fare paying passenger. Thus, the bus traveled the alleyways of Dali at the pace of a porter on the Ledo Road as the driver leaned from his cab to ask any unsuspecting local who had paused for even a fraction of second from his daily chores, whether he wanted to go to Lijiang or not.

Remarkably, the system worked and people who had popped out for half a dozen eggs, cheerfully hopped onto the bus, paid their five yuan and took their seat or threw a bundle on the floor and sat on it for the two hour journey north, except, what with all the fishing for fares and the stop for gas and the pause while the driver had a smoke and the steepness of the roads, two hours soon turned to three and slipped inexorably into four.

But this was alright since the scenery around here is as ruggedly attractive as Claire Chennault and the occasional singing of the passengers was not entirely tuneless. There was a momentary drama when the milk bottle that had been rushed into service by a woman to encourage her small boy to pass water slipped from her grasp and spread its sticky contents like a miniature Yellow River across the floor and onto bags, but I was safe at the back of the bus and able to view the whole shrieking episode with the amused detachment of a man whose bag was safe and dry, though a little crushed beneath a toothless farmer whose wind scoured face sat incongruous beneath a Rolling Stones baseball cap.

I resisted the temptation to ask if the farmer preferred early or late period Stones or whether he felt Mick Jagger's acceptance of an OBE had irreparably damaged the rebellious raison d'être of the band, and before long our stop start, wee stained party had arrived in Lijiang. The town's evolution and need to adapt has been necessary because of tourists like me. For such is the fame of this architectural gem, that visitors have come to Lijiang in their millions, a new airport has been built and the cobbled streets and canal side bridges are groaning under the weight of all those tramping feet.

You see, Lijiang is just too damn pretty. China's industrial boom has put paid to most places like this and as a consequence, the town has become a big favourite of the nascent Chinese tourist industry. Word has spread among the denizens of distant Eastern Mega cities of a place where it's possible to see what China was once like or at least what people *think* China once was. Its known as a honey pot in the tourist trade and certainly the bees were buzzing around on the day that I arrived, though I suppose they always are in a town of 25 000 souls that receives three million visitors each year.

My first impressions were of a broad boulevard, shopping mall, white tile architecture kind of town that can be found all over China and hardly merits a four hour bus ride. But this is the new city, decimated by the 1996 earthquake that killed 300 and injured 16 000 more. The old town is surrounded by all this functional modernity and survived the earthquake almost intact which speaks volumes for the traditional building styles of the local Naxi people and much about the quality of modern Chinese buildings too.

Old Lijiang is known as 'The Eastern Venice' and it's hard to choose the most appealing part of this place where the grey stone houses are topped by roofs and where curved tiles converge into dragons tails over shadowed eaves. Here the cobbled streets are polished to a honey coloured patina by the passage of endless feet and an intricate system of canals bring fresh water along a delightful maze of streets and provide a tinkling, gurgling backdrop to daily life.

I fled the crowds and climbed Lion Hill on the edge of town which is crowned by one of China's tallest wooden pagodas. From here, the grid patterned streets are laid out like a huge printing block and the absence of town walls is clear since the Mu family who ruled the town for 500 years were reluctant to place their name inside a frame or wall, since this would spell `kun` or siege or predicament, an inauspicious message indeed.

Jade Dragon Snow Mountain is visible from Lion Hill too. This 5596 metre hill has been climbed only once though a large proportion of Lijiang's visitors take Asia's highest cable car to a dizzying 4680 metres where chain smoking tourists can buy plastic bags of oxygen to alleviate the effects of altitude for a very reasonable 20 yuan and enjoy the view.

I lingered on Lion Hill until I could see that the crowds had dispersed even from Sifanjie town square and red lanterns were being lit on every cobbled street. Of course, not all tourists leave Lijiang after nightfall, but many are of the baseball hatted huge group, flag following day trip variety who depart to who knows which soulless hotel and leave the town with room to breathe. Lijiang continues to buzz after dark with Western bars (my favourite was called `Sexy Tractor`) outside of which local girls compete in singing contests and stall holders continue to peddle their genuine Lijiang tea, flutes and clocks sporting a view of Jade Dragon Snow Mountain. But the town does get quieter and a semblance of normal life begins to reappear. Fruit and vegetable stalls begin to trade though I was helpfully warned by a sign here that advised me `not to buy the small red fruit shaped like a coconut – it is just a coconut painted red and sold for a high price`, so instead bought a custard apple whose ugly, warty skin conceals sweet flesh inside.

Best of all, locals – real genuine Lijiang residents – sniff the air and emerge blinking into the lantern light. Many of these are from the local Naxi people since two thirds of the town's population are from this tribe. The Naxi might be the most famous of all Yunnan's minority groups and are unmistakable in their blue bonnets and deep blue top with white apron and quilted cape that is tied by two pale blue crossed ribbons. They wear white fur on their backs to represent the day and dark cloth above for the night and use a hieroglyphic script called Dongba that is the only picture board system of writing extant in the world today.

Language and script represent the matriarchal nature of Naxi society where children belong to their mother and village councils are controlled by women. The addition of 'female' to common words lends gravitas and 'male' renders the word insignificant and puny; thus female stone is boulder and male stone a pebble. Such matrilineal societies are not uncommon in Yunnan. Further north, 20 000 Musuo women take as many male partners as they want into their 'flower chamber' and exercise the right of a walking marriage, where men visit their partner at night and leave in the morning. Women visit the local 'penis cave' on nearby Geimu Goddess Peak where phallic rocks lend fecundity to women who want a child that will bear their name and inherit her wealth if it too is female. A 2001 Survey found that 21% of Musuo women are in walking marriages but that these relationships are rather more stable than they appear. Such inconvenient news is no doubt a disappointment to male Chinese tourists who flock to Lugu Lake in the hope of a one night stand with a Musuo woman in this apparently promiscuous tribe. But sex sells, or rather the idea of sex, and a number of flower chambers have been helpfully established and populated by Shanghai whores to satisfy the needs of these titillated tourists.

Both Naxi and Musuo are shamanistic societies where priests engage in trance-like dances to cast out evil and illness. If this fails the Naxi can turn to their traditional firewater boiled with black aconite as a cure all. This potent brew no doubt takes the edge off a difficult day but can also cause paralysis of the larynx and death and many a Naxi has no doubt slipped away on the comfort of a salted and sealed pig carcass which are traditionally used as mattresses, under the influence of this drink.

I took an early bus from Lijiang to the nearby village of Baisha in search of my own curative for my excesses in the Sexy Tractor the previous night. I knew that I would find He Shixiu there. This old man is best known as Dr Ho and has treated 300 000 patients in 40 countries and achieved a degree of fame by securing the signatures of John Cleese, Michael Palin and Bruce Chatwin among others in his visitors book.

The doctor's surgery does not inspire instant confidence in his remedies since it is a chaotic jumble of books, plants, jars of herbs and the occasional mewing Yunnanese cat. The walls are decorated with a remarkably disparate collection of luminaries; nowhere else in the world do Princess Diana and Chairman Mao appear side by side in a frame beneath a clock that tells the time somewhere on earth, though certainly not in Baisha. The sign inside the surgery announces that Dr Ho has 'many friends' and very soon the well-connected man shuffled through the door dressed in a white lab coat and with a wispy beard, greeted me and grabbed my wrist. My pulse revealed that I overindulged in food and drink but was of sound good health, that the simplest infusion of Yunnan herbs would restore my chi and leave me feeling brand new.

Consultation over and herbs carefully measured into a plastic bag, Dr Ho advised me to pay what my heart told me. I thanked him and left the room. Outside I was accosted by a man who pointed to Jade Dragon Snow Mountain, looming massive behind the village. "Have you climbed it?" he asked and I said that I had not. "Then let me provide you with a mule", he said. "180 yuan to 3800 metres and 350 yuan to 4600 metres, though I must charge more for passengers over 100 kg."

This all seemed remarkably business like and precise, though I was injured by his suspicion that my weight might be sufficient to incur a penalty. I was most intrigued by his further offer of 'insurance' at a bargain five yuan, though he was unable to furnish details of what this budget insurance policy might entail. I cannot imagine mule collapse or helicopter rescue were covered by such a nominal sum; perhaps he meant that he would personally undertake to carry me down should I be overcome by altitude – a not insignificant feat since I apparently weigh in excess of 100kg.

Dr Ho is not the only man with a fascination for the plant kingdom that is Yunnan. The British explorer Joseph Rock was sent here in 1922 to hunt for the Chaulmoogra tree and its rumoured cure for leprosy and stayed for 27 years before his forcible removable by the Communists in 1949. Rock is an intriguing character who became fluent in Dongba and lived in Nguluko village just outside Lijiang. He compiled an English-Naxi dictionary and sent 80 000 botanical specimens home, though heartbreakingly his collection of Naxi manuscripts were destroyed when the ship carrying them was sunk by a Japanese torpedo in 1944.

Rock is the ultimate China hand who went native and wandered his curmudgeonly way all over Yunnan. So intimately did he know Yunnan that he was commissioned to design the maps used by the Flying Tigers over the Hump in World War 2. Yet, he remained satisfyingly British, grumpy and aloof and always traveled with a complete set of silverware, a rubber bath tub and a battery powered gramophone. There are many photos of Rock with his porters wheezing and grimacing under their loads as he made his way to still more remote regions in the search for new flowers and herbs; the man himself sepia distant and cross looking, like some latter day Livingstone or Cecil Rhodes.

North of Lijiang, Yunnan becomes more mountainously dramatic and beautiful as Tibet draws closer and China becomes more remote. I rode another broken hearted old bus and skirted Jade Dragon Snow Mountain which by now had become a permanent fixture on my skyline and soon found myself in Qiaotou village beside the Jinsha Jiang and nestled at the entrance to the dramatic defile between the mountain and 5396 metre Haba Shan, its neighbour to the north. This might be the deepest chasm in the world and is known as Tiger Leaping Gorge and I was here to walk its 15 km length to Walnut Grove at the other end.

Margot comes from Australia and owns the guesthouse at the eastern edge of the gorge, dispensing fried eggs, coffee and advice to prospective gorge walkers in a mad melee of perpetual motion, imprecations, profanities and 'you can't go off dressed like that' advice. I hoisted my bag and set off up the steep and stony path with my family and shadowed by a man trailing a pony who despite my insistence that we wanted to walk, remained dogged in pursuit for two hours in the belief that one of us must crack eventually. But no matter how tired, the last thing you'd want to do on this precipitous path that plunges hundreds of feet to the foaming, thrashing Yangtze below, is to ride a stumbling and swaying old nag led by a man in slip on dress shoes.

Four hours of steady effort brought us to a tiny Naxi village perched on a bluff and surrounded everywhere by fields of rape seed and by towering, mountainous magnificence. We stayed in the simplest of rooms for 10 yuan, played badminton in the courtyard and ate fresh garden produce beneath racks of corncobs drying in the late afternoon sun. The sense of off the beaten track satisfaction is high here, though the scenery and drama improved still further the next day.

Beyond the Naxi village, the path climbs steeply up the 28 bends; a misnomer that fails to prepare the unwary traveler for the near 50 bends that lie in wait, before emerging onto a path that becomes narrower and cut out of the rock and below which the river is further away and seems angrier than ever. The Yangtze drops 700 feet in 12 miles in these parts, and this descent coupled with the narrowness of the gorge has resulted in a cataract that is fast flowing in the extreme. No chance of a game of Pooh sticks here, though remarkably men have tried to raft through here on a journey down the Yangtze from its source on the Gelandandong glacier high on the Tibetan plateau to the sea. Less remarkably, the men engaged in this venture were all killed, though a successful trip was made later by a team that decided to forgo their rafts on this section and bounced and ballooned their way down the gorge entirely sealed in a rubber capsule.

Such foolhardy souls clearly failed to spot the sign at the narrowest point of the gorge which explains that this is 'one of the dangerous gorges in the world which is not convenient to sail. However there is a kind of beauty making magnificence tugging at people's heartstrings'. 'Inconvenient' hardly seems to do justice to the power of the river here, though my heart strings were indeed yanked at this narrow point that gives the gorge its name since here a mythical tiger with hunters in hot pursuit crossed the river in one prodigious leap and made good his escape.

As ever in China, progress and change is encroaching on what seems unchangeable. A road has been blasted near the base of the gorge and there are plans to dam and harness its power to feed the demands of Kunming to the south and Chinese cities further east. Provincial governors in China love such large scale infrastructure projects that provide quick revenue from the giant east coast corporations. A popular saying goes 'Build a bridge and you'll get silver, build a road and you'll get gold, but construct a dam and you'll be counting diamonds' and China, long gripped by dam fever, is currently the owner of 85 000 dams, fully 46% of the world's total.

Such projects are an expression of the triumph of man over nature but have a heavy human cost too, since these 85 000 dams have led to the displacement of 12 million people. The people of Yunnan are protesting against such a project and know that displacement will give them a choice of becoming marginalised urban residents with no land or will move them to more mountainous areas where all the best land is already farmed. The movement against the dam has become the focal point for China's fledgling environmental action groups. Such has been the strength of this voice that the project has for now been shelved, pending further consultation. This marks a change in China even greater than the construction of the cycle path at Dian Chi lake, since environmental concern and the voice of the people do not rank high on governmental priorities here. The knowledge that Li Xiaopeng, the son of former Prime Minister Li Peng who pushed through the Three

Gorges Dam project, is one of the major backers of the Tiger Leaping Gorge dam, provides less of a rosy glow.

My route continued high above the Yangtze and past the Halfway House with its `Number one toilet in heaven and earth` and I can confirm that the view from this room is sufficiently good to detain the visitor for much longer than one would normally wish to tarry in a Chinese toilet. Finally the path began to descend gently to its finish at Walnut Grove; a hamlet as pretty as its name suggests and I left this land of dragons, tigers and Tolkien grandeur and was back in the real world.

The path by no means finishes in the village. For Tiger Leaping Gorge is just a tiny portion of the Cha Ma Dao or 'Tea Horse Trail' that stretches over two thousand kilometres from Sichuan to Tibet, traversing 78 mountains over three thousand metres, with 51 river crossings, 15 rope bridges and 10 iron bridges along its way. The trail was established as a form of political control over Tibet due to the Chinese desire for the fine Pu`er tea that is native to Yunnan and grows on bushes up to one thousand years old, and was exchanged for Tibetan steeds at the rate of 50kg per beast, which doesn't seem bad value for a whole horse.

The trade really took off during the Tang Dynasty in the 7th century and soon two thousand porters a day were carrying up to 150kg each (150kg!) across mountains and streams and presumably developing spines of steel and calves like melons in the process. Every year 7500 tons of tea was carried by these remarkable men who were the original coolies from the term 'ku-li` meaning `bitter strength`. The phrase `ku` has particular resonance in China where the ability to eat bitterness, to endure all manner of hardship is highly prized. This helps to explain the regard for the Long Marchers of 1935 and for the leadership of the earthy peasant revolutionary Deng Xiaopeng in the 1980s, a man who spent years in re-education camps and whose son was paralysed when thrown from a window during the Cultural Revolution and who had therefore eaten bitterness in spades.

One can only imagine the bitter lives of the coolies though at times their hardship takes physical form as the visitor climbs yet another hill and imagines 150kg on his back or looks at photos of these men dwarfed by their preposterous loads. Most poignant are the small holes by the side of the stone slab paths formed by the T-shaped walking sticks used by the coolies to counterbalance their loads as they tip tapped along or took a breather, and which remain as a testament to their ordeal. Remarkably, since the trade only petered out following the Japanese surrender in 1945, there are some survivors of the trade who can describe the wild route over the Hengduan Shan and the deep gorges of the Jinsha and the Cha ma si 'tea and horse offices' along the way which were established in 1074 to control, regulate and tax the trade.

Tea is not the only commodity to have been strapped to men's backs along the Cha Ma Dao. The trail has also been used to transport textiles, cigarettes, whisky, musk, furs and the intriguing Cordyceps Sinensis or Caterpillar Fungus that grows only at altitude in Tibet. This fungus feeds off a caterpillar that mummifies it and has earned the name `dong chang xia chao` or 'winter worm, summer fruit'. It's a highly valued ingredient in Chinese medicine, a treatment for cancer and an aphrodisiac since it has a unique balance of ying and yang due to its animal and vegetable quality. The amazing properties of these mummified worms was further enhanced by the victories of Wang Junxia and Qu Yunxia at the 1993 World Championships in Stuttgart where they broke the World Record in the 1500, 3000 and 10000 metre races. Their coach claimed it was all down to Cordyceps, though their failure to repeat the feat suggests that other substances may also have come into play.

I congratulated myself that my efforts through Tiger Leaping Gorge were entirely non-Cordyceps assisted though admittedly my efforts pale in comparison to those of the Times correspondent George Ernest Morrison who in 1895 wrote a book called 'An Australian in China' detailing his three thousand kilometre walk from Shanghai to Rangoon. A good deal of this hike traced the old Tea Horse Trail and was completed according to George at a total outlay of 18 pounds sterling.

Contrary to George's good example, I spurned the pedestrian route and declined another troublesome Chinese bus journey for the final leg of my Yunnan journey north. George would have been mystified as I handed over fully 100 yuan for the two hour taxi ride to Zhongdian but I felt as comfortable as Mao in his palanquin as the road slipped past houses that became more solidly Tibetan in shape, faces became more weather beaten and less Chinese and even the cows turned into hairy yaks.

Zhongdian or its Tibetan name Gyalthang are hard to find on a modern map since the town changed its name in 2001. A November 1997 China Daily report said that the Yunnan Economy and Technology Research Centre had established with 'certainty' that Deqin county, of which Zhongdian is a part, is the legendary valley identified by James Hilton as 'Shangri-La' in his 1933 novel Lost Horizon. According to this august research body, the region exactly matches the descriptions that Hilton gave, though the author almost certainly never visited this part of Northern Yunnan and at least six other Asian destinations claim that they are Shangri-La too. The pronouncement is of course in no way connected to the Yunnan Tourist Board who were represented at the Research centre and who by happy coincidence have seen a huge increase in tourist traffic and the building of Shangri-La airport whose name is so much more likely to drag in tourist dollars than plain old Deqin.

Hitler was much less sure of the location of Shangri-La. In 1935, his SS leader Himmler established the Ahnenerbe organization, a think tank for the study of intellectual history to research the history of the Aryan master race and in 1938, SS Gruppenfuhrer Ernst Schafer was sent to find Shangri-La in the hope of finding the master race there. There is no record of Schafer pitching up in Deqin but what the Yunnan Economy and Technology Research Centre and the German National Socialist Party have in common (and that's not a sentence you'll hear every day) is that they fail to grasp that Shangri-La, based on an old Tibetan notion of Shambala, probably doesn't exist on a map. It's merely a concept, a conceit or an aspiration. Anyway, having read Lost Horizon with its gloomy lamasery, ancient scary monks and sense of foreboding, I'm not sure I'd want to go there anyway.

Zhongdian town is cobbled and ancient like Lijiang but has none of that town's manufactured sterility, artificial joviality or pressing crowds. These cobbled streets sit at 3500 metres and its *cold* up here a long way from anywhere. I arrived to find the whole population of the town keeping warm with a two-step around a giant brazier in the town square under the shouted instructions of what appeared to be a yak, but on closer inspection was a man in a very hairy coat. This dancing happens every evening in Zhongdian and is a wonderful display of community and conviviality where teenagers in leather jackets, families and old men in traditional tribal wear join hands in a huge concentric waltz around the square.

It feels like a privilege to watch, though slightly intrusive because this is not designed for the tourists; it's just what happens around here of an evening. Nevertheless, I was spotted huddled on the stone steps of a restaurant (hot yak milk tea available inside) and dragged onto the square into the thick of the action where I shuffled and clapped my circular way around the fire too.

If tourists come at all to Zhongdian it is to see the Songzanlin Si. Known as Sumtseling Gompa in Tibetan, its most affectionate moniker is 'Little Potala' and is an admirable alternative for those who don't possess the wherewithal to get to the real Potala palace in Lhasa. This was my first real Tibetan temple and I visited with the expectation that it would be not too dissimilar from all those dozens of Chinese temples I had visited further east. How wrong I was.

The first impression inside this 300 year old temple is of darkness. The rooms are lit by yak butter lamps and as a consequence, the temple is all flickering yellow light and soot covered walls. Noise and smells hit the visitor next and almost simultaneously since the lamps give off a rich and creamy and slightly rancid aroma and the monks in serried ranks, near invisible in their red robes in the dim light chant, hum in a monotonous and hypnotic tone. This wasn't like China at all.

The assault on the senses of all this Tibetan culture should come as no surprise since this region really *is* part of Tibet but had been separated along with parts of Sichuan and all of Qinghai province further north by communist cartographers, eager to lessen the geographical and therefore the spiritual and cultural scope of that ancient region.

So, I really was in Tibet. But my journey north wasn't finished yet. The next day amidst flurries of snow, I climbed aboard a four wheel drive bound for Deqin town five hours distant over the 4300 metre Hong-la Pass and within sight of the border of modern Tibet which lies on the other side of giant Meili Xue Shan. This extraordinary, glorious triangular snow-capped mountain is called Kawa Karpo in Tibet and is like the mountains you would have drawn as a child. It's nearly seven thousand metres high, one of eight holy Tibetan mountains and has never been climbed despite the efforts of a joint Chinese/Japanese team who perished in a huge avalanche here in 1991. The journey over the pass through snow, edging past lorries and trying to ignore the huge drop below was a trial but the views of Meili framed by prayer flags sending their messages skywards in a stiff northerly breeze felt like an epiphany.

China's lowest glacier Mingyong is here as well, curling serpent like and silver to the valley floor, though its 200 metre retreat in the last four years is a reminder that even in this remote place the climate is on the turn. China Daily reassuringly reports that 'with efficient measures and continuous efforts from the government and people, preservation of glacier characteristics in the region will be realised', though it's not clear how these measures and efforts are being implemented. The problem is that like Dian Chi and Tiger Leaping Gorge, Mingyong is so vast that it looks indestructible no matter what humankind throws its way, and thus preservation seems unnecessary.

Yunnan's beauty will endure of course and as I flew from Shangri-la, I could see the immensity of the landscape below through fluffy good weather clouds. There were the Western Himalayas and the road to Tibet and sparkling in the last of the evening sunshine, the mighty rivers flowing north to south. And there at last, a great silver curve at Shigu sending the Yangtze River east before the clouds closed in and it was gone.

INNER MONGOLIA

內蒙古

1,178,755 sq km
Population 23.9 million

'The greatest happiness is to scatter your enemy, to drive him before you, to see his cities reduced to ashes, to see those who love him shrouded in tears, and to gather into your bosom his wives and daughters'

Genghis Khan

There was a purple glow in the sky as my train clanked into Baotou and I thrilled to see the first rays of dawn as the sun rose over the million square kilometres of Inner Mongolia.[52] But this was a man-made industrial glow from the foundries of a steel town that sprawls over the steppes for miles, disfiguring the landscape and sending fiery sparks into the predawn sky. Romantic notions of grasslands, horses and nomads are destroyed in Baotou; melted, incinerated, burned by the demand for steel, steel, steel.

My maths teacher sleeping compartment companion was getting off here. She extolled the virtues of her hometown, no doubt enthralled by the empiricism of production, the brute logic of the foundries and the symmetry of cooling towers. But I could only stare mutely from the window, awed by the devastation of industry and glad to be moving on to a part of Inner Mongolia that might look more Mongolian and less like the gates of hell.

Yet outside Baotou is the most symbolically Mongolian place of all. For it was at nearby Dongsheng that the great Genghis Khan is said to have died and was buried in 1227. The Chinese constructed a great mausoleum here in 1955 to commemorate the life of Mongolia's 'Universal King' and to curry favour with the locals who might be expected to shovel coal to make steel.

It's impossible to separate fact from legend in the life of Genghis Khan. Born in 1162, he is said to have been clutching a clot of blood as he entered the world and to have killed his stepbrother at an age when I was more worried about finishing my maths homework. By 1210, Genghis had conquered a huge swathe of territory in Asia with the use of tough cavalry who slit the veins in their horse's neck and drank their blood in order to travel light and reduce the problems of supplying an army over such huge distances. The ruthlessness of Khan's legions would put Hitler to shame. Genghis insisted that towns must be destroyed so thoroughly that by dusk he should be able to ride across the remains without his horse stumbling. The cavalry raped and pillaged and burned and drank warm horse neck blood then burned some more, destroying villages and cities and in one instance, a whole civilisation

---

52   Inner Mongolia is 12% of China's total landmass; one of the giant provinces in the north and west of the country that dwarf the small crowded Han provinces further east in everything but population.

called the Xixia in Northern China (see Ningxia chapter) so completely that historians have difficulty piecing together anything that happened there.

When Genghis died, 10,000 soldiers accompanied the cortege back to Mongolia and everyone within 10 miles of the procession on either side of the road was killed so that his death couldn't be prematurely reported back at his royal court. A grand funeral indeed, though there is no record that he had GENGHIS spelt out in flowers along the side of the hearse like proper gangsters. But where he died and where he is buried is unknown - no one even seems sure *how* he died.[53] It seems certain that wherever he was buried it's not at Dongsheng since the site has been thoroughly excavated and only a few weapons found. Genghis left testament that his burial place should be kept secret; all the emperors of the subsequent Yuan Dynasty followed suit and those who constructed their tombs were always killed so that they could not disclose their whereabouts.

Of course none of this is allowed to spoil a good tourist opportunity. Thousands of travelers make the pilgrimage to Dongsheng every year, though not me because I could not face the prospect of getting off at Baotou. So I stayed on the train and watched the town recede to the horizon and the scenery revert to a wide expanse of stones and dirt framed by wrinkled brown mountains, though the glow and orange smoke from the furnaces remained in view long after Baotou had gone.

Inner Mongolia's provincial capital is called Hohhot which means 'green city'. This sounded much nicer than Baotou so I got off there. Mongolian myths thrive in Hohhot too with soaring eagles painted on Communist concrete office blocks, beer and cigarettes sold from concrete Mongolian tents in car parks and 'genuine' Mongolian leather goods available in shops throughout the city. But this is really a Chinese town where 80% of the population is Han with little interest in Mongolian culture other than as a means to sell Genghis Khan wooden swords to the tourists.

---

53   The most common account involves Genghis falling from his horse, but battle wounds, pneumonia, even murder by a captured Xixia Princess who concealed a weapon in her vagina are rumoured.

There are traces of Tibetan culture in Hohhot too since Altan Khan who founded the town in the 16th century invited Tibetan monk Sonyam Gyatso to Lake Kokoner in 1578, gave him the title Dalai Lama and introduced Tibetan Gelugpa sect Buddhism to Inner Mongolia.[54] I walked through town past clothes shops and fast-food cafes under a blistering sun to the Tibetan corner of Hohhot. Two temples called Da and Xilitu Zhao are separated by streaming traffic along the wide Danan Jie Highway here. The temples resonated with bells and the low murmuring chant of Tibetan monks, but though the buildings are theoretically 500 years old, they'd been restored to within an inch of their lives and the chants seemed inauthentic so close to sea level and with the cars thundering by outside.

Most of Hohhot had this counterfeit quality, like a film set that might fall over in the next big gust of wind. Modern buildings were topped by Islamic cupolas so that the streets looked like those of a city in Kazakhstan and Chinese were crowding the Mongolian hotpot cafes eating mutton and nailao white cheese, but I was at a loss how to find any genuine Mongolian people, a theme that recurred throughout my time in the province.

The Qing Dynasty recreated hutong beside the temples was inauthentic too but I wandered down where every vendor was selling pictures of Genghis Khan and a myriad of leather goods - saddles, camels, hats and sheaths for extravagant knives - for the Chinese view of Mongolia appears to assume that this is a people who exist only to charge around on horseback and skin wild animals.

The faux Mongolian shop fronts led to a huge new Guanyin Temple and I was ready to be an unmoved by this too. But though the paint was barely dry on its intricate eaves and big studded red doors, the temple is so huge that I couldn't help but be impressed. Inside is a massive Guanyin statue, painted luridly gold and in the temple grounds sat a huge squat stupa painted with Buddha eyes like the traditional ones in Kathmandu and Tibet and around which locals were shuffling and chanting as they span prayer wheels. This was a religious version of the industrial gigantomania in China that inspired dams on the Yangtze

---

54   See Tibet chapter. Lake Kokoner is now called Qinghai Lake.

and steel works in Baotou, but it was good to see something built that had no economic rationale; driven by the needs of the soul instead of export figures. It's just that temple and statue and stupa needed to *weather* a bit so they didn't look so new; go to Hohhot in 500 years and they'll look just fine.

The streets around the temple were lined with more leather shops and I began to wonder if there were any sheep or cows with skins left in Mongolia. No one was buying the Genghis Khan hunting bow and broadsword set, but the cowboy hats (made of leather of course) were going down a storm. These were the holiday headgear of choice for Chinese tourists in Hohhot and they wore them in groups, determinedly having a good time. Hawaiian shirts serve the same purpose on Hainan Island and in Beijing, 'I heart BJ' T-shirts are popular, though I am confused whether this means the wearer loves China's ancient northern capital or is devoted to oral sex.

Hohhot's green city boast must be partly due to the large area of parkland in the city centre. Hyde Park or Central Park it isn't; Qingcheng Park is a rather dry and windswept place with sparse trees, grass trampled to dirt and flurries of dust blown across the concrete paths and into my face. But local families and tourists, their cowboy hats worn at a jaunty angle, were having a great time as they ran screaming from the fibre glass ghost train or pedaled boats shaped like swans around the expansive lake.

It all seemed very unexciting and provincial which is what Hohhot is, so many miles from the sophistication and economic drive further east. Yet as I wandered the back streets of the town, past cafes selling flatbread and sweet boiled milk naipi biscuits, I did at last find something old and authentic in Hohhot. There is an 18th century five tower pagoda hidden in the nothing to see centre of town, the oldest part of Hohhot but where the high-rises could be anywhere in China, notwithstanding the eagles painted on the side and the Mongolian tents in the yards outside. The tower is all that remains of the temple that stood here and is inexpressibly beautiful. The pagoda's beauty is partly due to its incongruity. Curved and sinuous and covered in carved Buddhas and with a rare celestial map chiselled into the wall, its form is much more Indian than Mongolian or Chinese. The spindly Qingcheng trees offered little shade so I rested from the hard summer sun in the cool of the pagoda's shrine room, the calm face of a Sakyamuni Buddha watching me and feeling pleased at last to have found something in Hohhot that was truly old.

Hohhot is proud of its Mongolian heritage though it has been repackaged and Genghis'd into a cliché. A huge museum, looking like an airport terminal, has been constructed outside town to celebrate Mongolian culture and to remind the city of its roots. The building is a wonderful Mongolian tent built of steel and glass, though the exhibits are rather less impressive than the building itself. Mongolian hunting, conquests, flora and fauna are commemorated here, though the shop window dummies dressed as Genghis Khan, the stuffed bears and wolves became tiresome after a while and the display on Mongolian landforms and geology was unspeakably dull.

Part of the dullness of the place was down to the overwrought and portentous language of the exhibit information. This was usually grammatically correct but possessed such an amount of formal and scientific detail that it became meaningless. 'The museum systematically portraying the distinctive and fascinating image of Inner Mongolia from microscopic to macroscopic aspect' droned my museum leaflet guide as I excitedly deliberated whether to look at macroscopic or microscopic Mongolia first.

The information became rabidly nationalist when it wasn't plain dull. A whole room was given over to China's space programme though this display was more exciting with burnt pieces of rocket fuselage and the suits of astronauts returned as heroes from space. The space program was imposed on Inner Mongolia because of the province's size and secrecy though the information suggested it was the thrill of the local Mongolians at taking part in this heroic endeavour 'an important mark of the integrated national power getting more and more puissant' that was the key to the government's choice. 'All nationalities in Inner Mongolia actively support the Motherland's space undertakings' trumpeted the information, 'to make an even greater contribution for the great renaissance of the Chinese nation' which suggests that the sending of men into space has more to do with patriotism than with scientific necessity.

The astronauts were in on the nationalist programme too. Their excited recollections of the view of Earth from the spaceship were not of the vast blue planet, its seas and oceans veiled in gossamer cloud but of China. "When the spaceship entered outer space, I saw my beautiful homeland", said Yang Liwei, Senior Colonel on the 2003 Shenzhou 5 mission. Like an infatuated lover, the view made him think of "the greatness of the Chinese nation and the greatness of our nation's power in science and technology" as if the other nations, the stars and the great infinite expanse of the cosmos were not even there.

Inner Mongolia has terrestrial as well as cosmic discoveries. More dinosaur bones have been found here than anywhere else in China since the vast grasslands north of Hohhot were a paradise of lakes, marshes and forests a mere 70 million years ago. Bones, skeletons and reconstructions littered the museum - huge long necked herbivores, woolly mammoths, razor toothed lizards and a model of a Gigantoraptor, an eight metre long birdlike predator that is the most famous discovery, dug up and reassembled in 2005. The exhibits climaxed in a eulogy to the planet, how we should protect and preserve our world to prevent further extinctions. The dinosaurs had a 'refulgent and solemn history' said the signs. 'Let us sing a coronach for the mournful life of those species who used to live on the earth to arouse that man should have the misery feeling of their living environment' it continued. 'Man has only one earth, man belongs to the earth, however the earth does not belong to man alone!' The sign boards were nearly hysterical by now and I wondered if any tourists in leather cowboy hats had read this who came from the horribly polluted coal towns of Shanxi.

Hohhot is host to the annual Mongolian Nadaam Festival, when men race horses, shoot arrows and dress in ludicrously short pants to wrestle with each other. I was too early for this year's games but took a taxi to the racecourse to see where it all takes place. It's a nationally famous event so I'd expected something other than the decrepit concrete stands and untended dusty field sprinkled with wild grasses and prickly bushes upon which a few desultory nags grazed, looking too thin and completely unlike the descendants of Genghis Khan's great cavalry.

Hohhot's fake Mongolianisms had run riot in the race ground too. Every cafe was a concrete patterned approximation of a Mongolian tent and Chinese staff swept the floor dressed in bright nylon versions of the jackets worn by traditional Mongolian horsemen. The sweepers were very happy to leave their brooms and pose for photos, but as a record of Mongolia the pictures felt false, like passing a Beefeater costume or a pearly queen off as the typical apparel of a Londoner.

The problem with Hohhot I had decided in my deep travelers wisdom, is that it is a film set, a falsehood; a Mongolian city with no Mongolians (though with plenty of Chinese *pretending* to be Mongolian). I was scouring the city with notebook and pen searching desperately for something authentic but found only cowboy hats, newly painted ancient temples and men urging me to have my photo taken with an eagle on a street corner.

So, although Hohhot was pleasant and green, I'd written it off until at last the city showed me something beautiful when the sun went down. Like most Chinese towns, Hohhot has a city square surrounded by roaring traffic and called something suitably strident and revolutionary. Hohhot's is 'New Republic Square' and after dark became the throbbing heart of the city. The public square almost always serves as meeting place, entertainment and bazaar for Chinese city dwellers; only Tiananmen Square in Beijing is a sterile place, policed and videoed so heavily that it has no purpose other than as a statement of party power. I determined to go to the town square of the city after dark in the hope of seeing local families having fun after a day tending shop, selling hats or posing as Genghis Khan soldiers. Hohhot town square was crowded with thousands of people. The main event this evening was a low-budget kung fu movie on a screen the size of a tennis court, on which so many pixels had burned out that the audience occasionally missed a foot or fist connect with a villain's face.

Ball games were popular too. Where in some towns, teenagers sit on motorbikes and look threatening or carry guns and *are* threatening, in Hohhot they preferred to bounce large green fluorescent balls to each other, though the possibility of being hit on the back of the head by one of these as I walked around the square was quite threatening too. People were playing badminton and skipping and here at last were real Mongolians dancing not for the tourists or their appreciation of China's space programme, but because they wanted to dance and not dressed as extras from a low-budget Genghis Khan movie either.

Despite the traffic, the movie and the high rise twinkling neon, New Republic Square had a mediaeval feel. There were no benefits of new republicanism for the beggars who dotted the square, hand outstretched and displaying suppurating wounds and severed limbs.[55] Disabled orchestras sawed away at erhus and banged symbols and drums and midgets danced and tumbled for crumpled jiao notes, subdivisions of yuan that are almost worthless but who grabbed up their money and scurried away on little legs when the police came. The kung fu movie struck me as mediaeval too, the modern equivalent of minstrels or Shakespearean theatre, the communal experience as important as the art, the crowds booing or cheering with every kick and punch. In fact the very notion of a mass gathering instead of staying in one's own apartment to watch one's own TV is delightfully communal and oldfashioned, though I wondered about -30°C wintertime Hohhot when the winds blow across the steppes from Siberia, and whether the people still came then to bounce balls and applaud dancing dwarves in New Republic Square.

Of course none of this felt like the wide open Mongolia that I wanted to see so I left Hohhot the next morning. I never catch a plane in China when a sleeper train is available but the train from Hohhot to Inner Mongolia's far north would be nearly 50 hours, the first half dispiritingly in the wrong direction to Beijing. So I opted to fly three hours to the grasslands of Haila'er instead, though when I saw the plane parked on the airport tarmac, I wished I had caught the train.

Every breath of wind bounced our 1960s jet around the clouds like a luminous ball on New Republic Square and the engines mounted on the tail fin made such a din that it would have been impossible to hear the music or movie on board if such affectations had existed. It wasn't quite as bad as the 1950s Antonov I rode to Pyongyang in North Korea, where luggage bounced around the cabin and the absence of seat belts made it easier to stand and respect the anthem and Kim Jong Il's

---

55   There is no free healthcare in China since income tax is only 3%. The government prefers roads and space rockets to hospitals.

portrait as we entered North Korean airspace, but it was still pretty bad.

I could barely manage my complimentary bread roll and glass of water and the 30 passengers in single row on the cigar thin vehicle that looked more like a Long March space rocket than an aeroplane looked distinctly edgy. The woman in front of me had to request a bag from an attendant who in no way conformed to sylphlike, cherry lipped cabin crew clichés, and vomited copiously throughout the flight as the wind buffeted us from side to side over the nothingness of grassland below that I could helpfully see through windows on my left and right.

I hope that I maintained a measure of stoical calm throughout, though I didn't know it was possible for my palms to sweat this much. When the pilot walked to the back of the plane and queued for the toilet with the other passengers, my stiff upper lip began to wobble and when he announced that it was very windy and dangerous outside but we would 'have a go at landing anyway' I started to make my peace with God. But the landing was fine and softened by brief tourist details of the town below in English that were utterly indecipherable and therefore pointless since I was the only foreigner on the plane, and I barely resisted the temptation to kiss the tarmac when we got off at Haila'er.

From my airborne coffin the little rows of toy houses had been as an island in a sea of green grass, for here the steppes wash right against Haila'er; a car launched from the shacks beached on the edge of town would soon crest the horizon and be voyaging solitary for days until it discovered new lands. A road sign outside the airport said 'Haila'er 6km, Gagner Temple 188km' which suggested my early impressions of town from the plane had been right; there was nothing much here in Inner Mongolia's far north west to tempt the tourist and what little there is was far, far away.

It was tricky to dwell on the great spirituality - or was it terror - of such a huge empty space because the taxi foot to the floor fury drive from the airport to town became so nerve wracking that I forgot all about grasslands and wished I was back on the aeroplane. The driver overcharged me horribly too and wouldn't perform the dance I was accustomed to where passenger and driver bargain, pretend to be outraged at each other's price and eventually smile and agree on a fare that is agreeable to both. This fellow refused to budge from a price that was at least three times the going rate, but what was I to do six kilometres from town outside the tiny airport surrounded by nothing but grass? My irritation was exacerbated when he called his friend over for a lift into town at the expense of the dumb foreigner with the deep pockets before commencing our white knuckle ride, the friends filling the cab with cigarette smoke. There are times when you have to stand up for yourself in China and refuse to be pushed to the back of a bus queue, ignored by a shop assistant or patronised by petty bureaucrat in a cheap uniform and this was my Alamo. We screeched to a halt in the town centre, I extracted my bag and gave the driver precisely half of what we had agreed, telling him that his friend could pay the other half. The driver was furious and leapt from the taxi with the same speed as he drove, shouting and pushing and demanding his money. I explained my view and hoped that a crowd wouldn't form, but my problem vanished in an instant when I said I would fetch the police. My probably unlicensed assailant jumped back into his probably unlicensed cab and sped away with a screech of tyres and screeching imprecations.

The town's purpose seems only to refuel, eat and sleep on long journeys through the grasslands. There were more Mongolians here and I began to recognise their language, guttural and distinct from sing song Chinese. Improbably, the long reach of Japanese military ambition extended to remote Haila'er when the town became the furthest edge of their wartime empire, unmolested by the Soviets who were preoccupied by Hitler in the West. I took a friendlier taxi to the grandly named Memorial Park of the World Anti-Fascist War and my driver was Mongolian. She greeted me in Russian, naturally assuming a large Caucasian this close to the border must be from Vladivostok or Novosibirsk, and had a brave stab at English before we settled on stilted Chinese. She said English was an important language and was proud of her daughter's efforts to learn it at school. But she didn't like her daughter's teacher who never encouraged her and seized on the smallest mistake and this sounded suspiciously like my experience of learning Chinese when I longed for approval or even a hint of encouragement amongst the disapproval of my syntax and tones.

The driver was warm and kind and interesting and knocked two yuan of my fare because she said she had driven the wrong way and I marvelled at the extremes of taxi driving in Haila'er. The last part of the drive climbed the only hill of any size in a town, for this is where the final battles were fought for control of this wild and inhospitable place, though *true* control of the massive grasslands could never be achieved by mere soldiers.

I wandered a series of trenches and machine-gun posts that commanded a view of miles of grass and then down stone steps into cold and damp tunnels that had been dug by slave labour and from where the Japanese organised and consolidated their control. The information boards were understandably sympathetic to the poor locals enslaved with shovels in these tunnels and predictably outraged about the Japanese being here at all, though I had some sympathy for the poor young conscripts enduring Mongolian winters so far from Tokyo and Osaka, from sake and sakura.

'These solid Japanese fortifications could hardly resist justice nor could Japanese imperialism's sweet dream' said the same information boards. I was led past displays of rusting rifles and grenades to the tune of The Internationale, a song of equality and justice that I love but whose own sweet dream was so mangled and misappropriated by a series of unpalatable 20th century tyrants.

The Chinese resistance here was called the Salvation Army which conjures up images of soldiers dressed in bonnets armed with tambourines and guerrilla warfare with trombones, but it was the Soviets who finally liberated Haila'er. They invaded in July 1945 after Hitler's defeat and though the battle was hardly a cakewalk and 227 Soviets were killed[56], the victory had an air of inevitability as the elite Japanese troops had all been withdrawn to fight and die from American bullets in the Pacific. Japan surrendered after the tragedy of Hiroshima and Nagasaki, but the troops in Haila'er ignored or misunderstood Hirohito's order to do the unthinkable and surrender. So the fighting in Northeast Asia continued until September which gave the Soviets time

---

56 How galling for the families of these men who had battled their way to Berlin only to be killed in this obscure corner of Asia so close to the war's end.

to find and capture Manchuria's puppet emperor Pu-Yi (see Jilin chapter) and to impose a sympathetic communist regime in North Korea whose civil aviation would frighten me half to death some years later.

The fight for Inner Mongolia in the dying days of World War II was savage but merely the last in a long series of battles here, for so much grassy flat land is ideal for marching feet, horses hooves and tanks. Genghis Khan marauded through of course (Khan's movements should always be referred to as 'marauding' and never merely riding which does not evoke the necessary wild and abandoned bloodlust), but it was his grandson Kublai Khan who truly consolidated Mongol greatness and sweet imperial dreams by establishing the Yuan Dynasty in Beijing in 1271, part of the largest empire the world has seen.[57]

Kublai Khan's successful control of China was based on his willingness to assimilate and adopt Chinese customs which enabled 100,000 Mongols to control 200 million Chinese, though the Khan's preference for Chinese pastoralism over Mongolian nomadic traditions destroyed the very skills of horsemanship that had made the Mongols strong and by 1368 they had been chased out of China for good.

But Kublai Khan is best known not for his court in Beijing but for his Summer Palace in Inner Mongolia.

In Xanadu did Kublai Khan
A stately pleasure dome decree
Where Alph the sacred river ran
Through caverns measureless to man,
Down to a sunless sea.

So wrote Samuel Taylor Coleridge in an 18th-century haze of opium and whose 'Vision in a Dream' was inspired by the words of Marco Polo and inspired in turn the name of Citizen Kane's mansion in an Orson Welles movie, all manner of 1970s prog-rockers and Olivia Newton John to sing of a mythical Palace called Xanadu.

---

57 They called Beijing 'Dadu'. Chinese historians have little good to say about the Yuan dynasty today, though this has more to do with the indignity of foreign occupation than the achievements of the Mongol Yuan which included China's first occupation of Yunnan and Tibet. In the same way, British control brought only hardship to Hong Kong according to most Chinese historians.

Marco Polo visited the Khan's Palace in 1275 and was positively beside himself with the opulence and magnificence of the place. The traveler speaks of marble palaces, beasts and birds, the Khan hunting with leopards and generally living a life of absurd luxury that would put Led Zeppelin to shame and that his grandfather would have thoroughly disapproved of. Indeed, Xanadu has become a metaphor for foolish overindulgence; Michael Jackson's Neverland ranch was compared to the Khan's folly as is Bill Gates' huge mansion, nicknamed Xanadu 2.0 by the press, though I suspect all such criticism is rooted in envy; perhaps we would all hunt with leopards if we had a chance?

There is no suggestion of opulence in modern day Shangdu where nothing remains of Kublai Khan's summer palace - no walls, no statues, not even a leopard wandering forlornly around. All of which serves to emphasise the strange incongruity of these two centuries of Mongolian success. Unnoticed before Genghis Khan, the Mongolians reverted to their natural state of anonymity after the fall of the Yuan Dynasty and it's difficult in today's Inner Mongolia to notice them at all amidst the Chinese.

I tried again the following day to meet a Mongolian who was not a taxi driver or a shop assistant, by taking a trip to the grasslands outside town. This was a difficult thing to organise; no one in Haila'er seemed able to advise me where to go because no one appeared to have been. I was amazed at this parochialism, this lack of curiosity about the world outside the confines of this small town, but most people here seemed to find everything they needed in the shopping centre, the night market and the ubiquitous KFC. My taxi driver sucked his teeth when I asked him to drive the 50 kilometres out of town but, curious to see the grasslands for himself, was willing to put aside his fears that we might drive off the edge of the world and so we went.

It was all a bit disappointing at first. We drove past three huge power stations that stood like a massive monuments on the flat land and could be seen for miles. There were also several Mongolian camps for tourists - tents lined in neat rows, horse riding, fences made of wagon wheels and all you can eat mutton BBQs - and I wasn't happy until we had driven far enough so that camps and power station chimneys had disappeared from the rear view mirror.

The driver pulled over, stalled his engine, lit a cigarette and declared himself very impressed with what he saw and here at last, I too found what I had been looking for. Our road was narrow, arrow straight and deserted, the only blot on a perfect landscape of green. Small folds in the landscape occasionally rose from the steppes, threatened to turn into hills before subsiding again. A river bisected the view, but mostly the world was simply flat and green and endless, the driver and I the last men on Earth. Birdsong punctured the silence and the sky was immense with cotton wool clouds more massive even than the grasslands below. Since my head was the highest object for miles, I could see rain falling in the distance perhaps 50 miles away and then like a satisfying Mongolian cliche, an eagle rose and arched over my head, gliding on broad wings towards the rain.

We drove a little further and found Mongolian horseman, though my romantic horseback notions were dismissed as I watched them corral sheep on their motorbikes. Their homes are ancient and authentic though. Mongolian tents are called gers (the common name 'yurt' is actually a Turkish word) though I prefer the Chinese term 'Menggu Bao' or 'Mongolian Buns' since they sit squat and white as if recently baked and risen from the flat grass. They're an old and utilitarian form of accommodation, easy to assemble and dissemble, to make warm or cool and ideal for a nomadic life in a place where temperatures take dramatic swings through the year. The ger has great cultural and spiritual significance too. The door always faces south and the North East quarter of the ger is reserved for women. The man is traditionally prohibited from entering the woman's quarter or touching her when she is there in the case of family conflict; so the North East quarter is a kind of safe haven for the woman though she is allowed to throw hard objects and scissors at her husband from her sanctuary. Every item of the ger is expendable and dispensable apart from the wooden crown called a shangrak. This is usually intricately carved and remains intact, passed from father to son, the accumulation of smoke stains there an indicator of a family's heritage and longevity.

My taxi driver waited patiently as I stared at the clouds, photographed horses in the distance and walked off across the steppes for an hour, the swish of grass around my ankles, so that I could not see the road and imagined myself entirely alone. I suggested we should stay out here but he drew the line at sleeping so far from the familiarity of high-rise Haila'er. I was keen to approach a herder and ask to sleep in his ger, share his food and see if the stars over the steppes would be as bright as I imagined.

"I have to go back to see my friends" said the driver

"Just give them a call and say you'll be back tomorrow", I replied

"If I stay here it will cost you double the fare" he said

"No problem" I replied.

I was dismissing his objections one by one, so he resorted to his trump card;

"The Mongolians are very dangerous; they drink too much and will kill us" he warned.

There was no sensible reply to this. Clearly my driver would not stay and I had no discernible way of returning to town without him. Also I did not want to be killed by an inebriated Mongolian shepherd, so we drove back through the miles of grass and past the power stations to Haila'er. I had seen true Mongolian scenery but had not met a true Mongolian.

The most traditional inhabitants of the steppes are not Mongolian at all and I had even less chance of meeting them. There are less than 30,000 Ewenki left in China, most of who live on the grasslands of Inner Mongolia. They're the only ethnic group in China who herd reindeer and have a modern museum devoted to them in Haila'er that describes their lives and customs where most of the exhibits are things entirely devoted to keeping warm. No amount of fur hats and gloves would be sufficient to keep me cosy in -40°C winter temperatures, but the Ewenki dummies wrapped in layers of fur outside their reindeer skin tepees seemed cheerful enough and not at all chilly. Chinese museum standard nationalist text had crept into even this place. One display showed the Ewenki bravely fighting against the Japanese and in the history of the Ewenki protection of China's territory exhibit, the tribe were shown repelling pantomime villain Russians from the country's borders, though I'm sure the Ewenki were fighting for protection of Rudolph and his friends rather than for love of the motherland.

The Ewenki milk and ride their reindeers and with their elk skin leggings and moccasins, their bows and arrows, embroidery headdresses and facial tatoos, look remarkably like North American Indians. The museum gave details of their shamanism and respect for nature; all natural phenomena are spiritualised and personified by the Ewenki. 'It is forbidden to torment an animal, bird or insect' said the displays. 'Wounded animals must be finished off immediately'. Dead members of the tribe would be sent to the Great Spirit by wind burial, the body hung in a cradle between two trees and left to dry so that the spirit can reach heaven more quickly, carried on the breeze.

The lifestyle choices of the Inner Mongolian Ewenki are not dissimilar to the Apache or Sioux, and neither is the impact on this life by strong central government. China has moved most of the Ewenki from the steppe to the city, granting better access to medical services, education and jobs. But in confiscating their rifles and building houses, the government has turned hunters into shoppers and made nomads sedentary. The government says resettlement raises living standards and protects the grasslands from overgrazing and desertification, an argument that is remarkably similar to the justification for modernization in Tibet and which might contain a kernel of truth; those who protest the destruction of traditional culture usually live in a heated house with running water rather than a reindeer skin tent in the freezing forest. But inevitably, slowly, the Ewenki culture is being destroyed, preserved only in reindeer themed culture parks; as inauthentic as the Genghis Khan shopping centres I'd seen elsewhere.

Haila'er felt like the end of the line. I was a very long way from Beijing, Great Wall and rice fields in this empty land where Russians fought Japanese and nomadic tribes ride reindeer. But it was possible to go just a little further still on the branch line for three more hours to the absolute full stop in China, where the train track meets the Russian border.

China's last town is called Manzhouli. It owes its existence to the creation of the Manchurian line in 1903 which links here with the Trans-Siberian tracks that plunge on all the way to Moscow. The train is less important now though it offered that most wonderful thing in China; a carriage that was not crowded with people and in which I could spread out over four seats and watch the grasslands turn to twilight, an electrical storm flickering over the impossibly distant horizon.

Timber is king in Manzhouli, though there are politics attached to each of the wagons piled high with fresh cut logs that I saw queued in the sidings of the Russian Tsarist imperial style train station. Forests stretch from here north and east into Heilongjiang province and over the Russian border; a hostile winter place made accessible by the turning of the Earth, the melting of snow and the rising of a sub - Arctic summer sun.

Most of the trees are on the Russian side, a detail that causes China much regret since no other great nation is so well endowed with territory and people but so undersupplied with trees. This may have been the cause of the battles up here when Chinese and Russian troops clashed in 1969, though the nations refused to call it war. They fought over the exact position of the border yet in truth, borders are an irrelevance since the whole of Northern Heilongjiang, Inner Mongolia and eastern Russia is a vast, unpopulated and seamless landscape that does not change, though the language of its inhabitants and the colour of soldiers' uniforms does.

It's a landscape of big skies, wide rivers and a vast emptiness that is as intimidating in its way as the deserts of Xinjiang and the mountains of Tibet in China's far west. China's lust for wood was further exacerbated by the Great Dragon Forest Fire here in 1987 so brilliantly described by Pulitzer Prize winning journalist Harrison Evans Salisbury. Salisbury's life from 1908 to 1993 is an encapsulation of the cataclysmic events of the 20th century; he reported on the front line of World War II and Vietnam (Salisbury was among the earliest US journalists to oppose the Vietnam War after reporting from the communist North in 1966), battled Soviet censorship from Moscow in the 1950s, covered civil rights and the assassination of JFK in the 60s and reported extensively from communist China where in 1989 he witnessed the bloody suppression of students on Tiananmen Square. Salisbury's work is fascinating and inspiring though there are times when I read his fine words and feel inclined to put a match to my amateurish scribbling.

The Black Dragon Fire burned about 18 million acres of pristine conifer forest - an area as large as New England or Scotland - and when

Salisbury visited the devastated area, he described walking in 'a prehistoric forest of a long dead planet'. The fire wrought its inferno on both sides of the border; the Russians let it burn, the Chinese fought the blaze with soldiers, though it was rain and the cessation of high winds that did most to kill the flames.

The Chinese battle with the fire was reminiscent of the Great Leap Forward in the 1950s when workers built dams with their bare hands and manufactured backyard steel in improvised furnaces. There were no water dumping helicopters and few bulldozers, so the authorities put 60,000 men on the fire lines to beat back the blaze with swatters. 250 were burned or injured, a further 220 died. There was a great enquiry into the fire that was so disastrous to the Chinese economy. The Forestry Minister lost his job. A brush cutter whose carelessness set off one of the fires got a stiff prison sentence. Officials who had tried to flee the fire instead of staying to help were chastised.

But these were simply more sacrificial lambs, mere window dressing. Nothing was said about the nepotistic management, the Black Dragon 'family' who ran the forest reserves as a personal fiefdom with little regard for safety or knowledge of fire fighting techniques. There was obfuscation from the family; the fire wasn't as bad as it seemed, would soon be under control, reporters couldn't have access to the area because it was too dangerous, everything was fine.

As far as I know the root cause of the problem remains. The same people control the profits of China's timber industry, though these profits are somewhat reduced since the burned forest might take 200 years to regenerate. Safety procedures are still inadequate though some token modern fire fighting equipment from Canada and Germany has been installed. Salisbury argued that 'the idea that the forest problems were in-grown - that nepotism, featherbedding.... and cover-ups had something to do with the tragedy - was silently swept under the rug'. The trees will still burn because there is so little accountability, too much self-interest in China to make it otherwise.

The sheer number of trees on the railway siding mocked the history of fire. China has dealt with her timber shortage through illegal logging in Russia and every day dozens of freight trains roll east into Manzhouli from the Russian border town of Zaibaikalsk, laden with

Russian timber. No less a person than Vladimir Putin has become involved in the timber issues that threaten to decimate the supply of Russian wood. Putin has described the illegal logging and transport as akin to embezzlement, but his disapproval has made not a jot of difference, foiled by the size and distance of his country, and Manzhouli continues to grow and prosper from the trade.

What was once a dusty and insignificant border town is now a thriving metropolis, its shopping malls and high-rises sprouting incongruously from the grasslands. Just as Hohhot has become an ersatz Mongolia, so Manzhouli is a kind of Russian theme park. The town is a home away from home for the thousands of Russians who come here every year to shop for cheap furs, Russian dolls, cigarettes, sports gear and spirits and as I wandered the streets past parked cars covered in Russian dust and with Russian number plates, I was greeted and urged to buy in Russian.

It felt a little strange to be among so many western faces, though at least it stripped me of the novelty status I sometimes enjoy in China and no one shouted 'Hallo Waiguoren' from across the street. The buildings in Manzhouli have Russian facades and the lampposts are encircled by laughing cherubs so that visitors might think they are in 18th-century Saint Petersburg and not a small Mongolian town on the edge of Siberia and the Gobi desert.

There were Russian doll litter bins in the small park where the shops on Manzhouli's imitation of Nevsky Prospekt thinned out and the grasslands began to reappear. The park was filled with more dolls, these ones six feet tall and painted with Chinese and Russian heroes and there were yet more matryoshkas smiling beatifically in painted headscarves who had doors in their bellies from where Chinese women dressed as Russian peasant girls sold Coca-Cola. The centrepiece of the park was a blue painted onion domed Russian Orthodox church and a twenty metre high white model that was a copy of the Motherland statue outside Stalingrad. Further still from the shops and crowds was a sprinkling of old wooden houses lifted straight from a bucolic Tolstoy scene of the Russian countryside and where locals tended their gardens behind picket fences, teasing vegetables and flowers from the sandy soil.

It all looked most un-Chinese, though I should know by now that such a phrase is redundant since there are so many versions of China. But I had not come to see the wooden homes or the faux Saint Petersburg shop fronts, nor even the giant Russian dolls with cafes under their aprons. My trip to far-flung Manzhouli was all about the border.

So I rode a bus for 20 minutes to where China stops. There was an old black Chinese steam locomotive here beside the tracks that headed arrow straight for a further fifty metres to an arch that said 'China' and a few metres more to a second arch that said 'Russia' in Cyrillic script. I was naturally keen to walk the dirt track to the border to stare more closely at the grasslands of Russia from the grasslands of China. Perhaps I could pose for a hilarious one foot in China, one foot in Russia photo?

But although Chinese and Russians were free to explore, I was too foreign and had to be content with hanging from the fence and poking my camera lens between the links of the wire. There would have been no harm in letting me go of course, but the guards were immune to the charm of my stumbling Chinese. "No foreigners", they said and I was reduced to voyeur; an outsider as I often am in China, though their stubborn hostility was understandable since the Chinese have had trouble with foreigners here before. Still they might have given me the benefit of the doubt since I was clearly no Genghis Khan; I had not trampled on the shattered remains of a city and I was drinking coke from a Russian doll cafe, not the warm blood from a horse's neck. So I retreated from the border and the glare of the sun over the steppes to find my own Xanadu of a cold Russian beer in a quiet Mongolian cafe where I could ignore the thought of my long flight home.

QINGHAI

青海

722 797 sq km
Population 5.3 million

'Remember that not getting what you want is sometimes a wonderful stroke of luck.'

Dalai Lama

If I was a more experienced writer I would better convey to my readers a sense of the lonely desolation and wild open space in Qinghai. I mused upon this as I sat on the train from Xi`an and wondered how best to capture the view from my window; but the remoteness of China's fourth-largest province is partly a state of mind and you have to *be* here to really understand what its isolation means.

The hills outside the window were huge and empty, but there are often hills with no settlements in view from the window of the train in Shandong or Guangxi too and the sky was no more flawlessly blue and vast than it had been when I gazed from the window racing through the outskirts of Shanghai. But in Qinghai, you know you're alone and there is no town over the next range of hills or the next, nor probably over the one after that and this lend a different perspective entirely.

A little simple geography illustrates my point. Qinghai is bigger than Western Europe but has a population of a little over five million. There are only two cities of any size here; the provincial capital Xining with 750,000 people and Golmud in the centre of the province that supports a population of less than a quarter of a million. As a consequence, Qinghai has a very small economy - only 0.3% of China's total and its people have an average annual income of less than $2000. Xining lies in the east of the province - a low-lying temperate region and the only place in Qinghai that can support sustainable agriculture. The North West is an arid depression on the edge of the Taklamakan desert that is given over to mining. All the rest is barren grassland at least three kilometres above the sea.

So every sign of life, every lone horse, every tiny ger tent in the Mongolian style billowing a serpent of blue smoke from its chimney, and above all every nomad or drover or peasant trudging along a thin ribbon of road, assumes a special significance in Qinghai. Mostly, the view is empty but with the profound sense of emptiness that few places in China possess.

I found it unsettling to be looking at a view where nothing could be eaten and noticed that the Chinese in the train spent the journey hunched over bowls of noodles playing cards or conversing in loud voices of exaggerated mirth but with a hint of panic. Anything but look outside, for this remote land is too empty and too devoid of life; a terrifying place to which Chinese have been sent to exile from the east as punishment for hundreds of years.

My train journey took me right through Qinghai but it was only after Xining on the way to Tibet that the enormity of the place becomes apparent. We left Xining at 6:30 pm and by one o'clock the next afternoon we were still trundling past patches of snow and the occasional herd of hairy cows (mao niu) that were still in Qinghai and not Tibet. Yet all such demarcation is slightly artificial, for in many ways Qinghai yaks *are* Tibetan.

The province is a modern communist cartographic construction designed to reduce the size and thus the cultural importance of troublesome Tibet. Tibetans stubbornly call the region 'Amdo' but my map said 'Qinghai'. The name comes from the huge 4500 km² Qinghai Lake which is China's largest. Qinghai means 'blue sea', a vast breeding ground for geese, cranes and cormorants 300 kilometres from Xining, though the squawking birds and lapping waves were indiscernible as my train trundled past after dark.

I had noticed that travel agencies in Xining offered day trips to Qinghai Lake. 300 kilometres on a bus to admire the Nian Dao Bird Island where hundreds of birds can sometimes be seen, a cafe lunch of cold noodles and then 300 kilometres back to town, arrival at 10 pm. There may be a grim satisfaction in a trip somewhere so inaccessible and I have no doubt that sometimes the journey is the experience; a mind broadening and satisfying challenge. But 600 kilometres to see some birds fornicating and crapping on a rock seemed like an exercise in futility.

I could barely make out Golmud town in the gathering dawn too, though here there were definite signs of life, a smattering of orange streetlights and a few bedraggled passengers on the platform beneath the sign that announced the town's name in Chinese, Mongolian and Tibetan. Golmud is 14 hours from the nearest town, an astonishingly remote place in a remote province that exists simply for the minerals that are coaxed from the ground and the trains that used to terminate here but now pioneer their way a further 15 hours all the way to Lhasa. Xining had seemed a small and unimpressive city but a shopkeeper there had warned me that Golmud was 'primitive' when I told him that I was catching the train. This was probably an exercise in self reassurance from a man who knew that his town was not up to much, but I laughed when I saw that under 'places of interest' in my guidebook, Golmud had none.

My book was rather more complimentary about Xining, though the phrase 'gritty charm' is guidebook speak for 'underwhelming'. So I had broken my journey in Qinghai's capital for two days to get a feel for the place, to acclimatise a little before the high altitude train trip over the Tanggula pass to Tibet and to retrace the early life of the 14th Dalai Lama.

Jetsun Jamphel Ngawang Lobsung Yeshi Tenzin Gyatso was born in the village of Taktser 45 kilometres south-east of Xining. His grand name means 'Holy Lord, Gentle Glory, Eloquent, Compassionate, Learned Defender of the Faith, Ocean of Wisdom, but back in the day in tiny Taktser he had been just little Lhama Dhondrub. The title 'Dalai Lama' had been conferred by the Mongolian leader Altan Khan in 1578 at Qinghai Lake upon the head of the Tibetan Gelugpa Buddhist sect Sonam Gyatso. 'Dalai' is the Mongolian word for Ocean which pertains to boundless wisdom, and I fancy the great Khan imagined this name as he gazed upon the vast, untamed, boundless and infinite Lake. If the encounter had happened during breeding season, the head of Tibetan Buddhist might have been named 'goose' instead.

The choosing of a Dalai Lama is a damned complicated business. When the rakishly moustachioed 13th Holy Lord died in Lhasa in 1933 his head was facing east and no matter how often he was turned, his body would stubbornly turn eastward again. Now this might imply that the successor could come from anywhere from Lhasa to Tokyo but reports came of visitations of auspicious crows at the birth of a baby in tiny Taktser near Xining. Three Lamas set out from Lhasa and found a child with the requisite oversize ears, sorrowful eyes and 'tiger stripes' on his legs and who passed all of the tests by choosing the correct beads and so little Dhondrub became Holy Lord.

My visit to Taktser was cloaked in secrecy and subterfuge. A guide approached me on the steps of the train station and asked if I wanted to see Qinghai Lake. I explained that 12 hours on a bus to see some waterfowl didn't sound like fun, but could he take me to the Dalai Lama's birthplace? The man became confidential, put his arm around my shoulders and said he could, though it might be 'dangerous' which naturally made me still more determined to go.

His concern was not misplaced since Taktser and most of Qinghai had been closed to foreigners for the past month because of the sensitive anniversaries of the 1959 and 2008 Tibetan uprisings and the Dalai Lama's birthplace was still not officially open. 'I can take you' he said but on the journey to the hotel he glanced round at me, put his fingers to his lips conspiratorially and gave a theatrical 'Sssh!'

We took a public bus the next day through a bone dry beige valley and beneath a hot sun. Farmers stood on plough boards and floated around fields pulled by oxen as the dry earth was turned over, while infants took shelter and drowsed beneath trees that were spindly and slight and looked like children's drawings of trees. The vehicle played the usual Chinese game of stopping at every house or village in the hope of finding new passengers and some peasants who seemed to have no intention of catching the bus at all stopped their work and climbed on board anyway simply because the driver had asked.

My guide was from distant Henan province. He spent the spring and summer months in Xining but returned home to see his wife and child in the winter when there were few tourists and little prospect of work in freezing Qinghai. He no doubt missed his family but the blow was softened because he had a 'very nice' girlfriend in Xining and the money he earned helped to pay for a good school for his son. He told me that his wife had been pregnant again last year but "they had taken her to hospital where they cut her stomach and removed the child".

This routine and matter-of-fact story is reflected in China's one child policy which makes abortion rather routine and matter-of-fact too. The policy was implemented in 1979 and authorities claim 350 million births have been prevented since its implementation and a nominally independent survey in 2008 by the Pew research centre showed that three quarters of the Chinese population support the policy. 36% of the population of China is subject to fines and punishment if they break the one child rule, though rural Chinese and minorities are still permitted to have more than one child. Measured in raw statistics the policy seems to have been a success - 1.8 births per woman now compared to more than five in the early 1970s - but the thousands of forced abortions by local birth control units known as 'womb police' and the creation of an army of overindulged only children called 'Little Emperors' in China has been a high price to pay. The government formally disapproves of forced abortions especially late in pregnancy, but it is their quotas that set the stage for this terrifying ordeal for women.

The forbidding of more than one child has also led to a high level of female infanticide in China and there are now over 60 million more men than females in the country. And despite all the enforcement of the one child policy with its attendant human rights issues, China's population continues to grow by over 10 million every year. It seems that of all Mao's mistakes, his failure to regulate population growth in his country is the one that continues to have the most lasting repercussions of all.

As we climbed the potholed road up the valley, the settlements became fewer and donkeys more numerous. The number of donkeys is a good indicator of the poverty of the region in China - call it an 'income Ass-ometer'. Donkeys must be cheap and certainly seem hardy beasts and I had not seen so many in China since the harsh desert lands along the Silk Road in the west of Xinjiang. Here, doe eyed dusty beasts were pulling ploughs and carrying loads or standing tethered to a post with one hoof raised in that funny way that donkeys do. They're a strangely appealing animal - maybe because of the religious connotations that I remember from my Sunday School youth - and their patient calmness seems completely at odds with the rest of China.

We got off the bus on a lonely stretch of road since if we were seen in the main village before Taktser the guide was convinced we would be reported to the police. He explained that the sighting of a foreigner in an outlawed part of Qinghai would earn a dutiful citizen a reward of 50 yuan, so locals were falling over themselves to announce the presence of a barbarian. I stood for a moment in this desolate valley and wondered what happens next when a small van trailing a plume of dust roared up and we clambered in. My guide had thought of everything and I noticed that the driver had blacked out the windows of the van with old copies of the China Daily and the man at the wheel gave me a confidential wink as we sped past houses and up the final climb to Taktser. There would be no 50 yuan rewards in the village today.

It would be hard to picture a more unprepossessing birthplace for one of the world's most respected and revered moral and spiritual leaders. But sweeping boulevards and manicured lawns would be entirely inappropriate for the Dalai Lama. Here instead was a smattering of simple earth and brick houses clinging to the steep valley walls and with expansive views past rolling brown hills to massive snowy mountains beyond. How right that Lhama Dhondrub should be born with a view of Tibet.

By this stage our secret mission had taken a comic turn. We left the van and set out on foot along narrow brick alleys to approach the house from the rear. My guide ran ahead to the end of a lane, looked around the corner and called me on when he had established all was clear. This went on for a few hundred metres before we emerged in front of a house festooned with prayer flags and with a large golden chorten outside. Apart from this, it was exactly like the other brown brick dusty houses in the village and I stood on tiptoe and gazed over the wall at the little courtyard inside. The house had been rebuilt in 1986 after it was damaged along with seemingly every other thing of value in China during the Cultural Revolution. The Chinese official news agency Xinhua says it cost US$51,000 to rebuild and has 61 rooms but there were certainly no more than three or four. Still, what are 56 rooms between friends?

The guide entered the house and returned panting apologies. "I'm sorry we can't go in. The Dalai Lama's nephew lives here and he is too worried that he will get trouble from the police if a foreigner visits". I couldn't imagine what harm my visit would do, but clearly the authorities were very twitchy about this place and I became suddenly aware that this exciting game of hide and seek could have repercussions for me too if some 50 yuan informer turned me in.

China is excessively sensitive about the Dalai Lama and what is always referred to as his 'clique'. Even this small brown birthplace is a source of potential trouble. But the authorities should be thankful that Dhondrub's Big Brother didn't choose the correct beads and become Dalai Lama instead. He was also called Taktser which means 'roaring tiger' and criticised his little brother's unwavering adherence to non-violent protest in Tibet. Taktser fled in the 1950s and settled in Indiana from where he was a tireless advocate of the use of guerrilla warfare against the Chinese in Tibet. He became consultant to the CIA to help promote warfare against the communist party and died in 2008, still no doubt disapproving of his kid brother's softly, softly approach. Taktser's son Jigme Norbu has taken up the good fight and recently walked 900 miles from Indiana to Washington DC in memory of his father and to protest at Chinese oppression of his homeland.

We drove back down the hill and I asked what would happen if the police had caught us there. "There would have been big trouble for me" my guide explained, "but you would have been okay because you're English. If you were French it would have been serious for you too". China has not forgiven France for the disruption of the Olympic torch relay in Paris when a disabled Chinese athlete was wrestled in her wheelchair by a protester who tried to wrench the flame from her grasp. The prurient Chinese media had found this profoundly shocking and I remember seeing newspaper pictures of protesters outside a French supermarket in Shanghai. The outraged citizens had drawn swastikas on a French flag and written 'Free Corsica', 'Jeanne d'Arc = prostitute' and 'Napoleon = pervert' beneath. Such surrealism must have been an arrow to the heart of French patriots though they might have been relieved at least that this random flag had not called into question the morality of Charles de Gaulle, the sexuality of Jacques Cousteau or suggested that Camembert is an inferior cheese.

We trundled down the hill in our van with our anonymity less assured since the driver had opened a window to smoke a cigarette and the newspapers were now flapping uselessly on the window frames. The visit to Taktser was over so everyone seemed to relax and I was allowed to get out and meet some locals at the tiny monastery a few kilometres downhill.

The monastery was moving in its simplicity; a few squat Tibetan buildings, a bell whose sound resonated up the valley and startled a donkey on the road below and an ingenious circle of silver metal from which the high altitude sun's rays reflected and boiled the water in a big black kettle perched in front. (I was more impressed still at the same contraption used to power traffic lights wheeled onto the road intersections in Xining). The monks here were tall and powerful looking Amdo Tibetans with long plaits of black hair and sun scorched faces, who looked for the entire world like Sioux or Apache Indians in their furs and beads. They were quick to smile and press the solar kettle into action and they gave me my first ever glass of yak butter tea. This unsophisticated brew requires only a generous blob of yak butter dissolved in hot water. The salty taste and residue of grease on the lips are not intolerable but the rancid cheesy smell makes it a challenging drink indeed. Still, I held my breath, sipped away and smiled and imagined I was drinking a delicate china cup of Earl Grey.

My host raised his big handsome face and his earrings made of shell swayed as he asked where I was going next and did I want more tea? I answered 'Lhasa' and the monk was so pleased with this answer that he didn't seem to notice that I'd ignored the second question. "Lhasa is very good" he said and I asked him if he had been. He replied that he had visited as a pilgrim two years earlier. "I'm going on the train" I said and asked him how he had traveled, expecting him to say that he had journeyed by horse or perhaps walked in a gesture of humility and hardship that might earn Buddhist merit points. "The train is very slow" he replied "I flew from Xining and it only took one hour."

The Dalai Lama was taken from Taktser as a two year old to the Gelugpa lamasery at Kumbum, and didn't return to his home village until he stopped there in 1955 en route to his fruitless visit to Beijing to be patronised and humiliated by Chairman Mao. Jetsun Jamphel Ngawang Lobsang Yeshi Tenzin Gyatso rode a white yak but I sped along in another ramshackle bus along one of those massive four-lane highways that the government is so keen on building in remote parts of China, though there are so few cars to travel on them. The renaming of Kumbum as Ta`er Si is as much a symptom of Chinese control of this far-flung region as the stretch of asphalt we were on and I had chosen a Tibetan guide for my visit to get a little local perspective on all this sinocizing.

Joseph referred to Kumbum and Amdo throughout but seemed less interested in Tibetan Buddhism than Tibetan independence. I asked him the meaning of the symbols and flags, the halls and the pictures as we wandered around Kumbum, but not once did he know the answer. "I think it's something to do with the attaining of Nirvana" he would say or "that's definitely important but I'm not sure why". He was more animated at the old sandalwood tree in the centre of the main temple and showed me the carvings on the trunk - mystical symbols that were not made by man - though he had no idea what they said.

The tree grew in the 14th century at the place where the legendary Tsongkhapa was born and drops of blood from his umbilical cord fell and had 1000 leaves, upon each of which there was the face of a Buddha. Tsongkhapa founded the Gelugpa yellow sect of Tibetan Buddhism and two of his disciples became the Panchen and Dalai Lamas so Kumbum, where the current Dalai Lama was taught, is central to the whole story of Tibet.

Yet it is a rather dispiriting and soulless place. The main hall was dark and atmospheric enough and smelt gratifyingly of yak butter lamps but there are only 400 monks here now instead of the 4000 at the monastery's height before 1958. We walked around the complex and while the lack of people lent a certain peaceful charm, it hardly seemed like a monastery at all.

Joseph was dismissive of the place and said it was just a tourist trap now for the thousands of Chinese visitors who came in the summer. We wandered into the yak butter sculpture hall and the huge and smelly diorama of Bodhisattvas and gods, temples and trees looked impressive enough to me, though Joseph maintained that even this wasn't as good as it used to be.

I can't really tell a good yak butter sculpture when I see it but I'm inclined to agree with Joseph. My exorbitant 80 yuan entrance fee from the ticket booth next to the yak model, Buddhist thangka painting and prayer wheel gift shop had earned me a souvenir CD of the monastery handed over by an aged monk in purple robes who looked the most unlikely person on earth to be dishing out computer technology 'compatible with PC and Macintosh and guaranteed virus free'. Over one million Chinese tourists a year give their 80 yuan and get their souvenir CD too. They can also pay for a Chinese guide dressed as a local Tibetan to show them around or they can sit on a yak and wave a Chinese flag if they haven't spent all their money on the trinkets in the yard outside. Arjia Lobsang Thubter Rinpoche, the current abbot of Ta`er Si was so disillusioned by 1998 that he fled Tibet for California and it seemed to me that the tiny temple in the hills near Taktser with its yak butter tea, solar powered kettle and tolling bell was more representative of Tibetan Buddhism now than its more famous cousin at Kumbum.

I walked with Joseph past the Lesser Golden Roofed Hall which is dedicated to animals and from whose second-floor windows a collection of demented stuffed deer, sheep and goats peer with lopsided glass eyes and hysterical grins at visitors below. Joseph led me up the hill behind Kumbum for views of the golden roofs and as the view spread out he became more expansive in his views on Tibetan politics than he had been on Tibetan religion.

He said that he hated being treated like a baby and forbidden to send texts or to surf the Internet as he wished. This was a complaint that I have heard from Chinese as well - the authorities are particularly sensitive about the insidious influence of the World Wide Web and have established a series of sophisticated firewalls to control what the population can and can't see. Like all puritanical, insecure and bossy governments, the Communist party think they know what's best for everyone, even if they don't know it themselves, though the net is a peculiarly difficult thing to control and the morals of the people are still no doubt at terrible risk.

Joseph was most exercised by his lack of passport. Despite this, he had crossed illegally into India to see the Dalai Lama at his home in exile at Dharamsala. His voice cracked with emotion when he described this meeting as the most important moment of his life. The Dalai Lama had spoken to him and other fugitives and told them to create peace and harmony in the world and to help people remember the plight of Tibet and I suppose Joseph was doing exactly this with me now.

Qinghai is a vast and peaceful place and more than anywhere I had seen in China it seemed to lack the incursion of Chinese industry and progress and the blight of pollution that has affected so many cities further east. Yet there are layers and problems in Qinghai; nowhere else in China had I been driven in a van with newspaper on the windows so that I wouldn't be spotted by informers, and nowhere else had my guide asked me to not tell his story to the authorities since the punishment for crossing the border as he had was seven years in prison. Joseph said the Chinese control of Qinghai was getting tighter and tighter, 'like a wet yak hide".

This control is best exemplified by the network of prison camps throughout Qinghai called 'laogai'. The word means 'reform through labour' which sounds suspiciously similar to 'work makes you free' on the gates of Auschwitz, and many factories on the outskirts of Xining and Golmud are actually prison camps. There are probably over 100 labour camps in the province with a total population of 400,000 – one tenth of all the people in Qinghai - of whom 40,000 are political prisoners.

I gazed from the window of the Tibet train and it was clear why the authorities chose Qinghai as their Gulag Archipelago. Far from the world's eye, there is so much space here and I wondered if the occasional cement works or agricultural farm or scurrying groups of workers on the road outside were really what they seemed. But as the train chuffed and huffed for hour after hour uphill there were no factories or laogai or workers or prisoners anymore - up here were just the brown rolling hills buffeted by clouds and the silver ribbons of river.

Many of the great Asian rivers have their source on this high plateau; the Yellow River begins here and so does the Lancang Jiang which crashes south through the rice fields and jungles of Laos and Vietnam where it is called the Mekong. The Yangtze, the greatest Chinese river of all also bubbles to the surface on the high plateau, at the foot of the Geladandong glacier six and a half thousand metres above the sea it meets at Shanghai. The Chinese may flow into and control Qinghai, but it is the water that flows from Amdo that helps China to exist and which gives an economic importance to this place that is out of proportion to its population. I felt a thrill of excitement as my train crossed finally into Tibet but in truth I had spent hours in Tibet already since Qinghai is a source of Buddhism as well as water and which with its temples, monks, meditative calm, butter lamps and Dalai Lama may be lonely but is not God forsaken.

TIBET

西藏

1 221 700 sq km
Population 2.75 million

"I came prostrating from Amchok Tsenyi Gonpa in Amdo and I am going to Dharamsala. My mission is to seek an audience with our leader of Tibet and an apostle of world peace. I am prostrating for His long life, for world peace, for long life of all the righteous people of Tibet and the well-being of all sentient beings."

Zodpa Namgyal

One cold February morning Zodpa Namgyal stood outside a monastery in Amdo, pressed his palms together by his chest, throat and head and lowered himself to his knees. He lay fully prostrate on his chest, arms spread in front in a position of supplication before pressing his forehead to the floor. Zodpa then stood up, taking a pace forward and repeated the process all the way to Nepal. His mother had pushed a metal cart of his belongings alongside for two months but had become ill and returned home. Since then, Zodpa had prostrated 50 metres past his cart, and then returned to fetch it before carrying on with his prostrations. After two years and two months he had reached Kathmandu and earned a few columns in the Nepali newspaper I once read as I drunk Everest beer in one of the trendy bars there that have sprung up there in Thamel before I had I been to Tibet.

It's the otherworldliness; the blinkered Mediaeval obstinacy of men like Zodpa that means Tibet will never be the country that modern, industrialized China wants it to be and the reason why despite the bureaucracy and politics, the altitude and remoteness, I had to go.

There was a moment when I almost didn't get there at all. It took me months to arrange the entry permit, the aliens permit to allow me to travel beyond Lhasa and the Everest National Park permit. But in March, the whole of Tibet and neighbouring Qinghai were closed to foreigners as a precaution at a time of sensitive anniversaries of the 1959 and 2008 riots. Just a week before I went, entry was still forbidden, but with that glorious capriciousness of the Chinese military, and only three days before departure, 'social harmony' was deemed to have been restored in the streets of Lhasa and I was in.

So there I was in Xining, the provincial capital of Qinghai with my permit in hand and ready to catch the train over the high plateau on the long journey to Lhasa. But I was stuck in the lift of my guesthouse which clunked and wheezed to a halt halfway between floors and my train was leaving in half an hour and I pressed the emergency bell and nothing happened and I could see the nylon trousers and dirty shoes of the lift attendant who was telling me to wait but I had no time to wait and so I crawled out of the lift onto the dusty floor amid cigarette butts and the attendant was yelling at me now but there's no way I'm waiting after it took me so long to get those damn permits and get out of my way I've got a train to catch and why does China have to be so *difficult*?

I tried to look calm and assured in the police office at the train station but it was difficult after my elevator stress. Still, it was nearly impossible for the officers with their feet on the desk to see what I looked like through the pall of blue cigarette smoke in the room so they stamped my forms and I was through to the platform.

I like that Chinese trains always have a removable sign on the side that says where they come from and where they're going. This one said Beijingxi - Lasa, Beijing West station - Lhasa, four thousand kilometres and 48 hours of clacking points and rolling wheels, and though I was joining the route almost halfway through, it would still be 25 hours before I trundled into the Tibetan capital.

The train was more comfortable and commodious than any I had been on in China. The sheets were crisp, the corridor carpet clean and the window polished enough to offer an unhindered view of the vast rolling hills and yaks outside. And Oh the toilets! They were so fresh and without a half inch of fetid water covering the floor though they had been in service since distant Beijing. Heck, there was even a roll of super non-absorbent toilet paper with no perforations in the dispenser.

This was more like the hermetically sealed experience of flying but with way more legroom, and as we crossed the five thousand metre Tanggula Pass, the guard brought round oxygen masks and a health declaration form where we all confirmed that 'my health condition can adapt the three thousand metre above sea level' like we even knew. Chinese passengers greedily plumbed their masks into the dispenser on the wall and sucked in the oxygen but the foreigners on the train ascetically declined to use this aid to comfort since severe altitude headaches and nausea were surely part of an authentic Tibetan experience. I plugged mine in to have a go and couldn't get it unplugged so spent the rest of the journey with gas hissing and leaching into the cabin and creating the world's most oxygen rich environment outside of a rainforest in Brazil.

The train had an 'in-flight' magazine too. It was called 'China's Tibet' which reminded me that even 'Tintin in Tibet' was called 'Tintin in China's Tibet' when the book was first published in Shanghai. The magazine passed a couple of oxygen rich hours on board and was packed with accounts of local gratification for their liberation by the Chinese.

"Democratic reform spread like a flaming fire everywhere all over Tibet to burn completely the rubbish of feudal slavery" trumpeted the magazine. There were stories of pre-revolutionary Lamas gouging the eyes of put-upon peasants, of leg irons, torture and cages, beatings and the cutting of flesh from slaves who were then forced to eat what had been removed.

Hardly your typical complimentary read and not inclined to make my fifth cup-a-soup of the trip more palatable, but the publishers were on a roll. "I am having a wonderful life", grinned one grateful peasant. "We have nothing to worry about, we are living in a harmonious society and there is no reason to complain at all". The collection of features listed in the contents was enough to create eager anticipation in even the most discerning reader. Turn to page 10 for 'The democracy reform emancipated all serfs including me', page 15 for 'The ticking clock counts down the demise of feudalism', centre pages for 'Chairman Jiang Zemin encouraged me to cultivate more land' and who could resist 'Before 1959 all we possessed was the shadows of our bodies behind us' on page 24?

So much has been written about the politics of Tibet and by more learned men than me so I will try to concentrate on other matters as far as I can. Yet the issue needs to be addressed since to not mention Chinese control of Tibet would be like telling the story of the Titanic and failing to mention the iceberg.

China claims that the region is an inalienable part of the motherland since it was assimilated during the Yuan dynasty in the 13th century. This might be true, but it is true also that Tibet has enjoyed periods of freedom from Chinese control. Most notable of these was from the fall of the Qing dynasty in 1911 until the successful communist revolution of 1949. During this time Tibet had its own passports and foreign affairs bureau and suffered little interference from China battling with Japanese invasion and civil war.

Crucially, no major Western Power recognised Tibetan independence during this period and despite the best efforts of the 13th Dalai Lama, the country remained an unmodernised and unreformed approximation of a mediaeval serf society. The Chinese returned with a vengeance in 1951 and forced a 17 point agreement on Tibet which provided a degree of autonomy for the region. Subsequent land reform and collectivisation created such turmoil in Tibet that a huge uprising broke out in 1959 in which an estimated 87,000 were killed and it was at this point that the Dalai Lama fled to India.

China imposed the flawed Great Leap Forward policy after the suppression of the revolt. Tibetans were encouraged to grow rice and wheat instead of the staple barley, and 10% of the country starved, though China itself endured such misguided economic policies at this time too. Worse was to come during the Great Proletarian Cultural Revolution from 1966 to 1976 when fanatical Red Guards attacked the four olds - customs, habits, beliefs and ideas. And what could be older in Tibet than Buddhism? By 1976 the 2700 monasteries populated by 114,000 monks in Tibet had been reduced to just eight with a monastic population of 800.

Leaders since Mao have exercised a more moderate policy; monasteries have reopened and the Tibetan language can be taught and for a while at least, images of the Dalai Lama were permissible too. More riots in 1987 put paid to this temporary reprieve and now the Dalai Lama is an enemy of the State and accused of that most heinous of crimes, 'splittism' - an attempt to break up the immutable and sacred entity of China.

It's the damning of the Dalai Lama by China that is hardest to stomach amongst many Tibetans at home and abroad. The Nobel Peace Prize was conferred on Tibet's spiritual leader in 1989 and Tenzin Gyatso has become more Saint than man in the West. Chinese cultural revolutionary style rhetoric attacking the Dalai Lama 'clique' sounds clumsy and monstrous and contrasts sharply with their enemy's tolerance and spirituality. Some Chinese too are aware that this damages the image of China and in 2008 a group of scholars wrote an open letter to the government asking that the rabid criticism be stopped.

It's equally difficult to pass judgement on the heart of the Tibetan problem. But the impact of Chinese control on the region they call 'Xizang' or 'Western Treasure House' depends on perspective. The Chinese argue that since 1959 they have lavished 201.9 billion yuan on Tibet. Average annual per capita GDP has risen from 142 to 13,861 yuan in the same period and the GDP of the whole region has reached

39.5 billion yuan from a 1959 low of 174 million Yuan. Life expectancy has raised from 35.5 to 67 years, roads have been constructed, schools built, literacy raised, basic hygiene improved and in the more tolerant post-Mao era China, 1700 monasteries have reopened and 46,000 Tibetans have taken their monastic vows.

From the Tibetan perspective there are still 1000 monasteries and 60,000 monks less in modern Tibet than in the years before the takeover. Per capita income in the 1970s was just $60 a year which made Tibet the poorest country in the world at that time. Chinese immigration means that Tibetans are outnumbered in their own country and no amount of infrastructure or investment can compensate the cultural destruction that has taken place since 1959.

As I traveled around Tibet I was struck by the investment that had been made. The roads were good and even in rural communities Chinese flags were flying from the roofs of newly constructed and comfortable homes. I have a feeling that a good house or a new tractor might be more important to a Tibetan farmer than democracy and yet the Chinese emphasis on economics at the expense of all else misses the point, since to assume that only subsistence food and comfort matters to people is to reduce them to the level of animals.

Qinghai hills had turned to Tibetan hills when I awoke from my oxygen enriched sleep next day. One thousand kilometres of this line lies at four thousand metres above sea level or higher on a bed of permafrost and it is all so mind-bogglingly remote. Former Chinese Premier Zhu Rongji called the railway 'an unprecedented project in the history of mankind'; a typically unvarnished government boast that for once wasn't hyperbole.

The engineers took steps to protect the wildlife and ecosystem of the high plateau and designed dozens of man-made swamps to replicate those destroyed by the train and over 30 passageways that allow migrating antelope and other animals to pass beneath the tracks. One of these helpful thoroughfares was the subject of an award-winning picture by news photographer Liu Weiqing in 2006 that showed the train racing past a startled herd of majestic antelopes beneath a magnificent storm filled Tibetan sky. The photo seemed to sum up the peaceful coexistence of man and nature but careful examination revealed it as a fake where train and beasts had been clumsily spliced together. Liu claimed to have waited in a pit for eight days for the rare chiru antelope to pass at exactly the same moment as the train, but admitted to his deception in 2008 and resigned amid public outcry, announcing "I have no reason to continue my sacred career as a newsman".

Arrival in Lhasa felt no less emotional for me than it must have done for foreign visitors to this most remote and mystical city in centuries past. Pilgrims were prostrating on the road parallel to our rails with tens of miles to go before their destination, and there at last, perched on its rocky outcrop, unmistakably squat and muscular above the rest of the city was the Potala Palace, that place which had seemed remote enough to be almost mythical in the encyclopedias I had pawed over in my youth as I dreamed of Tibet.

Entering most cities doesn't create such a sense of excitement and I couldn't take my eyes off the Potala. I'd arrived less than a week after the newly created Serfs Emancipation day and the bunting was still out at the huge station that is probably a symbol of China's greatness and permanence, though it is built in Tibetan style and rather tastefully done. The new holiday celebrates the defeat of the 1959 uprising when the serfs of Tibet were released from the eye gouging, flesh eating bondage that my train magazine described so graphically. The annual celebration of China seizure/liberation of Tibet is no doubt a provocation for many locals, though there was a poster of a craggy 73-year-old sun weathered peasant called Yixi Luozhou on the station forecourt who pronounced that 'the people say the party's policies are like the sun on a clear day in Lhasa'. So that's all right then.

The sky was wintry and blue and this contrasted delightfully with the green uniforms of the soldiers who stood outside the station and on every street corner in Lhasa with weapons and riot shields waiting for something to happen. Locals seemed oblivious to these 18-year-olds with huge guns that were like so many statues, impassive and bored. It might have been more fun for them if they'd chatted to the street vendors, the shopkeepers and pilgrims as they walked past. But there was to be no winning hearts and minds here and the young boys had clearly been told that interaction was tantamount to treason, though I did see one soldier reach into his pocket and carefully pass a sweetie to a little girl with dirty face and pigtails.

My hotel window had a glorious view of the Potala so I was able to sit on my bed, gaze at its vermilion and white walls and pantingly recover from my three flights of stairs high altitude expedition. The hotel was almost deserted and I spoke to the Nepali owner to ask if business was good. "It's very bad" he said "because foreigners have been banned from Tibet for so many months". But 90% of tourists to Tibet are Chinese so surely they provided the bulk of his customers? "We don't take Chinese guests" he explained, "business is bad but they are too noisy and they smoke everywhere even when we tell them not to" and I reflected on my journeys on Chinese buses and trains and my visits to Chinese restaurants and third-rate provincial hotels and decided there was some truth in what he said.

I was in the heart of the old Tibetan quarter and here it was easy to believe the Chinese claim that the population of Lhasa is 87% Tibetan and 13% Chinese, though the drive from the train station through untidy Chinese urban sprawl suggested that this was certainly not the case. Lhasa means 'ground of the gods' and there is no more holy place in this divine city than the Jokhang Temple.

I wandered past stalls selling prayer wheels and yak butter to the holiest spot in Lhasa and it seemed that all those prostrating pilgrims I'd seen on the road had arrived at once. The prostrators were joined by hundreds of other pilgrims who counted prayer beads, muttered mantras and led dogs and in one case a goat wearing a hat in a clockwise shuffling circumambulation of the Jokhang. Here were Chamdo Tibetans in long sleeved chuba sheepskin coats; women who wore their wealth in turquoise and coral jewelled necklaces and earrings; Tibetan Rongpa farmers in cowboy hats and with the toes on their boots turned up so they killed less bugs as they walked; Amdo girls, their hair braided into an auspiciously precise 108 plaits and Drokpa nomads from the great North West Chang Tang wilderness.

I had been afraid that Lhasa wouldn't survive my weight of expectation. Turning glossy pages of National Geographic magazines as a boy I had seen the city and read 19th-century traveler's tales of this forbidden town and imagined it the most exotic and strangest place on earth. As

I was washed along with this wave of pilgrims on their kora through the stink of yak butter lamps past the bulbous incense burners coiling juniper smoke to connect Earth and Heaven, I delighted in the feeling that my boyhood imaginings were not disappointed. This really *was* the strangest place on earth.

The Jokhang was built by King Songsten Gampo in the seventh century as a repository for the Buddha statue that his Tang Chinese wife had brought from her home. The story of Princess Wencheng is famous throughout China; it was she who converted the King to Buddhism and thus lay the foundations of this new religion in Tibet which had formerly followed the animistic, demon taming religion called Bon.

Wencheng's Jowo Sakyamuni statue is Tibet's most sacred object and I followed the pilgrims into the dark and devout temple feeling fraudulent as I bowed to the icon while others reverently wept or kissed the Sakyamuni's feet, though I might have wept too if I had reached my goal after prostrating for a month or more. The seventh century Tibetans believed a huge sleeping demoness lay beneath Lhasa. Monasteries were built over the foul beast's hips, shoulders, elbows and knees and she was so big that the temples pinning her hands and feet were erected in Bhutan and Sichuan. When she had been as thoroughly restrained as Gulliver by the Lilliputian monks, Lake Wothang was drained and filled with a sacred goat and a final temple was built over the foul Demon's heart and that temple was the Jokhang.

There were a host of pilgrims prostrating outside the main gates of the temple in a feverish display of devotion, the flagstones worn smooth by their supplication. I wandered past and up to the second floor for a view past the gilded deer and Buddhist wheel of life across Lhasa and found some monks debating the finer points of Buddhism. These are no ordinary arguments but involve one saffron robed monk sitting squat on the floor in quiet contemplation like the Buddha under a bodhi tree. His partner would approach, stamp his feet and clap his hands close to the other's face as he made a point about the beneficence of Bodhisattvas, the merits of kora or eternity of Avalokatishevera and then back off before beginning his assault again with a stamp and a clap.

Buddhism is a confusing religion to the uninitiated and there seems a lot to debate. Every temple I saw in Tibet was filled with images of gods and saints, smoking lamps, lessons in the samsara of illimitable rebirth and thangka paintings where the world's three evils of anger, ignorance and desire represented by a snake, pig and cockerel chased each other's tails in an eternal paradigm of futility. I began to dispense with a guide over time and preferred by far to remain ignorant of what I was seeing and simply to immerse in the smoke and chants, the worn stones or a shaft of sunlight bursting through glass and lighting up the gilded paint of a single seated Buddha.

I returned with a bump to the temporal world when a plainclothes police officer asked to see my camera. He was concerned that I might have taken pictures of the groups of soldiers parading on the Barkhor Square below and studied all of my shots in great detail until finally he spotted a tiny group of uniformed figures in a distant corner of a picture of the hills behind Lhasa upon the summits of which prayer flags fluttered their imprecations to heaven. The officer frowned and deleted the picture and I apologised since I knew that pictures of soldiers were not allowed, but how strange that China should be so sensitive about something that is a secret to none, and the deletion of my picture seemed like nothing so much as an admission of guilt.

It snowed in Lhasa that afternoon and I almost felt sorry for the teenage soldiers holding their semi automatic weapons in gloveless, godless hands. The pilgrims continued their kora around the Jokhang oblivious to the weather since all life is suffering until a cessation of desires. They shuffled past yangdrung swastikas and spun big brass prayer wheels which, like prayer flags and sky burials, have their roots in the earlier Bon religion, though the few Bonpos in Lhasa circumambulated anti-clockwise and against the tide. They paraded too past the ninth century stone marker which says 'Tibet and China shall abide by the frontiers of which they now in occupation.... on neither side shall there be waging of war or seizing of territory' but the irony seemed lost on the soldiers who sat on top of the Barkhor buildings with guns and binoculars and who took photographs of the throng below but who must not be photographed themselves.

It's tempting to the traveler to rush to the Potala that dominates the town on Marpo Ri Red Mountain and begins to dominate and pre-occupy the visitor's mindset too. Every walk and restaurant seems to have a backdrop of the Potala and every time I stopped to browse at a Barkhor side stall, the Palace brooded magnificently in my eye line. But Lhasa's centre piece was once the tallest building in the world and those 13 stories of steps require a period of acclimatisation before they are tackled.

So I stared up at the Palace for two days before finally paying my 100 yuan and going in. For that high price a guide was inevitable and I quickly learned that 'the Palace has over one thousand rooms and took seven thousand craftsmen 50 years to build in the 17th century and that the fifth to the 13th Dalai Lamas are buried here and here is the grandest burial chorten which is three stories high and contains 3700 kg grams of gold and was built for the fifth Dalai Lama since he was a great man and the most famous Dalai Lama of all', the details delivered in a rapid and breathless tone.

Lobsang Gyatso is often referred to as 'The Great Fifth' since it was he who united Tibet under the Gelugpa Buddhist School and began construction of the Potala. But it is the Dalai Lama who is not buried in the Potala Palace that most interests me.

Tsangyang Gyatso didn't really want to be Dalai Lama at all and after years of rebellion scandalously refused to take his final vows as a monk. Tsangyang was a tearaway who preferred the wine and brothels of Shol village below his palace to spirituality and Buddhist doctrine. He dressed as a layman, took the name Norsang Wangpo and such was his nocturnal pursuit of pleasure that one Jesuit monk in Lhasa at the time wrote "no good-looking person of either sex was safe from his unbridled licentiousness". It's nice that he only chose handsome lovers.

When he wasn't making the beast with two backs, the spiritual leader of all Tibet was writing about it. His poetry reads like the love-lorn ramblings of a teenage boy whose hormones are out of control since this is what he was, but maybe it loses something in translation.

I incline myself
To the teachings of my Lama
But my heart secretly escapes
To the thoughts of my sweetheart

Even if meditated upon,
The face of my Lama comes not to me,
But again and again comes to me
The smiling face of my beloved

If I could meditate upon the dharma
As intensely as I muse on my beloved
I would certainly attain enlightenment
Surely in this one lifetime

When my luck was good
I hoisted auspicious prayer flags
And the young lady of noble birth
Hoisted me at her home

Sweetheart awaiting me in my bed
Yielding tenderly her sweet soft body,
Has she come to cheat me
And disrobe me of my virtues?

People gossip about me.
I am sorry for what I have done;
I have taken three thin steps
And landed myself in the tavern of my mistress.

But for all his brothel creeping impropriety, Norsang Wangpo was still Tsangyang Gyatso. The Dalai Lama was kidnapped by Mongols and taken to Beijing but disappeared on the way, probably murdered near Kokonor in modern Qinghai and hence his bodily remains are not interred in the Potala with the other Dalai Lamas. It was the Ming Chinese who entered Lhasa, removed the Mongols and helped reinstate the new Dalai Lama and they've hardly been away from Tibet since. So there is a direct link between that 17th-century lovelorn fornicating poet-monk and the soldiers on Barkhor Square today.

The rest of the Potala was an anti-climax; a magnificent gilded and empty museum. It was great to have the place to myself since it is usually so busy with Chinese tourists in the summer that a timed ticket system has to operate to accommodate all those guests and they probably smoke and make too much noise too. But I was desperate to see some life, some evidence that the Palace has a function other than as a place of wonderment for gawping tourists like me. There was certainly no life in the careful reconstruction of the Dalai Lamas bedroom where pictures of other Dalai Lamas hung but there was no space for the current 'splittist' incumbent. No sign of life on the copper roofs either, but the views of Lhasa were certainly fine, though back in the maze of corridors at last I met some monks. "Where are you from?" they asked. "Oh England is a great country; best football premiership in the world" they nodded. I was thankful at least that there were no Manchester United team badges sewn on their red robes.

The Potala is aloof and empty all year now, and in the past the Dalai Lama was absent for half of the year too. His procession to the Norbulingka with his retinue traditionally marked the start of summer in Tibet and he would stay in the informal and verdant Jewel Park where 20 pound radishes and three foot wide cabbages were said to grow, until the cold autumn wind from the high plateau returned and he retreated back to the Potala. The Dalai Lama had been in the Norbulingka when the 1959 revolt broke out but escaped before the Chinese shelling began and the dead bodies were buried beneath the willow trees of the Summer Palace.

Norbulingka was just the first ancient site to be damaged by the liberators. There is a string of monasteries on the outskirts of Lhasa, all founded in the early 15th century which were seen by China as the cradle of Dalai Lama clique splittism and came under sustained attack as a result. Ganden or 'Joyous' monastery was a particular target for the Red Guards. A chorten had been raised there to contain the remains of Tsongkhapa, the founder of the Gelugpa yellow hat sect who came to dominate Tibetan political and cultural life. The Guards waved their

Little Red Books and broke into the tomb, supposedly finding the body perfectly preserved and with finger nails and hair still growing. The few pieces of bone that survived the destruction are in a newly built chorten around which pilgrims traditionally hop on one leg.

Drepung or 'Rice Heap' had been the largest monastery in the world with 10,000 monks and nuns but was almost completely destroyed, along with the neighbouring Nechung monastery where the State Oracle lived and whose name 'Immutable island of melodious sound' contains a poetry to which the bawdy 6th Dalai Lama could only aspire. The Oracle had played a vital part in decision-making in Tibet for 1300 years since no great policy was made by the Dalai Lama without reference to his advice. He would put on eight layers of clothes and an elaborate headdress, so heavy it took two men to lift, and to the accompaniment of cymbals, drums and blasts from long thungchen horns, would enter into a trance. His face would contort and his eyes roll before gasping out prophetic answers to the Dalai Lamas questions and falling into a dead faint. The Oracle could surely never have predicted the silence that has fallen on his monastery at Nechung where only the images of skulls in a sea of blood, body parts and Demons suggest that extraordinary events happened there once.

Ganden, Drepung and Nechung were all closed to foreigners when I was in Lhasa, but I did go to Sera, the monastery on the hill overlooking town below the Hermitage where Tsongkhapa had spent years in retreat. Sera too is a shadow of its former self and where once there were five thousand now I hardly saw a monk at all and the famous debating garden was closed. Worship and spirituality on the streets of the Barkhor and in the Jokhang seem indestructible. But for the time being, Tibetan Buddhism has been stifled in the great monasteries of Lhasa and as I drove past the noodle shops and karaoke bars on the outskirts of town, I wondered if the rest of Tibet would be the same.

I was being driven from Lhasa through the southern region of Tsang skirting the Himalayas and then finally plunging through a gap in the Mountains to the border town of Zhangmu and onto Nepal. This high level one thousand kilometre route is called the Friendship Highway and is one of the very few places that the Himalayas can be breached. The road is a rolling slideshow; almost a parody of a Tibetan experience with vast open views, snowcapped massive mountains, inquisitive and colourful locals and photogenic yaks lining the route and jostling for attention.

We sped along the road parallel to the nascent Brahmaputra River and climbed steeply to the five thousand metre Karo la Pass above Yamdrok-Tso Lake where I sat on a yak. It was a tourist yak, a yak that had sold his soul and abandoned a wild existence on the high plateau to pose for photos with idiots like me sitting on his back with my thumbs aloft. But it was a yak nonetheless and I liked his smell and the feeling of his broad hairy back between my thighs and the mysterious rumbling from his stomach that sounded like a portent of disaster.

This was a real yak too called a Drong which are bigger than most hairy beasts I'd seen called Dzo that are really the result when a cow falls in love with a yak and altogether inferior to a Drung. Like so many things in Tibet, the Drung is perfectly adapted to life halfway to the stratosphere with his huge lungs and extravagant red blood cell count. In fact, a yak wouldn't thank you to be taken on a visit to the seaside since he would be hot, uncomfortable and over oxygenated and would look daft in a 'kiss me quick' hat.

The Tibetan people have adapted equally well to their environment and know that only barley grows really well up here despite the Chinese attempt to switch to a wheat and rice crop which led to starvation for over 70,000 Tibetans between 1959 and 1961. Tibetan sky burials, where bodies are chopped up and fed to vultures, have a spiritual basis but are also well suited to an environment where there is little wood to spare for funeral pyres. The traditional practice of polyandry and monastic celibacy are good forms of population control in a land of little sustainable agriculture or surplus food.

The Tibetans know how to exist up here which can make Chinese interference, for all their road building and increased GDP such an irritation. The huge Yamdrok-Tso Lake, turquoise blue and framed by the Mount Nojin Kangtang massif that I was gazing down upon from my hairy perch is a case in point. The lake has a spiritual significance to locals but let us for a moment dismiss this objection to the Chinese hydroelectric scheme that has been established here as so much backward superstition. The scheme doesn't make sense on a more practical level too since there is no outlet or source into Yamdrok-Tso so water that is drained cannot be replaced. Locals say the lake will be drained in 20 years and a vital water supply irretrievably lost. Like the barley and the yaks, everything is finely balanced up here and somebody should really listen to the people who know.

The roads are impossibly remote on the plateau and we drove for mile after mile passing an occasional Chaktsal prostrating pilgrim on the way. Everyone we passed was an event and I wondered at their strength of purpose and wavered between puzzlement, admiration and thinking they were insane. These few Chaktsel were heading west like me and were probably standing up and lying down all the way to distant Mount Kailash, the most holy mountain of all to Buddhists, Hindus and Bonpos in the far west of Tibet. A circuit or kora of Kailash gives liberation within three lifetimes but there are any number of circuits and routes open to the devout who travel by truck, by foot and by prostrations to all the corners of Tibet. They often carry pilgrim guidebooks - a sort of Lonely Planet for the divine – that lists Tibet's 24 'power places' and help to maximise the merit. For the rules are quite complex; a circuit of Manasarovar Lake gives spontaneous Buddhahood, but is more auspicious in certain months. Three, 13 or 108 koras are particularly worthy and there is also instruction on the earth, herbs and rocks that should be best taken home as a blessing or a wish you were here holiday souvenir for those unfortunates who had been unable to go.

We arrived at last, after hours of dusty roads in the town of Gyantse where I settled down to a Tibetan meal of thukpa noodle soup, Momo steamed dough meat parcels and sweet yellow Chang beer in a restaurant beneath the town dzong or fort. The dzong is perched on a precipitous cliff and contains an anti-British imperialism Museum that commemorates the 'heroic battle fought to defend the Chinese motherland' at Gyantse in 1904, though Tibet was certainly not part of the motherland then.

The British had long harboured ambitions to enter Tibet in the 19th century but were forbidden, as all foreigners were, from entering the mysterious land. By the early 20th century, unused to being stymied in their imperial ambition, the British could wait no more and a body of one thousand men accompanied by ten thousand servants and four thousand yaks were led by Francis Younghusband, whose house-maid Gladys Aylward later embarked on a very different expedition to the Far East (see Shaanxi chapter) from Sikkim to the strategic town of Gyantse.

Younghusband fought a Tibetan force of 1500 at Yatung outside Gyantse and killed 700 of them in four minutes. The Tibetans wore garwu silver charm boxes blessed by the Dalai Lama, but these were no protection against the British Maxim guns, just as they weren't against Chinese mortars in Lhasa in 1959. The British force marched onto Gyantse and took the dzong from defenders who threw rocks at the cost of 300 Tibetan and four British dead and so ended the highest altitude battle that the British have ever fought.

This fairly typical episode of British imperial bullying and sabre rattling has a rather untypical ending. Younghusband marched onto Lhasa and established a trade agency there as instructed, but then something strange happened to the Colonel. He was at first unimpressed with the town which one of his journalists described as 'an insanitary slum', but the mustachioed stiff upper lipped old duffer seems to have had a mystical experience there.

He returned from Tibet convinced that 'men are at heart divine', renounced the invasion and established the World Congress of Faiths in 1936. Younghusband went on to publish a number of increasingly eccentric and spiritual books such as 'Mother World' and 'Life in the stars; an exposition of the view that on some planets or some stars exist beings higher than ourselves and on one a World Leader, the supreme embodiment of the Eternal Spirit which animates the whole' where he outlined the Gaia hypothesis in which a Christ-like figure exists on the planet Altair and radiates spiritual guidance by means of telepathy. From colonial native basher to new age hippy; Lhasa can have that effect on people.

Gyantse is famed for the Pelkor Chode monastery and Kumbum more than battles with the Brits. The monastery dates from the same era as Ganden, Drepung, Nechung and Sera but is less controlled and compromised than its contemporaries in Lhasa. This place feels vibrant and alive with the banging of drums and ringing of bells and most of all with the hypnotic chanting of monks. The Kumbum is a remarkable eight level chorten tower that houses 77 chapels. Kumbum means 100,000 images and though this is an exaggeration it's probably not too far wide of the mark since the interior is covered in deities, images, gods and saints and a fantastic jewel vomiting mongoose at its entrance.

I ascended the tower by ladder and stairs and emerged on a narrow ledge with a plummeting drop to the courtyard of Pelkor Chode below. Giant Buddha eyes are painted up here and we gazed together at the picture postcard old town with the dzong behind. This view of Gyantse is remarkable and is as ramshackle and picturesque as it must have been when the Kumbum was built. I scanned the view, but there were simply no signs of modern life here at all; no TV aerials, no machines, no tarmac and no plastic and the only sign of life was a dzo calf padding towards me. This was the Tibet that China was working so hard to liberate and change and it took little imagination to see that life must be hard in small towns like these on the high plateau, regardless of how photogenic they look. A little liberating would go a long way here.

My Hotel in Shigatse was new but already the sink drain and the heater were broken and there was no hot water. When one visits a three star Chinese hotel it's hard to understand how a nation where all toilet paper has to be put in a basket since it's impossible to flush anything away, is capable of controlling Tibet at all. Shigatse is Tibet's second city and for all the kitsch appeal of its scale model of the Potala, would be little more than a place to refuel, restock and collect the next permit if it wasn't for Tashilunpo.

My driver told me that Tibetans in Shigatse are friendlier than in Lhasa because they follow the Panchen instead of the Dalai Lama here. Certainly there was conspicuous Chinese flag flying, but then what other flag could be raised since the Tibetan one is banned? The difference in flags sums up the difference in the mentality of Chinese and Tibetans. The Chinese flag is bureaucratic and functional; the biggest star a representation of the Communist Party that prevails over the lives of all the nations of the motherland represented by the smaller stars and the bold red an assertive statement of socialist control and sacrifice. Tibet's flag is a flight of fancy. A snow peaked mountain is crested by a sun whose rays shine in all directions to represent spiritual and material happiness and freedom, below which two mythical snow lions with blazing eyes support a radiant three coloured jewel. All is surrounded by a border that is gold and purified as the teachings of the Buddha. It's a thoroughly subversive flag and it's no wonder the Chinese have banned it.

It would take days to fully explore the monastery at Tashilunpo founded by Tsongkhapa's nephew Genden Drup in 1447 and perched below Drolma Ridge. It's a maze of cobblestoned alleys that link temple to school to courtyard and finally to the steep hill where a massive whitewashed wall provides hanging space for the 40 meter appliquéd Thangka painting that is unfurled on the 15th day of the fifth lunar month.

Tashilunpo knows that size is everything and houses Tibet's biggest statue, a 26 meter image of Jampa the future Buddha built in 1914 that took four years to complete and is covered in 300 kg of gold. I'm pleased that at almost exactly the same time that Europe was tearing itself to pieces in the trenches of the First World War, one thousand craftsmen were quietly toiling on this massive tribute to God and I fervently hope that they neither knew or cared about man's madness at Verdun, Gallipoli and The Somme.

In 1642 the Great 5th Dalai Lama declared the Abbot of Tashilunpo to be the Panchen Lama or 'Great Precious Teacher' and second only in spiritual authority to himself. The Chinese have tried to use the Panchen Lama in opposition to the Dalai Lama since 1728 when they gave him sovereignty of Western Tibet, though like much of China's policy with Tibet, control of the Panchen Lama has reached new heights in recent years.

The 10th Panchen Lama fell into Communist hands in 1950 and became a fervent supporter of Mao. But following the violent suppression of the 1959 revolt changed his mind and issued a 70,000 character criticism of Chinese policy that announced that the Dalai Lama was the true leader of Tibet. In 1964 he spoke out at a huge rally in Lhasa and concluded his speech with a rousing 'Long live the Dalai Lama!'

This was too much for the Chinese who announced in typically colourful rhetoric that the Panchen Lama was 'a big rock on the road to socialism' and launched the 'thoroughly smash the Panchen Lama reactionary clique' movement. The errant monk was sent to Qin Cheng prison north of Beijing for 14 years where he was apparently tortured and attempted suicide. He was released in 1978 and never spoke out again and died on a visit to Tashilunpo aged 50 from a heart attack, though poisoning is just as likely.

There then followed the awkward question of succession. The Dalai Lama chose Gendun Choekyi Nyima, the son of a doctor from central Tibet, from his exile in Dharamsala, but the Chinese decreed that selection should be made by drawing lots from an 18th century golden urn that the Qing Emperor Qianlong had used to resolve disputes. The Golden receptacle was brought with much pomp to the Jokhang and the name of Gyaincain Norbu, the son of Communist Party members was drawn. Meanwhile the doctor's son was taken to Beijing where the authorities are holding him for 'protection' and he has not been seen since.

The new Panchen Lama is China's rival to the Dalai Lama. Like the Dalai Lama he preaches peace, but he insists that there is already freedom in Tibet. Norbu stood up blinking through his thick glasses under the bright lights of the Great Hall of the People in Beijing on the first official Serf Emancipation day and said "I want to thank the communist party for giving me a pair of clear eyes so I can tell right from wrong" and the delegates applause lingered long after he took his seat.

Leaving Shigatse it felt good to be leaving behind the politics of Tibet too. Now it would be raw nature, vast landscapes and scudding clouds all the way to the border with Nepal. Despite all the troubles and contradictions, the Dalai Lama urges "all open-minded people to discover what is the reality of Tibet for themselves" and the reality beyond Shigatse is of a landscape whose remoteness and grandeur is breathtaking and a little intimidating. But the land is never completely barren and empty, and often from my window, a small village of squat flat roofed Tibetan houses, a yak decorated with ribbons or a traveler in dusty robes and with a creased face could be seen hopefully flagging a lift from the middle of nowhere to the back of beyond.

We stopped at the Mongol style grey white and red Sakya monastery where my permit was checked by a boy with a gun who looked 15 and where the pit toilet surpassed even that at the Potala in foulness as the contents of visitors bowels were projected 30 feet onto the rocks of the Marpo Ri below. The main chapel of Sakya is supported by 40 wooden columns, one donated by Kublai Khan and carried by hand from China. A friendly monk left off carving butter from an enormous lamp and told me that another of the buttresses had been fetched from India on the back of a tiger, another on the horns of a yak while a fourth weeps black blood of the naga snake spirit that had lived in the tree that was felled so that Sakya's roof would not fall down.

But my head was in the Mountains now and I didn't look inside another monastery in Tibet after Sakya. We climbed the Lhakpa La Pass and I marvelled at the 5220 metre marker sign at the top since I've never been so high above sea level without being in an aeroplane. I marveled too at the group of beggars who emerged from behind a mound where they were sheltered from the bitter 5220m above sea level wind. They sent their children as advance guard, all ribbons of green snot, matted hair and outstretched hand and I wished that I knew Tibetan for 'surely there's a better place to beg than this?'

Beyond Lhakpa La, I stayed in the 'best hotel in Shekar' which was terrible and possessed all the essential requirements of the soulless Chinese hotel; deserted freezing lobby, apathetic staff, range of clocks telling the wrong time in five different world cities and a plastic basket next to the toilet. I wandered into Shekar below the Shekar Dzong Crystal Fort that climbed astonishingly on razor cliffs above and was followed around by a gang of kids who asked for money. They were soon joined by an old man who insisted on posing for photos though his dirty Adidas cap and nylon suit were not especially photogenic. He asked for money but was chased off by other locals who told me that although their village was poor they would never beg, though the children seemed to disagree as they laughed and danced and shouted 'gei qian' 'give money' and threw lumps of the Himalayas after me as I did a high altitude shuffle back to the 'luxury' of the hotel.

The hotel was so cold that it was little hardship to rise before dawn the next day and take refuge in the heat of the four-wheel-drive on the next leg of the journey. I wanted to crest the next pass at Pang La at sunrise where my first view of Everest and the massive peaks surrounding it would be tinged pink and magnificent under a brightening dawn sky.

The stars were bright and my spirits high as we drove towards the final checkpoint that gives access to the Qomolongma National Park but my dawn raid was foiled by the soldier behind a bare desk in a spartan room in remotest Tibet where access to the world's highest peak is granted or declined. Rural Tibet must surely be a hardship posting for an 18-year-old recruit in the People's Liberation Army who might be hoping to turn a lady's eye in his new uniform in Shanghai. Only the unluckiest recruit would be posted to Lhasa and how unfortunate or incapable must this soldier be to have landed in a glorified Portakabin on frozen tundra thousands of miles from home?

Incapable hardly did him justice as he pawed my passport, held it upside down millimetres from his nose and compared it to the permit, glancing from one to the other and trying to make sense of it all. His tongue was sticking out in concentration throughout the procedure and by the time he had grasped the pen and scrawled the necessary details down, the sun was a golden orb in a cloudless sky outside and my dawn view was gone.

The soldier was essentially illiterate but unwilling or unable to ask for help and I consoled myself that Everest would look just as fine under a full sun and at least there were no clouds and as we breasted the pass how could I be anything but overcome at the panorama of peaks spread before me, even if dawn had long passed?

I was surprised at the distance to Everest since it was our intention to drive to the foot of the mountain that day but we pressed gamely ahead down the switchback road of hairpin bends and I flung myself from side to side in the car so that Everest would not leave my sight. It seemed inconceivable from here that anyone could ever have doubted that the peak that Tibetans call Qomolongma Goddess Mother of the Universe, but British cartographers prosaically named Peak XV, could be anything other than the biggest on Earth.

Makalu, Cho Oyo and Lhotse were huge and brooding too, but Everest dominated them all. It was the British who accurately measured the mountain, ignored the beautiful Tibetan name, and dedicated Everest to an extravagantly bearded bureaucrat. But the confusion over heights and distance throughout Tibet is excusable since no explorers or surveyors were allowed in for so long.

The British solved their problem by sneaking Indian civil servants into Tibet who conducted laborious linear route surveys. These cartographical spies were called 'Pundits' and the most famous was a Sikkim schoolteacher called Nain Singh. Singh walked 1200 miles through Tibet in the employ of the British Secret Service. Dressed as a pilgrim, he was trained to walk every pace at exactly 33 inches and he counted millions of these paces on a specially adapted rosary that had only 100 beads instead of the usual 108. Singh's gadgets were very James Bond for the 19th Century. His bowl was used to hold mercury to find the horizon, his walking stick held a thermometer which he dipped into tea water as it came to the boil and thus determined altitude. His prayer wheel contained not the sacred Tibetan mantra 'Om Mane Padme Hum' (hail jewel in the Lotus) but his route survey - a careful record of the distance and altitude he had walked. Singh's meticulous route finding meant that Tibet was a mystery no more and paved the way for Younghusband's advance on Lhasa 40 years later. Thus the Indian pundit marching for miles in 33 inch increments across Tibet on 20 rupees a day can be held directly responsible for our knowledge of the Christ figure on the planet Altair and all the benefits that this discovery has brought mankind.

We bumped our way down the rough track from Pang La and through idyllic villages in a wide and stony river valley. My driver blared his horn like Toad of Toad Hall if a villager or a yak strayed within 10 yards of his road which seemed boorish and arrogant and I asked him to stop. He raised his eyebrows in surprise and desisted for a time but such is the ingrained use of the horn by Chinese drivers to warn of approach, overtake and to announce the manoeuvre complete, that he was soon disturbing the serenity of this remote place again.

Qomolongma had disappeared behind a low range of hills and we continued right up a side valley and almost to the foot of the mountain before we saw it again. Then, as we turned a corner (horn blast), the goddess was in front of us. How to describe the experience of seeing Everest up so close? I'd read stories of Mallory and Irvine, Tenzing Norgay and Edmund Hillary and now on this crystal clear day, there was the North Col and there the final approach to the summit. The approach from the north is so much more satisfying than from Nepal where trekkers climb the Khumbu Valley but Everest remains hidden in a confusing jumble of peaks. From the Tibetan side, the mountain's north face is unimpeded and gigantic, a huge triangular mass of rock and ice and today framed by a cobalt blue sky.

My driver said that he had never seen the mountain so clear and I felt blessed indeed and in this weather the route looked deceptively achievable – up that ice patch on the right; follow the shallow ridge to the col to the hands in pockets last stretch to the top. Such hubris dissolved as I walked one hundred metres to the top of a rocky lump in front for an unobstructed view and was left gasping through a raw throat in the thin, cold air. So I sat down instead and watched the play of light on the rock and the tiny flurries of spindrift whipped by a high altitude wind and looked at the splashes of red and yellow tents of early-season expeditions at base camp below and decided that I had no desire to climb the mountain at all, for my journey by train and road through Tibet had been adventure enough.

There is a monastery at base camp at 4980 metres that is of course the highest in the world and we stopped in the guest house for a lunch of roasted barley mixed with yak butter called tsampa that is a staple of the Tibetan diet. Rongphu monastery is small and lacks interest compared to the brilliance of Tashilunpo or the Jokhang but the stone chorten outside made a great photo with Qomolongma brooding and magnificent behind. Rongphu is a relatively new place founded in 1902, though hardy nuns have lived in meditation huts here for 200 years. The monastery has been repaired and restored since Cultural Revolutionary Red Guards found even this remote place in their search for the insidious four olds though such was the dedication and fanaticism of these communist disciples that I suppose they were pilgrims too. Their Little Red Books said that revolution is no picnic or garden party and that good revolutionaries must endure hardship and eat bitterness to earn socialist merit just as Chaktsel prostraters can earn merit from God. It's just that the Red Guard god who lies in a crystal coffin in Beijing turned out to be so much more flawed and unsatisfactory than the Buddha.

As if our route wasn't challenging enough, my driver decided to go off road for the next leg from Everest to Old Tingri. We drove through streams and over sparse featureless hillsides as I pondered the consequences of a breakdown out here where there was no one; but I loved the risk and the sense that we were a tiny pinprick on this land where perhaps no one had been before.

I was wrong of course and we soon came to a tented army post that was so extravagantly remote that it might have been a mirage. Four Army cadets, their faces as smooth as the barrel of the machine gun over their shoulders, shouted us down and ran to the car no doubt excited by the prospect of someone other than a yak to talk to. They checked passports and we exchanged pleasantries; "you like your job?" "It's very quiet up here" and we were waved on our way.

What I really wanted to ask was 'what is the point of you being here, since we have already had all of our documents checked by an illiterate boy at the National Park entrance post and there's no way out except through the checkpoints and we must be the only car you've seen in days?' But I was put off by the size of their gun. So I asked the driver instead who laughed and said he didn't know why China has so many army posts.

What he meant I think is they do it because they can. The point is that a huddle of green tents on a remote pass shows ownership. We had passed hundreds of road markers on our trip from Lhasa which marked our distance in kilometres from Beijing and they showed ownership too. Streets in Lhasa, Shigatse and Gyantse had all been named after Chinese towns and provinces to remind Tibetans living on Shanghai Street or Guangdong Avenue that they are part of the motherland too.

Yet ownership is a nebulous concept up here and when we finally hit a smoother road again in Old Tingri, the town seemed hardly Chinese at all. In fact I was reminded more of pictures of villages in the Andes in South America where leather faced locals in wide brimmed hats sat in the shade of geometric houses that could have been constructed by Incas or Aztecs. Old Tingri is a tumbledown sort of place but the views of Everest and Cho Oyo are sublime, though I suppose even this view would become mundane if you walked past it every day to a barebones field and tried to coax barley from the soil.

I stayed in the best hotel in town again which had two plastic baskets by the toilet but no running water at all and I woke to that view the next morning. We drove the last leg of the journey along a road lined by ruins of buildings, though these were destroyed by 18th-century Gurkhas from Nepal and not by Red Guards, and finally over the La Lung Pass. The views on this stretch of the road were the best of all and I annoyed my driver with dozens of pauses for photos and stops where I got out and walked a hundred metres along the road and pretended I was all alone and just stared. I had been eased into this extraordinary panorama of massive hills by the view at Everest base camp and along the road from Lhasa to Shigatse, but I would think that visitors who come straight up from the valleys of Nepal to this place might suffer from sensory overload as much as altitude sickness.

Then finally we began to descend from the plateau that had been my home and where my lungs had changed and my blood thickened over the last two weeks. We charged through Nyalam town whose name means 'gateway to hell' and then into the jaws of Hades itself on the improbable descent to the border 30 kilometres distant at Zhangmu.

The road here greedily seeks out a massive vertical rift in the mountainous barrier and plunges into it, clinging to the side for hairpin after hairpin bend, every swing of the car revealing a yawning chasm below. The route has a Tolkien grandeur and it was surprising to see trees, waterfalls and wisps of cloud that had become a rumour during my time in Tibet.

The road has been improved but repairs are a never ending job on this precipitous terrain. In places Chinese Dong Feng and Nepali Tata trucks edged past each other while the road crumbled like biscuit at the edge of the void beneath their wheels. Further down the valley, gangs of workmen live in makeshift tents on platforms that jut into space and battle rock fall and landslide and pouring rain in the Sisyphean task of keeping the road open. I chatted to one in stilted Chinese as we waited in a jam and drivers shouted, honked their horns and reversed, oblivious to the possibility of plummeting death. He said that he came from Sichuan, "like most of the workers here" and that he enjoyed the work "because the pay was good and anyway Sichuanese people are used to hardship". He said I was lucky to come from England because the economy was good and the roads are excellent over there.

Finally we rolled into Zhangmu, green and lush with it's ostentatiously thick oxygen, though this was a moot point as the air was thick with the fumes of revving diesel engines queueing at the border. We passed two further sets of customs where an official asked if my two dollar prayer wheel from a stall on the Barkhor was an antique and I shook my driver's hand in farewell, feeling sorry at the enormity of his drive back to Lhasa.

I walked from the car and marvelled that I didn't feel breathless as I strode over the boundary line on the Friendship Bridge that links Nepal with China. Here was a final reminder of Chinese ownership under a huge flag as I changed my watch by two hours because of the clumsy insistence that Tibet live on Beijing time. But there is timelessness about Tibet and a patient disregard for the unfairness and injustice of this temporal existence. I reflected that the Chinese should not mistake prostration for submission there, shouldered my bag and walked downhill towards Kathmandu.

Printed in Great Britain
by Amazon.co.uk, Ltd.,
Marston Gate.